Crime and Punishment
in Contemporary Greece

Crime and Punishment in Contemporary Greece

International Comparative Perspectives

edited by

Leonidas K. Cheliotis and Sappho Xenakis

PETER LANG

Oxford • Bern • Berlin • Bruxelles • Frankfurt am Main • New York • Wien

Bibliographic information published by Die Deutsche Nationalbibliothek.
Die Deutsche Nationalbibliothek lists this publication in the Deutsche National-
bibliografie; detailed bibliographic data is available on the Internet at
http://dnb.d-nb.de.

Library of Congress Cataloging-in-Publication Data:

Crime and punishment in contemporary Greece : international comparative
perspectives / Leonidas K. Cheliotis and Sappho Xenakis, (eds).
    p. cm.
  Includes bibliographical references.
  ISBN 978-3-03911-562-4 (alk. paper)
  1. Crime--Greece--History--21st century. 2. Criminal justice,
Administration of--Greece--History--21st century. 3.
Punishment--Greece--History--21st century. I. Cheliotis, Leonidas K.,
1977- II. Xenakis, Sappho, 1976-
  HV7075.5.C75 2011
  364.9495--dc23

                         2011026373

ISBN 978-3-03911-562-4

© Peter Lang AG, International Academic Publishers, Bern 2011
Hochfeldstrasse 32, CH-3012 Bern, Switzerland
info@peterlang.com, www.peterlang.com, www.peterlang.net

Printed in Germany

Contents

vi

MICHAEL TONRY

Foreword

Crime and Punishment in Contemporary Greece is a *tour de force*, an ingenious, useful, and important book on crime, criminal justice, and thinking about both in Greece, as seen from inside by Greek scholars and from outside by subject matter specialists from other Western countries. The ingenuity is to have developed a bifocaled methodology in which topics are discussed by people who see them up close in contexts of national history, culture, and values, and by people who see them from far away in contexts of personal experience and a broader international literature. The usefulness is in providing a comprehensive look at a single country's practices, policies, and politics at levels of expertise and sophistication no single writer could achieve. The importance is in showing that such a venture is possible and provides richness and nuance that comparative scholarship on the criminal law and its institutions seldom achieves.

The writers tell their stories and the commentators offer praise, elaboration, or disagreement. People interested in, say, the evolution of drug policy, the nature of organised crime, or the influence of the media on public attitudes and beliefs should read and learn what the writers and commentators have to say. There is no point in my attempting to summarise or comment on the individual chapters and commentaries. Instead, I comment on a few themes that emerge from the book. Four themes leap out.

One concerns the effects of shifting, as Greece recently did, from being an emigration country to being an immigration country (or, perhaps, from being a relatively homogeneous country to one having sizable ethnic minorities). Greeks are more fearful of crime than are citizens of most European countries, and they identify Albanians and members of a few other groups as the source of their fears, as the crux of the organised crime problem, and as the villains behind human smuggling. In one sense, there is nothing unusual about this. In every country, some ethnic group is stereotyped in that way, but the phenomenon is new, or more prominent than before, in Greece.

A second theme is the existence and power of befuddled public opinion and misconceptions that create social and political pressures in favour of repressive policies. Greeks believe that serious crime in general and serious youth crime in particular have been rising rapidly when they have not been. Steeply rising prison populations are one result, but Greeks believe there are many fewer people in prisons than are really there. The media promote and reify mistaken beliefs, simultaneously creating and reinforcing them, and building support for harsher practices and policies. Here, too, the Greek experience is not unusual. It is paralleled in every country concerning which there is relevant literature. In some countries, conspicuously England and Wales, New Zealand, and the United States, public misinformation and punitiveness have influenced the adoption of harsher punishment policies and practices. In others, for example Canada, Belgium, and the Scandinavian countries, they have not. An important question to be addressed is why Greece appears to be following the English rather than the Canadian, Belgian, or Scandinavian pattern.

A third theme is the inexorable influence of external pressures on national laws and policies. Examples include EU mandates and treaties aimed at the harmonisation of laws and procedures, international and especially American pressures to adopt repressive drug policies and common approaches to combating organised crime, the adoption of unprecedented forms of surveillance to reassure visitors to the 2004 Olympics, and more benignly, the influence of international treaties and conventions on the juvenile justice system. In the last respect, Greece is in the European mainstream: international human rights standards matter. In England and Wales and the United States, they do not. Another important question is why in this respect – in contrast to its adoption of repressive policies – Greece resembles Belgium (and the rest of Europe) more than England and Wales and the United States.

A contradictory fourth theme is the power of national history and culture. The Greek government has invested hugely in surveillance methods and technology, and Greek citizens, remembering life under the colonels, have resisted their use. One Greek government adopted US-modelled organised crime legislation, to external approbation. A successor government repealed it. Greek governments have changed laws in response to international commitments and pressures, but often reluctantly, partially, and belatedly.

The details of the stories told in *Crime and Punishment in Contemporary Greece* are uniquely Greek, but the stories are, if not universal, common. All developed Western countries are wrestling with the effects of immigration and increased ethnic diversity; public ignorance, fears, and attitudes; external pressures on traditional policies and practices; and the power of national history and culture.

Two features of this book warrant special mention. It is the first major English-language work on crime, criminal justice, and criminology in Greece. That is important. The comparative and cross-national literatures are growing, but so far they deal mostly with Northern and Western Europe and the English-speaking countries. Southern, Central, and Eastern Europe are seldom written about and almost never at length. Publication of a major, high-quality book on Greece is an important step towards broadening the literature, and, I hope, a harbinger of things to come from elsewhere. The book is written in strong, clear, idiomatic English. This is a major accomplishment which is likely to extend the book's reach and influence. For good or ill (I am of mixed views), English has become the international language of scholarship. Most ambitious European scholars speak and write in English. Even so, it is deucedly difficult to write fluently in a second or third language. The editors of this volume appear to have invested extraordinary (and, I assume, exhausting) effort in converting substantively strong articles into accessible English. Commendations are due.

The great strength of *Crime and Punishment in Contemporary Greece* is that it tells a common story with rich Greek details. I hope its bifocaled approach is emulated by others willing to undertake the daunting effort this book represents. Comparative and cross-national research on criminal justice systems is less rare than it once was, but comparative studies remain confined mostly to case studies, sometimes done in parallel, and genuinely cross-national studies remain somewhere between uncommon and non-existent. The approach Cheliotis, Xenakis, and their colleagues have taken will enable readers to know more about the Greek system than was heretofore possible, and illustrates a promising new way to learn more about their own and other countries.

SAPPHO XENAKIS AND LEONIDAS K. CHELIOTIS

Introduction

In recent months and years, media reports spanning topics such as financial corruption and economic turmoil, political violence and social unrest, and illegal immigration and migrant detention, have brought the themes of crime and punishment in Greece to the centre-stage of international attention. At the same time, the turn of the media spotlight onto Greek realities has exposed the apparent failure of pertinent knowledge to be adequately harnessed and disseminated. One obvious reason for this has been the language barrier, which has left many Greek experiences outside the scope of deeper insights and assessments from foreign perspectives, and goes some way towards explaining the country's common absence from international comparative studies of crime and punishment. Another reason has been the lack of any systematic introductory volume on these themes within Greece itself.

Aiming to address this important deficiency, but also to encourage greater and deeper engagement between scholars of Greece and of other jurisdictions, this collection presents and discusses key trends of crime and punishment in contemporary Greece. Rather than offering an exhaustive guide, the ambition here is to combine essential empirical information with an analytical exchange designed to stimulate further research. The structural novelty of the collection – which features chapters from specialists on Greece, followed by commentaries from international experts – is intended to encourage substantive dialogue for the benefit of both domestic and international comparative research.

The collection is divided into three sections. Respectively, these address the experience of crime, topical crime issues, and state reactions to crime. The collection comprises fifteen primary chapters and accompanying commentaries. Requirements have meant that certain chapters cover more than one key issue (hence also one chapter is followed by two commentaries).

Opening Part I of the collection, the chapter on crime, fear of crime and punitiveness, by Leonidas K. Cheliotis and Sappho Xenakis, introduces a number of core themes that are reprised in many of the contributions that follow, from crime rates and the criminalisation of immigrants to policing and the use of imprisonment. The chapter also proposes a theoretical framework through which these themes can be understood. In their ensuing commentary, Jonathan Jackson, Monica Gerber and Carolyn Côté-Lussier use international survey data to compare trends in fear of crime and punitive sentiment in Greece and the UK, with particular reference to the ideological roots of each. The following chapter, by Giannis Panousis, addresses media representations of crime and criminal justice in Greece, raising the difficulty of disentangling the effects of the media upon public opinion. Robert Reiner in turn places the discussion within the context of research on British and North American experiences. Immigration and crime is the focus of the next chapter, written by Vassilis Karydis, which challenges the widespread stereotyping of immigrants as crime-prone by reference to biases they face in the criminal justice process. Drawing parallels between the Greek experience and international trends, Didier Bigo situates concerns about immigrants and crime within a continuum of threats apparent in contemporary security discourses at the European level. In the last chapter of Part I, Ioannis Papageorgiou provides a review of the literature on crime and youth in Greece. The review sheds light on those aspects of the relationship between youth and crime that have attracted most research interest in the country, such as sports-related violence, bullying in schools, and gang involvement. The apparent absence of a focus in the Greek literature on the role of the family in causing or preventing delinquency is discussed by Leonidas K. Cheliotis in his commentary.

Part II of the collection, on topical crime issues, begins with a chapter by Effi Lambropoulou on corruption. Lambropoulou addresses the legal and institutional framework against corruption in Greece, and presents empirical findings and theoretical analysis that challenges preconceptions about the nature of the problem in the country. This is complemented by the critical approach to the theorisation of corruption presented in the commentary by Peter Bratsis. In the chapter which follows, Joanna Tsiganou offers a historical overview of the development of Greek drug control policies, emphasising the role played by international influences in shaping them. In his commentary, Trevor Bennett draws out the competing pressures that weigh upon drug policies, and especially the tensions between political imperatives and evidence-based responses. The intertwining of organised crime and political violence in Greece is then considered by Sappho Xenakis, who highlights the political debates that have accompanied the evolution of both concerns. Vincenzo Ruggiero ties the Greek experience to a critical appraisal of the way in which organised crime and political violence have been increasingly bound together in international security discourses. Margaret E. Beare elaborates the theme of US influence in organised crime policy internationally, making a striking comparison of the Greek experience with that of Canada. In their chapter on sex, trafficking and crime policy, Georgios Papanicolaou and Paraskevi S. Bouklis account for the transformation of sex trafficking into a leading concern of the Greek state. Examining the discursive associations of trafficking with organised crime and prostitution, Papanicolaou and Bouklis argue that the anti-trafficking agenda has served to marginalise and obscure the exploitation of immigrant labour in the country. Claudia Aradau sets this debate within the framework of international anti-trafficking regimes, problematising their relationship with empirical realities. Part II closes with a chapter by Efi Avdela on honour-related violence and crime, a topic that has long attracted anthropological scrutiny in Greece. Taking an historical approach, Avdela links the demise of honour-related violence and crime in the country by the 1960s to a range of cultural and socio-economic transformations. In his commentary, Pieter Spierenburg draws attention to the differences and similarities of the Greek case with those of other societies across Europe.

Part III of the collection, which addresses state reactions to crime, starts with a chapter by Valsamis Mitsilegas, who addresses the problems that have been encountered in implementing European Union criminal law measures into the Greek criminal justice system. In her commentary, Monica den Boer sets Greek experiences alongside those of other EU member-states, questioning the specificities and similarities of Greece's trajectory. Minas Samatas then provides an overview of surveillance modernisation in contemporary Greece, with particular reference to the country's authoritarian legacy, the role of 9/11, and the 2004 Olympic Games in Athens. Drawing on Samatas' account, Kevin D. Haggerty underlines the importance of historical memory to appreciating the dynamics of contemporary surveillance cultures. A chapter on the development and controversies surrounding the police and policing in Greece is then offered by Sophie Vidali. Rob I. Mawby follows with a rich commentary that reveals the commonalities which have historically existed between the Greek police and what he calls the 'continental European model'. Youth justice and probation is the subject of the next chapter, written by Angelika Pitsela. Pitsela gives a historical outline of the treatment of juveniles under Greek law, and points to continuing discrepancies between legal provisions and their implementation. The response by John Muncie, which takes an international comparative perspective, elaborates on the crucial distinctions to be made between policy as rhetoric, policy as codified, and policy as implemented. Charis Papacharalambous discusses Greek legal doctrine as a prism through which to examine very similar disjunctures between written law and its application with reference to the adult judicial system. Commenting on Papacharalambous' chapter, Nicola Padfield identifies a range of intriguing avenues for future research, especially on the subject of sentencing. In the final chapter of the collection, Leonidas K. Cheliotis illustrates the scope of, and explains some of the reasons for, the growth of imprisonment and the simultaneous decline in the use of parole in Greece over the last three decades. In his commentary, Roy D. King draws revealing comparisons – quantitative as well as qualitative – between the Greek case and jurisdictions elsewhere, including Russia, Brazil, and England and Wales.

Reflecting the interdisciplinary nature of the subject matter, this collection brings together analyses of crime and punishment across the fields of criminology, law, history, sociology, political science, and anthropology. We hope that the outcome will not only be of value to scholars concerned with developments in Greece from a national or comparativist perspective, but also to a wider audience interested in the social ramifications of politico-economic developments that the country has experienced over recent decades. In fact, a focus on crime and punishment may well serve to open up new ways of thinking about those politico-economic developments themselves.

The ambitions of this project meant that it was bound to be time-consuming. Indeed, from the commissioning of papers, drafting and negotiating content outlines and submission deadlines, and soliciting revised drafts following detailed reviews, to editing revised drafts, seeking author agreement on those drafts and sending them to other contributors for their commentaries, as well as editing the commentaries themselves, the preparation of the manuscript duly took longer than we originally anticipated. Neither our native grasp of Greek and English nor our familiarity with pertinent Greek and Anglophone literatures appeared to make the editorial process any less challenging.

We would like to thank all the participants in this book for their contributions and patience in the development of the collection, and Graham Speake for embracing the project at its outset. Thanks are also due to Lucy Melville, Gemma Lewis, and Mette Bundgaard, who skilfully led the manuscript to publication. We are particularly grateful to Michael Tonry for his encouragement, guidance, and generous words of introduction to the collection. We sincerely thank Julian Roberts for his invaluable advice on navigating the editorial challenges that the project posed. We would like to acknowledge support for this project provided by funding from the European Community's Seventh Framework Programme (*FP7/2007–2013*) under grant agreement number 237163. Finally, we would like to thank our families and friends for supplying much tea and sympathy along the way...

PART I

Experiencing Crime

LEONIDAS K. CHELIOTIS AND SAPPHO XENAKIS[1]

Crime, Fear of Crime and Punitiveness

Over the last the three decades, punitiveness on the part of the state in Greece in the field of law and order has been on the ascent. The most obvious indicator of this has been the steeply rising use of imprisonment. A striking accompaniment of state punitiveness has been punitive public opinion. As soon as one broaches the question of why this is the case, however, one is confronted with at least two puzzling findings. First, the prevalence of crime has only risen modestly, in sharp disproportion to the high recorded levels of fear of criminal victimisation, of distrust in the police and judicial authorities, and of public punitiveness. And second, fear of criminal victimisation itself does not axiomatically bear a positive correlation with expressed public support for state punitiveness, though it does predict lack of confidence in criminal justice authorities. This chapter sets out to review these contradictions and the limits of available explanations, placing them within the context of the country's legacy of authoritarianism. To the extent that space allows, the chapter goes on to argue for the development of a richer substantive and epistemological framework.

We begin by outlining the different ways in which Greece's authoritarian past and the dictatorship of 1967–1974 in particular are thought to have influenced state and public punitiveness in the years that have followed. Despite common assertions that the authoritarian legacy has functioned to restrict state and public punitiveness, the evidence reviewed suggests that any such impact has been limited. The next section summarises scholarly and commercial research on the levels and patterns of fear of crime and public punitiveness in contemporary Greece, as both distinct and

---

1   Thanks are due to Julian Roberts for his constructively critical comments on an earlier version of this chapter.

interrelated themes. Attention is then drawn to the disconnect between crime and imprisonment rates as an illustrative example of the irrational foundations of state punitiveness and its degree of public support; a disconnect that is all the more prominent when examined with reference to nationality. As subsequently discussed, research has increasingly sought to address the public dimension of punitive irrationality in conjunction with indicators other than crime or fear of crime without, however, interrogating the socio-economic and political environment within which punitiveness evolves. Taking inspiration from political economies of punishment in jurisdictions elsewhere, the remainder of the chapter points to state deployment of a law-and-order discourse and the use of punishment as symbolic devices by which social insecurities, generated in large part by the state itself, are displaced and discharged onto suitably weak subsections of the population.

The Legacy of Authoritarianism

The legacy of the Greek military dictatorship of 1967–1974 has overtly and steadfastly remained a key frame of reference within which public discussions have addressed the punitiveness or leniency of the Greek state. The junta employed a brutal system of repression that, notwithstanding its support from the United States, stimulated an international outcry. During the junta's seven-year rule, aside from some 10,000 Leftists that were banished to islands, and 1,700 that were sentenced to prison terms on political grounds, many more were subjected to short and violent detention (Cheliotis and Xenakis, 2010: 361). The use of torture by the state against resisters was routine and institutionalised, press censorship was tight, and surveillance measures were comprehensive (see further Athenian, 1972; Haritos-Fatouros, 2003). There have been assertions that the Greek public rapidly lost memory of the junta after its downfall, and evidence from opinion surveys that the specifics of the junta period are no longer easily recalled in detail (see, e.g., Sotiropoulos, 2010). But mention of the junta's legacy has persistently accompanied public debate about crime and punishment in contemporary Greece, as much as the language of the junta and pre-junta authoritarian eras has repeatedly been recycled in political discourse (see, e.g., discussion in Panourgiá, 2009: 175–176). Just what this legacy involves, on the other hand, remains a matter of debate.

Heightened public sensitivity towards particular manifestations of punitiveness on the part of the state has commonly been considered part and parcel of Greece's post-authoritarian legacy. The powerful impact of this legacy has been cited, for example, in explanations of the low level of trust accorded to the police by Greek citizens (see discussion in Lambropoulou, 2004: 98), and of the degree of public resistance displayed to the expansion of surveillance measures by the state (Samatas, 2004: 154–157). The fall of the country's military dictatorship in 1974 has been identified as a crucial turning point in the ideological make-up of Greek public opinion, which at that juncture allegedly saw its longstanding dominant conservatism del-egitimised and replaced by a 'left-wing ideological hegemony' (Kioukias, 1993; see also Dimitras, 1990). Whilst successive decades have reared gen-erations often believed to be less politically knowledgeable or committed than their predecessors (see Lyrintzis, 2006: 30–31), the broader destabil-ising influence of the 'permissive' socio-political culture heralded by the end of the junta has been a recurrent cause of concern for conservatives. This concern is well illustrated by the familiar critique that the romantici-sation of the anti-dictatorship struggle by the Greek Left has irresponsibly fuelled contemporary forms of rebelliousness which should be considered illegitimate (including repeated labour strikes or frequent public demon-strations that are obstructive of trade or traffic; see, e.g., *Kathimerini*, 11 May 2010, 10 June 2010).[2] Equally, this concern has been directly referenced in complaints that continuing political sensitivities concerning the junta have led the state to be unacceptably lenient in acting against crime (such as restricting police action against demonstrators, and maintaining the law which prevents the police from entering university buildings and campuses; see indicatively *Kathimerini*, 27 February 2009; and later).

2　Indeed, reflecting such concerns, a new law against 'persistent' labour strikers was passed on 30 September 2010 (on which see discussion in *Kathimerini*, 1 October 2010).

In terms of state punitiveness, the end of the dictatorship in Greece signalled a significant moment of catharsis in which the country belatedly experienced a discrediting of the type of exclusionary and highly coercive forms of government that had already been rejected by other states across the continent in the aftermath of the Second World War (see further Mazower, 2000: 219; on the history of coercion by the Greek state against the labour movement and Leftists, see Mazower, 1997; Rigakos and Papanicolaou, 2003; Seferiades, 2005; Cheliotis and Xenakis, 2010). The renunciation of authoritarian rule in Greece quickly appeared definitive: the country's elite-managed transition to democracy after 1974 was bloodless and relatively swift (Karakatsanis, 2001; Sotiropoulos, 2010) according to the standards of the so-called 'third wave' of democratisation experienced by a number of countries between 1974 and 1990 (Huntington, 1991), including those of Southern Europe more particularly (Diamandouros, 1997).[3] The length of the parliamentary tradition in Greece may provide some explanation for the comparatively short (seven-year) period of dictatorship in question (Bermeo, 1995). This should not detract from the point that the army had a history of directly meddling in Greek politics, and that it finally relinquished this role in 1974.

The transition from dictatorial to democratic structures and practices was by no means as abrupt as has often been assumed, however. As Samatas points out, politicians soon quietly reneged on their pledges to revoke authoritarian surveillance measures in the post-junta era; instead, surveillance practices were modernised and their accompanying anti-communist and anti-leftist terminologies replaced with an anti-anarchist lexicon (Samatas, 2004: 51–54). It was not until 1989 that the state finally destroyed 16.5 million intelligence files that had been compiled by police and intelligence services on the political and private affiliations of Greek citizens since 1944. Yet these constituted less than half of the 41.2 million police files that had been created since 1981 (ibid.: 64; see also Samatas, this collection).

---

3   According to Huntington (1991), the first and second 'waves' of democratisation experienced by states across the globe began in the early 1880s and during the Second World War, respectively.

Where policing and surveillance practices showed more signs of super-ficial adaptation than rupture after 1974, the use of imprisonment saw an all-too-brief reduction, followed by an accelerating rise. Between 1975 and 1979, the annual caseload of convicted and remand prisoners fell by 16.1 percent, from 9,650 (or 107 per 100,000 inhabitants) to 8,088 (or 85 per 100,000 inhabitants), whilst the caseload of prisoners sentenced to a year or more remained stable. Although the 1980s saw a modest overall decline of 6 percent in the annual caseload of convicted and remand prisoners (from 11,455, or 119 per 100,000 inhabitants, in 1980 to 10,763, or 107 per 100,000 inhabitants, in 1989), the average length of stay in prison under conviction saw a 47 percent rise (from 3.8 months to 5.6 months). Over this time, there was a large increase in the annual caseload of prisoners sen-tenced to longer custodial terms, and a 35.3 percent decrease in the annual caseload of convicted prisoners being discharged for any reason. Between 1990 and 2006, the total annual caseload of convicted and remand pris-oners underwent a sharp 52.6 percent rise (from 11,835, or 116 per 100,000 inhabitants, to 18,070, or 162 per 100,000 inhabitants), accompanied by a meteoric increase of 1,337 percent in the average length of stay in prison under conviction (from 5.1 months to 73.3 months). During this period, there was a huge expansion in the annual caseload of prisoners sentenced to longer terms – indeed, by 2006, the annual caseload of prisoners sentenced to a year or more was rapidly approaching parity with the historically peak levels recorded from the interwar years (see further Cheliotis and Xenakis, 2010) –, whilst the annual caseload of convicted prisoners discharged for any reason fell in proportion to the annual caseload of convicted prisoners, from 52.9 percent to 44.6 percent (see further Cheliotis, this collection).

Many of the continuities of punitive state practices in Greece in the immediate aftermath of the dictatorship have been directly attributed to the secretive or closed decision-making of political and security-sector elites, more than to public opinion (see, e.g., Samatas, 2004: 51–58). Over the longer term, however, the persistence and extension of punitive state prac-tices logically required the support of a sufficient segment of the population. Sympathetic attitudes towards state punitiveness may well have been facili-tated by the significant rehabilitation of the junta's record in Greek public opinion over the past quarter-century, and the corresponding ascription of the intervening years as a period of excessive leniency. In fact, if one were to accept the dominant academic interpretation of the *absence* of public support for the junta during its rule (see Sotiropoulos, 2010: 451; Bermeo, 1995; contrast Psomiades, 2004; see further Kassimeris, 2010: 55–56; and on the absence of mass opposition to the dictatorship, Clogg, 1986: 195–196), positive public appreciation for the dictatorship emerged subsequent to its demise and has progressively grown since. In 1985, a comparative international survey involving three other post-dictatorial countries of Southern Europe (Italy, Portugal, and Spain) found that whilst 59 percent of Greek respondents knew or remembered the junta to have been 'only bad', 31 percent believed its record to have been mixed ('in part good and in part bad'), and 6 percent that 'all considered, it was good' (see further Montero and Torcal, 1990: 128). A subsequent survey carried out in 1997 (cited by Sotiropoulos, 2010: 460) found that the proportion of Greek respondents considering the regime to have been wholly negative had dropped to around 40 percent, the proportion of those perceiving its record to have been mixed had risen to just under 50 percent, and those viewing it as entirely positive had risen to 11 percent. By 2007, a further opinion poll carried out in Greece found that 50.9 percent of respondents agreed that 'despite the negative characteristics that accompany a dictatorship, the junta also had, after all, benefits for Greece' (*To Vima*, 22 April 2007).

Whilst the growth in favourable memories of the junta has not been accompanied by evidence of any explicit preference for a return to authoritarian rule, calls for strong political leadership and the censuring of dissent within and outside parliament have become more vocal over recent years, and especially since the onset of the country's financial crisis. An opinion poll in April 2007 found that 60.2 percent of respondents preferred a system other than the country's parliamentary democracy: 48.6 percent a presidential democracy, and 11.6 percent a monarchical democracy (ibid.). One leading centre-right newspaper suggested the need for a bipartisan 'emergency administration' to manage the structural reforms outlined by the International Monetary Fund (*Kathimerini*, 8 November 2010), expressing the public's 'need to see a strong hand at the helm of the country' and 'for a government that will defend what needs to be done and an opposition that will stop behaving like a backbench naysayer' (*Kathimerini*, 21 June 2010). It is certainly true that the experience of the junta has often been critically evoked by protestors to condemn financial and physical punitiveness on the part of the state (e.g., with regard to the imposition of economic reforms and instances of police brutality; see protest imagery in Charitatou-Synodinou, 2010: 35, 58). That there has even been public discussion of the option of using the army to quell unrest during the upheavals of December 2008 (see further *Prin*, 6 December 2010), however, illustrates the extent to which the boundaries of acceptable state punitiveness have become untethered from the presumed liberal constraints of the junta legacy.

The concerns explicitly underpinning this evolution are discussed in the following section, which explores more particularly the relationship between fear of criminal victimisation and public punitiveness.

Fear of Crime and Punitiveness in Contemporary Greece

As Bakalaki (2003: 211) notes, Europeans and Americans have long seen the Greeks as the living embodiments of a Zorba-esque indifference to danger or even a proclivity to risk. Albeit discreetly, Greeks themselves also tend to endorse this stereotype, construing it as a positive national trait akin to agonistic masculinity that distinguishes them from an overly disciplined West. In recent years, however, and at least as concerns crime, Greeks have been characterised by a heightened consciousness of safety, not only matching but indeed exceeding their Western counterparts. The irony is that Greeks often only choose to see their heightened levels of safety consciousness as a process of convergence with the Western norm.

Fear of Crime and Confidence in the Police and Judicial Authorities

Ever since its inclusion in pertinent international comparative analyses in the early 2000s, Greece has ranked amongst the most crime-fearing nations in Europe and beyond. Juxtaposing the results of a nationwide survey conducted in Greece in 2001 with those of the International Crime Victimisation Survey (ICVS) of 2000 (in which Greece did not participate), Karydis found the perceived likelihood of burglary victimisation over the coming year to be by far the highest in Greece. In particular, 66 percent of respondents thought burglary victimisation was likely or very likely, a rate over twice as high as the international average of 31 percent, more than quadruple the US rate of 16 percent, and higher than any rate ever to have been recorded in the ICVS since it was first launched in 1989. Also, 35 percent of respondents in Greece reported feeling unsafe or very unsafe walking alone in their neighbourhood during the night, which was again the highest rate internationally, substantially higher than the international average of 23 percent, and more than double the US rate of 15 percent (Karydis, 2004: 152–156). The comparison with the US is telling, given that Greeks so often exclaim 'We have become like Chicago' or 'This is Texas' to describe their experience of increased insecurity (Bakalaki, 2003: 213).

More recently, the European Crime and Safety Survey (EU ICS) of 2005 found the public in Greece to be the most fearful of criminal victimisation on the continent. One in every two individuals surveyed (49 percent) considered burglary victimisation within the coming year to be likely or very likely. This rate, although lower than that recorded in 2001, was much higher than the European average of 30 percent, but also the fifth highest ever to have been recorded on the continent since the first sweep of the ICVS (the precursor of EU ICS) in 1989 (van Dijk et al., 2007a: 64–65, 117–118). Indeed, Greece ranked first even by global standards, as illustrated by van Dijk et al. in their synthesis of findings from the latest ICVS and EU ICS sweeps, which included countries such as the US, Japan, Mexico, New Zealand, Australia, Canada, and Bulgaria (see van Dijk et al., 2007b: 127–128). Moreover, four out of ten individuals in Greece (42 percent) reported feeling unsafe or very unsafe walking alone in their area of domicile after dark. This rate, which exceeded that recorded in 2001, was far higher than the European average (28 percent) and the third highest ever to have been recorded on the continent since the ICVS started running (van Dijk et al., 2007a: 66–67, 117–118). At a global level, it was the second highest rate after that of Bulgaria (see van Dijk et al., 2007b: 131–132). Some variation notwithstanding, prior and subsequent nationwide and local-level surveys have produced similar results (see, e.g.,

Panousis and Karydis, 1999; Zarafonitou, 2002; Vakiari and Kontargyri, 2009; Zarafonitou *et al.*, 2009; *Eleftherotypia*, 14 May 2009; Public Issue, 2009b; Hummelsheim *et al.*, 2010).

Unsurprisingly, people in Greece feel less safe living in areas where they think that types of crime such as burglary and vehicle theft are a serious problem (Christakopoulou *et al.*, 2001), and fear of crime tends to be greater amongst those who believe that crime rates have been rising (Zarafonitou, 2002). Consistently high levels of fear of crime may thus be linked to the prevailing and ever-spreading notion that the problem of crime has seriously worsened with time, both in terms of levels and patterns. In a nationwide survey conducted in 2005, for instance, 41 percent of respondents agreed that 'the state of crime' worsened over the past year. When the survey was repeated in 2009, the rate of respondents who expressed this view was more than double, at 88 percent, whilst 72 percent thought that 'the state of crime' had worsened 'a lot'. In this latter sweep, 61 percent of respondents felt unsafe in their area of domicile (Public Issue, 2009b; see also Public Issue, 2008; *Eleftherotypia*, 14 May 2009). From a qualitative point of view, meanwhile, crime is thought in Greece to have become more unpredictable and violent (Bakalaki, 2003; see also Public Issue, 2009b).

There is also evidence to suggest that fear of crime in Greece is significantly positively correlated with prior experience of victimisation (Tseloni, 2002; Tseloni and Zarafonitou, 2008; see additionally Karydis, 2004), whilst insufficient policing is the most common reason reported by Greeks to explain their lack of safety (Zarafonitou *et al.*, 2009; compare Vakiari and Kontargyri, 2009). Indeed, levels of fear of crime in the country are significantly negatively correlated with levels of perceived effectiveness of the police in controlling crime (see Kääriäinen, 2007: 421–422; Van de Walle and Raine, 2008: 27). Thus, in the EU ICS of 2005, only 57 percent of respondents gave a positive assessment of police effectiveness, a rate markedly below the European average of 67 percent and the third lowest on the continent (only Estonia and Poland ranked lower than Greece by this measure) (van Dijk *et al.*, 2007a: 79–80, 115–116). This was also the fifth lowest rate at a global level, with only Bulgaria, Estonia, Mexico, and Poland scoring lower than Greece (van Dijk *et al.*, 2007b: 142) (see also Lambropoulou *et al.*, 1996; Karydis, 2004; Lambropoulou, 2004; Zarafonitou *et al.*, 2009; *Eleftherotypia*, 14 May 2009).

In Greece, both fear of crime and perceived effectiveness of the police are significantly correlated (the former negatively and the latter positively) with citizen confidence in the national justice system (Van de Walle and Raine, 2008: 27, 22). It therefore comes as no surprise that the public in Greece expresses low levels of confidence in the justice system of the country: only 43.7 percent expressed 'a great deal or quite a lot of confidence' in the justice system in the World Values Survey of 1999–2000 (the fourth lowest rate amongst the EU-15 and below the median in global comparison), and 55 percent stated they tend to trust the justice system in the Eurobarometer Survey of spring 2006 (though this rate was above the EU-15 average of 50 percent) (ibid.: 59–61; Van de Walle, 2009: 25; see also *Eleftherotypia*, 14 May 2009). Domestic research also shows a high level of public dissatisfaction in Greece with what is perceived as 'lenient or very lenient' treatment of offenders by the judiciary, especially as concerns 'drug traffickers' (Zarafonitou *et al.*, 2009).

As far as trends over time are concerned, recent years have seen an overall increase in the number of individuals in Greece who believe that the effectiveness of neighbourhood policing has dropped. In a nationwide survey conducted in 2006, 31 percent stated that the quality of neighbourhood policing over the last year had deteriorated, 54 percent that it had remained the same, and 15 percent that it had undergone improvement. When the survey was repeated in 2009, the rate of respondents who saw deterioration in the quality of neighbourhood policing had gone up to 46 percent, those who saw stagnation amounted to 47 percent, and those who saw improvement only comprised 6 percent (Public Issue, 2009b; see also Public Issue, 2008). More generally, public confidence in the police 'in the fight against crime' has fallen. In a nationwide survey conducted in 2005, 54 percent expressed little or no confidence in the police, a rate that went up to 59 percent when the survey was repeated in 2009 (Public Issue, 2009b). Turning to the levels of public confidence in the justice system in Greece, Eurobarometer data for the period 1997–2006 reveal an overall decline, from 63 percent of respondents in the autumn of 1997 to 55 percent in the spring of 2006 (Van de Walle and Raine, 2008: 61). A comparison of data from the 2002 and 2004 rounds of the European Social Survey reveals a more impressive downward trend, from 62.3 percent in 2002 to

48 percent in 2004. Indeed, this downward trend was substantially starker in Greece than in any other surveyed country where public confidence in the justice system also fell during the period under consideration (ibid.: 19; for a discussion see Tsiganou, 2007).

At the same time that fear of crime has been rising and confidence in the police and judicial authorities has been dropping, citizens in Greece have been increasingly adopting situational crime prevention measures, from avoiding particular locales and making sure to keep house doors locked (Bakalaki, 2003) to investing in the hardware and services of the booming private security industry. For instance, nearly one in every two individuals (46 percent) surveyed in the EU ICS of 2005 stated that their home had a special (high-grade) door lock (van Dijk *et al.*, 2007a: 84, 117; see also van Dijk *et al.*, 2007b: 135–138; read further Yannakopoulos, 2007).

Public Punitiveness

Not unlike elsewhere in the West, citizens in Greece express support for a 'get tough' approach to crime control at a highly significant level, as Unnever and Cullen (2010) showed recently in their analysis of data from the 2006 Eurobarometer Survey of European Values and Societal Issues. According to more specific measurements, significant segments of the public in Greece tend to be supportive of punitive criminal justice policies and practices such as patrol policing (see, e.g., Karydis, 2004; Zarafonitou, 2008) and the use of imprisonment. At least as concerns the latter, comparison with other European jurisdictions puts Greece in a rather unflattering light. In the EU ICS of 2005, for example, Greece was the only European country other than the UK where more respondents opted for imprisonment as opposed to a community service order for recidivist burglars (30 percent chose the former and 27 percent the latter). Greece's rate of support for imprisonment placed it amongst the most punitive European nations by this measure (van Kesteren, 2009: 28; see also van Dijk *et al.*, 2007a: 87, 117), though not above the pertinent median in global comparison (see van Dijk *et al.*, 2007b: 148). More starkly still, the public in Greece was found to be the least likely in Europe to view a community service order as the most appropriate sentence for recidivist burglars (van Dijk *et al.*, 2007a: 89), with the second lowest rate of preference for a community service order ever to have been recorded on the continent since the first sweep of the ICVS in 1989 (ibid.: 117–118). In global comparison, only Mexico and Japan scored lower than Greece on this measure (van Dijk *et al.*, 2007b: 148).

Kühnrich and Kania (2005) present a methodologically different analysis of data from the EU ICS of 2005. Having first duly excluded true missing values, they demonstrate that 34.1 percent of the public in Greece favoured imprisoning recidivist burglars, which was the third highest rate in Europe (only the UK and Ireland ranked higher). Public support for a community service order stood at 46 percent, the third lowest rate after the UK and the Netherlands. Kühnrich and Kania also examine public punitiveness with reference to the duration of imprisonment, itself an important 'qualitative' indicator that usually goes unnoticed (Frost, 2008), even though it bears a significant positive correlation with support for imprisonment as such (van Dijk *et al.*, 2007b: 151–153), but also one with great relevance to the Greek case (see further Cheliotis, this collection). The proportion of respondents who opted for the longest possible custodial sentence (i.e., 'over ten years') in the same recidivist burglar scenario was higher in Greece than anywhere else on the continent (Kühnrich and Kania, 2005: 15–17; see further van Dijk *et al.*, 2007b: 151–153).

Greeks are more likely to favour stricter police treatment for immigrants than for natives (e.g., Panousis and Karydis, 1999), just as they are more likely to favour imprisoning immigrant offenders (Albanians in particular) than offenders from other socio-demographic categories (e.g., male juveniles, fathers of multiple children, unemployed young adults, and young women) (Zarafonitou *et al.*, 2009). Such attitudes, not unlike racist victimisation (van Dijk *et al.*, 2007a; Petoussi-Douli, 2008) and increased consent to situational crime control measures that compromise personal convenience and liberties since immigration into the country started rising in the early 1990s (Bakalaki, 2003; Figgou *et al.*, 2011), are linked to the widespread perception of immigrants as the major source of criminal danger and associated insecurities (Figgou *et al.*, 2011; see also Fakiolas, 1999; *To Vima*, 20 February 2000; *Eleftherotypia*, 14 May 2009,

20 February 2011; Karydis, this collection; Xenakis, this collection). This view is itself typically premised on one of two essentialist assumptions: either that immigrants are naturally prone to crime or that their poor conditions of living unavoidably push them into a life of illegality (ibid.; see also Figgou and Condor, 2007). Albanians are especially likely to be seen as dangerous, hence the term 'Albanian' is often used derogatorily by Greeks to describe immigrants in their entirety (Bakalaki, 2003; but see also Hatziprokopiou, 2006; Antonopoulos *et al.*, 2008).

Public punitiveness in Greece is also gauged with reference to the primary goal attributed to judicial punishment, with individuals selecting retribution qualifying as punitive. This approach, it should be noted parenthetically, has been rightly criticised by Maruna and King (2009) for missing that retributivists may well support minimal punishment; that harsh punishment may be justified on non-retributivist grounds such as incapacitation and deterrence; and that focusing on the goals people consciously attribute to punishment tends to obscure its unconscious expressive functions (see further Cheliotis, 2011; and later). In any case, the majority of Greeks surveyed choose an 'instrumentalist' response, whether in the form of incapacitation or general deterrence, although retributive and rehabilitative sentiments are far from absent. When operationalised as support for enhanced patrol policing, punitiveness bears a significant positive correlation with prior experience of victimisation. Conversely, when punitiveness is operationalised as support for imprisonment, it bears a significant positive correlation with fear of crime. Finally, when punitiveness is operationalised as support for retribution, it is significantly predicted by the experience of indirect victimisation (i.e., through knowing a victim) (see further Zarafonitou, 2008; Zarafonitou *et al.*, 2009).

Although not calling it as such, Papastamou *et al.* (2005) have measured punitiveness by reference to two other indicators, both of which are highly apposite to contemporary Greek realities: first, support for a range of 'anti-terrorist' policies, from surveillance of the citizenry in its entirety (including phone-tapping) and the tightening of border controls to the use of psychological or physical force during the questioning of suspects; and second, support for the denial of a range of human rights and civil liberties to individuals accused of terrorism, from the rights to a fair trial and protection from torture to the rights to vote and privacy of correspondence. Nearly a fifth of the sample surveyed (university students) supported such measures as the use of psychological or physical force during questioning, whilst two-fifths supported control measures specifically oriented against foreigners (i.e., simplification of extradition proceedings, denial of political asylum, and enhanced border controls) (ibid.: 253–254).[4] Also, half of the sample surveyed agreed with depriving individuals accused of terrorism of rights related either to privacy and individual physical integrity or to fair institutional treatment (ibid.: 253–255; for an older and somewhat similar survey see Lambropoulou *et al.*, 1996).

Other, seemingly less pertinent indicators of punitiveness in Greece have included support for the death penalty (which has long been abolished in the country, a caveat discussed below); support for vigilantism; support for carrying guns; and support for the use of truth serum on suspects by the police (which is not provided for by the law). Significant minorities have expressed support for the death penalty and vigilantism, but very few are those who have supported the carrying of guns, whilst views as to the use of truth serum by the police have been divided (Zarafonitou *et al.*, 2009: 99–109). Using data from the 2001 Eurobarometer Young Europeans Survey, Unnever and Cullen (2010) recently focused specifically on public support for the death penalty amongst youths aged 15–21 years old. In Greece, like in Belgium and Finland (but also in line with the broader international trend reported), support for the death penalty was found to be substantial and bore a significant positive correlation with the belief that crime rates are on the rise (see also Papastamou *et al.*, 2005). Unnever and Cullen explain that, even though the death penalty is unlikely to reappear in European jurisdictions in the foreseeable future given the pertinent constitutional ban imposed by the EU, it is still important to gauge public opinion on the use of this sanction around the continent. This is because

---

4   Three recent opinion polls showed very high levels of support amongst the public in Greece (from 59 to 80 percent) for the announced construction of a fence along a section of the country's borders with Turkey in the prefecture of Evros to prevent illegal immigration (Public Issue, 2011; *Proto Thema*, 16 January 2011; *Ethnos*, 17 January 2011).

reactive policies excluded by law are not unlikely to acquire symbolic significance in populist 'wars on crime'. For example, 'opposition to capital punishment may render political officials vulnerable. Such officials could be attacked as being elitist and "soft on crime" for not endorsing the use of the ultimate form of state legal power in the community's defence against an impending social collapse' (Unnever and Cullen, 2010: 851).

A number of further indicators of public punitiveness can be found in polling company research, including support for law and order over citizens' rights and liberties (Public Issue, 2007, 2009a, 2009b); support for the use of CCTV cameras in public places for security purposes (Public Issue, 2007, 2009b; see also Samatas, this collection); support for the establishment of neighbourhood watch schemes (Panousis and Karydis, 1999); support for a rise in the size of the police force (ibid.); support for police intervention during demonstrations and university occupations (Public Issue, 2009a, 2009b); support for the abolition of the university asylum law that forbids police from entering university buildings and campuses (ibid.; see also *Eleftherotypia*, 6 April 2009); support for mass arrests and prosecutions at times of urban disorder (Public Issue, 2009a); and support for punishing hood-wearing demonstrators (Public Issue, 2009b). The majority of people surveyed were commonly supportive of these measures. There is also short-term time series data on support for the abolition of the university asylum law and support for police intervention during demonstrations and university occupations, with an important increase having been recorded in both cases (measurements were taken before and after the December 2008 riots) (ibid.).

Another way of gauging trends in public punitiveness in Greece consists in looking directly at developments on the fronts of criminal justice policy and practice. This is not to say that criminal justice ever accurately reflects public views and desires (see, for example, van Kesteren, 2009). But if, as political psychologists suggest of representative democracies, the perceptions and preferences of citizens set limits to the design and implementation of governmental policies (see, e.g., Page and Shapiro, 1983; Gibson, 1992), then it is reasonable to infer a sufficient degree of correspondence between criminal justice policies and practices, on the one hand, and public attitudes, on the other. To take what is the most characteristic example in the Greek context, high levels of public support for imprisonment and its concomitant focus on immigrants have coincided with a significant rise in the actual use of imprisonment, with the numbers of non-Greeks kept behind bars swelling (see also van Dijk *et al.*, 2007b: 150–151).

In the section that follows, however, levels and patterns of public and state punitiveness as expressed through imprisonment are juxtaposed with levels and patterns of their purported antecedent – that is, of crime –, in order to bring into relief an emergent rationalist gap.

The Relationship between Crime and Imprisonment[5]

With a few exceptions (e.g., Kranidioti, 2003), the norm amongst criminologists of Greece is to ignore that a large proportion of the total volume of police-recorded crime in the country consists in traffic violations, namely, offences of little criminological interest that only very rarely result in imprisonment (see further Karydis, 2004: 39–40). It is not merely that crime rates are thereby inflated as such, but also that rising levels of imprisonment – and punitiveness, more generally – are unduly legitimated in response. The disconnect between trends in crime and imprisonment has been further obscured by a broader context of opposition to measuring the relationship between police-recorded crime and patterns of punishment, on the grounds that heavy court caseloads aggravate the time lag between the recording of the offence by the police and the adjudication of cases (see, e.g., Courakis, 2000: 345). The thematic and temporal scope of available data, in the following analysis extending to pre-trial detention and covering multi-year periods, clearly renders such argument redundant.

5   Our analysis in this section draws on crime data compiled by the Greek police and on imprisonment data compiled by the National Statistical Service of Greece (NSSG). Our findings as to the rates of crime in Greece are largely consistent with findings from self-reported victimisation surveys (see, e.g., Karydis, 2004; van Dijk *et al.*, 2005, 2007).

During the period 1980–2006, the annual total of police-recorded offences (including traffic offences such as speeding and illegal parking) increased by 57 percent, from 295,353 to 463,750. Expressed as a rate per 100,000 inhabitants, the volume of crime rose by 35.8 percent, from 3,063 in 1980 to 4,160 in 2006. During the same period, the annual total of traffic offences increased by 95.1 percent, from 114,138 to 222,720, and by 68.8 percent as a rate per 100,000 inhabitants, from 1,184 to 1,998. It follows that, in good part, the rise in the total volume of offences was because of the rise in the volume of traffic offences. Indeed, once one deducts the volume of traffic offences from the total volume of offences, one observes that the annual number of police-recorded crimes rose by 33 percent (from 181,215 to 241,030), and by a modest 15 percent as a rate per 100,000 inhabitants (from 1,879 to 2,161).

In any case, the rise in police-recorded offences cannot account for the fact that the annual total caseload of convicted and remand prisoners rose concurrently by 65.6 percent as an absolute number (from 10,703 in 1980 to 17,726 in 2006), by 43.2 percent as a rate per 100,000 inhabitants (from 111 to 159), and by 24.5 percent as a rate per 1,000 police-recorded offences (from 59 to 73.5).[6] To express the point differently, the likelihood of dealing with crime by way of imprisonment grew by a quarter during the period 1980–2006. The likelihood of imprisonment under conviction grew even stronger: by 29.7 percent as such (i.e., from 41 to 53.2 as a ratio per 1,000 police-recorded offences), by 129.5 percent for convictions of a year or more (i.e., from 19.3 to 44.3 as a ratio per 1,000 police-recorded offences), and by 246.1 percent for convictions of three years or more (i.e., from 10.4 to 36 as a ratio per 1,000 police-recorded offences). At the same time, the likelihood of pre-trial detention rose by 29.4 percent as a rate per 100,000 inhabitants (from 34 to 44), and by 12.7 percent as a rate per 1,000 police-recorded offences (from 18 to 20.3).

The rise in the use of imprisonment under conviction and especially for longer terms is commonly attributed to a rise in the caseload of prisoners

6   The imprisonment figures reported in this section do not take account of prisoners held in connection with traffic offences (see further Cheliotis, this collection).

convicted of a drug-related offence. Indeed, in 2006, drug offenders comprised the largest cohort in the total caseload of convicted prisoners (32.3 percent, up from 8 percent in 1980), in the caseload of convicted prisoners serving a term of a year or more (37.8 percent), and in the caseload of convicted prisoners serving a term of three years or more (43.2 percent) (see further Cheliotis, this collection). There is broad consensus that underpinning this development has been a mix of harsh reforms of sentencing and parole laws (e.g., providing that possession of small amounts of cannabis be punished more severely than possession of small amounts of heroin, and tightening the eligibility criteria for release of drug offenders on parole) and arbitrary punitive practices of sentencing (e.g., punishing petty drug possession according to the provisions for serious organised drug dealing) (see Lambropoulou, 2003; Cheliotis, this collection). None of the above trends, however, may be adequately understood unless close attention is paid to the nationality of those caught in the criminal justice net.

Regarding the nationality of convicted prisoners, official data collection only began in 1996. Between then and 2006, the annual total caseload of non-Greek convicts rose by 140.5 percent, from 2,253 (or 404 per 100,000 non-Greek inhabitants) to 5,420 (or 559 per 100,000 non-Greek inhabitants). Correspondingly, the proportion of non-Greeks amongst the total caseload of convicts increased from 25.3 percent to 41.1 percent. In 2006, and reflecting a long-standing upward trend, the majority (52.4 percent) of non-Greek convicted prisoners were Albanian. During the same period, the annual total caseload of Greek convicts increased by 16.8 percent, from 6,632 (or 65 per 100,000 Greek inhabitants) to 7,750 (or 76 per 100,000 Greek inhabitants), yet fell in reference to the annual total of cases of convicted prisoners, from 74.6 percent to 58.8 percent (see further Cheliotis, this collection).

The proportion of non-Greeks amongst the total caseload of convicts grew to become four times higher than the estimated proportion of non-Greeks in the general population of the country,[7] whilst the average

---

7   According to a recent snapshot of the prison population (including both convicted and remand prisoners) on 1 January 2010, non-Greeks comprised 55.5 percent of the total (6,307 out of 11,364). The data are available from the website of the Ministry of Justice, Transparency and Human Rights.

likelihood that a non-Greek is held in prison under conviction was 8.1 times higher than the equivalent likelihood for a Greek between 1996 and 2006. The discrepancy holds up (and indeed, widens) when one looks at the caseload of long-term convicts. In 2006, for instance, the proportion of non-Greeks amongst the total caseload of convicts serving a term of a year or more was 40.7 percent, and rose to 41.6 percent for terms of three years and beyond. Expressed as a ratio of rates per 100,000, between 1996 and 2006, the average likelihood that a non-Greek adult is in prison serving a term of a year or more was 7.9 times higher than the equivalent likelihood for a Greek adult, and 8.8 times higher for terms of three years and beyond.

The level and nature of non-Greeks' criminal involvement leave a lot unanswered as to the driving forces behind the overrepresentation of non-Greeks in the total caseload of convicted prisoners. Between 2000 and 2006, for example, the police-recorded rate of non-Greeks amongst offenders was 1.6 times higher than the rate of Greeks, but the likelihood of imprisonment under conviction was 7.9 times higher for non-Greeks than the equivalent likelihood for Greeks. Over the same period, non-Greeks represented an average of 43.2 percent in the total caseload of prisoners convicted of a drug-related offence, but secondary analysis of police data reveals that the average proportion of non-Greeks amongst the perpetrators of drug offences only stood at 10.9 percent (which was also equal to the estimated share of non-Greeks in the general population of the country). Expressed in terms of the ratio of rates per 100,000 population, the average likelihood that a non-Greek is held in prison under conviction for a drug offence was 9.4 times higher than the equivalent likelihood for a Greek, but the police-recorded rate of non-Greeks amongst the perpetrators of drug offences was only 1.5 times higher than the rate of Greeks.[8]

---

8   Not dissimilarly to their Greek counterparts, the most common main offence of which non-Greek prisoners had been convicted fell under the category of drug-related crimes (an average of 30.5 percent in the total caseload of non-Greek convicts). This was followed closely by the category of illegal entry into, departure from, and stay in the country (30.1 percent), and then by property offences (21.7 percent), whilst crimes against life and bodily harm were both rare (4.3 percent and 1.3 percent, respectively). These findings cast considerable doubt on the widespread stereotype that

Much more than in levels and patterns of offending, the reason why non-Greeks are over-represented behind bars is to be sought in the sentencing behaviour of judges. An emerging body of research evidence on drug-related (and other) court adjudications suggests that Greek judges are significantly more likely to order pre-trial detention or pass a custodial sentence – and indeed, a longer custodial sentence, whether in the first or second instance – when the defendant is non-Greek (see, e.g., Kalamatianou and Kosmatos, 2007; also Karydis, this collection).[9] Such findings chime with a survey conducted by Vagena-Palaiologou with members of the judiciary in the late 1990s and early 2000s. Of the 250 members of the judiciary surveyed, 99.6 percent stated that 'crime has been on the rise in recent years'; 35.6 percent that 'foreigners currently residing in Greece are exclusively responsible for the rise in crime'; 54.8 percent that 'there is racism in Greek society' (but 52.6 percent also stated that racism is due to foreigners' own conduct); 17 percent that 'foreign identity impacts negatively upon sentencing decisions'; and 61 percent that 'foreigners currently residing in Greece are too many' (Vagena-Palaiologou, 2006: 17–67).

But discrimination against non-Greeks must also be taken into account when interpreting crime rates as such, despite longstanding claims about low rates of reporting, recording, and clearing up crimes committed by non-Greek individuals and groups (see, e.g., *Kathimerini*, 22 November 1998). To begin with, the rate at which Greek citizens report crimes to the police exceeds the international average, as demonstrated by van Dijk *et al.*

---

foreigners are especially and even inherently prone to violence (see also Karasavoglou and Kiourktsoglou, 2006; Tsiganou, 2009). Not much more can be said here about imprisonment under conviction for illegal entry into, departure from, and stay in the country, only that this conviction offence category is of an administrative nature and concerns almost exclusively non-Greeks (but see also Xenakis, this collection).

9   In a study of appellate court rulings on cases of convicted felons, Koulouris and Spyrou (2009) found, first, that the majority of vindications concerned non-Greeks, which hints at unfairness in first-instance rulings, and second, that the waiting time for rulings on cases of non-Greeks was longer, which might as well be the outcome of discriminatory treatment against them. Whilst Koulouris and Spyrou report that nearly half of the felons in the sample had been convicted of a drug-related offence, and that the majority of them were non-Greeks, it is not clear what proportion of Greek and non-Greek drug felons were vindicated by second-instance courts.

(2007b: 110) in their synthesis of the latest data from the ICVS and EU ICS. In fact, frivolous incidents are also commonly reported, according to a study of calls to the police emergency service (see Panousis, 2001). Most crucially, Greek citizens are significantly more likely to report crimes to the police when offenders are believed – rightly or wrongly – to be immigrants (see, e.g., Antonopoulos, 2006).

Research has yet to focus specifically on the rates of reporting drug-related crimes, but it is known that the rate of reported exposure to drug-related problems in one's area of residence (i.e., seeing people dealing or using drugs, or finding syringes left by drug addicts) is far higher in Greece than anywhere else in Europe, but also the US, Canada, Australia, and New Zealand (see, respectively, van Dijk *et al.*, 2007a: 59–60, 112–113; van Dijk *et al.*, 2007b: 95–97); that the statistically significant positive correlation between reported exposure to drug-related problems in one's area of residence and levels of fear of crime is stronger in Greece than anywhere else on the continent (van Dijk *et al.*, 2007a: 68); and that the perceived rise in drug trafficking is attributed by the Greek public to the influx of migrants, especially Albanians (see, e.g., Antonopoulos, 2006: 149). It is reasonable to assume that a nation which rushes to report illegal parking and ringing car alarms to the police (Panousis, 2001: 131), tends to report drug-related crimes as well, even more so when drug-related crimes are blamed on immigrants.

The police, for their part, claim that recent years have seen a rise in both the quality of recording practices and the rates of clearing up crime (the latter also reaching 'above the international average', according to the Hellenic Police Headquarters (2009: 3)). In this context, organised crime in general and drug trafficking in particular have long been identified amongst the top priorities (Central Anti-Drug Coordinative Unit/ National Intelligence Unit, 2008). Whatever the progress made, however, it is bound to have been distorted, given that immigrant communities are systematically subject to over-policing, including a greater likelihood of being stopped and searched (Papandreou, 2009; EU-MIDIS, 2010) and so-called 'sweep' or 'cleaning operations' launched in the name of fighting illegal immigration, drug-related criminality, and prostitution (Petoussi-Douli, 2008). Immigrant individuals are also significantly more likely to be brought to a police station than Greek persons (see, e.g., Papantoniou *et al.*, 1998), and immigrant offenders remain easier to arrest due to the comparatively unsupportive social and physical environment in which they find themselves (a commonsensical finding shared openly by senior police officials; see, e.g., Tsandrizos (2008)). Indeed, non-Greeks are much more likely than Greeks to be arrested by the police regardless of whether the large number of arrests for deportation due to illegal stay in the country are accounted for (see further Papantoniou *et al.*, 1998: 29; Moschopoulou, 2005: 66–69; also Kranidioti, 2003: 155–156).[10]

Such findings also cohere with a survey conducted by Vagena-Palaiologou with police officers in the early 2000s. Of the 412 police officers surveyed, 92.2 percent stated that 'crime has been on the rise in recent years'; 35.9 percent that 'foreigners currently residing in Greece are exclusively responsible for the rise in crime'; 21.8 percent that 'criminal involvement amongst foreigners and especially Albanians is high due to their disrespect towards other humans' (some also stated that 'foreigners are born criminals'); 50 percent that 'there is racism in Greek society' (but 55 percent also stated that racism is due to foreigners' own conduct); 13.6 percent that foreigners are subject to discrimination by the authorities of formal social control; and 74 percent that the number of foreigners to remain in the country should not exceed that necessary for the economy (Vagena-Palaiologou, 2006: 68–109; see also Karydis, 1996; Papakonstantis, 2000; Antonopoulos *et al.*, 2008).

How to Account for Punitiveness?

The analysis up to this point exposes the irrationality underlying the levels and patterns of public and state punitiveness in Greece. That is to say, crime rates at best only bear a tenuous correlation with public support for punitive

---

10   No wonder many immigrants view the Greek police as hostile (Hatziprokopiou, 2003). Moreover, their experiences of discriminatory treatment by police authorities are negatively correlated with trust in the police (EU-MIDIS, 2010).

state interventions, even more so when targeting immigrants. Equally, levels of criminal victimisation as suggested by crime rates fall far short of adequately explaining trends in fear of crime (whether in terms of levels or 'objects') and the degree to which judicial punishment is associated with the 'instrumentalist' goals of incapacitation and deterrence. To top it all off, the ever-widening disconnect between crime trends, on the one hand, and the scope and nature of punitive policies and practices, on the other hand, problematises widespread public assessments of the criminal justice system as ineffective or lenient. (To anticipate crime-control champions: the point here is emphatically not that increased state punitiveness has helped keep crime rates low in Greece, though one might have expected the Greek public to be more persuaded that this is the case.)

Findings from survey research complicate things even further. Prior experience of victimisation does not significantly predict support for imprisonment, and is a negative correlate of support for retribution as the primary goal of judicial punishment. Also, fear of crime does not predict support for enhanced patrol policing nor for imprisoning immigrant offenders over offenders from other socio-demographic categories (see further Zarafonitou, 2008; Zarafonitou *et al.*, 2009). If still within the narrow context of statistical correlations, the emerging rationalist gaps have in recent years started to be addressed by academic researchers, who stretch their analyses beyond crime to include self-defined political standpoints (including voting behaviour) and broader social attitudes and concerns. Important material towards this direction has also been generated by commercial research. Several examples from both sources follow.

Fear of crime has been found to be greater amongst centrists and right-wingers (Panousis and Karydis, 1999), whilst perceiving immigrants as a 'life threat' has been shown to bear a significant positive correlation with religiosity (Karyotis and Patrikios, 2010). Meanwhile, confidence in the police 'in the fight against crime' has been found to be twice as high amongst those voting for the centre-right New Democracy party as for the centre-left 'Panhellenic Socialist Movement' (widely known as PASOK by its initials in Greek) (Public Issue, 2009b; but see also Panousis and Karydis, 1999). As in other European countries such as the Czech Republic, Estonia, Finland, Ireland, and Ukraine, so too in Greece, confidence in the justice system is greater amongst individuals who see themselves at the right end of the political left-right scale. Interest in politics, by contrast, is not a significant correlate of confidence in the justice system (Van de Walle and Raine, 2008).

As concerns punitiveness, holding a right-wing standpoint has been found to bear a significant positive correlation with support for imprisonment, support for the death penalty, and support for vigilantism. Interestingly, support for retribution as the primary goal of judicial punishment has been found to be greater amongst those holding a centrist or left-wing standpoint, whilst support for the use of truth serum by the police has been found to be greater amongst centre-leftists (Zarafonitou *et al.*, 2009). In line with trends observed more widely in the Western world, support for the death penalty in Greece is significantly lower amongst citizens who endorse egalitarian beliefs, and significantly higher amongst citizens who specifically express greater racial and ethnic intolerance (or 'animus towards immigrants'). Racially or ethnically intolerant citizens are also significantly more likely to support severely punishing criminals (even after such variables as age, gender, educational level, and marital status are controlled for) (Unnever and Cullen, 2010).

Support for 'anti-terrorist' measures, meanwhile, has been found to span all moderate political affiliations from Left to Right (including the Centre), but agreement with enhanced control measures specifically oriented against foreigners is greater amongst right-wingers and centrists (Papastamou *et al.*, 2005), as is support for mass arrests and prosecutions at times of urban disorder (Public Issue, 2009a). Surprisingly, perhaps, moderate left-wingers tend to agree with the denial of political participation rights to individuals accused of terrorism (Papastamou *et al.*, 2005). Support for punishing hood-wearing demonstrators has been found amongst the majority of those voting for the centre-left PASOK party and, even more so, the centre-right New Democracy party (Public Issue, 2009b). Finally, supporters of New Democracy appear far more likely than supporters of any other party to view the use of CCTV cameras in public places as protecting rather than infringing citizens' rights. Parties aside, individuals who position themselves on the Left are more likely than those who position themselves on the Right to view the use of CCTV cameras in public places as infringing rather than protecting citizens' rights (Public Issue, 2007).

Turning to the role of broader social concerns, a positive link has been found between fear of crime and various indicators of perceived decline in 'community well-being' or 'quality of life', from dissatisfaction with the built environment (e.g., cleanliness, greenery and parks, condition of the roads) and environmental quality (e.g., amount of traffic, parking facilities, quality of air), to other 'adverse neighbourhood' characteristics such as street begging and drug trafficking, to a sensed lack of social cohesion (e.g., the indifference of neighbours and passers-by in the event of a criminal attack), to rising rates of unemployment and immigration, to low rates of welfare provision (see further Christakopoulou *et al.*, 2001; van Dijk *et al.*, 2007a; van Dijk *et al.*, 2007b; Tseloni and Zarafonitou, 2008; Vakiari and Kontargyri, 2009; Public Issue, 2008; Hummelsheim *et al.*, 2010). It itself, immigration tends to be seen as a threat to the economic and cultural life of the country by individuals who exhibit greater religiosity (as measured by frequency of church attendance) (Karyotis and Patrikios, 2010). 'Quality of life' has been associated with public punitiveness, too. There is some evidence, for instance, that support for the use of imprisonment is significantly greater amongst citizens who rank immigration into the country as the most important social problem; those who rank unemployment as the most important social problem also tend to support the use of imprisonment, though this correlation has not been found to be statistically significant (Zarafonitou *et al.*, 2009).

Virtually no attempt has been made to date to account for the role of political standpoint, whilst attempts to theorise the role of broader social attitudes and concerns are scant and commonly limited to brief references to Durkheimian functionalism. Public and state punitiveness in the field of law and order, it is argued, serve to reaffirm moral order and promote social solidarity, both of which are challenged in the face of fundamental changes in the general structure of society and the experience of everyday life therein. Greece's transition to modernity and its constituent phenomena of urbanisation and immigration are thereby viewed as partaking of the psychosocial context of complexity and insecurity within which Greeks exhibit greater propensity towards punitiveness (see, e.g., ibid.; Unnever and Cullen, 2010).

A more nuanced perspective (and one that might well be applied to Durkheimian explanations themselves) is offered by Bakalaki. Rather than looking at the modernisation of Greece as a more or less completed process, Bakalaki invites us to consider the way in which Greeks openly attribute their enhanced safety consciousness and associated attitudes to a break with 'tradition' in favour of modernisation as a means by which they unconsciously convince themselves that the country is actually on the way to assimilation to an already modernised West. Thus, for example, the anxiety over the rise in burglaries and the various imperfect efforts to crack down on them are strangely reassuring in that they point to 'fulfilment of a longstanding collective dream – that Greece transcends poverty and backwardness and integrates itself into the modern world' (Bakalaki, 2003: 214). Whatever the viewpoint taken, insofar as punitiveness fulfils latent expressive functions, conscious beliefs about rising crime rates, about ineffective and lenient criminal justice agencies, and about the instrumental and moral missions of penality, may best be understood as rationalisations of otherwise irrational attitudes linked to the inherent human need for ontological security (see further Cheliotis, 2011).

Arguably, the expressive functions of punitiveness may be further elucidated by carefully disentangling the subtleties of general punitive attitudes. For instance, what has failed thus far to attract interpretative interest beyond the reporting of mere statistical correlations is that, whereas the effect of quality of life on fear of crime appears linear, this is not the case as regards punitiveness, where the relationship appears mediated by class. Recent survey research associating the latter (referred to as 'socio-economic level') with area of residence has shown that lower socioeconomic classes are more punitive than the upper class. But lower-middle-class respondents tend to be more punitive than their lower-class counterparts when it comes to such issues as support for the use of imprisonment and support for the imprisonment of immigrant offenders over those of other sociodemographic categories (Zarafonitou et al., 2009).

This brings us to a further and crucial point: just as public attitudes are never formed in a socio-cultural vacuum, so too social and cultural conditions are never plucked out of thin air. To put it differently, serious attention needs to be paid to the man-made, political processes by which social and cultural arrangements are produced in the first place. Once this analytic operation is performed, a whole new vista opens up for the explanation of punitiveness, attending simultaneously to the political functionality of punitive state action and the political processes that generate and reproduce one of its necessary prerequisites; a sufficient degree of punitive sentiment amongst the public (Cheliotis, 2011). Thus, for example, the role of the mass media in galvanising or inflaming public punitiveness cannot be adequately grasped just by reference to the levels and patterns of media production or consumption, however interesting and arguably important these may be. Whilst the media constitute a field with its own rules, these rules are defined both by its position in the world at large and by the attractions and repulsions to which it is subject from the 'meta-fields' of politics and the economy (Bourdieu, 1998). It is in this spirit that Hall *et al.* (1978) argue that sensationalised media reporting on crime, on the one hand, and harsh penal measures by the capitalist state and its agencies, on the other hand, combine to displace mass economic and ontological insecurities onto powerless minorities, thereby perpetuating and strengthening class rule (see further Cheliotis, 2010).[11] In short, accounting for trends in punitiveness requires no less than a political economy perspective that points to the material efficacy of symbolic power and the symbolic efficacy of material power, as these stand to one another in a relationship of mutual constitution (Wacquant, 2009).

This perspective has yet to be developed in the contemporary Greek context. As a step towards this direction, we revisit below the question begged by any claim that punitiveness performs an expressive function: 'expressive of what?' (Maruna and King, 2004: 93). In so doing, we take our cue from political economies of punishment in jurisdictions elsewhere (see further De Giorgi, 2007) and point to insecurities stemming from domestic trends in poverty and social inequality, the labour market, and welfare provision. These trends, we suggest, should not only constitute a basis for enriched empirical inquiries into the causes of punitiveness, but also serve as the framework within which past and future data are to be interpreted.

11   One could develop a similar argument in relation to the role played by religious elites in Greece (on which see further Karyotis and Patrikios, 2010).

The Roots of Social Insecurity

In Greece, lower- and middle-class anxieties are rooted in the social, political, and economic tensions typical of semi-peripheral societies: the particularly strained dynamics of social rights and mobility, political representation and state provision, and labour relations and profit-making. According to world-systems theory, 'core' and 'peripheral' states denote the winners and losers of international commodity exchange. Greece is a semi-peripheral state because it hosts a fairly even combination of high- and low-profit production processes employing both capital-intensive and labour-intensive techniques, and involving both skilled and highly-paid labour as well as coerced low-wage labour. It is this divided nature of production processes that, in semi-peripheral states such as Greece, tends to generate sharp struggles between higher and lower socioeconomic classes (and external economic actors), as each seek to influence state structures and policies in their favour (see further Tayfur, 2003; Featherstone and Papadimitriou, 2008). Whilst the vagaries of international commodity exchange have exerted strong pressures over the evolution of socio-economic conditions in Greece, national elites have played a crucial role in determining the shape of those conditions and their trajectories.

Since the mid-1980s, the country has seen the persistence of high levels of poverty and inequality. Although there was a significant drop in absolute poverty in Greece between the early 1960s and early 1980s, it has hovered at around 20 percent thereafter, one of the highest rates amongst EU and OECD member-states (see further Balourdos, 2004; Tsakloglou and Mitrakos, 2006; Lampousaki, 2010a; NSSG, 2010a; OECD, 2010). The country also saw an overall reduction in income inequality from the mid-1980s to the mid-2000s (OECD, 2009), but this slowed between 2001 and 2004 (Medgyesi, 2008) and here, too, levels have remained amongst the highest of the EU-27 (NSSG, 2010b). A number of factors have served to consolidate high levels of poverty and inequality, including the underlying structural weaknesses of the Greek economy (which stimulated the emergence of mass unemployment in the 1980s; see below), a weak labour force as indicated by low average wage levels and high levels of worker pauperisation, high levels of clientelism and corruption, and regressive tax and highly inadequate welfare systems (Papadimitriou, 2006; Tikos, 2008; Wolff, 2010).

The last three decades have also seen the national levels of unemployment undergo a significant rise. The rate of unemployment rose over the 1980s and 1990s, reaching a high of 12 percent in 1999 and henceforth overtaking the European average (Eurostat, 2009). The rate fell as of 2000 and, by the second half of the decade, had returned to levels of the late 1980s and early 1990s (IMF World Economic Outlook Database). Following the unveiling of the Greek financial crisis in late 2009, however, unemployment leapt from 8.5 percent to over 12 percent in 2010, with youth unemployment standing at over 32 percent (see *The Guardian*, 13 August 2010). Whilst aggravated by the onset of neoliberal policies over the 1990s, the problem of mass unemployment in Greece has emerged from the comparative weaknesses of the national economy and its semi-peripheral character. Over the past thirty years, this character was increasingly veiled by investment from, and market access to, the EU, which paved the way to the enlargement of the national labour force, attracting more women (Kanellopoulos and Mavromaras, 1999), immigrants, and Greeks who would otherwise emigrate (Mihail, 1996). Nevertheless, stubbornly low levels of investment in research and development activities (amongst the lowest in the EU; Seferiades, 2006), coupled with deep-seated features of the business sector (i.e., its composition by small and medium-sized enterprises specialising in low-tech industry or service activities; Liagouras *et al.*, 2003), ensured that Greeks would increasingly find their aspirations – heightened in the meantime by expanding education and media consumption – unmet by the domestic job market.

Reflective of this semi-peripheral environment, the Greek labour force has historically been weak, as illustrated by the low level of average wages and the inadequate structures of welfare protection and union representation (Seferiades, 1999, 2003; Petmesidou, 2006). Indeed, and despite allegations to the contrary (including by the OECD, 2010; and IMF, 2009), the Greek labour market has long been characterised by low wages, low indirect labour costs, and high flexibility (e.g., seasonal and part-time work, inadequate provisions for compensation and notice of job redundancies, and high wage elasticity; European Committee of Social Rights, 2010; Livanos, 2010; see further Mihail, 1996; Seferiades, 1999, 2003; Papadimitriou, 2006). From the 1990s, the relatively slow and stilted introduction of policies such as the dismantling of employment safeguards, the lowering of labour costs, the reduction of protectionism, the expansion of credit liberalisation, the deregulation of the market, and the privatisation of public services, primarily constituted a challenge to the middle-class workforce (see Staikouras, 2004; Pagoulatos, 2003; Tsakalotos, 2008; Spanou, 2008; OECD, 2010). Equally, the reforms introduced in 2010 that halved the severance pay of white-collar workers, lowered the threshold for collective dismissals, and reduced the minimum wage for young people under the ages of 25 and 18 to 84 percent and 70 percent of the national minimum wage, respectively (Lampousaki, 2010b), worked largely to formalise an already flexible market and extend its ramifications for the middle classes.

To date, the disproportionate impact of high informal flexibility in the labour market on lower socio-economic classes has been exacerbated by the state-sanctioned particularism of welfare provision, such as the differential provisions made for social insurance for specific professional sectors of the workforce. These arrangements have left a durable legacy of uneven distribution and a large proportion of the population entirely uncovered (Petmesidou, 2006; Tikos, 2008). Particularly vulnerable have been the self-employed and, of course, those working in the informal economy, both very sizeable sectors in EU comparison and both lacking union representation. The self-employed comprised over 21 percent of the total workforce in 2007, which was more than twice the EU-27 average (see Pedersini and Coletto, 2009), whilst the informal economy has been one of the largest in the EU (Schneider and Buehn, 2009; Matsaganis and Flevotomou, 2010). Amongst the most vulnerable groups of workers are immigrants, the majority of whom are confined to low-paid, menial, and technical labour in the informal economy by the overshadowing pincer pressures of exploitative immigration policies and selective repression by law enforcement (see Lawrence, 2005; and earlier).

On the one hand, social inequalities have been exacerbated by the minimalist and ineffective provision of welfare by the Greek state (for example, despite rising social expenditure over the past half-century, social transfers by the state have been amongst the least successful in reducing the risk of poverty by European comparison; see Seferiades, 2006; Wolff, 2010; Lampousaki, 2010a). On the other hand, inequalities have been compounded by a system of taxation that redistributes wealth regressively, by the prevalence of tax evasion (most common amongst the decile of the population with the highest level of income), and by entrenched practices of clientelism that sustain the power of state elites (see Papatheodorou, 2006; Matsaganis and Flevotomou, 2010; Pagoulatos, 2003; Petmesidou, 2006). Since the 1980s, this conjunction of low levels of social transfers, rising tax ratios, and mass unemployment, has functioned to offset labour gains from increases in real wages, ensuring that Greek workers face a far higher risk of poverty than the vast majority of their European counterparts (Maniatis, 2003; Tsakalotos, 2008; Papadimitriou, 2006; Tikos, 2008; Wolff, 2010).

This is not to say that living standards did not rise from the 1980s onwards; there was significant growth in household consumption from the 1990s onwards (by 22 percent between 1993/4 and 1998/9, and by 12.1 percent between 1998/9 and 2004/5; NSSG, 2001a). But this was facilitated by the deregulation of both consumer and housing credit, which in turn produced a steep rise in household indebtedness from the 1990s onwards (particularly amongst higher-income groups; see Mitrakos *et al.*, 2005). Although the ratio of household debt to national income has been comparatively low by European standards, the average annual rise in loans for housing and consumer goods has far outstripped that of the Eurozone in recent years (see Athanassiou, 2007). In 2009, a pan-European public opinion survey placed Greeks amongst those most likely to report serious financial problems and difficulties in keeping up with the payment of bills and credit commitments (Eurobarometer, 2010). Thus, consumerist expectations have advanced at a considerably faster pace than poverty and inequality have declined. Moreover, consumerism has expanded upon the shaky foundation of indebtedness, set against the background of rising unemployment.

Conclusion: Towards a Political Economy of Punitiveness

Given the above trends, it seems likely that what lies behind ever-rising levels of public and state punitiveness in Greece is, in good part, a growing sense of insecurity amongst the middle classes. Whilst lower socio-economic classes have long faced severe and multifaceted insecurities, it is the middle classes that have increasingly found themselves subjected to a range of new pressures over the last three decades, pressures that have combined to fuel the experience known as 'fear of falling'. This, as Jock Young has theorised, involves the dread of an 'ever-present possibility of downward mobility, of a descent into the underclass, a loss of control, of dignity' (Young, 2007: 44; see also Young, 1999). This is not to imply that the process by which fear of falling translates into punitiveness is unmediated (nor indeed that punitiveness is absent amongst other socioeconomic classes, though there it can take different forms).

Insofar as the pressures exerted upon the middle classes and the attendant fear of falling have been the outcome of state policy – and it is our argument that the state has played a major role in this respect –, they cannot but pose grave challenges to the authority of elected governments. Indeed, whether out of retributive impulse or purely instrumentally, middle-class citizens may adopt a 'punitive' stance against political elites thought to bear responsibility for the predicaments at issue, the mildest and most common example of which is the voting out of incumbent parties. In the continuing absence of concrete solutions, discourses meant to absolve domestic elites from blame (for example, the fatalistic rhetoric of globalisation and its positive promise of eventual prosperity for citizens and nation-states alike; Bourdieu and Wacquant, 1999; Harcourt, 2009), may only provide partial and, at any rate, temporary relief.

With a view to alleviating the mounting deficit in the legitimacy of their authority, as well as its potential consequences, but without practically addressing its root causes, state elites have deployed a law-and-order discourse and the use of punishment as symbolic devices by which middle-class anxieties are consecutively displaced onto 'actionable' fractions of the population and are 'acted out' against them. It seems no coincidence that state and middle-class punitiveness are so closely aligned, as illustrated by the way in which the use of imprisonment in general and against non-Greeks in particular has found greatest support amongst the middle classes. It seems no coincidence, either, that the middle classes concurrently display the strongest conviction that unemployment constitutes the gravest social problem in the country, and are most adamant that rising unemployment has been caused by the 'mass influx of immigrants' (see, e.g., Zarafonitou *et al.*, 2009). To the extent that the twin processes of displacement and 'acting out' may be successful, this is due to the nature of the anxieties they seek to manipulate. Indeed, a constant finding in pertinent international scholarship is that, when feeling trapped in situations of intense insecurity as to their actual life prospects, humans exhibit greater susceptibility to political myths which refocus danger and call for harsh reaction (see further Cheliotis, 2011).

The thesis developed in this chapter requires both thematic elaboration and thorough empirical testing. As concerns the former, future work should encompass such issues as the mechanisms by which public attitudes towards crime and punishment are shaped, the reasons why crime is selected over other risks, and the influence of political institutions on levels and patterns of state punitiveness (ibid.). Turning to the matter of testing our thesis empirically, the relationship between class and public punitiveness has been understudied in the Greek context. Research has tended to make limited use of proxies for class and without necessarily recognising them as such, whilst there has been little systematic attempt to provide an account of the evolution in punitive attitudes over time, let alone from a political economy perspective.

References

Antonopoulos, G.A. (2006) 'Public Reporting of Criminal Activities to the Police in Greece: Is there a Difference when the Offender is Migrant?', *European Journal of Crime, Criminal Law and Criminal Justice* 14(2): 135–160.

Antonopoulos, G.A., Tierney, J. and C. Webster (2008) 'Police Perception of Migra-
    tion and Migrants in Greece', *European Journal of Crime, Criminal Law and
    Criminal Justice* 16(4): 353–378.
Athanassiou, E. (2007) 'Prospects for Household Borrowing in Greece and Their
    Importance for Growth', *South-Eastern Europe Journal of Economics* 5(1):
    89–101.
Athenian (1972) *Inside the Colonels' Greece.* London: Chatto & Windus.
Bakalaki, A. (2003) 'Locked into Security, Keyed into Modernity: The Selection of
    Burglaries as Source of Risk in Greece', *Ethnos* 68(2): 209–229.
Balourdos, D. (2004) 'Poverty', in D. Charalambis, L. Maratou-Alipranti and A. Had-
    jiyanni (eds) *Recent Social Trends in Greece: 1960–2000*, pp. 660–668. Montreal:
    McGill-Queen's University Press.
Bermeo, N. (1995) 'Classification and Consolidation: Some Lessons from the Greek
    Dictatorship', *Political Science Quarterly* 110(3): 435–452.
Bourdieu, P. (1998) *Acts of Resistance: Against the Tyranny of the Market.* New York:
    The New Press.
Bourdieu, P. and L. Wacquant (1999) 'On the Cunning of Imperialist Reason', *Theory,
    Culture & Society* 16(1): 41–58.
Central Anti-Drug Coordinative Unit/National Intelligence Unit (2008) *Report
    on Drugs in Greece for the Year 2007* [in Greek]. Available online at: http://
    www.astynomia.gr/images/stories/NEW/SODN%20ENTYPO%202008%20
    upload.pdf
Charitatou-Synodinou, M. (2010) *Ash and... Burberry: December 2008 through Slo-
    gans, Images and Texts* [in Greek]. Athens: ΚΨΜ.
Cheliotis, L.K. (2010) 'The Ambivalent Consequences of Visibility: Crime and Pris-
    ons in the Mass Media', *Crime, Media, Culture* 6(2): 169–184.
Cheliotis, L.K. (2011) 'Governing through the Looking-Glass: Neoliberalism, Mana-
    gerialism and the Psychopolitics of Crime Control' [in Italian], *Studi sulla
    questione criminale* 6(1): 47–94.
Cheliotis, L.K. and S. Xenakis (2010) 'What's Neoliberalism Got to Do With It?
    Towards a Political Economy of Punishment in Greece', *Criminology & Crimi-
    nal Justice* 10(4): 353–373.
Christakopoulou, S., Dawson, J. and A. Gari (2001) 'The Community Well-Being
    Questionnaire: Theoretical Context and Initial Assessment of its Reliability
    and Validity', *Social Indicators Research* 56(3): 321–351.
Clogg, R. (1986) *A Short History of Modern Greece.* Cambridge: Cambridge Uni-
    versity Press.
Courakis, N. (2000) 'Juvenile Delinquency and Values in Contemporary Greece', in
    I. Daskalaki, P. Papadopoulou, D. Tsamparli, I. Tsiganou and E. Fronimou (eds)
    Offenders and Victims at the Doorstep of the 21st Century [in Greek], pp. 335–357.
    Athens: EKKE.

De Giorgi, A. (2006) *Re-Thinking the Political Economy of Punishment: Perspectives on Post-Fordism and Penal Politics*. Aldershot: Ashgate.

Diamandouros, P.N. (1997) 'Southern Europe: A Third Wave Success Story', in L.J. Diamond (ed.) *Consolidating the Third Wave Democracies: Regional Challenges*, pp. 3–25. Baltimore and London: The Johns Hopkins University Press.

Dimitras, P.E. (1990) 'Greek Public Attitudes: Continuity and Change', *International Journal of Public Opinion Research* 2(2): 92–115.

Eleftherotypia (6 April 2009) 'Polls Show a Sense of Insecurity' [in Greek].

Eleftherotypia (14 May 2009) 'Only 10 percent of Cretans Trust the Greek Police and the Justice System' [in Greek].

Eleftherotypia (20 February 2011) 'Racism in Numbers' [in Greek].

Ethnos (17 January 2011) '80 percent Vote "Yes" to the Construction of a Wall in Evros' [in Greek].

Eurobarometer (2010) *Poverty and Social Exclusion*. Brussels: European Commission.

European Committee of Social Rights (2010) *European Social Charter: Conclusions XIX-2 (2009) (Greece): Articles 3, 11, 12, 13, 14 and Article 4 of the Additional Protocol of the Charter*. Strasbourg: Council of Europe.

EU-MIDIS (European Union Minorities and Discrimination Survey) (2010) *Data in Focus Report: Police Stops and Minorities*. Vienna: European Union Agency for Fundamental Rights.

Eurostat (2009) *Europe in Figures: Eurostat Yearbook 2009*. Luxemburg: Office for Offical Publications of the European Union.

Fakiolas, R. (1999) 'Socio-Economic Effects of Immigration in Greece', *Journal of European Social Policy* 9(3): 211–229.

Featherstone, K. and D. Papadimitriou (2008) *The Limits of Europeanisation: Reform Capacity and Policy Conflict in Greece*. Basingstoke: Palgrave Macmillan.

Figgou, L. and S. Condor (2007) 'Categorising Category Labels in Interview Accounts about the "Muslim Minority" in Greece', *Journal of Ethnic and Migration Studies* 33(3): 439–459.

Figgou, L., Sapountzis, A., Bozatzis, N., Gardikiotis, A. and P.P. Pantazis (2011) 'Constructing the Stereotype of Immigrants' Criminality: Accounts of Fear and Risk in Talk about Immigration to Greece', *Journal of Community & Applied Social Psychology* (DOI: 10.1002/casp.1073).

Frost, N.A. (2008) 'The Mismeasure of Punishment: Alternative Measures of Punitiveness and Their (Substantial) Consequences', *Punishment & Society* 10(3): 277–300.

Gibson, J.L. (1992) 'The Political Consequences of Intolerance: Cultural Conformity and Political Freedom', *American Political Science Review* 86(2): 338–356.

Hall, S., Critcher, C., Jefferson, T., Clarke, J. and B. Roberts (1978) *Policing the Crisis: Mugging, the State, and Law and Order*. London: Macmillan.

Harcourt, B.E. (2009) 'Neoliberal Penality: A Brief Genealogy', *Theoretical Criminology* 14(1): 74–92.

Haritos-Fatouros, M. (2003) *The Psychological Origins of Institutionalised Torture*. London: Routledge.

Hatziprokopiou, P.A. (2006) *Globalisation, Migration and Socio-Economic Change in Contemporary Greece: Processes of Social Incorporation of Balkan Immigrants in Thessaloniki*. Amsterdam: Amsterdam University Press.

Hellenic Police Headquarters (2009) *Criminality during the First Six Months of 2009: Effectiveness of Police Services* [in Greek], Public Report. Available online at: http://www.astynomia.gr/images/stories/2009/DIAFOR09/120809_sxolia_egklhmat_Aexam2009.pdf

Hummelsheim, D., Hirtenlehner, H., Jackson, J. and D. Oberwittler (2010) 'Social Insecurities and Fear of Crime: A Cross-National Study on the Impact of Welfare State Policies on Crime-Related Anxieties', *European Sociological Review* (doi: 10.1093/esr/jcq010).

Huntington, S. (1991) *The Third Wave: Democratisation in the Late Twentieth Century*. Oklahoma: University of Oklahoma Press.

IMF (International Monetary Fund) (2009) *Greece: Selected Issues*: IMF Country Report 9/245. Available online at: http://www.imf.org/external/pubs/ft/scr/2009/cr09245.pdf

Kääriäinen, J.T. (2007) 'Trust in the Police in 16 European Countries: A Multilevel Analysis', *European Journal of Criminology* 4(4): 409–435.

Kalamatianou, K. and K. Kosmatos (2007) 'The Treatment of Foreigners by the Penal Justice System: A Comparative Study of Decisions by the Five-membered Appelate Court of Thessaloniki', in S. Georgoulas (ed.) *Criminology in Greece Today: A Volume in Honour of Stergios Alexiadis* [in Greek], pp. 281–304. Athens: KYM.

Kanellopoulos, C.N. and K.G. Mavromaras (1999) *Male-Female Labour Market Participation and Wage Differentials in Greece*, Discussion Paper No. 70. Athens: Centre of Planning and Economic Research (KEPE).

Karakatsanis, N.M. (2001) *The Politics of Elite Transformation: The Consolidation of Greek Democracy in Theoretical Perspective*. Westport, CT: Praeger.

Karasavoglou, A.G. and C. Kiourktsoglou (2006) *Foreigners' Lawbreaking in the Periphery of Eastern Macedonia and Thrace: A Empirical Study of the Years 2003 and 2004* [in Greek]. Kavala: Technological Educational Institute of Kavala.

Karydis, V. (1996) *The Criminality of Immigrants in Greece: Issues of Theory and Anti-Crime Policy* [in Greek]. Athens: Papazissis.

Karydis, V. (2004) *Hidden Criminality: A National Victimological Survey* [in Greek]. Athens-Komotini: Ant. N. Sakkoulas Publishers.

Karyotis, G. and S. Patrikios (2010) 'Religion, Securitisation and Anti-Immigration Attitudes: The Case of Greece', *Journal of Peace Research* 47(1): 43–57.

Kassimeris, C. (2010) *Greece and the American Embrace: Greek Foreign Policy Towards the US and the Western Alliance*. London: I.B. Tauris.

Kathimerini (22 November 1998) 'Lawbreakers have become more professional' [in Greek].

Kathimerini (27 February 2009) 'When Inmates Take Over the Asylum'.

Kathimerini (11 May 2010) 'Democracy Will Pay the Price'.

Kathimerini (10 June 2010) 'While the State Simply Looks On'.

Kathimerini (21 June 2010) 'Need for Responsible Leadership'.

Kathimerini (1 October 2010) 'Truckers Hint at Compromise Deal'.

Kathimerini (8 November 2010) 'Time to Rise to the Occasion'.

Kioukias, D. (1993) 'Political Ideology in Post-Dictatorial Greece: The Experience of Socialist Dominance', *Journal of Modern Greek Studies* 11(1): 51–73.

Koulouris, N. and S. Spyrou (2009) 'A Chronographic Analysis of the Administration of Penal Justice: The Effects of Appellate Decisions on the Serving of Custodial Sentences' [in Greek], in N. Koulouris (ed.) *On Standby: Korydallos Prison*, pp. 197–235. Athens-Komotini: Ant. N. Sakkoulas Publishers.

Kranidioti, M. (2003) 'Foreigners' Criminality in Greece: Theory, Research and Stances on Anti-crime Policy' [in Greek], in N.E. Courakis (ed.) *Anti-crime Policy, Vol. IV*, pp. 147–190. Athens-Komotini: Ant. N. Sakkoulas Publishers.

Kühnrich, B. and H. Kania (2005) *Attitudes towards Punishment in the European Union: Results from the 2005 European Crime Survey (ECSS) with Focus on Germany*, EU ICS Working Paper Series. Brussels: Gallup Europe.

Lambropoulou, E. (2003) 'Drug Policy in Greece: A Balance between Enforcement and Persuasion', *European Journal of Crime, Criminal Law and Criminal Justice* 11(1): 18–39.

Lambropoulou, E. (2004) 'Citizens' Safety, Business Trust and Greek Police', *International Review of Administrative Sciences* 70(1): 89–110.

Lambropoulou, E., Tsouramanis, C., Koulouris, N. and R. Soustiel (1996) 'An Inquiry into the "Situation of Opinion" of Law School Students about Crime, its Protagonists, Criminality, and the System of Penal Justice' [in Greek], *Chronicles* 10: 39–67.

Lampousaki, S. (2010a) *Working Poor in Europe: Greece. INE/GSEE Submission to a Comparative Study by the European Working Conditions Observatory (EWCO)*. Available online at: http://wew.eurofound.europa.eu/ewco/studies/tn0910026s/index.htm

Lampousaki, S. (2010b) *New Law Facilitates Dismissals and Cuts Labour Costs. INE/GSEE Submission to the European Industrial Relations Observatory (EIRO)*. Available online at: http://www.eurofound.europa.eu/eiro/2010/07/articles/gr1007019i.htm

Lawrence, C. (2005) 'Re-Bordering the Nation: Neoliberalism and Racism in Rural Greece', *Dialectical Anthropology* 29(3–4): 315–334.

Liagouras, G., Protogerou, A. and Y. Caloghirou (2003) 'Exploring Mismatches Between Higher Education and the Labour Market in Greece', *European Journal of Education* 38(4): 413–426.

Livanos, I. (2010) 'The Wage-Local Unemployment Relationship in a Highly Regulated Labour Market: Greece', *Regional Studies* 44(4): 389–400.

Lyrintzis, C. (2006) 'The Changing Party System: Stable Democracy, Contested "Modernisation"', in K. Featherstone (ed.) *Politics and Policy in Greece: The Challenge of Modernisation*, pp. 20–37. London: Routledge.

Maniatis, T. (2003) 'The Net Social Wage in Greece 1958–1995', *International Review of Applied Economics* 17(4): 377–398.

Maruna, S. and A. King (2004) 'Public Opinion and Community Penalties', in A.E. Bottoms, S. Rex and G. Robinson (eds) *Alternatives to Prison: Options for an Insecure Society*, pp. 83–112. Cullompton: Willan.

Maruna, S. and A. King (2009) 'Once a Criminal, Always a Criminal?: "Redeemability" and the Psychology of Punitive Public Attitudes', *European Journal on Criminal Policy and Research* 15(1–2): 7–24.

Matsaganis, M. and M. Flevotomou (2010) *Distributional Implications of Tax Evasion in Greece*, GreeSE Paper 31. London: Hellenic Observatory, London School of Economics.

Mazower, M. (1997) 'Policing the Anti-Communist State in Greece, 1922–1974', in M. Mazower (ed.) *The Policing of Politics in the Twentieth Century: Historical Perspectives*, pp. 129–150. Oxford: Berghahn Books.

Mazower, M. (2000) 'The Cold War and the Appropriation of Memory: Greece after Liberation', in I. Deák, J.T. Gross and T. Judt (eds) *The Politics of Retribution in Europe: World War II and its Aftermath*, pp. 212–232. Princeton, NJ: Princeton University Press.

Medgyesi, M. (2008) 'Income Distribution in European Countries: First Reflections on the Basis of EU-SILC, 2005', in I.G. Tóth (ed.) *Tárki European Social Report*, pp. 88–105. Budapest: Tárki.

Mihail, D.M. (1996) 'Unemployment and Labour Market Policies in Greece', *Spoudai* 46(1–2): 16–30.

Mitrakos, T.M., Simigiannis, G.T. and P.T. Tzamourani (2005) 'Indebtedness of Greek Households: Evidence from a Survey', *Bank of Greece: Economic Bulletin* 25: 13–35.

Montero, J.R. and M. Torcal (1990) 'Voters and Citizens in a New Democracy: Some Trend Data on Political Attitudes in Spain', *International Journal of Public Opinion Research* 2(2): 116–140.

Moschopoulou, A.G. (2005) *Immigrants' Criminality: Representations of the Phenomenon in the Afternoon Press: 1990–1999* [in Greek]. Athens-Komotini: Ant. N. Sakkoulas Publishers.

NSSG (2010a) 'Statistics on Income and Living Conditions 2008: Risk of Poverty'. Piraeus: NSSG [Press Release].

NSSG (2010b) 'Statistics on Income and Living Conditions 2008: Income Inequality'. Piraeus: NSSG [Press Release].

OECD (2009) *OECD Factbook 2009: Economic, Environmental and Social Statistics.* Paris: OECD.

OECD (2010) *Greece at a Glance: Policies for a Sustainable Recovery.* Paris: OECD.

Page, B.I. and R.Y. Shapiro (1983) 'Effects of Public Opinion on Public Policy', *American Political Science Review* 77(1): 175–190.

Pagoulatos, G. (2003) *Greece's New Political Economy: State, Finance and Growth from Postwar to EMU.* Basingstoke: Palgrave Macmillan.

Panourgiá, N. (2009) *Dangerous Citizens: The Greek Left and the Terror of the State.* New York: Fordham University Press.

Panousis, G. (2001) '"100": Facts and a First Approach to the Operation of the Emergency Police Service' [in Greek], in G. Panousis and S. Vidali (eds) *Texts on the Police and Policing*, pp. 129–139. Athens-Komotini: Ant. N. Sakkoulas Publishers.

Panousis, G. and V. Karydis (1999) 'Fear of Victimisation, Insecurity and Police Effectiveness' [in Greek], in Institute V Project Research Consulting, *Public Opinion in Greece: Studies-Opinion Polls 1999–2000*, pp. 247–259. Athens: Nea Synora – A.A. Livanis Publications.

Papadimitriou, D. (2006) 'The Limits of Engineering Collective Escape: The 2000 Reform of the Greek Labour Market', in K. Featherstone (ed.) *Politics and Policy in Greece*, pp. 159–179. London and New York: Routledge.

Papakonstantis, G.B. (2000) 'Police Officers and Immigrants' [in Greek], *Astynomiki Epitheorisi* (February Issue): 86–90.

Papandreou, P. (2009) *Children of Immigrants in Central Athens at the Turn of the 21st Century: A Study of Inferiorisation, Ethnicised Conflict, Criminalisation, and Substance Misuse*, Unpublished PhD dissertation. Department of Social Policy: London School of Economics and Political Science.

Papantoniou, A., Frangouli, M. and A. Kalavanou (1998) *Illegal Migration and the Problem of Crime*, Research Report. Athens: TSER Project.

Papastamou, S., Prodromitis, G. and T. Iatridis (2005) 'Perceived Threats to Democracy: An Examination of Political Affiliation and Beliefs about Terrorism, State Control, and Human Rights', *Analyses of Social Issues and Public Policy* 5(1): 249–262.

Papatheodorou, C. (2006) 'The Structure of Household Income and the Distribu-
    tional Impact of Income Taxes and Social Security Contributions', in M. Pet-
    mesidou and E. Mossialos (eds) *Social Policy Developments in Greece*, pp. 99–125.
    Aldershot: Ashgate.
Pedersini, R. and D. Coletto (2009) *Self-Employed Workers: Industrial Relations and
    Working Conditions*. Dublin: European Foundation for the Improvement of
    Living and Working Conditions (Eurofound). Available online at: http://www.
    eurofound.europa.eu/comparative/tno801018s/tno801018s_2.htm
Petmesidou, M. (2006) 'Tracking Social Protection: Origins, Path Peculiarity, Impasses
    and Prospects', in M. Petmesidou and E. Mossialos (eds) *Social Policy Develop-
    ments in Greece*, pp. 25–54. Aldershot: Ashgate.
Petoussi-Douli, V. (2008) 'Greece', in J. Winterdyk and G. Antonopoulos (eds) *Racist
    Victimisation: International Reflections and Perspectives*, pp. 139–168. Aldershot
    and Burlington, VT: Ashgate.
Prin (6 December 2010) 'December: Korkoneas is Still Shooting, Two Years Later...'
    [in Greek].
Proto Thema (16 January 2011) '73 Percent Yes to the Wall Against Illegal Immigrants'
    [in Greek].
Psomiades, H.J. (2004) 'Preface', in T.A. Couloumbis, *The Greek Junta Phenomenon:
    A Professor's Notes*, pp. 9–14. New York: Pella.
Public Issue (2007) *Barometer, November 2007* [in Greek]. Available online at: http://
    www.publicissue.gr/37/barometer-2007-november/
Public Issue (2008) *Problems, Life Conditions and Assessment of Municipal Work in
    the Municipality of Athens*. Available online at: http://www.publicissue.gr/155/
    athina/
Public Issue (2009a) *Attitudes of the Greek Public Towards the University Asylum
    and the Police* [in Greek]. Available online at: http://www.publicissue.gr/1365/
    asilo-2009/
Public Issue (2009b) *Research on Criminality, the University Asylum and Policing
    Measures* [in Greek]. Available online at: http://www.publicissue.gr/1088/
    univercity-asylum-police/
Public Issue (2011) *Public Opinion Towards the 'Wall' in Evros* [in Greek]. Available
    online at: http://www.publicissue.gr/1619/wall-survey-2011/
Rigakos, G.S. and G. Papanicolaou (2003) 'The Political Economy of Greek Polic-
    ing: Between Neo-Liberalism and the Sovereign State', *Policing and Society*
    13(3): 271–304.
Samatas, M. (2004) *Surveillance in Greece: From Anticommunist to Consumer Surveil-
    lance*. New York: Pella.

Schneider, F. and A. Buehn (2009) 'Shadow Economies and Corruption All Over the World: Revised Estimates for 120 Countries', *Economics: The Open-Access, Open-Assessment E-Journal*.

Seferiades, S. (1999) *Low Union Density amidst a Conflictive Contentious Repertoire: Flexible Labour Markets, Unemployment, and Trade Union Decline in Contemporary Greece*, EUI Working Paper No. 99/6. Florence: European University Institute.

Seferiades, S. (2003) 'The European Employment Strategy Against a Greek Benchmark: A Critique', *European Journal of Industrial Relations* 9(2): 189–203.

Seferiades, S. (2005) 'The Coercive Impulse: Policing Labour in Interwar Greece', *Journal of Contemporary History* 40(1): 55–78.

Seferiades, S. (2006) 'Employment Policy in the "European Employment Strategy" Era: What Prospects?', in M. Petmesidou and E. Mossialos (eds) *Social Policy Developments in Greece*, pp. 194–218. Aldershot: Ashgate.

Sotiropoulos, D.A. (2010) 'The Authoritarian Past and Contemporary Greek Democracy', *South European Society and Politics* 15(3): 449–465.

Spanou, C. (2008) 'State Reform in Greece: Responding to Old and New Challenges', *International Journal of Public Sector Management* 21(2): 150–173.

Staikouras, P.K. (2004) 'Structural Reform Policy: Privatisation and Beyond – The Case of Greece', *European Journal of Law and Economics* 17(3): 373–398.

Tayfur, M.F. (2003) *Semiperipheral Development and Foreign Policy: The Cases of Greece and Spain*. Aldershot: Ashgate.

The Guardian (13 August 2010) 'Greece's Economy Deeper in Recession than Forecast'.

Tikos, S. (2008) *Social Partners and Opposition Parties Oppose Government Reforms of the Pension System*, Submission by INE/GSEE to the European Industrial Relations Observatory (EIRO). Available online at: http://www.eurofound. europa.eu/eiro/2008/05/articles/gr0805029i.htm

To Vima (20 February 2000) 'Ministry of Internal Affairs: IDs and Passports Are Changing' [in Greek].

To Vima (22 April 2007) 'Greeks Are Searching for a New Strong Leader' [in Greek].

Tsakalotos, E. (2008) *Modernisation and Centre-Left Dilemmas in Greece: The Revenge of the Underdogs*, GreeSE Paper No. 13. London: Hellenic Observatory, London School of Economics.

Tsakloglou, P. and T. Mitrakos (2006) 'Inequality and Poverty in the Last Quarter of the 20th Century', in M. Petmesidou and E. Mossialos (eds) *Social Policy Developments in Greece*, pp. 126–143. Aldershot: Ashgate.

Tsandrizos, C. (2008) 'Foreigners' Criminality in Greece' [in Greek], in A.P. Sykiotou (ed.) *Foreigners in Greece: Integration or Marginalisation?*, pp. 149–152. Athens-Komotini: Ant. N. Sakkoulas Publishers.

Tseloni, A. (2002) 'Fear of Walking Alone in One's Own Neighbourhood: Regression and Multilevel Analysis' [in Greek and English], in C. Zarafonitou, *Fear of Crime: A Criminological Approach and Inquiry based on an Empirical Study of the Phenomenon within the City of Athens*, pp. 155–207. Athens-Komotini: Ant. N. Sakkoulas Publishers.

Tseloni, A. and C. Zarafonitou (2008) 'Fear of Crime and Victimisation: A Multivariate Multilevel Analysis of Competing Measurements', *European Journal of Criminology* 5(4): 387–409.

Tsiganou, J. (2007) 'Fear of Crime: Data and Methodological Gaps' [in Greek], in P. Kafetzis, T. Maloutas and J. Tsiganou (eds) *Politics, Society, Citizens: Analyses of Data from the European Social Survey*, pp. 194–217. Athens: EKKE.

Tsiganou, J. (2009) *Immigration and Criminality: Myths and Reality* [in Greek]. Athens: EKKE.

Unnever, J.D. and F.T. Cullen (2010) 'Racial-Ethnic Intolerance and Support for Capital Punishment: A Cross-National Comparison', *Criminology* 48(3): 831–864.

Vagena-Palaiologou, E. (2006) *Racism and Xenophobia: A Study of the Judiciary and the Police* [in Greek]. Athens: Nomiki Vivliothiki.

Vakiari, G. and K. Kontargyri (2009) *A Study of the Influence of Urban Space Planning on Citizens' Sense of Security* [in Greek], Unpublished BA dissertation. School of Business Administration and Economics: Technological Educational Institute of Thessaloniki.

Van de Walle, S. (2009) 'Trust in the Justice System: A Comparative View Across Europe', *Prison Service Journal* 183: 22–26.

Van de Walle, S. and J.W. Raine (2008) *Explaining Attitudes Towards the Justice System in the UK and Europe*, Ministry of Justice Research Series 9/08. London: Ministry of Justice.

van Dijk, J., Manchin, R., van Kesteren, J., Nevala, S. and G. Hideg (2007a) *The Burden of Crime in the EU. Research Report: A Comparative Analysis of the European Crime and Safety Survey (EU ICS) 2005*. Brussels: Gallup Europe.

van Dijk, J., van Kesteren, J. and P. Smit (2007b) *Criminal Victimisation in International Perspective: Key Findings from the 2004–2005 ICVS and EU ICS*. Den Haag: WODC.

van Kesteren, J. (2009) 'Public Attitudes and Sentencing Policies Across the World', *European Journal on Criminal Policy and Research* 15(1–2): 25–46.

Wacquant, L. (2009) *Punishing the Poor: The Neoliberal Government of Social Insecurity*. Durham and London: Duke University Press.

Wolff, P. (2010) *Population and Social Conditions: Statistics in Focus 9*. Luxembourg: Eurostat. Available online at: http://epp.eurostat.ec.europa.eu/cache/ITY_OFFPUB/KS-SF-10-009/EN/KS-SF-10-009-EN.PDF

Yannakopoulos, C. (2007) 'The "Other" as Spectacle: Spatial Policies of Distinction and Rennovation in Keramikos and Gazi' [in Greek], paper presentation at the conference 'Revisions of the Political: Anthropological and Historical Research in Greek Society' (Mytilini, 8–11 November). Available online at: http://www.sa.aegean.gr/Synedrio/Yannakopoulos.doc

Young, J. (1999) *The Exclusive Society: Social Exclusion, Crime and Difference in Late Modernity*. London: Sage.

Young, J. (2007) *The Vertigo of Late Modernity*. London: Sage.

Zarafonitou, C. (2002) *Fear of Crime: A Criminological Approach and Inquiry based on an Empirical Study of the Phenomenon within the City of Athens* [in Greek and English]. Athens-Komotini: Ant. N. Sakkoulas Publishers.

Zarafonitou, C. (2008) *Punitiveness: Contemporary Trends, Dimensions and Criminological Concerns* [in Greek]. Athens-Komotini: Ant. N. Sakkoulas Publishers.

Zarafonitou, C., Courakis, N.E., Gouseti, I., Kagelari, R., Chainas, E. and G. Kitsos (2009) *(In)Security, Punitiveness, and Anti-crime Policy: Presentation and Findings of a Study* [in Greek]. Athens-Komotini: Ant. N. Sakkoulas Publishers.

JONATHAN JACKSON, MONICA GERBER AND
CAROLYN CÔTÉ-LUSSIER

Commentary

Ideological Roots of Fear of Crime and Punitive Sentiment in Greece and the UK

The social sciences thrive on variation. Explaining the naturally occurring diversity we see across the continent, European cross-national research can address the psychological and sociological mechanisms that underpin complex and multi-layered social and political phenomena. But before carrying out meaningful cross-national work, it is imperative to be cognisant of national research literatures and to appreciate diverse social, cultural, and political settings. It follows that national accounts are vital if we are to develop a truly comparative European criminology; an understanding of contexts motivates and informs more powerful cross-national analyses. Cheliotis and Xenakis provide a fascinating account of fear of crime and punitiveness in contemporary Greece. They analyse the meaning and measurement of public insecurities about crime, summarise historical trends, consider the impact of insecurities about crime on the quality of life of citizens, and unpick some of the complex links between fear of crime, confidence in policing, and punitive sentiment. Their review forms an important basis for comparative research in this field of criminological enquiry.

In our commentary, we make some early comparisons between Greece and the UK. We focus on the point Cheliotis and Xenakis raise about the importance of broader social attitudes and ideological positions in fear of crime, confidence in policing, and punitiveness. We examine a range of instrumental and relational concerns, and we address the roles of ideology and psychological needs and motivations. We find that relational concerns are more important than insecurities about crime in predicting levels of punitivity and confidence in policing in some London data. But we also argue that the links between fear of crime, confidence in policing, and punitive sentiment – in both Greece and the UK – can profitably be brought together through a motivated social cognition (MSC) perspective. The MSC perspective suggests that ideological systems (and relational concerns) are partly rooted in psychological needs and motivations (Jost *et al.*, 2003). We present data from Round 4 of the European Social Survey (ESS) that are consistent with some aspects of this framework.

Punitive Attitudes and Trust in the Police: Instrumental or Relational Motives?

The Greek findings that Cheliotis and Xenakis review chime with prior work from the US and UK (e.g., Tyler and Boeckmann, 1997; Jackson and Sunshine, 2007; King and Maruna, 2009) on two perspectives on why people support the harsh punishment of law-breakers and express low levels of confidence in the police. One perspective lies in self-interested or 'instrumental' concerns about crime and future harm. Individuals, in this case, look to the police and harsh criminal sentencing to incapacitate offenders and deter would-be offenders. It follows that faith in the police and courts is lost when individuals experience and see crime around them, and worry for their safety and the safety of loved ones. Another answer lies in public concerns about social order, control, and moral decline, typically referred to as 'relational' concerns. Here individuals look to the police and harsh criminal sentencing to symbolically defend and re-establish social values and moral boundaries. Conversely, people lose faith in the courts and the police when they believe that social bonds are in decline.

Numerous UK and US studies have supported the idea that public anxieties about crime, policing, and punishment have less to do with the experience of crime and personal concerns about victimisation, and more to do with relational concerns about social cohesion and moral consensus. First, citizens who express support for harsher sentences for law-breakers typically also express concern about weakening social bonds (Tyler and Boeckmann, 1997) and economic stability (King and Maruna, 2008). Second, citizens who report low confidence in the police and high worry about crime also tend to express anxiety about neighbourhood breakdown and stability (Jackson and Bradford, 2009); once these more foundational relationships are taken into account, the correlation between confidence in the police and fear of crime is diminished.

The studies reviewed by Cheliotis and Xenakis largely support the relational perspective. Public concerns about social cohesion and moral consensus may be more important in explaining punitive attitudes in Greece. But thus far, the role of ideology has been underexplored. By way of contribution, we turn to London to test the two models, and in line with Cheliotis and Xenakis' comment on the importance of ideological positions in punitive sentiment in Greece, we add a measure of ideology into our analysis. We do not have comparable data for Greece; but these findings can be pertinent to future studies that develop our understanding of instrumental and relational motives in Greek attitudes towards crime and justice. Then, as a more concrete comparative contribution, we turn to the ESS for a comparable picture of the ideological basis of public attitudes in Greece and the UK.

The Story in London

To provide some empirical evidence, we first draw upon data from the 2007/2008 sweep of the London Metropolitan Police Public Attitudes Survey (PAS), which is a rolling representative-sample survey of 20,480 Londoners through face-to-face interview. Multinomial logistic regression (with standard errors clustered at the level of London Borough to account for the hierarchical nature of the dataset[1]) examined the predictors of (a) public confidence in policing (measured by answers to 'Taking everything into account, how good a job do you think the police in this area are doing?') and (b) public attitudes towards punishment (measured by agreement with the statement 'People who break the law should be given stiffer sentences'). We tested two models: the first concerning instrumental concerns, and the second concerning relational concerns. In Model I, covariates included age, gender, ethnicity, neighbourhood levels of crime and deprivation, and direct and indirect experience of crime. Model II then also included perceptions of disorder, collective efficacy, and long-term social change. For reasons of space, we only summarise here the findings (see Gerber *et al.* (unpublished results) for full details).

Without holding constant people's relational concerns, fear of crime was related negatively and significantly to public confidence in the police (Model I). Once relational concerns were taken into account, however, fear of crime lost its statistical significance (Model II). This finding is consistent with prior research that suggests that relational concerns predict both fear of crime and public confidence in policing, and that the effect of fear of crime on confidence in policing is reduced once one holds constant core social perception (e.g., Jackson *et al.*, 2009). To help visualise key effect sizes, Figure 1 provides fitted probabilities of Model II. The most predictive factor of confidence in the police was perception of long-term social change. Note how the predicted probability of respondents being in the 'good' category declines more steeply in the bottom right-hand plot (Figure 1) than in the other three plots. Stronger concerns about long-term social change were associated with lower levels of confidence in the police.

According to Cheliotis and Xenakis' review, a sensed lack of social cohesion is positively correlated with fear of crime in Greece. The findings from Greece are thus consistent with ours; they also accord with previous research that suggests that fear of crime emerges out of a set of interlinked

1   We also used ordinal and binary logistic regression. With ordinal logistic regression, the proportional odds assumption did not hold. With binary logistic regression, information on the response variable was lost. The results remained consistent across the three modelling strategies, however.

relational concerns in the UK and US (Ferraro, 1995; Girling *et al.*, 2000; Jackson, 2004; Farrall *et al.*, 2009). But what about punitive sentiment? We used the same statistical techniques to explain variation in punitive sentiment. Without holding constant relational concerns (Model I), fear of crime was a positive and significant predictor of punitivity. By contrast to public confidence in policing, the predictive power of fear of crime diminished ever-so slightly holding constant relational concerns (Model II). Figure 2 shows that concerns about disorder and social change were also significant and positive predictors of punitivity. As with public confidence in policing, this is controlling for factors such as direct and indirect victimisation.

We can expand on these findings by testing a mediational model using the London data. This model brings both public confidence in police and punitive sentiment into one framework. It also accounts for indirect effects between the variables of interest. Figure 3 shows the results from structural equation modelling with categorical indicators (using MPlus 5.2). Starting from the left, perception of social change predicted people's perception of disorder in their environment. This is consistent with the idea that perception of disorder is not just about material circumstances, but also about prior concerns about the need to restore morality, order, control, and a lost sense of solidarity (Jackson *et al.*, 2010). Perceived disorder and concerns about social change both predicted perceptions of collective efficacy, which is here measured as the sum of (1) mutual trust and shared expectations among residents, and (2) the shared willingness to intervene to defend social order (Sampson *et al.*, 1997). Worry about crime was also predicted by perceptions of disorder and concerns about long-term social change. Confidence in policing was predicted by fear of crime, disorder and collective efficacy, and also by a direct and indirect effect of concerns about long-term social change. The same was true for punitiveness, with fear of crime also being a more important predictor in this case.

As seems to be the case in Greece as well, we found that in London perceived disorder had direct effects on punitiveness and confidence in the police, but also indirect effects through collective efficacy (and fear of crime for punitive sentiment). In the next section, we pick up on these findings as well as on findings in the US to consider the role of ideological positions in perceptions and attitudes toward crime and justice.

The Ideological Roots of Public Attitudes towards Crime and Justice

We have shown that – in London at least – the observed association between fear of crime and confidence in the police disappears once prior social concerns are held constant. For punitive sentiment, however, fear of crime remains a significant predictor. Comparatively, there is evidence from Greece that when linked to politico-ideological beliefs, punitiveness is not necessarily predicted by fear of crime, but is rather dependent on the perception of particular cohorts of the population as dangerous. We therefore turn to the role of politico-ideological beliefs in predicting punitivity in London.

We added to the model (Figure 3) ideological concerns about authority and discipline in society (somewhat similar to items regularly used in scales of authoritarianism). We found that the strongest predictor behind endorsing harsh punishment of law-breakers was a sense of lost morality and authority in society (Figure 4). Controlling for these concerns rendered perceived disorder and collective efficacy not statistically significant – although fear of crime and perceived social change remained important predictors of punitiveness. This finding is in line with the Greek case, but also to some degree with findings in the US. Tyler and Boeckmann's (1997) California study, for instance, found a strong association between punitiveness and what they called 'social values' (i.e., a combination of measures of ideology and social values).

It has been shown that punitiveness in Greece is most strongly linked to perceiving immigration and crime as important social problems. Victimisation and fear of crime are also associated with punitiveness, although this latter association does not hold when taking into consideration factors such as politico-ideological beliefs. In this respect, evidence from the UK and Greece suggests that punitiveness is strongly linked to ideological and political concerns or preferences.

A More Formal Comparison of the UK and Greece

These findings are interesting, but they are only a starting point. In particular, our understanding can benefit from emerging research in political psychology on the association between psychological needs and motivations, and political ideology. Consider Jost and colleagues' (2003) motivated social cognition framework on political conservatism. This work seeks to integrate diverse findings on the antecedents of conservatism which include dispositional factors (e.g., psychological needs and motivations, such as need for order and openness to change) and situational factors (e.g., threat to the social system or to the self). We finish our commentary by testing whether there is a resonance (or elective affinity) in the UK and Greece between, on the one hand, resistance to change, need for order, and need for security, and, on the other hand, conservatism, fear of crime, confidence in policing, and punitive sentiment. To do so, we draw on representative-sample data from Round 4 of the ESS (Greece: N=2,072; and United Kingdom: N=2,352).

Ideological positions – or 'beliefs about the proper order of society and how it can be achieved' (Erikson and Tedin, 2003: 64, quoted in Jost *et al.*, 2009: 309) – reflect individuals' assumptions about the right and proper way of achieving a desired society. Reflecting developments over the past few decades in political research, our measure of political conservatism distinguishes between two dimensions: economic and cultural conservatism. Economic conservatism concerns acceptance or rejection of inequality, measured here in the ESS as agreement or disagreement to three statements: 'The government should take measures to reduce differences in income levels', 'Large differences in people's incomes are acceptable to properly reward differences in talents and efforts', and 'For a society to be fair, differences in people's standard of living should be small'. Cultural conservatism concerns acceptance or rejection of social change, measured in the ESS as agreement or disagreement with three statements: 'Gay men and lesbians should be free to live their own life as they wish', 'Schools must teach children to obey authority', and 'A woman should be prepared to cut down on her paid work for the sake of her family'.

If cultural conservatism is rooted in resistance to social change, and if economic conservatism is rooted in acceptance of inequality, then there may be a resonance between conservative ideologies and a deeper psychological motive to reduce uncertainty and threat. Accepting the status quo allows individuals to 'maintain what is familiar and known while rejecting the risky, uncertain prospect of social change' (Jost et al., 2007: 990), but also to justify the current (at times inegalitarian) social system which can have palliative effects (Jost et al., 2009). Like the analysis by Thorisdottir et al. (2007) of the ESS, we focus on three psychological needs and motivations: (1) the need for order (or rule-following), (2) the need for security, and (3) openness to new experiences. We address not just the links between psychological needs and conservative ideology, but also the extent to which confidence in the police and punitive sentiment are explained by psychological needs, both as direct effects and as mediated through conservative ideology. We test the model separately for the UK and Greece.

We found, examining the Greek data, that while psychological needs have small but significant effects on trust in the police, these effects were considerably weakened once individuals' political ideology was taken into consideration (see Figure 5). However, need for order (or rule-following) and openness to experience strongly predicted cultural conservatism, which was in turn the strongest predictor of trust in the police. Fear of crime, on the other hand, was not a significant predictor of trust in the police. In the UK, we saw a slightly different picture, with psychological needs having no significant direct effects on trust in the police (the exception being need for order). Moreover, in the UK, fear of crime remains a predictor of trust in the police (see Figure 6). Lastly, while cultural conservatism positively predicted trust in the police in Greece, it negatively, albeit weakly, predicted trust in the police in the UK.

For punitiveness, Greece and the UK were more similar. In both countries psychological needs had direct and indirect effects on punitiveness, which were mediated both by political ideology and fear of crime. Controlling for political ideology and fear of crime partly weakened the effect of psychological needs, though in both cases a need for security remained a comparatively strong predictor of punitiveness, especially in the UK. While a need for order had a direct effect on punitiveness, it also had a considerable indirect effect through cultural conservatism. The strongest predictor in both countries was cultural conservatism, particularly in Greece, with fear of crime having smaller but comparable effects in Greece and the UK (see Figure 7 and Figure 8, respectively).

Together, these findings suggest that psychological needs predict trust in the police and punitiveness both directly and indirectly, even after controlling for political ideology and fear of crime. Individuals' need for order was a strong predictor of trust in the police (with a direct effect in the case of the UK and an indirect effect mediated by cultural conservatism in Greece). This effect may partly be explained by a preference for rule-following and a decreased tendency to be critical towards rule-enforcers in general, and the police in particular. Punitiveness was strongly predicted by needs for security and order in the UK and Greece (both directly and indirectly, through ideology). Individuals' need for security can lead to punitiveness because of a need to incapacitate and deter criminals, in order to feel safe. Individuals who place greater importance on conformity and strong norms are likely to perceive crime as reflecting a lack of conformity with norms and values, and will thus endorse cultural conservatism and punitive measures which support stable values and norms, and a strong reaction to deviance and law-breaking.

Final Comments

A growing number of datasets on crime and justice provide comparability across many European countries. By capitalising on such data, we, as a community of scholars, can reinvigorate criminological research. On fear of crime, for example, we can examine whether public insecurities and attitudes are associated with national-level characteristics (e.g., levels of crime, the political economy, normative and social arrangements of a country) and individual-level factors (e.g., experiences of crime, feelings of vulnerability and threat, perceptions of neighbourhood breakdown and stability). Some of this work has already begun (see, for example, Hummelsheim *et al.*, 2010). Yet, one of the barriers to building a foundation for comparative research in Europe is language. It is difficult to learn about research findings and assess the social, cultural, and political contexts if one cannot read accounts written in the native tongue. The current chapter is therefore especially welcome.

In this short commentary, we have only been able to develop one or two points. We have first drawn comparisons to findings in London and the UK, and second sought to integrate and expand findings in Greece and the UK by applying the motivated social cognition perspective. Findings from Greece and ours suggest that criminologists should recognise the ideological significance of crime (to the extent that crime represents change, threat to order, and a lack of social cohesion). Ideological positions can tint the social and political meaning attributed to crime and partly explain the variance in public feelings of safety, trust in the police, and punitiveness.

Moreover, the motivated social cognition perspective suggests that both dispositional factors (e.g., psychological needs) and situational factors (e.g., influx of immigrants, economic instability, traumatic social events) should be brought into the picture. In this study, we found that in Greece and in the UK psychological needs have both direct and indirect effects – mediated mainly by cultural conservatism – on confidence in the police and punitive attitudes. We encourage future work to use this framework to tie together findings on various facets of crime and justice which at times appear disparate.

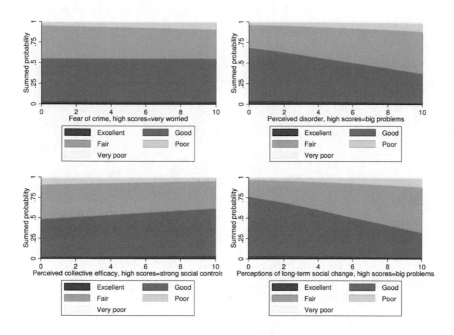

Figure 1 Predicted levels of public confidence in the police
Source: 2007/2008 METPAS

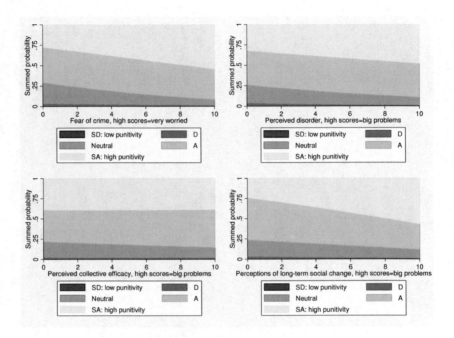

Figure 2 Predicted levels of punitivity
Source: 2007/2008 METPAS

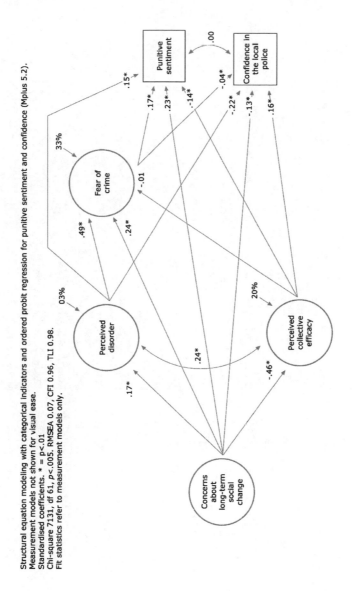

Structural equation modeling with categorical indicators and ordered probit regression for punitive sentiment and confidence (Mplus 5.2).
Measurement models not shown for visual ease.
Standardised coefficients. * = p<.01
Chi-square 7131, df 61, p<.005. RMSEA 0.07, CFI 0.96, TLI 0.98.
Fit statistics refer to measurement models only.

Figure 3 Mediational model of confidence in policing and punitivity
Source: 2007/2008 METPAS

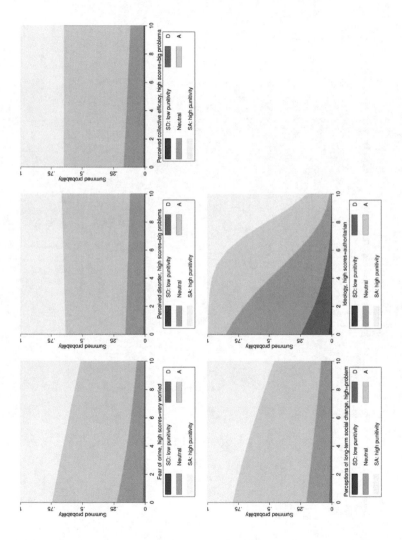

Figure 4   Predicted levels of punitivity controlling for ideology. Source: 2007/2008 METPAS

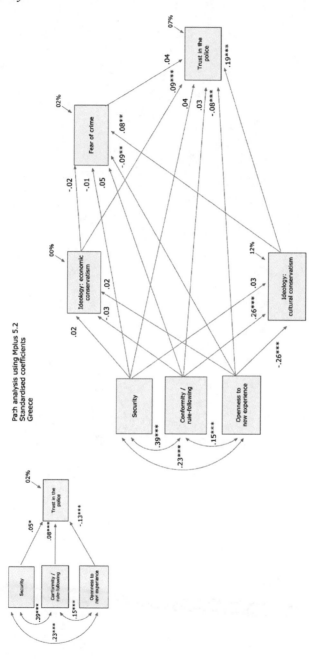

Figure 5   Trust in the police in Greece

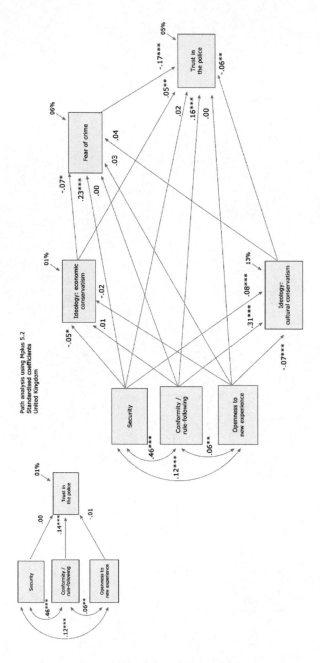

Figure 6 Trust in the police in the UK

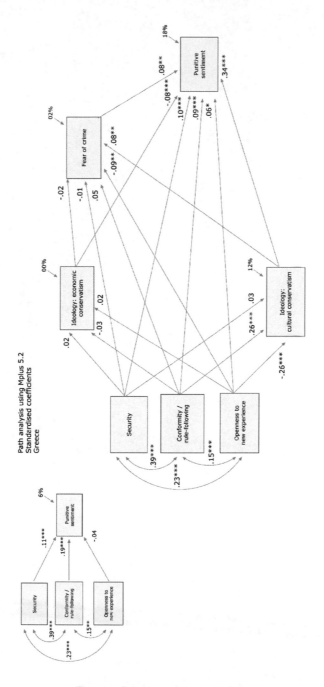

Figure 7   Punitive sentiment in Greece

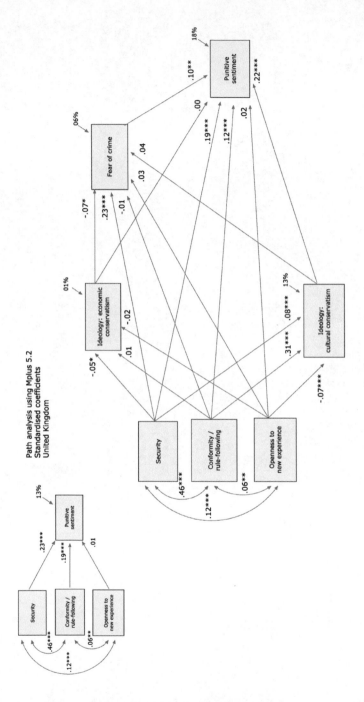

Figure 8 Punitive sentiment in the UK

References

Conover, P.J. and S. Feldman (1984) 'How People Organise the Political World: A Schematic Model', *American Journal of Political Science* 28(1): 95–126.

Erikson, R.S. and K.L. Tedin (2003) *American Public Opinion*, 6th edn. New York: Longman.

Farrall, S., Jackson, J. and E. Gray (2009) *Social Order and the Fear of Crime in Contemporary Times*. Oxford: Oxford University Press.

Ferraro, K.F. (1995) *Fear of Crime: Interpreting Victimisation Risk*. New York: SUNY Press.

Gerber, M., Côté-Lussier, C. and J. Jackson. *The Punitive Sentiment: Relational Concerns and Motivated Social Cognition*. Unpublished LSE working paper.

Gerber, M., Hirtenlehner, H. and J. Jackson (2010) 'Insecurities About Crime in Germany, Austria and Switzerland: A Review of Research Findings', *European Journal of Criminology* 7(2): 141–157.

Girling, E., Loader, I. and R. Sparks (2000) *Crime and Social Control in Middle England: Questions of Order in an English Town*. London: Routledge.

Hummelsheim, D., Hirtenlehner, H., Jackson, J. and D. Oberwittler (2010) 'Social Insecurities and Fear of Crime: A Cross-National Study on the Impact of Welfare State Policies on Crime-Related Anxieties', *European Sociological Review* (doi: 10.1093/esr/jcq010).

Jackson, J. (2004) 'Experience and Expression: Social and Cultural Significance in the Fear of Crime', *British Journal of Criminology* 44(6): 946–966.

Jackson, J. and B. Bradford (2009) 'Crime, Policing and Social Order: On the Expressive Nature of Public Confidence in Policing', *British Journal of Sociology* 60(3): 493–521.

Jackson, J., Bradford, B., Hohl, K. and S. Farrall (2009) 'Does the Fear of Crime Erode Public Confidence in Policing?', *Policing* 3(1): 100–111.

Jackson, J., Gray, E. and I. Brunton-Smith (2010) 'Decoding Disorder: On Public Sensitivity to Low-Level Deviance'. Available online at: http://ssrn.com/abstract=1567953

Jackson, J. and J. Sunshine (2007) 'Public Confidence in Policing: A Neo-Durkheimian Perspective', *British Journal of Criminology* 47(2): 214–233.

Jacoby, W.G. (1991) 'Ideological Identification and Issue Attitudes', *American Journal of Political Science* 35(1): 178–205.

Jost, J.T., Federico, C.M. and J.L. Napier (2009) 'Political Ideology: Its Structure, Functions and Elective Affinities', *Annual Review of Psychology* 60: 307–337.

Jost, J.T., Glaser, J., Kruglanski, A.W. and F.J. Sulloway (2003) 'Political Conservatism as Motivated Social Cognition', *Psychological Bulletin* 129(3): 339–375.

Jost, J.T., Napier, J.L., Thorisdottir, H., Gosling, S.D., Palfai, T.P. and B. Ostafin (2007) 'Are Needs to Manage Uncertainty and Threat Associated with Political Conservatism or Ideological Extremity?', *Personality and Social Psychology Bulletin* 33(7): 989–1007.

King, A. and S. Maruna (2009) 'Is a Conservative Just a Liberal who Has Been Mugged? Exploring the Origins of Punitive Views', *Punishment & Society* 11(2): 147–169.

Sampson, R.J., Raudenbush, R. and F. Earls (1997) 'Neighbourhoods and Violent Crime: A Multi-Level Study of Collective Efficacy', *Science* 277: 918–924.

Thorisdottir, H., Jost, J.T., Liviatan, I. and P.E. Shrout (2007) 'Psychological Needs and Values Underlying Left-Right Political Orientation: Cross-National Evidence from Eastern and Western Europe', *Public Opinion Quarterly* 71(2): 175–203.

Treier, S. and D.S. Hillygus (2009) 'The Nature of Political Ideology in the Contemporary Electorate', *Public Opinion Quarterly* 73(4): 679–703.

Tyler, T.R. and R.J. Boeckmann (1997) 'Three Strikes and You are Out, But Why? The Psychology of Public Support for Punishing Rule Breakers', *Law & Society Review* 31(2): 237–265.

GIANNIS PANOUSIS

Media, Crime and Criminal Justice

The influence of the mass media, and especially of television, on public opinion in Greece is an issue complicated by the low credibility of the media in
the eyes of the public. On the one hand, nearly half of the population believes
that public television is more independent from the government than it was
in the past. Indeed, it is the media that has appeared to increasingly encroach
upon the state's sphere of authority (see further Demertzis, 1996: 540). An
illustrative example of such encroachment was presented by the kidnapping
of a bus containing passengers in May 1999. The kidnappers chose to com-
municate their messages and demands live via the media rather than directly
to the police, in a spectacle which lasted more than 24 hours. On the other
hand, a significant minority (one in four) considers the independence of
public television to have decreased, whilst levels of public trust are, in any
case, greater towards private television (Papathanassopoulos, 2000; see also
Darzanou, 2002; compare Deliyanni, 2004). Moreover, a significant proportion of journalists themselves believe that Greek TV is 'hostage' to economic
interests (19 percent), that it promotes the abuse of power (15 percent), and
that it is governed irresponsibly (14 percent) (Papathanassopoulos, 2000).
Much, then, as the mass media may constitute a platform for the presentation and diffusion of party-political and materialist agendas, the extent to
which the latter are accepted by the public as a result of media consumption
remains unclear. It has been argued, for example, that only 10 percent of
viewers are influenced by televised political debates (Kakepaki, 2002: 166;
see also Mendrinou, 2002). From fuelling crime to fuelling fear of crime, and
from hindering the work that the police and the judiciary are expected to
undertake, to reproducing stereotypes, the media play a highly contentious
role in discourses about crime in Greece. This chapter suggests that, whilst
the progressive potential of the media has been little explored, responsibility
for media output cannot be left in the hands of the media alone.

The Mass Media, Crime and Fear of Crime

The public in Greece receives information about deviance and crime in the country (and elsewhere) mainly through television and radio, as well as through newspapers and magazines (see further Zarafonitou, 2002, 2006, 2008). Media regulation by the state has been characteristically weak over the past twenty years (see, e.g., discussion in Pleios, 2002: 259). The independent authority charged with monitoring the output of radio and television (the 'National Council of Radio-Television', or 'ESR'), has typically been handicapped in its administration of appropriate financial sanctions by bureaucratic complexities, the inadequate experience of its personnel, and political pressure.[1]

The extensiveness and forms of Greek media representations of violence has been the subject of considerable criminological interest, not least since the frequency of such images is believed to have significantly increased over recent years (Papathanassopoulos, 1997, 1999, 2004; Papathanassopoulos and Giannakoulopoulos, 2006). In particular, a number of criminological studies have focused on the extent and variety of media consumption reported by children (see, e.g., Papathanassopoulos, 1998: 505) and by convicted prisoners (see, e.g., Symeonidou-Kastanidou, et al., 2003: 364; Kodellas, 2006), with particular attention paid to the consumption of violent media formats (such as thrillers and action or martial arts films). In the case of juvenile convicts (surveyed in the prisons of Korydallos and Kassavetia), the relation between the media consumption habits of prisoners before and after conviction has also been explored (Courakis et al., 1995).

---

1   The existence of ESR is mandated by the Hellenic Constitution (Article 15) to regulate radio and television output. ESR operates in accordance with its own Code of Ethics, in addition to professional standards set by journalists' associations (see further Karakostas, 2005). There are three public TV channels in Greece (ERT, NET, and ET3), and various private ones (e.g., STAR, ANTENNA, MEGA, and ALTER), two of which are run by political parties: 902, by the Greek Communist Party (or 'KKE'), and Tele-Asty, by the nationalist party 'Popular Orthodox Rally' (or 'LAOS').

Beyond concerns about the criminogenic potential of the media are those related to its role in generating social panics. As regards the coverage of crime in news reports, it has been noted that homicides and drug-related crimes are reported more frequently than any other type of crime in the Greek media (Lambropoulou *et al.*, 2000). With respect to homicides, reporting tends to be extensive (e.g., up to three pages in newspapers) and focused mainly on offenders and their profile, often also including their photographic identification (Koukoutsaki, 2000; Varvaressos, 2000). As a general rule, and as the public and even journalists themselves commonly point out (see, for example, discussion in Panousis, 1991), media representations of deviance and crime are inaccurate in the sense of exaggerating the extent of the problem at issue, being selective in their content, reproducing stereotypes, and misconstruing the profile of offenders (Paraskevopoulos *et al.*, 1990; Ploumpidis, 1990; Artinopoulou, 1995; Lambropoulou, 1997; Papaioannou, 2001; Zarafonitou, 2002; Moschopoulou, 2005; Roussis, 2006; Tsalikoglou, 2007). As illustrated by a study of the way in which six Athenian newspapers reported anarchist activities in 1980, 1985, and 1995, above and beyond the common reproduction of associated stereotypical notions such as 'vandalism', 'enemies of democracy and morality', 'menace for public security', 'conspiracy', and 'moral panic', media representations were also shown to be significantly influenced by the political standpoints of the newspapers in which they appeared (Kalamatianou, 2007: 263–265).

Their low credibility notwithstanding, media representations of deviance and crime are said to generate, boost, or at least sustain alarmist and exclusive attitudes amongst the public (Pleios, 2004; Panousis, 2006a, 2008). And nowhere appears this paradox to be more pronounced than in the cases of school violence, immigration, and drug abuse and addiction. By way of dramatising isolated incidents and grossly exaggerating pertinent statistical data, the Greek mass media present violence as widespread in schools across the country (Beze, 1998; Artinopoulou, 2001). Indeed, such headlines as 'When school becomes a nightmare', 'Violence goes to school', and 'Crash course in violence at schools' help give rise to moral panics (see further Panousis, 2004b). That violence is shrouded in conceptual ambiguities makes schoolchildren prone to reproduce and legitimate its myth, as when they respond to survey questions by interpreting otherwise normal (if not necessarily welcome) behaviours as instances of bullying (ibid.).

As for the immigration-crime nexus (on which see further Karydis, this collection; and Cheliotis and Xenakis, this collection), this is more often than not presented in the Greek media by non-specialist journalists whose main sources of information are the Internet and their colleagues. The offences most commonly reported in connection with immigrants span illegal entry into the country, human trafficking, prostitution, theft, and robbery (Tsiakalos, 1997/1998). A content analysis of two daily nation-wide newspapers for the period 1990–1999 showed that immigrants were deemed responsible for nearly half of the crimes reported – a proportion far larger than the actual representation of immigrants in official crime statistics. Headlines were invariably negative when they referred to immi-grants and Albanians in particular ('Albanians kill without mercy' being but one example; Giannarou, 2008), also presenting victims as gravely angry, and demanding more and harsher measures of crime control in response (Moschopoulou, 2005; see also Karydis, 1996; Konstantinidou, 2001; Tsoukala, 2001; Galanis and Triantafyllidou-Galani, 2002).

Turning to drug abuse and addiction, and in stark contrast with per-tinent statistics, media reports regularly speak of 'waves of crisis', even though they shed scant light on the risks of drug abuse as such (Roussis, 2006). Furthermore, in line with the dominant policy-making mindset, drug abuse and addiction are associated in the media with immorality and lawbreaking. Drug-related lawbreaking itself is attributed to the pursuit of hedonistic pleasure, and arbitrarily linked to a range of activities such as anarchism, organised crime, or terrorism, hence also the urgent calls for further and more effective measures of penal control for drug abuse and addiction (Panousis, 2006b).

Challenges for Criminal Justice

The power of media spectacle to negatively influence criminal justice proc-esses (see further Demertzis 1996: 540), as a consequence of its proclivity for exaggeration and titillation in crime reporting, has been recognised as a significant challenge by diverse voices from the state bureaucracy, politicians, and civil society. Studies of Greek police personnel carried out in 1995 (Panousis, 2001) and in 1998 (Georgoulas, 2003: 26–71) indicate that they are as much influenced by negative media distortions of the realities of crime as are the rest of the general public. Equally, however, the media commonly reproduce a stereotypical image of Greek police officers as a force bedevilled by political partisanship, corruption, and a lack of meritocracy (see further Panousis, 2001: 103–110). This stereotype serves to reinforce public assumptions of police ineffectiveness – a problem of representation of which the police are themselves only too aware (Leandros, 2000), given low levels of public trust in the police (see further Vidali, 2007; and Cheliotis and Xenakis, this collection). As underlined by a survey carried out in 1994 of 465 police officers, 49 percent felt that the public regarded them as 'batsous' – a derogatory term akin to 'cops' (Tsalikoglou *et al.*, 1999). Thus, an overwhelming majority of police officers surveyed in 1995 believed that alongside the influx of immigrants and the role of contemptuous public attitudes towards law-abiding behaviour, the media also played a role in fuelling crime (Panousis, 2001).

Turning to the administration of justice, the mass media in Greece have a reputation for generating endless reports and debates concerning criminal trials which are ongoing, in which the goal of exciting public passions clearly surpasses that of neutrally elucidating the subject matter. The influence of the media in this field has not been entirely unchecked, however. A key example of the contrary came in 2002, when members of the terrorist organisation 'November 17' were identified, and newspaper and television coverage were replete with commentaries on the group. The entire criminal process (from arrest and preliminary judicial proceedings onwards) swiftly became reminiscent of a Hollywood production (see further Panousis, 2005; on discussion of such 'virtual justice' processes, see Kardara, 2003). There was nevertheless a sufficient degree of political consensus that making a spectacle of terrorism would not be conducive to a fair or orderly trial (Panousis, 2004a). Law 3090/2002 was therefore passed in order to prohibit any televised transmission or video-recording of the trial, in part or in whole (even for archival purposes). Interestingly, whilst both the state (i.e., government, judiciary, and other elements of the state bureaucracy) and the accused opposed the televising of the trial, a small number of academics specialising in Constitutional Law and Criminology supported such use of the media (see Lambropoulou, 2005: 239).

More generally, however, the vast majority of the mass media in Greece has been almost exclusively oriented towards the support of victims of crime. For example, even when the notoriously overcrowded Greek prisons have been the subject of media attention (see further Cheliotis, this collection), reporting typically reproduces the stigmatisation of prisoners by focusing upon their deviant behaviour and minority or subcultural identities, and endlessly characterising their prison environment in such terms as 'violence', 'chaos', 'hell', 'a jungle', full of 'fear', 'blood', and 'anarchy' (Nikolaides, 2006: 274–283; see also Kartalou, 2006: 238).[2] In stark contrast, a study published by the independent media website *Indymedia Athens* offered a qualitative analysis of discourses by the electronic media on prison, which focused upon the complaints of inmates concerning living conditions, institutional violence, and the demands and rights of prisoners (Vatikiotis, 2006: 306). Such latter perspectives have shone an entirely different media light on the predicament of those imprisoned.

Conclusion

Greek criminology has only recently begun to concern itself with the mass media and the influence they exert on public attitudes in the country towards crime and criminal justice. An accumulating throng of studies support the notion that the Greek media legitimate and reproduce widespread exclusive attitudes amongst the public (Kaytatzi-Whitlock, 2005). Public susceptibility to distorted media content is tightly linked to what Beck (1992) has famously described as the rise of the 'risk society', whereby

2   This study, conducted in 1995, analysed the coverage by four Athenian newspapers
     of a riot at Korydallos prison (see further Nikolaides, 2006).

the insecurities of everyday life are projected onto scapegoated targets. This, however, is not to say that the socio-political role played by the mass media is unavoidably negative. The mass media, much like technology more generally, are merely means of communication, and it is their use that should constitute our ultimate concern. To the extent that the media may deter crime by constituting a conduit for awareness-raising and knowledge-building, studies on the effects of reporting on drug use (Roussis, 2006: 88–90) and rape (see Artinopoulou, 1995: 295–298; Alygizakis 2007), for example, show that the Greek media has scarcely met such expectations. The challenge for criminologists is to acknowledge and act upon the fact that responsibility for media output on crime extends beyond media professionals, the ESR, or even the state, but also to themselves as well. Acting upon this fact means forsaking academic isolationism in order to dispel public myths and to accurately reconstruct reality (see further Melossi, 1999; Deliyanni, 2004; Barak, 2007).

References

Alygizakis, E. (2007) *Rape as Public Spectacle: Videotaping and Publicisation of Women's Rape* [in Greek]. Athens: Ant. N. Sakkoulas Publishers.

Artinopoulou, V. (1995) 'Social Representations of Rape in the Press' [in Greek], *Elliniki Epitheorisi Eglimatologias* 11–16: 285–306.

Artinopoulou, V. (2001) *Violence at School: Studies and Policies in Europe* [in Greek]. Athens: Metaihmio.

Barak, G. (2007) 'Mediatising Law and Order: Applying Cottle's architecture of Communicative Frames to the Social Construction of Crime and Justice', *Crime, Media, Culture* 3(1): 101–109.

Beck, U. (1992) *Risk Society: Towards a New Modernity*. London: Sage.

Beze, L. (ed.) (1998) *Violence at School and School' Violence* [in Greek]. Athens: Ellinika Grammata.

Courakis, N., Milioni, F. and associates (1995) *Survey in Greek Prisons* [in Greek]. Athens: Ant. N. Sakkoulas Publishers.

Darzanou, A. (2002) 'Journalism and Media: A Different Reading of Research', in
    C. Vernardakis (ed.) *Public Opinion in Greece* [in Greek], pp. 244–268. Athens:
    A.A. Livanis.
Deliyanni, E. (2004) *Media Ethics* [in Greek]. Athens: I. Sideris.
Demertzis, N. (1996) 'Political Publicity, Persons and TV', in Foundation S. Kara-
    giorgas (ed.) *Limits and Relations between the Public and the Private* [in Greek],
    pp. 539–553. Athens: Foundation S. Karagiorgas.
Galanis, G. and S. Triantaffylidou-Galani (2002) 'Immigrants and the Mass Media',
    in M. Kaila (ed.) *Educational, Family and Political Psychopathology* [in Greek],
    pp. 363–385. Athens: Atrapos.
Georgoulas, S. (2003) 'Police Discourse and "Images" of Criminological Statistics',
    in N. Courakis (ed.) *Anti-crime Policy III* [in Greek], pp. 23–72. Athens: Ant.
    N. Sakkoulas Publishers.
Giannarou, L. (27 September 2008) 'The Greek media "Favour" Racism',
    Kathimerini.
Kakepaki, M. (2002) 'Television and Electoral Behaviour', in N. Demertzis (ed.) *Politi-
    cal Communication in Greece* [in Greek], pp. 141–171. Athens: Papazissis.
Kalamatianou, K. (2007) 'Representations of Anarchists' Action in the Press: Research
    Difficulties and Findings', in S. Georgoulas (ed.) *Criminology in Greece Today*
    [in Greek], pp. 262–271. Athens: KYM.
Karakostas, I. (2005) *Media Law* [in Greek]. Athens: Ant. N. Sakkoulas Publishers.
Kardara, A. (2003) *Terrorism and the Mass Media* [in Greek]. Athens: Ant. N. Sak-
    koulas Publishers.
Kartalou, A. (2006) 'Imprisonment and Television: Conditions of Representation
    and Reading of the Medium', in A. Koukoutsaki (ed.) *Images of the Prison* [in
    Greek], pp. 237–260. Athens: Patakis.
Karydis, V. (1996) *The Criminality of Immigrants in Greece: Issues of Theory and Anti-
    Crime Policy* [in Greek]. Athens: Papazissis.
Kaytatzi-Whitlock (2005) 'Public Dialogue, Citizens and the Media' [in Greek],
    Zitimata Epikoinonias 3: 81–103.
Kodellas, S. (2006) *A Condemned Audience? A Study of Media Use by Prisoners* [in
    Greek]. Athens: Ant. N. Sakkoulas Publishers.
Konstantinidou, C. (2001) *Social Representations of Crime* [in Greek]. Athens: Ant.
    N. Sakkoulas Publishers.
Koukoutsaki, A. (2000) 'Criminal Stereotype and Mass Media', in I. Daskalaki, P. Papa-
    dopoulou, D. Tsamparli, I. Tsiganou and E. Fronimou (eds) *Criminals and Victims
    at the Doorstep of 21st Century* [in Greek], pp. 445–462. Athens: EKKE.
Lambropoulou, E. (1997) *The Construction of Social Reality and the Mass Media: The
    Case of Violence and Criminality* [in Greek]. Athens: Ellinika Grammata.

Lambropoulou, E. and A. Arfaras (2000) 'The Press and Criminality', in I. Daskalaki, P. Papadopoulou, D. Tsamparli, I. Tsiganou and E. Fronimou (eds) *Criminals and Victims at the Doorstep of the 21st Century* [in Greek], pp. 431–444. Athens: EKKE.

Lambropoulou, E. (2005) 'Crime, Criminal Justice and Criminology in Greece', *European Journal of Criminology* 2(2): 211–247.

Leandros, N. (2000) *Political Economy and the Mass Media* [in Greek]. Athens: Kastaniotis.

Melossi, D. (1999) 'Social Theory and Changing Representations of the Criminal', in A. Koukoutsaki (ed.) *Images of Crime* [in Greek], pp. 21–59. Athens: Plethron.

Mendrinou, M. (2002) 'Public Opinion in Greece: Symptoms of Discontent', in C. Vernardakis (ed.) *Public opinion in Greece* [in Greek], pp. 35–67. Athens: A.A. Livanis.

Moschopoulou, A. (2005) *Immigrants' Criminality* [in Greek]. Athens: Ant. N. Sakkoulas Publishers.

Nikolaides, A. (2006) 'Mass Media and the Prison: The Case of the Revolt in the Prison of Korydallos in November 1995', in A. Koukoutsaki (ed.) *Images of the Prison* [in Greek], pp. 261–303. Athens: Patakis.

Panousis, G. (1991) 'The Criminal Stereotype: Social Poison Transmitted via the Press?', in G. Panousis (ed.) *Criminological Studies* [in Greek], pp. 125–158. Athens: Ant. N. Sakkoulas Publishers.

Panousis, G. and V. Karydis (1999) 'Fear of Victimisation, Insecurity and Police Efficiency', in C. Vernardakis (ed.) *Public Opinion in Greece* [in Greek], pp. 247–259. Athens: Livanis.

Panousis, G. (2001) 'Police and the Mass Media: Dangerous Relations?', in G. Panousis and S. Vidali (eds) *Texts on the Police and Policing* [in Greek], pp. 103–111. Athens: Ant. N. Sakkoulas Publishers.

Panousis, G. (2004a) *The Trial of N17 on TV* [in Greek]. Athens: Ant. N. Sakkoulas Publishers.

Panousis, G. (ed.) (2004b) *About Criminals: Rhetoric and Counter-rhetoric* [in Greek]. Athens: Ant. N. Sakkoulas Publishers.

Panousis, G. (ed.) (2005) *The Trial of N17 through Newspaper Columns* [in Greek]. Athens: Ant. N. Sakkoulas Publishers.

Panousis, G. (2006a) 'Mass Media, TV Enemies and Immigration', in G. Panousis (ed.) *Mass Media and Contemporary Problems* [in Greek], pp. 135–161. Athens: Ant. N. Sakkoulas Publishers.

Panousis, G. (2006b) 'Mass Media and Drugs', in G. Panousis (ed.) *Mass Media and Contemporary Problems* [in Greek], pp. 11–34. Athens: Ant. N. Sakkoulas Publishers.

Panousis, G. (2008) *To Excess* [in Greek]. Athens: Nomiki Vivliothiki.

Papaioannou, P. (2001) *Crimes of Jealousy* [in Greek]. Athens: Nomiki Vivliothiki.

Papathanassopoulos, S. (1997) *The Power of Television* [in Greek]. Athens: Kastaniotis.

Papathanassopoulos, S. (1998) 'Television and Violence', in R. Panayotopoulou *et al.* (eds) *The 'Construction' of Reality and the Mass Media* [in Greek], pp. 503–514. Athens: Alexandria.

Papathanassopoulos, S. (1999) *Violence on Greek Television* [in Greek]. Athens: Kastaniotis.

Papathanassopoulos, S. (2001) 'The Impression of Public Television amongst the Greek public', in C. Vernardakis (ed.) *Public Opinion in Greece* [in Greek], pp. 187–201. Athens: A.A. Livanis.

Papathanassopoulos, S. and A. Giannakoulopoulos (2006) 'Television and Violence: Representation of Violent Scenes on Greek Television' [in Greek], *Zitimata Epoikoinonias* 4: 69–85.

Paraskevopoulos, N., Grigoriadou, E. and E. Koi (1990) 'The Presentation of the Penal Phenomenon in the Press: Representation or Distortion', *Dikaio kai Politiki*: 117–133.

Pleios, G. (2002) 'The Privatisation of the Mass Media and the Formation of Televised Political Discourse', in N. Demertzis (ed.) *Political Communication in Greece* [in Greek], pp. 235–280. Athens: Papazissis.

Pleios, G. (2004) 'The Racism of Televised Discourse', in G. Panousis (ed.) *Youth, Violence and Racism* [in Greek], pp. 105–128. Athens: Papazissis.

Pleios, G. and S. Papathanassopoulos (2008) 'The Publicisation of Political Institutions through Television News' [in Greek], *Zitimata Epikoinonias* 7: 55–77.

Ploumpidis, D. (1990) 'Psychiatry and the Mass Media' [in Greek], *Tetradia Psychiatrikis*: 65–68.

Roussis, A. (2006) 'The role of the Mass Media in Youth Drug Addiction', in G. Panousis (ed.) *Mass Media and Contemporary Problems* [in Greek], pp. 35–106. Athens: Ant. N. Sakkoulas Publishers.

Symeonidou-Kastanidou, E., Kaiafa-Gbanti, M. and A. Pitsela (2003) 'Anti-crime Policy and Youth', in N. Courakis (ed.) *Anti-crime Policy III* [in Greek], pp. 327–376. Athens: Ant. N. Sakkoulas Publishers.

Tsalikoglou, F. *et al.* (1999) *Police Officers' Perceptions of the Criminal Phenomenon* [in Greek]. Athens: Panteion University.

Tsalikoglou, F. (2007) *Schizophrenia and Murder* [in Greek]. Athens: A.A. Livanis.

Tsiakalos, G. (ed.) (1997–98) *Origins and Conditions of the Emergence of Racist Discourse and Racism in Greece: Daily Press and Elements of Racist Discourse* [in Greek]. Thessaloniki: University of Thessaloniki.

Tsoukala, A. (2001) *Immigration and Criminality in Europe* [in Greek]. Athens: Ant. N. Sakkoulas Publishers.

Varvaressos, C. (2000) 'Representations of the Perpetrator and the Victim', in I. Daskalaki, P. Papadopoulou, D. Tsamparli, I. Tsiganou and E. Fronimou (eds) *Criminals and Victims at the Doorstep of 21st Century* [in Greek], pp. 463–480. Athens: EKKE.

Vatikiotis, P. (2006) 'Releasing "Images"', in A. Koukoutsaki (ed.) *Images of the Prison* [in Greek], pp. 304–333. Athens: Patakis.

Vidali, S. (2007) *Crime Control and Public Police* [in Greek]. Athens: Ant. N. Sakkoulas Publishers.

Zarafonitou, C. (2002) *Fear of Crime: A Criminological Approach and Inquiry based on an Empirical Study of the Phenomenon within the City of Athens* [in Greek and English]. Athens-Komotini: Ant. N. Sakkoulas Publishers.

Zarafonitou, C. (2006) 'La peur du crime parmi les immigrés et leurs attitudes face aux institutions de la justice pénale', in T. Papatheodorou and P. Mary (eds) *Mutations des politiques criminelles en Europe*, pp. 91–113. Athens: Papazissis.

Zarafonitou, C. (2008) *Punitiveness: Contemporary Trends, Dimensions and Criminological Concerns* [in Greek]. Athens-Komotini: Ant. N. Sakkoulas Publishers.

ROBERT REINER

Commentary

The chapter by Giannis Panousis offers a stimulating overview of research and discussions about the significance of media representation of crime and criminal justice in Greece. I have no knowledge about the content of media representations in Greece other than what I have learned from his informative account. In what follows, I will comment on his points in terms of how they compare with research and analysis in Britain and North America (for recent overviews, see Reiner, 2007a; Greer, 2010).

The Crime-Media Debate

As Panousis states, concerns about media representations have been both about 'the criminogenic potential of the media' and 'those related to its role in generating social panics'. Indeed, conservatives frequently claim that the media subvert authority and exacerbate deviance, while liberals and radicals have suggested that the media undermine the rule of law and legitimise authoritarian policing (and even vigilantism) by exaggerating the extent and seriousness of crime. The systematic tendency of the media to encourage tough policing and other law-and-order solutions to crime is usually attributed by radical analyses to the interests that the elites who dominate media industries have in maintaining the socioeconomic and political status quo. Media demonisation of offenders diverts public anxiety away from other sources of insecurity, and solutions to the crime problem are portrayed in terms of strengthening the forces of order rather than reform of the social system.

During the twentieth century, these polar anxieties stimulated a veritable industry of research attempting to assess the content, effects, and sources of media representations. Much of the research on media content and effects has been conducted within a positivist psychological perspective. Positivistic content analysis purports to be an objective quantitative method of studying the meaning of media texts and images. But there are major problems with the claim that traditional quantitative content analysis is objective. While the categories used to quantify message attributes may be free of conscious or intentional subjective bias, they are neither randomly plucked out of thin air, nor do they necessarily reflect a structure of meaning objectively inherent in the texts analysed. They always embody theoretical presuppositions by the researcher about criteria of significance. Thus, traditional content analysis may be rigorous in the precision of its statistical manipulation of data, but the categories used necessarily presuppose some theory of meaning, usually about likely consequences.

Most research on media effects has also been conducted within a positivist psychological frame of reference, seeking to establish whether exposure to particular images has clearly identifiable consequences either for 'anti-social' attitudes or actions, or for fear of crime. These prodigious efforts to isolate a 'pure' media effect tend to result in masterpieces of inconsequentiality, such as the conclusion of one major study that 'for some children, under some conditions, some television is harmful. For some children under the same conditions, or for the same children under [different] conditions, it may be beneficial. For most children, under most conditions, most television is probably neither particularly harmful nor particularly beneficial' (Schramm *et al.*, 1961: 11).

It is not surprising that the vast positivist research enterprise on media effects has been rather inconclusive. The implicit model behind such anxieties is unbelievably simplistic: the media purportedly operate as an autonomous and powerful ideological hypodermic syringe, injecting ideas and values into a passive public of cultural dopes. It is far more plausible to suggest that media images do indeed have profound consequences, but not in a pure and directly deterministic manner. Audiences interpret media images in differing ways, according to their particular social experiences and interests. The media themselves do not change autonomously, but reflect developments in social perceptions and practices that have other origins. The media-society relationship is dialectical: each develops in interaction with the other, in a complex loop of interdependence. Media representations have significant consequences, although the hunt for pure effects that can be experimentally isolated is chimerical.

However complex and hard to measure the relationship might be, it is undeniable that media representations are a major source of popular perceptions of crime and criminal justice in contemporary societies, and frame public discourse about them (as Panousis shows for Greece). This is indeed recognised by most people themselves. In a major survey of Londoners, for example, 80 percent said the news media were their principal source of information about the police, contrasted with only 20 percent citing 'direct experience'. Whilst 'word of mouth' was the second most prominent source of information (43 percent), it is striking that 29 percent mentioned 'media fiction' as their main source (Fitzgerald *et al.*, 2003). This suggests a major source of the so-called 'reassurance gap', the contrast between rising fear of crime and falling crime levels in the last fifteen years: how could flesh-and-blood coppers compete with their never-failing fictional comrades who can be relied upon to solve the most puzzling crimes in an hour or so?

The Content of Media Representations of Crime and Criminal Justice

The results of research on media representations of crime and criminal justice obviously vary in detail between the numerous studies conducted over the last sixty years or so in a great variety of countries. They differ according to methodology, media studied, the market the media are pitched at ('quality' vs. mass market, for example), where and when the data were gathered, and whether 'factual' or 'fictional' representations are examined. Nonetheless, there is a broad convergence of results despite the variations in the period and place in which content was studied (see further Reiner, 2007a: 304–315). This repeated pattern discerned in media representations of crime includes the features outlined below.

News and fiction crime stories feature prominently in all media, through-out media history. There are, of course, variations in this prominence according to the methods of the research (the broader the definition of crime adopted by a study, obviously the higher the number of crime stories it will find in the media). There are also variations over time (a general trend towards a higher proportion of crime stories in all media), between societies, and according to the level of the market the particular media studied are targeting, with other things being equal more popular levels carrying more crime stories.

In terms of structural features of crime stories, whether purportedly factual or fictional, they tend to follow what has been called the 'law of opposites' (Surette, 2007). The pattern of depiction of what crimes occur, how serious and threatening they are, who are the victims and perpetrators, and how successful and ethical the police and criminal justice system are, is the opposite of the picture given by official statistics (which, of course, are themselves highly problematic; see Reiner, 2007b). In the media, there is an overemphasis on serious violent crime against individuals; the risks of crime are exaggerated quantitatively and qualitatively, though property crime is relatively downplayed; there is a disproportionate concentration on older, higher-status victims and offenders (except in the growing sub-genre of 'reality' programming); a generally positive image of the effective-ness and integrity of policing and criminal justice is presented (e.g., most cases are cleared-up, whilst there is relatively little focus on corruption or abuse, although there is a clearly discernible trend to increasing criticism; see Reiner 2007a: 309, 314; 2007b: 140–151; 2008: 323–329); and most stories are about individual cases, rather than general trends.

Thus, the overall picture of crime and control presented in the media is highly favourable to the criminal justice perspective and the police image. Crime is represented as a serious threat to vulnerable individual victims, but one that the police routinely tackle successfully because of their prowess and heroism. The police accordingly appear as the seldom-failing guardians of the public, essential bulwarks of the social order. One striking feature in Panousis' account of the Greek media is that this pattern is different from the predominant UK or North American one, corresponding to much lower levels of public trust in the police (although public confidence in them has declined in the UK in recent decades, the police remain more trusted than most other institutions).

The Consequences of Media Representations of Crime and Criminal Justice

As shown earlier, most of the huge volume of research on media 'effects' has been conducted within a positivist paradigm. An experimental and a control group are exposed to some media content, and their behaviour, biochemistry, attitudes or other variables are measured before and after for 'effects'. As indicated above, the results of this mass of studies is rather inconclusive, largely because of the artificial nature of the experimental setting, and the implausible model that is implicitly being tested, the media as ideological syringe. But that the media do have some criminogenic effects as well as consequences for public perceptions of crime is very likely. The media figure in most explanatory accounts in criminological theory of the elements shaping crime:

Labelling

The media are an important factor shaping the conceptual boundaries and recorded volume of crime. News and fiction stories stimulate public anxiety, producing changes in policing, criminal justice policy, and public perceptions that become a self-fulfilling spiral of deviancy amplification. Many studies document media-amplified 'crime waves' and 'moral panics' about law and order, and Panousis examines several contemporary Greek examples. Thus, increases and decreases in recorded crime levels may be due in part to the deviance construction and amplifying activities of the media.

Motive

The media feature in many of the most commonly offered social and psychological theories of the formation of criminal dispositions. Probably the most influential sociological theory of how criminal motives are formed is Merton's version of *anomie* theory (Merton, 1938; see also Messner and

Rosenfeld, 2000; Reiner, 2007b). The media are pivotal in presenting for universal emulation images of affluent life-styles and a consumerist culture, accentuating relative deprivation and generating pressures to acquire ever higher levels of material success regardless of the legitimacy of the means used. Psychological theories of the formation of motives to commit offences also often feature media effects as part of the process. For example, the images of crime and violence presented by the media are a form of social learning, and may encourage crime by imitation or arousal effects.

Means

It has often been alleged that the media act as an open university of crime, spreading knowledge of criminal techniques. A notorious instance was the allegation that the murderers of Jamie Bulger had been influenced by the video *Child's Play 3* in the manner in which they killed the unfortunate toddler. A related line of argument is the 'copycat' theory of crime and rioting. Video games such as *Grand Theft Auto* have been accused of being an especially potent source of learning about crime, as the player is placed in the subject position of a criminal (Hayward, 2004: 172–173, 193–194), although the evidence is disputed. New forms of media have sometimes been seen as creating new means to commit crime. This concern has been particularly stimulated recently by fears that the Internet facilitates all sorts of offences, from fraud, identity theft, child pornography, and grooming children for sex, to organising transnational crime and terrorism (Wall, 2007).

Opportunity

The media may increase opportunities to commit offences by contributing to the development of a consumerist ethos, in which the availability of tempting targets of theft proliferates (Hayward, 2004; Hallsworth, 2005: 62–63). They can also alter 'routine activities', especially in relation to the use of leisure time, which structure opportunities for offending (Cohen and Felson, 1979). The domestic hardware and software of mass media use

– TVs, videos, radios, CDs, personal computers, mobile phones – are the common currency of routine property crime, and their proliferation has been an important aspect of the spread of criminal opportunities.

Controls

Motivated would-be offenders, with the means and opportunities to commit offences, will not be able to carry out these crimes if effective social controls are in place. These might be *external* (the deterrent threat of sanctions represented in the first place by the police) or *internal* (the still, small voice of conscience – what Eysenck famously called the 'inner policeman'). A regularly recurring theme of respectable anxieties about the criminogenic consequences of media images of crime is that they erode the efficacy of both external and internal controls. They may undermine external controls by derogatory representations of criminal justice (e.g., ridiculing its agents, a key complaint at least since the days of Shakespeare's Dogberry, resuscitated in this century by the popularity of comic images of the police, from the Keystone Cops onwards). Serious representations of criminal justice might undermine its legitimacy by becoming more critical as they have done in the UK in recent decades, questioning the integrity and fairness, or the efficiency and effectiveness of the police. Negative representations of criminal justice could lessen public cooperation with the system, or potential offenders' perception of the probability of sanctions, with the consequence of increasing crime. Probably the most frequently suggested line of causation between media representations and criminal behaviour is the allegation that the media undermine *internalised* controls, by regularly presenting sympathetic or glamorous images of offending. This is a common trope of conservative discourse, quintessentially illustrated by Tony Blair's many diatribes against the baleful legacy of 60s 'permissiveness' for crime and criminal justice (Reiner, 2007b: 77–80).

Despite these theoretical reasons for expecting the criminogenic consequences of media representations to be significant, the plethora of positivist attempts to measure media effects have not yielded clear support for this, as noted earlier. The few studies conducted in the 'field' of the impact of new media developments on crime patterns also suggest some effects, though only small ones (see, e.g., Hennigan *et al.*'s 1982 econometric study of the spread of TV across the USA in the early 1950s). So the measurable *direct* short-term effects of the media on crime are small. But this is because of the somewhat simplistic stimulus-response model underlying such research. The deeper, more subtle, longer-term, and reciprocal ways in which media influence culture need a different approach. 'The study of enculturation processes, which work over long time periods, and which are integral to rather than separate from other forms of social determination, would not ask how the media make us act or think, but rather how the media contribute to making us who we are' (Livingstone, 1996: 31–32).

As many studies of the formation of public perceptions show, the media are the principal source of information about crime and criminal justice for most people. They crucially frame debate about 'law and order' (Sasson, 1995; Cavender, 2004), in conjunction with politicians' campaigning and broader shifts in culture, social structure, and political economy (Garland, 2001). Fluctuations in public concern *follow* media and political campaigns, not crime trends (Beckett, 1997; Reiner, 2007b: 139–154).

Panousis confirms this clearly in his analysis of the Greek media. He is right to deny, however, that 'the socio-political role played by the mass media is unavoidably negative'. His concluding call 'for criminologists to acknowledge and act upon the fact that responsibility for media output on crime extends... to themselves as well' by 'forsaking academic isolationism in order to dispel public myths and to accurately reconstruct reality' deserves our full support. But we must acknowledge the formidable obstacles, too. Certainly, contemporary developments – the increasing mediatisation of life in a globalised 24-hour news culture, and the proliferation of citizen recording devices that can capture images of official misconduct such as police brutality – vastly complicate the vexed question of how images and narratives that are felt to be undesirable can be regulated or influenced. Perhaps hope lies precisely in the greater openness of the media to a diversity of inputs and influences. Past experience, on the other hand, suggests the more pessimistic prediction that, although contemporary mass communications present 'an appreciably open terrain for struggles for justice' (Ericson, 1991: 242), the dice are loaded in favour of dominant interests – even if they have to struggle harder for their hegemony.

References

Beckett, K. (1997) *Making Crime Pay*. New York: Oxford University Press.

Cavender, G. (2004) 'Media and Crime Policy', *Punishment and Society* 6: 335–348.

Cohen, L. and S. Felson (1979) 'Social Change and Crime Rate Trends: A Routine Activities Approach', *American Sociological Review* 44: 588–608.

Ericson, R. (1991) 'Mass Media, Crime, Law and Justice', *British Journal of Criminology* 31: 219–249.

Fitzgerald, M., Hough, M., Joseph, I. and T. Quereshi (2003) *Policing for London*. Cullompton: Willan.

Garland, D. (2001) *The Culture of Control*. Oxford: Oxford University Press.

Greer, C. (2010) *Crime and Media*. London: Routledge.

Hallsworth, S. (2005) *Street Crime*. Cullompton: Willan.

Hayward, K. (2004) *City Limits*. London: Glasshouse.

Hennigan, K.M., Delrosario, M.L., Heath, L., Cook, J.D. and B.J. Calder (1982) 'Impact of the Introduction of Television on Crime in the United States: Empirical Findings and Theoretical Implications', *Journal of Personality and Social Psychology* 42: 461–477.

Livingstone, S. (1996) 'On the Continuing Problem of Media Effects', in J. Curran and M. Gurevitch (eds) *Mass Media and Society*, pp. 305–324. London: Arnold.

Merton, R. (1938/1957) 'Social Structure and Anomie', *American Sociological Review* 3: 672–682.

Messner, S.F. and R. Rosenfield (2000) *Crime and the American Dream*, 3rd edn. Belmont: Wadsworth.

Reiner, R. (2007a) 'Media-made Criminality', in M. Maguire, R. Morgan and R. Reiner (eds) *The Oxford Handbook of Criminology*, 4th edn., pp. 302–337. Oxford: Oxford University Press.

Reiner, R. (2007b) *Law and Order: An Honest Citizen's Guide to Crime and Control*. Cambridge: Polity.

Sasson, T. (1995) *Crime Talk: How Citizens Construct a Social Problem*. New York: Aldine De Gruyter.

Schramm, W., Lyle, J. and E.B. Parker (1961) *Television in the Lives of Our Children*. Stanford, CA: Stanford University Press.

Surette, R. (2007) *Media, Crime and Criminal Justice: Images and Realities*, 3rd edn. Belmont: Wadsworth.

Wall, D. (2007) *Cybercrime*. Cambridge: Polity.

VASSILIS KARYDIS

Immigration and Crime

There is a joke that a famous artist with an ambivalent life dies and meets Saint Peter, the Gatekeeper of Paradise. Peter informs him that, despite his sins, he can enter paradise as a distinguished person, and also that he has the privilege to pay a visit to Hell and then decide where he wants to stay. Our man spends a week in paradise with the usual serenity and boredom, so he soon asks Peter to visit Hell. When he arrives there, demons escort him to a hall with music, dance, women, and drink, and he spends a very pleasant evening before returning late to paradise. After a few days, the artist goes to Peter and announces that he decided to move to Hell. Peter warns him that the decision is final and it is impossible to change his mind again. He answers that 'paradise is nice, but Hell surely suits me better'. He thus finds himself in Hell, but this time it looks like Dante's Inferno, replete with fires, tortures, and other horrors. Very surprised and indeed terrified, he asks the demons of the whereabouts of all the amusements he had enjoyed during his previous visit. 'Ah, my friend', a demon says, 'those are for the tourists, not the immigrants'.

The joke reflects the social history of Greece concerning migration, as both a sending and a receiving country. A country of emigration for almost a century (from 1890s until 1970s), it was suddenly transformed into a host country during the 1990s. It is indicative that, until relatively recently, the law regulating the status of aliens in Greece dated back to 1929 (Law 4310). Until the 1990s, the majority of aliens established in the country were Europeans and Americans who resided legally and usually worked in enterprises or military bases. In 1989, Greece was hosting some 50,000 citizens from EU countries, 40,000 citizens from other European countries, 23,000 US citizens, 16,000 Africans, and 43,000 citizens from other countries (Petrinioti, 1993: 15–20). At the beginning of the 1990s, changes in the international environment and in large part stemming from the collapse of socialist regimes in Eastern Europe and the Balkans, Greece faced an unexpected and massive influx of mostly irregular immigrants.

This chapter presents an outline of the demography of the immigrant population in Greece, before examining the philosophy and transformation of the legal framework governing immigration since 1991, and the basic characteristics of immigration policies as both 'law in books' and 'law in action'. The chapter moves on to consider the connections made between the presence of the immigrants in the country and crime, exploring the reliability of official criminal statistics, and presenting empirical data that demonstrate the way in which the penal system discriminates against immigrants. Such discrimination is associated with the demonisation of immigrants, and primarily of Albanians (who constitute the overwhelming majority of immigrants), which in turn is related to the particularities of the Greek case as a country of 'new immigration', as well as to certain historical and political parameters. In the conclusion, it is argued that a complex of social and political factors (from stereotyping to inadequate immigration policy) may be preparing the ground for serious tensions involving second-generation immigrants in the not-too-distant future.

Immigrants and Immigration

Demographics of Immigration

According to the 2001 census of the National Statistical Service of Greece, the size of the immigrant population in the country amounted to approximately 800,000, of whom 750,000 were citizens from non-EU (i.e., not of the EU-15) states. Not included in this number were 300,000–330,000 Greek co-ethnics (either Albanian citizens belonging to the Greek-Orthodox minority located in South Albania – known as 'Voreioipeirotes' – or Greek Pontians from the states of the former USSR (mainly Georgia,

Kazakhstan, and Russia)). Co-ethnics have a different and more privileged legal status, but they face more or less similar problems as other immigrants. According to estimates based on information from police sources and immigrant associations, an additional 180,000–220,000 irregular immigrants also reside in Greece (Triandafyllidou, 2008; Lianos *et al.*, 2008). It is therefore reasonable to assume that today Greece is host to around one million immigrants (in addition to over 300,000 co-ethnics), constituting over 10 percent of the total population.

According to the ethnic distribution of valid residency permits, over 60 percent of immigrants are Albanian citizens, with Bulgarians as the second largest group (at around 6 percent of the immigrant population), followed by Romanians (4 percent), Russians (3 percent), Africans (3 percent), and Poles (2 percent) (Ministry of Interior, 2007; Kotzamanis, 2008: 12–17). Overall, the country is host to immigrants belonging to approximately thirty national groups, but is the only EU member-state with such a significant majority of immigrants from one country (the significance of which for migration policy will be considered below). Over 60 percent of the immigrant population is male, the majority of whom belong to the 25–34 age group (in contrast with the Greek population, which is more or less evenly distributed amongst every age group).[1] As will be discussed further below, age is an important factor in the evaluation of criminality indices.

Legal Framework and Immigration Policies

As indicated above, Greece – along with other South European countries such as Italy and Spain – belongs to a group of host countries that have experienced so-called 'new immigration'. 'Old immigration' was directed primarily towards Western Europe, was largely legal, and was a response to

---

1   There are considerable differences between certain ethnic groups, however: over 90 percent of Indian and Pakistani are males, while the majority of Filipinos and Bulgarians are female, for example.

the need for additions to the labour force in receiving countries (the 'pull' factor; Marshall, 1997). In contrast, 'new immigration' has mainly been provoked by the 'push factor' of economic collapse and impoverishment, persecution, and war, and has been characterised by considerable irregularity, the formation of illegal trafficking networks, the high absorption of immigrants by the informal economy, and the serious deficit of social and legal rights of immigrants (Baldwin-Edwards, 2004: 11–18). Given these conditions, it does not come as a surprise that, almost from the outset, 'new immigration' has encountered distrust and hostility all over Europe, and has been linked to organised crime and, subsequently, to terrorism (Albrecht, 1991; Killias, 1997).

Nancy Green has made the interesting remark that in all countries and languages, the movement of people is often associated with the sea and with fluidity in general. The newcomers are described as 'waves', 'flows', 'streams', a 'human tide', for example (Green, 2004: 15–18). These powerful metaphors remind us of the fluid and spontaneous character of the phenomenon of migration as well as the complexities of attempts to manage these 'oceanic' human movements. Facing such a phenomenon, Greece proved to be totally unprepared, administratively and psychologically, to address and manage it. Greek society developed defensive reflexes towards the massive influx of immigrants, and a new Law for the Aliens was soon enacted (Law 1975/1991). The defensive and punitive philosophy and aims of the new legal framework were clearly stated in its preamble:

> Suddenly, Greece began to be flooded by aliens, who entering, staying, and working illegally, create enormous social problems to the state, while they inevitably try to solve their own problems by engaging in criminality (drugs, robberies, thefts, etc.). (Minutes of Parliament, Session of 10 October 1991)[2]

---

2   It is indicative that the Speaker of the Socialist Opposition (the Panhellenic Socialist Movement, or 'PASOK'), Theofilos Kotsonis, also stated that '[t]he presence of suspicious characters amongst the unfortunate illegal economic refugees, and the commission of illegal acts by these elements, created a psychology of defence in Greek society' (ibid.).

This perception of the presence of the immigrants as an 'historical accident' that is solvable by policing, is reflected in the provisions of the law, which are dominated by the spirit of deterrence for almost all aspects of immigrant activity. In particular, three main groups of provisions are discernible according to the different goals they try to serve (Karydis, 2001: 134–139): firstly, the drastic reduction of the number of petitions for asylum by curtailing the rights of asylum-seekers; secondly, the deterrence of those entering illegally or staying irregularly in the country, by threatening serious penalties both against them and any Greek citizen who helps them find work, hosts or hires them, and by excluding irregular immigrants from access to public services; and thirdly, the control of immigrants who enter and stay legally in the country, by the wide discretion accorded to the police and administrative authorities to impose serious restrictions upon them.

Regularisation and Rights

The adoption of a penal response to this serious social and political problem was destined to fail. The acceptance of this fact came first with the ratification of two Presidential Decrees (358/1997 and 359/1997, respectively) which allowed for the regularisation of 200,000 out of an estimated total of 600,000 irregular immigrants. This was a partial measure, intended to ease social tensions that had been caused by the presence of so many immigrants in the country. A new law was enacted in 2001 (Law 2910/2001), which reluctantly moved away from institutional hostility towards a system more tolerant of basic rights for immigrants.[3] In this direction, there were provisions for the regulation of family reunions, legal remedies against deportation decisions, the explicit recognition of equal social security rights and benefits to those of nationals, and official acceptance of foreign minors in the public education system irrespective of their families' legal status. Despite setting strict conditions, the Law also allowed for the regularisation of another large swathe of the immigrant population (Vrellis, 2003).

3   It should, of course, be noted that that the legislation is decisively influenced each
     time by the institutional framework of the European Union (see Nikolopoulos,
     2008; also Mitsilegas, this collection).

On the other hand, institutional distrust and the spirit of surveillance and control were left intact. Consider, for example, the short duration of residence permits (three months), the narrow deadlines allowed for pursuing legal remedies (just a few days), continued burdens upon employers, the prohibition of free movement and residency in certain areas of the country, the arbitrary criteria used to determine 'undesirable' aliens, and, most importantly, the wide discretionary powers and lack of accountability of police and administrative authorities in these areas (Karydis, 2000). At the same time, 'law in action', i.e., the actual function of the administration in the everyday interaction with the immigrants, made the proper exercise of their rights almost untenable. Amongst the immigrant community, the rights provided by the new legal framework were felt to be temporary and insecure. Indicatively, and confirming the validity of this interpretation in surveying the administrative practices and bureaucratic pathologies of the state, a Deputy of the Greek Ombudsman comments:

> It is safely assumed that the regime of temporariness is not simply a bureaucratic symptom, it is what characterises the whole attitude of the Greek state towards immigrants, an attitude of immobility and embarrassment against the course of the immigrant wave and the transformation of Greece into a country receiving immigrants. (Chatzi, 2004: 236)

After falling under this kind of criticism (with which the vast majority of the academic community agreed) and its obvious malfunctions, a new legal framework was introduced with Law 3386/2005 (amended by Law 3536/2007). Certain provisions moved towards rationalisation and simplification of administrative procedures, especially regarding the issuance of stay and work permits, which were henceforth combined in a single permit issued by the Department for Aliens of the Region. Law 3386/2005 also provided better safeguards against deportation and the revocation of permits, as well as the right to appeal against administrative decisions (Filippou, 2008: 365–390). However, the Law retained strict conditions for the issuance of permits and petitions for family reunion, e.g., the high cost of the relevant fee (at 1,500 euros, the highest fee levied in the EU). The requirement that the immigrant is professionally active remains, as does the wide discretion of the authorities. At the time of writing, there also remains a lack of any regulations concerning irregular second-generation immigrants who are nevertheless integrated within the national education system. Furthermore, strict penalties are provided for illegal entry to, and stay in, Greece (a minimum three months of imprisonment and a fine of 3,000–10,000 Euros, without the right to request a suspension of the sentence), as well as repatriation for those considered 'undesirable aliens'. The blanket provision forbidding access to any public service for irregular immigrants has also been retained, with the exception of hospitalisation in cases of emergency (Papatheodorou, 2007: 68–153; Greek Ombudsman, 2007: 17–24).

Naturalisation

The legal framework for the naturalisation of immigrants is very restrictive. Greek nationality follows *ius sanguinis* (the principle of ancestral or 'blood' connections) and, to that extent, at first sight resembles the German model of 'differential exclusion' (following the classification by Castles (1997)). However, the peculiarity of the Greek case is symptomatic rather of a 'Balkan syndrome' concerning minorities. The history of the Balkans is full of wars among nation-states that emerged from the disintegrating Ottoman Empire and sought neighbouring territories where co-ethnic (and/or co-religious) groups were based (see Mazower, 2002). This has left legacies of insecurity and suspicion, of which the political tension between Greece and FYROM (the Former Yugoslav Republic of Macedonia) concerning the constitutional name of the latter, is characteristic. It is equally indicative that, according to the Code of Greek Citizenship (Law 3284/2004), the prerequisites for a naturalisation petition include adulthood, permanent legal stay in the country for at least ten years during the 12 years preceding the petition, and lack of a criminal record (no conviction that brings over a year of imprisonment). Most importantly, the state has absolute discretion in its treatment of the petition and has no obligation to give reasons for a rejection, to which there is no judicial redress (Christopoulos, 2004: 338–366). Administrative delays in addressing petitions may last many years, and often more than ten. In practice, some ethnic groups, such as immigrants of Albanian origin, appear to be excluded from naturalisation. There is even a reluctance to grant naturalisation to Albanian citizens of Greek origin (Voreioipeirotes) since they would thereby lose Albanian citzenship and consequently their minority status within Albania. Instead, Voreioipeirotes tend only to be provided with a Special Identity Card, renewable after ten years, granting them and their families a special status amongst the immigrant community in Greece (Baltsiotis, 2004: 303–337).

By the ways outlined above, including the high cost of applications in particular, most immigrants are deterred from petitioning for naturalisation. As a result, almost no non-ethnic immigrants were naturalised before 1997, and only 10,000 of them were granted citizenship between 1997 and 2004 (Pavlou, 2004: 395–399). To the extent that it is possible to talk about a 'model' of immigration policy in Greece (something not at all certain), it seems to be a peculiar hybrid of 'differential exclusion' and a *sui generis* 'assimilation', not allowing adequate space for the identity, citizenship, and political rights of immigrants (unlike the assimilation model of *ius soli* in France). This approach inevitably affects and reinforces public attitudes towards the presence of immigrants in the country, and especially the characterisation of ethnic Albanians as threatening and problematic.

Criminality, or Criminalisation, of Immigrants?

The question arising at this point is whether, or to what extent, negative perceptions concerning the involvement of immigrants in crime reflect reality. To address this question, the starting point must be the official indices of criminality, notwithstanding the well-known deficiencies regarding the validity and reliability of criminal statistics (see, e.g., Maguire, 1994; Coleman and Moynihan, 1996).

Official Indices of Crime

The number of foreign offenders known to the police during the period 2000–2006 constituted approximately 8 percent of the total number of offenders, according to publicly available official police statistics. As mentioned above, immigrants in Greece comprise over 10 percent of the total population. At the same time, however, aliens make up close to half of the prison population (see further Cheliotis and Xenakis, this collection) – a fact which for many simply confirms their assumptions of the criminality of immigrants. How can these apparent paradoxes be explained? Collective national indices of criminality do not provide a clear picture about the qualitative features of criminal activity by immigrants, but it is clear that a significant segment of immigrant deviancy is related to 'status offences' such as violations of the Law on Aliens (i.e., concerning illegal entry and stay) and other similar crimes (e.g., the use of false identity or permit documentation), whilst immigrants are underrepresented in forms of crime from which their largely disadvantaged status (economic and educational) precludes their participation (see Triantafyllidou, 2008). Such offences include, for example, traffic offences, violation of labour and tax laws by employers, and other 'white-collar' offences (from issuing bad cheques to committing embezzlement), which have been increasing over recent years. To address the alleged nexus between immigrants and crime in Greece, it is important to return to the official indices and focus upon three indicative serious felonies of the 'street crime' variety: intentional homicide, robbery, and rape. These particular crimes are highlighted here because they involve violence, are serious in their consequences for the victims, are highly visible and attract publicity, fuel public fear and insecurity, and their alleged rise has largely been attributed to the presence of the immigrants and has thus contributed decisively to their demonisation.

According to data gathered at the Headquarters of the Greek police between 2000 and 2006, foreigners (the huge majority of whom are immigrants) accounted for 43 percent of known homicide offenders, and over 70 percent of these were Albanians. On average, only about 15 percent of homicide cases were not cleared, which means that statistics here provide a more or less objective and representative picture of the ethnicity of homicide offenders (taking into account that the 'dark figure' of crime in the case of homicide is minimal). Given that their percentage of the total population is 10 percent, this impressive overrepresentation of immigrants may be qualified by the age factor. As mentioned above, the age and gender distribution of the immigrant population is very different from that of the Greek population. According to the 2001 Census, approximately 60 percent of the (largely male) immigrant community belongs to the 20–44 age range, whilst, in contrast, 40 percent of Greek nationals (for whom the gender distribution is equal) fall in the same age range. The significance of this distribution is grounded in the fact that over 90 percent of homicide offenders – as with perpetrators of robbery and rape – belong to precisely the same group (males between 20–44 years old).

During the same period (2000–2006), immigrant robbery offenders accounted for approximately 40 percent of the total number, with Albanians and Romanians being the most prevalent amongst these. As with the case of homicides, immigrant offenders were highly overrepresented in cases of robbery (and also in other predatory crimes such as theft and burglary), notwithstanding the factors of age and gender. The low rate of clearance in robbery cases (35 percent on average) and the heavy policing of the immigrant community may nevertheless have resulted in the distortion of the statistical records regarding this particular crime. It is widely acknowledged that the focus of police activities upon certain groups of the population, certain areas of the city or categories of crime, may lead to the disclosure of more hidden crime, turning the labeling of such groups or areas as 'criminogenic' into a self-fulfilling prophecy (Cook and Hudson, 1993; Solomos, 1993; Courakis, 2003). The immigrant community in Greece undoubtedly lives under constant and heavy policing; research shows that immigrants are fifteen times more likely to be brought to a police station than Greeks (Papantoniou et al., 1998), not taking into account the large military-type operations to apprehend irregular immigrants. Also, because of the aforementioned prejudices, victims are also more willing to report crime to the police where the offender is suspected to be an immigrant. Again, over the same period, an average 42 percent of known rape offenders were immigrants. Whilst assessments similar to those above may be applied to the case of immigrant involvement in rape offences, it should additionally be borne in mind that the 'dark figure' – or non-reporting – of this particular crime is thought to be over 90 percent, and there are many different criteria influencing a victim's decision to report the incident (Tsigris, 1996).

From serious street crimes, to other serious crimes such as drug and people trafficking and sexual exploitation, immigrants are overrepresented in the official figures of known offenders. To explore why this is the case, and in particular why different crimes are associated with particular foreign ethnicities rather than others (e.g., why Albanians and Romanians are over-represented in official crime statistics whilst Filipinos and Egyptians are almost absent from them), further research is required. A first step towards explaining the overrepresentation of immigrants in particular forms of crime such as these, however, is to examine the practices and attitudes of those working in the field of law enforcement.

Attitudes and Practices of Law Enforcement

As concerns the administrators of policing, a study of police attitudes has shown that many officers believe in a direct link between immigration and serious criminality (Alexias, 2001). There have been many reported deaths of migrants at and near the borders by police and army patrols. Many incidents of torture – at times resulting in death – have been reported in places of immigrant detention, actions which appear to take place in a general environment of impunity.[4] There are regular reports by the press, immigrant organisations, and NGOs, citing incidents of harassment, use of arbitrary force, unlawful search and custody, and humiliation of immigrants on the part of the police, but almost no officers alleged to be involved have ever been punished. As submitted by Greece in its 19th periodic report to the UN Committee on the Elimination of Racial Discrimination, between 2003–2007, of 238 cases where police employees had been accused of maltreating individuals, only one was expelled from the force.[5] According to a Special Report of the Greek Ombudsman investigating decunciations by citizens of police employees,

---

4   See further the 2008 report of the CPT (European Committee for the Prevention of Torture and Inhuman or Degrading Treatment or Punishment).
5   The report, from 2008, is available online at: http://www2.ohchr.org/english/bodies/cerd/docs/CERD.C.GRC.19EN.doc

> The use of force, abusive or illegal behaviour, is linked to particular actions of members of the police during the course of their duty, and emerge with a high incidence and intensity in certain police practices or activities, especially during police controls, arrests, escort to the police station, and custody. [...] In particular, in many cases, individuals allege that arbitrary conclusions have been deduced by the classification of individuals into categories of suspects according to their racial origin, [...] their sexual preference [...], or their ethnic origin [...], a fact which is often accompanied, according to allegations, by barbaric or improper behaviour. (Greek Ombudsman, 2004: 28, 35)[6]

Furthermore, in the few detention centres created to retain irregular migrants apprehended at the country's borders, conditions are unbearable. The detention centre on the island of Lesbos, for example, has a capacity of 400 places but is currently housing over 800 immigrants. The sanitary conditions are terrible: for instance, a doctor of the NGO 'Doctors Without Borders' who inspected the site, reported that for one chamber of the centre there was only one toilet for over a hundred people (*Ta Nea*, 13 July 2008).

Judges also share the view that the overrepresentation of immigrants in the prison system accurately reflects their level of involvement in serious crime. A survey (which was conducted by a judge) of 250 judges and 412 police employees in the wider area of Athens (the prefecture of Attica), carried out between 1998–2003, found that the majority of judges believed there to be 'too many' foreigners in the country and that foreigners were – at least partly – responsible for rising criminality. Foreigners were also far more likely to be portrayed by judges as 'offenders' rather than as 'victims'. At the same time, however, respondents declared that, despite holding certain negative attitudes towards the presence of immigrants in the country, they did not consider such sentiments to influence the execution of their duties in delivering justice. Confirming the results of these interviews, the survey concluded that judges are not biased against immigrants in their judicial work, and treat them equally and objectively, as any other offender (Vagena-Palaiologou, 2008: 98–117).

6   It is important to note, however, that the number of immigrants who file a report to the Greek Ombudsman is still quite small, with the exception of the office addressing the protection of human rights, and mainly in respect to the implementation of the Law for Aliens. Nevertheless, the number of reports submitted by immigrants to the Ombudsman is increasing each year (Pavlou, 2004: 400–402).

In order to examine the objectivity of this claim, archival research was conducted upon convictions handed out between 2004 and 2006 by the Felonies Court (of the First and Second Instance) in Athens. The study sought to assess whether judicial treatment of offenders in similar cases was the same or was differentiated according to the ethnicity of the offender (ethnicity being the only significant variable of the cases under comparison). The convictions selected concerned drug offences (drug trafficking), in part since they constituted the majority of the cases of that particular court, but also since with this category of offences the judiciary sets sentences that are fixed according largely to the quantity and the kind of the drug involved. The total sample under study consisted of 767 offenders; 385 Greeks (50.2 percent) and 382 foreigners (49.8 percent).[7] The large majority of the defendants were male (there were only 81 female defendants), while almost 80 percent of the defendants were between 22–50 years old (49 percent were between 22–35, and 38.2 percent were between 36–50). As regards profession, 47 percent were employees, 20.3 percent were unemployed, and 20.1 percent were self-employed. Approximately 9 percent of the Greek offenders were Roma, who were thus overrepresented in comparison to their proportion in the general population.

By examining the length of imprisonment to which different ethnic groups of offenders were sentenced on average, a clear differentiation in the degree of gravity of the imposed sentences was evident. In the 29 cases where life sentences were imposed, 24 of the offenders were foreigners, one was of the Greek-Roma community, and only four were ethnically Greek. It is also indicative that all four Greeks were charged with trafficking large quantities of 'hard' drugs (over 1.5 kg), whereas in at least four of the other cases of the rest 25, the charge was for quantities less than 200 grammes. Where similar drug offences (of hard/soft drugs and their amounts) were compared, it was found that the length of sentences imposed upon foreigners were little affected by the severity of the crimes and were consistently almost double those awarded to Greeks. Moreover, Albanians were found to receive longer sentences than other foreign offenders. It was thus clear

7   The sample was formed by picking at random every fourth file. The data were gathered by Dimitra Yiazintzi (University of Athens) and Danai Kassimati (University of the Peloponnese) under the supervision of the author.

from the findings that, as a rule, immigrant offenders are treated differently, and more harshly, than Greek offenders, receiving more severe sentences in similar cases (Karydis, 2010: 228–244).

In light of these findings, the over-representation of immigrants in crime statistics and amongst the prison population in Greece is explainable by the influence of judicial bias against immigrants which in turn affects sentencing. This serves to compound other factors which militate against immigrant defendants, such as poor knowledge of the language, financial inability to secure adequate legal representation, and inability to draw on 'reliable' witnesses for their defence. It is also not unrelated that immigrants constitute 60 percent of defendants kept in prison awaiting trial (upon the joint decision of the Investigating Judge and the Prosecutor), and that defendants awaiting trial constitute a third of the total prison population (see further Cheliotis, this collection).

The Significance and Social Construction of Stereotypes

The attitudes and practices of Greek law enforcement authorities do not exist within a vacuum, and there is no doubt that immigrants in the country are victimised by broader formal and informal mechanisms of social control. The economic exploitation of immigrants has been enormous, especially during the 1990s, when their wages were typically set at a third of the amount received by nationals (Katseli *et al.*, 1996). In 1996, the then Minister of Finance Stefanos Manos (who remains politically prominent today) publicly stated: 'I am enthusiastic about Albanians! It is, of course, illegal work, but this is a prerequisite in order for their labour to be provided at a low price' (*Rizospastis*, 31 March 1996). One study of the discrepancies between wages in four categories of different professions (skilled professionals, service workers, skilled workers, unskilled workers) over the period 2004–2005, found an average salary differential of 48 percent, which was only explainable by the variable of the ethnic origin of the employees, thus underlining the clearly disadvantageous position of immigrants (Demoussis *et al.*, 2008: 132–153).

Laying the groundwork for such exploitation has been the rise of xenophobia in the country. A Eurostat survey in 1989 – i.e., just before the first immigrant wave – found that Greek people expressed a high level of tolerance about the presence of foreigners in the country and support for their rights. Three years later, Greek respondents proved more xenophobic than those of many other European member-states, including both those of 'old' and 'new' immigration (e.g., Britain and the Nertherlands, and Spain and Portugal, respectively; Dodos *et al.*, 1996: 321–343). Another survey found that the percentage of people believing there were 'too many' foreigners in the country rose every year, from 29 percent in 1991 to 69 percent in 1994 (see Voulgaris *et al.*, 1995), despite the fact that the number of immigrants had not seen an outstanding rise during that period.

A content analysis of the Greek press during the period 1990–1992, conducted on behalf of the Council of Europe to assess the protection of human rights for immigrants in Greece, revealed that unemployment and criminality were the main concerns raised about the presence of immigrants in the country (Spinelli *et al.*, 1992). Ten years later, research showed that criminality remained the primary justification cited by Greek respondents for xenophobic attitudes, in addition to the perceived negative impact of immigrants upon Greek levels of unemployment and national cultural life (EKKE, 2003). Newspaper reports and headlines usually characterised immigrants as 'killers' and 'assassins'. The most frequently mentioned ethnic group were the Albanians, who were mainly held responsible for property crimes and drug law violations (Konstantinidou, 2001; Moschopoulou, 2005). During the 1990s, therefore, it is possible to trace the development of a typical moral panic (Goode and Ben-Yehuda, 1994), which directly linked an alleged significant increase in serious criminality with the presence of immigrants in Greece. As recent research has shown, the same pattern of media reporting concerning the presence of the immigrants in the country is still evident today, fuelled further on occasion by exciting crime incidents.[8]

---

8   See, for example, the research conducted by Louisa Tsaliki at the University of Athens, as described in the report 'Greek Media Favour Racism' in *Kathimerini*, 27 September 2008. See also Panousis, this collection.

The Albanian 'Other'

To focus on the particularly prominent phenomenon of the 'othering' of Albanians, one explanation for its emergence has undoubtedly been the particular circumstances of Greece's transformation into a country of immigration and the sheer size of the Albanian community amongst the immigrant population. Once Albanians started emigrating to Greece in their masses, moreover, there were no established networks within the country to support them, which swiftly made them a highly visible presence in public spaces. The discomfort which this caused may in part be attributable to the resurrection of older stereotypes that had arisen around poor relations between Greece and Albania over previous decades (which included the issue of the rights of a Greek-Orthodox minority in southern Albania). Cultural prejudices constituted another parameter of this discomfort, wherein Albanian origin was regarded as synonymous with the uncivilised, savage 'Balkans', in contrast to the 'civilised West' to which Greeks believe that they culturally belong (Karydis, 1998: 354–356).

In a survey conducted amongst first-year Law School students at the Democritus University of Thrace in February 1996 (with 151 fully completed questionnaires from a pool of 211 students), the four most significant attributes of Albanians, according to the respondents, were: 'dirty' (74 percent), 'thieves' (70.7 percent), 'dangerous' (70 percent), and 'impoverished' (67 percent). The vast majority of respondents sampled (97 percent) believed that a large increase in serious criminality in Greece was due to the presence of the immigrants, and when asked which ethnic group was responsible for such a rise, overwhelmingly blamed Albanians. Amongst ethnic groups in Greece, the respondents also recorded feeling least sympathy towards Albanians (Karydis, 1996: 138–155). More interestingly, a follow-up survey ten years later (in June 2006), did not show any material change to the attitudes and perceptions of the student respondents, apart from the development that 'dangerous' and 'unreliable' had replaced 'dirty' and 'impoverished' amongst the four most significant attributes reported (Karydis, 2010: 66–116).

As these findings indicate, negative stereotypes of immigrants have become embedded in the collective consciousness of Greeks, despite the evolution of the experience of immigration over the course of almost two decades, the regularisation of a majority of immigrants, and their absorption into the labour market and national education system. The findings of the first National Victim Survey (published in Karydis, 2004), conducted in 2001, confirm that the public continued to perceive a connection between crime and the presence of immigrants in Greece. In comparison with the International Crime Victims Survey of 2000 (van Kesteren *et al.*, 2000), whose methodology was followed for the Greek survey, the Greek scores placed the country amongst the most insecure internationally. In response to being asked which aspects of criminality the respondents had discussed over the last two weeks, the issue of drugs came first (19.4 percent), and the issue of foreigners/immigrants came second (14.1 percent). The survey illustrated the abstract and general way in which immigrants are identified with crime by the Greek public. Furthermore, 72 percent of the sample agreed with the position that 'the police must be stricter towards immigrants', while 81 percent rejected the proposition that immigrants be employed by the police force (ibid.; see also Cheliotis and Xenakis, this collection).

Instead of an Epilogue, a Foreword: The Issue of the Second Generation

Experiences of discrimination and their internalisation serve the construction of a collective identity amongst many of the immigrant communities. Bitterness and discontent emerge from their sense of inferior social and legal status and the negative stereotyping of their community (Kranidioti, 2002: 171–176; Karydis, 2004b: 224–228). In the vicious circle of 'deviance amplification' (Wilkins, 1971), immigrants may in their turn construct a stereotype of an unjust, hostile, and cruel 'Greek Other', as indicated by the findings of a survey using 'life history' interviews with

Albanian immigrants (Nitsiakos, 2003). As I argued over ten years ago, '[i]f the present situation remains the same, the processes of marginalisation [...] will eventually produce an alienated "underclass" consisting mainly of massively deprived migrants. Moreover, the potential for second-generation migrants to self-identify as personally or collectively deprived will facilitate their participation in deviant subcultures or even organised criminal networks, contrary to any anticipated improvement in the material conditions of their lives' (Karydis, 1998: 363–364). What is, indeed, at stake now is the integration of second-generation immigrants. These minors, who have been born or brought up in Greece, attend school, talk the language, and participate in youth culture, are not granted naturalisation, and by eighteen years of age are treated as any other immigrant. Indicatively, the rate of school drop-outs is much higher amongst immigrant students than Greek nationals, especially at the level of secondary education (Yianitsas et al., 2008: 178–195).

In Athens, of the minors known to the police as offenders, 25 percent are Greek, 65 percent are Albanian, and 10 percent are of other foreign ethnicity. According to police statistics, amongst minors known to be responsible for offences against property, 35 percent are Greek, 50 percent are Albanian, and 15 percent are of other foreign ethnicity. Approximately half of the offences perpetrated by minors are cases of begging, and 90 percent of begging offences are committed by Albanian minors. An illustrative example of dominant attitudes towards this phenomenon is provided in the findings of a study carried out by the University of Thessaloniki, during summer 2002, on behalf of the Ministry of Public Order:

> They are usually boys, but lately many girls also appear, aged 5–15 years. ... The children usually sell cheap objects or beg or steal. They are solicited, use drugs and/or even take part in homicides. A case of a child from Albania is reported who, in gratitude, told a Greek who had helped him: 'Uncle, do you have any "friend" you would like me to kill?' (Vidali, 2002)

As a country of 'new immigration', young immigrants in Greece still belong to the so-called 'one-and-a-half generation', in the sense that most were not born in the country but have been brought up in Greece. It may be possible to discern trends, but not to predict the modes, of their adaptation to Greek society. Precisely for this reason, it is important to give serious consideration to the experiences of countries of 'old immigration', and to the warnings they offer. In particular, it is instructive here to recall the words of Jock Young: 'The grand irony of "cultural othering" is that, as migrant groups become more like the majority culture, they experience higher levels of relative deprivation and discontent in response to their poverty, and their level of crime increases. [...] Finally, of course, some minority groups take up the negative characteristics projected upon them, while others evolve cultures of difference and fundamentalism to cope with, and make sense of, their rejection. Having summoned forth false demons we find, in front of our eyes, real demons arising' (Young, 2007: 143).

References

Greek Ombudsman (2004) *Special Report: Disciplinary-Administrative Investigation Against Police Employees* [in Greek]. Athens: National Publishing Office.

Greek Ombudsman (2007) *Annual Report 2007* [in Greek]. Athens: National Publishing Office.

Albrecht, H.-J. (1997) 'Minorities, Crime and Criminal Justice in the Federal Republic of Germany', in I.H. Marshall (ed.) *Minorities, Migrants and Crime*, pp. 86–109. London and New York: Sage.

Alexias, A. (2001) 'The Social Perception and Study of the Phenomenon of Immigration', in Y. Amitsis and Y. Lazaridi (eds) *Legal and Sociopolitical Dimensions of Immigration in Greece and the European Union* [in Greek], pp. 287–302. Athens: Papazissis.

Baldwin-Edwards, M. (2004) 'Immigration, Immigrants and Socialisation in Southern Europe: Patterns, Problems and Contradistinctions', in C. Inglessi, A. Lyberaki, H. Vermeulen and G.J. Van Wijngaarden (eds) *Immigration and Integration in Northern Versus Southern Europe*, pp. 11–26. Athens: The Netherlands Institute in Athens.

Baltsiotis, L. (2004) 'Citizenship and Naturalisation in Greece', in M. Pavlou and D. Christopoulos (eds) *The Greece of Immigration: Social Participation, Rights and Citizenship* [in Greek], pp. 303–337. Athens: Kritiki.

Castles, S. (1997) 'Multicultural Citizenship: The Australian Experience', in V. Bader (ed.) *Citizenship and Exclusion*, pp. 113–138. Basingstoke: MacMillan Press.

Chatzi, C. (2004) 'The Foreigner as Bearer of Rights in the Greek Legal System', in M. Pavlou and D. Christopoulos (eds) *The Greece of Immigration: Social Participation, Rights and Citizenship* [in Greek], pp. 233–252. Athens: Kritiki.

Christopoulos, D. (2004) 'Immigrants in the Greek Political Community', in M. Pavlou and D. Christopoulos (eds) *The Greece of Immigration: Social Participation, Rights and Citizenship* [in Greek], pp. 338–366. Athens: Kritiki.

Coleman, C. and J. Moynihan (1996) *Understanding Crime Data*. Buckingham: Open University Press.

Committee for the Prevention of Torture and Inhuman or Degrading Treatment (CPT) (2008) *Report on Greece*. Strasbourg: Council of Europe.

Courakis, N. (2003) 'Foreigners, Immigration Policy and Criminality' [in Greek], *Poinika Chronika* 53: 577–583.

Demoussis, M., Yiannakopoulos, N. and S. Zografakis (2008) 'A Study of Wage Differentials between Greek and Immigrant Employees in Greece', in J. Kavounidi, A. Kontis, T. Lianos and R. Fakiolas (eds) *Immigration in Greece: Experiences, Policies, Prospects, Volume 1* [in Greek], pp. 132–153. Athens: Hellenic Migration Policy Institute (IMEPO).

Dodos, D., Kafetzis, P., Michalopoulou, A. and E. Nikolakopoulos (1996) 'Xenophobia and Racism in Greece, 1988–1992', in EKKE (ed.) *Dimensions of Social Exclusion in Greece: Report for the European Social Fund*, pp. 321–343. Athens: EKKE.

Filippou, D. (2008) 'Administrative Deportation and Judicial Protection according to Law 3386/2005', in A. Sikiotou (ed.) *Foreigners in Greece: Inclusion or Marginalisation?* [in Greek], pp. 365–392. Athens-Komotini: Ant. N. Sakkoulas Publishers.

Goode, E. and N. Ben-Yehuda (1994) *Moral Panics: The Social Control of Deviance*. Oxford: Blackwell.

Green, N.L. (2004) *The Roads of Immigration: Contemporary Theoretical Approaches*. Athens: Savallas.

Cook, D. and B. Hudson (1993) 'Racism and Criminology: Concepts and Controversies', in D. Cook and B. Hudson (eds) *Racism and Criminology*, pp. 1–27. London: Sage.

Karydis, V. (1996) *The Criminality of Immigrants in Greece: Issues of Theory and Crime Policy* [in Greek]. Athens: Papazissis.

Karydis, V. (1998) 'Criminality of Criminalisation of Migrants in Greece? An Attempt at Synthesis', in V. Ruggiero, N. South and I. Taylor (eds) *The New European Criminology*, pp. 350–367. London and New York: Routledge.

Karydis, V. (2000) 'The New Draft Law on Immigration Policy' [in Greek], *Poiniki Dikaiosyni* 11: 1126–1129.

Karydis, V. (2001) 'Social and Legal Aspects of Migration Policies in Greece', in P. Marry and T. Papatheodorou (eds) *Crime and Insecurity in Europe*, pp. 129–142. Brussels: Bruylant.

Karydis, V. (2004) *Invisible Criminality: A National Victim Survey* [in Greek]. Athens-Komotini: Ant. N. Sakkoulas Publishers.

Karydis, V. (2004b) 'The Issue of the Second Generation: Crime and Immigration', in M. Pavlou and D. Christopoulos (eds) *The Greece of Immigration: Social Participation, Rights and Citizenship* [in Greek], pp. 205–232. Athens: Kritiki.

Karydis, V. (2010) *Visions of Social Control in Greece: Moral Panics, Criminal Justice* [in Greek]. Athens-Komotini: Ant. N. Sakkoulas Publishers.

Killias, M. (1997) 'Ethnicity, Crime and Immigration: Comparative and Cross-National Perspectives', *Crime and Justice: A Review of Research* 21: 375–405.

Konstantinidou, C. (2001) *Social Representations of Crime* [in Greek]. Athens-Komotini: Ant. N. Sakkoulas Publishers.

Kotzamanis, V. (2008) 'Foreigners in Greece, 1991–2001', in J. Kavounidi, A. Kontis, T. Lianos and R. Fakiolas (eds) *Immigration in Greece: Experiences, Policies, Prospects, Volume 1* [in Greek], pp. 12–37. Athens: Hellenic Migration Policy Institute (IMEPO).

Kranidioti, M. (2002) 'Foreigners' Criminality in Greece: Theory, Research and Views on Anti-crime Policy', in N. Courakis (ed.) *Anti-crime Policy IV* [in Greek], pp. 147–190. Athens: Ant. N. Sakkoulas Publishers.

Maguire, M. (1997) 'Crime Statistics, Patterns and Trends: Changing Perceptions and their Implications', in M. Maguire, R. Morgan and R. Reiner (eds) *The Oxford Handbook of Criminology*, pp. 135–188. Oxford: Oxford University Press.

Marshall, I.H. (ed.) (1997) *Minorities, Migrants, and Crime*. London and New York: Sage.

Mazower, M. (2002) *The Balkans* [in Greek]. Athens: Patakis.

Moschopoulou, A. (2005) *Immigrants' Criminality* [in Greek]. Athens: Ant. N. Sakkoulas Publishers.

Lianos, T., Kanelopoulos, K., Gregou, M., Gemi, E. and P. Papakonstantinou (2008) *Estimation of the Illegal Immigrant Population in Greece* [in Greek]. Athens: Hellenic Migration Policy Institute (IMEPO).

Greek Parliament, *Minutes, Session of 10 October 1991* [in Greek]. Athens: National Publishing Office.

National Center for Social Research (EKKE) (2003) *Greece-Europe: Society, Politics, Values* [in Greek]. Athens: EKKE.

Nikolopoulos, G. (2008) *The European Union as Bearer of Anti-crime Policy: The 'Hague Programme' and its Implementation* [in Greek]. Athens: Nomiki Vivliothiki.

Nitsiakos, V. (2003) *Testimonies of Albanian Immigrants* [in Greek]. Athens: Odysseas.

Papantoniou, A., Frangouli M. and A. Kalavanou (1998) *Illegal Migration and the Problem of Crime*. Research Report. Athens: TSER Project.

Papatheodorou, T. (2007) *Foreigners' Legal Status* [in Greek]. Athens: Nomiki Vivliothiki.

Pavlou, M. (2004) 'The Greece of Immigration in Numbers', in M. Pavlou and D. Christopoulos (eds) *The Greece of Immigration: Social Participation, Rights and Citizenship* [in Greek], pp. 367–402. Athens: Kritiki.

Petrinioti, C. (1993) *Immigration to Greece* [in Greek]. Athens: Odysseas.

Said, E.W. (1996) *Orientalism* [in Greek]. Athens: Nefeli.

Solomos, J. (1993) 'Constructions of Black Criminality: Racialisation and Criminalisation in Perspective', in D. Cook and B. Hudson (eds) *Racism and Criminology*, pp. 118–135. London: Sage.

Spinelli, C.D., Vidali, S., Dermati, S., Koulouris, N. and M. Tavoulari (1992) *Protection of Human Rights of Recent Migrant Groups in Greece with Emphasis on Those Deprived of Their Freedom*. Report to the Council of Europe.

Triantaffylidou, A. (2008) *The Immigrant Population of Greece: Size, Sociodemographic Features and Labour Market Integration* [in Greek]. Paper presented at the Sixth Annual Symposium of the Aristovoulos Manessis Association, Ioannina, Greece, 4–5 April.

Tsigris, A. (1996) *Rape: The Invisible Crime* [in Greek]. Athens: Ant. N. Sakkoulas Publishers.

Van Kesteren, J., Mayhew, P. and P. Nieuwbeerta (2000) *Criminal Victimisation in Seventeen Industrialised Countries*. The Hague: NSCR/WODC.

Vayena-Palaiologou, E. (2008) 'Racism and Xenophobia in Greece Today: Attitudes of the Bearers of Formal Social Control (Justice-Police)', in J. Kavounidi, A. Kontis, T. Lianos and R. Fakiolas (eds) *Immigration in Greece: Experiences, Policies, Prospects, Volume 2* [in Greek], pp. 98–117. Athens: Hellenic Migration Policy Institute (IMEPO).

Veikou, M. (2001) 'The Construction of Ethnic Identity', in A. Marvakis, D. Parsanoglou and M. Pavlou (eds) *Immigrants in Greece* [in Greek], pp. 350–361. Athens: Ellinika Grammata.

Vidali, S. (2002) *A Study and Proposals of Anti-crime Policy for the Control of Deviance and Victimisation of Minors* [in Greek]. Unpublished report submitted to the Ministry of Public Order.

Voulgaris, Y., Dodos, D., Kafetzis, P., Lyrintzis, C., Michalopoulou, K., Nikolakopoulos, E., Spourdalakis, M. and K. Tsoukalas (1995) 'Perception and Treatment of
the Other in Today's Greece: Findings from an Empirical Study' [in Greek],
Greek Review of Political Science 5: 81–100.

Vrellis, S. (2003) *Foreigners' Law* [in Greek]. Athens: Nomiki Vivliothiki.

Wilkins, L.T. (1971) 'The Deviance Amplifying System', in W.G. Carson and P.N. Wiles
(eds) *The Sociology of Crime and Delinquency in Britain: Sociological Readings*,
pp. 219–225. London: Martin Robertson.

Yianitsas, D., Mavromatis, G. and T. Avramidi (2008) 'The Presence of Foreign Pupils
in Second-grade Education', in J. Kavounidi, A. Kontis, T. Lianos and R. Fakiolas
(eds) *Immigration in Greece: Experiences, Policies, Prospects, Volume 2* [in Greek],
pp. 178–195. Athens: Hellenic Migration Policy Institute (IMEPO).

Young, J. (1992) 'Ten Points of Realism', in J. Young and R. Matthews (eds) *Rethinking
Criminology: The Realist Debate*, pp. 24–68. London: Sage.

Young, J. (2007) *The Vertigo of Late Modernity*. London: Sage.

DIDIER BIGO

Commentary

Crime, Violence, Migration:
An (In)security Continuum Led by Institutional Struggles?

The chapter by Vassilis Karydis on immigration and crime is central to our understanding of the processes through which an (in)security continuum has been built, enunciated, and practiced, and how it works today in Greece. As analysed by Karydis, in the case of Greece the narrative transforming the migrant into a potential enemy has focused on the role of Albanians. In other countries, it has been the Roma, the Algerians, the Moroccans, and/or the home-grown 'radical' Muslims. Clearly, the target may move, but the *de facto* rationale against foreigners, other EU citizens or even national citizens of a different background, is that they are all seen as disenfranchised from the society they live in, and that they may be ready to attack it, as a 'fifth column' of invisible enemies, if they receive an order to do so. This phenomenon of what my colleagues and I have called the 'strategisation of intolerance' (or, as labelled by military and intelligence think-tanks, 'fourth-generation conflict' or 'inner counter-subversive operations') is very often the key argument justifying suspicion and derogatory measures against these categories of populations. It often explains the different judicial and political biases that operate against migrants (and not only against foreigners, as noted above), and constructs them as 'useful enemies' through a process of criminalisation which associates them with illegality and violence. This process, if successful, allows those who fall victim to the structural policies of governments (e.g., determining where they live, their health conditions, and their lack of language skills) to be deemed responsible for their own fate when they are attacked or despised by large segments of population:

the stigma becoming in itself a reinforcement of the belief that suspicion was 'legitimate'. In the UK, the discourse associating radicalisation of violence with religious belief and Muslims with terrorists is certainly one of the most obvious cases of this strategisation of intolerance, even if only one amongst many examples. Karydis shows that Greece participates in this phenomenon, if with its own specificities.

In conjunction with the contribution to this collection by Sappho Xenakis on organised crime and political violence, these chapters address key aspects of the (in)security continuum as experienced in Greece. Many professionals of politics (from the government or the opposition) and some academics in tune with the former have developed the idea of a 'symbiosis' between organised crime and terrorism, and they have often related the notion to foreigners or migrants. The Greek narrative shares many characteristics with other versions developed in the UK, Netherlands, Italy, Austria, Hungary, and France. The common feature is to first declare that organised crime has recently expanded and, via corruption, has entered the realm of politics. It is claimed that, in tandem, the de-ideologisation of clandestine organisations and their recruitment procedures in prisons has allowed terrorism to merge into organised crime, or vice versa. In a second step, the narrative explains that the violence associated with such groups comes from foreigners. Precise variations are of less importance than the diverse manifestations of a new form of conflict in which war and crime merge – conflict characterised by violence done by dangerous others attacking the identity of society in either a spectacular manner (terrorism) or more insidiously (organised crime).

One familiar account of the genesis of such narratives turns our attention to the cottage industry of journalists and academics born after the Cold War and which expanded after September 2001. Experts on terrorism, counter-insurrection, and strategy converted themselves into specialists of cultural identities and 'new wars', and, in order to exploit their own vein of fear propagation and pave the way to presenting their tailored 'security solutions', sought to marginalise the influence of anthropologists and sociologists of minorities. Coming from different countries, often strongly interconnected but also in competition with one another, these authors have nevertheless largely played the role of transmitting to the broader public interpretations developed and pursued by different bureaucratic institutions. Such writers have contributed to the belief in the veracity of the narrative about the fusion of war and crime at the same time as making a profit from selling books re-affirming every couple of years that the world is on the verge of a catastrophe: from repeated genocides to nuclear terrorism, to the rise of organised crime and massive flows of migrants and refugees, and now, beyond human actors, to climate change and epidemics of new viruses. Contrary to common perceptions, however, this is not a narrative born after September 11. It predates the end of the Cold War and is related to a certain type of institutional discourse prevalent amongst professions strongly affected by the idea of the removal of border controls and the possibility of freedom of movement inside the European Union (Bigo, 1996). It has, then, old roots and many different local versions. It is not a 'true' narrative, but it performs the function of creating a space for competition between different agencies in order to define understandings of reality for themselves, for politicians, and for the general public (Bigo, 2008).

This narrative concerning the fusion of war and crime, its connection with migration, and finally the strategisation of intolerance and fear of the future which it encompasses, has been developed from a heterogeneous group I have called the 'neo-moderns', in opposition to more a 'classic' group who want to uphold traditional narratives of borders (in terms of sovereignty, territory, and institutional missions). It connects strongly the fear of crime, violence, and social change with the fear of majorities becoming minorities as foreigners become insiders (Appadurai, 2006). Even more importantly, it transforms fear – or, more exactly, unease – into a liquidity which can be exported and globalised. And it is this 'liquid fear' or unease which has invaded our lives (Bauman, 2006; Haine, 1995; Robin, 2004). In my brief discussion below, I explore further the genesis of this narrative in its European trajectory, how it operates and cements the field of professionals of (in)security managers, and what possible avenues exist for counteracting it.

The Genesis of the Discursive Continuum of Threats

In Europe, this insecurity continuum has taken a specific path defined by the fear – which emerged in the mid-eighties – of open borders within the region, and by the discourse of the security deficit related to the removal of internal border controls (a discourse including such concerns as the arrival of the Italian mafia in France and the UK, Turkish migrants moving to the UK, British hooligans appearing at football matches across Europe, and the constitution of a European *internationale* of far-left terrorism) (Bigo, 1992). The German and Austrian terminology of *Inhere Sicherheit* (internal security) in the early eighties certainly took one of the first steps in connecting fear of crime and fear of migration. It grew out of an effort on the part of various European Ministries of the Interior to extend their activities to border surveillance and the control of minorities, reacting against the insistence of professionals from the field of politics upon the free movement of persons and the removal of internal border controls. Once the new internal border regime was in place, various groups of police officers, customs officers, and intelligence services swiftly met at the European level and pronounced the new conditions to be creating a 'security deficit'. By developing a series of 'warnings' and talking of the necessity of 'safeguard measures', the Trevi group (especially Trevi '92), was one of the propagators of this fear.

Under the banner of European internal security, the control of the transnational flow of people was added to the top of the traditional policing tasks of combating crime, and served to reframe the missions – and sometimes the professions – of customs authorities, border guards, and police officers. The exchange of information about people on the move thus became obligatory and gave impetus to such European databases as the Schengen Information System and the SIRENE system (see further Samatas, this collection). The British Conservatives, who were opposed to Schengen, portrayed the removal of internal border controls as a catastrophe and predicted a rise in violence and crime throughout continental Europe. The Schengen agreements, which were forged without the UK, were premised upon the idea of building 'compensatory measures' at the external borders of the EU; these would function by ensuring that the internal freedom of movement enjoyed by EU citizens would be compensated by the imposition of limits upon the freedom of movement outside the Union. After long discussions, and mainly for practical considerations, freedom of movement was extended to third-country nationals holding residence permits. This framework nevertheless created differentiation between third-country nationals and EU citizens, leaving space for the growth of 'racism under another name' (to such an extent that US citizens working in the EU now try to refuse the appellation of third-country nationals and migrants, and ask to be called 'impatriates', having well understood the possible stigma associated with the term 'third-country national').

The expansionary effect upon policing driven by the use of the term 'internal security' at the European level was also to draw together wildly disparate phenomena – the fight on terrorism, drugs, organised crime, cross-border criminality, and illegal immigration – as if they were the same phenomenon, linked by the mobility of persons. That is why control of the transnational movement of persons, whether in the form of migrants, asylum-seekers, or other border-crossers (such as tourists), and, even more broadly, the control of any citizen not corresponding to the *a priori* social image held of their national identity (such as the children of first-generation immigrants, or minority groups), became a 'police' task, if one extending beyond traditional crime policing and law-and-order concerns.

Special squads formed to combat illicit drugs traffic imported their techniques of undercover operations and data-gathering into other domains of policing activities by linking organised crime, terrorism, and illegal migration. These techniques led to the open derogation of laws protecting the rights of the defendant, and to the development of both categories of suspicion and arguments for more proactive and preventive policing methods involving the large-scale use of databases and social categorisation. Enforcement efforts were thus stretched beyond the parameters of conventional crime control measures and the policing of foreigners to include also the control of persons living in zones labelled 'at risk' (from the *banlieues* to declining city centres) and put under surveillance because they corresponded to a type of identity or behaviour supposed to derive from these predispositions of risk. The enablement of this body of expertise on extra-territorial matters saw the remit of those sections of Ministries of Interior in charge of internal security internationalised. It also saw the launch of competition between Ministries of Interior and Ministries of Foreign Affairs over whose model of foreign diplomacy would prevail. Various international negotiations about visa policies and extradition or readmission agreements were to be shaped by the preoccupations of Ministries of the Interior.

Responding to the threat was not simply a matter of policing, or even of 'internal security'; it was a matter of 'survival' of the 'societal identity' of nations. Whether one by one or together, in different institutional arenas, military and intelligence services decided it was also their task to consider the 'flow of migrants' as a danger. To this were added their preoccupations concerning their own future (endangered by the discourse of the peace dividend and the reduction of their budgets). For them, the question was no longer the legality of missions or respecting the divide between domestically-focused police forces and externally-focused military forces (constructed to avoid coups against civilian rule), but rather the new nature of the threat. As a senior French army official stated in an interview with Emmanuel Guittet, 'the problem is not to know whether the army has a role, but to know what the threats are that we are talking about'. And another added, 'the threats are now transversal; with our technology we are better equipped to follow them [than the police], and it is our duty to protect our own citizenry. We will not stop at the borders of our own country' (Bigo *et al.*, 1999; Guittet, 2006). Military doctrines have increasingly included terrorism amongst the core of their attentions, whilst their views about it have changed. From an indirect and peripheral activity linked to great power strategies, terrorism has become an autonomous category; one linked to foreigners and, more importantly, to migrants. In France, discourse on 'urban warfare' has relied on the scenario of a massive upheaval in the suburbs linked with terrorist groups coming from abroad or which are even homegrown. The bombings of 1995 were a catalyst for this doctrine. Even without the materialisation of such scenarios (no mass migration from Russia, no foreign invasion by the Italian mafia, no generalised terrorism), and despite the tremendous success of opened borders in Europe, the narrative of liquid fear only continued to unfurl after September 2001.

After 2001, any form of mobility was considered dangerous. The so-called war on terror 'perfected' the belief of the merging of war and crime, of internal and external threats, of transversal threats and their globalisation, of globalised insecurity and the world as a place of perpetual risk and danger in which organised crime, terrorism, and even migration were taken as 'proof' of an approaching Armageddon (Bigo and Walker, 2008). This 'militarisation' of the mind, this appeal to suspicion between citizen and 'migrant' or 'citizen of other origins' (as if it were possible to detect the *autochthones* and the *allochtones* from first sight), is evident amongst military personnel who believe their future to be the fight against subversives inside their own countries, rather than awaiting the military uniforms of the enemy at the border to stop their invasion. Their missions have changed as much as their 'terrain of operation'. To conduct a war inside liberal democracies, however, is possible only if it is not considered as a war, but as a policing operation designed to protect. Legitimacy comes only if state borders are considered obsolete and if the enemy is considered to be everywhere and to be multifaceted.

The incursion by military and intelligence services into the fields of policing, justice, and foreign affairs, has not always been welcome, and has created tensions. Equally, however, the police insist not only that they are better equipped for domestic mandates, but that police missions are performable outside national boundaries. The roar of this (administrative) battle has been strong. In response, many mainstream political declarations and academic works have often attempted to dismiss these extremist and (overly) explicit bureaucratic approaches in order to promote political versions that are more attentive to community sensitivities about folk devil mechanisms, but such lighter versions often adapt similar grammars of exclusion. Official discourses may position themselves in favour of an integrationist solution and against flagrant exclusion by normalising individuals instead of rejecting them, but they often construct a form of 'Ban', too (Bigo, 2007; Rajaram and Grundy-Warr, 2008). Indeed, after the end of the Cold War, the narrative of the security deficit was particularly prevalent in media and political discourses. This time it was the Polish mafia, and then the Chechen mafia, which would transform our civilised countries into barbarian realms. The Russians would not send their army, but their refugees – fleeing in their millions – would invade us. A tidal wave of migrants would submerge the EU. It would come from the East, but also from the South, because of the proliferation of failed states and grey areas controlled by organised crime in Colombia, Nigeria, and along the diverse routes of drug trafficking. Traffickers would not only smuggle drugs but also illegal migrants.

Countering the (In)Security Continuum Discourses

Facing such an overwhelming series of discourses that repeat, if with local variations, the same basic kinds of arguments, and given that localised research shows the discourse of a fusion of war and crime to be a useful simplification for journalists as much as a useful resource for bureaucratic infighting, rather than a serious starting point for investigating actual practices of violence, what can one possibly do? One option is to develop a counter-narrative which would multiply examples of differences between organised crime and terrorism, and would insist on the political element inherent to so-called terrorism. A different historical narrative would show the focus upon foreigners and migrants to be generally erroneous and disproportionate, that their participation in both crime and political violence is minimal even if they are more often overrepresented in prison. This would be an important advance against the ideological view of the fusion between war and crime. Nevertheless, my worry with this strategy is that the inverted image of the globalist discourse of 'fusion' would mirror it by simply reaffirming the existence of categories (such as terrorism or organised crime) that might be explanatory of specific local realities. This narrative of local complexities is, then, certainly critical and important, but can lead one to forget that we have not one narrative, but multiple narratives of insecurity, including those traditional types that also differentiate between crime, terrorism, and migration, but propose very coercive measures on all fronts in response (those referred to above as 'classic' narratives of insecurity). So, in my view, this first option, albeit critical, does not sufficiently address the reason why the first narrative of the fusion of migration, war and crime through terrorism, is so powerful and so prevalent, even though it is mistaken. Are our governments ignorant? Will they change their minds if we provide the right statistics? Are the public naturally racist, or are they misled by an elite? Are education and better knowledge the solutions to rectify misrepresentation?

I have tried to show in my own work, as well as in collaboration with my colleagues of *Cultures et Conflits*, that better knowledge will not create a change of attitude so long as the state continues to see like a state, professionals of politics to see like politicians, and professionals of (in)security as technicians of struggles against threats (Bigo, 2002). So, whilst I recognise that dominant discourse today presents rising global insecurity as originating from the merging of major external and internal threats, leading to the demand that these are combated, I also try to show that a counter-narrative constructed through the traditional categories of organised crime and terrorism will not succeed in convincing a large public, nor will it serve to change the discursive practices of professionals of politics given that they often know perfectly well what they are doing. The question is, therefore, displaced from a refutation of the narrative of the fusion of war and crime to an explanation of what this discourse permits, and the critique moves from what this discourse means to what this discourse does.

This second option analyses the positions of the different actors enunciating discourses of fear and insecurity, as well as their struggles. What looks, at first sight, as 'one' ideology becomes more adequately analysed as a field of struggles between different discourses and different spokespersons of institutions. This approach takes seriously the controversies of actors, and by doing so demonstrates that this narrative of the insecurity continuum emanating from the merging of war and crime (and whose counteraction is necessary) is a product, the 'doxa', hiding a deeper structural insecurity continuum arising from the de-differentiation of police and military universes and the reframing of the boundaries of security by intelligence services and other intermediary agencies. It is this continuum that we have to address. To put it differently, the narrative of the insecurity continuum of threats, although empirically erroneous, is the strong symbolic product of an (in)security continuum, or spectrum of bureaucratic agencies (public and private), that are competing over the definition of what constitutes a threat, what does not constitute a threat, and what is fate. What has merged is not war and crime, but police and military universes.

This implies that the continuum of war and crime is the result of multiple and contradictory strategies and not the product of one dominant group, or of one dominant ideology. It implies also that this is not a truth, a shared knowledge, but rather a discursive space with possibilities for competition over missions, status, and budgets between public and private professionals of (in)security management. The fusion of war and crime is not the result of one line of thought, privileged only by far-right parties or by some den of intelligence services. It is a 'discursive formation' in itself, containing a multiplicity of competing discourses, which may be one of the primary reasons for its popularity. Diversity and competition nevertheless dissolve the idea of a homogeneous securitarian discourse, of a uniform ideology of security. We need to be aware of this multiplicity of different (in)security discourses coming from very different spokespersons who disagree strongly about solutions even if, or because, they share the same primary assumptions. Thus, instead of seeing complicity, or ideological hegemony, it is better to view this (in)security continuum of threats as the result of competition amongst professionals of (in)security, who are struggling to impose their interpretation of the hierarchy of threats and who often portray their specific mission as key to addressing those most important (especially in a world of limited resources).

Furthermore, the discursive existence of this argument about the fusion between war, crime, and migration creates the possibility for police and military universes to enter into competition over the best instruments, techniques, strategies, and ideologies, by constructing connections between their own specialisations and the missions of others via the renaming of threats as new. To the extent that everyone insists on the novelty of the threats, it is because this novelty allows them to be 'colonised' as 'new territories', as new missions. The bridge-building of these universes after the Cold War has worked, then, because it has produced a doxa of the field about the violence and undesirability stemming from the very existence of migrants. This has favoured a shift of attention to 'global' terrorism as the point of convergence between crime and war, and has facilitated the claims of 'intermediary agencies' that they are the most efficient. Once built, this doxa in return has acted as a magnet, attracting different agencies from the margins of the field, and obliging them also to participate in the social construction of fear and unease concerning migrants, and to enter into the competition for preventive actions, including the accumulation of personal data through specific databases. Even social services addressing the needs of migrants and asylum seekers have now been drawn into this narrative of globalisation of (in)security, and have had to position themselves within it, implying alliances with other more central actors of the field. As for the case of Greece, it is certainly not the most 'advanced' country in this (in)security field, and it may thus be that resistance from within the country is still possible.

References

Appadurai, A. (2006) *Fear of Small Numbers: An Essay on the Geography of Anger*. Durham: Duke University Press.

Bauman, Z. (2006) *Liquid Fear*. Cambridge: Polity Press.

Bigo, D. (1992) *L'Europe Des Polices Et De La Sécurité Intérieure*. Bruxelles: Éditions Complexe.

Bigo, D. (1996) *Polices En Réseaux: L'expérience Européenne*. Paris: Presses de Sciences Po.

Bigo, D. (2002) 'Security and Immigration: Towards a Governmentality of Unease', *Alternatives/Culture & Conflits* 27: 63–92.

Bigo, D. (2007) 'Exception et Ban: À Propos de l' 'État D'Exception'', *Erytheis-Revue Éléctronique d'Études en Sciences de l'Homme et de la Société* 2.

Bigo, D. (2008) 'The Emergence of a Consensus: Global Terrorism, Global Insecurity, and Global Security', in A. Chebel d'Appollonia and S. Reich (eds) *Immigration, Integration and Security: America and Europe in Comparative Perspective*, pp. 67–94. Pittsburgh: University of Pittsburgh Press.

Bigo, D., Hanon, J. and A. Tsoukala (1999) *La Participation Des Militaires À La Sécurité Intérieure: France, Italie, Allemagne, Etats-Unis*. Paris: Centre d'Etudes sur les Conflits pour la DAS.

Bigo, D. and R.B.J. Walker (2008) 'Le Régime Du Contre-Terrorisme Global', in D. Bigo, L. Bonelli and T. Deltombe (eds) *Au Nom Du 11 Septembre... Les Démocraties À L'épreuve De L'antiterrorisme*, pp. 13–35. Paris: LA Découverte.

Guittet, E.-P. (2006) 'Military Activities inside National Territory: The French Case', in A. Tsoukala and D. Bigo (eds) *Illiberal Practices in Liberal Regimes*, pp. 137–162. Paris: L'Harmattan.

Haine, J. (1995) 'Troubler Et Inquiéter: Les Discours Du Désordre International', *Cultures & Conflits* 19–20: 3–5.

Rajaram, P.K. and C.W. Grundy-Warr (2008) *Borderscapes: Hidden Geographies and Politics at Territory's Edge*. Minneapolis and London: University of Minnesota Press.

Robin, C. (2004) *Fear: The History of a Political Idea*. New York: Oxford University Press.

IOANNIS PAPAGEORGIOU

Youth and Crime

This chapter seeks to provide an overview of key themes pertaining to the field of crime and the Greek youth population, as well as information about the range of studies that have been undertaken to date in this area. The chapter begins with a discussion of trends in youth offending in Greece from the 1970s onwards, drawing on data from the National Statistical Service of Greece (NSSG), the Hellenic Police, and the Ministry of Justice (the latter as found in the Statistical Yearbook of Greece), as well as pertinent academic studies. The focus then turns to the key themes of sports-related violence, bullying in schools, deviant youth gangs, drug use, and youth victimisation. The chapter ends with comments on the portrayal of the relationship between youth and crime in the media, and public attitudes towards youth crime.

The Young Offender

The main sources of statistical data on delinquency in Greece have always been police and judicial statistics, with self-report and victimisation studies peripheral until recently. What follows is a discussion of general delinquency trends, starting with police statistics and proceeding with a brief assessment of the relevant judicial and self-report delinquency studies.

Police Statistics

Police statistics refer to felonies and misdemeanours for which police officers were in charge of first-instance interrogation or for which police officers lodged a complaint.[1] In terms of offenders, police statistical tables include those known to them the month that the offence took place. In 2003, the law changed in relation to the age limits of criminal responsibility; from 7–12 years old to 8–12 years old for children, and from 13–17 to 13–18 for juveniles (see further Pitsela, this collection). In 2010, a further change in the law took place, allowing for the confinement of those aged 15 years and above. Police statistics have not yet taken these changes into account. Further problems with the data include lack of reference to complicity in the crime, which means that each and every participant constitutes a new entry, and disregard for the 'principle of the genuine offender', which practically means that, if the same offender commits more than one crime in a year, each act will be a new entry (Pitsela *et al.*, 2005). Finally, it is not uncommon that police authorities revise the data (see, e.g., Courakis, 1999; Nova-Kaltsouni, 2001a), which is, perhaps, why secondary analyses do not always produce consistent results. Magganas (1996) and Courakis (1998), for example, report different data for the years 1980, 1981, and 1982, with the differences ranging from slight (e.g., 220 child offenders instead of 213 in 1981) to extensive (e.g., 8,574 juvenile offenders instead of 7,392 in 1981).

Indeed, there has long been a lack of consensus amongst criminologists in Greece as to the trends in youth offending. Courakis (1999), for instance, speaks of a substantial increase in the rates of juvenile delinquency over the 1990s (see also Pitsela *et al.*, 2005), whereas Georgoulas argues that juvenile offending only increased slightly, mainly due to offences committed by children (Georgoulas, 2003). Nova-Kaltsouni (2001a, 2001b), for her part, agrees that juvenile offending rates have undergone an increase, but also identifies a decrease in the rate of offending by children.

---

1   This includes all crimes that require direct action from an authority (such as violent crimes, thefts, or robberies) along with a large percentage of the rest. It is possible to lodge a complaint at the prosecutor's office for such crimes, but this is rare and the prosecutor will usually send the case to the police headquarters for first-instance interrogation.

As can be seen in Figures 1 and 2, which are based on official records of the numbers of young people known as offenders to the police during the period 1979–2007, youth involvement in crime should be no cause for major concern in Greece. More specifically, as concerns children, the rise in the total caseload of offenders is counterbalanced by the consistently low absolute numbers. At the same time, the intense fluctuations from year to year may well be attributed to police practices. As concerns juveniles, and excluding traffic offences, there was a remarkable stability in the total caseload of offenders (as also reported by Pitsela, this collection).

Table 1 presents official data on the caseload of young offenders known to the police according to particular types of offence during the period 1984–2007. Once again, the numbers are strikingly reassuring, particularly when one considers that theft and robbery are the most common serious offences amongst the youth (Courakis, 1999; Pitsela *et al.*, 2005). For example, there was a 23 percent drop in the caseload of children who committed theft or robbery, and only four children were known to the police in 2007 in connection with bodily harm. Similarly, there was a 19 percent drop in the caseload of juveniles who committed theft or robbery, and a mere 61 were known to the police in connection with bodily harm.

Police statistics do not categorise young offenders by sex, nor are there official data on immigrant young offenders.[2] Particularly as regards the latter, some information may be found in scholarly research. For the year 1993, for example, Karydis (1996) has argued that immigrants amounted to 25 percent of all young offenders, and that the majority of their offences included vagrancy, begging, and drug-related and traffic offences. More recent years have seen some local-level studies on this issue (e.g., Papatheodorou, 1999), but nationwide research has been absent, thereby disallowing firm conclusions.

2   Other official sources such as judicial statistics and tables from 'reformatory' institutions do include information on girls. Nova-Kaltsouni (2001a: 161) has argued that boys far exceed girls in the commission of offences.

Judicial Statistics

Turning to judicial statistics, Table 2 shows the penalties imposed by juvenile tribunals over an extended period of time (1965–2004).[3] Generally speaking, courts decide on the nature of measures to be imposed upon young offenders ('reformative' or 'therapeutic'), whilst juvenile offenders (over 15 years old) may receive a custodial sentence (though the category 'confinement' in Table 2 does not account for suspended sentences) (see further Pitsela, this collection). NSSG provides data on juvenile confinement by gender from 1973 onwards. As with police statistics, there is a substantial portion – at least in earlier years – of prosecuted persons of unknown age not included here. There are also a number of cases where the penalty has not been recorded at all. At any rate, one needs to note that the data largely reflect the sentencing behaviour of judges, and are also influenced by 'extra-judicial' factors such as lengthy delays of hearings and lawyers' abstentions (see, e.g., Courakis, 2000b: 339). Particularly as concerns the great time lapses between the actual occurrence of offences and the corresponding court hearings, they prohibit comparison between judicial data and the data recorded by the police (according to Courakis, 2000a).

In sharp contrast with how adult offenders are treated in the criminal justice system (see further Cheliotis, this collection), the period 1980–2004 saw a 26.5 percent drop in the caseload of young offenders subjected to 'reformative' measures, from 4,720 in 1980 to 3,466 in 2004; the caseload of juvenile offenders sentenced to imprisonment rose by a meteoric 1,277 percent, from 13 in 1980 to 179 in 2004, but it is obvious that absolute numbers remained very low (and, as mentioned earlier, suspended sentences are not accounted for in the dataset under consideration). As one might expect, males are overrepresented in all categories (see Table 2).

3   Extensive analysis of judicial statistics has been made by Mpakatsoulas (1984) for the years 1959–1978, Tsaousis *et al.* (1974) for the years 1960–1964, Andrianakis (1982) and Zafiriou (1979) for the years 1965–1979, Courakis (1999, 2000a) for the years 1983–1996, Pitsela *et al.* (2005) for the years 1995–1997, and Efstratiadis (2004) for the years 2001–2003.

Self-report Studies

Moving from secondary analyses of official data to self-report delinquency studies, the first such survey in Greece was conducted in 1984 with a sample of 3,795 urban students aged between 14 and 17. As one might expect, the findings revealed a discrepancy between official data and self-reported delinquency, with the latter exceeding the former, particularly in relation to offences not recorded by the police unless reported by victims (e.g., minor bodily harm, vandalism of private property, and theft amongst relatives). Less expectedly, perhaps, girls contributed substantially to the overall rate of minor bodily harm and vandalism in schools, and exceeded boys in terms of theft amongst relatives (Beze, 1991). The highest overall rates of self-reported delinquency were recorded in Thessaloniki (for metropolitan cities) and Kalamata (for non-metropolitan cities). Shoplifting was more prevalent in metropolitan cities, whilst physical violence and joyriding were more prevalent in non-metropolitan cities (see Panousis, 1990, 1995).

Based on face-to-face interviews, and following the International Self-Report Delinquency Study protocol, another survey of self-reported delinquency was conducted in Athens in 1992 with a sample of 200 boys and 100 girls aged between 14 and 21. Shoplifting and burglary were found to be the most common offences, followed by vandalism, fare-dodging, and driving without a licence. In terms of overall rates, boys exceeded girls, and younger interviewees were more delinquent than their older counterparts (Spinellis *et al.*, 1994). The method followed in this survey, however, poses some questions regarding sampling and data-gathering procedures, which are reflected, amongst other things, in the low rate of response to certain questions. In 1996, the National Centre for Social Research carried out a survey of 400 students in their last three years of high school in Thessaloniki. There was a high prevalence of traffic offences and interpersonal violence, especially amongst boys, whilst girls were significantly involved in running away from home and vandalism. Offending (particularly driving without a licence) was most common in the last year of high school amongst boys and girls (Papadopoulou *et al.*, 2000).

Self-report surveys have shown that, alongside long-term trends as presented in official statistics, the proportion of offences committed by young people and especially boys is not insignificant. Girls' participation is also important but qualitatively different. Overall, self-report surveys have revealed a higher prevalence of property offences, vandalism, and interpersonal violence than reported by the police.

Sports-related Violence

Particularly prominent concerns in Greece pertaining to youth crime have been sports-related violence, violence at school, and gang involvement. As regards sports-related violence, empirical research was initiated in the mid-1980s. Using a range of methods, the first study took place between 1986 and 1988, and focused on a sample of 319 hardcore supporters of sports clubs based in Athens and Thessaloniki. The average age in the sample was 20 years old. Nearly half had used drugs at least once, and 84 percent admitted to having been involved in fighting or having hurled objects in a stadium at least once. Furthermore, 59 percent stated that they had fought or committed acts of vandalism at least once while travelling to or from a stadium. The most common reason respondents gave for their engagement in violent behaviour was the provocative behaviour of fans supporting the opponent team, followed by the wrong decisions of referees and the presence or provocative attitude of the police. Over a quarter of respondents had been convicted of offences related to sport violence, and the vast majority also knew someone else who had been, or had witnessed vandalism or fighting. In addressing the causes of sports-related violence, the study pointed to a variety of factors, from personal and social problems to mass psychology (Courakis, 2002). Not all operational definitions are clear in this study, however, and the apparent mixing of symptoms with causes hinders any firm explanatory conclusion.

Another study, conducted in a working-class area of Athens between 1991 and 1993 and focused on 'sub-cultural' groups such as fans of heavy metal music and rockabilly, found that sports-related violence was the exception in a generally non-violent social environment. According to the same study, however, stadiums had grown to be arenas for a broader range of delinquent acts, including drug-dealing and robbery. Sport violence was accounted for primarily by reference to the experiences of social exclusion and cultural deprivation (Astrinakis *et al.*, 1996). A similar explanation has been offered by Panousis (2004a); whilst not treating sport violence itself as an alarming social issue, he links it to a search for personal identity in an alienating world (see also Panousis, 1987, 2000).

Bullying in School

It is important to note that, whilst there is no term in Greek for 'bullying', this should not be interpreted as a sign that there is no need for such a term, either because the phenomenon does not exist in Greece or because it is not perceived as remarkable. As outlined below, a number of studies argue that bullying does indeed exist in Greek schools, but it may be viewed more as an annoyance than as an example of intolerable and deviant behaviour (the obvious exceptions being damage to school buildings and property).

An ever-increasing number of studies have been undertaken in Greece since the 1990s on school violence. In 1994, a survey conducted in Athens with a sample of 3,774 pupils aged between 12 and 19 found that 6 percent engaged in physical and verbal abuse on a regular basis, whilst boys were significantly more violent than girls (Fakiolas and Armenakis, 1995; see further Artinopoulou, 2000; also Houndoumadi *et al.*, 2003). Another self-report survey was conducted during the same period, though in Ioannina and Corfu, with a sample of 2,545 pupils aged between 12 and 16. Of them, 40 percent were aware of violent incidents having taken place at school; 23 percent reported having been physically victimised themselves; 52 percent had used physical violence against weaker students; and 57 percent had been involved in fighting. Again, boys were more violent than girls, and were more likely to be victims of bullying. In terms of age, younger students were more frequently victimised than older ones (Gotovos, 1996; see further Artinopoulou, 2000; also Houndoumadi *et al.*, 2003).

A few years later, in 1999, the General Secretariat of Youth undertook a countrywide survey of 350 students attending the last three grades of high school. Of those, 82 percent reported having witnessed violence (mainly in the form of beating) between same-age students, and 69 percent between students of different ages. The prevalence of violence was three times as high in urban areas as in semi-urban and rural areas, and younger students identified twice as many incidents as their older counterparts. In terms of self-reported violent behaviour, 23 percent admitted participation in physical or verbal abuse (36.5 percent of boys and 10 percent of girls), but the rate rose to 29 percent in relation to violence against non-Greek students. As far as victimisation is concerned, physical and verbal violence had been experienced by 12 percent of all students surveyed; 17 percent of boys and a mere 3.5 percent of girls (General Secretariat of Youth, 2000; see further Artinopoulou, 2000; also Houndoumadi et al., 2003; Panousis, 2006).

A series of studies conducted by the Pedagogical Institute of the Greek Ministry of Education towards the end of the 1990s confirmed the findings from previous studies regarding the distribution of school violence according to gender. A link was also found between victimisation at school and the experience of corporal punishment at home (Petropoulos et al., 2000; see further Houndoumadi et al., 2003). A further series of surveys carried out during the 1990s in central Greece set out to identify personality traits in bullies and non-bullies at primary school. It was found that bullying children suffered low levels of social acceptance, self-esteem, and problem-solving competence, and tended to be 'manipulative' (Andreou, 2000; see also Andreou, 2001, 2004).

A pilot study in 1994 of 117 primary school children in East Attica confirmed the general finding that girls are victimised to a lesser extent than boys (Kalliotis, 2000). The main study took place in 1996 with a sample of 677 students aged between 8 and 16. It was concluded that bullying amongst schoolchildren is mainly physical, though girls tended to find verbal abuse more threatening than boys did. Furthermore, younger children showed greater tolerance towards aggressive behaviour than their older counterparts (Kalliotis, 2001). Similar results were reported in a larger-scale study in Athens in the late 1990s with a sample of 1,312 children aged between 7 and 11. Physical abuse, for example, was found to be more frequent amongst boys, but also to recede with age (Pateraki et al., 2001).

Between 1999 and 2000, moreover, the National Centre for Social Research (EKKE) surveyed 4,967 secondary school students and 1,075 teachers from 100 schools across Greece. The study reported that a high proportion of the students were in denial of violent victimisation (Tsiganou *et al.*, 2004). In 2005, a study of 1,843 urban and rural secondary school children focused on perceptions of violence; in particular, respondents were asked to rate tolerance towards various forms of violent conduct. Physical molestation was found to be the least tolerable form of victimisation, followed by physical assault and damage to personal property. These, however, were also the least commonly experienced types of victimisation (being teased, which was included in the study as a possible type of victimisation, was the most common) (Psalti *et al.*, 2007).

In profiling the perpetrator of the intimidation, victims stated that it is usually committed by a boy of the same age as the victim, acting alone or in a small group. Girls reported more frequent bullying by other girls. On the other hand, more boys reported being bullied by students of a different religion, and more non-Greeks reported bullying by students of a different nationality to their own. Interestingly, a large percentage of the students (30 percent) noted that teachers and parents do not intervene to stop acts of intimidation (ibid.). A study of 1,758 children in Thessaloniki drew similar conclusions, with boys outnumbering girls in all categories (the sole exception being primary school children) and a gradual decrease of physical bullying in older children. Boys were victimised more than girls, and experienced more verbal than physical abuse as they got older (Sapouna, 2008).

There is clearly a tension between the need to combat aggressiveness in schools to ensure the healthy psychological development of the young, and the logic of associating aggressive behaviour at school with deviance outside school, which could, in turn, become a self-fulfilling prophecy. Some studies have nevertheless insisted that it is important to examine the connection between school-based aggressiveness and external factors such as dysfunction in the home (see, e.g., Dimakos, 2002). Other assessments of aggressive behaviour at school have pointed out that, since school is a porous institution and not an isolated one, it is to be expected that aggression reflects wider social phenomena (Panousis, 2006). Conflict-focused approaches, meanwhile, have pointed to evidence of aggression and factionalism between teachers and the didactic teaching style employed in schools, which may be experienced by students as aggressiveness, serving to reproduce the status conflicts being played out beyond the narrow confines of the school environment (Panousis, 2004b). Indeed, it seems convincing that school violence cannot be separated from broader social developments.

Deviant Youth Gangs

A relatively recent field of interest in Greek as well as European criminology is that of youth gangs. The following analysis employs the Eurogang Network definition as a benchmark: 'A youth gang is a durable, street-oriented youth group whose involvement in illegal activity is part of their group identity.' 'Durable' here means that the group is not formed incidentally to commit a particular crime, but rather with a view to continuous offending. Members are usually young individuals of up to 24 years of age (Apospori, 2002).

As mentioned earlier, an ethnographic study of subcultures in Athens has associated particular music fans and delinquency. Researchers claimed, for example, that heavy metal fans presented three types of delinquent behaviour. The first revolved around conflict between groups or persons, the second was associated with sexual delinquency, and the third was characterised by a total rejection of societal values. The study also addressed a series of crimes carried out in 1994 involving rape and murder that attracted much media attention. That year it emerged that a group of Satanists, led by a pair of heavy metal fans, were committing ritualistic crimes of 'human sacrifice'. Because the group lacked a characteristic crucial to the Eurogang definition of a 'youth gang' – namely, that they were not street-oriented –, the study judged that the group instead fell into the category of a 'criminal organisation', as defined in the Greek Penal Code. However, the study also concluded that the criminal behaviour of this group could not be considered characteristic of heavy metal sub-culture more generally, in large part because information about offending was only disseminated amongst members of the group itself (Astrinakis *et al.*, 1996). The same study also recorded incidences of delinquency amongst rockabilly music fans, with inter-group rivalries sometimes leading to conflict amongst different groups of fans, and between rockabilly fans and skinheads. Given that, in the mid-1990s, the two rockabilly groups of Athens spent much time in public places (e.g., bars and cafes), it might have been possible to characterise them as youth gangs, but it is not clear from the data available whether criminal offending was actually part of their identity or whether any violence was merely incidental and a consequence of antagonism.

Using different definitions of a 'youth gang', other researchers have also concluded that there is no problem of criminal youth gangs in Greece at the time of their writing. According to Panousis (2004c), for example, evidence of such a group would require an area of operation, a specific type of criminal behaviour, and specified relations inside the groups as well as with other gangs. The fact that this phenomenon has not yet appeared in Greece is because certain required conditions – slum areas within big cities, the presence of ethnic minorities, inter-family violence, and societal tolerance towards violence – are still emergent (ibid.). A different perspective has been offered by Manoudaki (1998). Her study, involving self-report surveys with 126 students aged between 15 and 19, operationalised a delinquent youth group as a group of young people that commits crimes, and is characterised by strong ties amongst its members (mutual support and solidarity), organised operation, and lax hierarchy. The findings revealed that less than a fifth of the sample were involved in vandalism, fighting with other groups, breaching anti-drug legislation, and stealing and dealing in stolen goods (mainly in order to fund drug use) in groups. This proportion nevertheless included respondents that committed such offences within the framework of a group of youngsters that corresponded neither to the Eurogang nor to the researchers' own operational definition of a 'delinquent youth gang'. More specifically, around 7 percent of the respondents fell into the latter category. According to the study, offenders were overwhelmingly boys, but they did do not conform to the stereotype of being low-achievers from poor or broken homes, even if many did report problematic relationships with their parents (ibid.).

Another study set out to identify the number of crimes committed by two or more juvenile perpetrators, drawing on decisions taken by the Court of Juvenile Justice in Athens during the year 2000, and on self-report surveys in schools (Courakis *et al.*, 2003). The study concluded that, although there was evidence of a pattern of delinquent youths working together, the phenomenon was not sufficiently widespread to cause concern. After offences irrelevant to the study (e.g., traffic or procedural) were discounted from the total of 3,595 court decisions taken, only 148 were left for analysis. These were committed by 264 offenders, 53.8 percent of whom were Greeks, and the majority of them boys between the ages of 14 and 16. In less than half the cases did the perpetrator act alone (46 percent), and 41 percent operated in pairs. The majority of the crimes committed were thefts (37.5 percent), followed by robberies (7 percent), assaults (6 percent), and vandalism (5 percent). Offenders were convicted of belonging to a criminal organisation in only ten of the cases, however; this may be explained by the fact that the legal definition of criminal gang membership is much narrower than that commonly employed by criminologists in Greece. Peer relations and relations between parents and the peer group were found to be very important. Members of delinquent groups were more likely than non-group members to report feelings of mutual support and solidarity amongst their peers, and more likely to socialise in public places than non-group members (who were more likely to spend free time at the homes of friends) (Courakis *et al.*, 2003).

Drug Use

Estimating levels of drug use in the general population of Greece has been a focus of scientific research since the 1980s (see also Tsiganou, this collection). Research into drug-taking by the student population began in 1983–1984, and was repeated in 1993 and 1998. The first nationwide epidemiological surveys were conducted by the Psychiatric Clinic of the University of Athens from 1984 onwards, and later by the University Mental Health Research Institute (UMHRI), which became the focal point for the European Monitoring Centre for Drugs and Drug Addiction (EMCDDA). Further surveys were carried out in 1999, 2003, and 2007 (ESPAD, 2000, 2004, 2009), but these used a different research method.

There is a tendency inherent in surveys based either in the home or in school to obscure the true number of heavy drug users because they are hardly ever at school or at home when trying to obtain illicit substances (UMHRI, 1996). To compensate for this, EMCDDA uses as indirect indicators arrest and conviction rates, as well as data on the confiscation of drugs, drug-related deaths, applications for treatment, and drug-related infections.[4] Epidemiological studies and household and school surveys provide direct quantitative indicators of drug use, whilst EMCDDA also employs qualitative indicators based on ethnographic research.

School Population Surveys

The surveys of 1984, 1993, and 1998 covered children between the ages of 13 and 18 from all types of schools (public, private, inner-city, and rural). Together, these surveys revealed that drug use amongst students followed a steeply increasing trend, with many more boys taking drugs than girls, especially as they get older. Solvents were the most prevalent substance used in 1993 and 1998. The use of licit but non-prescribed medicines declined over the years to be overtaken by cannabis. Finally, the overall use of synthetic drugs increased dramatically due to the introduction of ecstasy in the mid-1990s and an increase in the use of LSD (Kokkevi *et al.*, 1991, 1992, 2000).

The method employed in the second set of national surveys (1999, 2003, and 2007) was based on the protocol issued by the European School Survey Project on Alcohol and other Drugs (ESPAD, 2000, 2004, 2009, respectively). The samples (4,909 students in 1999, 3,775 in 2003, and 3,060 in 2007) consisted of students aged between 16 and 18 years, and

---

4   Greek police statistics are not helpful in measuring drug use; apart from shifting police attitudes and changing policies, the relevant tables only refer to general breaches of anti-drug legislation with reference to known offenders, so it is impossible to tell the difference between drug users and facilitators of drug use. Pertinent Greek legislation (Law 3459/2006) provides an exhaustive description of the illegal acts and the relevant penalties in case of breach (see further Tsiganou, this collection).

were stratified and random so as to enhance reliability. Results were reflective of the first surveys carried out in the late 1990s, apart from a notable decline in the use of illicit drugs, mainly attributed to the decreased use of cannabis. Data for 2007 suggest a stabilisation in the use of cannabis and other drugs, and decreasing solvent abuse.

General Population Surveys

General population surveys were conducted by the UMHRI in 1984, 1998, and 2004, and the sample ranged from 12 to 64 years, selected at random from greater Athens, Thessaloniki, other urban areas, and semi-urban and rural areas. The data were gathered after a structured face-to-face interview in the participant's home, based on a pre-piloted structured questionnaire (Madianos *et al.*, 1995). Use of illicit drugs was measured separately from that of licit but non-prescribed medicines, whilst solvent abuse was not measured at all. The rates of drug use revealed were strikingly lower than the rates found in school surveys, and can be partially explained by the different method of data collection. All school surveys were based upon a self-completion questionnaire completed in the classrooms without the presence of a teacher, but the general population surveys were conducted through face-to-face interview in the home, where respondents may have been more reluctant to reveal drug use (Kokkevi *et al.*, 2007).

Amongst other important indicators to consider are statistics relating to the number of heavy users, treatment for drug abuse, and fatalities from drug abuse. As regards the latter, available statistical data referring to drug-related deaths, as issued by Greek police, appear to confirm the general trends of epidemiological surveys (see UMHRI reports, especially of 2004, 2005, and 2006).[5]

---

5   In 1998, UMHRI conducted an ethnographic study to uncover the relationship between entertainment patterns and drug use amongst young people. Ecstasy, LSD, and cocaine were shown to have high percentages of use among trance music fans (UMHRI, 1998; see also UMHRI, 2001).

Youth Victims

The systematic study of youth victimisation is relatively new in Greece, and to date it has principally received attention from scholarship with a legal perspective (see, e.g., discussion of the legal framework for dealing with juvenile victimisers by Adrianakis, 1982: 104–109). Lack of funding has prohibited investment in regular victimisation studies.

The first national victimisation study took place in 1991, and basically followed the protocol of the 1990 International Crime Victimisation Survey (ICVS). Although it covered 16 to 19 year-olds, it seems that the study did not include a particular analysis of youth victimisation (as judged on the basis of the resulting publication: Spinellis, 1997). The second national victimisation study was conducted in 2001. The sample comprised 6,095 people over 15 years of age throughout Greece, and was designed according to the demographic characteristics of the Greek population as represented in the census of 1991. The instrument of the survey was a structured, piloted questionnaire, which was based on that of the 2000 ICVS. The survey of 2001 used face-to-face structured interviews at the respondent's home, since the researchers believed that this method would be better suited to the Greek mentality than telephone interviews, even if this was perhaps not ideal for gathering data on the more sensitive issues which were addressed by the survey. Crimes reported were divided into two groups for analysis. The first referred to crimes against household property, whilst the other group referred to violent crimes, including mugging, assault, and sexual attack. The results confirmed that juveniles are as much victims of theft as all other age groups, but are far more likely to be victims of mugging than other age groups. Experience of sexual crime and violent attack were highest amongst 18 to 24 year-olds. The researchers noted that results were skewed by varying degrees of tolerance; for example, sexual crimes were highly reported amongst students and private sector employees, where higher levels of education appeared correlated with lower tolerance of unwanted sexual attention, whilst youth were the age group least interested in crime (only a quarter amongst them having discussed crime issues with a relative) (Karydis, 2004).

Sexual Crimes

There is a substantial lack of quantitative studies of sexual crime against youths in Greece. Some quantitative data have been presented on crimes such as pornography, prostitution, sexual assault, rape, and incest, for the periods 1980–1985 and 1990–1995 (though the source of data is not clear; see Panousis, 2004: 147–149).[6] In a series of studies using police and judicial records to profile the youth victims of sexual crimes, Tsigris (1999) considered rape, prostitution, and sexual assault, and found the rates of youth rape to be worryingly high, and incestual rape to be more common in rural areas. The Greek Institute for Child Health has also conducted studies concerning the sexual abuse of children. Of 743 university students who took part in a survey in 1992, 17 percent of women and 7 percent of men reported having experienced some form of sexual abuse in adolescence. For this study, 'sexual abuse' included rape or sexual assault, as well as both physical contact and other incidents such as exposure to an exhibitionist. Offenders were equally divided between relatives, other persons known to the victim, and offenders with no relationship to the victim at all (Agathonos and Fereti, 1992; see further Stavrianaki *et al.*, 2008).

Intrafamilial Violence

Whilst the exact definition of intrafamilial violence is still a matter of debate in Greece, there is agreement that corporal maltreatment carried out by a parent or guardian is a form of child abuse that could be legally described as aggravated assault. Corporal punishment was criminalised by Law 3500/2006. Legally, it is considered a mitigated form of child abuse, but the boundaries remain obscure; child abuse may begin as corporal punishment, but include or develop into psychological violence, neglect, or sexual abuse (Fereti, 2008). Even as early as the 1970s, some research

6   Some additional data regarding adolescent victimisation and prostitution is presented by Lazos (in Magganas, 1999).

considered neglect, physical abuse, and corporal punishment of children, all to be forms of abuse (Marouli, 1977). Nevertheless, corporal punishment is still widely tolerated in Greek society and, indeed, is a common phenomenon (Paritsis *et al.*, 1987; Bakoula *et al.*, 1993; see further Agathonos-Georgopoulou, 1997). In 1997, for example, a study of 591 Athenian families with both younger and older children revealed that 65.5 percent of the mothers interviewed had smacked their children at least once. Nevertheless, less than 20 percent of the parents believed smacking to be effective, and 78 percent claimed to support the complete abolition of corporal punishment (Fereti, 2000).[7]

Towards a Conclusion: Youths and Crime in the Media and Public Opinion

There is evidently considerable scope for further research into youth crime in Greece, and one key dimension that has been understudied to date is the relationship between juveniles and crime in the media and public opinion. Studies that do exist point to the fact that press coverage of youth victims and offenders has tended to be more emotive than informative, and to focus more on offenders than on victims. In a local, small-scale study of the press in Rhodes between 1984 and 1990, for example, it was found that media sources were usually police reports, and that the nature of the crime and the character of its perpetrator were often subject to distortion (Tsopotos, 1990). Similarly, a study of national printed media in Greece between 1992

---

7   Reference has also been made in the Greek criminological literature to voluntary abandonment of home by children. Whilst doing so does not in itself constitute an offence, unattended adolescents are vulnerable to exploitation, and may have already suffered from a dysfunctional family environment (Spinellis 1997; Nova-Kaltsouni, 2001a, 2001b). Both missing and runaway children and unattended refugee and immigrant children lack permanent residence and risk criminal exploitation (see further Dionysiou, 1998; Spinellis, 1997).

and 1996 found that coverage of sexual crimes against juveniles and children was characterised by exaggerated headlines and provocative content (Tsigris, 1999). In a further small-scale study in 2007 of the representation of children in television news, the selection and construction of news was found to focus on persons (and on victims more particularly) rather than on institutions or social and political contexts, such simplification serving to reinforce negative stereotypes (Kourti, 2001; see also Tsili, 1987).

One important suggestion that may be extrapolated from opinion research, however, is that media portrayals of youths and crime do not necessarily determine public attitudes (a point also raised by Panousis, this collection). One such study, conducted between 1996 and 1997, interviewed court reporters in Athens and Piraeus, students of the Police Academy in Athens, and students of sociology at Panteion University in Athens, in an exploration of public perceptions of pre-offending youth undergoing reformative or therapeutic treatment.[8] All four sets of respondents more or less agreed with a stereotypical image; that of a boy, from a broken family, who has abandoned schooling, is strongly influenced by the mass media, is led astray by a peer group, and is a user of drugs or alcohol. Respondents tended to agree with a sympathetic interpretation of the stereotype; that the figure represented a victim of neglect or of other maltreatment. They tended to disagree on the root cause of the problems generating such youth; educational, psychological, and welfare deficiencies were prominent alternative suggestions. Additionally, however, the majority held a negative opinion as to the admission of juveniles to reformatory institutions, whilst views were slightly more positive towards therapeutic institutions (Georgoulas, 1998, 2001).

---

8   According to Laws 2724/1940 and 2298/1995, adolescents who live in conditions that could lead them to crime (e.g., in a family of known offenders) may receive 'reformative' or 'therapeutic' treatment even though they have not yet committed a crime. The most punitive measure taken is admission to a 'reformatory' institution (see further Pitsela, this collection).

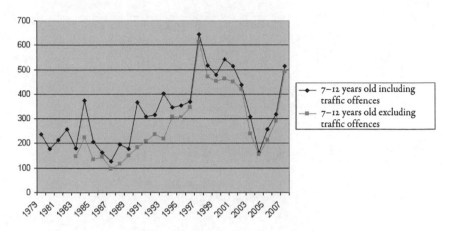

Figure 1   Caseload of children known as offenders to the police, 1979–2007
Source: Statistical Yearbook of the Greek Police

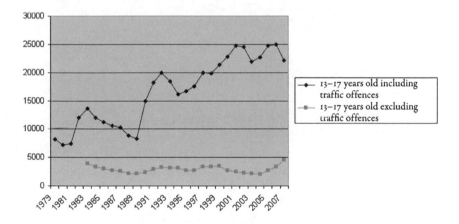

Figure 2   Caseload of juveniles known as offenders to the police, 1979–2007
Source: Statistical Yearbook of the Greek Police

| | Offence category | | | | | | | |
| Year | Theft/Robbery | | Bodily harm | | Homicide | | Rape | |
	Children	Juveniles	Children	Juveniles	Children	Juveniles	Children	Juveniles
1984	120	1,172	8	80	2	12	-	-
1987	42	956	7	78	0	6	-	-
1988	50	705	1	85	0	3	0	8
1989	82	699	3	46	1	7	0	5
1990	55	755	4	60	0	6	0	11
1991	64	1,116	6	52	5	6	0	8
1993	113	1,382	2	66	0	9	3	10
1994	137	1,282	1	73	0	6	0	9
1995	94	1,066	0	74	1	12	0	9
1996	106	737	0	57	1	11	0	8
1997	138	932	4	64	0	13	0	20
1998	106	968	2	78	1	10	0	19
1999	113	1,120	3	75	1	11	3	18
2000	101	945	5	58	0	8	4	6
2001	92	894	4	57	1	2	2	5
2002	183	872	1	55	0	7	1	13
2003	144	801	2	66	0	7	0	11
2004	91	767	3	56	0	5	0	5
2005	80	797	3	57	0	6	0	11
2006	98	764	2	68	0	12	3	18
2007	92	948	4	61	0	2	0	8

Table 1   Annual caseload (absolute number) of young offenders by type of offence, 1984–2007
Source: Statistical Yearbook of the Greek Police

	Type of punishment Males			Type of punishment Females			Type of punishment Males and Females	
Year	Ref.	Sent.	Conf.	Ref.	Sent.	Conf.	Ref.	Conf.
1965	2,367	369	-	103	27		2,470	184
1966	2,461	396	-	93	33		2,559	326
1967	2,408	355	-	103	27		2,512	281
1968	1,814	288	-	88	34		1,902	270
1969	1,823	386	-	85	44		1,908	184
1970	1,994	351	-	80	52		2,074	173
1971	2,580	419	-	98	33		2,678	119
1972	4,539	797	-	105	27		4,644	83
1973	4,640	881	70	123	41	14	4,773*	84
1974	3,798	780	58	93	63	3	3,891	61
1975	5,252	820	105	123	41	1	5,373	106
1976	5,657	757	61	150	28	2	5,807	63
1977	5,344	729	57	135	30	4	5,479	61
1978	4,942	876	32	125	35	2	5,067	34
1979	4,379	884	12	97	31	2	4,475	14
1980	4,616	939	13	100	34	0	4,720	13
1981	4,492	997	24	100	35	2	4,592	26
1982	5,715	1,119	35	122	30	2	5,837	37
1983	6,783	1,104	47	132	34	0	6,915	47
1984	7,578	1,107	66	160	33	4	7,738	70
1985	6,875	706	77	151	34	1	7,026	78
1986	7,046	736	82	169	29	1	7,215	83
1987	6,150	2,090	94	161	122	2	6,311	96
1988	4,952	1,412	32	187	132	0	5,139	32
1989	4,304	809	34	128	40	1	4,432	35

	Type of punishment Males			Type of punishment Females			Type of punishment Males and Females	
1990	5,133	1,519	31	154	110	1	5,287	32
1991	5,709	489	16	176	26	0	5,885	16
1992	7,263	505	30	243	14	1	7,506	31
1993	5,368	646	58	186	30	2	5,554	60
1994	4,560	846	85	181	24	3	4,741	88
1995	5,670	815	134	242	25	3	5,912	137
1996	4,841	794	156	195	54	8	5,036	164
1997	6,507	892	139	262	56	4	6,769	143
1998	4,128	760	32	283	66	0	4,411	32
1999	3,441	682	147	230	62	5	3,671	152
2000	3,278	744	78	258	58	7	3,536	26
2001	3,304	1,002	87	254	51	6	3,555	88
2002	3,270	886	99	248	66	9	3,518	108
2003	2,897	803	51	222	50	1	3,119	52
2004	3,292	790	170	174	44	9	3,466	179

Table 2   Annual judicial caseload (absolute number) of punishments, by offender
gender, 1965–2004
Source: National Statistical Service of Greece (NSSG)
Notes: 'Ref.' stands for 'reformative', 'Sent.' for 'sentenced', and 'Conf.' for 'confinement'.
The total for the year 1980 does not accurately correspond to the sum of the respective
subtotals for males and females.

References

Agathonos-Georgopoulou, H. (1997) 'Child Maltreatment in Greece: A Review of Research', *Child Abuse Review* 6: 257–271.

Agathonos, H. and I. Fereti (1992) 'A Retrospective Study of Child Sexual Abuse Experiences among Greek College Students', paper presented at the IX ISPCAN Congress, Chicago, U.S.A.

Andreou, E. (2000) 'Bully/Victim problems and their Association with Psychological Constructs in 8- to 12-year-old Greek Schoolchildren', *Aggressive Behaviour* 26: 49–56.

Andreou, E. (2001) 'Bully/Victim Problems and their Association with Coping Behaviour in Conflictual Peer Interactions among School-age Children', *Educational Psychology* 21: 59–66.

Andreou, E. (2004) 'Bully/Victim Problems and their Association with Machiavellianism and Self-efficacy in Greek Primary School Children', *British Journal of Educational Psychology* 74: 297–309.

Andrianakis, E. (1982) *The Age Effect on Criminal Deviance* [in Greek]. Athens: Kentro Egklimatologikon Ereunon.

Apospori, E. (2002) 'The Eurogang Network and Troublesome Youth Groups: An Attempt at an Interdisciplinary, Multi-methodological International Comparative Study' [in Greek], *Poinikos Logos* 2: 2679–2685.

Artinopoulou, V. (2000) 'School Violence in Greece: Review of Studies and Coping Strategies' [in Greek], *Poiniki Dikaiosini* 3: 1035–1041.

Astrinakis, A. and L. Stylianoudi (1996) *Heavy Metal, Rockabilly, Fans, Youth cultures and Subcultures in Western Attica* [in Greek]. Athens: Ellinika Grammata.

Bakoula, C., Kavadias, G. and N. Matsaniotis (1993) 'Contradictions in the Greek Family related to their Children's Upbringing', paper presented at the 31st Panhellenic Pediatric Conference, Kassandra, Greece.

Beze, L. (1991) *Juveniles* [in Greek]. Athens-Komotini: Ant. N. Sakkoulas Publishers.

Courakis, N. (1998) 'Report on the Development of Criminality in Contemporary Greece' [in Greek], *Poiniki Dikaiosini* 1: 239–248.

Courakis, N. (1999) *Juvenile Delinquents and Society: A Study of the Fundamental Values, Institutions and Juvenile Delinquency in Greece* [in Greek]. Athens-Komotini: Ant. N. Sakkoulas Publishers.

Courakis, N. (2000a) 'Juvenile Delinquency and Values in Modern Greece', in I. Daskalaki, P. Papadopoulou, D. Tsamparli, I. Tsiganou and E. Fronimou (eds) *Criminals and Victims at the Doorstep of the 21st Century* [in Greek], pp. 335–357. Athens: EKKE.

Courakis, N. (2000b) 'Juvenile Delinquency, 1983–1996: Conclusions of a Study' [in Greek], *Poiniki Dikaiosini* 3: 185–186.

Courakis, N. (2002) 'Violence in Greek Stadiums: Between Theory and Reality', in Elliniki Etairia Thymatologias (ed.) *Sports, Violence, Victimisation, Protection* [in Greek], pp. 23–177. Athens: Elliniki Etairia Thymatologias.

Courakis, N., Zagoura, P. and M. Galanou (2003) 'Youth Gangs in Greece: Conclusions from the Decisions of Juvenile Justice Court in Athens' [in Greek], *Poinikos Logos* 3: 2205–2218.

Dimakos, I. (2002) *The Role of the Family in the Prevention of Students' Aggressive Behaviour* [in Greek]. Available online at: http://vchristinakis.googlepages.com/family_violence_prevention.pdf

Dionysiou, I. (1998) 'The Need for Criminological Research on the Extent of the Phenomenon of "Street Children" in Athens' [in Greek], *Poiniki Dikaiosini* 1: 1033–1035.

Efstratiadis, S. (2004) 'Adolescent Criminality: Judicial Years 2001–2002, 2002–2003' [in Greek], *Poiniki Dikaiosini* 7: 1415–1427.

ESPAD (2000) *The 1999 ESPAD Report: Alcohol and Other Drug Use Among Students in 35 Countries*. Stockholm: CAN and Pompidou Group.

ESPAD (2004) *The 2003 ESPAD Report: Alcohol and Other Drug Use Among Students in 35 Countries*. Stockholm: CAN and Pompidou Group.

ESPAD (2009) *The 2007 ESPAD Report: Substance Use Among Students in 35 European Countries*. Stockholm: CAN, EMCDDA and Pompidou Group.

Fakiolas, N. and A. Armenakis (1995) 'Delinquency and Aggressiveness among Juvenile Students' [in Greek], *Syghroni Ekpaideusi* 81: 42–50.

Fereti, E. (2000) 'The Use of Violence in Children's Education: Research Data and Perspectives', in I. Daskalaki, P. Papadopoulou, D. Tsamparli, I. Tsiganou, E. Fronimou (eds) *Criminals and Victims at the Doorstep of the 21st Century* [in Greek], pp. 543–552. Athens: EKKE.

General Secretariat of Youth (2000) *Phenomena of Violence in School Life (October 1991-November 1999)* [in Greek]. Unpublished manuscript.

Georgoulas, S. (1998) *Social Representation and Treatment of the Pre-delinquent Adolescent in Greece*, PhD dissertation [in Greek]. Athens: Panteion University.

Georgoulas, S. (2001) 'New Methods of Adolescent Crime Prevention and Public Perceptions: Findings from a Study' [in Greek], *Chronika Ergastiriou Egklimatologikon Epistimon Tmimatos Nomikis Panepistimiou Thrakis* 11–12: 103–112.

Georgoulas, S. (2003) 'Adolescent Delinquency as a Problematic Situation: The Children's Ombudsman from an Abolitionist Policy Perspective' [in Greek], *Poiniki Dikaiosini* 6: 986–989.

Gotovos, A. (1996) *Youth and Social Change: Values, Experiences and Prospects* [in Greek]. Athens: Gutenberg.

Houndoumadi, A., Pateraki, L. and M. Doanidou (2003) *Tackling Violence in Schools: A Report from Greece.* Available online at: http://old.gold.ac.uk/connect/report-greece.html

Kalliotis, P. (2000) 'Bullying as a Special Case of Aggression: Procedures for Cross-Cultural Assessment', *School Psychology International* 21: 47–64.

Kalliotis, P. (2001) *School Violence from a Globalisation Perspective: The Nature and Extent of the Problem in our Country* [in Greek]. Available online at: http://www.pee.gr/pr_syn/s_nay/c/3/mer_g_th_en_3/kalliotis.htm

Karydis, V. (1996) *The Criminality of Immigrants in Greece: Issues of Theory and Crime Policy* [in Greek]. Athens: Papazissis.

Karydis, V. (2004) *Invisible Criminality: A National Victim Survey* [in Greek]. Athens-Komotini: Ant. N. Sakkoulas Publishers.

Kokkevi, A., Fotiou, A. and Richardson, C. (2007) 'Drug Use in the General Population of Greece over the Last 20 years: Results from Nationwide Household Surveys', *European Addiction Research* 13: 167–176.

Kokkevi, A., Loukadakis, M., Plagianakou, S., Politikou, K. and C. Stefanis (2000a) 'Sharp Increase in Illicit Drug Use in Greece: Trends from a General Population Survey on Licit and Illicit Drug Use', *European Addiction Research* 6: 42–49.

Kokkevi, A., Madianou, D. and C. Stefanis (1992) *Drugs in Greece, Volume 2: Drug Use in the Student Population* [in Greek]. Athens: Psychiatriki Vivliothiki.

Kokkevi, A. and C. Stefanis (1991) 'The Epidemiology of Licit and Illicit Substance Use among High-school Students in Greece', *American Journal of Public Health* 81: 48–52.

Kokkevi, A., Terzidou, M., Politikou, K. and C. Stefanis (2000b) 'Substance Use among High-school Students in Greece: Outburst of Illicit Drug Use in a Society Under Change', *Drug and Alcohol Dependence* 58: 181–188.

Kourti, E. (2001) 'The Child in Television News: The Process of Selection and Construction of News in Greek Television' [in Greek], *To Vima ton Koinonikon Epistimon* 30: 91–117.

Lazos, G. (1997) *Prostitution in Modern Greece* [in Greek]. Research report submitted to Panteion University.

Madianos, M., Gefou-Madianou, D. and C. Stefanis (1995) 'The Epidemiology of Illicit and Licit Drug Use in Greece: A Nationwide General Population Survey', *European Psychiatry* 10: 175–182.

Magganas, A. (1996) 'Children Protagonists in a New Form of Violence: Offenders or Victims?', in V. Artinopoulou and A. Magganas (eds) *Victimology and Aspects of Victimisation* [in Greek], pp. 123–144. Athens: Nomiki Vivliothiki.

Magganas, A. (1999) 'Who is Responsible for Adolescent Prostitution?' [in Greek], *Poiniki Dikaiosini* 2: 497–499.

Manoudaki, T. (1998) 'Youth Gangs in Greece Today: Findings from a Study' [in Greek], *Poiniki Dikaiosini* 1: 1144–1145.

Mpakatsoulas, M. (1984) *Criminology Volume II* [in Greek]. Athens-Komotini: Ant. N. Sakkoulas Publishers.

Marouli, E. (1977) 'Retrospective Research on the Abused Child Syndrome' [in Greek], *Epitheorisi Koinonikon Ereunon* 9: 275–284.

Nova-Kaltsouni, H. (2001a) *Forms of Juvenile Deviant Behaviour: The Role of the Family and the School* [in Greek]. Athens: Gutenberg.

Nova-Kaltsouni, H. (2001b) 'Adolescent Delinquent Behaviour: The Role of the Family' [in Greek], *Chronika Ergastiriou Egklimatologikon Ereunon Tmimatos Nomikis Panepistimiou Thrakis* 11–12: 63–83.

Panousis, G. (1987) 'Hooliganism: A Social Phenomenon with Two Faces' [in Greek], *Athlitiki Psychologia* 1: 39–42.

Panousis, G. (1990) 'Youth Criminality: The "Game" and the "Challenge"', in L. Beze (ed.) *Prevention and Treatment of Youth Criminality (Retraining-Integration)* [in Greek], pp. 61–79. Athens-Komotini: Ant. N. Sakkoulas Publishers.

Panousis, G. (1995) 'Self-reported Delinquency by Adolescents', in *In Honour of Ilias Krispis* [in Greek], pp. 341–366. Athens-Komotini: Ant. N. Sakkoulas Publishers.

Panousis, G. (2000) 'Is the Violent Fan a Sports Fan?' [in Greek], *Yperaspisi* 10: 515–520.

Panousis, G. (2004a) 'Hooliganism', in G. Panousis (ed.) *About Criminals: Rhetoric and Counter-rhetoric* [in Greek], pp. 135–141. Athens: Ant. N. Sakkoulas Publishers.

Panousis, G. (2004b) 'Violence at School', in G. Panousis (ed.) *About Criminals: Rhetoric and Counter-rhetoric* [in Greek], pp. 159–163. Athens: Ant. N. Sakkoulas Publishers.

Panousis, G. (2004c) 'Adolescent Offenders and Victims', in G. Panousis (ed.) *About Criminals: Rhetoric and Counter-rhetoric* [in Greek], pp. 143–157. Athens: Ant. N. Sakkoulas Publishers.

Panousis, G. (2006) 'School Struggles With or Without a Referee? Violence at Schools' [in Greek], *Poiniki Dikaiosini* 9: 75–84.

Papadopoulou, P., Teperoglou, A. and D. Tsamparli (2000) 'Delinquence: Juveniles and Accountability', in I. Daskalaki, P. Papadopoulou, D. Tsamparli, I. Tsiganou and E. Fronimou (eds) *Criminals and Victims at the Doorstep of the 21st Century* [in Greek], pp. 319–333. Athens: EKKE.

Papatheodorou, T. (1999) 'Crime and the Local Community: Evident Criminality in Corfu between 1995 and 1998' [in Greek], *Poiniki Dikaiosini* 2: 1155–1162.

Paritsis, N., Pallis, D.J., Lyketsos, G., Phylactou, C., Sarafidou, E. and F. Vrachni (1987) 'School Delinquent and Deviant behaviour in Adolescence: The Role of Children's Personality and Attitudes' [in Greek], paper presented at the 1st European Conference on Child Abuse and Neglect, Rhodes, Greece.

Pateraki, L. and A. Houndoumadi (2001) 'Bullying Among Primary School Children in Athens, Greece', *Educational Psychology* 21: 167–175.

Petropoulos, N., Papastylianou, A., Katerelos, P. and H. Harisis (2000) 'Antisocial Behaviour of Children and Juveniles', in A. Kalantzi-Azizi and H. Bezevekis (eds) *Issues of Physical Health of Children and Adolescents* [in Greek]. Athens: Ellinika Grammata.

Pitsela, A., Filou, M., Neubacher, F. and M. Walter (2005) 'A Comparative Study of Adolescent Criminality in Greece and Germany' [in Greek], *Poiniki Dikaiosini* 8: 469–479.

Psalti, A. and K. Konstantinou (2007) 'The Phenomenon of Intimidation in Secondary Education Schools: The Influence of Gender and National-Cultural Origins' [in Greek], *Psychology* 14: 329–345.

Sapouna, M. (2008) 'Bullying in Greek Primary and Secondary Schools', *School Psychology International* 29: 199–213.

Spinellis, C. (1997) *Crime in Greece in Perspective*. Athens-Komotini: Ant. N. Sakkoulas Publishers.

Spinellis, C., Apospori, E., Kranidioti, M., Simiyianni, Y. and N. Angelopoulou (1994) 'Key Findings of a Preliminary Self-report Delinquency Study in Athens, Greece', in J. Junger-Tas, G. Terlouw, M. Klein (eds) *Delinquent Behaviour among Young People in the Western World: First Results of the International Self-report Delinquency Study*, pp. 288–318. Amsterdam-New York: Kugler.

Stavrianaki, M., Kyriakopoulou, A., Rigka, A. and G. Nikolaidis (2008) *Delphi Methodology: A Qualitative Approach to the Phenomenon of Violence against Adolescents* [in Greek]. Available online at: http://ich-mhsw.gr/uploads/progs/delphi.pdf

Tsaousis, D. and E. Korre-Grueger (1974) *Adolescent Criminality in the Athens Region* [in Greek]. Athens: EKKE.

Tsiganou, I., Daskalaki, K.-I. and D. Tsamparli (2004) *Images and Representations of Violence in the Greek School* [in Greek]. Athens: Nomiki Vivliothiki.

Tsigris, A. (1999) *Sexual Molestation of the Child: Perspectives of Social Control* [in Greek]. Athens-Komotini: Ant. N. Sakkoulas Publishers.

Tsili, S. (1987) 'Drug Addiction: A Different Approach' [in Greek], *Epitheorisi Koinonikon Ereunon* 66: 226–239.

Tsopotos, D. (1990) 'Adolescent Offenders and the Local Press in Rhodes', in L. Beze
    (ed.) *Prevention and Treatment of Youth Criminality (Retraining-Integration)* [in
    Greek], pp. 213–215. Athens-Komotini: Ant. N. Sakkoulas Publishers.
University Mental Health Research Institute (UMHRI) (1996–2008) *Yearly Reports
    by EMCDDA's Focal point on Drugs in Greece* [in Greek]. Athens: UMHRI.
Zafiriou, E. (1979) 'Criminality by Minors' [in Greek], *Nomiko Vima* 27:
    1541–1545.

LEONIDAS K. CHELIOTIS[1]

Commentary

The chapter by Papageorgiou offers a useful overview of research on youth and crime in contemporary Greece. Police-recorded data reveal that, unlike what is commonly suggested by the national media and populist politicians, at times proposed by scholarly research, and often believed amongst the public, youth involvement in delinquent and criminal acts has neither grown in numerical terms nor has it become more violent over the last three decades. This notwithstanding, recent years have seen the expansion of pertinent research, increasingly including focus on such themes as school bullying and gang involvement. It is interesting that, despite the continuing centrality of the family in Greek society (see, e.g., Halkias, 2004), its role – whether in causing or preventing delinquency – appears to have been largely overlooked. One wonders whether this is because family factors in Greece are seen as unrelated to juvenile delinquency, or because the family remains a taboo subject.

This commentary therefore aims to provide a critical excursus to the ways in which international criminological research accounts for the importance of family factors in the aetiology of delinquent conduct. More specifically, the discussion addresses three categories of variables that are considered to be amongst the strongest family predictors of juvenile offending: criminal and antisocial parents and siblings; large family size; and child-rearing methods (poor supervision, poor discipline, coldness and rejection, and low parental involvement).[2] Each category is reviewed below

---

1   Thanks are due to Sappho Xenakis for her substantive feedback on this commentary.
2   Following Farrington (2002a), delinquent siblings are grouped with criminal parents, and parental discipline is included in the child-rearing methods category. Other family factors associated with delinquency risk include parental conflict and disrupted

with reference to the major relevant studies (especially longitudinal studies) and their primary theoretical explanations. The commentary concludes with an overall assessment of the significance of the family factors under scrutiny in effecting delinquency, also sketching some research questions that consequently emerge for the Greek case.

Family Factors and Delinquency: A Brief International Review of Longitudinal Research

Ever since criminologists set out to study systematically the influence of family factors on juvenile offending, one of the most robust predictors of delinquency has proved to be *criminal or antisocial parents and siblings*. Robins *et al.* (1975) followed up over 200 black males in St Louis and reported that arrested parents tended to have arrested children, while the juvenile records of the former were mirrored in those of the offspring with regard to both rates and types of offending. Also, in the Cambridge Study of Delinquent Development, which is a prospective longitudinal survey of 411 South London working-class males from ages 8 to 46, only 6 percent of all families accounted for half of the criminal convictions of all parents and children surveyed (Farrington, 2002b). Within that context, having a convicted father, mother, brother, or sister were all, independently from one another, strong predictors of a boy's own convictions, while also relating to his self-reported offending (Farrington, 1979). Moreover, same-sex relationships were stronger than opposite-sex relationships, and older siblings were stronger predictors than younger siblings (Farrington *et al.*, 1996; see also Farrington *et al.*, 1975; Farrington and West, 1990). The Pittsburgh

---

families, physical/sexual abuse of children, socio-economic conditions like poor housing and poverty, and certain parental characteristics such as young age, substance abuse, or working mothers (see Loeber and Dishion, 1983; Loeber and Stouthamer-Loeber, 1986; Snyder and Patterson, 1987; Utting *et al.*, 1993).

Youth Study – a longitudinal study of 1,517 male students from ages 7 to 13 – yielded similar results: 43 percent of all arrested family members aggregated in just 8 percent of the families, while arrests of fathers, mothers, brothers and sisters all predicted the boys' own delinquent involvement. Moreover, arrested fathers were the strongest independent precursor (Farrington, 1992; Loeber *et al.*, 1998a). The robust father-son link was also found in a 30-year follow-up of approximately 250 boys in the Cambridge-Somerville (Boston) Youth Study, where convicted males tended to have convicted fathers (McCord, 1977; see also Ferguson, 1952; Glueck and Glueck, 1950; Offord *et al.*, 1979; Wilson, 1987).

Several tentative explanations, interrelated to a great extent, have been offered with regard to the concentration of offending in certain families and its transmission from one generation to the next. *First*, and most plausibly, the phenomenon is seen as stemming from the common deprivations and problems experienced during juvenility by parents and, later on, by their children. In this respect, as West and Farrington (1977) found in the Cambridge study, parental criminality is only part of a perpetual chain entailing exposure of juveniles to multiple risk factors like poverty, large family size, parental conflict, family disruption, and poor child-rearing, that, when aggregated, give rise to antisocial behaviour, including offending. In a similar vein, the Pittsburgh study showed that many types of risk factors predict multiple child problems and, within that context, delinquent behaviour (Loeber *et al.*, 1998a). A *second* explanation emphasises the role of environmental mechanisms in linking parental criminality to children's delinquency, rather than (co)effecting the latter directly. Sampson and Laub (1993) have argued that most effects of parental criminality are engendered by intervening family processes. Similarly, the Cambridge study suggested that poor parental supervision by criminal parents mediated, along with other factors, their children's delinquency (West and Farrington, 1977). Later on, however, Rowe and Farrington (1997) showed that the impact of parental criminality could not be accounted for by the poor child-rearing environment. According to a *third*, also environmentally-oriented view, children may witness and, in turn, imitate the antisocial behaviour of older siblings and/or parents. Yet, empirical findings with regard to this explanation are mixed. For example, while co-offending by brothers was a strikingly common phenomenon in the Cambridge study, co-offending with parents was disproportionately rare. Furthermore, contrary to the view that criminal parents tolerate their children's deviant behaviour, 89 percent of convicted men at age 32 expressed their disapproval of offending by the offspring (Reiss and Farrington, 1991). Finally, a *fourth* explanation suggests that juvenile delinquency reflects genetic influences (Mednick and Volavka, 1980; Rowe and Osgood, 1984). Indeed, a plethora of adoption and twin studies suggest that the intergenerational transmission of offending is, at least partially, due to heredity (Carey, 1994; Grove *et al.*, 1990, Raine, 1993; Rutter *et al.*, 1998). However, considerable doubt has been cast over this view due to the concurrent impact of environmental factors on delinquent conduct (see Farrington, 2002a: 133–134), but also the questionable methodological quality of most such studies (see Rutter *et al.*, 1998: 195).

Another strong predictor of delinquency is *large family size*, namely, a large number – usually interpreted as *at least four* – of children in the family (Rutter and Giller, 1983). This factor proved similarly important in the Cambridge and Pittsburgh studies (Farrington, 2002b). In the former, for example, boys who had four or more siblings by their tenth birthday were twice as likely to be convicted as juveniles (West and Farrington, 1973). Furthermore, large family size was the most important independent predictor of convictions up to age 32. Indeed, 58 percent of boys from such families were convicted up to that age (Farrington, 1993). In the National Survey of Health and Development, which is a longitudinal study of 5,362 children born in England, Scotland, and Wales in 1946, Wadsworth (1979) also found that the proportion of officially delinquent boys increased from 9 percent for single-child families to 24 percent for families containing four or more children. Moreover, almost half of the male recidivists (with two or more convictions) came from large families with three or more brothers and sisters. Similarly, a survey of approximately 700 children in Nottingham concluded that large family size was one of the most important precursors of delinquency (Newson *et al.*, 1993; see also Capaldi and Patterson, 1996; Kolvin *et al.*, 1988; Ouston, 1984).

There exist several possible explanations of this link, but large family size can only be part of causal chains, rather than engendering unlawful conduct by itself. Both the Cambridge and Pittsburgh studies, for example, have suggested that large family size tends to be associated with poor supervision of children because of the problem of dividing attention between them, thus indirectly enhancing their likelihood of delinquent involvement (Farrington and Loeber, 1999; see also Wilson, 1980). Another potential explanation is that proposed by Ferguson (1952) in his study of over 1,300 Glasgow boys: large family size usually creates overcrowding which, functioning as an intervening factor, may effect criminogenic conditions like frustration, irritation, and conflict (see also West and Farrington, 1973). Also, as Offord (1982) and Jones *et al.* (1980) maintain, delinquency risk increases with the number of brothers in the family who, unlike sisters, tend to encourage boys' antisocial behaviour. Other explanations present large family size as either giving rise to risk factors like family poverty, stress, and disruption (Rutter *et al.*, 1998; see also Rowe and Farrington, 1997).

As follows from some of the above-mentioned propositions, *child-rearing methods* are also associated with the likelihood of a child's delinquent involvement. Indeed, there is abundant empirical evidence, particularly through observations and interviews, that the main dimensions of child-rearing, namely *parental supervision, discipline, attitude*, and *involvement*, are strong, albeit not independent, predictors of delinquency (Farrington, 1979; Rothbaum and Weisz, 1994). Poor parental supervision – that is, inadequate monitoring of the child's activities, and insufficient watchfulness or vigilance (Farrington, 1994) – is usually the most important child-rearing risk factor. For example, in studying 400 boys in Birmingham, Wilson (1980) found that the strongest correlate of conviction cautions and self-reported delinquency was lax parental supervision at age 10. Moreover, the Cambridge-Somerville study showed that poor parental supervision was the best predictor of both violent and property crimes (McCord, 1979; see also Cortés and Gatti, 1972; Farrington and Loeber, 1999; Gladstone, 1978; Hirschi, 1969; Jephcott and Carter, 1955; Riley and Shaw, 1985). At a protective level, the Newcastle 1,000 Family Study, which examined the delinquent involvement of children born in Newcastle upon Tyne in 1947, demonstrated that those who avoided having a criminal record by the age of 33 had enjoyed good parental supervision during childhood (Kolvin *et al.*, 1988; see also Laybourn, 1986).

Parental discipline, on the other hand, refers to the ways in which parents discourage (or, more generally, respond to) their children's misbehaviour. At a pre-offending stage, poor discipline usually takes the form of failing to accurately and consistently define and label certain behaviours as excessive or antisocial (Snyder and Patterson, 1987). Once delinquency occurs, as West and Farrington (1973) found in the Cambridge study, ineffective disciplinary action may translate into either erratic treatment by one parent, ranging from bypassing the child's bad behaviour to punishing it severely, or inconsistency between the parents, with one being tolerant or even indulgent and the other adopting a punitive stance (see also Loeber and Stouthamer-Loeber, 1986; Olweus, 1980; Rowe and Farrington, 1997). Also, it may involve unusually harsh or even physical punishment, which often overlaps with parental violence and child abuse (Steinmetz, 1979). In the Cambridge study, harsh discipline predicted both violent and persistent offending up to age 32 (Farrington, 1991). In a follow-up study of approximately 900 children in New York State, Eron *et al.* (1991) demonstrated that harsh parental punishment at age 8 predicted a man's arrests for violence, the severity of punishment he imposed on his children, and his history of spouse assault, all up to age 30. In their survey in Nottingham, the Newsons (1989) also found that physical punishment at ages 7 and 11 was largely associated with later convictions. Similarly, in a retrospective study of 908 abused or neglected children and a 667-membered comparison group in Indianapolis, Widom (1989) demonstrated that physical abuse up to age 11 doubled the risk of becoming a violent offender within the next 15 years. In revisiting the cohorts six years later, Maxfield and Widom (1996) found that early childhood victimisation continued to have significant long-term consequences for delinquency, adult criminality, and violent criminal behaviour.

There is also much empirical support for the notion that parental attitude towards offspring, whether this translates into warmth and affection or coldness and rejection, relates to the likelihood of children's delinquent conduct. One of the main conclusions reached by Glueck and Glueck (1950, 1968) in their longitudinal study of 500 male delinquents in Massachusetts correctional institutions and 500 matched non-delinquents in 1939–1944 was that indifference, rejection, and outright hostility were very commonly displayed by the parents of delinquents. In contrast, most of the non-delinquents enjoyed parental warmth and affection. Similarly, Bandura and Walters (1959) found that aggressive boys were loved less and rejected more than non-aggressive children, especially by their fathers. The Cambridge-Somerville study also demonstrated a tendency of cold and rejecting parents to have unlawful children (McCord, 1979), whereas parental warmth acted protectively against physical punishment (McCord, 1997, cited in Farrington, 2002b; see also Andry, 1960; Lewis, 1954; Nye, 1958).

Finally, low parental involvement in the children's activities also predicts delinquency. As Loeber and Stouthamer-Loeber (1986) demonstrated in their detailed concurrent analyses of family factors, lack of parental involvement is strongly related to children's official delinquency and aggression, while also predicting, although to a relatively lesser extent, their self-reported indices of lawbreaking. In the US National Youth Survey of 1,725 adolescents aged 11 to 17, Canter (1982) found that delinquents' parents spent less time with their children. Moreover, in the Chicago Youth Development Study, which examined 362 African-American and Latino boys aged 11 to 13, low family cohesiveness proved to be the most important precursor of violence (Gorman-Smith *et al.*, 1996). In a similar vein, the Pittsburgh and Nottingham studies showed, respectively, that poor parent-child communication and low parental involvement were robustly associated with delinquent conduct (Farrington and Loeber, 1999; Newson and Newson, 1989; see also Farrington, 1989; Farrington and Hawkins, 1991; West and Farrington, 1973).

Insofar as the theoretical explanation of the link between child-rearing patterns and delinquency is concerned, it is mostly focused on the models proposed by the *social learning, attachment,* and *social bonding theories.* Social learning theories attribute delinquent behaviour to juveniles' improper socialisation and their consequent lack of internal conscience or inhibitions against offending. This may be due to the lack of close supervision, low reinforcement of prosocial acts (see, for example, Farrington and Loeber, 1999; Patterson *et al.*, 1989), the antisocial models provided by the parents, or the failure of the latter to disapprove their children's transgressions in an appropriate and consistent manner (Trasler, 1962; see also Akers, 1990, 1999; Bandura, 1977). Attachment theory, on the other hand, proposes that low psycho-emotional ties with warm, loving, and law-abiding parents enhance the risk of delinquent involvement (Carlson and Sroufe, 1995, cited by Farrington, 2002b). In a similar vein, social bonding theory suggests that, in order for juveniles to abstain from delinquency, they should be tightly bonded with 'conventional others' and society in general, thus being controlled into the direction of conformity (Hirschi, 1969).[3] To this goal, parents – like the rest of socialisation agents (e.g., school teachers) – should care about the child, devote time and energy in monitoring his or her behaviour, and non-oppressively correct misdeeds when they occur (Hirschi and Gottfredson, 2003).

Concluding Remarks:
Knowledge Gaps and Future Directions

Criminological research has made considerable advances in deepening our knowledge with regard to the relationship between family factors and delinquent behaviour. Indeed, there is substantial consistency in the preponderance of studies as to the family characteristics which correlate with juvenile offending. However, developing a watertight theoretical explanation on the basis of those findings is not nearly as straightforward as their (relative) uniformity suggests. In fact, perplexing questions about precisely how family factors are causally related to delinquency remain unanswered. A major limitation is the potential correlation between causally linked

---

3   More recently, Hirschi, along with Gottfredson, shifted his focus to self-control, namely to 'the differential tendency of people to avoid criminal acts whatever the circumstances in which they find themselves' (Hirschi and Gottfredson, 1990: 87). According to the self-control theory, delinquency is due to low self-control, as this stems from poor parental supervision, particularly in large families, with single or criminal parents (see Akers, 1999: 90–95).

variables. That is, family factors that are thought to engender delinquency also tend to be correlated with each other (see Loeber and Stouthamer-Loeber, 1986: 40–41). For example, brothers in the Cambridge study were more likely to co-offend when they came from large families (Rowe and Farrington, 1997). Similarly, family risk factors may be correlated with other, not necessarily familial, adversities (e.g., poor school attainment) that also predict offending (Farrington, 1992). In both cases, causal inferences are inevitably weak. According to McCord *et al.* (1969), it is more likely that multiple causes and various developmental paths lead to the same results. In that case, delinquent behaviour may well be the product, at least partially, of some third variables that have not been put under parallel scrutiny. Moreover, it may also be giving rise to the very factors that have been (mis) interpreted as its causes (Rutter, 1981; Larzelere and Patterson, 1990). For instance, Rutter and Giller (1983) have argued that some of the putatively criminogenic parental factors (e.g., excessively harsh discipline, poor supervision) can sometimes be the consequences of rearing disruptive and difficult children (see also Campbell *et al.*, 1996; Kandel and Wu, 1995; Lytton, 1990; Paternoster, 1988). Thus, it is hard to disentangle causes from effects, let alone to establish what family factors predict delinquency independently of other possible causal variables, whether familial or non-familial.

In addition, family factors have different effects on children of different ages. Unfortunately, however, most researchers have contented themselves with studying family influences on the child's onset of offending, rather than expanding their research horizons to the family impact on his or her later criminal career, whether this translates into persistence of or desistance from unlawful conduct (Farrington, 2002a). It is also important to study the ways in which family factors affect gender differences in delinquency. For example, past findings have shown, although not consistently, that boys in patriarchal families exhibit more antisocial behaviour than their sisters due to their risk-prone socialisation, as this stems from the gender-related imbalanced power relations between parents (Hagan *et al.*, 1987; for relevant discussions, see Canter, 1982; Hagan *et al.*, 1985; Hill and Atkinson, 1988; Morash and Chesney-Lind, 1991; Moffitt *et al.*, 2001; Singer and Levine, 1988). Moreover, as Wikström and Loeber (2000) maintain, the effects of family risk factors on delinquency also have to be tested in relation to the neighbourhoods where children reside. Indeed, socio-economic factors such as poor housing or low income may indirectly effect delinquency by causing familial handicaps like poor child-rearing (Farrington *et al.*, 1993; Wikström *et al.*, 1995; Larzelere and Patterson, 1990; Loeber *et al.*, 1998b). Finally, it is crucial to examine in more depth how the links between family factors and delinquency might vary between different ethnic groups (Farrington *et al.*, 2003). For instance, the delinquency risk associated with physical punishment does not seem to apply to African American samples (Deater-Deckard *et al.*, 1996).

Turning back to the case of Greece in light of the above, a number of questions emerge. Could it be the case that the high cohesiveness of the family unit – as typified by the crucial provision of welfare support to family members in the absence of sufficient state provision (see Cheliotis and Xenakis, 2010) – has served to limit the development of juvenile delinquency in the country? This, indeed, would suggest one very positive but underappreciated product of the much-maligned trope of 'familism' in Mediterranean societies like Greece (see further Xenakis, 2010), although any such inquiry also needs to take into account changes in the family sphere (e.g., single parenthood, female-headed households, increased participation of mothers in the labour force, and divorce rates; see Coltrane and Collins, 2001). Might the relative absence of focus on the family within Greek research on juvenile delinquency indicate, not so much its taboo status, but its weaker relevance in contrast to neighbourhood effects (see, e.g., Sampson (1997)? Moreover, given the changing ethnic composition of Greek society over the past twenty years, is it now possible to identify any variation in risk or, indeed, protective factors associated with particular ethnic groups and their concentration in given neighbourhoods, as has been recorded elsewhere (e.g., by Graif and Sampson, 2009)?

References

Akers, R.L. (1990) 'Rational Choice, Deterrence, and Social Learning Theory in Criminology: The Path Not Taken', *Journal of Criminal Law and Criminology* 81: 653–676.

Akers, R.L. (1999) *Criminological Theories: Introduction and Evaluation*, 2nd edn. Chicago: Fitzroy Dearborn.

Andry, R.G. (1960) *Delinquency and Parental Pathology: A Study in Forensic and Clinical Psychology*. London: Methuen.

Bandura, A. (1977) *Social Learning Theory*. Englewood Cliffs: Prentice-Hall.

Bandura, A. and R.H. Walters (1959) *Adolescent Aggression*. New York: Ronald Press.

Brownfield, D. and A.M. Sorenson (1994) 'Sibship Size and Sibling Delinquency', *Deviant Behaviour* 15: 45–61.

Campbell, S.B., Pierce, E.W., Moore, G., Marakowitz, S. and K. Newby (1996) 'Boys' Externalising Problems at Elementary School Age: Pathways from Early Behaviour Problems, Maternal Control, and Family Stress', *Development and Psychopathology* 8: 701–719.

Canter, R.J. (1982) 'Family Correlates of Male and Female Delinquency', *Criminology* 20: 149–167.

Capaldi, D.M. and G.R. Patterson (1996) 'Can Violent Offenders Be Distinguished from Frequent Offenders: Prediction from Childhood to Adolescence', *Journal of Research in Crime and Delinquency* 33: 206–231.

Carey, G. (1994) 'Genetics and Violence', in A.J. Reiss, K.A. Miezek and J.A. Roth (eds) *Understanding and Preventing Violence, Vol. 2: Biobehavioural Influences*, pp. 21–58. Washington, DC: National Academy Press.

Carlson, E.A. and L.A. Sroufe (1995) 'Contribution of Attachment Theory to Developmental Psychopathology', in D. Cicchetti and D.J. Cohen (eds) *Developmental Psychopathology, Vol. 1: Theory and Methods*, pp. 581–617. New York: Wiley.

Cheliotis, L.K. and S. Xenakis (2010) 'What's Neoliberalism Got to Do With It? Towards a Political Economy of Punishment in Greece', *Criminology & Criminal Justice* 10: 353–373.

Coltrane, S. and R. Collins (2001) *Sociology of Marriage and the Family: Gender, Love, and Property*, 5th edn. Belmont: Wadsworth.

Cortés, J.B. and F.M. Gatti (1972) *Delinquency and Crime: A Biopsychosocial Approach*. New York: Seminar Press.

Deater-Deckard, K., Dodge, K.A., Bates, J.E. and G.S. Pettit (1996) 'Physical Discipline among African American and European American Mothers: Links to Children's Externalising Behaviours', *Developmental Psychology* 32: 1065–1072.

Eron, L.D., Huesmann, L.R. and A. Zelli (1991) 'The Role of Parental Variables in the Learning of Aggression', in D.J. Pepler and K.J. Rubin (eds) *The Development and Treatment of Childhood Aggression*, pp. 169–188. Hillsdale: Lawrence Erlbaum.

Farrington, D.P. (1979) 'Environmental Stress, Delinquent Behaviour, and Convictions', in G. Sarason and C.D. Spielberger (eds) *Stress and Anxiety, Vol. 6*, pp. 93–107. Washington, DC: Hemisphere.

Farrington, D.P. (1989) 'Early Predictors of Adolescent Aggression and Adult Violence', *Violence and Victims* 4: 79–100.

Farrington, D.P. (1992) 'Juvenile Delinquency', in J.C. Coleman (ed.) *The School Years: Current Issues in Socialisation of Youth People*, 2nd edn., pp. 123–163. London: Routledge.

Farrington, D.P. (1993) 'Childhood Origins of Teenage Antisocial Behaviour and Adult Social Dysfunction', *Journal of the Royal Society of Medicine* 86: 13–17.

Farrington, D.P. (1994) 'The Influence of the Family on Delinquent Development', in C. Henricson (ed.) *Crime and the Family: Conference Report*, pp. 9–17. London: Family Policy Studies Centre.

Farrington, D.P. (1998) 'Predictors, Causes and Correlates of Male Youth Violence', in M. Tonry and M.H. Moore (eds) *Crime and Justice, Vol. 24: Youth Violence*, pp. 421–475. Chicago: University of Chicago Press.

Farrington, D.P. (2002a) 'Families and Crime', in J.Q. Wilson and J. Petersilia (eds) *Crime: Public Policies for Crime Control*, pp. 129–148. Oakland: Institute for Contemporary Studies Press.

Farrington, D.P. (2002b) 'Developmental Criminology and Risk-Focused Prevention', in M. Maguire, R. Morgan and R. Reiner (eds) *The Oxford Handbook of Criminology*, pp. 657–701. Oxford: Oxford University Press.

Farrington, D.P., Gundry, G. and D.J. West (1975) 'The Familial Transmission of Criminality', *Medicine, Science, and the Law* 15: 177–186.

Farrington, D.P. and D.J. West (1990) 'The Cambridge Study in Delinquent Development: A Long-Term Follow-Up of 411 London Males', in G. Kaiser and H.-J. Kerner (eds) *Criminality: Personality, Behaviour, Life History*, pp. 117–138. Berling: Springer-Verlag.

Farrington, D.P. and J.D. Hawkins (1991) 'Predicting Participation, Early Onset, and Later Persistence in Officially Recorded Offending', *Criminal Behaviour and Mental Health* 1: 1–33.

Farrington, D.P., Sampson, R.J. and P.-O. Wikström (eds) (1993) *Integrating Individual and Ecological Aspects of Crime*. Stockholm: National Council for Crime Prevention.

Farrington, D.P., Barnes, G.C. and S. Lambert (1996) 'The Concentration of Offending in Families', *Legal and Criminological Psychology* 1: 47–63.

Farrington, D.P. and R. Loeber (1999) 'Transatlantic Replicability of Risk Factors in the Development of Delinquency', in P. Cohen, C. Slomkowski and L.N. Robins (eds) *Historical and Geographical Influences on Psychopathology*, pp. 299–329. Mahwah: Lawrence Erlbaum.

Farrington, D.P., R. Loeber and M. Stouthamer-Loeber (2003) 'How Can the Relationship between Race and Violence be Explained?', in D.F. Hawkins (ed.) *Violent Crime: Assessing Race and Ethnic Differences*, pp. 213–237. New York: Cambridge University Press.

Ferguson, T. (1952) *The Young Delinquent in his Social Setting*. London: Oxford University Press.

Forehand, R., Biggar, H. and B.A. Kotchick (1998) 'Cumulative Risk across Family Stressors: Short and Long Term Effects for Adolescents', *Journal of Abnormal Child Psychology* 26: 119–128.

Gladstone, F. (1978) 'Vandalism among Adolescent Boys', in R.V.G. Clarke (ed.) *Tackling Vandalism, Home Office Research Study 47*, pp. 19–39. London: HMSO.

Glueck, S. and E.T. Glueck (1950) *Unraveling Juvenile Delinquency*. Cambridge, MA: Harvard University Press.

Glueck, S. and E.T. Glueck (1968) *Delinquents and Non-Delinquents in Perspective*. Cambridge, MA: Harvard University Press.

Gorman-Smith, D., Tolan, P.H., Zelli, A. and L.R. Huesmann (1996) 'The Relation of Family Functioning to Violence among Inner-City Minority Youths', *Journal of Family Psychology* 10: 115–129.

Gottfredson, M. and T. Hirschi (1990) *A General Theory of Crime*. Palo Alto: Stanford University Press.

Graif, C. and R.J. Sampson (2009) 'Spatial Heterogeneity in the Effects of Immigration and Diversity on Neighbourhood Homicide Rates', *Homicide Studies* 13: 242–260.

Grove, W.M., Eckert, E.D., Heston, L., Bouchard, T.J., Segal, N. and D.T. Lykken (1990) 'Heritability of Substance Abuse and Antisocial Behaviour: A Study of Monozygotic Twins Reared Apart', *Biological Psychiatry* 27: 1293–1304.

Haapasalo, J. and E. Pokela (1999) 'Child-rearing and Child Abuse: Antecedents of Criminality', *Aggression and Violent Behaviour* 1: 107–127.

Hagan, J., Gillis, A.R. and J. Simpson (1985) 'The Class Structure of Gender and Delinquency: Toward a Power-Control Theory of Common Delinquent Behaviour', *American Journal of Sociology* 90: 1151–1178.

Hagan, J., Simpson, J. and A.R. Gillis (1987) 'Class in the Household: A Power-Control Theory of Gender and Delinquency', *American Journal of Sociology* 92: 788–816.

Halkias, A. (2004) *The Empty Cradle of Democracy: Sex, Abortion and Nationalism in Modern Greece*. Durham, NC: Duke University Press.

Hawkins, J.D., Catalano, R.F., Morrison, D.M., O'Donell, J., Abbott, R.D. and L.E. Day (1992) 'The Seattle Social Development Project: Effects of the First Four Years on Protective Factors and Problem Behaviours', in J. McCord and R. Tremblay (eds) *Preventing Antisocial Behaviour: Interventions from Birth through Adolescence*, pp. 139–161. New York: Guilford Press.

Hill, G.D. and M.P. Atkinson (1988) 'Gender, Familial Control, and Delinquency', *Criminology* 26: 127–149.

Hirschi, T. (1969) *Causes of Delinquency*. Berkeley, CA: University of California Press.

Hirschi, T. and M.R. Gottfredson (2003) 'Punishment of Children from the Perspective of Control Theory', in C.L. Britt and M.R. Gottfredson (eds) *Advances in Criminological Theories Vol. 12: Control Theories of Crime and Delinquency*, pp. 151–160. New Brunswick: Transaction.

Jephcott, A.P. and M.P. Carter (1955) *The Social Background of Delinquency*. Nottingham: Nottingham University.

Jones, M.B., Offord, D.R. and N. Abrams (1980) 'Brothers, Sisters and Antisocial Behaviour', *British Journal of Psychiatry* 136: 139–145.

Kandel, D.B. and P. Wu (1995) 'Disentangling Mother-Child Effects in the Development of Antisocial Behaviour', in J. McCord (ed.) *Coercion and Punishment in Long-Time Perspectives*, pp. 106–123. Cambridge: Cambridge University Press.

Kolvin, I., Miller, F.J.W., Fleeting, M. and P.A. Kolvin (1988) 'Social and Parenting Factors Affecting Criminal-Offence Rates: Findings from the Newcastle Thousand Family Study (1947–1980)', *British Journal of Psychiatry* 152: 80–90.

Larzelere, R.E. and G.R. Patterson (1990) 'Parental Management: Mediator of the Effect of Socio-economic Status on Early Delinquency', *Criminology* 28: 301–324.

Laybourn, A. (1986) 'Traditional Working Class Parenting: An Undervalued System', *British Journal of Social Work* 16: 625–644.

Lewis, H.S. (1954) *Deprived Children*. Oxford: Oxford University Press.

Lipsey, M.W. and J.H. Derzon (1998) 'Predictors of Violent or Serious Delinquency in Adolescence and Early Adulthood: A Synthesis of Longitudinal Research', in R. Loeber and D.P. Farrington (eds) *Serious and Violent Juvenile Offenders: Risk Factors and Successful Interventions*, pp. 86–105. Thousand Oaks: Sage.

Loeber, R. and T. Dishion (1983) 'Early Predictors of Male Delinquency: A Review', *Psychological Bulletin* 94: 68–99.

Loeber, R. and M. Stouthamer-Loeber (1986) 'Family Factors as Correlates and Predictors of Juvenile Conduct Problems and Delinquency', in M. Tonry and N. Morris (eds) *Crime and Justice, Vol. 7*, pp. 29–149. Chicago: University of Chicago Press.

Loeber, R. and D.P. Farrington (1997) 'Strategies and Yields of Longitudinal Studies of Antisocial Behaviour', in D.M. Stoff, M. Breiling and J.D. Maser (eds) *Handbook of Antisocial Behaviour*, pp. 125–139. New York: Wiley.

Loeber, R., Farrington, D.P., Stouthamer-Loeber, M. and W.B. van Kammen (1998a) 'Multiple Risk Factors for Multi-Problem Boys: Co-occurrence of Delinquency, Substance Use, Attention Deficit, Conduct Problems, Physical Aggression, Covert Behaviour, Depressed Mood, and Shy/Withdrawn Behaviour', in R. Jessor (ed.) *New Perspectives in Adolescent Risk Behaviour*, pp. 90–149. Cambridge: Cambridge University Press.

Loeber, R., Farrington, D.P., Stouthamer-Loeber, M. and W. van Kammen (1998b) *Antisocial Behaviour and Mental Health Problems: Explanatory Factors in Childhood and Adolescence*. London: Lawrence Erlbaum.

Lytton, H. (1990) 'Child and Parent Effects in Boys' Conduct Disorder: A Reinterpretation', *Developmental Psychology* 26: 683–697.

Maxfield, M. and C. Widom (1996) 'The Cycle of Violence: Revisited 6 Years Later', *Archives of Pediatrics and Adolescent Medicine* 150: 390–395.

McCord, J. (1977) 'A Comparative Study of Two Generations of Native Americans', in R.F. Meier (ed.) *Theory in Criminology*, pp. 83–92. Beverly Hills: Sage.

McCord, J. (1979) 'Some Child-Rearing Antecedents of Criminal Behaviour in Adult Men', *Journal of Personality and Social Psychology* 37: 1477–1486.

McCord, J. (1997) 'On Discipline', *Psychological Inquiry* 8: 215–217.

McCord, W., McCord, J. and I.K. Zola (1969) *Origins of Crime*. Montclair: Patterson Smith.

Mednick, S.A. and J. Volavka (1980) 'Biology and Crime', in N. Morris and M. Tonry (eds) *Crime and Justice, Vol. 2*, pp. 85–158. Chicago: University of Chicago Press.

Moffitt, T.E., Avshalom, C., Rutter, M. and P.A. Silva (2001) *Sex Differences in Antisocial Behaviour: Conduct, Disorder, Delinquency, and Violence in the Dunedin Longitudinal Study*. Cambridge: Cambridge University Press.

Morash, M. and M. Chesney-Lind (1991) 'A Reformulation and Partial Test of the Power Control Theory of Delinquency', *Justice Quarterly* 8: 347–377.

Newson, J. and E. Newson (1989) *The Extent of Parental Physical Punishment in the UK*. London: Approach.

Newson, J., Newson, E. and M. Adams (1993) 'The Social Origins of Delinquency', *Criminal Behaviour and Mental Health* 3: 19–29.

Nye, F.I. (1958) *Family Relations and Delinquent Behaviour*. New York: Wiley.

Offord, D.R., Abrams, N., Allen, N. and M. Poushinsky (1979) 'Broken Homes, Parental Psychiatric Illness, and Female Delinquency', *American Journal of Orthopsychiatry* 49: 252–264.

Olweus, D. (1980) 'Familial and Temperamental Determinants of Aggressive Behaviour in Adolescents: A Causal Analysis', *Developmental Psychology* 14: 644–660.

Ouston, J. (1984) 'Delinquency, Family Background, and Educational Attainment', *British Journal of Criminology* 24: 2–6.

Paternoster, R. (1988) 'Examining Three Wave Deterrence Models: A Question of Temporal Order and Specification', *Journal of Criminal Law and Criminology* 79: 135–179.

Patterson, G.R., DeBaryshe, B.D. and E. Ramsey (1989) 'A Developmental Perspective on Antisocial Behaviour', *American Psychologist* 44: 329–335.

Patterson, G.R., Reid, G.B. and T.J. Dishion (1992) *Antisocial Boys*. Oregon: Castalia.

Plomin, R. (1994) *Genetics and Experience: The Interplay between Nature and Nurture*. Thousand Oaks: Sage.

Raine, A. (1993) *The Psychopathology of Crime: Criminal Behaviour as a Clinical Disorder*. San Diego: Academic Press.

Raine, A., Brennan, P.A. and D.P. Farrington (1997) 'Biosocial Bases of Violence: Conceptual and Theoretical Issues', in A. Raine, P.A. Brennan, D.P. Farrington and S.A. Mednick (eds) *Biosocial Bases of Violence*, pp. 1–20. New York: Plenum.

Reiss, A.J. and D.P. Farrington (1991) 'Advancing Knowledge about Co-Offending: Results from a Prospective Longitudinal Survey of London Males', *Journal of Criminal Law and Criminology* 82: 360–395.

Riley, D. and M. Shaw (1985) *Parental Supervision and Juvenile Delinquency*. London: HMSO.

Robins, L.N. and R.G. Lewis (1966) 'The Role of the Antisocial Family in School Completion and Delinquency: A Three-Generation Study', *Sociology Quarterly* 7: 500–514.

Robins, L.N., West, P.J. and B.L. Herjanic (1975) 'Arrests and Delinquency in Two Generations: A Study of Black Urban Families and Their Children', *Journal of Child Psychology and Psychiatry* 16: 125–140.

Rothbaum, F. and J.R. Weisz (1994) 'Parental Caregiving and Child Externalising Behaviour in Nonclinical Samples: A Meta-Analysis', *Psychological Bulletin* 116: 55–74.

Rowe, D.C. and D.W. Osgood (1984) 'Sociological Theories of Delinquency and Heredity: A Reconsideration', *American Sociological Review* 49: 526–540.

Rowe, D.C. and D.P. Farrington (1997) 'The Familial Transmission of Criminal Convictions', *Criminology* 35: 177–201.

Rutter, M. (1981) 'Epidemiological-Longitudinal Strategies and Causal Research in Child Psychiatry', *Journal of the American Academy of Child Psychiatry* 20: 513–544.

Rutter, M. and H. Giller (1983) *Juvenile Delinquency: Trends and Perspectives*. Harmondsworth: Penguin.

Rutter, M., Giller, H. and A. Hagell (1998) *Antisocial Behaviour by Young People*. Cambridge: Cambridge University Press.

Sampson, R.J. (1997) 'Collective Regulation of Adolescent Misbehaviour: Validation Results from Eighty Chicago Neighbourhoods', *Journal of Adolescent Research* 12: 227–244.

Sampson, R.J. and J.H. Laub (1993) *Crime in the Making: Pathways and Turning Points though Life*. Cambridge, MA: Harvard University Press.

Singer, S.I. and M. Levine (1988) 'Power-Control Theory, Gender, and Delinquency: A Partial Replication with Additional Evidence on the Effects of Peers', *Criminology* 26: 627–647.

Snyder, J. and G.R. Patterson (1987) 'Family Interaction and Delinquent Behaviour', in H.C. Quay (ed.) *Handbook of Juvenile Delinquency*, pp. 216–243. New York: Wiley.

Steinmetz, S.K. (1979) 'Disciplinary Techniques and Their Relationship to Aggressiveness, Dependency, and Conscience', in W.R. Burr, R. Hill, F.I. Nye and I.L. Reiss (eds) *Contemporary Theories about the Family, Vol. 1*, pp. 405–438. New York: Free Press.

Trasler, G.B. (1962) *The Explanation of Criminality*. London: Routledge and Kegan Paul.

Utting, D., Bright, J. and C. Henricson (1993) *Crime and the Family*. London: Family Policy Studies Centre.

Wadsworth, M.E.J. (1979) *Roots of Delinquency: Infancy, Adolescence and Crime*. Oxford: Martin Robertson.

West, D.J. and D.P. Farrington (1973) *Who Becomes Delinquent?* London: Heinemann.

West, D.J. and D.P. Farrington (1977) *The Delinquent Way of Life*. London: Heinemann.

Wikström, P.-O., Clarke, R.V. and J. McCord (eds) (1995) *Integrating Crime Prevention Strategies: Propensity and Opportunity*. Stockholm: National Council for Crime Prevention.

Wikstöm, P.-O. and R. Loeber (2000) 'Do Disadvantaged Neighbourhoods Cause Well-Adjusted Children to Become Adolescent Delinquents? A Study of Male Juvenile Serious Offending, Individual Risk and Protective Factors, and Neighbourhood Context', *Criminology* 38: 1109–1142.

Widom, C.S. (1989) 'The Cycle of Violence', *Science* 244: 160–166.

Wilson, H. (1980) 'Parental Supervision: A Neglected Aspect of Delinquency', *British Journal of Criminology* 20: 203–235.

Wilson, H. (1987) 'Parental Supervision Re-examined', *British Journal of Criminology* 27: 275–301.

Xenakis, S. (2010) 'Resisting Submission? The Obstinacy of "Balkanist" Characteristics in Greece as Dissidence against "The West"', in L.K. Cheliotis (ed.) *Roots, Rites and Sites of Resistance: The Banality of Good*, pp. 178–196. Basingstoke: Palgrave Macmillan.

PART II

Topical Crime Issues

EFFI LAMBROPOULOU

Corruption

Since the 1990s, corruption in Greece has increasingly attracted the attention of the media, become an issue of public concern, and provoked political intervention and the creation of new legislation. These national developments have unfolded against the backdrop of a growing global movement against corruption that has involved major international organisations, such as the European Union (CoE, 25 June 1997, 1999a, 1999b), the World Bank (1997), the IMF and OECD (2010), the United Nations (28 January 1997, 1998), and the World Trade Organisation, as well as affected countries all around the world. The emergence of this movement was in turn stimulated by the 'eruption of corruption' in the mid-1990s, the end of Cold War, and the setting of new priorities in global politics, the expansion of international trade, and the negative consequences which corruption was widely assumed to have for development. Corruption thereby emerged as a central feature of good governance initiatives.

In the early 1990s, the trust of the Greek citizenry in politics and justice was shattered. In large part, this loss was the result of the commitment to trial of the then Greek Prime Minister, Andreas Papandreou, and a number of ministers of the PASOK (Panhellenic Socialist Movement) government. Papandreou was linked to a multi-million-dollar embezzlement scandal involving a private bank, and was accused of facilitating the embezzlement by ordering state corporations to transfer their holdings to this bank, where the interest was allegedly skimmed off to benefit his government party.[1] Public faith was further undermined by the repeated

---

1   In November 1988, a shortfall of US$132 million was discovered by the Bank of Crete. The discovery took place some months after bank chairman, Giorgos Koskotas, a Greek-American millionaire entrepreneur under investigation for large-scale financial

statements of political leaders about the legal issues surrounding the scandal long before the decision of the Special Court whose investigation had been ordered by the Greek parliament with the support of the principal party of the conservative opposition – New Democracy – and the Coalition of Left parties. These statements created the impression that Greek justice lacked independence and impartiality (Manoledakis, 1992: 24). In parliament, the Prime Minister accepted political responsibility for the case, as well as the financial consequences for the bank, but denied criminal responsibility. The judicial process, which began in March 1991 and finished in January, concluded with the Prime Minister being acquitted of all charges by a vote of seven to six. Subsequently, over the course of time, it was argued that accusations of the involvement of the Prime Minister in 'passive bribery' had been orchestrated by the leader of New Democracy for party-political reasons.

This chapter will present the national legislation and the institutional framework against corruption, trends in crimes of corruption and their punishment from 1980 to 2004, findings of research into perceptions of corruption, and an overview of the key theoretical approaches to, and research carried out into, the subject in Greece.

An Overview of the Legal and Institutional Anti-Corruption Framework

In older Greek legal texts and especially case-law, 'corruption' referred to the stimulation of feelings which 'corrupt the soul or cause sexual desire' (Staikos, 1961/1963: 652; Paraskevopoulos, 1979: 183; see also Bratsis, 2003:

---

crime (forgery and embezzlement), had fled the country. Greek officials charged that the banker forged documents belonging to Merrill Lynch & Company and the Irving Trust Company, using them to buy control of the Bank of Crete and subsequently steal at least $135 million from depositors.

10–11, 14–15). In the recently abolished Criminal Law Article 349 (Law 3064/2002), 'corruption' concerned the procuring and the instigation of corruption of young girls. The term has also occasionally been included in the disciplinary law of authorities responsible for crime control, i.e., *Disciplinary Law of Police Personnel*, Presidential Decree 22/1996, where activities indicating the 'corruption of character, ruined character', and 'quality as persons', and penal offences relating to the fulfilment of the duties of police officers, would result in their dismissal from the agency. Since the morally loaded nature of the term has not been regarded as helpful in the enforcement of the law, the term was not used in court decisions or the findings of the investigations of public prosecutors until recently. This is related to the fact that the country shares the continental tradition of legal positivism, with the consequence that law must be written and its implementation cannot be based on subsequent ethical, emotional, political, or cultural interpretations. Greece is a civil law country, in which jurisprudence is not considered the main source of law, and the Constitution is the supreme law of the land.

The complex of offences that constitute 'corruption' today is set out in the chapter of Greek Criminal Law concerning duties and service. Regarding the public sector, Criminal Law refers specifically to bribery in both passive and active forms, breaches of duty and of trust, oppression, illicit participation in auctions and leases, and embezzlement. Members of Parliament and Local Authorities are subject to Criminal Law; civil servants, on the other hand, are subject to both Disciplinary and Criminal Law. Furthermore, for several years now, all civil servants, police officers, and parliamentarians have been obliged to submit a declaration of their assets, in addition to the standard private annual tax form. As concerns the private sector, special regulations are set out for entities such as athletic associations, shared or limited liability companies, and unions, which are subject to both Private Law (including civil, contract, commercial, corporation, and competition law) and Public Law (i.e., constitutional, administrative, and criminal law).

Greece has also ratified all the relevant conventions of the EU, the Council of Europe, the OECD, and the United Nations, and has begun integrating their conditions into national legislation (see Laws 2656/1998;

2802/2000; 2803/2000; 2957/2001; 3560/2007, 3666/2008). With the ratification of international conventions against corruption, and in particular the Civil Law Convention on Corruption (CoE, 1999), the definition of corruption contained therein was adopted by Greece:

> requesting, offering, giving or accepting, directly or indirectly, a bribe or any other undue advantage or prospect thereof, which distorts the proper performance of any duty or behaviour required of the recipient of the bribe, the undue advantage or the prospect thereof. (Law 2957/2001, Article 2)

Law 3251/2004, which imported the Framework Decision 2002/584/ JHA of the European Council on the European Arrest Warrant (CoE, 13 June 2002), foresaw its application to 'crimes of corruption and bribery' without necessitating verification of the 'double criminality' of the act. Consequently, corruption was included amongst the most serious crimes (e.g., terrorism, trafficking in human beings, participation in a criminal organisation, and fraud including acts affecting the financial interests of the Communities), for which special conditions pertain, such as the removal of the requirement that the specific act is punishable under national law (the principle of 'double criminality'; see Fytrakis, 2007: 1–2). The abolishment of double criminality in combination with the importation of crimes, such as corruption, to the Greek legal system provoked serious objections because of its vagueness and breadth (Report of the Scientific Board of the Greek Parliament on the Bill for a 'European Arrest Warrant and Surrender Procedures', 20 June 2004: 4–5).

Furthermore, institutional reforms have been introduced to promote transparency, such as the Inspectors-Controllers Body for Public Administration (established in April 1997), the Police Service of Internal Affairs (established in September 1999), and the Office of the General Inspector of Public Administration (set up in November 2002). In October 2006, the responsibilities of the Office were expanded, empowering it with the authority of investigations. Its remit is to attend to, support, and evaluate the work of the entire gamut of inspectorate agencies and offices of public administration, including the Financial and Economic Crimes Office (SDOE) and the Inspectors-Controllers Body for Public Administration of the Ministry of the Interior, Public Administration, and Decentralisation. The General Inspector is the head of all first-degree inspection bodies, including the disciplinary councils, of the public sector. In January 2003, the passing of Law 3094 extended the authority of the Ombudsman to investigate allegations of corruption pertaining to public service departments. Another Law (3103/2003) extended the authority of the police to investigate charges of bribery and extortion against all categories of civil servants.

Explanations for Greece's shortcomings in combating corruption have tended to point to the non-enforcement and/or the fragmentary or inefficient implementation of laws, although further elaboration is rarely provided. An evaluation of implemented policies should draw upon quantitative as well as qualitative data concerning the measures and laws issued and ratified (see further Lambiri-Dimaki, 1987: 32–38, 45–48). Since there are no reliable data to be used for such an analysis, the most prevalent lay theories can often prevail.

Trends in Crime and Punishment for Corruption[2]

Analysts usually derive their information from the National Statistical Service of Greece (NSSG) and police records (the Statistical Bulletins of the Greek Police) as also presented in the *European Sourcebook of Crime and Criminal Justice Statistics* and the Council of Europe's *Penological Information Bulletin*. Concerning 'corruption', crime and justice statistics contain data of arrests and convictions for 'crimes against duties and service'. The disciplinary law of public servants, as referred to in the previous section, offers additional punitive instruments aside from or irrespective of

2   The data for this section were collected by Ms Erifyli Bakirli, to whom I am thankful.

criminal law.[3] In the event of an irrevocable conviction from the criminal court of appeal, the public servant is dismissed from service. Since 2003, data for accusations and arrests of public servants and police officers have also been held by the Police Division of Internal Affairs (DEY) and the Office of the General Inspector of Public Administration. Data from the latter, however, are case-based and confidential, whilst DEY is not responsible for keeping data on convictions, only on those cases of complaints and investigations referred to it.

To summarise the existing data from DEY, according to its Annual Report (2006: 36–44), between 25 October 1999 to 31 December 2006, the Service dealt with 4,053 cases, of which 3,697 (91.2 percent) related to police personnel, 189 (4.7 percent) to public servants, 102 (2.5 percent) to both groups for aiding and abetting, and 65 (1.6 percent) to private individuals. Charges were brought in 32 percent (1,299) of cases, and in 10 percent (412) of cases the accused were caught red-handed. Allowing that not all cases have been adjudicated and closed after revocation in the court of appeal, it appears that 125 (7.3 percent) of prosecuted persons were acquitted (54.4 percent of police officers, 8.8 percent of other public

3   Measurement of the number of public servants has depended upon the definition given by different governments and what has been included at any particular time. Until 1986, the number of public servants *stricto sensu* stood at 200,000–260,000; in 1986, the employees of public enterprises were included in the total official figure. Up to that point, such employees had been working under contracts without tenure. Teachers from all levels of education were also included, as were priests, judges, and police personnel, amongst others. Thus, the number of employees in the public sector *lato sensu* rose to 600,000. In the late 1990s, regional civil servants were also included, so the total number rose further to 700,000. However, the absolute number of public servants in the stricter sense fluctuated after 1986 from between 260,000 and 300,000, which means that it increased by around 40,000. Today, however, the employees of public enterprises are once again excluded from public sector status, since a large number of the former have been privatised. According to the recent registration (of summer 2010), the number of employees in the public sector *lato sensu* had risen to 768,000, representing 15 percent of the economically active population of the country at the time (Ministry of Interior, Decentralisation, and E-Government and Ministry of Finance, 30 July 2010).

servants, and 36.8 percent of private individuals), whilst 173 (10.1 percent) were convicted. Of those convicted, 6.3 percent received prison sentences of over 5 years (41.3 percent of which were police officers and 5 percent public servants), and 93.6 percent received prison sentences of up to five years (72.8 percent of which were police officers).

DEY also has the authority to exert administrative control across the police service, similar to the authority of a director of any public organisation; namely, to collect data about the activities of any member of the organisation which might be illegal or in contravention of the organisation's regulations. In the case of public services, however, there are further instruments of control (e.g., the Office of the General Inspector of Public Administration, DEY, and Inspectors-Controllers). DEY carried out 934 administrative checks and imposed disciplinary penalties in 42.5 percent (or 397) of cases, of which 228 (57.4 percent) comprised either the dismissal or the temporary suspension of the individual from the police corps, and 42.5 percent (169) involved a reprimand or fine. In 5.6 percent (53) of the cases, accused police officers were acquitted, and in 41.2 percent (385) of the cases the charges were filed. From the post-2003 data, when DEY's authority extended to public services, only a small part of prosecutions concern 'corruption'; for police personnel, prosecutions primarily related to breach of duty, followed by acts of forgery, fraud, bribery, and extortion. In contrast, for public servants, prosecutions related mostly to bribery, followed by breach of duty (DEY, 2004/2005).

As regards NSSG statistics, since 1988, offences have been divided into three categories: *bribery of judges*, *violation of home/shelter asylum*, and *other*. The number of crimes falling within the first two categories ranged in absolute numbers from 0 to 4, with one exception in 1998, when 20 convictions of Justice personnel were recorded, representing 30.3 percent of the total number of offences against duties and service that year (sixty six). Figure 1 shows the volume of recorded crimes against duties and service, and the convictions for the period 1980 to 2004. The total recorded offences within this category are divided into more serious felonies and misdemeanours. Felonies, i.e., crimes punishable by a prison sentence of between 5 and 20 years or by a life sentence, constituted 1.1 percent of all relevant offences. Misdemeanours, i.e., crimes punishable by a prison sentence of ten days to 5 years, comprised the remaining 98.9 percent. In terms of numbers, there were, in total, 16 recorded felonies between 1980 and 2004, compared with 1,431 misdemeanours. Taking into account the total number of recorded crimes in Greece, and choosing randomly three years – 1980 (295,353), 1989 (287,177), and 2004 (405,627) –, the offences against duties and service represent an extremely small proportion (1980: 34 or 0.01 percent; 1989: 65 or 0.02 percent; 2004: 69 or 0.01 percent).

Nevertheless, there has been an increase in the number of these offences and the corresponding convictions since the 1980s, although their proportion amongst general crime rates and in absolute numbers has remained at a low level. Playing a role in the increasing number of offences and convictions have been new control bodies instituted after 1997. Between 1980 and 2004, there was an average annual increase of 1,14 offences and 1,06 convictions secured (on imprisonment rates, see further Cheliotis, this collection). The highest registered increases in offences were in 1987 (135.3 percent), 1993 (232.3 percent), and 2002 (126.4 percent). The highest number of convictions were registered in 1988 (119), 1989 (100), 1993 (127), and 2004 (114). The largest drops in the number of convictions were in 1983, 1996, and 2003 (see Figure 1).

Secondary analysis of official judicial data published by the National Statistical Service of Greece reveals that, over the period 1980–2004, the vast majority (between 49.3 and 86.6 percent) of defendants found guilty of crimes against duties and service received a prison sentence of up to six months, which was convertible into a fine. The next most common penalty was a suspended prison sentence (accorded to between 11 and 40.7 percent). From 1994, when the data for sentences converted into fines began to be recorded separately, converted penalties constituted 9 to 32 percent of the total, with a steady drop in fines as such (from 4.6 to 0.6 percent).

Under the Greek Penal Code, short prison sentences are convertible into fines. The conversion of a prison sentence into a fine commonly depends upon the nature of the crime. Where the individual convicted with a prison sentence that is convertible into a fine is initially unable to pay, there is an option of paying the fine at a later time in order to be released. Conversion and suspension limits were extended several times since the mid-1980s in order, at least in part, to bring prison overcrowding under control (Spinellis, 1998). Thus, the total number of suspended sentences doubled from the 1980s to the 1990s, rising from 10 to 20 percent (but see also Cheliotis, this collection). For the group of crimes and offenders examined here, however, the rates of suspended prison sentences have remained more or less the same, despite some fluctuations, being applied to approximately one fourth of total convictions, although seeing a significant increase between 1999 and 2003. After peaking in 1999, there has been a downward trend in the use of suspended prison sentences for these crimes, but the proportion remains higher than that before 1999. Figure 2 shows that all forms of imposed prison sentence for crimes against duty and service have followed a similar pattern. However, as calculated by linear regression, the highest rate of increase has been recorded for longer prison sentences (of one to five years (+1)), followed by sentences of six to twelve months (+0.3); a picture which corresponds to the general trend of crime politics in Greece (see further Cheliotis and Xenakis, this collection). As also shown in Figure 2, the proportion of offenders admitted to prison for crimes against duty and service underwent a steady downward trend of 0.7 prisoners per year (1980: 36; 1988: 12; 1996, 1997: 1; 2001: 10), with a sudden increase to 19 prisoners in 2005.

Perceptions of Corruption

According to the European Values Survey of 1999/2000 (Halman, 2001), the vast majority of Greeks placed 'corruption-bribery' in the category of highly disapproved behaviours (1,116 out of 1,142 respondents; see also World Values Survey, 1999–2004, 2000). Moreover, 83.3 percent of Greeks agreed that citizens must always abide by the law, a level of response that placed Greece first amongst the UK (76.5 percent), Portugal (65.5 percent), Spain (62.1 percent) and the Netherlands (55.4 percent) (EKKE, 2003: 29). However, in an EU-wide opinion survey published in 2005 (van Dijk *et al.*, 2007), the results placed the country in the highest position of perceived corrupt practices amongst the 18 countries sampled (880 or 43.6 percent of 2,020 residents over 16 years old (EU ICS, 2005: 14)). Between 1988 and 1996, Greece's scores on the Transparency International Corruption Perceptions Index (CPI) decreased from 5.05 to 5.01, and further to 4.3 in 2003 and 2005, with a slight increase after 2006, which has not influenced its overall ranking, and a further decline in 2010 to 3.5 after the intervention of the IMF in the country (Transparency International, 1996–1998; 2003–2010). As far as this author knows, empirical research into the distinctions between private and public perceptions as well as into the discourse concerning corruption from a sociological perspective has only recently appeared. This was in an international project coordinated by the University of Konstanz in Germany between 2006 and 2009, in which Greece also participated, examining the perceptions of not only politicians, administrative decision-makers, and representatives of the private sector, but also of other authorities such as the police and the judiciary, as well as the media and civil society.[4] The project focused on identifying the cultural patterns underlying perception of corruption amongst the various target groups. By analysing documents and interviews with target group representatives, the project reconstructed commonsense definitions of corruption and revealed that these extend well beyond legal definitions. Noteworthy findings including, but not restricted to, Greece were that expert perceptions differed strongly from those held by people in their daily life (Lambropoulou *et al.*, 2008). Experts were more likely to focus on grand corruption involving public officials, whilst respondents from the general public displayed a more diverse interpretation of corruption, varying from widespread and socially tolerated forms of petty corruption to truly condemnable acts that violate public interests (Lambropoulou *et al.*, 2007).

4   This research project was funded under the Sixth Framework Research Programme of the European Commission, Priority 7, FP6–2004-CITIZENS-5, and involved the EU candidate states Croatia and Turkey, and the EU member states Germany, Greece, United Kingdom, Bulgaria, and Romania. For further information, see www. unikonstanz.de/crimeandculture/index.htm.

Some studies have noted that moral disapproval of corruption is not necessarily associated with a willingness to make a complaint about it (Killias, 1998), and that followed behaviour does not necessarily coincide with the degree to which corruption is perceived to be legitimate (Karstedt, 2004: 389–390, 397–408; WVS, 1989–1993). Perceptions may be influenced by a complex range of factors, such as unending media furores over corruption that shape citizens' perceptions (see, e.g., the coverage of the 2005 EU International Crime Survey in *Eleftherotypia*, 7 February 2007). Notwithstanding criticism of corruption perception indicators relating to their breadth, methodology, quality, and role in fashioning a new orthodoxy, few can dismiss the impact of corruption in terms of economic development and its relationship to political and economic liberalisation (Sklias, 2005). Nevertheless, in the case of Greece it is striking that the more the country has improved its normative and administrative instruments in both the public and private sectors to prevent corruption and promote transparency, the lower has been its score on the TI CPI. In order to sensationalise these scores and attract attention, pertinent reports by the mass media are exaggerated.[5] The diffusion of these reports affects the perceptions of the citizenry in that the latter accept media portrayals as accurate, and reproduce and overstate them in turn. From both quarters emerges a false image concerning the size and seriousness of the problem in the country.

5   See, for example, how the newspaper *To Vima* (8 February 2009) reported the findings of a public opinion research carried out by the polling company Public Issue on behalf of Transparency International-Hellas. Note, in this regard, the mutually supportive relationship between the mass media and the research carried out for Transparency International-Hellas. Although 27.6 percent (1,684) from a sample of 6,105 people had experienced 'corruption' (bribery) in their life, and 79 percent had never faced any such demand from a civil servant (Public Issue, 2009a), these findings were understated. It was instead overstressed that 91 percent of a subsample (comprising 51 percent of the total, or 3,060) regarded corruption as a serious problem in society (Public Issue, 2009b), as if this proportion had paid a bribe.

Theory and Research

Although a number of historians have argued against the extended use of patronage as an explanatory concept of Greek politics (Hatziiosif, 1994; Hering, 2004), the notion of patron-client relations has remained central to Greek academic discourse on corruption (for an overview of academic approaches to the subject of corruption in Greece, see Koutsoukis and Sklias, 2005). Research has included analysis of the meaning of 'corruption' and its scope, the effectiveness of existing control systems, and proposals for their improvement. Most assessments concentrate upon the issue of political corruption, namely, the use of state power by officials or their representatives for illegitimate private gain (see further Bratsis, 2003; Kontoyiorgis, 2005), and its relationship to a series of phenomena such as public distrust of the political system, the reproduction and reinforcement of social inequality, the erosion of certain socio-political values, and the violation of democratic principles in particular.

Clientelism may be best understood as a form of interpersonal, dyadic exchange characterised by a sense of obligation and often also by an unequal balance between those involved (Hopkin, 2006; see also Stokes, 2007). The term of 'old' clientelism connotes that form found principally in developing countries, involving patron-client proximity and exclusively selective benefits (Hopkin, 2006: 8). In contrast, 'new' clientelism has been said to entail less proximity in patron-client relations, and is characteristic of more advanced capitalist countries. Moreover, in new clientelism the patron is a less autonomous actor, an integral unit of the party organisation and bureaucracy. Indeed, according to the model of new clientelism, the patron is ultimately the party organisation itself.

Clientelist relations in Greece have been defined in a number of different and at times contradictory ways. For several Greek authors (e.g., Sotiropoulos, 1996: 60–62; Lyrintzis, 2005: 248), clientelism in contemporary Greece has been characterised by organised interests that constitute the ultimate patrons. It is organised interests that provide political or financial support to politicians or parties in exchange for privileged access to goods such as public works projects and licenses. In such cases, clientelism has been regarded as an instrumental relationship between patron and client that operates to the benefit of both sides of the exchange (Mavrogordatos, 1988). In contrast, clientelism has also been interpreted to be a means of political participation by the masses (Lyrintzis, 1984). Mouzelis (1987) distinguishes between 'horizontal' and 'vertical' relations between citizens and the state; 'horizontal' being political participation based on collective forms of social access (e.g., professional unions and political parties), and 'vertical' that based upon personal or family bonds with members of local and national elites, which thus connect the citizen to the political and power system in general (see also Tsoukalas, 1987).

Institutional and Cultural Explanations of Corruption in Greece

The Greek sociopolitical system has tended to be approached from the basis of its differences rather than of its similarities with other developed countries in Western Europe. The starting point of such approaches consists in the peculiarities of Greek state development following its liberation from Ottoman rule. Accordingly, emphasis has been placed on the fact that the establishment of parliamentarianism preceded industrialisation in Greece, contrary to other European countries. The 'premature' institution of parliamentarianism in the country, without the respective development of productive forces, is thought by some writers to have led to the formation of a strong state and a weak civil society (interest groups, social movements, voluntary associations, cultural and religious organisations; see further Sotiropoulos, 1995), thereby facilitating the growth of corruption (Komninou, 1989; Lyrintzis, 1984). Even though the concept of civil society is a relatively recent construction, analysts have considered it to be well-rooted in western states (Benhard, 1993: 310), contrary to the experience of Greece (Voulgaris, 2006; from a different viewpoint, see Pantazopoulos, 1993, 1994). In turn, however, weak civil society has been argued to be the outcome of either 'state corporatism' (Mavrogordatos, 1988: 198–201), 'clientelism' and 'populism' ('incorporatism') (Mouzelis, 1987: 73–75; 1995: 24), or 'clientelistic corporatism' (Tsoukalas, 1987: 92–5; 1993: 20–1; see further Sotiropoulos, 2007b). Alternatively, weak forms of civil society in Greece have been explained in terms of low levels of 'social capital', considered to have been caused by low levels of confidence in the state (see further Jones *et al.*, 2008: 177–182, 187–188), a condition which favours corruption. Clientelist relations, in this conception, are regarded as a negative form of social capital (Iosifides *et al.*, 2007: 1344–1345).

The analysis of Thermos (2005) focuses upon the role of electoral systems and political corruption in post-war Greece. He suggests that, after 1952, electoral systems based on 'reinforced proportional representation' predominated in the country, which supported the exchange of power between the two largest parties and discouraged the formation of splinter parties. This made parliamentary majorities possible even when the leading party fell short of winning an overall majority, and has been regarded as a means to enhance governmental stability.[6] According to Thermos, however, these systems have created deficits and failings in representation, fuelling clientelistic relations and opacity in the political system and the operation of public administration. Additionally, they have facilitated the merging of *status quo* interests that serve to provide cover to illegal and corrupt practices. Rantis (2005), meanwhile, draws on Horkheimer and Adorno (1969), and on Pollock's conceptualisation of *Rackettheorie* (Schmidt and Noerr, 1985), to analyse corruption in capitalist societies, Greece included. Politics, in this view, is dominant over the economy, and this dominance is promoted through its organisation via networks, rackets, and gangs (Rantis, 2005: 194–198). The main type of power in capitalism is the racket and the network. Using the approach above, Rantis distinguishes three periods of corruption experienced by Greece over the twentieth century (see also Koutsoukis, 1998: 67–77). The first period, 1944–1966, is one of political corruption, when clientelistic relations appeared dominant. The second, 1967–1974, is a period of authoritative rule and characterised by the cynicism of bureaucratic corruption. The third, from 1974–1987, which could be interpreted as continuing to date, has been a period of gradual expansion of the public sector and the establishment of 'new ethics of authority'.

6   The law in its current form favours the first-past-the-post party to achieve an absolute majority (151 parliamentary seats), provided that it receives over 41 percent of the votes nationwide (Law 3231/2004).

Rantis nevertheless concludes that, for the time being, we cannot formulate an integrated theory about corruption in Greek society. Despite his inspired use of *Rackettheorie* for explaining corruption, its application is not convincing, and many questions are left unanswered.

Koutsoukis (1998, 2005), one of the most prolific writers on corruption in the country, proposes that the causes of corruption in Greece are not only related to the development of the country, but are also pathological. He accepts the existence of definitional problems and difficulties of data collection, which, as he writes, account for his preference to describe the situation 'theoretically' (Koutsoukis, 2005: 105). He questions whether corruption is a symptom either of development, moral decay of authority, or a crisis of society, although the term 'corruption' and its forms are not disputed at all. Koutsoukis' position is that developing countries produce more corruption than their developed counterparts, and that the level of political development of a country is determined by the degree to which democratic processes are consolidated, and there is social control, diffusion of information, and effective state institutions. Accordingly, there are three types of society: civil society (a responsive society); apathetic-unresponsive society (which is law-abiding but does not show any interest in common issues and goods); and the self-interested society, to which Greece belongs (Koutsoukis, 2005: 105–113). The citizens of the latter use the state or exploit its shortcomings for their own advantage. The self-interested society is flexible and opportunistic; persons and groups use their power positions exclusively for their own good.

How exactly the three types of societies may be measured or transformed remains unclear, whilst historical variables that could affect the development of state-societal relations are not treated as significant to the analytical framework (for a critique, see Bratsis, 2003). Similarly, Kontoyiorgis (2005, 2007) argues that corruption can be analysed either morally or politically. The moral approach to corruption presupposes a system of rules which rely on individuals' natural moral capacity and self-commitment to abide by the rules. Society uses the moral approach because it cannot understand corruption in political terms. Kontoyiorgis underlines that politicians are not the beneficiaries of politics; they operate instead for the benefit of the citizenry. Their liability cannot be counterbalanced by the revocation of their mandate, because only the principle (i.e., the citizen) and not the trustee-agent (i.e., the politician) can change the content of the mandate. In modern states, however, a parliamentary majority controls parliament, the government, and the state mechanism. The identity of the controller and the controlled coincides in the same persons. The leading element of the party in government becomes the political master of state authority and state power. The transformation of political responsibility from a law-and-justice issue to an issue of political succession in power produces a fiction of responsibility, because the elections are a means of selection for future governance and not a means of dispensing justice and law enforcement. For Kontoyiorgis, as far as concerns Greece, the party has been identified with the state and the political system since the inception of the modern Greek state (i.e., producing a hegemony of party politics). This means that the goals of the party have been transformed into the goals of politics, and the citizen into a voter.

Nevertheless, clientelism has also been interpreted as a functional product of particular historical events, political structures, and state development, turning it into a rational mechanism of redistributing social wealth, welfare benefits, and social protection that were lacking, rather than constituting an intrinsic national cultural value or attribute (Petmesidou, 1996; Sotiropoulos, 1996: 60–62; 2007a: 100; Lyrintzis, 2005: 248). At the same time, however, according to a different perspective, this mechanism has generated a mentality that reproduces corruption and petty corruption in particular (Koutsoukis, 1998). These viewpoints often contrast the countries of the South with those of the North (Lambropoulou *et al.*, 2008: 27–28; see further Hallin and Papathanassopoulos, 2002), though clientelist relationships exist to some degree and in various forms in all modern societies (Legg, 1975). In these societies, overt political patronage, whether reviewed or approved by the legislature, is seen as a tool for rewarding and enforcing loyalty. Loyalty rather than merit is the criterion for selecting an office-holder. This selection process may be seen as questionable.

Finally, the very meaning and ascription of the term in and to Greece has been challenged by Bratsis (2003). Bratsis argues that two interrelated factors account for the generation of perceptions of Greek politics as corrupt. Firstly, Bratsis suggests that the way in which the 'public' and 'private' spheres have been defined within advanced capitalist societies has shaped perceptions of the 'normal' and the 'pathological'. Secondly, he points to the way in which institutions of global capital have equated the idea of *corruption* with that of *opacity*, and have promoted this perception through the media and international organisations. At the same time, he highlights the role of all those who have unthinkingly imported such approaches into Greece, despite their negative ramifications for the perceived legitimacy of the Greek state.

Concluding Thoughts

Thousands of books and journal articles have been published on corruption in more than fifty languages over recent decades. Defining corruption and its contributing factors is not an easy task. Every definition of the phenomenon is partial and incomplete, reflecting the legal and socio-cultural context within which relevant legislation is produced. Definitions also reflect the agencies and interests that participate in identifying various phenomena as 'corrupt'. Corruption is more a social construction than a concrete, universal phenomenon which needs a proper definition in technical terms (i.e., an operational definition). Furthermore, it is rather an evolving construction of certain social groups and interests than an act of determining the 'objective reality' of corruption, which leads necessarily to specific policy measures to confront it. This is not to imply that certain practices such as 'bribery' or 'political patron-client exchange' are a 'social construct' composed by dominant interests and rhetoric. What is meant instead is that the labelling of some acts as 'corrupt' serves certain political and economic goals (Lambropoulou *et al.*, 2008: 10, 107).

In addition, the relationship between culture and corruption is more complex than it often appears; many scholars follow a line of thought which associates certain cultural traits in developing countries and in countries of the semi-periphery, including Greece, with corruption. As already noted, the Greek sociopolitical system has been approached from the basis of its differences rather than of its similarities with other developed countries in

Western Europe, highlighting the peculiarities of the Greek state's development following liberation from Ottoman rule. The starting point of any analysis, however, gives meaning to the issues under examination. We understand different things when, for example, we study deviance as one of the products of change in power relations, or as a crisis of values, or as a threat to domestic and public safety. Different diagnoses thereby give rise to different methods for confronting and dealing with the problem. The relationship between state and society, as well as between the economy and the state, is often treated in an over-simplistic way that serves (whether unconsciously or not) certain (economic) interests. Informal networks embedded in national social structures have not been studied systematically, but there now do appear to be moves to reassess the 'weak' nature of Greek civil society, which may also bear implications for research into corruption and its confrontation. It remains to be seen whether the social, political, and economic reforms taking place in the context of contemporary 'good governance' agendas will overturn the counterbalance achieved by 'corrupt practices' in Greece.

Many questions are yet to be answered: How important are informal structures and social networks when implementing reforms? To what extent are 'clean', dominant states (on which see Lambsdorff, 1998), international organisations, or multinational companies responsible for fostering corruption or for facilitating its combat?[7] Such an approach cannot fit justifica-

---

7   A scandal involving Siemens broke in November 2006, and evidence has since mounted that officials, eventually with the covert connivance of senior managers, used bribes (drawing from a slush fund of at least €1.3 billion) across the globe (e.g., the US, Italy, Greece, Russia, Libya, and Nigeria) to obtain lucrative foreign contracts and secure foreign tenders. Prosecutors in Germany, Liechtenstein, Switzerland, Italy, and Greece have looked at the claims. The public prosecutor's office in Munich has also investigated Siemens projects, including some relating to the 2004 Olympics in Athens (see further Samatas, this collection). Siemens has stated that it was involved with 65,000 products and systems in various projects for the Olympics, from security systems to the reconstruction of twenty stadiums and the modernisation of the Greek telecommunications system. Siemens also carried out more sensitive work such as the establishment of a telecommunications network amongst the police, the fire brigade, the coast guard, and several ministries. Political party financing, politicians, executives of Siemens Hellas, and the National Telecommunications Organisation have been embroiled in a scandal involving bribery and embezzlement. As far as is known, in Greece investigations are still in progress, whilst they have ended in Germany (see also Xenakis, this collection).

tions of corruption grounded on national tradition, culture, geographic area, transition in market economy etc., since they seem over-simplified, if not reproducing stereotypes, and finally have no effect. Because if corruption is reduced in one system, it does not necessary preclude its transfer to or increase in another social system. Corruption is neither an issue of morals nor of embedded attitudes, whilst successful anti-corruption strategies must involve much more besides. It is the result of serious social or organisational problems, for which there does not exist 'a solution'.

However improbable any solution may seem, problems of corruption are unlikely to be alleviated without the achievement of certain sociopolitical changes, such as securing more meaningful public participation in political life as well as fairer and more stable systems of both taxation and law enforcement. If this does not happen, legislation, conventions, and measures such as sensitisation campaigns and punishment will be nothing more than an attempt to reduce the impact of the problem.

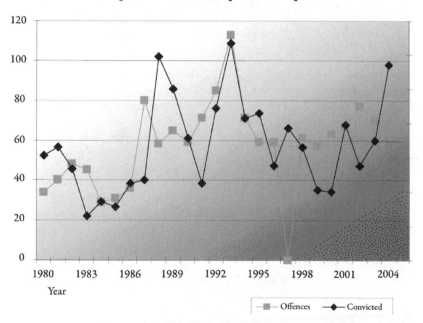

Figure 1 Annual caseload (absolute number) of offences against duties and service, 1980–2004; Annual caseload (absolute number) of persons convicted of offences against duties and service, 1980–2004
Source: National Statistical Service of Greece (NSSG)

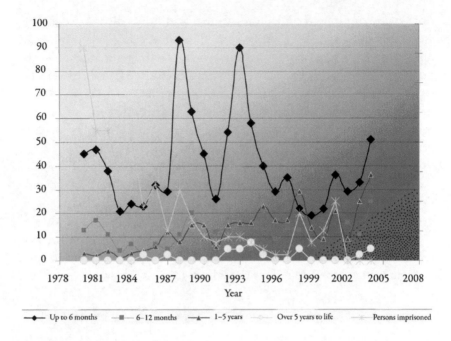

Figure 2: Annual caseload (absolute number) of persons sentenced to imprisonment for offences against duties and service, by sentence length, 1980–2004; Annual caseload (absolute number) of persons actually imprisoned for offences against duties and service, 1980–2004
Source: National Statistical Service of Greece (NSSG)

References

Bernhard, M. (1993) 'Civil Society and Democratic Transition in East Central Europe', *Political Science Quarterly* 108(2): 307–326.

Bratsis, P. (2003) *Corrupt Compared to What? Greece, Capitalist Interests, and the Specular Purity of the State*, Discussion Paper No. 8. London: Hellenic Observatory & European Institute, London School of Economics and Political Science.

Council of Europe (CoE) (1992–2002) *Penological Information Bulletin*, Nos. 17–24. Strasbourg: Council of Europe.

CoE (25 June 1997) *Convention on the Fight against Corruption involving Officials of the European Communities or Officials of Member States of the European Union*. Strasbourg: Official Journal of the European Union C 195.

CoE (1999a) *Criminal Law Convention on Corruption*. Strasbourg: European Treaty Series No. 173.

CoE (1999b) *Civil Law Convention on Corruption*. Strasbourg: European Treaty Series No. 174.

CoE (13 June 2002). *Framework Decision 2002/584/JHA on the European Arrest Warrant and the Surrender Procedures between Member States*. Strasbourg: Official Journal of the European Union L 190.

Division of Internal Affairs of the Greek Police (DEY) (2005, 2007) *Annual Reports 2004, 2006* [in Greek]. Athens: Greek Police Headquarters.

National Centre for Social Research (EKKE) (2003) *Greece-Europe: Society, Politics, Values* [in Greek]. Athens: EKKE.

Eleftherotypia (7 February 2007) 'Greece: European Champion in Corruption and Bag-Snatching' [in Greek].

Fytrakis, E. (2010) *The Controller Bodies of Public Administration: Theory, Legislation, Case Law* [in Greek]. Athens: Nomiki Vivliothiki.

Hallin, D.C. and S. Papathanassopoulos (2002) 'Political Clientelism and the Media: Southern Europe and Latin America in Comparative Perspective', *Media, Culture and Society* 24(2): 169–189.

Halman, L. (2001) *The European Values Study: A Third Wave. Sourcebook of the 1999/2000 European Values Study Surveys*. Tilburg: Tilburg University. Available online at: http://spitswww.uvt.nl/web/fsw/evs/documents/Publications/Sourcebook/EVS_SourceBook.pdf.

Hatziiosif, C. (1994) 'Democracy and Clientelist Relationships: Three Recent Analyses of Greek politics of the 19th Century' [in Greek], *Mnimon* 19: 167–197.

Hering, G. (2004) *The Greek Political Parties* [in Greek]. Athens: MIET.

Hopkin, J. (2006) 'Conceptualising Political Clientelism: Political Exchange and Democratic Theory', paper presentation at the American Political Studies Association Annual Meeting, Philadelphia, USA, 31 August.

Schmidt, A. and G.S. Noerr (eds) (1985) *Max Horkheimer: Collected Works, Volume 12. Posthumous Writings, 1931–1949* [in German]. Frankfurt: Fischer.

Horkheimer, M. and T.W. Adorno (1969) *Dialectic of Enlightenment: Philosophical Fragments, 1944–1947* [in German]. Frankfurt: Fischer.

Iosifides, T., Lavrentiadou, M., Petracou, E. and A. Kontis (2007) 'Forms of Social Capital and the Incorporation of Albanian Immigrants in Greece', *Journal of Ethnic and Migration Studies* 33(8): 1343–1361.

Jones, N., Malesios, C., Iosifides, T. and C.M. Sophoulis (2008) 'Social Capital in Greece: Measurement and Comparative Perspectives', *South European Society and Politics* 13(2): 175–193.

Karstedt, S. (2004) 'Power, Inequality and Corruption: Structural and Cultural Determinants in International Comparison', in D. Oberwittler and S. Karstedt (eds) *Sociology of Crime* [in German], pp. 384–412. Wiesbaden: Verlag für Sozialwissenschaften.

Killias, M. (1998) 'Corruption: Vive la Repression!– Or Something Else? Blindness of the Criminal Policy of Causes and Nuances', in H.-D. Schwind, H.-H. Kühne and E. Kube (eds) *Festschrift for Hans Joachim Schneider at 70* [in German], pp. 239–254. Berlin: de Gruyter.

Komninou, M. (1989) 'Critical Dialogue or Crisis of Discourse? An Interpretation for a Different Theoretical Approach to the Mass Media in the West and in Greece', in C. Lyrintzis and M. Komninou (eds) *Society, Power and Mass Media* [in Greek], pp. 360–389. Athens: Papazissis.

Kontoyiorgis, G. (2005) 'Corruption and Political System', in K. Koutsoukis and S. Sklias (eds) *Corruption and Scandals in Public Administration and Politics* [in Greek], pp. 131–143. Athens: Sideris.

Kontoyiorgis, G. (2007) *Democracy as Freedom: Democracy and Representation* [in Greek]. Athens: Patakis.

Koutsoukis, K. (1998) *The Pathology of Politics. Dimensions of Corruption in the Modern Greek State* [in Greek]. Athens: Papazissis.

Koutsoukis, K. (2005) 'Self-Interested Society and Corruption', in K. Koutsoukis and P. Sklias (eds) *Corruption and Scandals in Public Administration and Politics* [in Greek], pp. 101–114. Athens: Sideris.

Koutsoukis, K. and P. Sklias (eds) (2005) *Corruption and Scandals in Public Administration and Politics* [in Greek]. Athens: Sideris.

Lambiri-Dimaki, I. (1987) *Sociology in Greece Today* [in Greek]. Athens: Papazissis.

Lambropoulou, E., Iosifidis, T., Papamanolis, N., Bakali, E., Aggeli, S., Bakirli, E. and G. Massouri (2008) *A Comparison of Findings of the First (Documents Analysis) and Second (Interviews Analysis) Project Phase in Greece: Report 3*. Available online at: http://www.unikonstanz.de/crimeandculture/docs/scientificreport2008/ CRIME_AND_CULTURE_Scientific_Report_Greece_2008.pdf

Lambropoulou, E., Papamanolis, N., Aggeli, S. and E. Bakali (2007) *Perceptions of Corruption in Greece. A Content Analysis of Interviews from Politics, Judiciary, Police, Media, Civil Society and Economy*. Report for the research project 'Crime and Culture' funded under the 7th Framework Programme of the European Commission. Available online at: http://www.unikonstanz.de/crimeandcul-ture/docs/scientificreports2007/STREP%20Crime%20and%20Culture%20 Scientific%20Report%20PU%202007.pdf

Lambsdorff, J.G. (1998) 'An Empirical Investigation of Bribery in International Trade', *European Journal for Development Research* 10(1): 40–59.

Legg, K.R. (1975) *Patrons, Clients and Politicians: New Perspectives on Clientelism*, Working Papers on Development, Series No. 3. Berkeley, CA: Institute of International Studies.

Lyrintzis, C. (1984) 'Political Parties in Post-Junta Greece: A Case of Bureaucratic Clientelism?', *West European Politics* 7(2): 99–118.

Lyrintzis, C. (2005) 'The Changing Party System: Stable Democracy, Contested "Modernisation"', *West European Politics* 28(2): 242–259.

Manoledakis, I. (1992) 'Judicial Dependence on the Executive', in The Society of Greek Judges for Democracy and Freedoms (ed.) *Patterns of Justice Dependence on Executive Power* [in Greek], pp. 12–29. Thessaloniki: Sakkoulas Publishers.

Mavrogordatos, G. (1988) *Between Pityocamptes and Procroustes: Corporate Interests in Contemporary Greece* [in Greek]. Athens: Odysseas.

Ministry of Interior, Decentralisation, and E-Government and Ministry of Finance (30 July 2010) *Information Notice: Registration Results* [in Greek]. Available online at: http://www.apografi.gov.gr/2010/07/379

Mouzelis, N.P. (1987) *Politics in the Semi-Periphery: Early Parliamentarism and Late Industrialisation in the Balkans and Latin America* [in Greek]. Athens: Themelio.

Mouzelis, N. (1995) 'Greece in the Twenty-First Century: Instructions and Political Culture', in D. Constas and T. Stavrou (eds) *Greece Prepares for the 21st Century*, pp. 17–34. Washington, D.C.: The Woodrow Wilson Center Press.

National Statistical Service of Greece (NSSG) (1980–1996) *Crime and Justice Statistics*. Athens: NSSG.

Organisation for Economic Co-operation and Development (OECD) (2010) *Convention on Combating Bribery of Foreign Public Officials in International Business Transactions and Related Documents*. Paris: OECD.

Pantazopoulos, N. (1993). *Greek Communitarianism and the Modern Greek Communal Tradition* [in Greek]. Athens: Paroussia.

Pantazopoulos, N. (1994) 'Communitarianism Today: Origins and Perspectives' [in Greek], *New Sociology* 17: 13–32.

Paraskevopoulos, N. (1979) *The Meaning of Morals and Lechery in Sex-related Crimes: Historical, Comparative, Case-Law and Doctrinal Research* [in Greek]. Thessaloniki: [s.n.].

Petmesidou, M. (1996) 'Social Protection in Southern Europe: Trends and Prospects', *Journal of Contemporary European Studies* 4(9): 95–125.

Public Issue (2009a) *National Research on Corruption in Greece 2008* [in Greek]. Available online at: http://www.publicissue.gr/wpcontent/uploads/2009/02/diafthora_1.pdf

Public Issue (2009b) *National Research on Corruption in Greece 2008: Scales for Measuring Attitudes and Perceptions about Corruption in Greece* [in Greek]. Available online at: http://www.publicissue.gr/1070/corruption-2008/

Rantis, K. (2005) 'Rackettheory and Corruption' [in Greek], in K. Koutsoukis and P. Sklias (eds) *Corruption and Scandals in Public Administration and Politics* [in Greek], pp. 193–212. Athens: Sideris.

Scientific Board of the Greek Parliament (20 June 2004) *Report on the Law Concerning the European Arrest Warrant and the Surrender Procedures: Change of Law 2928/2001 Concering Criminal Organisations and Other Regulations.*

Sklias, P. (2005) 'The Consequences of the Phenomenon of Corruption on the Viable Development of Economies in Transition: A Comparative Study of the Western Balkans and the Third World', in K. Koutsoukis and P. Sklias (eds) *Corruption and Scandals in Public Administration and Politics* [in Greek], pp. 585–606. Athens: Sideris.

Sotiropoulos, D. (1995) 'The Remains of Authoritarianism: Bureaucracy and Civil Society in Post-Authoritarian Greece', *Cemoti* 20. Available online at: http://cemoti.revues.org/document1674.html

Sotiropoulos, D.A. (1996) *Bureaucracy and Political Power: Sociological Analysis of the Relations between Public Administration and Politics in Greece during the 1980s* [in Greek]. Athens-Komotini: Ant. N. Sakkoulas Publishers.

Sotiropoulos, D.A. (2007a) *State and Reform in Contemporary Southern Europe: Greece, Spain, Italy, Portugal* [in Greek]. Athens: Potamos.

Sotiropoulos, D.A. (2007b) 'Working Hypotheses and Open Questions in the Literature on Greek Civil Society' [in Greek], paper presentation at the conference in honour of Dimitris T. Tsatsos, Goethe Institute, Athens, 14 March.

Spinellis, C.D. (1998) 'Attacking Prison Overcrowding in Greece: A Task of Sysiphus?', in H.-J. Albrecht, F. Conceit, H.-J. Kerner, J. Kürzinger, H. Schoech and K. Sessar (eds) *International Perspectives in Criminology and Criminal Law* [in German], pp. 1273–1289. Berlin: Duncker & Humblot.

Staikos, A.G. (1961) *Abridged Interpretation of the Greek Penal Code: Law 1492 of 17 August 1950* [in Greek]. Athens: M. Frangoulis.

Stokes, S.C. (2007) 'Political Clientelism', in C. Boix and S. Stokes (eds) *Handbook of Comparative Politics*, pp. 604–627. New York: Oxford University Press.

Thermos, I. (2005) 'Electoral Systems and Political Corruption in Postwar Greece', in K. Koutsoukis and P. Sklias (eds) *Corruption and Scandals in Public Administration and Politics* [in Greek], pp. 623–631. Athens: Sideris.

Transparency International (1996–2010) *Corruption Perceptions Index Survey Results: 1996–2010*. Available online at: http://www.transparency.org/policy_research/surveys_indices/cpi/2010

Tsoukalas, K. (1987) *State, Society, Labour in Post-war Greece* [in Greek]. Athens: Themelio.

Tsoukalas, K. (1993) '"Free-riders" in Wonderland: On Greeks in Greece' [in Greek], *Greek Review of Political Science* 1: 18–26.

United Nations (1998) *Corruption and Integrity Improvement Initiatives in Developing Countries*. New York and Paris: United Nations Development Program and the OECD.

United Nations, General Assembly (28 January 1997) *Resolution on Corruption*. Fifty-First Session, Agenda Item 101. A/RES/51/59.

van Dijk, J., van Kesteren, J., Nevala, S. and G. Hideg (2007) *The Burden of Crime in the EU. A Research Report. A Comparative Analysis of the European Crime and Safety Survey (EU ICS) 2005*. Brussels: Gallup Europe.

Voulgaris, G. (2006) 'State and Civil Society in Greece: A Relationship under Re-Examination?' [in Greek], *Greek Review of Political Science* 28: 5–33.

World Bank (1997) *Helping Countries Combat Corruption: The Role of the World Bank*. Report by the Poverty Reduction and Economic Management (PREM) Network of the World Bank. Washington DC: World Bank.

World Values Survey (1989–1993, 1994–1999) *World Values Survey, Online Data Analysis, Greece*. Available online at: http://www.worldvaluessurvey.org/

PETER BRATSIS

Commentary

Greek Corruption in Context

Effi Lambropoulou has provided us with an extremely well written and researched review of three key overlapping areas of inquiry regarding corruption in Greece: administrative and criminal statutes and procedures, perceptions of corruption, and the ways that the academic literature has attempted to understand and explain the question of corruption in Greece. All three sets of questions contain fundamental points that are relevant to the broader analytical and practical concerns involving corruption. Indeed, corruption in Greece has itself become a global concern and has been making front-page headlines in major newspapers around the world since the Greek debt crisis emerged. Between the time that Lambropoulou completed her chapter and my writing of this commentary, Greek corruption has become a topic that is discussed in cafés and classrooms around the world. In fact, according to some formulations, corruption in Greece is the source of recent problems on Wall Street, the possible collapse of the Euro, and the reason why the retirement age for Germans may need to be raised (see, for example, Walder, 2010). In this commentary, I will depart from Lambropoulou's chapter to focus on three overarching questions: the limits of criminology as a way of approaching the question of corruption, the centrality of perceptions to the question of corruption, and, most importantly, how the current crisis in Greece and beyond has driven the question of corruption and what it teaches us about the political content of the moment as well as the value of existing approaches to the question of corruption.

Corruption is Not a Crime

The attempt to address corruption from the standpoint of criminology quickly runs into a significant problem; there is no law or statute against political corruption as such. As shocking as this may first appear, 'political corruption' is not illegal anywhere, not Greece, not Norway, not Sweden, not Germany, not the United States. What may be illegal (or, more often, against administrative regulations) are some instances of what may be regarded as 'corruption', for example bribery or nepotism. Lambropoulou tackles this question directly when she notes that most uses of the term corruption (*diaphthora*) within Greek case law are related to questions of sexual conduct and the perversion of morals. More recently, she notes, the term has, at times, been used in the context of breaches of trust by public servants. The relative lack of the use of the term *diaphthora* in court proceedings is explained by Lambropoulou as a product of the legal positivist tradition in Greece, the fact that courts must rely upon written laws rather than ethical or political interpretations. This begs the question, however, as to why there is not a law against political corruption.

I believe that the answer to this question gets to the heart of much of the fuzziness in the idea of political corruption. The typical textbook definitions of political corruption stress the subversion of the public good by private interests (see Heidenheimer *et al.*, 1989). As I have previously argued, it is impossible to develop a law against corruption that comes close to this general understanding given that contemporary politics is all about the centrality and rationality of these self-interests and their conflicts (Bratsis, 2006: 25–74). It would imply, for example, that voters were corrupt for voting according to their economic self-interests or that members of parliament were corrupt for acting on behalf of the interests of their political party or constituents. Indeed, much of what laws and rules against specific modalities of 'corruption' do is to normalise all of these other presences of private interests amongst the public.

Accordingly, the key question with regard to Greece, as well as other societies, when it comes to crime and rules is how the law codifies the distinction between what is a pathological presence of private interests amongst the public and what are normal presences of private interests. According to Lambropoulou, the key Greek laws with regard to corruption are set out in the section of the criminal code dealing with public service (which includes laws against bribery, breach of duty, embezzlement, and so on). In addition to these laws, which everyone is subject to, civil servants are also subject to administrative laws. From the very general contours and description of these laws, it is hard to know what may constitute 'corruption' in each case. If, for example, a public servant is caught moonlighting and charged with a crime of 'breach of duty', is that corruption? In the Greek context, this is made doubly confusing because the term *diaphthora* still retains its original meaning, decay and corrosion, as well as the idea of the subversion of the public by the private. Thus, a politician who lies or is involved in a sex scandal may be seen as guilty of *diaphthora*, but it would not be political corruption as it is typically understood.

Perceptions of Corruption

The foregoing leads directly to the question of perceptions of corruption. For one, the expansive meaning of the term *diaphthora* in Greek leads to a great many more examples of behaviour being perceived as 'corrupt' when compared to most other societies. More importantly, there is a fundamental conflation between bureaucratic corruption and political corruption. This is not unique to the Greek case, but the implications are very severe when it comes to perceptions of corruption. Corruption in relation to politicians and high officials is very different from corruption with regard to rank-and-file civil servants.[1] When it comes to the implementation of laws, civil servants typically have very little autonomy and are held to strict standards

---

1   This distinction is a slightly modified variation of an idea first developed by Tsoukalas (2006).

and regulations. Most importantly, they are expected to act in a disinterested way, to treat all citizens equally.[2] When it comes to the policy-making process, there is a much broader range of behaviour that is allowable. In fact, anything short of direct bribery is usually acceptable. When we are dealing with the interests of groups, industries, regions or other parties in the policy-making process, there is no presumption of being 'disinterested'. It is perfectly allowable, most of the time, for a politician or high-ranking bureaucrat to act in ways that favour one part of society over another. In this domain, as noted earlier, it is impossible to eliminate private interests since all of politics in liberal societies is about the promotion of self-interests. When it comes to concrete individuals, as is the case with the normal day-to-day implementation of laws and policies by civil servants, any lack of indifference is likely to be perceived as a form of corruption.

The typical Western strategy has been to minimise bureaucratic corruption while leaving political corruption intact. This has the great advantage of creating the perception of the state somehow being 'clean' and free from corruption, even though private corruption continues unfazed.[3] This not only plays off the difference between individual interests and those of broader social categories, but also creates experiences through which citizens live the 'objectivity' and 'fairness' of the state. All of those instances of being treated equally poorly or well at the hands of civil servants and the state (from waiting in line at public agencies to receiving parking tickets, serving on juries, and voting in elections) provide a sensual and material

---

2   See Herzfeld (1992) on the production of the bureaucratic ethos in Greece.

3   This point also ties very directly to the constant mantra of the need for 'transparency', a favourite refrain of current Prime Minister George Papandreou. As with the ways that political corruption is hidden in plain sight by the focus on bureaucratic corruption, transparency can achieve little more in this endeavour. As Lacan demonstrated for us in his seminal analysis (2005) of Poe's *The Purloined Letter*, making something visible is no more than an attempt to hide its core truth. Such is the fundamental purpose of second-marking and external examiners in British academia, for example, hiding in plain sight the truth that marks are always subjective and capricious. So too with state policy-making, meticulous record-keeping and procedural formalism hide in plain sight the role that self-interests and collusion play in politics today. Can there be a greater folly than assuming that new accounting and record-keeping procedures could transform the character of Greek politics?

confirmation of the fundamental equality of all citizens as claimed by the liberal state as well as the state's own professed neutrality and mission of serving the 'public interest'.[4]

The core problem with Greece in this context stems from its clientelist political networks and the continued existence of petty bribery. The lack of bureaucratic indifference this demonstrates is in direct conflict with the production of the perception of a state that is objective and treats all citizens equally. From petty bribes for preferential service at the hands of doctors or tax agents to the continuing efforts of political parties to find public employment for their supporters, most of the many stories we hear today regarding how corrupt Greece is are examples of this bureaucratic corruption. Unsurprisingly, this form of corruption is also the most amenable to criminalisation under modern law as it is individualised and subject to measures and control.

Comparing the question of corruption in Greece to broader conceptual concerns demonstrates the centrality of the bureaucratic form and the indifference it presupposes to the legitimacy of the capitalist state and the paradoxical belief in some form of 'general will' or public good while, at the same time, all of us know full well that public policies are the outcomes of struggles and conflicts of interest. Thus, the perception of corruption in Greece does present a limit to the capacity of the state to present itself as neutral and objective, but it does not in any way at all differ from other states in its complete constitution by private interests. What does vary from state to state and historical conjuncture to historical conjuncture is the degree to which the state may have some autonomy from the interests of some set of specific individuals or corporation, what Poulantzas (1974) referred to as the relative autonomy of the state. Never is it the case, however, that state power is anything other than an institutionally mediated articulation of social power, class or 'private' struggles. In this sense, there can never be a society or state that is more or less corrupt than its neighbour, even though the perception of corruption may – and does – vary

4   See Nicos Poulantzas' (1974) idea of the 'isolation effect' for more on how this aspect
     of the capitalist state and bourgeois law separate the working class into juridical and
     abstract individuals.

radically. Similarly, although the state is always a product of social struggles and power, its form does impact upon these struggles and its capacity
to fulfill its functions of engendering legitimacy as well as regulating and
coordinating economic accumulation.

The New 'White Man's Burden'

I have so far offered a rushed review of some conceptual touchstones necessary for addressing what I think is the key question regarding Greek corruption today. As we currently sit in the midst of the fiscal meltdown of
Greece and its concurrent political crisis, we are constantly told that Greek
corruption has been a fundamental source of the Greek state's inability
to develop sufficient fiscal prudence and successful policies for economic
development. The narrative is common to Greeks of all walks of life as
well as to those outside Greece. Is this narrative correct? How can we
understand the relation of corruption to economic and political development in Greece?

    In this regard, Lambropoulou notes two fundamentally opposed poles
in the study of development and corruption in Greece. On the right, thinkers grounded in some version of modernisation theory, represented most
clearly by Koutsoukis and Mavrogordatos, presuppose a chronic weakness of
civil society in Greece (given some pathological cultural/historical retarda-
tion or backwardness within Greek political development), this weakness
serving as the key cause of Greek corruption. On the other hand, more
critical leftist thinkers, represented by Tsoukalas and myself, have argued
that corruption in Greece is not a product of political development, or lack
thereof, but is simply a function of perception, an increasing tendency to
judge the less abstract and nebulous form through which private interests
exist within the Greek public sphere as corruption.[5]

5   Many other thinkers, such as Lyrintzis, Mouzelis, and Sotiropoulos, occupy positions
     somewhere between these two extremes.

The current political crisis brings the stakes and differences of the two positions into stark relief. The divide is no less than either a warm embrace and acceptance of Northern European and American political institutions and cultures as superior, as a normative and historical end for development, or a rejection of the idea that any global or regional inequalities can be explained by the failure of some societies to live up to the proper 'western' cultural and political norms. The argument that corruption in Greece is a key source of its economic crisis is simply a repetition of the typical colonial viewpoint that the peoples of the south are poorer and disadvantaged because they are not disciplined or civilised enough.[6] As much as it can be dressed up in the tattered clothes of behaviourist social science, the idea that Greek culture is to blame for the crisis leads to no more than a new version of the white man's burden. The key idea is that Greeks, together with their fellow 'PIGS' (Portugal, Ireland, Greece and Spain), are not sufficiently civilised in the fundamental sense of the term, as capable of controlling their urges and immediate self interests in order to secure longer-term and collective goods (see further Elias, 2000). We are continually presented with either blatant lies (e.g., that the average retirement age in Greece is 53)[7] or with general metaphors regarding the corrupt, lazy, and unruly nature of Greeks.[8]

This current moment of anti-Greek sentiment was prefaced by frequent reports from organisations such as Transparency International, which has consistently placed Greece as by far the most corrupt of states in the Euro-zone, and has continually argued that corruption is the primary cause of poverty and lack of development around the world (see, e.g., Transparency

6　This emphasis on Greek culture and corruption also tends to crowd out any more serious discussion of the economic structures and arrangements that have led to the present situation.

7　This has been reported extensively in the media. For just one example, see Nixon (2010). In fact, for 2005, the average age of withdrawal from the labour market was 58.4 for women and 61.7 for men, while the EU average was 59.4 for women and 60.7 for men (Romans, 2007).

8　This is obvious in the now infamous cover of the German magazine *Focus*, but is also internalised by Greeks themselves, as evidenced in the popular position that having a German coach for the national football team was thought necessary for organising the Greek players and leading them to victory in the 2004 Euro Cup; the Greeks believing they needed German organisation and discipline.

International, 2009). Here we are faced with a number of anomalies or contradictions. For one, we see that many of the most corrupt countries, as designated by Transparency International, have some of the highest rates of economic growth in the world, China, Russia, India, and Brazil being key examples. Indeed, if Greece's problem is that tax collectors and other regulators are easily corrupted, one would expect Greece to be a capitalist paradise with few taxes paid and few regulations followed. Secondly, we are faced with the idea that the Greek masses are completely vulgar and corrupt for aggressively furthering their self-interests, whether in the form of securing generous wages and benefits and not paying taxes, or in the form of bribing officials for preferential treatment. At the same time, the pursuit of self-interests by investors or banks are always seen as perfectly legitimate as is the idea that Germans, for example, should not sacrifice their own short-term economic well-being for the sake of more collective or long-term interests (defending the long-term stability of the EU by providing loans to Greece). Self-interested behaviour is good for business and 'hard-working' Anglo-Saxons, but becomes pathological when done by workers and 'lazy' not-quite whites.

Here we see the real stakes of the two divergent academic views on corruption in Greece. Either we adopt a normative position from the standpoint of the liberal heartland and judge all other political cultures in terms of how closely they conform to these standards or we understand the key disconnection between the substance of contemporary politics and the ways in which it is experienced and categorised. In this regard, what I have claimed is that the substance of Greek politics, struggles of private interests, is exactly the same as the substance of liberal politics everywhere. What may be different are the ways that it is perceived and experienced. There are also potential differences in terms of which sets of interests are most dominant and represented within the state. In this context, the strong linkages between local elites and clientelist networks may make Greece more autonomous from transnational capital than it would be otherwise.

The emphasis on Greek corruption tells us nothing, absolutely and totally nothing, about how and why the present crisis has come about. However, looking to the Greek case does allow us to see how the focus on bureaucratic corruption allows for political corruption to continue unfettered. It also shows how we have not moved very far from the political sensibilities of the 19th century. Rather than arguing that the Greeks are poorer and inferior because of biological or religious reasons, it is now a matter of cultural and ethical defects. Traditional approaches, such as those of Koutsoukis and Mavrogordatos, do little to overcome these cultural hierarchies and the popular perception of Greeks and other Mediterranean peoples as inferior to whites; reconfirmed every year when Transparency International measures *perceptions* of corruption.

When it comes to corruption, the Greek case is probably the most fundamental today, both because of how much is being written about it and its status as, presumably, a key source of global economic decline. It may also be because of how comparative analysis of Greek corruption shows us just how corrupt all contemporary societies are. The distinction between political and bureaucratic corruption is key here, as is the question of how our lived experiences lead to our belief in the equality of citizens and the state's dedication to the public good. Unless we take academic work to be at the service of the state and of dominant classes and interests (which, of course, it most often is), our analytical task is to understand and explain how we have gotten to the point that the claim of corruption and the moralism that accompanies it have come to comprise the guiding ethos of the new financialised and technocratic colonisers. Rather than sticking to the narrow boundaries of criminology or even to the slightly broader contours of functionalist sociology and modernisation theory, we must now take corruption to be a phenomenon understood through conceptually rigorous and imaginative theoretical and empirical studies that allow us to go beyond the self-presentations and common-sense notions that plague us. This is not simply a matter of analytical finess, but goes directly to the core of contemporary schisms within Europe, the unfolding crisis within Greece, and the many muted ways in which racism and colonialism live on today.

References

Bratsis, P. (2006) *Everyday Life and the State*. Boulder: Paradigm Publishers.

Elias, N. (2000) *The Civilising Process*. Oxford: Blackwell.

Heidenheimer, A.J., Johnston, M. and V.T. LeVine (1989) 'Terms, Concepts, and Definitions: An Introduction' in A.J. Heidenheimer, M. Johnston and V.T. LeVine (eds) *Political Corruption: A Handbook*. New Jersey: Transaction.

Herzfeld, M. (1992) *The Social Production of Indifference*. Chicago: University of Chicago Press.

Lacan, J. (2005) *Ecrits*. New York: W.W. Norton.

Nixon, S. (7 May 2010) 'Greek Lessons for the New UK Prime Minister', *Wall Street Journal*.

Poulantzas, N. (1974) *Political Power and Social Classes*. London: New Left Books.

Romans, F. (2007) *Statistics in Focus: Populations and Social Conditions*. Luxemburg: European Communities.

Transparency International (2009) *Corruptions Perception Index*. Berlin.

Tsoukalas, K. (2006) *On Political Corruption*, Unpublished manuscript.

Walder, M. (15 April, 2010) 'Tragic Flaw: Graft Feeds Greek Crisis', *Wall Street Journal*.

JOANNA TSIGANOU

Drugs, Crime and Criminal Justice

Introduction: International Drug Control Policies and National Law

The latter part of the twentieth century has seen drugs emerge as an increasingly important aspect of both criminology and criminal justice systems around the world (see, e.g., discussion in Pearson, 1999: 477). Greece it is not an exception to this trend. As historical studies bear witness (e.g., Berridge, 1977; Musto, 1973; Courtwright, 1982), it is not that the trade and use of drugs such as opiates, cocaine, their derivatives, and a number of chemically produced psychotropic substances, had been previously unknown. What has changed through the centuries, however, is the imposition of large-scale international and domestic prohibitive controls on practices previously considered to be both common and permissable (Duster, 1970; Stein, 1985). Greece did not escape such global developments, either (Grivas, 1990, 1991; Paraskevopoulos, 1993; Tsiganou, 2003). Most importantly, as concerns the issue of 'human casualties', whilst this was undoubtedly present under the vague and largely unregulated conditions of previous centuries, it had become a serious matter of public concern by the early decades of the twentieth century. As a result, 'addiction went from being a pathetic condition to being a stigmatised one' (Courtwright *et al.*, 1989: 5). This was the case in Greece, too (Koukoutsaki, 1999).

Indeed, the 20th century saw very energetic and persistent efforts to bring about international and domestic prohibitory controls on narcotic drugs, worldwide. It also gave birth to a variety of strategies and machineries of control that were shaped by different circumstances of enforcement, as illustrated by the much-discussed policy divide between, on the one hand, the successful (if to a historical point) benign British system of medical treatment of addiction, and, on the other hand, the strict penal controls of the US over the illegal use or abuse of narcotic drugs (Schur, 1962; Lindesmith, 1965; Strang and Gossop, 1993; South, 1994). One doubt has remained persistent, however; whether the adoption of the latter means – namely, crime control measures – have not created as many problems as they have sought to solve (Kleiman, 1992). As 'labelling theorists' have claimed, social control may itself fuel deviant conduct and its attendant social difficulties, producing spirals of 'deviance amplification' far larger than the original problem against which the control measures had been designed (see further Pearson, 1999: 478).

A brief review of the history of narcotics control in Greece provides further empirical support to the above critiques. The Greek experience bears witness to the ways and means that global and local legal machineries of control may transform a social situation to a social problem, and to how drug problems may become a matter of heightened public concern for reasons other than the dimensions of drug use or experimentation themselves. The development of Greek drug control policies serves as an illustrative example of the way in which the legal system of a contemporary Western state can be subordinated to, or powerfully influenced by, supranational legal regimes. In so doing, it contributes to the debate concerning the extent to which the growing importance and internationalisation of law bears upon corresponding national legal and socio-cultural processes (Tsiganou, 2003). At the same time, the Greek experience underlines the importance of investigating the political nature of the deployment of danger as a notion (see Douglas, 1992), as well as the conditions in which a nation-state is driven to accept solutions to conflicts and dilemmas that are foreign in their origins (see Chambliss and Zatz, 1993; Garland, 1996). This chapter offers an overview of the socio-political history of legal controls upon illegal drugs in Greece. A review of current practices in confronting the drug scene and evidence concerning the emerging trends in Greece then follows, as well as a discussion of the relationship between drugs, crime, and criminal justice (further information on which is also provided in Papageorgiou's chapter in this collection). In the conclusion, a critical view is offered on the politics and policies of drugs regulation.

The Origin and Development of Drug Control Policies in Greece

The Greek experience provides an insight into the means and ways by which bilateral, international, and regional considerations, rather than domestic drug predicaments, directly impinge on the emergence of national drug control policies: archival research has made clear that decision-making and law-creation with respect to domestic 'narcotics' legislation have always been by-products of considerations involving external demands, inter-state rivalries, or international obligations, rather than domestic conflicts of interests or internal major 'drug problems' (Tsiganou, 2003). The Greek experience also illustrates the limits to intra-state public decision-making and law-creation, and the role of domestic economic, national, cultural, and political values in creating certain grounds for resistance against bilateral and international arrangements. As the Greek case indicates, however, such resistance may delay or modify but not nullify outcomes.

With regard to the issue of cannabis, until the end of the 19th century, Greece was a country producing hashish legally and profitably trading this product around the Mediterranean as well as further overseas. The enactment of prohibitory domestic laws and regulations against all practices related to this product, making legal practices illegal and gradually penalising its production, trade, distribution, and use, did not emerge in response to domestic considerations. Instead, controls were by-products of inter-state rivalries between Britain, Egypt, and Greece, and were introduced in compliance with dictated terms of bilateral agreements in order to resolve important national, political, and commercial disputes between Greece and Egypt, and which were backed by British aid and support. By means of bilateral diplomatic negotiations between Greece and Egypt, prohibition was initially destined to regulate hashish cultivation and trade between the two countries. It was gradually advanced, however, through successive intra-state arguments and agreements (1884–1920), to full-scale prohibitive controls against cannabis in Greece in 1920.

Thus, unlike the case in most Western nations, the ban against cannabis was introduced in Greece prior to any attempt for its international regulation (Geneva Conventions, 1925, 1931), by machineries distinct to those destined for narcotics. Also, unlike cases such as that of Egypt and Persia, the ban did not originate in response to a major domestic problem. Domestic theorisation of the habit of hashish-use – widespread among certain low-class social categories and within prisons –, which occasionally stressed its deleterious effects upon society as a whole (Chatziantoniou, 2002; Striggaris, 1937), did not affect official responses at that particular time, although it was used to legitimise their outcome. As far as domestic conflicts of interests were involved, they managed to generate domestic resistance to the bilateral arrangements which, to an extent, impeded the machinery of enforcement. By the mid-1930s, however, Greece had ratified and brought into force the Geneva Conventions of 1925 and 1931, which included hashish on the list of the prohibited narcotic drugs. Until today, identical to those international treaty stipulations, domestic laws and regulations still provide for the prohibitive legal treatment of hashish and narcotics alike. As a result, the previous domestic differential legal treatment of hashish, on the one hand, and narcotics, on the other, based upon particular socio-political circumstances, was abruptly substituted by legal documents and texts that unified them. Such a development, apart from its consequences for the intent of the law, had a significant symbolic impact – as a legal norm affecting domestic systems of meaning – upon the social image of drug-users and addicts (Chatziantoniou, 2002; Tsiganou, 2003).

As concerns opium, a broad overview of the processes which led to the development of prohibitive policies regulating opium (and narcotics more generally) also indicates that domestic laws and regulations have always been inaugurated in response to international directives or to comply with stipulations included in international conventions. Greece's participation in increasingly powerful international agencies, such as the League of Nations, the United Nations, and the European Union, as well as associated conferences and conventions, made her susceptible to the influence of international administrative bodies and control machineries. As and when expedient, bilateral diplomatic bargaining (initially with Britain, later on with the US – patronage politics possibly playing a role (see Mouzelis, 1978;

Grivas, 1997) –, and currently with European counterparts as well) was also employed to secure Greek compliance with international directives.

The main factor which ignited the law-making process with respect to narcotics controls in Greece was the signing and ratification of the treaties ending World War I, which included a simultaneous ratification of the International Opium Convention. The Act of 1920, however, which brought into force the Hague Opium Convention (1912), met with serious impediments at the level of enforcement, especially with the control of opium production and trade. With the annexation of Macedonia, Greece had inherited an opium harvest and a significant and flourishing opium market in Salonica, which had raised expectations of an increase to State revenue. Greek reluctance to enforce controls, however, was soon curbed by intense British diplomatic 'enlightenment' and administrative action by the League. Subsequent developments were also profoundly influenced by the stipulations of the Geneva Conventions of 1925 and 1931, and the highly energetic role of international diplomats and administrations within the League. The domestic legal reorganisation of the 1930s (especially the promulgation of Acts 5539 and 6169/1934) set the basis for a control structure much as we know it today, with the common regulation of cannabis and narcotics, and the treatment of addiction within the apparatus of criminal law. Once again, legal controls cannot be viewed as an institutionalised reaction to a major domestic addiction problem. International technologies, guidance, and 'enlightenment' contributed to this effect.

Domestic drug control policies during the first decades after World War II, developed, again, in accordance with successive treaty obligations of the Greek state from signing the Protocols of 1946, 1948, and 1953, the Single Convention of 1961, and the Protocol of 1972, all of which gradually increased legal controls over a huge list of prohibited substances of a narcotic, psychotropic, or hallucinogenic nature. Under the auspices of the United Nations, the international community intensified its efforts to combating the drug problem. 'Recalcitrant' countries were transformed into 'delinquent' countries, and tolerance of unilateral actions by nation-states in opposition to international objectives declined, even though governments were warned that addicts 'should not be lost sight of' by United Nations Commission on Narcotic Drugs (CND) (itself appointed by the United

Nations Council) in the report of its 1961 session to the United Nations Economic and Social Council (ECOSOC) (see further Mangone, 1958).[1]

In 1934, the Greek Government had concluded a special agreement with the United States for co-operation and exchange of information and experiences between the Greek agencies of control and the US Federal Narcotics Bureau, thus establishing a close and direct communication between the police authorities in Greece and those under Commissioner of Narcotics, Harry J. Aslinger. The rise of more advanced systems of sanctioning non-compliance (e.g., publicity and embargoes) by the United Nations and its organs, the advent of the Nixon Administration and its War on Drugs (see Epstein, 1977), and the influence of the US administration upon the military dictatorship in Greece (1967–1974), combined to effectively stimulate eager compliance on the part of Greece. Strict new legislation was introduced in the 1970s (Decrees 743/1970 and 1176/1972) which intensified pre-existing penal controls domestically. As a result, domestic statutes once more provided for the legal management of the narcotics problem within the larger context of crime, and presented the drug user as a criminal on the basis of drug use alone. This characterisation included occasional users and those addicted to prohibited drugs, with no differential treatment for the consumers of cannabis or opiates. Heavy sentences and incarceration were used as the ultimate weapon against any illicit transaction (Vougioukas, 1971; Tsiganou, 2003).

In turn, the country's return to democracy and its entrance to the European Union shaped domestic policy-making and law-creation. Without abandoning compliance to successive United Nations and international agreements, the last decades saw law-making and implementation processes vastly influenced by the European Drugs Strategy and Action

---

1   ECOSOC was entrusted with supervising national enforcement of the international
     treaties on narcotic drugs, and was empowered to decide upon recommendations
     and resolutions, and to call for the adoption of new domestic drug control policies
     (Mangone, 1958). Further information on the CND is available on its website, at:
     http://www.unodc.org/unodc/en/commissions/CND/.

Plans.[2] Despite the explosion of ideas undermining the foundations of the penal confrontation of drug addicts, and the unprecedented advance of the medical profession in the treatment of addiction (Daskalaki and Tsiganou, 2000; Koukoutsaki, 2002), successive legal amendments (Acts 1729/1987, 1990/1991, 2161/1993, 2331/1995, 2408/1996, 2479/1997, 2721/1999, 2943/2001, 3189/2003) have little altered the character of prohibitive controls. As the national report for EMCDDA (the European Monitoring Centre for Drugs and Drug Addiction) indicates (Terzidou, 2005: 6), the most recent modification came with Law 3189/2003, which provided for more lenient penal treatment of drug users.[3] The law now provides for the voluntary medical treatment of drug addicts, and sanctions the operation of state-run or non-profit therapeutic establishments. Meanwhile, it has reaffirmed the compulsory treatment of addiction within legal constraints, and positions against the hedonistic and ameliorative consumption of cannabis, opiates and psychotropics alike. The law treats all prohibited substances in the same way, and no differential treatment is provided between 'soft' and 'hard' drugs.

2   On which see the annual reports of the EMCDDA, 'The State of the Drugs Problem in Europe', available online at: http://www.emcdda.europa.eu/publications. The EMCDDA processes data and information across European member-states and publishes annual reports on policy issues and agendas at the European level.

3   The EMCDDA commissions annual national reports on Greece from the national focal point of the Reitox network, the University Mental Health Research Institute. The national focal point collects information from all relevant authorities (police, courts, prisons, medical centres, private or public research centres, etc.) and, amongst other work, drafts annual reports on the developments in Greek policy, expert opinions of the field, and the progress of the European action plans. The focal point processes all information relevant to the issue of drugs in Greece and holds a more useful database than those partial collections held by specific national agencies, allowing it to provide data otherwise hard to collect and access (e.g., information on finance distribution and expenditures of treatment centres, special action plans by treatment institutions or within prisons, survey data).

The Relationship between Theorisation,
Legislation, and Practice

International instruments have left the treatment of addiction to the discretion of individual governments on the condition that legal constraints
should underpin all approaches, including those medical. The exchange
of policy knowledge between Greece and its international counterparts,
meanwhile, has helped the transfer of ideas across national borders. Thus, a
fruitful re-interpretation of domestic experiences has proceeded through a
process of communication by means of awareness-raising by external agents
that also draws on domestic knowledge and professional ideas, but which
nonetheless places the treatment of addiction under the apparatus of criminal law rather than of the medical profession. Domestic (re-)interpretations
of theories of drug use have been able to exert a tremendous impact on the
official handling of drug addiction in Greece. They have offered grounds
by which policies adopted are legitimised, and have contributed to the
continuous swinging between punitive and medical-oriented approaches
(although policies are always resolved in favour of the former). As a result,
drug addiction has been transformed from an individual indulgence into
a national problem.

When early narcotics control measures were introduced to Greece,
authoritative, official, and independent Greek knowledge on this subject
was limited. No precautions had been taken to stop deliveries of cocaine
from Germany – as war compensation to Greece – being distributed in
public auctions (see the 'Report on Narcotic Drugs' in Greek Police Chronicles, 1963). Opium, its tinctures and derivatives, were sold at grocery shops
(Agioutandes, 1969: 96). Opium preparations were administered to babies
to induce them to sleep, or as medicines for coughing, respiratory, and
intestinal problems. Such practices were quite widespread and sometimes
resulted in accidental deaths. Doctors and pharmacists did not devote much
attention to the 'dangerous' properties of opium and its derivatives. Medical Examiners had repeatedly identified improper medical administration
of opium preparations as an important cause of death (Georgiades, 1926),

but it was only during the mid-twenties, after the full-scale imposition of controls, that broader public light was shed on these practices and they became a subject of debate within medical circles. It was only then that some medical experts, in influential administrative and academic positions, urged the introduction of special regulations against careless medical prescription and pharmaceutical distribution of prohibited substances.

The Greek Law of 1920 clearly intended to prevent the use of the prohibited drugs for 'hedonistic purposes', and to remove these substances entirely from ordinary, non-medical channels of commerce, restricting their sale to therapeutic (rather than recreational) purposes. Nevertheless, there was no intent to interfere with existing medical practices in the treatment of the physically ill. The 1920s thus witnessed collaboration between medical practitioners and enforcement agents in the treatment of addiction. Greek physicians remained more or less independent in their practice, while enforcement agents were mainly preoccupied with the repression of illicit drug traffic and the inspection of hashish dens, prosecuting drug users who were caught red-handed. As a result, there is no mention of any heroin addict being treated in public hospitals during the 1920s, and few members of the middle and upper classes were arrested and prosecuted for using narcotic drugs for hedonistic purposes (Striggaris, 1937).

By the 1930s, however, expertise on drug addiction had become diffused and widespread. A number of theories had surfaced, if based to a large extent on faith rather than science. Expert medical opinions, in concert, viewed the addict as a psychopath, addiction being a manifestation of 'physical inclination' or 'psychological predisposition'. Certain voices went further, to stress that addiction to controlled drugs (i.e., hashish and narcotics such as opium) 'ravaged the body', 'destroyed morality', and 'deteriorated character', making drug users 'weak, sinful, and evil' members of society, a 'criminal and sexual' menace, their criminality being a manifestation of their addiction. Repeated administration of opium and hashish alike was understood to produce dependence upon the use of the drug. Those 'addicted' developed a 'craving' for the continuation of their habit, which ceased only on administration of new dosages. Drug addiction produced not only severe psychic disturbances and chronic mental illness, but also various 'perversions' such as an 'inclination for gambling, fabulism, homosexuality, prostitution' and 'released criminal instincts' (Georgantas, 1889; Dondas, 1925; Joakimoglou, 1934; Georgiades, 1926; Kouretas and Skouras, 1928; Mitaftsis, 1932; Striggaris, 1937). Despite the emphasis on such 'criminogenic' elements, however, Greek physicians almost unanimously maintained that the treatment of addiction was difficult, if not impossible, to be effected domiciliary, rather than in special therapeutic environments suitable for alleviating withdrawal symptoms and provide proper medical care. They were also mostly in favour of abstinence and after-care rather than maintenance programmes.

Nevertheless, prohibitory legislation against non-medical drug consumption transformed recreational users into targets for law enforcement agencies. Consequently, by the early 1930s, law enforcement agencies had developed their own conception of hashish and narcotics use, and established an unquestionable causal link between addiction and crime. In their view, hashish users and opiates addicts were evidently criminals; 'involved in illegal activities especially under the influence of the drug. ... [T]hey often commit property crimes, violent assaults, thefts and burglaries' (Koutsoumaris, 1932). They were portrayed as a tremendous threat to the well-being of society, not only because of their alleged identity as criminal public enemies, but also because of the notion that their addition was contagious. It was mostly because of this latter factor that enforcement agents promoted and supported the compulsory incarceration and isolation of drug addicts in prisons and special penitentiaries (Archimandritis, 1954; Stamatis, 1963, 1965).

This is not the place to reiterate the counter-arguments produced in numerous studies, but it is important to note that these early theorisations were not the exclusive inventions of Greek scientists and professionals. In the United States, for example, the early campaign against the 'heroin epidemic' advertised a number of 'evil' effects associated with heroin, matching those developed in Greece. Experts argued that heroin, even marijuana, 'undoubtedly' caused insanity, that it propelled the users towards violent criminal activity, it destroyed their sense of moral responsibility and appropriate behaviour, their ethos and fear of punishment, it caused organ damage, producing significantly harmful side-effects, and was an ineffective pain-killer. Early theories on addiction, developed in both Europe and

America, also provided an explanation of this 'phenomenon', attributing its origins to physiological, biological, or psychological defects and predispositions (see further Terry and Pellens, 1928; Trebach, 1982; Kolb, 1925; Ausubel, 1958; Walton, 1938; Henderson, 1939; Rado, 1933; Lindesmith, 1940, 1968; Stimson, 1973; Young, 1971). With such expert ideas, it is not surprising that the evolution of controls and the treatment of addiction proceeded in Greece in the way it did.

Later developments did nothing but reaffirm early conceptualisations (Gardikas, 1950, 1957; Kanatsios, 1957; Karanikas, 1960; Vougioukas, 1971). Especially during the dictatorship, interpretations went further in theorising addicts as both public enemies and as potential criminals. The media and state authorities (as well as other individuals) projected a mirror image of the drug addict as found elsewhere in the western world. There was no account of drug addiction without references to heroin addicts and LSD users all over the world, if not in Greece. Yet, as stated, the public image of the drug addict was constructed through narrations and myths promoted by the social status quo and its institutions which went even further in stressing the use or abuse of drugs by representatives of the Hippy movement in America, and cycles of drug use within the protests of May 1968 in France, thereby underlying the stimulant effects of prohibited drugs and their contribution to sentiments of generalised euphoria and revolution (Tsili, 1995: 33). Official statements reflected the rationalisation offered by international drug control agents, diplomats, administrators, and bureaucrats acting as 'moral entrepreneurs' (Becker, 1973), in recognising the sporadic nature of addiction in Greece whilst simultaneously asserting the need for strict law enforcement to protect the country (as well as friendly or neighbouring countries) from the 'contagious threat of the disease' (Vougioukas, 1971).

It was only with the return to democracy in 1974 that official and independent rhetoric gradually changed. A study of Greek parliamentary archives has shown that, from 1975 onwards, the 'drug problem' began to make a marked appearance, and on occasion claimed a prominent position, in public discourse. The number of parliamentary debates on the subject tripled from 1979 to 1980, and doubled again from 1980 to 1982, since which point they have continued to attract high levels of interest. Meanwhile, the number of parliamentary deputies questioning official policy on the 'drug problem' multiplied by five over the course of the 1980s, and has also continued to rise (Daskalaki and Tsiganou, 2000). At the same time, through the electoral brochures of political parties, civil society campaigning, interest group petitions, and press commentaries, drug addiction has been promoted to the status of an 'ideological hazard, a social catalyst cast in moral language and used to motivate and reinforce traditional values, symbols and stereotypes' (Tsili, 1995: 276). Following these developments has been a dramatic change in public attitudes towards the 'drug problem', as evidenced by the prominent position this issue holds in repeated opinion surveys of the most serious threats facing Greek society. It is also evidenced by the great difficulty faced by those who have successfully undergone addiction rehabilitation in becoming re-integrated into society (see further Marselos *et al.*, 1988; Tsili, 1999; Fakiolas *et al.*, 1999).

The above developments coincided with public realisation that Greece was no longer immune to drug addiction. The numbers of known drug addicts were increasing, and the authorities had to confront a growing drug problem which was no longer restricted by age or class. As the police records testify, whereas 1,000 individuals were charged for drug offences in 1982, this number had tripled by 1992, and re-doubled by the mid-1990s. Equally, whilst there had been negligible drug-related deaths in the early 1980s, fatalities had multiplied almost twenty times by the early 1990s, and re-doubled by the turn of the century. The heroin market has strengthened, as have those for cannabis, cocaine, and hallucinogens, in a trade which enters the country for local consumption and in transit from the East towards Western Europe and the US (Tsili, 1999; see also EMCDDA Annual Reports on 'The State of the Drug Problem in Greece' since 1995). As a result, questions related to non-medical drug consumption have been subject to political and scholarly debates. Greek scientists, politicians, enforcement agents, party political activists, administrative entities and pressure groups, journalists and other commentators, have all played an important role in keeping some of these issues before the wider public (Daskalaki and Tsiganou, 2000). Much of such exchanges have challenged the intellectual foundations of uniform prohibitive control over cannabis and opiates, while proposals have stressed the need for the criminal treatment of drug addicts to be substituted by medical rehabilitation, after-care, and social re-integration programmes (Tsilichristos, 1984; Economopoulos, 1988; Farsedakis and Sylikos, 1996; Pavlou, 1997; Grivas, 1995, 1997; Koukoutsaki, 2002; Panousis, 1981; Karabelas, 1985; Paraskevopoulos, 1993; Zarafonitou and Tsiganou, 2002). Official recognition was eventually forthcoming that enforcement of the existing control system had resulted in the imprisonment of drug users almost to the exclusion of drug traffickers, and had led to improper efforts of accused individuals to be incarcerated in clinics rather than prisons by illegitimate means (i.e., corruption; see Paraskevopoulos, 1993; Koukoutsaki, 2002).

Greek policy-makers soon decided that it was time to adopt not only the harsh features of the American system, but also its benign and therapeutic measures. Thus, the Synanon and Daytop programmes – two of the most celebrated examples of communal, self-managed, and drug-free therapeutic communities in the US (Eldridge 1967) – provided a basis for the birth of Greek therapeutic community programmes (between 1983–1984). The first Greek attempts operated in a mode similar, if not identical, to the above programmes; run by medical experts, with provision for treatment, support, and reintegration, for employment amongst the community of rehabilitated individuals, and for the continual training of professionals in therapeutic communities abroad. Legislative measures legitimised the voluntary medical treatment of drug addicts and the operation of state-run or non-profit therapeutic communities and establishments. However, they also reaffirmed the compulsory treatment of addiction in accordance with legal constraints and criminal procedures, and continued to oppose hedonistic and ameliorative consumption of cannabis, opiates, and psychotropics alike. Once more, international developments shed important light upon the range of constraints facing domestic decision-makers; the CND had urged governments to reject policies that might lead to the legalisation of any prohibited substance, for example (see the 1984 annual report of the UN International Narcotics Control Board (INCB) to the ECOSOC).[4] Overall, and despite an obvious shift in official policy towards the medicali-

---

4 The INCB is an independent and quasi-judicial control organ responsible for monitoring the implementation of UN drug control conventions, and is accountable to the United Nations Commission of Narcotic Drugs (CND). Further information about the INCB is available on its website, at: http://www.incb.org/

sation of drug addiction, Greek treatment of the drug-addicted individual as an offender under criminal law remains in place; contemporary social practices associated with drug addiction are still prohibitively regulated according to a penal criminal-medical framework.

Drug Scenes in Greece:
Past and Present-day 'States of the Art'

To a large extent, crime statistics on lawbreaking and drug-taking are based on data available from the administration of criminal justice, the police, prisons, and medical establishments. Arguments about *dark figures* concerning the scale of the phenomena, as well as those referring to pitfalls in crime reporting and crime recording more generally, hold true (Lambropoulou, 2005; Tsiganou, 2005; but see also Cheliotis and Xenakis, this collection). Furthermore, data collection tends to focus on pre-determined and pre-structured targets, as defined by local and international government agencies. As these targets alter in response to shifting official policies, data collection becomes harder to compare across time and subject matter. The following interpretation of the available data of lawbreaking and drug-taking in Greece is offered with these limitations in mind.

Drug Use and Control in the Interwar Period

The availability of cannabis in the domestic market and the permissiveness of its trade constituted prerequisites of its abundant and cheap distribution. During the 1920s, hashish was available in variety of forms; cakes, leaves, powder, and cigarettes. Several different qualities of product were available for domestic consumption, some of them produced locally and others imported from Turkey. The legal trade in cannabis had created subsidiary illicit networks of distribution, from producers to merchants, and from merchants to intermediaries who distributed hashish to customers together with the paraphernalia for its use. Despite the existence of pro-hibitory measures, hashish dens flourished in Syra, Piraeus, and Athens, although their permanent clients became more cautious. Cannabis use was seen expanding amongst seamen, soldiers, prisoners, and refugees, as well as amongst middle-class citizens. Existing data suggest that introduction to drug use was affected by social, professional, and familial associations, and, for the majority of habitual users, began in adolescence (Striggaris, 1937; Kotaridis, 1996; Petropoulos, 1987, 1991).

Following the reorganisation of the police force in the early 1920s, efforts intensified to close hashish dens and suppress and eliminate the illicit trade in heroin, opium, and opiates (Archimandritis, 1954; Stamatis, 1963, 1965). Policing zeal led to the closure of 28 of the 66 known hash-ish dens, as well as to high numbers of arrests of the respective owners of such establishments and their customers who had been caught in the act of hashish-smoking. Efforts to combat the spread of drug use were directed primarily against its public consumption. Those targeted were the persistent clients of hashish dens, who also belonged to the Greek underworld and who were stigmatised due to their involvement in a variety of contraband activities. Data available on hashish use, although highly imperfect and controversial, suggest that the number of hashish users were estimated to be more than 2,000 across Greece by the 1930s (Striggaris, 1937). Hashish use appears to have been increasing at the turn of the 1930s, in a trend similar to that of heroin consumption. The vast majority of those convicted were male; half were residents of the capital, whilst most of the rest lived either in Macedonia or in refugee settlements. Official crime and judicial statistics show that only a small number of persons were arrested and convicted for hashish cultivation, while the bulk of convictions involved hashish use. Nevertheless, the penalties imposed by the Courts were extremely lenient (less than three months for drug use, although drug production was gener-ally dealt with more severely), and were much lower than the fixed sanctions the law provided. There was little scope for rehabilitation accompanying imprisonment for drug use, however, given that cannabis consumption was very popular amongst inmates in both civil and army prisons and proved impossible to control (Koutsoumaris, 1932).

Very little is known about the number of opium and opiates addicts in Greece during the same period. Highly imperfect and irregular official statistics also suggest that the vast majority of convicted drug addicts and drug sellers were young, male, lower-class residents of major cities or refugee settlements. From 1928 onwards, there was a rapid increase in the rate of convictions for violations of narcotics laws with penalties ranging from less than three months of imprisonment to little over a year. The illicit production, trade, and distribution of narcotics were sanctioned more severely than corresponding activities related to hashish. The sentences imposed, however, were far more lenient than those legally provided. From 1932 onwards, controls appeared to become more severe, with a higher percentage of offenders sentenced to more than three months of imprisonment (see further the 'Statistics of Justice' produced by the National Statistical Service of Greece between 1926 and 1937). There is little explanation in the official documentation for this shift, however.

In the years before the Second World War, Greek authorities had to confront a serious rise in heroin use. The number of known heroin addicts by the late thirties was 5,000 people (Gardikas, 1957), and although the actual number of drug users might not have increased, the nature of drug use had altered substantially. A large number of morphine and cocaine addicts who could otherwise have maintained their habit through legitimate medical sources, had converted to illegal narcotics by the mid-thirties. There were repeated official statements that heroin use was spreading alarmingly (see, for example, the *Police Chronicles* for the years 1953–1957), and drug-related deaths started to make notable appearances in the daily press. The maintenance and expansion of drug use was supported by the flow of heroin from Turkey westwards (see the Reports to the Council of the Advisory Committee on Opium Traffic between 1935 and 1940), the ineffectiveness of the control system in combating the illicit traffic, and the continuation of drug use within prisons.

The Postwar Environment

In the years immediately following the Second World War, local opium production under government licence was negligible, and had ceased entirely
by the end of the 1960s. Greece nevertheless remained both a transit point
for trade between the Middle East and the West, and a producer of contraband raw materials (opium and hashish) which also supplied the local black
market. By 1954, heightened repression by enforcement agencies had an
effect in stabilising, if not reducing, illicit transactions.[5] Official data and
press reporting suggested that the drug 'epidemics' of the pre-war period
had subsided. The main drug of preference amongst the few drug users
arrested was hashish, and use of opiates and cocaine appeared extremely
limited.[6] Until the mid-1970s, the extent and form of drug addiction did
not raise alarms. The number of estimated drug users was low (less than
2,000) and the addicted population consisted almost exclusively of cannabis users.[7] Raw opium production was controlled severely, and the main
concern of Greek authorities remained the suppression of the illicit trade.
Various forms of cannabis, and to a limited extent heroin also, left the country either by sea or by land, primarily across the Greco-Turkish frontier,
and in transit to the West.[8] Increased police activity revealed thousands of
cannabis plants growing 'wild' or 'illicitly cultivated', and official seizures

5   See further UN Commission on Narcotic Drugs, *Summary of Annual Reports Series,
     1945–1954*; also, UN ECOSOC and Commission on Narcotic Drugs, *Regulations
     Series: Greece, 1947–1954*.

6   See further UN Commission on Narcotic Drugs, *Summary of Annual Reports Series,
     1945–1954*; UN Commission on Narcotic Drugs, *Summary of Illicit Transactions and
     Seizures Series, 1947–1954*.

7   See further UN Commission on Narcotic Drugs, *Summary of Annual Reports Series,
     1954–1970*; UN INCB, *Statistics on Narcotic Drugs: Greece, 1969–1985*; and UN
     ECOSOC, *Annual Reports on Narcotic Drugs, 1945–1984*.

8   See further the *Confidential Official Records* of the Narcotics Committee of the
     Greek Ministry of Health for the years 1961–1973; UN Commission on Narcotic
     Drugs, *Summary of Annual Reports Series*, 1954–1970; UN Commission on Narcotic
     Drugs, *Summary of Illicit Transactions and Seizures Series, 1954–1970*.

amounting to a yearly average of 1,000,000 to 1,200,000 plants (see the section on Indian hemp in the Summary of the Annual Reports on Greece, between 1954–1969, produced by the CND).

In the early 1980s, however, the numbers of known drug addicts began to gradually increase. The black market grew both for local consumption and for transit from East to Western Europe and the US, in heroin, cannabis, cocaine, and hallucinogens (see the Annual Reports on the State of the Drugs Problem in Greece, between 1997–2007, produced by the EMCDDA). Trafficking patterns have remained similar since. Albania has been the main source of cannabis and heroin trafficking, while cocaine originates mainly from the Caribbean. Psychotropic substances come either via the classic Balkan route (Albania, Bulgaria) or from other European countries (i.e., the Netherlands, Germany). Drug seizure rates have remained almost at the same levels as those during the 1990s. At the same time, drug prices in Greece have remained fairly stable, despite falling prices in the rest of Europe (EMCDDA, 2007: 87). Whilst drug use in Greece has shown an overall upward trend over the past 20 years (EMCDDA, 2004: 14), Greece still holds one of the lowest positions in almost all trends of drug consumption across Europe and the US (see further the Annual Reports on the State of the Drugs Problem in Europe, since 2000, produced by the EMCDDA).

Domestic mass prevention interventions inspired by European Strategic Action Plans became 'a key priority for the policy and philosophy of prevention in Greece' (EMCDDA, 2004: 16), leading to the establishment of addiction therapy institutions with drug-free or substitution programmes, with not even kindergartens escaping the provision of counselling, but services were overwhelmingly concentrated in major cities, which led to long waiting lists (especially in dosage substitution centres). Comparative data nevertheless suggest that drug use patterns in Greece (i.e., with regard to cannabis and cocaine) follow European trends, although in lower numbers and percentages. The development of drug use within recreational settings has re-emerged with the growth of clubbing as a fashionable form of youth entertainment (see EMCDDA, 2005: 94). By 2007, the number of heroin users and addicts aged 15–64 was estimated to have risen to around the 20,000 persons (see further Papageorgiou, this collection).

In 2006, the last year for which data are available as to the number of users approaching drug services, showed that 4,847 individuals made use of an increased provision of services that year. A slight increase was also evidenced in the number of drug users who reported cocaine as their primary substance of abuse, and in those reporting inhaling than injecting as the main route of administration (EMCDDA, 2007). The majority of users approaching treatment facilities are men (about 85 percent), in their twenties (63 percent), of Greek nationality (98 percent), and with low educational attainment. Whilst, in the main, they are unemployed, they report stable accommodation and family or spousal support. Although a very high proportion of users report polydrug use, the favoured substance by far is heroin, followed by cannabis, sedatives, and cocaine. Less common are stimulants, hallucinogens, and other opiates. According to reports by male and female users, both tend to first experiment with drugs at the age of 16, and the vast majority report cannabis as the first substance used. Time-trends in the patterns of use indicate that, more recently, those who demand treatment have, for the first time, a younger and less socially-excluded profile; have permanent accommodation, employment, and are largely cannabis users; report less polydrug and/or intravenous use; and have a shorter drug history. Harm reduction policies appear to have had an effect on drug-related deaths, since they are moving downwards (see further Xenakis, this collection). But the majority of victims reaffirm consumption trends, since they remain young men, of Greek nationality (96 percent), single (91 percent), and unemployed (80 percent). Available data also point to the fact that such deaths are overwhelmingly related to heroin use (approximately 98 percent in 2007), the ratio between men and women being 10:1 (EMCDDA, 2007: 70, 75–82).

Data on the penal confrontation of addiction, although under-studied, show that 6,961 individuals were prosecuted on drug-law violations in 1996, 12,543 individuals in 2000, a peak of 16,195 individuals in 2003, and a fall to 13,948 persons in 2006, the majority of whom were male and Greek nationals (EMCDDA, 2007: 83). Nevertheless, high numbers of imprisoned drug law offenders are non-Greek nationals: in 2005, for example, almost 47 percent of the total number of drug offenders in prison were foreigners (see further Cheliotis and Xenakis, this collection). In the same year, data

on drug use in prisons indicated the use of illicit drugs – especially cannabis – to be running high (see further EMCDDA, 2005: 63, 68). Sentences
for illegal drug use involve up to a year of imprisonment, illegal possession
and possession for use are sentenced more severely (between 1–3 years of
imprisonment), and convictions for illegal transactions or trade may receive
life sentences. The only commutable sentences are those related to illegal
use. Female and juvenile offenders tend to receive more lenient treatment
by the Greek Criminal Courts (EMCDDA, 2007: 83–84). Pending legal
proceedings may seriously obstruct the process of drug dependence treatment, however, and research findings suggest that a large number of former
or recovering drug users (40 percent) are awaiting trial or court decision
(EMCDDA, 2005: 67).

Concluding Remarks

Whilst drug use in Greece has fluctuated, the prohibitory system of control has essentially remained unchanged. The more progressive outlook of
recent policy in the area still operates within the framework of a criminal
law approach, which serves to reinforce stigmatisation. Instead of examining
the determinants of drug consumption (whether macro-social, economic,
or cultural) and their impact on addiction trends, authoritative knowledge
in the field has focused on penal controls, ignoring the historical lessons of
patterns of drug use, abuse, and trade. One of the most interesting facets
of Greek drug policy is the lack of a notable moral panic, crusade, or even
simply a consensus amongst Greek society for action to be taken against the
prohibited practices, prior to the imposition of controls (compare Duster,
1970). Rather, the design and implementation of controls have primarily
been influenced by international policy developments as well as the active
engagement of international diplomats, administrators, and bureaucrats.
This, then, is an invitation to consider both the ways in which domestic
and international politics shape policies, but also those by which law acts
upon societies (Anleu, 2000).

References

Agioutandes, G. (1969) *Issues of Toxicology and Medical Examination* [in Greek]. Athens: Parisianos.

Anleu, S.L.R. (2000) *Law and Social Change*. London: Sage.

Arcalides, N. (1928) 'Drug Addicts in Greece', in M. Katsaras (ed.) *Medical Issues* [in Greek]. Athens: [s.n.].

Archimandritis, N. (1928) 'The History of the Police: 1921–1954' [in Greek], *Police Chronicles*.

Ausubel, D.P. (1958) *Drug Addiction: Physiological, Psychological and Sociological Aspects*. New York: Random House.

Becker, H. (1973) *Outsiders*. Glencoe: Free Press.

Berridge, V. (1977) 'Fenland Opium Eating in the Nineteenth Century', *British Journal of Addiction* 72: 275–284.

Chambliss, W. and M. Zatz (eds) (1993) *Making Law: The State, the Law, and Structural Contradictions*. Indiana: Indiana University Press.

Chatziantoniou, T. (2002) 'The Hashish User and the Opium Addict', in C. Zarafonitou and J. Tsiganou (eds) *Narcotic Drugs* [in Greek], pp. 297–335. Athens: Nomiki Vivliothiki.

Courtwright, D. (1982) *Dark Paradise: Opiate Addiction in America before 1940*. Cambridge, MA: Harvard University Press.

Courtwright, D., Joseph, H. and D. Des Jarlais (1989) *Addicts Who Survived: An Oral History of Narcotic Use in America, 1932–1965*. Knoxville: University of Tennessee Press.

Daskalaki, I. and J. Tsiganou (2000) 'The "Political Paradigm" in Griminology and the Prohibited Abuse in Drugs', in I. Daskalaki, P. Papadopoulou, D. Tsabarli, J. Tsiganou and E. Fronimou (eds) *Criminals and Victims at the Doorstep of the 21st Century* [in Greek], pp. 305–317. Athens: EKKE.

Dondas, S. (1925) *Pharmacology* [in Greek]. Athens: [s.n.].

Douglas, M. (1992) *Risk and Blame: Essays in Cultural Theory*. London: Routledge.

Duster, T. (1970) *The Legislation of Morality*. London: Collier-Macmillan.

Economopoulos, G. (1988) *Narcosis and De-Addiction* [in Greek]. Athens: Koinotita.

Eldridge, W.B. (1967) *Narcotics and the Law*. Chicago: University of Chicago Press.

Epstein, E.J. (1977) *Agency of Fear*. New York: Putnam.

Fakiolas, N., Styliaras, G. and K. Moula (1999) 'De-addicted Persons and Social Exclusion', in E. Katsoulis, D. Karantinos, L. Maratou and E. Fronimou (eds)

Dimensions of Social Exclusion in Greece [in Greek], pp. 331–366. Athens: EKKE.

Farsedakis, I. and G. Sylikos (1996) *Narcotic Drugs: Legal and Criminological Aspects in Greece and the EU* [in Greek]. Athens: Ant. N. Sakkoulas Publishers.

Gardikas, K. (1950) 'Criminals, Alcoholics, Drug-Addicts' [in Greek], *Review of the Correctional System*: 2–3.

Gardikas, K. (1957) *Criminology* [in Greek]. Athens: Tzaka.

Garland, D. (1996) 'The Limits of the Sovereign State', *British Journal of Criminology* 36: 445–471.

Georgandas, A. (1889) *Issues of Toxicology and Medical Examination* [in Greek]. Athens: [s.n.].

Georgiades, J. (1926) *Toxicology* [in Greek]. Athens: Estia.

Grivas, K. (1990) *Narcotic Drugs and Power* [in Greek]. Thessaloniki: Ekdotiki.

Grivas, K. (1991) *Narcotic Drugs: The Price of Repression* [in Greek]. Thessaloniki: Ekdotiki.

Grivas, K. (1995) *Opiates: Morphine, Heroin, Methadone* [in Greek]. Athens: Nea Synora-Livanis.

Grivas, K. (1997) *Global Governance and Drugs: The Role of Drugs in American Internal and Foreign Affairs* [in Greek]. Athens: Nea Synora-Livanis.

Henderson, D.K. (1939) *Psychopathic States*. London: Chapman and Hall.

Joakimoglou, G. (1934) *Pharmacology* [in Greek]. Athens: [s.n.].

Kanatsios, G. (1957) *Alcoholism and Drug-Addiction* [in Greek]. Athens: [s.n.].

Karabelas, L. (1985) *The Legislative Management of the Drug Problem* [in Greek]. Athens: Ant. N. Sakkoulas Publishers.

Karanikas, D. (1960) *Penal Law* [in Greek]. Athens: [s.n.].

Kleiman, M.A.R. (1992) *Against Excess: Drug Policy for Results*. New York: Basic Books.

Kolb, L. (1925) 'Drug-Addiction in its Relation to Crime', *Mental Hygiene* 9: 74–89.

Kotaridis, N. (1996) *Rebetes and Rebetika Songs* [in Greek]. Athens: Plethron.

Koukoutsaki, A. (ed.) (1999) *Images of Crime* [in Greek]. Athens: Plethron.

Koukoutsaki, A. (2002) *Use of Drugs and Homosexuality* [in Greek]. Athens: Kritiki.

Kouretas, D. and F. Skouras (1928) *Issues of Psychiatry: Studies in the Armed Forces* [in Greek]. Athens: [s.n.].

Koutsoumaris, A. (1932) 'The International Control on Illicit Drug Traffic and Greek Anti-narcotic Legislation' [in Greek], *Medical Journal*.

Lambropoulou, E. (2005) 'Crime, Criminal Justice and Criminology in Greece', *European Journal of Criminology* 2: 211–247.

Lindersmith, A.R. (1940) 'The Drug Addict as a Psychopath', *American Sociological Review* 5: 914–920.

Lindersmith, A.R. (1965) *The Addict and the Law*. New York: Vintage Books.

Mangone, G. J. (1958/1954) *A Short History of International Organisation*. New York: McGraw-Hill.

Marselos, M., Koutras, B., Yfantis, T., Kafetzopoulos, E., Fragidis, C. and M. Malamas (1988) 'Use and Abuse of Psychotropic Substances by High School Students' [in Greek], *Greek Review of Social Research* 71: 102–124.

May, H.L. (1958) 'The Evolution of the International Control of Narcotic Drugs', *United Nations Bulletin of Narcotics* IV.

Mitaftsis, K. (1932) *Textbook of Psychiatry* [in Greek]. Athens: [s.n.].

Mouzelis, N. (1978) *Modern Greece: Facets of Underdevelopment*. London: Macmillan.

Musto, D. (1973) *The American Disease: Origins of Narcotics Control*. New Haven: Yale University Press.

Panousis, G. (1981) *Narcotic Drugs* [in Greek]. Athens: Diogenes.

Paraskevopoulos, N. (1993) *Penal Repression of Drug Use in Greece* [in Greek]. Athens: Exandas.

Pavlou, S. (1997) *Narcotic Drugs* [in Greek]. Athens: Ant. N. Sakkoulas Publishers.

Pearson, G. (1999) 'Drugs at the End of the Century', *British Journal of Criminology* 39: 476–487.

Petropoulos, E. (1987) *Holy Hashish* [in Greek]. Athens: Nefeli.

Petropoulos, E. (1991) *Rebetika Songs* [in Greek]. Athens: Kedros.

Rado, S. (1933) 'The Psychoanalysis of Pharmacothymia', *Psychoanalytic Quarterly* 2: 1–23.

Schur, E. (1962) *Narcotics Addiction in Britain and America*. Bloomington, IN: Indiana University Press.

South, N. (1994) 'Drugs: Control, Crime and Criminological Studies', in M. Maguire, R. Morgan and R. Reiner (eds) *The Oxford Handbook of Criminology*, pp. 393–440. Oxford: Oxford University Press.

Stamatis, C. (1963) 'The Police in Piraeus: 1923–63' [in Greek], *Police Chronicles*.

Stamatis, C. (1965) 'The Police in Athens: 1925–65' [in Greek], *Police Chronicles*.

Stein, S. (1985) *International Diplomacy, State Administrators and Narcotics Control: The Origins of a Social Problem*. Aldershot: Gower.

Stimson, G. (1973) *Heroin and Behaviour*. Shannon: Irish University Press.

Strang, J. and M. Gossop (eds) (1993) *Responding to Drug Misuse: The British System*. Oxford: Oxford University Press.

Striggaris, M. (1937) *Hashish* [in Greek]. Athens: Saliveros.

Terry, C.E. and M. Pellens (1928) *The Opium Problem*. New York: The Committee on Drug Addictions, Bureau of Social Hygiene.

Terzidou, M. (2005) *2005 National Report to the EMCDDA: Greece – New Developments, Trends and In-depth Information on Selected Issues*. Athens: University Mental Health Research Institute.

Trebach, A. (1982) *The Heroin Solution*. Yale: Yale University Press.

Tsiganou, J. (2003) *Lawmaking on Drugs and Politics in Greece* [in Greek]. Athens: EKKE.

Tsiganou, J. (2005) 'Recording and Interpreting Crime Statistics: The Greek Case', in J. Kallas (ed.) *The Node for Secondary Processing: A Comparative Research Infrastructure* [in Greek], pp. 129–144. Athens: EKKE.

Tsili, S. (1995) *Drug Addiction as Ideological Hazard: The Case of Greece* [in Greek]. Athens: EKKE.

Tsili, S. (1999) 'Drug Addicts and Social Exclusion', in E. Katsoulis, D. Karantinos, L. Maratou and E. Fronimou (eds) *Dimensions of Social Exclusion in Greece* [in Greek], pp. 113–132. Athens: EKKE.

Tsilichristos, N. (1984) *Narcotic Drugs* [in Greek]. Athens: Theoria.

Walton, R.P. (1938) *Marihuana: America's New Drug Problem*. Philadelpia: Lippincott.

Young, J. (1971) *The Drugtakers*. London: Granada.

Zarafonitou, C. and J. Tsiganou (eds) (2002) *Narcotic Drugs* [in Greek]. Athens: Nomiki Vivliothiki.

TREVOR BENNETT

Commentary

The chapter by Joanna Tsiganou is a thought-provoking exposition of the recent history of drug policy in Greece. The main argument of the chapter is that domestic drugs policy in Greece has been shaped not so much by problems and harms caused by local drug misuse, but by global concerns and international controls relating to the world-wide drug trade. This is not an insignificant point. It raises all sorts of questions relating to the basis and integrity of local drug policies generally, and the extent to which they can be justified on the grounds of domestic concerns.

The first section of the argument discusses the history of drug control policy in Greece and the way in which it has been guided by the expansion in global technologies, guidance, and (with a possible touch of irony on the part of the author) 'enlightenment'. As a result of these and other forces, Greece transformed from a mildly tolerant society, which for much of the 19th century was a major producer and trader in hashish, to a country which criminalised drug misuse and sale, and administered heavy prison sentences to the most serious offenders. The second section looks more closely at the way in which the conventional response to drug use changed from the domain of the medical profession to that of the legal profession and the courts. Drug users had been fairly rapidly reconceptualised from being sick and needing medical help, to being criminals and needing punishment. The third section examines the rise, during the 20th century, in heroin use and the growth of the black market. The fourth section concludes with an appeal for better information on the way in which international controls impact on domestic policy and the extent to which they shape the attitudes and behaviours of people and their societies. The following will identify some of the discussion points raised in the chapter and consider what these might mean for our understanding of domestic and international drug policies.

Globalisation of Drug Policy

The first discussion point is the main argument of the chapter that domestic drugs policies are, at least in part, a product of international policies and concerns about the global drugs market. One implication of this is that domestic drugs policies are not wholly a reflection of the local drugs problems and needs of the individual countries. This raises questions about the factors that influence policy and the effect that these have on individual countries. Another implication is that the internationalisation and globalisation of drug policy is likely to result in a convergence of response with countries becoming more similar over time as global conceptions and practices begin to dominate. This, in turn, has the implication that local problems and policies become subordinated to the objectives and motives of global interests.

There is considerable evidence that domestic drug control policy is strongly informed by international controls. This can be seen through the lists of countries that sign up to the international treaties governing the distribution and trade in illegal drugs. Globalisation of technology also means that many countries have access to the latest intervention and treatment methods including drug testing, methadone treatment, and the use of opiate antagonists such as naltrexone and naloxone in the treatment of drug misuse. Global philosophies and perspectives also can be imported into the policy-making processes such as the international trend towards harm reduction and the rehabilitation and reintegration of drug offenders. In some senses, the drugs policies of individual Western countries are strikingly similar in the nature of the problems identified (focusing on heroin and cocaine as well as the other major stimulants), the prolific use of imprisonment for offences relating to the possession, sale, and distribution of these drugs, and the types of treatment programmes available ranging from methadone treatment to residential rehabilitation. This consensus is unlikely to have occurred without some kind of influence from external sources.

It is perhaps not surprising that there are also some differences between countries in their responses. Bennett and Holloway (2005) recently examined drug policies across several Western countries and found important differences. Sweden and the United States could be regarded as being at the 'tough' end of the spectrum. Sweden has made all forms of involvement with illegal drugs prohibited in law, including personal use. The United States invented the notion of a 'war on drugs', and gives particular emphasis to penal responses including interdiction, arrest, prosecution, and incarceration of users (Drug Policy Alliance, 2010). In contrast, Switzerland has a more 'lenient' approach and places its focus on drug users and reintegrating them back into society. The Netherlands has a similar approach based on the principle of harm reduction and the need to rehabilitate drug users and to integrate them into mainstream society.

As Tsiganou suggests, more needs to be known about the ways in which international policies are generated and the way in which they impact on domestic policies and more generally on the people and societies that implement them.

The Triumph of Criminalisation?

As with most histories of drugs control, the author draws on the concepts of 'criminalisation' and 'medicalisation' to explain policy developments, and notes in relation to Greece 'the continuous swinging between punitive and medical-oriented approaches (although policies are always resolved in favour of the former)'. The current discussion point takes the argument outside of Greece, and considers whether drug misuse and drug control policy in Western societies has generally become 'criminalised'.

It should first be mentioned that the distinction between criminalisation and medicalisation has a long history and it has not always been used to describe the way in which ostensibly medical problems have become criminalised. In its earliest forms, the concepts were used to describe the way in which ostensibly criminal problems became medicalised. This was particularly apparent in the increasing involvement of the medical profession in the criminal justice process in relation to mentally disordered offenders, sex offenders, and the early history of the changing aims of the prison system which gradually became more treatment-oriented (Conrad and Snyder, 1980). In the realm of drug policy, the concepts have been used predominantly to explain the increasing involvement of governments in taking control of drug misuse away from the medical profession by defining it as a criminal activity (Bennett and Holloway, 2005).

As Tsiganou's chapter points out, there is clear evidence of an expansion in the number of international agreements promoting legal controls and penalties as a means of controlling drug distribution and trade. There is also a substantial body of academic literature (especially from the US and the UK as well as other European countries) documenting the domestic expansion in the number of laws relating to drugs misuse as well as the increase in the number of new drugs that are regularly added to the list of prohibited substances. At the same time, many countries have experienced increases in the severity of penalties relating to breaches of these laws. It is tempting to conclude on the basis of this evidence that 'criminalisation' has triumphed as the dominant conception of drug use and control.

The main problem with this conclusion is integrating into it the fact that medical approaches to drug misuse and treatment not only still exist, but are also a central and expanding part of national responses to drug misuse. Even the strictest societies provide some kind of medical support for drug users, through methadone prescribing or detoxification programmes. The US and the UK, which at one level can be viewed as strong advocates of criminalisation, both run comprehensive treatment programmes for drug offenders within the criminal justice system, including the drug courts programmes of rehabilitation and integration in the US and the Drugs Interventions Programme in the UK (Bennett and Holloway, 2005). In turn, both countries subscribe to the concept of harm reduction as an important element of their drug policies. One of the principles of the approach is to reduce the problems of drug misuse through medical interventions rather than to remove them entirely through punitive measures.

The distinction between criminalisation and medicalisation has worked well in the past to summarise and explain policy developments over time. The current combination of policies and the general broadening of approaches have made the distinction less clear, and most modern societies include elements of both criminal and medical responses. Nevertheless, the conceptual framework remains compelling and continues to be used in academic debate. It is perhaps most useful in the current context to view these concepts as philosophical orientations rather than specific programmes or methods. Viewed in this sense, there are stronger grounds to argue that criminalisation has triumphed. To a large extent, medical approaches have been incorporated into the criminal justice system rather than the other way around. The current situation is not too different from the early use of the concept of medicalisation as a means of describing involvement of the medical profession in the implementation of the law. This discussion is picked up again in the next section in considering the meaning and implications of the concepts of coercive and non-coercive treatment.

Coercive versus Non-coercive Treatment

One of the problems with the concept of 'criminalisation' of drug misuse (as mentioned above) is that it invariably includes some kind of drug treatment. This means that drug treatment is a feature of a policy of both 'criminalisation' and 'medicalisation'. In order to clarify the distinction and to differentiate treatment of drug-misusing offenders in the criminal justice system and in the community, two new concepts have been devised, commonly referred to as 'coercive' and 'non-coercive treatment'. Coercive treatment is provided as part of the criminal justice process, whereas non-coercive treatment is used in the case of voluntary referrals. The distinction raises all sorts of questions for theory and practice.

The first is whether coercive treatment is in fact coercive. It falls under the general heading of diversion in the criminal justice system, and, as with other forms of diversion, the offender is given a choice. Drug-misusing offenders are typically offered at various stages in the criminal justice process an option to continue to be processed as normal or to be diverted to some kind of drug treatment. In the UK, this provision is made possible through the Drug Interventions Programme, which offers diversion points at arrest, at charge, at conviction, and during imprisonment. In the US, it is operated primarily through the drug courts and through the Tiers of Rehabilitation programme. It could be argued, therefore, that coercive treatment is not a matter of coercion, but a matter of choice. The counter-argument is that, while it is a matter of choice, it is not a free choice as it is made under constraint, and the options given are not treatment or no treatment, but treatment or punishment.

The second point is whether coercive treatment is in any way different from non-coercive treatment. In some ways, the two forms of treatment are the same. In both cases, drug users are provided with help and support, and sometimes medication, to help them abstain or reduce their drug use. The kinds of programmes offered to drug users within the criminal justice system are very similar to those offered to voluntary patients. The UK criminal justice system is based on the principle (through its system of programme accreditation) of offering some of the best-quality programmes currently available to prisoners and drug-misusing offenders, including family support programmes, counselling, cognitive behavioural therapy, mentoring, and so on. In fact, it could be argued that the treatment provided for drug users in the criminal justice system is better (because of the accreditation programme) and more available (in terms of the referral process) than can be obtained by users in the community. There are even stories of desperate drug users committing a crime as a means of obtaining access to treatment through the criminal justice system (Bennett and Holloway, 2009).

The use of these new concepts to differentiate forms of treatment in terms of their source draws attention to the increasing difficulties involved in identifying and distinguishing between the broad philosophies and practices of drug policies. The final discussion point considers whether the rise in the concept of evidence-based policy can help understand contemporary developments in international drugs policies.

Is Drugs Policy Evidence-based?

In the UK, and many western countries, drug policies and other government policies are justified on the grounds that they are based on evidence.
In the UK, all public services are expected to produce evidence-based policies to ensure that they are shaped by facts rather than opinion (Cabinet
Office, 1999). If this were so, then it would provide weight to the influence
of domestic drug problems and local solutions in guiding national drug
policies. This leads to the question of whether drugs policies are in fact
evidence-based or influenced by other, perhaps external, concerns.

In 2008, the UK government launched its most recent drugs strategy
which aimed to reduce drug misuse and to protect families and communities. As with other policies at the time, it was required that the strategy be
based on evidence. The strategy document contained many references to
research evidence and development of an evidence base. However, concerns
have been expressed in the literature that the commitment to evidence
expressed in policy documents was not wholly matched by the reality of
policy-making. A review of the government's strategy concluded that the
government's commitment to evidence-based policy has been called into
question on many occasions and was concerned to hear 'allegations from
certain academics that departments have been commissioning and publishing research selectively in order to "prop up" policies' (Science and Technology Committee, 2006: 49). Another review of current drugs policy by
Bennett and Holloway (2010) concluded that the current policy documents
contained many references to evidence. However, there was some concern
about the way in which the research evidence was selected and interpreted.
In half of the cases investigated, there was bias in terms of research study
selection and misrepresentation of the research conclusions.

It is doubtful whether any drugs policy could be *wholly* evidence-
based, and there is some scepticism that it could be even *mainly* evidence-
based. The research suggests that government policy is a product of many
influences and objectives, and (as suggested in Tsiganou's chapter) political
pressures and processes will also play an important and sometimes overarching role in this process.

Conclusion

The primary chapter identifies key policy issues relating to Greece and embeds these into broader drugs policy debates. The main argument of the paper is that domestic drugs policy might be shaped not so much by local drug problems and responses, but by global concerns and international controls. This is an important point which raises many direct and indirect issues. The direct issues concern the extent to which the observations in Greece are applicable to other countries, the extent to which international policy shapes domestic responses, and the effect of the internationalisation of policy on the perceptions, attitudes, and behaviour of individuals and societies affected by them. The indirect issues include those raised in the discussion above, such as what does this mean for traditional methods of conceptualising drugs policy in terms of criminalisation and medicalisation, what is understood by, and known about, coercive drug treatment, how does it differ from non-coercive treatment, and what do the author's conclusions mean for the concept of evidence-based policy?

It is not the task of the discussant to answer all of the questions raised. This would be difficult in relation to the complexity of the topic and impossible in the space remaining in a conclusion. Nevertheless, it is worth mentioning some possible directions. The first has already been made by Tsiganou in that more needs to be known about the way in which international policies interact with domestic policies, and the ways in which these act upon societies and the individuals within them. The second is that these issues could be more profitably discussed if more research were done on the decision-making processes of governments at all levels of policy-making. Case studies of specific examples of policy generation would be useful in identifying the interplay between national and international interests as well as the role of evidence and politics in this process. The third concluding point is that more research needs to be done on the characteristics of post-modern societies, a strong feature of which is the trend towards globalisation and internationalism, as well as the subversion of local interests to broader concerns. A better understanding of the global context might be the key to taking forward the current debate relating to the origins and motives of international drugs policy and its assimilation into domestic controls.

References

Bennett, T.H. and K. Holloway (2005) *Understanding Drugs, Alcohol and Crime*. Buckingham: McGraw-Hill/Open University Press.

Bennett, T.H. and K. Holloway (2009) 'The Causal Connection Between Drug Use and Crime', *British Journal of Criminology* 49: 513–531.

Bennett, T.H. and K. Holloway (2010) 'Is UK Drug Policy Evidence-Based?', *International Journal of Drug Policy* 21: 411–417.

Cabinet Office (1999) *Modernising Government*. London: The Stationery Office.

Conrad, P. and J.W. Schneider (1980) *Deviance and Medicalisation: From Badness to Sickness*. St Louis: C.V. Mosby Company.

Drug Policy Alliance (2010) *Drug Policy Around the World: United States*. Available online at: www.lindesmith.org/global/drugpolicyby/northamerica/unitedstates/ (Accessed 6 June 2010)

Science and Technology Committee (2006) *Scientific Advice, Risk and Evidence Based Policy-Making. Seventh Report of Session 2005–06*. London: The Stationery Office.

SAPPHO XENAKIS

Organised Crime and Political Violence

Internationally and domestically, Greeks have long been bound by a reputation for unruliness (see discussion in Xenakis, 2010). Insidious, multi-dimensional forms of organised crime, as well as regular incidences of political violence perpetrated by non-state groups against property and, less frequently, against symbolic human targets, together embody the most extreme forms of illegality commonly believed to bedevil Greece. Additionally spurred by the intensification of international attention upon organised crime and terrorism in recent years, these issues have become prominent public concerns in Greece, alongside – if sometimes overshadowed by – foreign affairs, immigration, and public corruption. Given the overview of state legislative efforts to combat the phenomena as presented elsewhere in this collection (by Mitsilegas), this chapter aims to contextualise and review long-term trends and typologies of organised illicit economic and violent political activities, as well as practical state efforts to counter them. The chapter begins with an outline and explanation of the politics surrounding official efforts to characterise these two challenges as a single problem. The chapter moves on to provide overviews of the recent history of organised crime and political violence by non-state groups in contemporary Greece. It concludes with a comment on the debates that have surrounded the evolution of organised crime and political violence over the past twenty years.

A necessary prerequisite of this exploration is clarification of the subject parameters, given that both 'organised crime' and 'political violence' may be interpreted in so many different ways. This chapter will explore the applicability of two, overlapping interpretations of 'organised crime' to the Greek context. Firstly, the relevance to Greek realities of what could be called a 'traditional' notion of organised crime *qua* mafia will be addressed. Such an approach generally tends to privilege the role of geographically and socially rooted groups that straddle licit and illicit worlds, for whom shared identity constitutes an important plank of group cohesiveness, and who may enjoy a close, if hidden, relationship with key elite power-holders (official, political, and financial).[1] Secondly, the chapter will address the notion of organised crime *qua* illegal market activity, involving transnational networks that transport illicit cargo and corrupt lower-level state officials who facilitate (or 'tax') such trade. International and European agreements have favoured an expansive conceptual and legal definition of the phenomenon that encompasses 'structured group[s] of three or more persons existing for a period of time and acting in concert with the aim of committing one or more serious crimes [...] in order to obtain, directly or indirectly, a financial or other material benefit' (UN Convention against Transnational Crime, 2000, Article 2a). According to this definition, 'serious crime' denotes 'conduct constituting an offence punishable by a maximum deprivation of liberty of at least four years or a more serious penalty'. This approach has the quality of facilitating the study of the amorphous nature and breadth of criminal markets and their protagonists (as outlined by Edwards and Gill (2002), for example, it can encompass street-level, 'organised', and 'white collar' crimes). In practice, however, the approach has overwhelmingly been used to focus on the weaker, more evident and punishable participants in illicit markets, becoming practically fused in official analyses with the policing of small groups and gangs of ethnic subalterns. With regard to the Greek context in particular, the flexibility of this approach to organised crime has appeared to leave little that necessarily falls outside its definition, apart from crimes perpetrated by individuals or groups of two people, or those defined as terrorism.[2] Such approaches have

1   The closer the organised criminal group to state power, the stronger and more serious its potential political and financial impact. On the application of the term 'organised crime' to denote illicit entrepreneurial activity that is embedded in the legal economy and crucially operates with the support of corrupt government officials, legitimate businessmen, and politicians, see, e.g., Lyman and Potter (1997).

2   Greek Law (Law 2928/2001 and Article 187 of the Penal Code) characterises organised crime as 'a structured group with constant action consisting of three or more persons', in order to commit crimes (counterfeiting, forgery, grand theft, bribery,

fuelled fears of the reach and threat posed by organised crime (not least due to the high numbers of organised crime groups identified by the police each year), at the same time as reasserting the comfortable paradigm of its perpetration by society's more easily identifiable and punishable 'outsiders'. In this chapter, the costs to definitional clarity of seeking to straddle the mafia and enterprise definitions of organised crime will hopefully be outweighed by the enhanced potential for cross-national and theoretical comparability that this offers.

With regard to political violence, this term is used in order to maintain a wider scope for analysis than that suggested by 'terrorism' alone, and therefore uses both whilst seeking to circumvent unnecessary controversy. The aim here is to sketch the field of sub-state actors employing physical violence with overt political rationales, rather than to dwell upon the attachment of particular labels denoting gradations of illegitimacy or immorality to different groups. This chapter focuses primarily upon non-state groups involved in political violence in Greece (on the intersections of non-state and state violence in Greece, see further Xenakis, under review). Preliminary acknowledgement is due of the particular distinctions made between *political crime* and *terrorism* in Greek Law. The Greek Constitution offers elements of protection to 'political crime', if ones shrouded by legal opacity. Political crime is not defined in the Constitution itself, and has thus been a matter of considerable contention. As upheld by the Greek Courts in their judgment of 2003 that the crimes of the Revolutionary Organisation November 17 (17N) be considered 'common' rather than 'political', the consensus that spans the greater part of legal opinion in Greece is that the characterisation of a crime as 'political' is conditional upon both

---

arson and other broad forms of destruction – such as through flooding, the use of explosives, shipwrecking, mass poisoning – tampering with the security of public transport, murder, and other forms of serious physical violence, kidnap, rape, sexual assault, and sexual abuse of minors, as well as illicit trafficking of drugs, trafficking and use of arms, and explosive and radioactive materials), punishable with up to ten years of imprisonment. Further details of the legal provisions against organised crime are listed in the 2004 annual report on organised crime of the Hellenic Police (Hellenic Police, 2005: 36).

the means and the ends of the act in question (*Kathimerini*, 23 October 2003; on 17N see further Kassimeris (2001) and below). It is not enough for a crime to be perpetrated with a political goal in mind; firstly, the goal of those instigating the crime must be the overturning or undermining of the state; and secondly, with regard to the 'means', the 'victim' of the act can only be the state, and cannot comprise non-state, private actors, or individuals (see Symeonidou-Kastanidou, 2007: 147–152; Tsoulos, 2005: 117–120; and Manoledakis, 2002: 205–206). Constitutional protection for political crime consists of the right to trial by jury, and the potential for limiting the imposition of penalties for crimes committed.[3] In contrast, although political character may be admitted in the inspiration of terrorist acts, it is the targeting of non-state actors that legitimates a more punitive response from the state, including those provided more recently by the laws 2928/2001 and 3251/2004 on organised crime and terrorism, respectively (see further Kyritsis, 2005; and Mitsilegas, this collection).

Tying Organised Crime to Terrorism in Policy-Making

Tying organised crime to terrorism for the purposes of analysis and remedial policy-planning is, like so many aspects of these subjects, a hotly debated political issue. On the one hand, opponents of the effort to conjoin the two have argued that such steps conflate very different types of activities. From this critical perspective, organised crime and terrorism are clearly distinguishable by their primary motivations: material versus political. Furthermore, such a distinction is vital to the development of deeper understanding

---

3   Article 47 paragraph 3 of the Greek Constitution affords the Greek Parliament the power to offer amnesty to an individual convicted of a political crime, as determined by a stringent majority vote procedure; Article 62 extends the immunity of parliamentary deputies in cases of political crime; Article 97 provides that political crimes be judged by jury.

that necessarily underpins successful efforts to combat the phenomena. Indeed, such distinctions can be exploited by the state in order to reduce the challenges posed; for example, separating political from economically motivated interests was apparently part of a relatively successful strategy to bring about greater stability in Northern Ireland over the 1990s. Whilst fully congruent with other expansive trends in contemporary security theorising and policy-planning that are typically denoted by the epithet 'risk', and despite typically being cushioned by proclamations of fidelity to scientific methodologies, notions of a common symbiosis between organised crime and terrorism are challenged for their weak empirical bases and their fundamental disinterest in rigorous empirical underpinnings (see Hebenton and Thomas, 1995). As Edwards and Gill (2003) conclude, although in certain cases organised criminal and terrorist groups and activities are known to be intimately bound together, this is not so in much of the world.

Today, however, the reverse logic is increasingly privileged in dominant discourse on the subject; that organised crime and terrorism have become ever more intertwined since the 1990s, to the point where they should today be conceived of as poles of a continuum, rather than as characteristically different threats that only sporadically or superficially interact or converge (see, for example, Shelley, 2002; Makarenko, 2005). From this perspective, the assumption that such a continuum exists is a necessary precondition for successful state counter-operations. The Greek context appears to offer an interesting variation from this general trend. In Greece, the legitimacy of studying organised crime and terrorism together has not stemmed from any dominant consensus that the two are significantly interrelated in practice. Even whilst a consensus along these lines has been growing, it has largely been regarded as commonsensical that the two are, and have been, clearly distinguishable, even if it is also believed that they have overlapped at times and – according at least to some experts – should be appreciated as being more comparable than they have generally been (see, for example, *Kathimerini*, 8 July 2009, 27 October 2009). At the most basic level, organised crime and terrorism are distinguished by their symptomatic activities, whether those be in the profitable criminal fields of drugs, weapons, or people smuggling, for example, or in the execution of symbolic acts of violence against so-designated 'establishment' targets, respectively. And yet, organised crime and terrorism have been inextricably linked both in successive pieces of counter-legislation formulated by government and in the political debates that have accompanied them. Perhaps more interesting still is that the Greek state was initially motivated to link the two *before* strong international pressure for policy harmonisation along these lines gained momentum. The position of Greece was not determined at its outset by foreign pressure, but rather – as with other examples of Greek policy-making today – took policy inspiration from the international stage to a more dramatic end and with particular domestic objectives in mind.

A Brief Review of Policy

The first step taken towards the overt linking of organised crime and terrorism in Greek legislation was in 1990 with the passing of Law 1916 'For the Protection of Society from Organised Crime' under the government of the conservative New Democracy party. The introduction of the Law followed the steady growth in both anti-terrorist and anti-organised crime legislation and accords in and between other European jurisdictions since the late 1970s, and such precedents were cited in the explanations proffered by Greek officials of why the country needed to 'catch up' in this regard (see further Livos, 2007). The notion that Greek experiences of organised crime or terrorism could be deemed comparable with those of other European states was scorned by the legislation's critics, who pointed to radical differences between the respective histories of terrorism and organised crime of Greece, in contrast with those of such states as Germany, Italy, and France (Kassimeris, 2001: 173–181). Both the focus of the political furore that preceded its conception, as well as its key prescription criminalising the publishing of terrorist proclamations, demonstrated that the primary impetus and focus of the legislation was local political violence rather than organised crime *per se* (see also Mitsilegas, this collection; and Livos, 2007). Evident also was the futility of the attempt to court public support and avoid political controversies by forgoing counter-terrorism for counter-organised crime in the title of the legislation, that particular aspect of the public relations effort being immediately sidelined by supporters and opponents alike in the furious debate that erupted around the proposed measures. The backlash against the legislation was swift and comparatively durable; upon taking office in 1992, the government of the centre-left PASOK party (Panhellenic Socialist Movement) carried out its promise to annul the legislation, doing so in 1993. Until 2001, there were no further efforts to tie organised crime and terrorism in legislation. In 1997, indeed, Minister of Public Order Georgios Romaios not only rejected the notion of a connection between organised crime and terrorism in Greece, but also denied that there was serious organised crime in the country (*To Vima*, 12 October 1997; see also Livos, 2007: 64). Nevertheless, familiar steps continued to be taken by the government during this period, if with a somewhat lower profile, as demonstrated by the establishment of an official anti-terrorism think-thank titled 'The Scientific Committee for the Analysis, Investigation, and Planning against Organised Crime', by Minister of Order Stelios Papathemelis, which ran between 1994 and 1996.[4]

The next occasion that proposals for new legislation against both organised crime and terrorism were put forward, this time by a PASOK government, there was equally short-lived timidity about linking the issues. In late November 2000, the Ministry of Justice set up a Special Committee to draft the legislation, which at least two of the invited participants – professors of Law from the University of Thessaloniki – had been given to understand would address the penal suppression of organised crime. The latter were only acquainted with the broader scope of the Committee's work at the first meeting itself, stimulating their swift resignations in

---

4   The think-tank, which received support from the US Anti-Terrorism Assistance programme, was directed by the academic and government advisor Dr Mary Bossi. It was dissolved in September 1996, due (according to Bossi) to confusion and absence of a unified strategic plan, lapses in communication, and animosity between academics and law enforcement officers (see further Kassimeris, 2001: 196). Bossi was subsequently targeted by the group 'Fighting Rebel Formation' (*Mahomenos Antartikos Schimatismos*, or *M.A.S.*), which placed a bomb at her house for her role in 'legitimating' the counter-terror policy of the Greek state (Tsoulos, 2005: 8–10).

protest against what they saw as unnecessary legislative elaborations that would function to restrict civil rights (Manoledakis, 2002). Even following three further resignations from the Committee (by individuals who also apparently supported the development of legislation against organised crime but not additionally against terrorism), the last remaining cohort apparently *still* favoured a division in the treatment of organised crime and terrorism, despite accepting the need for new legislation on each.[5]

It was sheer pressure from the Minister of Justice, Michalis Stathopoulos, a former Dean of Athens University and Professor of Civil Law, that ensured a single piece of legislation combining both issues (what was to become Law 2928/2001) was drafted in the small timeframe accorded for the Committee's work (the Committee sitting only from December 2000 to February 2001, according to Manoledakis, 2002). That the Justice Minister held firm in the face of the significant public protest that ensued was all the more notable given his admission that he himself had frequently argued that Greece's legal framework on these issues should be regarded as adequate (see the interview of Stathopoulos in *Athens News*, 20 April 2001). But there was also reportedly great pressure placed on Stathopoulos by the Prime Minister, Costas Simitis, and by the Minister of Public Order, Michalis Chrysohoidis, to produce the desired legislative result swiftly, to such an extent that rumours briefly surfaced of an impeding resignation by the Justice Minister (*Athens News*, 3 March 2001). Likewise, Chrysohoidis, as with the overall administration of PASOK, had been under considerable sustained international pressure – particularly by the US and the UK – to the same end. Although the government, Stathopoulos, and members of the Special Committee responsible for drafting the legislation, all rejected the accusation of critics that policy was in any way either 'scripted' or significantly influenced by the lobbying of foreign governments, something akin to a 'domino effect' does appear to be fairly easily traceable along the path of policy pressure and legislative outcomes (see further Xenakis, 2004, 2006).

5   Interview with Nicholas Livos, one of the seven-member Committee that drafted the law, cited in Xenakis (2004, 2006).

By 2000, the desirability of new legislation against organised crime had become a point of consensus amongst experts and officials alike, and whilst the new legislation did introduce a detailed framework that largely focused upon countering the activities of criminal organisations, the principal target of Law 2928 'For the Protection of the Citizen from Punishable Offences of Criminal Organisations', was nevertheless widely interpreted to be political violence, as encapsulated in its popular renaming as the 'Tromonomos' ('terror-law') (Xenakis, 2004, 2006). The Law introduced to the Greek penal code the notion of equivalence between terrorism and organised crime by omitting the identification of secondary (motivational) aims in the characterisation of the criminal act, thus making irrelevant the act's underlying rationale, whether political or economic. This was an audacious legislative advance that exceeded the ambitions of European and UN Conventions, given that the latter did include secondary (financial) motivations in their definitions of organised crime. That the Law introduced trial by judge for such 'organised' crimes cemented common perceptions that its chief purpose was to lay the ground for the anticipated arrest and trial of members of 17N, which actually took place over the course of 2003. This procedural innovation was viewed by many as a direct challenge to the Constitutional proscription that political crimes be tried by mixed jury courts composed of regular judges and jurors (see also above). During the trial of 17N, despite the acknowledgement of the presiding judge that the defendants could not be labeled 'common criminals' because – as he concurred – they had been motivated by a certain 'vision', the court rejected the argument made by the defence that the group's crimes were political, since their acts were not directed explicitly against the state (see Xenakis, 2006: 180–181).

Whether or not 17N were an organised crime group, terrorists, or urban guerrillas – long a matter of contention in Greek political discourse – thus became a central debate enveloping their trial. Over its twenty-seven years of existence, 17N killed twenty-three people in targeted assassinations, in addition to carrying out dozens of small-scale attacks using rockets and improvised explosive devices. Its targets were chosen according to the relation they were judged to have with the forms of imperialism and corruption that the organisation sought to destabilise, whether Greek,

US, British, Turkish, or NATO. That the group avoided mass casualties and had no evident intent to terrorise the public, however, had served to foster apathy amongst both state officials and the general public, as well as the sympathies of a considerable minority, raising consequential questions about the validity of their labeling as terrorists (see, e.g., Pollis, 2002; Karyotis, 2007). According to a public opinion poll taken only a few months before the capture of 17N members, whilst nine out of ten disagreed with the 'tactics' and 'means' of 17N, one in four supported the positions of the organisation, and only two percent of those polled considered terrorism to be a 'real threat' in Greece (*Eleftherotypia*, 19 April 2002). In light of this poll, the government's choice of wording for Law 2928/2001 ('for the protection of the citizen') could thus be viewed as a striking, if not entirely effective, move to reshape and consolidate public perceptions of the threat posed by terrorism-as-organised-crime, as one directed primarily against themselves, the Greek citizenry, rather than against the more abstract and less intimate conceptions of Greek 'society' or the 'state'. After the capture of group members, and once it was revealed that they had robbed banks in order to raise funds for their activities, some felt that the question of the group's character was definitively answered; their commitment to revolutionary ideology was finally, demonstrably, moribund, and they could be regarded simply as pathological criminals (see, for example, *Kathimerini*, 9 June 2002). For others, even if materialism had not driven the group's actions (it was revealed that members had lived neither ostentatiously nor in significant wealth), ultimate testament to the shallowness of their convictions was provided by the way in which a number of the group had denied affiliation after arrest (see, e.g., *Kathimerini*, 23 July 2002).

The passing of Law 3251/2004 on the 'European Arrest Warrant, Amendment of Law 2989/2001 on Criminal Organisations and Other Legal Provisions', which introduced a separate definition and criminalisation of 'terrorism', did not appear to bring about a disentanglement of the two subjects in the eyes of the state. After the arrest and imprisonment of 17N members, the debate concerning the entrepreneurial character of political crime and the relations between politically- and profit-motivated criminals grew all the stronger as extreme forms of organised non-state political violence resurfaced. The terms of the debate shifted, too, with the relationship between organised illicit economic and political activities becoming more commonly considered. Indeed, a question underpinning much subsequent public discussion about the resurgence of organised non-state political violence has been the extent to which the same individuals or groups have carried out both economic and political illegal activities, or are distinguishable but co-operate as and when necessary (see also above). In July 2009, soon after reports of police investigations into connections between an organised crime gang involved in kidnaps and robberies, and the weaponry used by a number of small domestic terrorist groups, the government of New Democracy announced that the recently re-shaped National Intelligence Agency (EYP) would have a new focus on organised crime, terrorism, and the relationship between the two (*Kathimerini*, 8 July 2009, 20 July 2009). In November 2009, two months after a PASOK government had been elected, Michalis Chrysohoidis, heading the newly formed 'Citizen's Protection Ministry', signaled his intention to reform the police in such a way that would facilitate their investigation of 'organised crime and its connections to domestic terrorist groups'. This, he emphasised, would be 'the key focus' of their work (*Kathimerini*, 10 November 2009).

As this brief review illustrates, the Greek state has increasingly viewed domestic organised crime and terrorism as intertwined problems. The approach of Greek governments has appeared to evolve from superficial consideration of organised crime as a way in which to 'sell' counter-terror policies to the public in the early 1990s, to an enthusiasm, visible today, for addressing the particular challenges posed by each, as well as treating them as significantly interrelated phenomena. While such enthusiasm may have been constructed for the purpose of 'selling' the image of a modernised and effective Greek state to foreign and domestic audiences, it has also attracted a wide range of ideationally-committed supporters from the fields of the police, law, academia, and the media (see Xenakis, 2006). Furthermore (and despite criticisms of government reticence in some areas), that such support continued to grow in the aftermath of the Athens Olympics of 2004 – when the pressure placed by the demands of organisational planning, political prestige, and foreign governments, had largely subsided – demonstrates the state's success in normalising the notion that organised crime and terrorism be addressed together. The extent to which such an approach is appropriate in the Greek context will be examined below through discussion of the commonalities and dissimilarities of what is known of organised criminal and politically violent actors, with the caveat that so long as these groups remain at large, there is restricted scope for this question to be answered entirely reliably or comprehensively.

A Brief Overview of Organised Crime in Greece

One of the central debates over organised crime in Greece concerns the date and source of its emergence as a 'serious problem'. One oft-cited limitation in answering this conundrum is that official data on organised crime in Greece, which began to be collected in the mid-1990s, have not been regarded as particularly reliable in the early years, even by the police themselves (see Xenakis, 2004, 2006). Furthermore, independent analyses are rare; the Greek police have more frequently and easily passed details of their organised crime analyses to trusted journalists than made them available to researchers by standardised means (see further Lambropoulou, 2003; Papanicolaou, 2008).[6] Notwithstanding the potential critique posed by securitisation theory (Buzan *et al.*, 1998) – that the emergence of serious organised crime in Greece has owed more to subjective analytical constructions than to the accurate discovery of any new objective reality –, the debate is valuable in shedding light on the ways in which organised crime is understood, and feared, in the country. The Greek public has certainly demonstrated a striking level of concern about organised crime: results of the Eurobarometer public opinion surveys across EU member states between 1995 and 2003 indicate that Greek citizens were consistently and considerably more concerned about organised crime and drug trafficking than the average EU citizen, whilst in 2002 Greeks polled top

6   For example, only the 2004 and 2005 Annual Reports on Organised Crime in Greece are publicly available online.

amongst their EU counterparts in agreeing that organised crime had infil-
trated the national economy and society (see further discussion in Xenakis,
2006: 186–187). This trend was overturned in 2004, when Greek concerns
about crime dropped below the European average, and only saw sharp rise
again in 2009.[7]

For a country in which entrenched patronage, clientelism, and corruption more generally, have typically been used to characterise the relationship
between political, business, and media elites, one may well wonder how
'organised crime' emerged as such a prominent and widespread anxiety, and
how it has been understood. In short, the answer is that in distinction to
political corruption and financial crimes engaged in by members of Greek
elites, 'organised crime' has been popularly characterised as the crime of
foreigners *par excellence*. Just as with the reported pronouncement of the
newly-elected Prime Minister Costas Karamanlis in 2004 that he would
tackle the 'five davatzides' ('pimps') that were 'effectively running the country' – alluding to key moguls of Greek industry and media with close ties
to government –, so too with the recent pronouncement by Minister of
Citizens' Protection Chrysohoidis, that organised crime and corruption
should be treated as equivalent crimes by law, and that economic crimes
would become more significant in organised crime investigations by the
Greek police: such aspirations have evidently reflected popular acknowledgement of some overlap between the concepts of elite corruption and
'organised crime'.[8] Both aspirations and acknowledgement have nevertheless remained clearly overwhelmed by a primary concern with illegal
immigration and the networks of organised illegality that are believed to
be associated with it.

---

7   Full details of the surveys are available from the European Commission website at:
     http://ec.europa.eu/public_opinion/standard_en.htm. The sharp rise in recorded
     fear of crime in 2009 may have been propelled in large part by the unrest experienced
     across Greece in December 2008. For analysis of the reasons for comparatively high
     levels of reported fear of organised crime in Greece, see Xenakis (2006: 186–189)
8   Although Karamanlis' words were widely reported, his aides later denied he had used
     the term (*BBC*, 14 December 2008; *Kathimerini*, 7 October 2004). See further an
     interview with Michalis Chrysohoidis in *To Vima* (12 July 2009).

Thus it is that organised crime has so often been portrayed as a novel import brought to Greece by the influx of immigrants in the 1990s. Before that time it is often suggested that there was little or no 'ethnic Greek' organised crime within Greece, and this only developed – if it did so – as a response to the economic and security competition posed by criminal immigrant groups to local Greek businesses.[9] That this 'new' organised crime has also been portrayed as more 'serious' than prior forms of organised criminality in Greece seems to based upon the perception that the former involves unprecedented levels of violence (as apparently supported by official data; Lambropoulou, 2002).[10] There has been no appreciable evidence of any increased likelihood of violence being perpetrated against those who are not gang members. Nonetheless, official and public concerns appear to have been fortified by the thought that larger numbers of groups involved in the use of violence have increased the general level of threat posed to society.

9   E.g., Mary Bossi, interviewed by the author on 5 September 2002. The same year, Minister of Public Order Michalis Chrysohoidis also reportedly stated that 'organised crime was a problem imported into Greece' (*Athens News Agency*, 2002). See also Bossi (1999: 245–246), and further discussion and citation of other interviewees – from the media and the Greek state – with similar perspectives, in Xenakis (2006: 110) and Antonopoulos (2009).

10 Whilst earlier annual reports on organised crime by the Greek police, such as those of 1997 and 1999 (see further Lambropoulou, 2002: 263; Lambropoulou, 2003: 82), suggest that the use of violence by organised crime groups was rare and restricted to those comprised of 'ethnic Greeks' (see further below), later reports, such as that of 2004, also reported on the ruthlessness of physical violence perpetrated by Albanian, Bangladeshi, Chinese, Greek-Moldavian, Greek-Ukrainian, Greek-Romanian and Russian, Greek Iranian, and Pakistani, as well as Greek gangs (MPO, 2005: 28). More common, however, have been commentaries that under-emphasise the comparative violence of ethnic Greek organised crime groups. See, for example, the summary provided online by the Greek Embassy based in Washington D.C. of the 2004 Annual Report on Organised Crime, at: http://www.greekembassy.org/Embassy/Content/en/Article.aspx?office=3&folder=844&article=15348; and a summary outlining the threat of organised crime as advertised by a web-based company selling home and business security technologies in Greece, available online at: http://www.mat-security.com/news/ayxisi-toy-organomenou-eglimatos/

The 'absence' of organised crime in Greece prior to the influx of migrants that began in the 1990s – and, for some, the continued dearth of 'ethnic Greek' organised crime groups – may best be explained via the prism of securitisation. It is not that there has been any shortage of willingness on the part of commentators to entertain the notion that a criminal conspiracy, with specific if unknown figureheads, has lain behind public-sector scandals and failures alike. Whenever such scandals have broken, however, media revelations never seem to satisfy common expectations of what organised crime looks like, whether that be a mafia-style, close-knit group of kith and kin, or a durable, broad-spanned, centrally-planned business (see, for example, discussion in *To Vima*, 22 May 2005; and comment in Antonopoulos, 2009: 3). No insights into the workings of the famously 'intermeshed interests' of Greek elites have sufficiently conformed to one or other accepted image of 'organised crime'; neither scandals concerning the illicit monopolisation of markets though price-fixing (e.g., the MEVGAL affair), nor of public-private collusion through bribes-for-contracts over a number of years (such as the Siemens scandal), nor of networks of corruption involving the sale of state assets (e.g., the Vatopedi scandal), nor unsolved cases of apparently organised violence and intimidation against trade and prisoners' rights activists (as alleged in the Kuneva and Goulioni affairs).[11] For the majority of Greeks, none of the above has been obviously recognisable as organised crime.

---

11   In the MEVGAL scandal, seven Greek dairy companies were fined €50 million by the country's Competition Commission for forming a cartel. Two state officials from the Competition Commission and Customs, as well as a businessman, were also found guilty of colluding to secure a €2.5 million bribe so that MEVGAL could avoid being fined for price-fixing (*Kathimerini*, 14 April 2009). In the Siemens scandal, a former executive of the German firm testified at a trial in Germany that the company had paid in excess of €1 billion in bribes to both New Democracy and PASOK parties in order to secure contracts in which they would supply electronics equipment for the Greek state telecoms operator and for the security effort for the Athens Olympic Games (see *The Economist*, 11 September 2008). The Vatopedi scandal erupted when it was revealed that valuable state land had been traded for less valuable land held by a monastery on Mount Athos, at an estimated loss to the Greek state of €100 million (for a brief introduction to the scandal, see *BBC News*, 23 October 2008). Konstantina

'Greek' Organised Crime

To the extent that a notion of home-grown organised crime has been associated with Greeks in Greece, it has most typically been identified as extortion and smuggling rackets run by so-called 'godfathers of the night', particularly concentrated in the casino, clubland and brothel districts of Athens and its outskirts, but also affecting shops, restaurants, bars, and bouzouki music venues, as well as betting shops and football clubs across the capital and in Greece's second largest city of Thessaloniki (see Lambropoulou, 2003; *To Vima*, 6 April 2008). Since the end of the military dictatorship in 1974, police and media reports of such forms of criminal entrepreneurialism have been relatively common, and have outlined the fluctuating patterns of competition and co-operation between groups, their capture by the police, and replacement in the market by other gangs (*To Vima*, 13 September 2009). Recognition of the extensiveness of organised criminal activity in such markets has nevertheless been little reflected in the priorities of Greek law

---

Kuneva, a Bulgarian migrant worker and General Secretary of the Athens-based 'All Attica Union of Cleaners and Domestic Workers' (PEKOP), was the victim of an attack in December 2008, in which she was sprayed with, and made to drink, sulphuric acid, resulting in the loss of one eye and her larynx, as well as other permanent serious health problems. The attack followed an escalation in tensions with her employer (Oikomet, a cleaning firm subcontracted by the Athens-Piraeus Electric Railway Company 'ISAP'), including death threats against her, relating to her work in defending the rights of migrant workers and fighting for better conditions and pay (see her interview in Delorme, 2009). According to Amnesty International, the official investigation into the attack has been 'neither thorough nor objective' (AIUK, 2009). Katerina Goulioni was a prisoner activist for the improvement of prison conditions, particularly the abolition of mandatory vaginal inspections in jail. Following her campaigning on the issue, Goulioni was being transferred to another prison when, in transit, she died. According to witnesses, Goulioni's hands had been tied behind her back, and she had been instructed to sit apart from other prisoners during the journey by the police guard, but had subsequently been found dead, allegedly with blood on her face. According to a toxicology report commissioned by the State, she died of heart failure caused by drug use (*Eleftherotypia*, 14 April 2009). The Kuneva and Goulioni affairs appear reminiscent of the 1950s Italian experience of mafia involvement in the suppression of trade union activities, as outlined by Arlacchi (1986).

enforcement agencies in addressing organised crime (see Vidali, 2009). In 2007, the reported average 'protection fee' enforced by such gangs in Athens ranged from €600 per month for coffee shops, to €5,000 per month for bouzouki music clubs.[12] More significant sources of income have been said to include the smuggling of commodities such as drugs, oil, and contraband cigarettes, the supply of Eastern European women and adulterated alcoholic drinks to bars and nightclubs and match-fixing, whilst profits are laundered through the ownership of nightclubs, sports clubs, and other businesses (*BBC News*, 25 June 2011, Lambropoulou, 2006; *Kathimerini*, 12 July 2002, 2 February 2007). Groups have employed violence – from mistreatment and torture to arson to assassination – against gang members, rivals and extortion victims. By 2008, feuding between certain groups (variously portrayed as beginning in 1997, or being decades old), in which twenty-five people were said to have been killed, was thought to be intensifying (*Kathimerini*, 11 November 2008; *To Vima*, 6 April 2008).

Speculation has varied as to the numbers of individuals involved in such activities. According to some reports, considerably more 'godfathers' and their associate groups have been identified by the police than have been imprisoned. In 2002, in a move that was heralded as the end of four long-standing crime gangs in Attica (Athens and its outskirts), the police prosecuted forty-four individuals (*Kathimerini*, 12 July 2002). During the same period, criminologist Effi Lambropoulou suggested that seven gangs were estimated to be operating across Greece (Lambropoulou, 2003). By 2003, however, only 'two or three' related individuals were in prison. Explanations for the arguably low rate of imprisonment have included the difficulty of securing witness testimony against gang members, the practice of providing immunity from prosecution to informers, and the protection provided to gangs by corrupt members of the police. Even in cases where 'godfathers' have been jailed, reports commonly suggest that they often continue to run their criminal businesses from prison (*To Vima*, 21 September 2003; *To Vima*, 6 April 2008). Conversely, concerns about the low imprisonment

---

12 Figures provided by convicted gang member George Hatzopoulos during an interview he gave whilst in prison (*Kathimerini*, 2 February 2007).

rate may have been unduly exacerbated by the characterisation of *all* members of gangs as 'godfathers' (see, e.g., Lampropoulou, 2003). Interestingly, however, their corrupt official accomplices have rarely, if ever, been labelled godfathers themselves, underlining the way in which godfathers are perceived as distinct social outsiders.

The activities of the godfathers in Athens appear to have been enhanced by co-operation with the longstanding but increasingly sophisticated criminal operations of Cretan gangs (*To Vima*, 18 November 2007). The island of Crete, nationally renowned for its 'customary lawlessness' (see, for example, discussion in *The Independent*, 12 November 2007; *Kathimerini*, 6 November 2007), is home to gangs structured around kith and kin, which have been particularly active in the drugs and the light arms market, as well as associated crimes of corruption, money laundering, and occasional violence (as suggested by the arrests of whole families in police action against crimes perpetrated by a group based in the village of Zoniana; see *Eleftherotypia*, 22 December 2008). The geographical and cultural distinctness of Crete, however, has appeared to facilitate its portrayal as an all-too-easily-discounted anomaly of the Greek context with regard to organised crime.

Multi-Ethnic and Foreign Organised Crime Groups[13]

There has been some speculation as to the continued 'ethnic Greek' character of the godfathers and, moreover, of the ethnic integrity of organised crime groups in Greece more generally. Family connections do not appear to have defined or restricted group membership, and there has been broad acknowledgment of patterns of co-operation between Greek godfathers and partners of different ethnicities or nationalities. In recent years, for example, a number of ethnic Greeks from Georgia and other states of the

---

13   For further information on the way in which the Greek Police has distinguished between 'indigenous' and 'non-indigenous', 'homogeneous' and 'heterogeneous' organised crime groups, see MPO (2005).

former Soviet Union, with expertise in martial arts and body-building, are believed to have joined gangs run by Greek 'bosses', although a minority established their own, smaller, private protection rackets in areas that would not challenge the spheres of influence of larger groups (see, e.g., *Eleftherotypia*, 23 August 2004). The Greek media have commonly reported police assessments highlighting the role of foreign 'mafias' in Greek illicit markets; from the Italian mafia, to gangs from the former Soviet Union, to Albanian, Bulgarian, Romanian and, more recently, Chinese, Pakistani, and Iraqi groups. When, in 2000, the parliamentary leader of the opposition suggested that there were foreign 'godfathers' operating in Greece, however, Minister of Public Order, Michalis Chrysohoidis, reportedly called the notion 'laughable' ('asteia') (*in.gr*, 2 August 2000).

Greece is also often described as being a 'hub' of organised crime due to its geographical location – and vulnerability – on the borders of Europe, the Balkans, and the Mediterranean. Its position has certainly made it a valuable route for trade in and out of Europe, as well as a source and destination country, too (as argued with regard to the smuggling of cigarettes, by Antonopoulos, 2008). In 2000, the Greek police suggested to US authorities that the value to 'international crime syndicates' of criminal operations in Greece was $11.5 billion annually (*Athens News Agency*, 23 December 2000). The strength of such trade flows would logically enhance the likelihood and value of multi-ethnic networks of entrepreneurs co-operating to exploit such markets. It is in this sense that the reported 'transplantation' of Italian (*To Vima*, 14 January 2001) and other foreign mafia groups to Greece in the late 1990s (such as Albanian, Russian, Colombian, and Chinese; see also discussion in Antonopoulos, 2008) may be best understood; as rackets organised by a number of groups with different identities across a number of countries (e.g., see discussion in EUROPOL, 2009).

Threat Assessments

Since they began in 1994, official assessments of the threat posed by organised crime in Greece have typically been structured hierarchically according both to the number of individuals arrested, and to assumptions, or guesstimates, as to the profits associated with the activities concerned. At the outset of the 2000s, drugs, weapons, and trafficking in women, were widely cited as the most significant and lucrative illicit trades in the country (see *Athens News*, 14 December 2001; and, further, Xenakis, 2006: 122). With regard to the illicit arms market, in 2000 the Greek police reportedly estimated illicit gun ownership in Greece at 300,000 (*Athens News*, 30 August 2000). The relationship between the illicit arms market and organised crime groups was emphasised by Minister of Public Order Michalis Chrysohoidis in 2001: 'If you want to strike against organised crime in Greece, you have to strike heavy blows against the illegal arms trade' (cited in *To Vima*, 5 August 2001). However, the 2004 Annual Organised Crime Report of the Greek police noted that, as concerned the trafficking of firearms and explosives, no activities connected with organised crime groups in Greece had been found that year (MPO, 2005), implying a relatively insignificant level of market activity. Nor did arms trafficking receive particular attention in the report of the following year (MPO, 2006). The police nevertheless reportedly suggested that 1.5 million weapons were by that point illicitly circulating in Greece, although they also indicated that 800,000 of these were hunting rifles and were overwhelmingly based in Crete (*Kathimerini*, 14 August 2005).

Amongst organised criminal activities, 'illegal immigration', 'trafficking in people', and 'drug trafficking' have consistently proved to be by far the most common subjects of police investigations (see, e.g., MPO 2005, 2006), if of unclear market size in comparison with those for contraband such as cigarettes and oil, for example. While political tensions over immigration have mounted both domestically and in European politics, the US and Britain – historically influential actors in Greek security affairs – intensified their own focus and pressure for action regarding trafficking in women and children, and immigration and drugs, respectively. As much as these concerns appear to have been reflected in the similar focus of organisations such as EUROPOL (see for example EUROPOL, 2009), so have they been in Greek official threat assessments; people smuggling rose to the top of the anti-organised crime agenda of the Greek police, followed closely by people trafficking (see further Papanicolaou and Bouklis, this collection) and the illicit trade in narcotics (e.g., as illustrated in the Annual Organised Crime Reports of the Greek police: MPO, 2005, 2006).

Drug use increased significantly in Greece between 1984 and 1998, but began to decline over the following six years, whilst the estimated number of problematic drug users has remained stable since 2002 (at 2.7 per 1,000 inhabitants). The numbers of recorded deaths by drug overdose peaked in 2001, but were significantly reduced by 2006/7 (see further CADCU, 2004; EMCDDA, 2009; and Tsiganou, this collection). Furthermore, at the very time that immigration – legal, irregular, and trafficked – became an actionable issue of such high priority for the Greek government, it appears that the unprecedented influx of migrants to Greece of the post-Cold War era had started to wane. According to a study by the Mediterranean Migration Observatory at Panteion University in Athens, the numbers of those arrested whilst illegally entering the country actually declined dramatically from 2001 to 2004, despite the increased attention paid to policing illegal immigration during that period (Baldwin-Edwards *et al.*, 2004: 20).[14]

By July 2010, however, the European Union border-control agency FRONTEX reported that whilst irregular migration into the EU as a whole was continuing its decline, entries into Greece had risen to 75 percent of detected illegal border crossings in the EU (FRONTEX, 2010b). In 2008, detections of illegal border crossings between Albania and Greece and between FYROM and Albania stood at almost 40 percent of the EU total, and more than 90 percent of those intercepted were Albanians, the vast majority of whom were travelling for seasonal work in Greece (FRONTEX, 2010b: 17). As FRONTEX has noted, '[d]espite strengthened measures, border controls appear to have little effect on circular migration from Albanian nationals to Greece' (ibid.). In 2010, the interception of crossings between the Greek-Turkish land border for the first time exceeded detections of illegal crossings on the maritime border between Greece and Turkey (which themselves fell by more than 60 percent in early 2010; FRONTEX, 2010a). FRONTEX responded to a subsequent request by the Greek government for assistance in managing its land border by sending 175 guards to assist in patrolling, screening and interview procedures, and pronounced that this

---

14 According to the MMO study, the numbers of those arrested whilst illegally entering Greece had already decreased significantly since the late 1990s. In 2001, just under 7,000 individuals were arrested in this way; in 2002, 4,000 individuals; and in 2003, 2,400 individuals (Baldwin-Edwards *et al.*, 2004: 20).

had been effective in diminishing the number of interceptions at the land border by over 43 percent by late 2010 (FRONTEX, 2010c).

Because of the difficulty in immigrating to Greece legally, migrants entering the country have experienced an almost inevitable baptism in illegality over the past two decades. The country has maintained one of the lowest rates of refugee recognition in the EU, although it receives one of the highest rates of asylum applications amongst the community (see further Cheliotis and Xenakis, 2010: 363). The thousands of irregular migrants entering Greece from the country's northeastern and southern land and maritime borders each month have routinely found themselves facing internationally-notorious conditions in a range of formal and ad hoc detention centres (Amnesty International, 2010). By contrast, imprisonment stands as a looming threat for those immigrants (the majority of whom are Albanian) that manage to avoid detention and reach the Greek labour market. In disregard of calls made by international human rights experts that irregular immigration should not be criminalised by states (see Amnesty International, 2010: 18), one out of every three non-nationals in Greek prisons have been jailed for illegal entry into, departure from, or stay in the country (see further Cheliotis and Xenakis, this collection). Stringent immigration policies and infamously protracted and restrictive bureaucratic registration procedures have made the acquiring and renewal of work permits extremely difficult. In conjunction with a broader environment of targeted punitiveness by criminal justice authorities, the exploited status of such workers has been perpetuated (see, e.g., Lawrence, 2005; Baldwin-Edwards, 2001; Karydis, this collection). Indeed, even though the participation of immigrants in crime remains disproportionately low, foreigners outnumber nationals in Greek prisons (see Cheliotis and Xenakis, this collection).

Many of the irregular migrants that have remained in Greece have gradually been absorbed by the legal economy. Here too, however, the criminogenic label has remained in place; immigrants have increasingly been regarded with collective suspicion for 'laundering' the gains made – by them or others – in the licit economy, even if the notion of 'money laundering' tends to be associated with sophisticated organised crime groups.[15] Equally, this shift in the association of migrants from illict to licit markets has been mirrored by a growing concern on the part of the state about money laundering. In the late 1990s, Greece acknowledged that its weak banking controls might make it a target for money laundering, but there was little evidence or official interest in pursuing the issue. This was highlighted by the testimony provided by the head of the anti-money laundering team at the Ministry of Economy and Finance to a parliamentary committee in 2005, in which he stated that for ten years the team had been functioning with only two members of staff, one of whom had to bring his personal laptop to work in order that they have internet access (*Kathimerini*, 17 November 2005).

By 2005, international pressures had also mounted from the OECD, the Financial Action Task Force (FATF), and the European Commission, which combined to force some action from Greece (see further Xenakis, 2006: 134). By late 2009, it was clear that this action had been piecemeal; whilst announcing new anti-laundering measures, Deputy Finance Minister Philippos Sahinidis reportedly acknowledged that Greece had fulfilled only 13 of 49 anti-money laundering recommendations made by the FATF and faced being placed on a blacklist of high-risk countries if the situation were not remedied by February 2010 (*GR Reporter*, 2009). One possible explanation for the slow official response to this issue is that, by making financial transactions and banking practices easier to trace, record, and investigate, there might also be significant impact upon both corruption and the shadow economy, with potentially negative political and social ramifications for any government that might do so. The shadow economy, for example, was estimated by the government to stand at 25 percent of GDP in 2006 (*The Guardian*, 30 September 2006), and has been calculated as involving two out of three Greek households (Tsatsos, 2001). In sum, many questions remain unanswered with regard to the normative and legal frameworks underpinning data collection, the methodology and analysis that underpin official threat assessments, and, consequently, the accuracy of threat assessments of organised crime themselves.

15   E.g., as stated explicitly by Alvanou (2003: 3); see also *To Vima*, 22 November 1998; and as outlined by Dr Mary Bossi in an interview with the author on 5 September 2002.

An Outline of Organised Non-State Political Violence in Greece

Organised Political Violence: From the metapolitefsi to the 2000s

Over the past thirty years, Greeks have lived through an unprecedented degree of democratic stability. During the same period, however, a number of extra-parliamentary groups have engaged in organised acts of political violence, several of which have been accompanied by the explicit intention of sowing fear amongst particular segments of the population (on recurrent cycles of violence in Greece, see Xenakis, under review). During most of the twentieth century, Greece was riven by deep splits between right and left under governments dominated by the right, and experienced numerous periods of political instability; from a civil war (1944–1949), to military revolts, to periods of military and authoritarian rule. Following the military dictatorship of 1967–1974, Greece followed an idiosyncratic path towards democratic consolidation (the 'metapolitefsi') lacking the extensive negotiation or purging processes commonly engaged in by other democratising societies (see further Karakatsanis, 2001). Efforts at lustration of those within public bodies who had been involved in the abuses of the junta focused upon upper echelons rather than the main body of personnel.[16] State-led prosecutions appeared delayed and limited, leading many private citizens to file their own lawsuits against their former persecutors. Prosecutions for torture and human rights abuses against more than one thousand individuals were initiated almost exclusively by private citizens, and were judged by a panel composed largely of career military judges at the Athens Permanent Court Martial (see further Kofas, 2005; Close, 2002;

16   In 1975, in the aftermath of a reported coup conspiracy, the government retired 207 officers from the army, navy, and air forces, as well as a number of police officers (Roehrig, 2002). Kassimeris (2001), who concurs, cites a report by the newspaper *Eleftherotypia* in 1975 that 100,000 junta sympathisers had been removed from their posts, of which 200 were notable junta appointees and collaborators.

Kornetis, 2008; Roehrig, 2002). Forty-nine military and security officers were convicted for human rights abuses, but many known perpetrators of torture escaped prosecution, either by being granted immunity for testifying against other defendants, or as a result of a law past in 1976, which imposed time limits on the filing of civil suits. Due to the particular way in which the latter was interpreted by the courts, two-thirds of the lawsuits filed by private citizens – i.e., the majority of all filed – were dismissed (see Close, 2002; Alivizatos and Diamandouros, 2001; Roehrig, 2002).

In their search for justice and/or retribution from the state, leftists, who had been the primary persecuted subjects under the junta (see further Panourgia, 2009), thus found themselves considerably frustrated in its aftermath. Although Constantine Karamanlis, who led the country as Prime Minister after the military dictatorship, made notable reforms, including decriminalising the Greek communist parties in 1974 (which had been outlawed since 1947; see further Seferiades, 1986), there was little evidence that the traditions of political policing (on which see further, Mazower, 1997) were to be so easily dismantled. It was not until 1989, for example, that the Greek government finally took steps to destroy 16.5 million intelligence files that had been compiled by the Greek police and intelligence services since 1944 on the political and private sentiments of Greek citizens (Murtagh, 1994: 276; see further Samatas, this collection).

Post-Junta Violence of the Far-Right

The sense of frustration amongst the left was exacerbated not only by the presence of ministers tainted by association to fascism in the post-Junta government (Kassimeris, 2001), but also by the lenient treatment the state accorded to neo-fascist groups that had launched a programme of political violence in the years after the fall of the dictatorship, including physical attacks on journalists (McDonald, 1983: 187–188) and a series of bombings at bookshops, cinemas, trade union offices, and left-wing organisations. The 'basic nuclei of the extreme right' responsible for these attacks were arrested in 1979 and were sentenced to prison (*Kathimerini*, 26 August 2002). In the aftermath of the dictatorship, many of the far-right had been absorbed by the new centre-right New Democracy party of Constantine Karamanlis. A number also remained outside it, some supporting the pro-junta EP party ('Ethniki Parataxis', or 'National Alignment') established in 1977 (and known as EPEN –'Ethniki Politiki Enosis' or 'National Political Union' – after 1981; Seferiades, 1986) and, subsequently, the increasingly active neo-fascist party Chrysi Avyi ('Golden Dawn'). With links to a former right-wing terror group operating during the junta era (EOKA B, the 'National Organisation of Cypriot Struggle', formed in 1971) as well as to the junta itself, Chrysi Avyi was formed by former EPEN members in 1985 and was recognised as a political party in 1993 (*To Vima*, 11 September 2005; see further Kousoumvris, 2004). It constitutes the largest of far-right fringe groups, and has a reputation for intimidation and violence. In comparison to the well-documented history of right-wing terror in the pre-dictatorial era, however, organised violent activities by right-wing groups during and since the junta have received far less public attention or interest. Although overshadowed in documented lethality by the operations of the far-left 17N group, leftists have argued that right-wing violence has been systematically under-studied and under-reported by the police and much of the media (*Eleftherotypia*, 29 February 2002).[17]

Post-Junta Violence of the Far-Left

The far left emerged from the dictatorship divided, if dominated by the Stalinist KKE. Alongside the Eurocommunist KKE-Esoterikou, the entry of both these communist parties to parliament was interpreted by many as their acceptance of reformism and compromise with the existing political system. Other members of the far-left and emergent anarchist group-ings mobilised to raise public awareness and support for radical change,

---

17   The centre-right newspaper *Kathimerini* has proposed exactly the opposite thesis, that the rare actions of far-right fringe groups always 'overexcited the democratic sensibilities of those in the media who systematically underestimated the actions of real terrorists', implying those of the far-left 17N group and its well-documented lethality (*Kathimerini*, 26 August 2002). Nevertheless, from a search for publications on terrorism and extremism in Greece since the dictatorship, it is evident that the overwhelming focus has been on mobilisations by the far-left.

organising political demonstrations, occupations, and strikes. It was against this background that covert organisations also formed, with the specific purpose of carrying out violent campaigns of political protest against what they saw as a superficial democratic transformation, castigating others amongst the far-left for their disavowal of such methods. Those that gained greatest prominence amongst these organisations were ELA and 17N (see further Bossi, 1996; Kassimeris, 2001).

ELA

ELA ('Revolutionary Popular Struggle') was formed in 1975 and, until 1995 (when it declared an end to its activities), carried out over 100 low-level bombings aimed at symbolic targets of capitalist power (police, banks, government offices, and material and human targets linked to US interests; *Kathimerini*, 5 February 2003, 12 October 2004). It was associated with the killings of a former torturer of the junta, a Deputy Supreme Court prosecutor, and a riot policeman, and took direct responsibility for the latter (see further Xenakis, under review). In 2003, seven months after police began arresting suspected members of 17N – one of whom (the veteran trade unionist Yiannis Serifis) they also suspected of membership in ELA –, an additional five individuals suspected of ELA membership were arrested. An eight-month trial considered charges of 42 bombings and 48 murder attempts carried out between 1983 and 1995.

In August 2004, two months before the sentences were announced, the presiding judge was cited commenting that the evidence put forward by the prosecution was 'most insufficient' and that political pressure for the trial to conclude before the start of the Olympic Games (13–29 August 2004) had compromised the rights of the defendants (*Kathimerini*, 12 October 2004). Nevertheless, in October 2004, the court imposed the maximum possible sentence of 25 years of imprisonment to each of the four convicted, as well as imposing fines for the bombings, whilst the fifth suspect was acquitted. Only one of those convicted admitted to any involvement in the group, saying that, between 1976 and 1990, he had been a member of ELA, and had been responsible for a magazine produced by the group, had taken part in mass demonstrations, gathered funds and advised workers on practical issues, but had not played any part in the group's attacks (*Kathimerini*, 9 July 2004).

Following an appellate court decision that the statute of limitations should be extended from 15 to 20 years so that earlier ELA attacks could be included, a second trial of the six suspected ELA members began in February 2005 (*ERA*, 7 February 2005). Prosecutors eventually recommended that two individuals be exonerated (one of whom was Serifis; *Kathimerini*, 8 June 2005), but all six defendants at the second ELA trial were unanimously found not guilty of the killing of the riot policeman and were acquitted of the new charges in June 2005 (*ERA*, 1 July 2005). Subsequently, following a thirteen-month appeal, the four original convictions of 2004 were also overturned in December 2009, when the court acknowledged the lack of evidence against the convicted individuals and showed greater skepticism as to the credibility of the primary state witness in the 2004 trial, who was the former wife of one of the suspects (*Kathimerini*, 4 December 2009). In June 2009, whilst this appeal was ongoing, a plainclothes policeman guarding the house of the witness was shot and killed outside her property by three individuals on motorbikes. A group named 'Sect of Revolutionaries' claimed responsibility for the killing. Police later announced that cartridge casings from the scene were identified as having been emitted from a weapon already used by that organisation (*Ta Nea*, 22 June 2009; *Kathimerini*, 18 June 2009).

17N

Named after the student uprising whose crushing by the military heralded the waning of support for the dictatorship (subsequently commemorated by a national holiday; see Kornetis, 2008), the self-described Marxist-Leninist organisation November 17 was publically launched in 1975 with the murder of the CIA station chief in Athens. As noted above, 17N went on to kill a further twenty-two individuals (including a total of five US Embassy employees), in addition to numerous bombings (including improvised rocket attacks) and a number of bank robberies (see further Kassimeris, 2001). Skepticism persisted as to the true identity of the group across its lifetime; amongst a broad array of experts, officials, and the Greek public, were suspicions that 17N was a front organisation or pawn of foreign intelligence agencies or foreign terrorist groups (see further discussion in Kassimeris, 2001; Karyotis, 2007). Equally, the failure of the Greek state to make any apparent progress in apprehending 17N fuelled the belief held by some (Greeks and non-Greeks, and particularly Americans) that PASOK, which dominated government throughout the 1980s, 1990s, and early 2000s, had intentionally limited investigations in order to protect former comrades of its forerunner association, the anti-dictatorship organisation 'PAK' (Panhellenic Liberation Movement) (see further *Kathimerini*, 26 August 2002).

By 2000, Greek law enforcement announced it was following a number of suspects whose names had been gathered in collaboration with French authorities and the assistance of British law enforcement, including that of Alexandros Yiotopoulos, a suspected leader of the organisation. In June 2002, a bomb exploded prematurely in the hands of group member Savvas Xiros.[18] He was taken to hospital where, under questioning (and allegedly under the influence of drugs administered there), he provided information that led to a number of other arrests and the discovery of an arms cache (Kassimeris, 2006). The following month, the alleged ideological leader and mastermind of the group was seized by police. Sixty-three-year-old Alexandros Yiotopoulos, who had been living under an assumed name in Athens, had been convicted *in absentia* by court-martial in 1971 for participating in the establishment of, and recruitment for, a resistance group during the dictatorship (*Macedonian Press Agency*, 18 July 2002). He consistently denied any connection to 17N. On 5 September that year, the alleged 17N leader of operations, Dimitris Koufodinas, handed himself in to the police. Although he accepted responsibility for the group's legacy, he refused to provide any details of its organisation or membership, elaborating only upon its ideological positions.

Nineteen individuals were charged in total with membership of the group. On 31 July 2002, a day following the publication of photos of arrested

---

18 Kassimeris (2006) notes that early media reports of the incident speculated that Xiros was a member of 'Revolutionary Cells' or 'Popular Resistance', two other minor domestic groups that had been active around that time.

suspected members of 17N, a proclamation apparently authored by remaining members of 17N was sent to the media, which defended the record of 17N and asserted its continued existence and operational capabilities (*Eleftherotypia*, 31 July 2002). Amongst those arrested were two individuals who had also been involved in the anti-dictatorship struggle (Serifis and Theologos Psaradellis), and the charges against them heightened concerns that the anti-dictatorship struggle was purposefully being embroiled in the hunt for 17N by those individuals all too keen to see the former delegitimised and discredited (*Kathimerini*, 19 July 2002).

The record nine-month 'mother of all trials' concluded in December 2003, when the three-member jury convicted fifteen members of the group and acquitted four defendants (including Serifis and Psaradellis) on grounds of insufficient evidence. The twenty-five-year maximum imprisonment sentence was handed out to eleven of the convicted members, multiple life sentences being given to those considered by the Court to be core members of the group, whilst two of those convicted and two of those acquitted were tried again following an appeal lodged by the state prosecutor (Kassimeris, 2006). A collective appeal, which took 18 months to finally conclude, was launched for those convicted as well as for two of those who had been acquitted in December 2005 but who faced new charges by the prosecutor. In May 2006, the Court sentenced six members to imprisonment with 44 life sentences combined. Some of the charges against a further four members were dropped. A year later, following an appeal by the defendants, the Court ruled that the remaining convictions against a total of 13 individuals be upheld, including the life sentences imposed on six members (although the number of life terms imposed was reduced), whilst convictions against two individuals were quashed on the grounds that the crimes for which they had been found guilty now stood beyond the twenty-year statute of limitations (*Kathimerini*, 4 May 2007, 10 May 2007).

Until its capture, explanations of the failure on the part of the Greek state to apprehend any member of the group over a twenty-nine-year period had distributed blame between the historical legacy of the dictatorship which made more rigorous and effective counter-terrorism policies politically and socially unconscionable, the complicity or political embarrassment of PASOK politicians which led to their disinterest and disengagement from the issue, and police and intelligence agency incompetency, numerous examples of which left little space for confidence in their efforts (see Floros and Newsome, 2008; Karyotis, 2007; Kassimeris, 2001). After the successful capture, prosecution, and imprisonment of group members, the reputation of Greek law enforcement agencies saw significant rehabilitation (see further Floros and Newsome, 2008; Karyotis, 2007; Papahelas and Telloglou, 2002; Xenakis, under review). There have been dissenting voices, however, who have questioned the extent to which the capture of 17N members truly demonstrated either the defeat of the organisation, or the enhanced effectiveness of Greek counter-terrorism policy. Some have suggested that not all or even only relatively unimportant members of 17N had been arrested, and that other members might be involved in the new groups operating today (see further Xenakis, under review). These criticisms have proved persuasive; the file on 17N was re-opened in December 2009 in order to search for up to a dozen further members thought to be at large (*Athens News*, 18 January 2010). It has also been argued that the arrests owed more to an accident that befell a 17N member than to any superior competency of the Greek counter-terror division (e.g., by Anagnostopoulos-Melkiades, 2003). Moreover, the interpretation of the group as a collection of anachronistic and pathological individuals, set far apart from the rest of Greek society and broader social trends (e.g., Kassimeris, 2001; Konstandopoulos and Modis, 2005), has seemed to sit increasingly uncomfortably alongside the subsequent rise of new groups and the widespread social unrest of December 2008.

Organised Political Violence of the 2000s

Despite expectations of a decline in political violence after the apparent collapse of violent groups run by the generation of the anti-dictatorship struggles, Greece witnessed a resurgence in political violence by sub-state organisations of the left and right over the decade of the 2000s, as well as occasions (such as the protests of December 2008) in which political violence has drawn in a range of organisationally unaffiliated participants (see Schwarz, Sagris and Void Network, 2010). The unprecedented breadth of social mobilisation across Greece over December 2008 spurred perceptions that those who participated should be considered part and parcel of the challenge of political violence in the country. To the extent that violence has attracted broader public appeal in addressing political problems, this may be regarded as symptomatic of the intensifying pressures, fears, and frustrations generated by a highly problematic national political and economic environment, and which has placed the youth under particular stresses. Corruption, rising unemployment, and steeply increasing levels of household debt have together comprised a potent source of public anger and anxiety over recent years (see Cheliotis and Xenakis, 2010). Furthermore, the regularity with which political demonstrations descend into violence (a self-fulfilling expectation on the part of both the police and demonstrators) has, to an extent, served to normalise low-scale conflict.[19]

Amongst disparate groups of the left, the appeal of political violence has been stoked by violence and impunity on the part of front-line police officers, and violence perpetrated by far-right groups in open collusion with the police. Another important stimulus of political violence has been the broadening and escalation of law enforcement measures to include detentions, raids, and arrests of those participating in non-violent gatherings (from book launches to social clubs), as well as the introduction and widening of repressive measures (from punitive sanctions against those wearing hoodies, to prosecuting universities for hosting the independent media network *Indymedia*; see further Xenakis, under review). Indeed, the dangers of a broad-brush approach to identifying a symbiosis of organised crime and political violence (and with important ramifications for officially

19   Thus, for example, the visual impression of demonstrations that have become violent as a battleground in which different organised formations are involved. Organised protestors (such as students) that are not themselves engaging in violence will take precautions against attacks from others by making tight formations within such demonstrations. Groups of youths that are regularly involved in violence – spanning the breadth of the political spectrum – also tend to mobilise in formations during and after political demonstrations, but typically wear protective headgear (motorcycle helmets) in addition.

recorded levels of such crimes) have been illustrated by the alleged use of pre-formulated charge sheets by policemen in detaining and arresting youths they have encountered, even if alone, after demonstrations and riots. As detailed by Amnesty International (2009), for example, following a demonstration that turned violent in a town outside Athens in 2008, 21 out of 25 people arrested were charged under legislation relating to organised crime, including the uniform charge of forming a criminal organisation. Of the 21 so charged, 17 were youths aged between 15 and 17, and had been arrested at different times and locations throughout the evening (Amnesty International, 2009).

The New Generation of Far-Right Violence

Whilst political parties of the far-right such as LAOS and Chrysi Avyi have seen their electoral support increase over recent years, it has been suggested that political violence has spread beyond the activities of 'Chrysavyites' (groups of Chrysi Avyi supporters) to other organisations that have emerged across Greece. The number of organised and spontaneous politically symbolic attacks by groups of far-right activists appears to have climbed, reaching a new high in 2009. Underlying this growth has also been an apparent escalation over the 2000s in the number of reported and alleged cases of violence by police and other law enforcement officers against migrants and suspected anarchists or leftist activists. Violence perpetrated by smaller right-wing groups has also appeared to be on the increase. Attacks have overwhelmingly been directed against immigrants (there have been numerous raids and beatings of immigrants in their shops, for example), but have also included left-wing targets. A number of raids have been carried out by groups on the homes of immigrants, in which victims have been beaten and have had money and identification documents stolen from them. In May 2009, five Bangladeshis suffered injuries following arson attacks on a prayer room and a church basement hosting immigrants in Athens (see, e.g., *Avyi*, 9 September 2009).

'Chrysavyites'

Notable recent actions alleged to have been undertaken by Chrysavyites have included storming and holding hostage participants of a book launch relating to FYROM in central Athens at the offices of the Foreign Press Association (adjacent to the Ministry of Foreign Affairs), on 2 June 2009, and a caustic spray attack to the face of a female, who on exiting a metro station in Athens on 1 October 2009 had rejected Chrysi Avyi election flyers (the organisation denies the allegation; see further Xenakis, under review). Chrysavyites are thought to mobilise regularly against immigrants in Athens; recent footage (*Al Jazeera*, 2010) has indicated that such mobilisations can take the form of a platoon-like formation of around 30–40 people armed with flags (and the sticks attached to the flags), in which there is often little attempt made to hide individual identities. The close relationship between Chrysavyites and elements of the Greek police has been demonstrated to be at unparalleled levels given evidence that the former have emerged from, or alongside, police ranks, armed with molotof cocktails, batons, and knives, to attack anarchists and anti-establishment activists during demonstrations and riots, and even return for protection behind those lines (see, e.g., *Eleftherotypia*, 10 February 2008). One example of close relations between Chrysavyites and the riot police ('MAT') was the incident of 9 May 2009, when dozens of Chrysavyites passed by police lines to attack Asian refugees housed in Omonia, central Athens, armed with shields, batons, and grenades, leading to the injury of five immigrants. So blatant has been the relationship between Chrysavyites and segments of the police that, in October 2009, the incoming PASOK Minister of Protection for the Citizen, Michalis Chrysohoidis, acknowledged the relationship, vowing to seek an end to it, and drew attention to his efforts to see the Chrysi Avyi outlawed (*Eleftherotypia*, 21 October 2009). The Minister also talked publicly of the rise of new far-right violent groups, and the possibility that right-wing violence might reach terrorist proportions in the future (*To Vima*, 13 December 2009).

The New Generation of Violence from the Far-Left and Anarchists

The 2000s witnessed the emergence of self-named violent political groups whose activities ranged from minor acts of vandalism or arson to lethal attacks, both of which appeared to gather momentum after the social unrest of December 2008. A number of groups appeared to commit a few acts but faded soon after, whilst approximately ten organisations are thought to have proved durable (see *New York Times*, 12 January 2007). A smaller number have reached particular prominence due to the frequency and damage of their actions. Three such groups are addressed below: 'Revolutionary Struggle', 'Sect of Revolutionaries', and the 'Conspiracy of Fire Nuclei' ('SPF'). There is little certainty as to whether smaller, short-lived groups have been absorbed by larger, more permanent organisations, or whether they have been fronts for those seeking to cultivate the impression of a far more populous and politically diverse violent landscape. Law enforcement officers have also speculated as to the possible connections between the most prominent of the groups, arguing that there may be significant communication between them, or even that they may be 'branches' of a single organisation (see further *To Vima*, 6 September 2009; *Kathimerini*, 3 September 2009). Most recently, police have suggested that two of the most active groups (SPF and Sect of Revolutionaries) may have been led by the same individual (*To Vima*, 28 November 2010). The government has also pointed to evidence that anarchists and anti-establishment actors are forging novel bonds of cooperation with criminals, thereby creating a very dangerous climate of violence that is more brutal and less ideological than posed by past cases of politically violent organisations (see, e.g., *Athens News*, 29 November 2009).

Revolutionary Struggle ('Epanastatikos Agonas' or 'EA')

Revolutionary Struggle (EA) first announced its presence in October 2003, when it bombed a courthouse complex in Athens, injuring one policeman. Since then, it has attacked the police, ministries, banks, and, on one occasion, the petroleum firm Shell (*Eleftherotypia*, 13 March 2009). One of its most prominent and audacious attacks, footage of which made international news, was a fire rocket that hit the US Embassy in Athens just before dawn on 12 January 2007. Throughout 2007–2008, the group set off a number of low-level improvised incendiary devices, but increased the menace of its actions in late 2008, when it used a Kalashnikov to spray gunfire at a bus carrying riot police on 23 December. EA then claimed responsibility for the shooting of policemen on duty outside the Greek Ministry of Culture on 5 January 2009, which left one victim critically injured. In February and March 2009, the group also targeted two bombs at Citibank branches in Athens, one of which was so large that it could have leveled the building had it exploded (see *Athens News*, 18 April 2010).

In a manifesto published in 2005, the group proclaimed its actions to be a response to police violence and its impunity, stating that its attacks would continue if the Public Order Ministry were not to cease 'protecting rich thieves, criminal ministers and state officials' (see *Eleftherotypia*, 7 January 2009). In this and other proclamations, the group has set out its position as revolutionary, anti-capitalist, and anti-US hegemony; against the exploitative elitist classes, but also against the middle classes who support an exploitative system for their own consumerist, capitalist-defined ends. There are similarities between EA and 17N with regard to their proclaimed ideological bases, tactics, and targets. Yet EA has rebutted comparisons to 17N and emphasised that it takes precautions to avoid committing violence against bystanders (see *Athens News*, 13 March 2009).

Nevertheless, the group was suspected of planting the bomb which killed the Head of Security at the Ministry of Citizen Protection (formerly known as the Ministry of Public Order) in June 2010 (see *BBC News*, 25 June 2010). Following a shoot-out on 21 March 2010, which left one suspect dead, the police announced the discovery of a suspected hideout of the group in April 2010. Included in the cache was a sub-machine gun that had been stolen during a bank robbery in Thessaloniki in 2004 (*Kathimerini*, 22 April 2010), and police speculated that disgruntled members of EA had split to form the 'Sect of Revolutionaries' (on which further below). Three of six suspected members of the group subsequently accepted responsibility for a range of shootings and bombings which had taken place since 2003 (*Kathimerini*, 30 April 2010).

Sect of Revolutionaries (Sehta Epanastaton)

This group emerged in the aftermath of the fatal shooting of a fifteen-year-old in December 2008, the event which ignited a month of nationwide social unrest. Its first appearance was an attack in which grenades were thrown and a sub-machine gun was fired at a police station in the district of Korydallos outside Athens on 3 February 2009. It then issued a proclamation in February 2009, left on the grave of the teenager, threatening violence against the police and prominent establishment figures – from journalists to media stars, and businessmen to public officials and politicians –, whilst claiming responsibility for an attack on a police station that month (*BBC News*, 5 February 2009). It has espoused anarchist principles and its prominent ethos is anti-capitalism, but it has also repeatedly made threats involving targeted lethal violence in its public pronouncements. On 17 February 2009, the group fired shots and threw an explosive device (which failed to detonate) at a prominent private television station, 'Alter'. In June 2009, the group shot and killed the policeman guarding the house of a state witness in the case against ELA during the appeal case of ELA suspects. And in July 2010, they carried out a second lethal attack, on the investigative journalist Sokratis Giolias (see Xenakis, under review).

Conspiracy of Fire Nuclei
(or Conspiracy Cells of Fire, Synomosia Pyrinon tis Fotias)

Conspiracy of Fire Nuclei (SPF) emerged on 21 January 2008, when the group carried out a range of gas canister attacks against car dealerships, banks, and the Public Power Company in Athens and Thessaloniki, over the space of half an hour over midnight. Its actions were declared to be in support of the imprisoned anarchist Vangelis Voutsatzis. The group has also voiced support for the jailed member of 17N, Dimitris Koufodinas (see, e.g., *Ta Nea*, 12 January 2010). Ideologically, the organisation has described itself as an urban guerilla group, and has issued proclamations railing against consumer society and its ills. They have also rejected the notion that their acts of urban warfare are, or should be, a means to an end, claiming rather that they are an end in themselves.

SPF has committed numerous acts of arson, including, unusually, day-time strikes. In May 2009, the group used home-made explosives to strike at two police stations in Athens and issued a proclamation deliberating on 'revolutionary terrorism'. In June 2009, the group claimed joint responsibility with a lesser-known group, 'Nihilist Faction', for a home-made time bomb placed outside the home of a former Minister of Public Order. These two groups have since continued to cooperate. On 27 December 2009, Conspiracy of Fire Nuclei, in co-operation with the a newly emerged 'Guerilla Team of Terrorists', used a four-member unit to plant a bomb that destroyed the entrance to a prominent building on Syngrou Avenue (a central Athenian thoroughfare), preceding the attack with a warning call to newspapers. Conspiracy of Fire Nuclei also claimed responsibility for a bomb which exploded outside the Greek Parliament on 9 January 2010. Media report that the group commonly calls in warnings to the media before impending attacks (see, e.g., *Eleftherotypia*, 25 September 2009).

Following raids on apartments in the suburbs of Halandri and Galatsi outside Athens, Greek police arrested four suspected members of the group (and, in early 2010, one individual who had previously been arrested at demonstrations during the European Social Forum in Athens in 2006). All suspects were between the ages of 20–26. On 5 October, the organisation responded with a series of bombs across Athens and a statement vowing revenge and denying that those arrested had any connection with the group (*To Vima*, 5 October 2009). In March 2010, SPF carried out a further series of bomb attacks. After the anti-IMF and anti-austerity demonstration of 5 May 2010, during which three individuals died as a result of the fire-bombing of a bank, the organisation issued a text defending – but not claiming responsibility – for those who carry out political violence (see *Athens IMC*, 2010). The group did claim responsibility for the small packages of low-level explosives sent to a dozen foreign targets in November 2010, which led to the arrest of a number of suspected members of the group. In total, thirteen suspects accused of membership were due to stand trial in January 2011 (*Kathimerini*, 12 November 2010).

Concluding Remarks

Amongst official, media, and academic commentators in Greece, there has been considerable debate about the extent to which political violence today poses a greater threat than in previous generations. Concerns about the relationship between organised crime and organised political violence have steadily intensified since the 1990s, but their impact on public perceptions of the legitimacy of political violence remains unclear. As yet, it is also not evident whether the ideological, actional, and structural differences and similarities between the current generation of politically violent groups and their predecessors amount to a more violent present (see Xenakis, under review).

In more general terms, however, and whilst there is often more chauvinism than merit at the heart of essentialist assessments of political violence in Greece, suggestions that political violence has increasingly become delegitimised within Greek society over the past twenty years have been patently over-optimistic (ibid.). The latter thesis is still repeated today; that, for example, the unrest of December 2008 marked the end of an era in which political violence was regarded acceptable by Greek society (see *Kathimerini*, 5 December 2010). Yet instances of both disorganised and organised political violence continue to reappear, even if perpetrated by a minority, alongside peaceful mass political mobilisations (see, e.g., *Athens News*, 6 December 2010). Although public acceptance of austerity measures has been higher than expected, there are clear signs that related fears and frustrations remain intense and extensive. Rather than public attitudes changing, it may be that a stronger show of force by the state has thus far ensured that such attitudes are less able to manifest themselves (see, e.g. *To Vima*, 6 December 2010). Greece nevertheless remains one of the most highly politicised societies in Europe, and high levels of social politicisation have provided a context in which violence is more likely to demonstrate a political character.

References

Amnesty International UK (AIUK) (2009) *Konstantina Kuneva: Attacked for Defending Workers' Rights*. London: Amnesty International.

Alivizatos, N.C. and P.N. Diamandouros (2001) 'Politics and the Judiciary in the Greek Transition to Democracy', in A.J. McAdams (ed.) *Transitional Justice and the Rule of Law in New Democracies*, pp. 27–60. Indiana: University of Notre Dame.

Al Jazeera (4 December 2010) 'Racial Tension on the Rise in Greece'.

Alvanou, M. (2003) 'Money Laundering in Greece: A Problem for All Europe', paper presentation at the General Conference of the European Consortium for Political Research, Marburg. Available online at: http://www.essex.ac.uk/ecpr/events/generalconference/marburg/papers/19/6/Alvanou.pdf

Amnesty International (2010) *Greece: Irregular Migrants and Asylum-Seekers Routinely Detained in Substandard Conditions*. London: Amnesty International Publications.

Amnesty International (2009) *Greece: Alleged Abuses in the Policing of Demonstrations*. London: Amnesty International Publications.

Anagnostopoulos-Melkiades, V. (2003) *The Hardest Muscle is the Heart: I, Alekos, and the 'Others'* [in Greek]. Athens: Dodoni.

Antonopoulos, G.A. (2008) 'The Greek Connection(s): The Social Organisation of the Cigarette-Smuggling Business in Greece', *European Journal of Criminology* 5(3): 263–288.

Antonopoulos, G.A. (2009) '"Are the 'Others' Coming?": Evidence on "Alien Conspiracy" from Three Illegal Markets in Greece', *Crime, Law and Social Change* 52(5): 475–493.

Arlacchi, P. (1986) *Mafia Business: The Mafia Ethic and the Spirit of Capitalism*. London: Verso.

Athens IMC (19 May 2010) 'Announcement Concerning the Recent Events of 5/5' [in Greek].

Athens News (30 August 2000) 'Illegal Trade in Weapons a Thriving Industry in Greece'.

Athens News Agency (23 December 2000) 'US Government Publishes International Organised Crime Report on Greece, Cyprus, Turkey'.

Athens News (3 March 2001) 'Press Watch'.

Athens News (20 April 2001) 'Minister: Terror Bill Strikes Balance'.

Athens News (12 December 2001) 'Sex Slave Trade Bill Unveiled At Last'.

Athens News Agency (25 November 2002) 'Public Order Minister at UK Conference for Balkan Organised Crime'.

Athens News (13 March 2009) 'Terrorist Group Blasts the System'.

Athens News (29 November 2009) 'Chrysohoidis: Anarchist Violence Linked to Common Crime'.

Athens News (18 April 2010) 'Cracking Revolutionary Struggle'.

Athens News (6 December 2010) 'Three Injured in Protests on Alexis Murder Anniversary'.

Baldwin-Edwards, M. (2001) *Crime and Migrants: Some Myths and Realities*, paper presentation at the International Police Association, 17th Greek Section Conference, Samos, 4 May. Available online at: http://www.mmo.gr/pdf/publications/publications_by_mmo_staff/Police_Gazette2001_MBE_English_translation.pdf

Baldwin-Edwards, M., with the assistance of G. Kyriakou (2004) *Statistical Data on Immigrants in Greece: An Analytic Study of Available Data and Recommendations for Conformity with European Union Standards*. Athens: Mediterranean Migration Observatory.

BBC News (23 October 2008) 'Greek Minister Quits Over Scandal'.

BBC News (14 December 2008) 'New Generation Flexes its Muscles'.

BBC News (5 February 2009) 'New Greek Group Threatens Police'.

BBC News (25 June 2010) 'Bomb Blast Kills Aide to Greek Counter-Terrorism Minister'.

BBC News (25 June 2011) 'Dozens Named in Greece Football "Scandal"'.

Biliouri, D. and T. Makarenko (2002) 'Is This The End of 17N?', *Jane's Intelligence Review* 14(9): 6–10.

Bossi, M. (1996) *Greece and Terrorism: National and International Dimensions* [in Greek]. Athens: Ant. N. Sakkoulas Publishers.

Bossi, M. (1999) *Security Issues in the New Order of Things* [in Greek]. Athens: Papazissis.

Buzan, B., Waever, O. and J. de Wilde (1998) *Security: A New Framework for Analysis*. Boulder and London: Lynne Rienner.

CADCU (Central Anti-Drug Co-ordinating Unit) (2005) *Annual Report on Drugs in Greece, 2004*. Athens: CADCU.

Cheliotis, L.K. and S. Xenakis (2010) 'What's Neoliberalism Got to Do With It? Towards a Political Economy of Punishment in Greece', *Criminology & Criminal Justice* 10(4): 353–373.

Close, D.H. (2002) *Greece Since 1945: Politics, Economy and Society*. London: Pearson.

Delorme, J. (2009) 'Spotlight on Constantina Kuneva (PEKOP-Greece)', interview for the International Trades Union Confederation. Available online at: http:// www.ituc-csi.org/spotlight-on-constantina-kuneva.html?lang=en

Edwards, A. (2005) 'Transnational Organised Crime', in J. Sheptycki and A. Wardak (eds) *Transnational and Comparative Criminology*, pp. 211–225. London: Glasshouse.

Edwards, A. and P. Gill (2003) 'After Transnational Crime: The Politics of Public Safety', in A. Edwards and P. Gill (eds) *Transnational Organised Crime: Perspectives on Global Security*, pp. 264–281. Oxford: Routledge.

Edwards, A. and P. Gill (2002) 'Crime as Enterprise? The Case of "Transnational Organised Crime"', *Crime, Law & Social Change* 37(3): 203–223.

EMCDDA (European Monitoring Centre for Drugs and Drug Addiction) (2009) 'Country Overview: Greece'. Available online at: http://www.emcdda.europa. eu/publications/country-overviews/el

Eleftherotypia (19 April 2002) 'Revelation Gallop Poll on 17N' [in Greek].

Eleftherotypia (31 July 2002) 'The Police Hit the Centre but We Are Still Alive' [in Greek].

Eleftherotypia (29 September 2002) 'The Cache of Karamanlis: The Forgotten Terrorism' [in Greek].

Eleftherotypia (23 August 2004) 'The "Flowers" of the Night Bloom in Thessaloniki' [in Greek].

Eleftherotypia (10 February 2008) 'The Blackshirts of the Police' [in Greek].

Eleftherotypia (22 December 2008) '40 on Trial for 30 Felonies' [in Greek].

Eleftherotypia (7 January 2009) 'At War with the Police' [in Greek].

Eleftherotypia (13 March 2009) '"Struggle" on the Citibank Attacks' [in Greek].

Eleftherotypia (14 April 2009) 'Official Investigation for the Death of Katerina Goulioni' [in Greek].

Eleftherotypia (21 October 2009) 'I know About Chrysi Avyi – I will stop the Abuses' [in Greek].

ERA (Hellenic Radio) (7 February 2005) 'Accused of Eight Bomb Attacks: ELA Back in Court'.

ERA (1 July 2005) 'ELA Acquitted'.

EUROPOL (2009) *EU Organised Crime Threat Assessment*. The Hague: European Police Office.

Floros, C. and B. Newsome (2008) 'Building Counter-Terrorism Capacity Across Borders: Lessons from the Defeat of "Revolutionary Organisation November 17th"', *Journal of Security Sector Management* 6(2): 1–15.

FRONTEX (2010a) *FRAN Quarterly Update, Issue 1 (January–March)*. Warsaw: FRONTEX.

FRONTEX (2010b) *Extract from the Annual Risk Analysis 2010*. Warsaw: FRONTEX.

FRONTEX (2010c) *Frontex Estimates Illegal Border Crossings on the Greek-Turkish Border Have Diminished by 44% by the End of November*, Press Release, 30 November.

GR Reporter (17 November 2009) 'Greece Loses Fight Against "Dirty Money"'. Available online at: http://www.grreporter.info/en/greece_losing_against_money_laundering_fight/1506

Hebenton, B. and T. Thomas (1995) *Policing Europe: Co-operation, Conflict and Control*. London: Macmillan.

I Avyi (9 September 2009) 'Syriza: New Outbreaks of Racial Violence in Agios Panteleimonas' [in Greek].

In.Gr (2 August 2000) 'We Are At War with the Godfathers' [in Greek].

Karyotis, G. (2007) 'The Securitisation of Greek Terrorism and the Arrest of the Revolutionary Organisation November 17', *Cooperation and Conflict* 42(3): 271–293.

Kassimeris, G. (2001) *Europe's Last Red Terrorists: The Revolutionary Organisation 17 November*. London: Hurst.

Kassimeris, G. (2005) 'Urban Guerilla or Revolutionary Fantasist? Dimitris Koufodinas and the Revolutionary Organisation 17 November', *Studies in Conflict and Terrorism* 28(1): 21–31.

Kassimeris, G. (2006) 'Last Act in a Violent Drama? The Trial of Greece's Revolutionary Organisation 17 November', *Terrorism and Political Violence* 18(1): 137–157.

Kathimerini (9 June 2002) 'From Ideology to Robbery and Murder'.

Kathimerini (12 July 2002) 'Mass Prosecution of Athens Mobsters'.

Kathimerini (19 July 2002) 'Heroes and Villains'.

Kathimerini (23 July 2002) 'Irresponsible Cowardice'.

Kathimerini (26 August 2002) 'Terror Unfettered as Noone Took Charge'.

Kathimerini (5 February 2003) 'ELA Architect Behind Bars'.

Kathimerini (23 October 2003) 'Judge: 17N Defendants had "Vision"'.

Kathimerini (9 July 2004) 'Tsigaridas Describes ELA to Court'.

Kathimerini (7 October 2004) 'PM Vows War on Business Interests but "Pimp" Comment Is Denied'.

Kathimerini (12 October 2004) 'ELA Four Get 25 Years'.

Kathimerini (8 June 2005) 'Prosecutors Call for Kassimis, Serifis to be Freed, 4 Convicts to be Sentenced'.

Kathimerini (14 August 2005) 'Large-scale Illegal Possession of Firearms' [in Greek].

Kathimerini (17 November 2005) 'Only 2 Officials Hunt Dirty Cash'.

Kathimerini (2 February 2007) 'The "Godfathers" and Contract Killings' [in Greek].

Kathimerini (4 May 2007) '17N Appeal is Rejected'.

Kathimerini (10 May 2007) '17N Sentences'.

Kathimerini (6 November 2007) 'Crete Drug Raid Backfires'.

Kathimerini (11 November 2008) 'Arrests Point to Gangland Feud'.

Kathimerini (14 April 2009) 'Three Guilty of Mevgal Blackmail'.

Kathimerini (14 June 2009) 'Anti-Terror Officer Shot Dead'.

Kathimerini (8 July 2009) 'Police Probe Crime-Terror Link'.

Kathimerini (20 July 2009) 'EYP Planning Crime Crackdown'.

Kathimerini (27 October 2009) 'Reward offered for terror suspects'.

Kathimerini (10 November 2009) 'Police Shake-Up on Cards'.

Kathimerini (4 December 2009) 'Innocent: The Three Defendants of the ELA Trial'.

Kathimerini (22 April 2010) 'Terrorist Evidence Being Gathered'.

Kathimerini (30 April 2010) 'Revolutionary Trio Claim Terror Hits'.

Kathimerini (12 November 2010) 'Domestic Terrorism: Trial of Conspiracy Cells of Fire Suspects Set for January 17'.

Kathimerini (5 December 2010) 'Two Years Later' [in Greek].

Kofas, J.V. (2005) *Under the Eagle's Claw: Exceptionalism in Postwar US-Greek Relations*. Westport, Conneticut: Praeger.

Konstandopoulos, A.G. and T. Modis (2005) 'Urban Guerilla Activities in Greece', *Technological Forecasting and Social Change* 72(1): 49–58.

Kornetis, K. (2008) 'Spain and Greece', in M. Klimke and J. Scharlothe (eds) *1968 in Europe: A History of Protest and Activism, 1956–1977*, pp. 253–266. New York: Palgrave Macmillan.

Kousoumvris, C.J. (2004) *Demolishing the Myth of Chrysi Avyi*. Piraeus: Erevos.

Kyritsis, D. (2005) 'Terrorism and Political Crime: Proposals for a Categorisation' [in Greek], *Poinika Chronika*: 490–499.

Lambropoulou, E. (2003) '"Criminal 'Organisations" in Greece and Public Policy: From Non-Real to Hyper-Real?', *International Journal of the Sociology of Law* 31(1): 69–87.

Lambropoulou, E. (2002) 'Greece', in M. den Boer (ed.) *Organised Crime: Catalyst in the Europeanisation of National Police and Prosecution Agencies?*, pp. 261–307. Netherlands: European Institute of Public Administration.

Lawrence, C. (2005) 'Re-Bordering the Nation: Neoliberalism and Racism in Rural Greece', *Dialectical Anthropology* 29(3–4): 315–334.

Livos, N. (2007) *Organised Crime and Special Interrogation Acts* [in Greek]. Athens: P.N. Sakkoulas.

Lyman, M.D. and G.W. Potter (1997) *Organised Crime*. New Jersey: Prentice Hall.

Macedonian Press Agency (18 July 2002) 'Giotopoulos Convicted During the Dictatorship'.

Makarenko, T. (2005) 'The Crime-Terror Continuum: Tracing the Interplay between Transnational Organised Crime and Terrorism', in M. Galeotti (ed.) *Global Crime Today: The Changing Face of Organised Crime*, pp. 129–145. Oxford and New York: Routledge.

Manoledakis, I. (2002) *Security and Freedom* [in Greek]. Athens-Thessaloniki: Sakkoulas.

Mazower, M. (1997) 'Policing the Anti-Communist State in Greece, 1922–1974', in M. Mazower (ed.) *The Policing of Politics in the Twentieth Century: Historical Perspectives*, pp. 129–150. Oxford: Berghahn Books.

Ministry of Public Order (MPO) (2006) *Annual Report on Organised Crime in Greece for the Year 2005* [in Greek]. Athens: Public Security Division, Ministry of Public Order.

MPO (2005) *Annual Report on Organised Crime in Greece for the Year 2004*. Athens: Public Security Division, Ministry of Public Order.

Murtagh, P. (1994) *The Rape of Greece: The King, the Colonels and the Resistance*. London: Simon & Schuster.

New York Times (12 January 2007) 'US Embassy in Greece is Attacked'.

Panourgia, N. (2009) *Dangerous Citizens: The Greek Left and the Terror of the State*. New York: Fordham University Press.

Papahelas, A. and T. Telloglou (2002) *File on 17 November* [in Greek]. Athens: Estia.

Papanicolaou, G. (2008) 'The Sex Industry, Human Trafficking and the Global Prohibition Regime: A Cautionary Tale from Greece', *Trends in Organised Crime* 11(4): 379–409.

Pappas, T.S. (1999) *Making Party Democracy in Greece*. Hampshire: Macmillan.

Pollis, A. (2002) *Testimony on the Subject of Terrorism in Greece at the US Helsinki Commission Hearing 'Human Rights in Greece: A Snapshot of the Cradle of Democracy*, 20 June.

Roehrig, T. (2002) *The Prosecution of Former Military Leaders in Newly Democratic Nations: The Cases of Argentina, Greece, and South Korea*. Jefferson, NC: McFarland.

Schwarz, A.G., T. Sagris and Void Network (eds) (2010) *We Are an Image of the Future: The Greek Revolt of 2008*. Oakland, CA: A.K. Press.

Seferiades, S. (1986) 'Polarisation and Non-Proportionality: The Greek Party System in the Postwar Era', *Comparative Politics* 19(1): 69–93.

Shelley, L.L. (2002) 'The Nexus of Organised International Criminals and Terrorism', *International Annals of Criminology*. Available online at: http://pages-persoorange.fr/societe.internationale.de.criminologie/pdf/Intervention%20Shelley.pdf

Symeonidou-Kastanidou, E. (2007) *Organised Crime and Terrorism: Contemporary Developments in European and Greek Legal Orders* [in Greek]. Athens-Thessaloniki: Sakkoulas.

Ta Nea (22 June 2009) '"Sect of Revolutionaries" Claim Responsibility for Killing Officer' [in Greek].

Ta Nea (17 November 2009) 'Searching for Connections between Rizai and Terrorists' [in Greek].

Ta Nea (12 January 2010) 'The Text of the Proclamation' [in Greek].

The Economist (11 September 2008) 'Greece's Government: Schools for Scandal'.

The Guardian (30 September 2006) 'Greek Economy Up 25% – With a Little Help From Prostitutes'.

The Independent (12 November 2007) 'Greek Police Retreat after Ambush by Cretan Drug Gangsters'.

To Vima (22 November 1998) 'Who and How They Wash "Dirty Money" in Greece' [in Greek].

To Vima (14 January 2001) 'The Tentacles of the Italian Mafia in Greece' [in Greek].

To Vima (5 August 2001) 'The Arms Trade in Greece' [in Greek].

To Vima (21 September 2003) 'Why the Godfathers are Evading' [in Greek].

To Vima (22 May 2005) 'The Greek Mafia: Why Do We Not Have Obvious Examples of "Ethnic" Organised Crime? The Relations Between the State and the Financial Power of Parallel Centres' [in Greek].

To Vima (11 September 2005) 'Greek Right: The Rotten Egg of the Snake' [in Greek].

To Vima (18 November 2007) 'The "Footholds" of the Mafia in Athens' [in Greek].

To Vima (6 April 2008) 'Who is Involved in the (Deadly) War of the Godfathers' [in Greek].

To Vima (12 July 2009) 'I Worry Deeply About Organised Crime' [in Greek].

To Vima (13 September 2009) 'Bosses of the Godfathers Changed' [in Greek].

To Vima (13 December 2009) 'Michalis Chrysohoidis: "I Don't Pray in Front of the Icon of Stalin"' [in Greek].

To Vima (28 November 2010) 'The Human Key of the "Cells"' [in Greek].

To Vima (6 December 2010) 'Calm in the Centre; The Last Have Left from Exarchia: Overall, Police Detained 85, of which 42 Became Arrests' [in Greek].

Tsatsos, N. (2001) *The Black Economy and Tax Evasion in Greece* [in Greek]. Athens: Papazissis.

Tsoulos, N. (2005) *Terrorism: Criminological and Legislative Approaches, Views, Dimensions of the Phenomenon, and Problematisations* [in Greek]. Athens-Komotini: Ant. N. Sakkoulas Publishers.

UN Office for Drug Control and Crime Prevention (2000) *United Nations Convention against Transnational Organised Crime*, General Assembly Resolution 55/25.

US Department of State (2008) *Country Reports on Terrorism 2007*. Office for Counterterrorism.

Vidali, S. (2009) 'Greece', in P. Hadfield (ed.) *Nightlife and Crime: Social Order and Governance in International Perspective*, pp. 183–194. Oxford: Oxford University Press.

Xenakis, S. (2004) 'International Norm Diffusion and Organised Crime Policy: The Case of Greece', *Global Crime* 6(3–4): 345–373.

Xenakis, S. (2006) *International Norm Diffusion and the Development of Greek Policy against Organised Crime, 1989–2001*, Unpublished DPhil dissertation. Department of Politics and International Relations: University of Oxford.

Xenakis, S. (2010) 'Resisting Submission? The Obstinacy of "Balkanist" Characteristics in Greece as Dissidence Against "The West"', in L.K. Cheliotis (ed.) *The Banality of Good: Roots, Rites and Sites of Resistance*, pp. 178–196. Basingstoke: Palgrave Macmillan.

Xenakis, S. (under review) 'A New Dawn? Change and Continuity in Political Violence in Greece'.

VINCENZO RUGGIERO

Commentary

Organised Behaviour and Organised Identity

Sappho Xenakis proposes a very useful and comprehensive review of the concepts of organised crime and political violence, while documenting the official efforts to address such concepts jointly and treat them as a single issue. It would be intriguing to investigate how members of organised criminal groups and violent political groups respectively react to such official efforts. In my own memory, when the 'mafiosi' happened to share a prison institution with members of the Red Brigades, they would steer away from those idealist Communists who got nothing out of killing. The former, when overcoming the disgust they felt in the presence of those who in their eyes adopted an incomprehensible political stance, and perhaps even a disposable sexual lifestyle, would simply suggest: 'Don't make revolution, make money, you cretin!' The latter, in their turn, would deal with the former as one deals with yet a different version of the economic and political power against which they fought.

Sappho Xenakis examines how Greek courts have attempted to term 'common' rather than 'political' the offences attributed to the Revolutionary Organisation November 17, and discusses how in the dominant discourse, at the international level, organised crime and terrorism have become increasingly intertwined. She also gives a detailed account of the story and recent development of organised criminal groups in the country and of the plethora of armed, or otherwise, political organisations which continue the long Greek contentious tradition. The fact that organised crime is guided by material motivations and terrorism by political ones may be seen as irrelevant by official agencies pursuing the objective of degrading the 'enemy', whoever that might be. Therefore, the ceremonies of degradation, including the choice of an *ad hoc* vocabulary, may well serve the task, as the mad, the drug user, and the terrorist constitute an undistinguishable mob in the face of which quibbling differences may just obstruct the criminal justice process. The text written by Sappho Xenakis is so rich that it only requires some brief comments.

Let us start with the hypothesis that organised political groups, in order to finance their activity, are often forced to resort to forms of serious criminality. While such criminality may at times include drug trafficking, it is likely to be a general rule that political groups purporting to represent disadvantaged communities would avoid involvement in activities that might damage those very communities. Moralistic and Robin Hood-esque in their own self-perception, political groups will opt for 'robbing the robbers', namely, the wealthy who are favoured by the exploitative system against which political action is addressed. Lucrative hold-ups, for example, or kidnappings of tycoons, according to this logic, would be the preferred sources of financing for violent political organisations. But even when carrying out such financially rewarding exploits, are we sure that political organisations mimic their criminal organised counterparts? In order to answer this question, it is necessary to identify some peculiarities of organised crime and political violence, respectively.

Attempts to define organised crime through the type of activity this is adept in are, in my view, unconvincing. Drug trafficking, trafficking in human beings, and extortion, for example, may be carried out by large organisations as well as by small independent groups. What connotes large criminal organisations is their internal division of labour, which transcend the technical skills of their members, displaying a *social* differentiation between those enjoying decision-making power and those devoid of it. A provisional answer to the question posed above, therefore, is that, even when committing serious crimes, political organisations cannot be assimilated to organised crime, but rather to varieties of professional criminality. In this type of criminality, the distribution of roles is typically based on specific individual skills, while a relative collegiality presides over decision-making, so that the planning and execution of operations are enacted by individuals close or known to one another. On the contrary, contract killers or drug couriers working for large criminal organisations, for example, hardly know the identity of the final beneficiary of their acts. They may engage in a long-term career while ignoring the strategy, motivations, let alone the face, of their employers.

Considering that some organised criminal groups do not limit their activities to conventional offending, some supplementary observations are needed. Successful organised crime manages to establish partnerships with the official world, particularly with business people and political representatives. When unable to do so, it remains a form of pariah organised crime, operating in the underworld, and destined to exhaust its resources and energies within the restricted realm of illicit markets. Organisations leaping into the overworld, by contrast, are required to adopt a business style, a conduct, a strategy, and a 'vocabulary of meaning' helping them to blend in the environment receiving them. In an environment saturated with corruption, within the political as well as the economic sphere, organised criminals will learn the techniques and the justifications of white collar criminals, now their partners. They may still 'commute' between licit and illicit markets, but their new status will force them to identify allies, sponsors, mentors, and protectors. In brief, they will be required to develop the negotiation skills characterising an economic consortium or a political party. Even when groups, while operating in the official economy, find it opportune from time to time to use violence, this violence will still be inscribed in the 'vocabulary of meaning' belonging to political parties and competing economic actors. Killing, in this case, may thereby become part and parcel of the negotiation process.

Violent political groups, on the contrary, use violence as a signal of their unwillingness to negotiate with a system they would rather demolish. Their action transcends the immediate result they achieve, and prefigures, realistically or not, a different set of achievements which will be valued in a future, rather than in the current society. Of course, some political groups may use violence as a supplementary form of pressure to accelerate a specific negotiation and pursue a concrete, material objective. But in this case, the word 'terrorism' becomes inappropriate, and such groups might be described as engaging in 'armed trade unionism'. Are official governments prepared to do so? The *ad hoc* vocabulary alluded to above would prohibit it.

Finally, the evolution of organised crime into structures commonly described as networks may make comparisons between the two forms of violence increasingly far-fetched. Networks imply the alliance between highly heterogeneous groups and individuals, each with a distinctive cultural and ethnic background, who may establish common goals on an occasional or long-term basis. Actors operating in networks are socially 'fuzzy', in the sense that their exploits and careers overlap with those of others who are apparently radically different from them. Networks are a reflection of grey areas hosting diverse cultures, identities, values, and motivations, areas in which the diversity of activities results from the development of points of contact, common interests and strategies between licit, semi-licit, and overtly illicit economies. I am thinking of 'dirty economies' consisting in encounters which add to the respective cultural, social, and symbolic capital possessed by criminals, politicians, and entrepreneurs, who interlock their practices. Networks, mobility, and fluidity are metaphors that aptly describe the flows of people and groups engaged in some of the most successful forms of organised crime.

Such forms of organised crime, in sum, see the participation of diverse collective or individual entities, each pursuing their own goals in a style and against a set of values that are consistent with their own specific cultural, ethnic, and professional background. As collective actors, participants display a form of *organised behaviour* without showing signs of an *organised identity*.

Let us now shift to a set of considerations pertaining to political violence. Violent political groups do not pursue material gain, and when they do, this is related to the acquisition of symbolic status, namely, a capacity to step up their propaganda and hence their visibility. Although criminology does provide analytical tools to deal with symbolic or expressive violence, there are other characteristics in political violence which make this specific conduct hard to locate within a criminological framework. A short overview of theories will help clarify this point.

Anomie theorists may interpret the behaviour of armed groups as the effect of a lack of social integration and regulation, namely, of cohesion, collective beliefs, and mutually-binding constraints allowing smooth interactions. However, violent political groups claim to represent highly integrated and regulated groups, such as classes, political formations, or religious communities. In other words, their lack of solidarity with the dominant social groups is counter-balanced by a high degree of solidarity proffered to what are deemed dominated groups, thus describing a situation of anomie with respect to the former and one of strong normativeness with respect to the latter. In their case, therefore, it is not anomie, but its opposites, namely solidarity and integration, that provide crucial preconditions for action.

Adopting the concept of social disorganisation, it might be suggested that political violence is a possible solution to the dilemmas of exclusion and impotence. However, it should be noted that a similar solution is embedded in a process of empowerment in which 'boundary creation' is paramount. All social relations occur within boundaries between those involved, and while at the individual level these boundaries fall somewhere between *you and me*, at the collective level they fall between *us and them*. Boundary creation between *us and them* is crucial for the formation of identities, and in the case of social movements and groups it also involves the recognition of existing inequalities as unjust. The concept of disorganisation may explain 'oppositional behaviour', not 'oppositional identity'. The latter involves identifying with an unjustly subordinated group, recognising the injustice suffered by that group, opposing it, and forging a collective identity of interest in ending that injustice. This implies a high degree of organisation and purposefulness, rather than aimless social disorganisation. While it is useful to explain dysfunctional processes and behaviours, it is also important to describe how some processes are functional to the promotion of shared consciousness, the identification of collective interests, and the building of organisational capacity to act on those interests. Political violence is one of the outcomes of such functional processes.

From the perspective of learning theories, violent behaviour is transmitted in enclaves of peers and through mimetic processes triggered by role models. Learning opportunities, however, are accompanied by 'claim making' about social justice and the perception of viable ways of pursuing it. Such claims become political when groups and organisations holding means of coercion are addressed. On the other hand, strain theorists would posit that political violence is one of the possible deviant adaptations to an unsatisfactory situation. The impossibility of achieving goals through legitimate means, in this type of adaptation termed 'rebellion', is turned into the imagining of alternative goals and the promotion of alternative, including violent, means to achieve them. Rebellion, however, which implies a 'genuine transvaluation', namely, a full denunciation of officially prized values, also includes a sense of frustration, a degree of resentment, and ultimately the perception of one's impotence due to lack of resources. Although questioning the official monopoly of imagination, rebellion as described in strain theory remains anchored to a deprived social condition hampering the constitution of alternative reservoirs of imagination. Such a reservoir, on the contrary, can be regarded as an important resource without which movements as well as violent political groups could not produce action. Resource mobilisation theorists, for example, suggest that availability of resources, rather than absence of them, makes groups capable of undertaking concrete action. Resources include material and non-material items, such as finances, infrastructures, authority, moral commitment, political memory, organisations, networks, trust, skills, and so on. In brief, while strain theorists tend to see social action as the result of a deficit, organised social action, whether violent or not, can also be interpreted as the outcome of a surplus.

Political violence may be prevalent in contexts where control efforts eschew negotiation or accommodation, and are themselves characterised by violence. In this sense, the activity of some violent political groups could be understood as violence against the establishment, on the one hand, and as one of the effects of violence perpetrated by the establishment, on the other. If this relational dynamic seems to be successful in explaining political violence, conflict theory, which also contains relational elements, proves too general for the task. It is true that institutions do not represent the values and interests of society at large, and that norms of conduct may only reflect the norms of the dominant culture. But to state that political violence is a manifestation of two sets of norms violently clashing does not account for the fact that in most contexts, where the norms of conduct also only reflect the norms of the dominant culture, there is a negligible degree of contentious politics and political violence. The analysis of the specific context in which political violence occurs is crucial if the generalisations of conflict theory are to be avoided. The existence of repertoires of action, accumulated through long periods of conflict, is in this respect paramount. Repertoires consist of a legacy, made of cultural and political resources, available to political groups. They contain sets of action and identity deriving from shared understandings and meanings; they are cultural creations that take shape in social and political conflict.

Some of the techniques of neutralisation identified in criminology may well describe the ideological process whereby violent political groups come to terms with the effects of their acts. The denial of the victim is operated through the perception of the victim as wrongdoer, the condemnation of the condemners through their association with immorality, and finally the appeal to higher loyalties through the appropriation of the ideals and practices of one's political or religious creed. Techniques of neutralisation, however, seem to belong to an *ex post* repertoire of motivations mobilised by offenders in order to fill the moral void they presumably experience. They are, in sum, a defensive device which may temper moral disorientation. Political violence, instead, combines defensive and offensive strategies, a combination without which action could hardly be triggered. Such strategies may include ways of overcoming a presumed moral disorientation, but must provide, at the same time, strong, unequivocal orientation for individuals and groups to act. This combination of strategies coalesce in the form of collective identity, which transcends pure role or group identity, in that it refers to shared self-definitions and common efforts towards the production of social change. Collective identity offers orientation in a moral space and gives rise to a sense of self-esteem and self-efficacy; it also prompts what is worth doing and what is not in *organisational terms*, leading individuals to appreciate their capacity to change the surrounding environment.

Political violence, therefore, is one of the outcomes of *organised identity* and entails high degrees of subjectivity, so that some features of social life are no longer seen as part of misfortune, but of injustice. Along with techniques of neutralisation, political violence needs to elaborate an interpretive 'frame alignment' with the activists it intends to mobilise. Against the backdrop of control theories, political violence could be examined as the result of a lack of attachment, commitment, involvement, and belief.

On the contrary, most armed organisations possess all of these in exceeding measure. In turn, adopting 'propensity event theory' may prove problematic, as the violence of the organisation does not reveal a deficit in self-control and an inclination to impulsivity, but an extremely developed ability to postpone gratification (the perfect social system to come) and an equally patient capacity to plan actions.

In brief, what is 'organised' in political violence is not crime or behaviour, but identity. And yet one may opine that organised crime and political violence could still be analysed jointly, because both require scientific investigations and interpretations of their structure, their internal make up, their external interactions, their targets, and their changing physiognomy. The sociology of organisations, in this respect, could well be mobilised for such a joint examination. This specific branch of sociology is certainly useful for the analysis of other organisations, for example universities, companies, bureaucracies, and so on. Why, then, limit our joint analysis to organised crime and terrorism? One could propose that, say, the next edition of the *Oxford Handbook of Criminology* contains a chapter on 'Organised Crime and Universities', or 'Fundamentalist Violence and the Post Service'.

MARGARET E. BEARE

Commentary

The paper by Sappho Xenakis paints a fascinating picture of Greece, as befitting its 'reputation for unruliness'! Whether Greece is any more 'unruly' than other nations is, of course, debatable, and there are perhaps more themes in common than could be seen to separate Greece from either her European neighbours or from the North American experience with regard to both organised crime and forms of political violence and/or terrorism. Above all, what is accomplished by looking cross-jurisdictionally at these issues is to reconfirm that there is no uniform set of conditions or criteria that justifies a strictly uniform or 'harmonised' response. Cultural conditions and other factors that give rise to, or tolerate, or encourage criminality – be it 'organised crime', 'political violence', or 'terrorism' – can be quite different across jurisdictions. The differences demand that appropriate policies and legislative responses take the differences into account. The similarities across countries relate to the political use that is made of the 'threat' of organised crime and terrorism, more so than to the nature of these two concepts.

Xenakis mentions the 'unprecedented breadth of social mobilisation across Greece', and describes a society where a segment of the population appears to share a lack of trust in the political, judicial, health, and educational systems, and in the official mechanisms of law enforcement. Xenakis mentions the increasing cynicism towards politics due in part to major political scandals. If the official, organised structures are not and will not be there for you, frustration can, and is, expressed in many different ways – including 'militant' types of response, such as the ones coming from the right- and left-wing groups that Xenakis mentions in her chapter.[1]

---

1   Personal communication with Yota Vassou, former 'Nathanson Fellow' at the Centre for the Study of Organised Crime and Corruption, York University, Canada.

The debate, however, focuses on the nature of these groups and, therefore, the nature of their responses. While such groups in Greece may use violence and tend to have a set structure and an organisation, they may also have an ideological way of envisioning society. Therefore, are the groups engaged in 'terrorism' or 'organised crime' or this broader, and possibly even more vague term, 'political violence'?

The left-wing groups that Xenakis mentions have very much followed the same pattern as groups like the Red Brigades in Italy in their fight against capitalism, imperialism, and in their envisioning of an alternative type of society – a society based on their ideological principles. Their strategies include using violence against targets including CIA agents in Greece, allegedly corrupt prosecutors, people who were allegedly torturers during the dictatorship, and others that they consider to be representing stumbling blocks to this 'better' society; or, alternatively, against those who have never been subjected to adequate 'justice' through the official judicial mechanisms. However, the 'redeeming' characteristic of groups such as 17N, as discussed by Xenakis, is the fact that, while they were accused of some twenty-three assassinations, the group avoided 'mass casualties and had no evident intent to terrorise the public', the result being a degree of public ambivalence, apathy – or even support.

Extreme right-wing groups such as Chrysi Avyi, which Xenakis discusses in her chapter, want their interpretation of a nationalist, extreme law-and-order model of society, and, to the extent possible, prefer to blame immigrants for all kinds of evils. It is not unusual for the target of right-wing groups to see the problems of society as being caused by 'foreigners'. While the violence used by some of the Greek-based groups might be more extreme than some other groups, a review of the organised crime literature reveals a history of the labeling and targeting of ethnic groups as being 'the' organised crime threats within North America. As immigration into the United States changed from one country of origin to another, so did the focus of law enforcement. For example, there is a vast literature that debates the nature of the Italian Mafia – i.e., the merits or abuses of focusing on Italian criminals during the late 1960s and 1970s within the United States to the near exclusion of all other groups.

'Organised crime' has always been a powerfully stigmatising label since it can mean many different things depending on the inclinations of the state, the public, and the media. Groups of ethnic minorities (such as Albanians in Greece) are easier to target and to label as being 'organised crime'. Various EU organised crime reports and Greek internal reports refer to the 'immigrant' crime problem in Greece with mention made most often of Albanians, Bulgarians, Pakistani, and Turks. Less mention is made of the fact that Greece has one of the lowest crime rates in Europe! Xenakis states that, 'in distinction to political corruption and financial crimes engaged in by members of Greek elites, "organised crime" has been popularly characterised as the crime of foreigners *par excellence*.' Not only are organised criminals seen to be foreigners, but when there is evidence of the contrary (i.e., Greek businesses engaging in organised crime), the suggestion is made that those businesses were forced into crime by the competition imposed by criminal immigrant groups upon local Greek businesses. Therefore foreigners, including, of course, illegal migrants living within Greece, are thrice guilty: are seen as the main source of organised crime; became a significant cause of Greek nationals having to engage in organised crime themselves; and, finally, are seen to be significant money launderers.

One area where Greece was seen to tarry behind the demands of the Financial Action Task Force (FATF) was in terms of that country's response to money laundering. Xenakis suggests that this delay before taking any aggressive action into reducing money laundering had the advantageous consequence that identification of those corporate or otherwise elite criminals and/or corrupt officials who were benefiting from illicit profits from one source or another could remain below the gaze of the media at the level of 'rumour'. Policies stayed for as long as possible away from threatening the corrupt practices of government or the shadow economy of the much wider society.

Canada does not have the reputation of being 'an unruly' country (possibly to our discredit!). What characterises both our understanding of the issues pertaining to organised crime and terrorism in Canada *and* our response to these forms of criminality is our close proximity to the United States and the pressure that is perpetually exerted upon Canada to respond in a harmonised manner to their definitions of threats and in line with their responses. More recently, the pressure comes via international agreements. However, international pressures are also not devoid of US influence. Pertaining to both organised crime and terrorism, the merits of a harmonised global response is now 'dressed up' as a required response to money laundering and terrorist financing. What began under the double-pronged focus of prohibiting the infiltration of dirty money into legitimate business and the desire to 'take the profits out of criminal activity', has morphed into the global focus on preventing the laundering of money as well as the illegal use of clean money for evil deeds.

The history to this enforcement strategy goes back to the passage of the US Racketeering Influenced and Corrupt Organisations (RICO) statute, as drafted by Robert Blakey in 1970. Keeping organised criminals out of legitimate business was one of the statute's targets. The stated purpose of RICO was the 'elimination of the infiltration of organised crime and racketeering into legitimate organisations operating in interstate commerce' (Bradley, 1980). Criminal forfeiture, civil forfeiture, and triple damage relief for persons injured by violations that fell under RICO were aimed at financially 'putting the criminal out of business', be it a legitimate or an illegitimate business. The majority of the literature today refers to the various 'dangers' to legitimate societal institutions from the laundering of dirty money (Beare and Schneider, 2007).

While Xenakis speaks of the Greek response being 'ahead' of the international pressure for policy harmonisation at least in terms of linking organised crime rhetoric to terrorist rhetoric, both Greece and Canada were deemed to be 'behind' and were criticised by the FATF for failure to implement some of the 'recommendations' directed at anti-laundering. The FATF recommendations are 'recommendations' in name only! A mechanism to apply 'pressure on difficult countries via its Non-Cooperating Countries and Territories (NCCT) programme, which provides for listing countries that are non-cooperative with respect to internationally accepted anti-money laundering practices', serves to ensure 'voluntary' compliance (Wayne, 2005).

Through multilateral institutions like the FATF, the IMF, and the UN, compliance is assured. In his study of money laundering, Mitsilegas (2003) takes the reader though the 'securitisation' process that resulted in the European Union's three pillars in the fight against money laundering. These measures constitute what he calls a 'new paradigm of security governance', which are now integral to the dictates of the FATF. The pillars are: *criminalisation, responsibilisation*, and *centralisation*. US Assistant Secretary E. Anthony Wayne acknowledged the quick progress that has been made in ensuring international uniformity in national terrorist financing enforcement standards and laws:

> We have seen substantial progress in securing countries' commitment to strengthen their anti-money laundering laws and regulations, which is inextricably linked to combating the financing of terrorism. In large part due to FATF's focus and our technical assistance and diplomatic pressure, governments pass amendments to improve their ability to combat terrorist financing. (Wayne, 2005)

Canada followed suit and passed new laws, mandated 'policing' responsibilities to the private sector, and all of this information/intelligence is now supposed to flow into our Financial Transactions and Reports Analysis Centre (FINTRAC) in Ottawa.

Canadian organised crime legislation was changed in part to match the UN Convention against Transnational Crime, with the exception that we eliminated the 'pattern' aspect that originated with RICO. Our criminal organisations must have three or more members in their groups, but there is no requirement regarding the need to have been committing crimes over a fixed period of time. The definition of criminal organisation activities is broad enough to include any and all 'serious criminality' and a seemingly favourite target for our legislation is gangs; not only the Hells Angels who are seen to have 'required' this form of legislation, but also, and in fact more frequently, street gangs. Gang members, including 'participants' and those who knowingly or unknowingly have facilitated the activities of the criminal organisation, are rounded up and, after an initial arrest period, are duly culled, as it becomes obvious that our court system cannot manage the mega-trials that flow from these enthusiastic policing activities!

As with these anti-money laundering provisions, the more recent anti-terrorism amendments codified into law through the *Proceeds of Crime (Money Laundering) and Terrorism Financing Act* are a reflection of American enforcement priorities and approaches. One would be hard-pressed to identify any aspect of Canada's terrorist financing enforcement philosophy that has any originality. The global war on terrorist financing is being pursued through a foreign policy approach used by the United States to combat the proceeds of crime and money laundering: placing intense pressure on countries around the world – both bilaterally and multilaterally – to stop the funding of terrorist activities and to enact laws and regulations that force the private sector to play a role in detecting terrorist funds.

Given the disastrous collapse of the global economy, caused not by traditional criminals or even by terrorists, but rather more accurately by the wildly self-serving activities of crony capitalists, we can now appreciate the irony in the dire anti-laundering warnings issued by the United Nations' Global Programme Against Money Laundering following September 11, 2001, that summarised the anticipated negative financial effects of money laundering as follows:

> Left unchecked, money laundering can erode a nation's economy by largely increasing the demand for cash, making interest and exchange rates more volatile, and by causing high inflation in countries where criminal elements are doing business. The siphoning away of billions of dollars a year from normal economic growth poses a real danger at a time when the financial health of every country affects the stability of the global market. The consequences of money laundering are bad for business, development, government, and the rule of law.[2]

While Canadian terrorism enforcement strategies mimics our anti-organised crime legislation, and while we certainly have political corruption cases, the three are not as co-mingled as would appear to be the case in Greece. We bemoan political influence that gives advantage to certain individuals, but it is more on the individual level and is less 'political' as depicted by the numerous vying Greek organisations, whether criminal, terrorist, or politically violent.

As I read the paper by Xenakis, I recall working with a colleague, Rusby Chaparro, to co-author a presentation that compared Canada to

---

2   ODCCP Counters Money Laundering; no author provided. Press release provided
     to Jennifer Katrina Penman in e-mail exchange with Ms Solongo.

Colombia in terms of our two countries' responses to organised crime and terrorism. Because Canada is so boringly 'ruly', perhaps Colombia might be a better comparison with Greece. Looking at Colombia serves to highlight some of the issues that are less obvious in Canada. In Canada, one can see the influence of the United States; within Colombia, one sees both US 'influence' as well as direct operational involvement that go beyond the making of policies straight into US enforcement operations within Colombia. While we may debate in Canada how best to bring domestic terrorists to justice, there is not the same history of political protest and over-thrown governments that appear to have given birth to left- and right-wing organisations with extremists on both sides.

With reference to Colombia, Chaparro writes:

> The juxtaposition between organised crime and terrorism is unquestionable in contemporary Colombia, but the understanding of this juxtaposition is a contested matter among academics, policy makers, and law enforcement agencies. That conjunction has developed in a context of armed conflict in which guerrillas, paramilitary, and large-scale drug trafficking groups have co-existed as crucial players, ... are all involved in drug trafficking, have permeated the public administration and politics at various levels, and have engaged in severe crimes such as massacres, selective killings, forced displacement, forced disappearances, and bombings to a major or lesser extent. ... [I]t is agreed that neither organised crime nor terrorism could be understood without reference to the other. (Chaparro, n.d.)

Chaparro goes on to describe how, in Colombia, the understanding of organised crime and terrorism have evolved through history but drug trafficking has remained their element of intersection. Organised crime has been studied in reference to the dynamics of drug trafficking, while terrorism has been articulated in reference to the dynamics of political forces and military strategies of the various groups involved in the conflict.

As in Greece, there is, of course, disagreement as to what constitutes 'terrorism'. In the academic and activist literatures, any of the armed groups involved in the conflict could be deemed to be engaged in an act of terror, including the army and other official institutions. In fact, it has been argued that the severity of the actions undertaken by the Colombian government to implement the global wars on drugs and terrorism constitute state terrorism (Stokes, 2004: 122–123), and that a dominant method used by the government in that war has been the paramilitary strategy (Garcia-Pena Jaramillo, 2005: 59–74). While the groups most notably against the official 'state' establishment are the guerrillas, one must acknowledge (in terms of 'security' issues and harm to citizens) the role of the paramilitaries in the internal conflict and directly in drug trafficking. The problem lies in the fact that those groups are part of the politico-criminal connection, in whose creation government agents participated and continue to be involved.

It is reasonable to predict, and supported by analysis of arrests and court decisions, that laws passed with the professed objective being to bring greater security to the people, will somehow contrive to either benefit or leave untouched those groups that have impunity (earned in exchange for favours or benefits). This appears to echo the Greek experience, or at least the government and the political debates as described by Xenakis. She writes:

> In Greece, the legitimacy of studying organised crime and terrorism together has not stemmed from any dominant consensus that the two are significantly interrelated in practice. ... And yet, organised crime and terrorism have been inextricably linked both in successive pieces of counter-legislation formulated by government and by the political debates that have accompanied them. ... The position of Greece was not determined at the outset by foreign pressure, but rather... took policy inspiration from the international stage to a more dramatic end and with particular domestic objectives in mind.

What is or is not a terrorist group or, for that matter, what is or is not an organised criminal operation and how the activities of such groups are advanced by political interests are questions that are woven through the Greek, the Colombian, and, to some extent, the Canadian experience. Cynicism is a common response to legislation that may be seen to serve domestic political objectives that are quite far removed from any likely impact in terms of 'fighting' criminal acts. Once we accept the fact that criminal operations could involve both legitimate as well as illegitimate players, and that definitions of terrorism or organised crime may, in some cases, be too interlinked with politics, then we must look to other measurements of 'harm'. The impact from the actions, rather than the categories assigned to the organisations, must take precedence.

References

Anthony Wayne, E. (2005) 'Money Laundering and Terrorist Financing in the Middle East and South Asia', Testimony before the Senate Committee on Banking, Housing, and Urban Affairs, Washington DC, 13 July. Available online at: http://www.state.gov/e/eb/ rls/rm/2005/49564.htm

Bradley, C.M. (1980) 'Racketeers, Congress and the Courts: An Analysis of RICO', *Iowa Law Review* 65: 837–897.

Beare, M.E. and S. Schneider (2007) *Money Laundering in Canada: Chasing Dirty and Dangerous Dollars.* Toronto: University of Toronto Press.

Chaparro, R (2008) *Legalisation of Criminal Networks: The Case of the Colombian 'Justice and Peace Law' Law 975 of 2005*, Unpublished LLM dissertation. Toronto: Osgoode Hall Law School, York University.

Garcia-Peña, D.J. (2005) 'La Relación del Estado Colombiano con el Fenómeno Paramilitar: Por el Esclarecimiento Histórico', *Analisis Politico* 53: 59–74.

Mitsilegas, V. (2003) *Money Laundering Counter-measures in the European Union: A New Paradigm of Security Governance versus Fundamental Legal Principles.* The Hague: Kluwer Law International.

Stokes, D. (2004) *America's Other War: Terrorising Colombia.* London and New York: Zed Books.

GEORGIOS PAPANICOLAOU AND PARASKEVI S. BOUKLIS

Sex, Trafficking and Crime Policy

This chapter offers a critical account of developments in the issue area of human trafficking, and more particularly sex trafficking,[1] on which public attention, crime policy, and law enforcement efforts have focused preponderantly in the past twelve years approximately. We set out to accomplish more than a review of available data and of the legislation and policies that are currently in place with regard to human trafficking. We find that the developments in this issue area during this period, in so far as they constitute a break with a previously long existing situation on several counts, lend themselves to a case study in the formation of crime policy in contemporary Greece and to an interrogation of the objective nature of state strategies the latter embodies. We follow suit from a certain stream of work that understands crime policy as the result of wider, complex social and political processes, and is concerned with how change in Greek crime policy and criminal justice comes about (e.g., Lambropoulou, 2003; Xenakis, 2004; Papanicolaou, 2008). Thus, we are keen to investigate the process by which *sex* trafficking came to be registered in the public agenda as an issue, as well as its relation to and significance for wider contemporary transformations of Greek criminal justice.

---

1   The use of the term 'sex trafficking' aims to preserve the economy of our text while sacrificing little from the substance of the matter. In the literature, there can be found a variety of definitions and terms (e.g., 'trafficking of women for sexual exploitation', 'trafficking for prostitution') depending on one's position in the ongoing raging debates, whose outcomes even the officially adopted terms often reflect (see, e.g., Ditmore and Wijers, 2003; Doezema, 2005; Munro, 2005). Our analyses will make clear that we regard sex trafficking to be an issue of economic exploitation as much as it is a gendered one.

That sex trafficking came to dominate the agenda in Greece may appear as a paradox, because important conditions that would justify such prominence were absent in the beginning of the 1990s.[2] When one considers human trafficking in general,[3] there is no lack of evidence suggesting that, since the early 1990s, numerous sectors of the Greek economy, and not merely the sex industry, have become a site of extensive and intensive exploitation of migrants originating from Eastern and Southeast Europe, as well as from the greater middle East (Linardos-Rylmon, 1993; Kapsalis, 2004; *Ta Nea*, 21 April 2008). Furthermore, sexual labour and the conditions under which it is exploited had hardly ever been an issue in the past. The activities involved in commercial sex constituted a marginal and obscure area of Greek social life unlikely to be registered in public discourse, let alone occupy the forefront of policy agendas. This situation remained largely unchanged throughout the 1990s, and legislation introduced in 1999 (Law 2734/1999) made marginal changes to the regulationist regime that had been in place since the mid-1950s (Lazos, 2002a). Interestingly, sufficient indications about both the prevalence of migrant sexual labour and the conditions under which it was exploited did surface as a remarkably vibrant and multifaceted sex industry

2   The emergence of the sex trafficking debate in Greece coincided with the widely acknowledged shift of the 1990s in relation to the migration trends, more precisely until the early 1990s, and after the geopolitical changes of 1989, when Greece was transformed into a host country of mainly undocumented immigrants from eastern and central Europe, the former Soviet Union, as well as from Africa and Souteast Asia (see, e.g., Karydis, 1996 and this collection; Gropas and Triandafyllidou, 2005; Vasilikou, 2007).

3   See the definition introduced by Article 3(a) of relevant Protocol of the 2000 UN Convention against Transnational Organised Crime: '"Trafficking in persons" shall mean the recruitment, transportation, transfer, harbouring, or receipt of persons, by means of threat or use of force or other forms of coercion, of abduction, of fraud, of deception, of the abuse of power or of a position of vulnerability or of the giving or receiving of payments or benefits to achieve the consent of a person having control over another person, for the purpose of exploitation. Exploitation shall include, at the minimum, the exploitation of the prostitution of others or other forms of sexual exploitation, forced labour or services, slavery or practices similar to slavery, servitude or removal of organs' (United Nations, 2000).

began to emerge in the early 1990s (Roumeliotou and Kornarou, 1994; see also Lazos, 2002a). We are thus inclined to distance our analyses from the idea that the policy responses to the issue have been primarily underpinned by either human rights sensibilities or by considerations of gender and sensibilities regarding violence against women (e.g., Sykiotou, 2009). In fact, both the gamut of state responses to illegal migration and Greek criminal policy's record with regard to gender issues arguably make such an understanding untenable. This is not to deny that issue advocacy did not reflect genuine concerns about the conditions of exploitation in the sex industry. However, these conditions began to draw wider and official attention only at the turn of the century, and only when a certain notion of transnational organised crime that was *imported* to Greece (Xenakis, 2004; Papanicolaou, 2008) at the time began to serve as the organising logic of the state's punitive response to illegal migration. As notions of transnational mafias and ethnic criminal organisations gradually provided the ground where issue advocacy and state policy began to converge, prostitution, migration, and trafficking were fused into a single issue, triggering the developments leading to the introduction of special anti-trafficking legislation in 2002 (Law 3064/2002), and a series of readjustments in police organisation and procedures with a view to enforcing this legislation.

In short, what was accomplished within a relatively short period of time was that trafficking was transformed from a known and criminalised but not necessarily dominant (Hatzi, 1980; Roumeliotou and Kornarou, 1994) aspect of the marginal underworld of prostitution to the cornerstone of an official discourse wherein it mediates a regular and unproblematic association between prostitution and organised crime. What properly concerns us here, therefore, are the conditions that made the above process possible, as well as its contribution to wider changes in Greek criminal justice and crime policy. At the same time, we also want to offer a few suggestions regarding how the issue of trafficking could be situated within wider social and political developments in Greece. In what follows, we begin from an obvious point, by reviewing the legislative framework that currently applies to human trafficking, the data made available by the Hellenic police since the introduction of that legislation, and available information on the implementation of the relevant legislation. We then gradually widen our focus to investigate the ground on which the Greek anti-trafficking regime[4] has been built, focusing on issue advocacy and its protagonists, the question of illegal migration and the social organisation of its exploitation. The concluding section will relate these analyses with a brief discussion of wider transformations in contemporary Greek society.

The Legislative Framework and its Implementation

The backbone of the anti-trafficking regime in Greece consists of the special anti-trafficking legislation introduced in 2002, Law 3064/2002, as subsequently supplemented by delegated legislation and other specific provisions contained in Law 3386/2005 on the status of third-country nationals. The law in 2002 inserted human trafficking for the purpose of organ removal or for the exploitation of labour as a specific form of crime in the body of the Greek Penal Code (Article 323A). Furthermore, it amended extensively those provisions of Chapter 19 (Articles 336–353) of the Greek Penal Code dealing with crimes associated with prostitution, and which were in place since the enactment of the Code in the 1950s. No changes were made in the regulatory framework of prostitution itself, which remains legal in Greece, under the conditions laid out by Law 2934/1999.[5] It also introduced general

---

4   We understand the idea of regime as generally involving 'principles, norms, rules, and decision-making procedures around which actor expectations converge in a given issue-area' (Krasner, 1982: 185).

5   These involve: an obligation to obtain a work permit (Article 1); an obligation to undergo fortnighltly medical examinations (Article 2); and an obligation to obtain a licence for the use of the premises where the activity takes place – this licence is issued by local authorities provided that certain conditions regarding the location of the premises are fulfilled (Article 3). Furthermore, the law prohibits the use of the same dwelling by a group of prostitutes unless the members of the group, up to three prostitutes, work in different hours (Article 4). The violations of these conditions incur sentences of imprisonment up to two years accordingly, as well as a pecuniary sentence. As regards street prostitution, Article 5(4) also explicitly criminalises

provisions pertaining to the protection and assistance of victims, leaving the details to be laid out by delegated legislation, currently the Presidential Decree 233/2003 issued in August 2003.

The prohibitions of activities associated with 'crimes of economic exploitation of sexual life' unfold in the amended articles 348 to 353, and additional articles were inserted, pertaining to pornography featuring minors (Article 348A) and to the commission of indecent acts with or involving minors in exchange for money or gifts (Article 351A); the custodial sentences prescribed by the Law are in the latter case mandatory. To provide an overview of the revamped part of Chapter 19 of the Penal Code: Article 348 addresses the facilitation of sexual relations of others by trade or for profit (this includes the publication of personal advertisements, images, telephone numbers, or the use of other electronic messages if it involves sexual relations with minors); and Article 349 addresses procurement, distinguishing between procurement of a minor, which is punished with imprisonment of up to twenty years according to the circumstances of the case, and procurement of adult women, which incurs a sentence of imprisonment of at least eighteen months. Additionally, men who live off the earnings of a professional prostitute may also be punished by imprisonment of up to three years. The old Article 351 on procurement was replaced in its entirety by the new Law, and now punishes trafficking for sexual exploitation by imprisonment of up to ten years, or up to twenty years provided that certain circumstances are present, such as when the victim is a minor or when it can be deduced that the offender intends to earn income from the commission of these acts. The reformed article also provides for the punishment of a person who commits sexual acts in the knowledge that the other individual is a victim of trafficking (that is, knowledge of the conditions the law associates with trafficking).[6]

---

soliciting in public using indecent postures, talk or movements, which is punished by up to three months of imprisonment.

6   For a recent systematic commentary on the provisions of the Greek Penal Code, see Sykiotou (2009).

The wording of the new Article 351 follows generally the template offered by Article 3(a) of the UN Protocol to the Convention against Transnational Organised Crime (2000), an approach which was not entirely welcomed by Greek legal circles, due to potential issues regarding interpretation of the terms that were transplanted to the Criminal Code's text from the English original (e.g., 'harbouring' and 'position of vulnerability'; see Dimitrainas, 2003; Sykiotou, 2009). Generally speaking, the Greek academic community of criminal lawyers has been traditionally very wary of the Parliament's increasingly frequent, opportunistic, and piecemeal amendments of the Penal Code, and the majority, in this case, seems to have concurred with the view that the special anti-trafficking legislation did not add anything that the previously existing provisions of the Code did not address systematically (see Symeonidou-Kastanidou, 2003). The substantive changes that Law 3064/2002 brought about involve a more explicitly austere sentencing framework, but this has been accomplished with a simultaneous amendment of the substantive content of the relevant articles. This has been deemed likely to create confusion in the application of the law by the courts, and thus perpetuate the lack of effective enforcement of the legislation, to which commentators have pointed as the real problem surrounding most crimes of sexual exploitation. In other words, the desired changes could have been accomplished with minor amendments rather than a radical rewording of the law, and with added political emphasis on enforcement (Symeonidou-Kastanidou, 2003: 32). As Dimitrainas noted commenting on Law 3064/2002,

> [t]he specific legislative intervention ... ultimately creates the impression that the Greek legislator was more interested to use the specific words and descriptions of the international and European texts, so that he could exhibit the results of their identical transfer into national legislation, rather than deal with the phenomenon with the seriousness that it demanded. (Dimitrainas, 2003: 156)[7]

With the above, we are able to begin the indexing of several issues to be investigated further, and return to our claim that the legislative change of 2002 involved more specifically the institutionalisation of the equation

7   Quotations from texts in the Greek language have been translated by the authors.

of prostitution, trafficking (and illegal migration), and organised crime. It should be already clear that the major focus of the legislative changes of 2002 has been sex trafficking, rather than trafficking in general. But it should be also noted that Law 3064/2002 is not a stand-alone instrument: Article 11(3) of that law makes explicitly applicable for crimes of sexual exploitation the provisions of article 187 of the Penal Code, by means of which the special legislation on organised crime kicks in. Article 187 of the Penal Code had also been refurbished a little earlier by a legislative initiative, Law 2928/2001, whose reception by the academic community of criminal lawyers had been similar or worse on the basis of similar misgivings as the above; in fact, Law 2829/2001 caused wider and considerable political fury, especially among the parties of the Left, exactly because it was perceived as a hasty and over-reaching effort of the Greek government to provide a response to international pressures, particularly with regard to combating terrorism. The extensive and heated legal and political debates on Law 2928/2001 on organised crime cannot be discussed at length here.[8] The substance of the matter lies not only in the more severe sentencing framework for those found guilty under this legislation, but also, importantly, in the changes brought about in various aspects of the investigation process and the judicial procedure for organised crime suspects. Some of the investigative powers systematised by the 2001 law were not unknown in Greece, especially under the special legislation regarding drug control and drug-related investigation introduced as early as 1987. Yet this latest intervention made at once applicable for the entire range of the crimes named in Article 187 of the Penal Code an impressive gamut of powers, including DNA analysis, undercover policing, controlled deliveries, wiretapping, personal data processing, and the monitoring of financial transactions; furthermore, the law removed jurisdiction for the trial of these crimes from jury courts and reallocated it to higher courts composed exclu-

8   See the respective contributions of Mitsilegas and Xenakis to this collection. The reader may also refer to the minutes of the parliamentary procedure and the following indicative publications: Hellenic Parliament (2001a), Hellenic Parliament (2001d), Hellenic Parliament (2001b), Hellenic Parliament (2001c), Manoledakis (2002), and Symeonidou-Kastanidou (2007).

sively by professional judges; and finally, it introduced leniency policies for whistle-blowers and witness protection measures (see Hellenic Parliament, 2001e). For all practical purposes, therefore, the direct connection of the anti-trafficking legislation with legislation dealing with organised crime is bound to affect the position of the prostitute-victim in anti-trafficking investigations, as she represents a particular use-value for the conduct and results of the investigation as a witness; in other words, her (or his) position, in so far she is entangled in an enterprise that is inherently police business, is defined by that particular use-value and less by considerations of victim rights and support. This is evident in the police circular guiding the process of interrogation of identified victims, whose logical structure is that of a bargain-cooperation for assistance:

> [I]f you think that you were forced to suffer one of the things mentioned above, then do not hesitate to declare this to the police officers who carry out the inquiry (the preliminary investigation), [and] who will examine with sensitivity and respect your case, and will offer you the help and support that you are entitled to by law. (Hellenic Police, 2003: 7)

Finally, given the real changes that the influx of migrants brought about in the ethnic composition of the sex industry (Lazos, 2002a), it is very clear that the anti-trafficking legislation cannot be considered in separation from the legislation regulating the status of migrants, both women and men, as it applies, of course, to all forms of trafficking. The link is not merely notional, but rather is very much manifested by the fact that important components of the anti-trafficking framework are found in the body of legislation relevant to migration, currently Law 3385/2005 on third-country nationals. So while victims of trafficking are for the purposes of that legislation a special category of third-country nationals, the procedure established by Articles 46–52 remains at all times conditioned by the victim's use-value to the investigative procedure. For example, the issuing of the special stay permit for victims of trafficking depends in the first instance on the characterisation of the individual as 'victim' by the public prosecutor (Article 46); the reflection period of Article 48 is also granted by a special order of the public prosecution service, depending on the results of the police screening. The actual issuing of the stay permit depends on 'whether the extension of the stay of the said person is deemed expedient, in order to facilitate the ongoing investigation or penal process, whether 'the above person has demonstrated clear will to cooperate', or whether the individual 'has broken all relations with the alleged traffickers'. Conversely, according to Article 51, the stay permit is not extended or is recalled when the authorities (the prosecution service) considers that the cooperation or report of the victim is malevolent or abusive, or when the victim stops cooperating. The 'use-value' of the victim is not a metaphor, but an accurate description of what is involved.

In the symbolic hierarchy of illegal migrant identities instituted by the new legal apparatus, 'witness' is not followed by 'victim', but by 'alien'. The practical relevance of embedding the regime of protection and support within the regulatory framework of the position of migrants is that, when the behaviour expected by the individual does not materialise, the repressive state apparatuses can always regress to the original treatment of the migrant as an alien body. That this has been and remains the case is illustrated, firstly, by actions at the level of street policing and in the obscure spaces of migrant detention centres, and by the consistent and persistent ill-treatment of migrants, as documented by the recurrent reports of human rights activists (see, e.g., Amnesty International, 2005) and of agencies operating beyond the strictly repressive core of the state, such as the Greek Ombudsman (Greek Ombudsman, 2001). But it may also be visible in practices which manifest themselves as instances of discretionary non-compliance to the victim-centred layers of the regulatory regime. One may note, for example, the case of the foreign woman who was added, for reasons of 'public order and security', to the National Catalogue of Unwanted Aliens (Article 82 of Law 3386/2005) and was thus refused extension of her residence permit, as a consequence of her conviction for illegal prostitution – she had been sentenced to twenty days of imprisonment and a fine of €200. The police chose that course of action, despite indications that the woman had been a victim of trafficking, and despite the fact that she lived in Greece with her minor child, circumstances which, according to the Greek Ombudsman, could justify a discretionary decision of the authorities to exclude her from the Catalogue on humanitarian grounds (Greek Ombudsman, 2006).

Enforcement of the Regime

We now proceed to examine available information on the enforcement of this legislation. A cautionary note is due here, since the amount of information made available by the Hellenic police is frustratingly sparse. This is not a situation restricted to human trafficking, but rather reflects well-known and widely criticised problems with the poor quantity and quality of the flow of information released from the police to the public domain (Spinellis and Kranidioti, 1995; Papanicolaou, 2003, 2009). On the other hand, it has become standard practice that more detailed information is leaked and presented in the press rather than made available via official avenues, and some information about trafficking has indeed found its way to newspaper columns occasionally. For all practical purposes, what is officially known about the prevalence of trafficking in Greece is based on data that the Hellenic Police publishes on its official website (with some latency), and on information that was included in the yearly open edition of the Organised Crime Report of the Hellenic Police, a publication which has been discontinued since 2006 (Hellenic Police, 2000, 2004, 2005, 2006).

It is useful to draw a line between what can be inferred about the situation in the 1990s and what we began to learn after Law 3064/2002 was enacted, if only to highlight the contradictions that the focus of that legislation on sex trafficking has accentuated. What was probably the first extensive report of the problem of trafficking in the press drew information from an unpublished report of an interministerial committee in spring 1996 – probably the first official response towards trafficking (Nikolakopoulos, 1996). According to this report, 3,948 women were deported in 1995 on grounds of illegal entry or illegal stay (that is, after their visa expired). As reported, these women were 'engaging in the exercise of the oldest profession', but it is added at another point that 1,277 women were arrested for prostitution (and also 196 procurers) during the same year. Furthermore, it was also reported that, between 1990 and the first semester of 1995, 6,420 crimes against sexual freedom were committed in total, of which 1,094 were felonies and 4,297 misdemeanours; and of the offenders, 7,015 were Greek nationals and 466 were aliens (but, as the classification makes very clear, these data had been drawn from the official recorded crime series of the Hellenic Police, and are therefore not entirely relevant (e.g., rape and indecent assault are also included in these numbers)). Interestingly, what is also reported is the number of women who were allowed entry and work permit as performing artists; their number declined from 3,411 in 1991 to 2,021 in 1995, totalling 13,677 in the period between 1990 and 1995 (ibid.).

For 1996, Psimmenos (2000: 82) refers to media reports according to which 200 under-age and almost 1,000 adult female migrants were repatriated to their countries of origin. And for 1999, Emke-Poulopoulos (2001: 5) reports that 88 foreign women working in brothels without permit were arrested, as well a 1,341 'foreign women in Greece working illegally in bars and other establishments subject to health control' (e.g., cafeterias, bars, café-bars). This report asserted that the figures represented a fraction of the foreign women working under exploitative conditions, and more specifically 'hidden prostitution, which is covered by socially accepted professions such as waitresses, hostesses, and dancers in public and private establishments. Other forms of hidden prostitution are masseuses, strippers, pornographic video actresses, entertainers, and beauticians' (ibid.). It is doubtful, however, whether this assertion is warranted, since it equates the employment of *all* female illegal migrants in these establishments with sex trafficking. It is interesting to note that Emke-Poulopoulos' report concerned specifically sex trafficking.

The Hellenic Police began to report figures on trafficking victims only after the introduction of Law 3064/2002. It is interesting to contrast these numbers with those reported for the preceding period, because it becomes immediately evident that thousands of exploited migrant women who could not be identified as victims of trafficking had been (officially) invisible. Table 1 presents the data regarding all forms of human trafficking made available by the Hellenic Police, and also additional information on the course of action taken after the victims were identified.

These details are important because when the Hellenic Police reports 'victims' in general, they essentially report the total number of the women who were identified in connection with the cases recorded as trafficking in the first instance. Whether victimisation may have indeed taken place is established in the course of the preliminary investigation, during which the police are authorised to carry out a screening process, alongside the interrogation (Hellenic Police, 2003). Once this procedure has resulted in formal prosecution, the provisions of article 12.1 of Law 3064/2002 and of its executive Presidential Decree 233/2003 are activated, and the victim can be placed under arrangements of assistance and protection.[9] After the enactment of Law 3386/2005 on 'third-country nationals', depending on the results of police screening, a special order of the public prosecutor may grant the victim a month's reflection period before formal prosecution 'so that they recover and escape the influence of the offenders in order to make an unbiased decision regarding their cooperation with the authorities' (Article 48.1).

As Table 1 shows, just above one-third of the victims identified in connection with recorded trafficking cases were actually placed between 2003 and 2008 under the regime of assistance and protection laid down by the Greek law. While the official series does not differentiate by gender or by type of trafficking, it can be safely assumed that the vast majority of the individuals were involved in cases of sex trafficking and were women, something that reflects screening procedures, the development of special anti-trafficking units alongside regular vice squads, and the involvement of an array of public and private players all of which were concerned preponderantly with sex trafficking. But it is evident that, over six years, there has been no significant increase in the numbers of assisted and protected victims as a proportion of the total number of victims identified. The official note accompanying the publication of these data each year clarifies

---

9   Alternatively, assistance and protection are offered to victims once they have sought themselves help from the (public) services and establishments of assistance and protection (Article 2 of the Presidential Decree 233/2003). After the introduction of the Presidential Decree, the point of contention between the police and NGOs was the procedure by which the latter's expertise and shelters could be integrated in the process of providing assistance. Eventually, a memorandum of cooperation was signed in November 2005, and we comment on it in the following section.

that the majority of victims (in the first sense of 'identified victims') have stated upon contact with the police that 'they do not wish to be placed under the protection of the State', and, additionally, most of them reside legally in Greece (Hellenic Police, n.d.).

As regards victims, therefore, the examination of the officially available information generates reasonable doubt whether all of them can be considered as being trapped in forced prostitution – or forced labour, as the series do not discriminate. Furthermore, none of the annual Organised Crime reports of the Hellenic Police, which included a dedicated section on trafficking, despite references to the regimes of force and fraud that these women are subject to, have entirely or strongly affirmed the image of sex slavery that has become the mantra of many actors involved in contemporary issue advocacy campaigns (O'Connell Davidson, 2006).

The Hellenic Police also makes available information about the country of origin of the trafficking victims. Firstly, of note is the absence of any Greek victims; secondly, the vast majority of the victims came from Eastern European countries, particularly Romania, Russia, Ukraine, Bulgaria, Albania, and Moldova, about 80 percent of victims identified between 2003 and 2008 (Hellenic Police, n.d.). This pattern follows the wider trend of *migratory movements* to Greece in the 1990s and after, which primarily involved populations originating from Eastern European countries. But the data are also instructive about the exact focus of law enforcement efforts on foreign nationals.

Additional insights about the focus of law enforcement efforts on the issue can be derived from data regarding identified offenders. An upshot of changing priorities of the police towards the attainment of quantitatively tangible results after the introduction of Law 2928/2001 on organised crime has been an explicit concern about *criminal organisations*. As the 2005 Organised Crime report of the Hellenic Police noted with regard to the anti-trafficking results of the preceding year,

> the number of criminal organisations dismantled in 2004 is significantly increased with respect to the previous year. This fact is due mainly to the more substantive and efficient action of the investigating authorities. The dismantling of *criminal organisations* that commit human trafficking was among the priorities of the Hellenic Police in the year 2004. (Hellenic Police, 2005: 10, our emphasis)

The available data between 2003 and 2008 on identified trafficking offenders by country of origin are presented in Table 2. In the course of these years, the Hellenic Police encountered diverse forms such as labour trafficking or baby trafficking; the Organised Crime report for 2004 includes a particular mention to both these forms, as a number of criminal networks had been targeted and dismantled successfully in that year. But the majority of cases involved sex trafficking. With the above qualification, it can be observed that, while the data for the six-year period reveal an involvement of Romanian, Albanian Bulgarian, Russian, or Ukrainian nationals, the majority of trafficking offenders, almost 60 percent of the total number of investigated individuals, were Greek.

The Organised Crime reports provide additional information regarding the size, structure, and *modus operandi* of those criminal organisations. The reports offer information on the number of members of the criminal organisations that were targeted each year by the services of the Hellenic Police; the information from the available three reports is presented in Table 3. In connection to sex trafficking, the report for 2005[10] includes the standard review of the *modus operandi* of those criminal organisations, noting that the victims are recruited in the countries of origin by travel or 'work-abroad' agencies that advertise waitressing, care-taking, or housekeeping jobs in Greece. The transport of the victim to Greece is the job of foreign members of the groups, while the place of detention, the mode of transport, and contacts with clients are the job of the Greek members of the criminal organisations. The women are exchanged or sold, and are moved frequently by the traffickers in various places in Greece. Furthermore,

> nightclubs that offer strip shows continue to play an important role. There the victims are forced to be prostituted to clients by means of cover-labour as waitresses or dancers. Non-indigenous and indigenous criminal organisations cooperate with the owners of these clubs where the victims are prostituted, offering sexual services

10   For the economy of the text, we only refer to the 2006 report here, as the substance of the matter is not affected: the report noted that the *modus operandi* of the criminal organisations involved in trafficking in 2005 'has not differed from that of the previous years' (Hellenic Police, 2006: 10).

to the clients of these establishments, after secret arrangements of the clients with them [the criminal organisations] or the persons responsible for the establishment. (Hellenic Police, 2006: 11)

The report continues by making an explicit distinction between types of criminal organisations, and notes the existence of recruiting criminal organisations that in turn sell to 'indigenous' ones; recruiting and exploiting organisations who either exploit their victims in Greece or sell on to 'other indigenous criminal organisations'; 'indigenous organisations that sexually exploit the victims and traffic them within Greece'; at the same time, the structure of these organisations is found to be hierarchical in most cases, and there has been 'in recent years' a trend towards ethnic heterogeneity and increased participation of women in the recruiting process (Hellenic Police, 2006: 11).

When all the available data are put together, it is unclear whether this emphatic reference to 'criminal organisations' is fully justified. It certainly does not support any idea of large organisational structures, or transnational mafias, which, again, feature heavily in mainstream accounts of the criminal activity used for issue advocacy. The case may be that the authors of the Organised Crime reports strictly conform to the definition of criminal organisation found in Article 187 of the Penal Code, which was introduced by Law 2928/2001; this speaks of a 'structured and continuously active group (organisation)' of three or more members that purports to commit specifically named felonies (ibid.: 37; see also Hellenic Parliament, 2001e). But it can be seen clearly that the majority of investigated criminal organisations barely exceed the legislative threshold of three members. More than two-thirds of these groups involve six members or less, which appears to be approximately the average membership of human trafficking groups according to the Organised Crime reports (as a ratio of *suspects* to investigated groups) (Hellenic Police, 2004, 2005, 2006).

The discontinuation of the publication of the Organised Crime reports of the Hellenic Police has been an unfortunate event, because it has made it difficult to evaluate whether the institutionalised preoccupation with criminal organisations continues to constitute a powerful distortive lens in the counter-trafficking efforts of the police. It certainly has the potential to constitute such a distortive factor, because what is of interest here is the social profile of the business. In this respect, the indisputable analytical point of departure is no other than the strong Greek ('indigenous') presence exactly at the points where migrant sexual labour is exploited. Whereas standard accounts conjure up an image of all-powerful, control-hungry, mafia-type transnational organisations, the consideration of the available information so far points to rather small groups, which are perhaps inter-connected and heterogeneous overall, but which possess significant ties with legitimate end-points, such as bars, night clubs, or strip clubs, where a strong *indigenous* presence is indispensable to the whole process. In other words, not only are the exploiters primarily indigenous, but also the entire circuit of exploitation is embedded in their conditions of the economic and social existence as small business owners and legitimate entrepreneurs: the causes of victimisation are related to the structures of Greek social and economic life much more than to those of any 'transnational mafias'. But such conditions can scarcely be brought to the forefront of the analysis under the weight of terms such as 'sex slavery' and 'organised crime'.[11]

Understanding the Greek Anti-trafficking Regime

The preceding analyses should have made clear in what sense the anti-traffick-ing policy regime established after 2002 can be understood as the institu-tionalised conflation of prostitution, illegal migration, and organised crime.

11   Of note here is the small but emerging stream of empirical research we begin to pos-sess with regard to the exact question of the social organisation of trafficking itself, as well as of other illicit services in Greece, that depend on trafficked goods such as cigarettes, stolen cars, and car spares. This research has been successful in reveal-ing the significance of indigenous elements at the end-points of the process, and of the overlap of these end-points with activities and establishments associated with legitimate businesses and entrepreneurship (Antonopoulos and Winterdyk, 2005, 2006; Antonopoulos and Papanicolaou, 2008).

This particular result is not, of course, uniquely Greek; rather, developments in Greece fall within a wider international pattern wherein the implementation of the 2000 UNCTOC and its protocols has amounted to aggressive suppression of unregulated migratory flows, to an extent that it functions in its entirety as a tool for migration control. In the context of a recent international stock-taking exercise, Dottridge has openly acknowledged that 'the anti-trafficking framework has done little good for the trafficked person and great harm to migrants and women in the sex industry' (Dottridge, 2007: 17). In what follows, we are concerned with the investigation of the conditions that brought about this result within the particular context of Greece.

Actors in the anti-trafficking campaign

We begin our investigation from the more evident factor, which is none other than the character of issue advocacy in the years preceding the introduction of Law 3064/2002. Indeed, the particular colour of the regime owes much to the platform a multitude of NGOs and other organisations and actors developed in order to bring the issue of trafficking to public attention in the late 1990s.

While counter-trafficking in the Greek context after Law 3064/2002 has involved progressively numerous governmental organisations, including the Ministries of Public Order, Public Health, and Foreign Affairs, the backbone of the anti-trafficking campaign prior to the introduction of that law consisted primarily of NGOs and campaign groups of diverse orientation (anti-prostitution, pro-sex work, and anti-trafficking as such). When the issue of trafficking began to emerge, the organisational components of the campaign had very low levels of interconnection (Lazaridis, 2001), and its more robust points of reference had been the General Secretariat for Equality and its research centre, KETHI, as well as the research group around Grigoris Lazos at Panteion University in Athens. Lazos' work was a unique longitudinal study of the development of the Greek sex industry in the 1990s that offered a thorough view of the field through an unambiguously abolitionist feminist lens (Lazos, 2002a, 2002b), and which proved decisive in offering scientific legitimation to the conflation of prostitution and organised crime.[12] Additionally, the campaign successfully developed links with other organisations and international actors, which were in a position to support it in various ways, including diplomatic pressure on the Greek government (see Papanicolaou, 2008). Overall, those who joined the campaign found a convenient common ground in human rights and anti-slavery advocacy, heavily borrowing elements of rhetoric and practice from international anti-trafficking campaigns that unfolded around the time, and, accordingly, lobbied for, and been involved in, providing support to victims of sex trafficking (see, e.g., Ditmore and Wijers, 2003; Doezema, 2005; Outshoorn, 2005; Soderlund, 2005). 'Borrowing' is not an exaggeration: in contrast with the way the international and other national anti-trafficking campaigns have developed, the Greek one lacked an indigenous background of feminist theorisation around the commercialisation of sex and the objectification of the gendered body (Munro, 2006), and it failed just as much to develop an articulated feminist voice that clearly reflected the Greek situation. Additionally, important questions regarding the social position of women, including migrant women, in Greek society have begun to be explored only recently. For example, the issues of domestic violence and victimisation of women have only emerged in public and research agendas in the past decade (see, e.g., KETHI, 2003; Sklavou, 2008; Courakis, 2009).[13]

12   Lazos' research successfully charted the changes in the Greek sex industry that occurred in the 1990s. While groundbreaking in many respects, his work should nevertheless be best regarded as controversial, firstly because of the particular conceptual framework he explicitly adopted in the interpretation of his data, and secondly, relatedly, because of the significant methodological problems marring the production of his estimates of the number trafficking victims. For a thorough review and critique, see Papanicolaou (2008).

13   We are pointing here to the absence of a robust infrastructure on both intellectual and organisational counts. For a critical consideration of the development of the feminist movement in Greece, see, e.g., Varikas (1993) and Petoussi (2007). Relatedly, Halkias (2004) gives a thorough critique of conflicting cultural beliefs around female subjectivity, as this is constructed through narratives, cultural assumptions, and nationalist ideas of race, religion, freedom, resistance, and the fraught encounter

Ultimately, what emerged as the main carrier of the anti-trafficking campaign in Greece has been an initiative known as the Galatsi Group. The Group emerged in winter 2001–2002 and comprised a range of organisations, particularly NGOs from different cities and different activist fields (public health, human rights, women's movement, religious groups). Its fundamental objectives were the prevention of trafficking and advocacy for assistance to victims of trafficking, and to facilitate reintegration. Mainly because of the diversity of these organisations, the initiative did not develop an official face and was loosely organised on the basis of monthly meetings to discuss developments, exchange feedback on activities, and establish action plans. The formation of the Galatsi Group was itself the result of developments involving the activities of NGOs, and financial support from sources, such as the General Secretariat for International Relations and Development Cooperation (YDAS) of the Hellenic Ministry of Foreign Affairs. A core component of the Group was involved in the Stop Now project, launched by the Centre of Research and Action on Peace (KEDE) in December 2001. The project has been associated with an awareness campaign and the lobbying of public organisations that shared competence on the issue of trafficking at the time, and supported not only the works of the Galatsi Group, but also academic research on the issue of prostitution and trafficking (Lazos, n.d.). Stop Now's position on trafficking has perhaps been an exemplary specimen of the new slavery discourse in Greece, in terms of placing human trafficking within a broad field of knowledge around the category of organised crime and the narrative of enslavement (Papanicolaou, 2008; STOPNOW, n.d.).

Seen in retrospect, the weakness of this initiative has been the impressively divergent philosophies and positions of its members. For instance, the Centre for the Support of the Family (Kentro Stiriksis Oikogeneias

between the Greek modernity and tradition. Lastly, for an account of the evolution of the Greek feminist movement, considering the role of the PASOK socialist party, and the foundation of the 'Women's Union of Greece' in 1975 by Margaret Papandreou, see Van Steen (2003): this 'second-wave feminism' movement resulted in radical amendments to Greek women's legal status in the family and in the labour force in the early 1980s.

(KESO)), established by the Archdiocese of Athens and the Church of Greece, campaigned for support to trafficking victims on the basis of an unambiguously conservative position on issues such as the 'crisis of the Greek family, the foundation of the conservation and growth of the Nation', and the 'prevention of the biological annihilation of the Greek nation' (KESO, 2008). Quite in contrast, the Greek Helsinki Monitor (GHM) is known for its anti-conformist discourse in defending the rights of minorities in Greece, including ethnic, religious, and sexual minorities, and for its aggressive critique of discriminatory practices of the Greek authorities against these groups (Amnesty International, 2007; Papanicolaou, 2008).

Such divergence explains the underlying tensions between the different agencies which prevented not only the development of a consistent platform for action over time, but also agreement on defining trafficking and criteria for victim identification, or even the provision of specific services. The absence of a more robust organisational platform has also meant that NGO initiatives have remained crucially dependent on external funding, mainly from public sources, and also relatively isolated from other social movements, which could potentially offer support. The campaign reached a high point with the signing in 2005 of a 'Memorandum of Cooperation on combating trafficking in persons and for providing aid to the victims', by means of which the state authorities did acknowledge that civil society actors could play a role in the implementation of the regime established by Law 3064/2002, particularly as regarded its victim welfare aspects. Under the memorandum, the government's involvement would be reinforced by a committee of representatives from all the competent ministries (Justice, Interior, General Secretariat for Gender Equality, Foreign Affairs, Employment and Social Protection, Health and Social Solidarity, Public Order). Yet interestingly, not all the organisational components of the NGO antitrafficking initiative were included in the memorandum: while the International Organisation for Migration and a multifaceted group was part of it, including such organisations as the NGOs Arsis and Solidarity, the Centre of Rehabilitation of Victims of Torture and Other Forms of Abuse, the Centre for Defence of Human Rights (KEPAD), the Greek Council for Refugees, the European Women Network, the International Society for

Support to Families (DESO), StopNow, or the charity organisation Smile of the Child, other crucial actors in the campaign, such as the Greek Section of Amnesty International, were not signatories. Additionally, one should note the tendency of certain groups to develop an autonomous effort, such as the A21 Campaign, which has been developing infrastructure for victims services in Thessaloniki and is part of a wider international initiative with offices in the United States and in Australia (The A21 Campaign, n.d.), the anti-prostitution religious group 'Nea Zoi' (INVgr, n.d.) and international organisations with long-standing presence in Greece such as *Médecins Sans Frontières* and *Médecins du Monde*.

The mutable landscape of NGO involvement in counter-trafficking efforts and victim assistance in Greece is an indication of how ultimately the whole field exists under the domination of the state, which not only is able to offer legitimacy to 'civil society' initiatives as such, but also to determine their very material existence. As many activists in the field note, 2005 was not only a high, but also a turning point in the campaign, since in the period following the 2004 Athens Olympics funding has been less available, causing numerous efforts to stall. But there is little doubt that the causes for the current state of the Greek anti-trafficking campaign can be traced back to the fundamental weaknesses of its beginnings; namely, its dependence on a borrowed language and models of action that alienated the campaign from critical allies within Greece's contemporary social movements.

Mirages of exploitation and crime policy transitions

Our concern with the implications of the explicit focus of the Greek anti-trafficking campaign on sex trafficking mainly stems from the realisation that, ultimately, it functioned to sideline and obscure the wider issue of the over-exploitation of migrant labour in Greece. The changes in the sex industry and the influx of foreign women in the 1990s and after should be understood, not as an isolated phenomenon, but as an integral part of a wider trend in the participation of migrants in the labour market and Greek society in general. After the sociopolitical changes in Eastern

Europe, Greece became a migratory destination in a dramatic reversal of long-standing historical patterns (Linardos-Rylmon, 1993; Petriniotis, 1993). The vast majority of migrants were Eastern Europeans, who mostly entered the country and its labour market illegally, and, in fact, the Greek economy, in the 1990s and after, had the capacity to employ migrant labour in low-status, low-paid jobs in the primary and secondary sectors of the economy, and, in the case of women, domestic services (see, e.g., Karydis, 1996; INE/GSEE, 1999; Pavlou 2004; Vasilikou, 2007).

It is important to note certain qualitative characteristics of the migrants' situation in the Greek labour market and society. They have firstly constituted a reserve of cheap labour, which could be employed profitably *and* be held at ransom, since a simple report to the authorities by the employers themselves could lead to an individual's arrest and expulsion. As noted in an early report published by the General Confederation of Greek Workers (GSEE),

> the extension of illegal foreigners' employment in Greece has been combined with the spread of the black economy and in particular with the infringement of workers' rights and of the relevant legislation. Illegal foreigners constitute a cheap workforce used in those economic sectors where the trend towards a partial or total infringement of labour and social security laws is already obvious, as well as in those branches where cheap labour could offer new possibilities not existent before. ... It has been estimated that the contributions evasion, due to the illegal work of foreigners, reaches about 100 billion drachmas per year. (Linardos-Rylmon, 1993: 62)

Secondly, the entry of these populations has been associated with the formation of new, relatively isolated social spaces, particularly in central areas of Greece's urban centres, where migrants have congregated in search of housing, relative security from the persecution of the authorities, and easier access to employment. Psimmenos, in his study of the living conditions of migrant workers in Athens under a general problematic of social exclusion, has understood these areas of congregation as *periphractic spaces* (fenced-off spaces): hidden from the public eye and organised around the places where downgraded mass accommodation could be found, such collective spaces were 'an amorphous environment full of physical and moral humiliation and unable to care for the physical, spiritual, and emotional needs of the population' (Psimmenos, 2000: 92). This situation of social isolation uncovered ethnographically by Psimmenos' and subsequent studies in other cities (see, e.g., Labrianidis and Lyberaki, 2001) have confirmed, complemented, and substantially enriched the knowledge about the brutal economic exploitation of migrant labour which studies carried out from within the established structures of the Greek labour movement have repeatedly reported over time (Linardos-Rylmon, 1993; Kapsalis, 2004). The vulnerable position of migrant women, about which we have recently begun to learn more (Sklavou, 2008), is essentially embedded in the general conditions of an already vulnerable population.

These wider dimensions of change in Greece's workforce and the reconfiguration of relations in the labour market *were not registered in discussions about the sex industry*. Rather, questions about the participation of foreigners in commercial sex services, and women who followed homologous trajectories to those of men within Greece's new periphractic spaces (Lazaridis and Romaniszyn, 1998; Psimmenos, 2000; Lazaridis, 2001),[14] were framed around the existence of organised criminal networks, which were seen to exercise total control over the movement and conditions of work of those engaging in prostitution. The implications of this have been considerable.

Firstly, the focus on sex trafficking victims has, in fact, led to a human-rights policy focus on a severely marginalised but elusive category of migrants, whereas the real issue has been the general conditions under which migrant labour as a whole has made its significant contribution to Greece's rapid economic recovery in the 1990s. On one hand, the influx of migrant labour provided a unique opportunity for the satisfaction of demand for cheap labour in a series of productive sectors of the Greek economy; these included agriculture, with migrant workers being involved in the formation of a waged-labour category 'for the first time after several decades', as well as manufacture, construction, and services, where low wages played a role in the ability of these enterprises to sustain competitiveness.

14   Interestingly, the conditions of sexual exploitation of migrant women did *not* escape the attention of local trade unions (Linardos-Rylmon, 1993: 49).

Additionally, the redistribution of income in favour of certain social strata during the late 1980s made possible the employment of migrants in domestic services and the fledging night-time economy. But there is little doubt that exploitation in the sex industry is inscribed as a phenomenon in the generalised employment and exploitation of (primarily undocumented) migrant labour by means of the terrorisation (Kapsalis, 2004) and the thorough social marginalisation of this population. This situation has been directly connected to the prohibitions instituted by the state, as it involved a certain reliance on illegal networks in order to satisfy the demand for labour (Linardos-Rylmon, 1993: 25).

Secondly, the framing of the whole advocacy campaign along lines conjuring up the spectre of organised crime and transnational mafias normalised that discourse in the public domain (Karaiskaki, 2001; see also Tsarouchas, 2002) and ultimately offered credibility to policy approaches that had made particularly uneasy first steps in Greece (see Xenakis, 2004). It has to be remembered that the Greek state's prior strategy towards illegal migration control hardly went beyond fire-brigade-style management, and more particularly it involved purely police responses that were as repressive as they were unsystematic. The favourite measure implemented by the Hellenic Police were the so-called 'sweep operations', involving mass stop-and-search operations in public places, whereby any number of undocumented migrants arrested would be then forwarded to the border for expulsion (see, e.g., Petriniotis, 1993). The numbers of migrants who rode the unhappy merry-go-round of entry–deportation–re-entry in the 1990s are estimated to millions (Linardos-Rylmon, 1993; Karydis, 1996; Lambropoulou, 2000). The introduction of legislation on organised crime in 2001 brought into play an impressive gamut of powers that allow the police and other investigative authorities to be much more strategic in their approach, and Law 3064/2002 provided the first instance in which these powers were effortlessly extended to apply in domains that directly relate to the disruption of illegal migration. Essentially, the issue of sex trafficking acted as a lubricant towards that strategic transition in Greek crime policy.

Victims	2003	2004	2005	2006	2007	2008	Total
Identified	93	181	137	83	100	78	672
Assistance and protection	28	46	57	39	35	36	241
(by type of action)							
Prosecutor's Order	–	25	20	34	17	16	112
Cooperation with GOs and NGOs	–	31	19	37	29	26	142
Cooperation with diplomatic authorities	–	12	33	22	28	32	127
Cooperation with IOM	–	17	12	20	15	4	68

Table 1   Victims identified and victims assisted, 2003–2008
Source: Hellenic Police

	2003	2004	2005	2006	2007	2008	Total
Albania	22	22	13	28	4	13	102
Armenia	3	0	1	0	0	0	4
Belarus	0	2	0	0	0	0	2
Belgium	0	1	0	0	0	0	1
Bulgaria	1	15	12	12	26	10	76
Colombia	0	0	0	0	0	1	1
Egypt	0	7	0	0	0	0	7
Georgia	2	0	0	0	0	1	3
Greece	166	207	133	142	48	70	766
India	0	0	1	0	0	2	3
Iran	0	0	0	0	0	1	1
Iraq	0	0	0	3	0	1	4
Kazakhstan	3	1	0	1	2	1	8

Latvia	0	0	0	0	0	1	1
Lebanon	0	0	0	2	0	0	2
Lithuania	5	0	0	0	2	3	10
Moldova	8	4	3	0	2	4	21
Nigeria	0	0	5	4	0	6	15
Pakistan	0	0	1	0	0	0	1
Poland	2	0	0	0	0	1	3
Romania	20	5	28	9	18	32	112
Russia	30	10	3	4	12	7	66
Serbia	0	0	0	0	0	1	1
Sierra Leone	0	0	0	0	0	1	1
Slovakia	3	0	0	0	0	0	3
Syria	0	1	0	0	0	2	3
Turkey	4	4	1	0	0	0	9
Turkmenistan	0	0	0	0	0	1	1
Ukraine	12	5	1	1	7	1	27
UK	0	0	0	0	0	1	1
Unknown	0	64	0	0	0	0	64
Uzbekistan	3	4	0	0	0	1	8
Total	284	352	202	206	121	162	1327

Table 2   Human trafficking offenders, 2003–2008
Source: Hellenic Police

No. of members	2003	2004	2005	Total
2–3	35	38	26	99
4	36	40	32	108
5	32	25	20	77
6	20	17	20	57
7–10	21	37	30	88
11–15	8	12	8	28
16–20	4	2	3	9
>20	1	7	0	8
Total	157	178	139	474

Table 3 Number of members of criminal organisations under investigation, 2003–2005
Source: Hellenic Police (2004, 2005, 2006)
Note: The 2006 report includes a separate category for two-member criminal
organisations.

References

Amnesty International (5 October 2005) *Greece: Out of the Spotlight. The Rights of Foreigners and Minorities are Still a Grey Area, Report EUR 26/016/2005*. Available online at: http://web.amnesty.org/library/index/engeur250162005

Amnesty International (2007) *Greece: Protection of Rights of Women and Girls Victims of Trafficking for Sexual Exploitation* [in Greek]. Athens: Amnesty International Greek Section.

Antonopoulos, G.A. and G. Papanicolaou (2008) *Gone in 50 Seconds: The Social Organisation of the Stolen Cars Market in Greece*. Paper presented at the X Cross-border Crime Colloquium, Belgrade, November.

Antonopoulos, G.A. and J.A. Winterdyk (2005) 'Techniques of Neutralising the Trafficking of Women: A Case Study of an Active Trafficker in Greece', *European Journal of Crime, Criminal Law and Criminal Justice* 13: 136–147.

Antonopoulos, G.A. and J.A. Winterdyk (2006) 'The Smugggling of Migrants in Greece: An Examination of its Social Organisation', *European Journal of Criminology* 3: 439–461.

Courakis, N.E. (ed.) (2009) *Gendered Criminality: A Penal and Criminological Approach to Gender* [in Greek]. Athens: Ant. N. Sakkoulas Publishers.

Dimitrainas, G. (2003) 'Combating Human Trafficking After L.3064/2002', in E. Symeonidou-Kastanidou (ed.) *The New Law 3064/2002 on Human Trafficking* [in Greek], pp. 87–156. Thessaloniki: Sakkoulas.

Ditmore, M. and M. Wijers (2003) 'The Negotiation on the UN Protocol on Trafficking in Persons', *Nemesis* 19: 79–88.

Doezema, J. (2005) 'Now you see her, now you don't: Sex workers at the UN Trafficking Protocol Negotiations', *Social and Legal Studies* 14: 61–89.

Dottridge, M. (2007) 'Introduction', in GAATW (ed.) *Collateral Damage: The Impact of Anti-trafficking Measures on Human Rights around the World*, pp. 1–27. Bakgkok: Global Alliance Against Traffic in Women.

Emke-Poulopoulos, I. (2001) *Trafficking in Women and Children: Greece, A Country of Destination and Transit* [in Greek]. Athens: Institute for the Study of the Greek Economy and Greek Society of Demographic Studies.

Greek Ombudsman (2001) *Conditions of Detention in the Detention Rooms of the Police Directorate of Chios, of the General Police Directorate of Athens (Alexandras) and in the Detention Rooms of Illegally Entering Economic Migrants and Refugees in Kos* [in Greek]. Athens: Greek Ombudsman.

Greek Ombudsman (January 2006) *Deletion of a Victim of Trafficking from the National Database of Unwanted Aliens (E.K.AN.A.) on Humanitarian Grounds.* Available online at: http://www.synigoros.gr/reports/synopsi_diamesolavisis_diagrafh_trafficking.pdf (Accessed 10 July 2009)

Gropas, R. and A. Triandafyllidou (2005) *Migration in Greece at a Glance.* Athens: ELIAMEP-Hellenic Foundation for European and Foreign Policy.

Halkias, A. (2004) *The Empty Cradle of Democracy: Sex, Abortion and Nationalism in Modern Greece.* Durham and London: Duke University Press.

Hatzi, T. (1980) *'Poutana': A Woman's Fate, or the Misery of Being a Woman* [in Greek]. Athens: Odysseas.

Hellenic Parliament (2001a) *Minutes and Report of the Permanent Committee for Public Administration, Public Order and Justice on the Draft Law 'Amendments of Provisions of the Penal Code and Code of Criminal Procedure and Other Provisions on the Protection of the Citizen from Punishable Acts of Criminal Organisations'* [in Greek]. Athens: Hellenic Parliament.

Hellenic Parliament (2001b) *Minutes of the Hellenic Parliament, 10th Period (Parliamentary Republic), 1st Session, 185th sitting (Tuesday 5 June)* [in Greek]. Athens: Hellenic Parliament.

Hellenic Parliament (2001c). *Minutes of the Hellenic Parliament, 10th Period (Parliamentary Republic), 1st Session, 187th sitting (Thursday 7 June)* [in Greek]. Athens: Hellenic Parliament.

Hellenic Parliament (2001d) *Minutes of the Hellenic Parliament, 10th Period (Parliamentary Republic), 1st Session, 190th sitting (Tuesday 12 June)* [in Greek]. Athens: Hellenic Parliament.

Hellenic Parliament (2001e) *Report on Draft Law 'Amendment of Provisions of the Penal Code and Code of Criminal Procedure regarding the Protection of Citizens from Punishable Acts of Criminal Organisations* [in Greek]. Athens: Directorate of Scientific Studies, Hellenic Parliament.

Hellenic Police (2000) *Annual Report on Organised Crime in Greece 1999* [in Greek]. Athens: Hellenic Police, Hellenic Ministry of Public Order.

Hellenic Police (2004) *Annual Report on Organised Crime in Greece 2003, Open Edition* [in Greek]. Athens: Hellenic Police, Hellenic Ministry of Public Order.

Hellenic Police (2005) *Annual Report on Organised Crime in Greece 2004, Open Edition* [in Greek]. Athens: Hellenic Police, Hellenic Ministry of Public Order.

Hellenic Police (2006) *Annual Descriptive Report on Organised Crime in Greece 2005, Open Edition* [in Greek]. Athens: Hellenic Police, Hellenic Ministry of Public Order.

Hellenic Police (26 November 2003) *Combating Human Trafficking, and Assistance to Victims*, Circular 3007/38/90-κδ' [in Greek].

Hellenic Police (n.d.) *Cooperation of Hellenic Police with Other Agencies in the Framework of OKEA*. Available online at: http://www.ydt.gr/main/Article.jsp?ArticleID=94780 (Accessed 12 May 2008)

Hellenic Police (n.d.) *Statistical Data on Human Trafficking*. Available online at: http://www.ydt.gr/main/Section.jsp?SectionID=13438 (Accessed 2 May 2008)

Hindelang, M.J., Gottfredson, M.R. and J. Garofalo (1978) *Victims of Personal Crime: An Empirical Foundation for a Theory of Personal Victimisation*. Cambridge, MA: Ballinger.

INE/GSEE-ADEDY (1999) *Yearly Report 1999: Report of the Institute for Labour of the General Confederation of Workers of Greece* [in Greek]. Available online at: http://www.inegsee.gr/ekthesi-main.htm (Accessed 10 December 2005)

INVgr. (n.d.) *Selected Charities and NGOs in Greece*. Available online at: http://www.invgr.com/ngos_greece.htm (Accessed 5 June 2009)

Kapsalis, A. (2004) *Presentation of Results from Interviews with Target Groups of Immigrant Workers in the Construction, Fuel and Clothing Sectors* [in Greek]. Athens: EKA.

Karaiskaki, T. (16 December 2001) 'Women Slaves in the Greece of 2001'. *Kathimerini* [in Greek].

Karydis, V. (1996) *The Criminality of Immigrants in Greece: Issues of Theory and Anti-Crime Policy* [in Greek]. Athens: Papazissis.

KESO (2008) *KESO Report*. Available online at: http://www.simetexo.gr/index. php?view=article&id=69%3A2008-04-05-11-28-20&option=com_content&Itemid=63 (Accessed 5 June 2009)

KETHI (2003) *Domestic Violence against Women: 1st Panhellenic Epidemiological Research* [in Greek]. Athens: KETHI.

Krasner, S.D. (1982) 'Structural Causes and Regime Consequences: Regimes as Intervening Variables', *International Organisation* 36: 185–205.

Labrianidis, L. and A. Lyberaki (2001) *Albanian Immigrants in Thessaloniki: Journeys of Prosperity and Aberrations of Public Image* [in Greek]. Thessaloniki: Paratiritis.

Lambropoulou, E. (30 January 2000) 'The Routes of Mafia: The Geography of Organised Crime in Eastern Europe and the Balkans', *To Vima* [in Greek].

Lambropoulou, E. (2003) 'Criminal "Organisations" in Greece and Public Policy: From Non-Real to Hyper-Real?', *International Journal of the Sociology of Law* 31(1): 69–87.

Lazaridis, G. (2001) 'Trafficking and Prostitution: The Growing Exploitation of Migrant Women in Greece', *European Journal of Women's Studies* 8: 67–102.

Lazaridis, G. and K. Romaniszyn (1998) 'Albanian and Polish Undocumented Workers in Greece: A Comparative Analysis', *Journal of European Social Policy* 8: 5–22.

Lazos, G. (2002a) *Prostitution and Transnational Trafficking in Modern Greece, Vol. 1: The Prostitute* [in Greek]. Athens: Kastaniotis.

Lazos, G. (2002b) *Prostitution and Transnational Trafficking in Modern Greece, Vol. 2: The Client* [in Greek]. Athens: Kastaniotis.

Lazos, G. (n.d.). *Transnational Trafficking and Forced Prostitution in the Greece of 2002* [in Greek]. Available online at: http://www.stop-trafficking.org/database/STOPNOW_REPORT_en_2002.pdf (Accessed 26 March 2007)

Linardos-Rylmon, P. (1993) *Foreign Workers and the Labour Market in Greece* [in Greek]. Athens: INE/GSEE.

Manoledakis, I. (2002) *Security and Liberty: Interpretation of L.2928/2001 on Organised Crime* [in Greek]. Thessaloniki: Sakkoulas.

Munro, V. (2005) 'A Tale of Two Servitudes: Defining and Implementing a Domestic Response to Trafficking of Women for Prostitution in the UK and Australia', *Social and Legal Studies* 14: 91–114.

Munro, V. (2006) 'Stopping Traffic? A Comparative Study of Responses to the Trafficking in Women for Prostitution', *British Journal of Criminology* 46: 318–333.

Nikolakopoulos, D. (1996) 'Foreign Women in the Nets of Trafficking Networks' [in Greek], *To Vima*.

O'Connell Davidson, J. (2006) 'Will the Real Sex Slave Please Stand Up?', *Feminist Review* 83: 4–22.

Outshoorn, J. (2005) 'The Political Debates on Prostitution and Trafficking of Women', *Social Politics* 12: 141–155.

Papanicolaou, G. (2003) 'The American Police and Public Contact Survey: An Alternative Measure of Police Activity' [in Greek], *Poinika Chronika* 53: 583–591.

Papanicolaou, G. (2008) 'The Sex Industry, Human Trafficking and the Global Prohibition Regime: A Cautionary Tale from Greece', *Trends in Organised Crime* 11: 379–409.

Papanicolaou, G. (2009) 'Research in the Greek Police: Problems and Prospects' [in Greek], paper presented at the Conference celebrating 30 years of the Hellenic Society of Criminology, Athens.

Pavlou, M. (2004) 'Migrants "Like Us": Visions of the Response to the Migration Phenomenon in Greece and in Europe', in M. Pavlou and D. Christopoulos (eds) *The Greece of Migration* [in Greek], pp. 39–87. Athens: Kritiki.

Petoussi, V. (2007) 'Feminist Voices in the Law: Debating Equality, Neutrality, and Objectivity', in G. Papageorgiou (ed.) *Gendering Transformations* [in Greek], pp. 351–364. Rethymno: eMedia.

Petriniotis, C. (1993) *Migration to Greece: A First Recording, Classification and Analysis* [in Greek]. Athens: Odysseas.

Psimmenos, I. (2004) *Immigration from the Balkans: Social exclusion in Athens* [in Greek]. Athens: Papazissis.

Psimmenos, I. (2000) 'The Making of Periphractic Spaces: The Case of Albanian Undocumented Migrants in the Sex Industry of Athens', in F. Anthias and G. Lazaridis (eds) *Gender and Migration in Southern Europe: Women on the Move* [in Greek], pp. 81–101. Oxford: Berg.

Roumeliotou, A. and H. Kornarou (1994) *Final report EUROPAP. Country report of Greece*. Available online at: http://www.europap.net/dl/archive/reports/country/COUNTRY%20REPORT%20OF%20GREECE.pdf (Accessed 30 March 2005)

Sklavou, K.V. (2008) *Domestic Violence and Social Integration of Migrant Women* [in Greek]. Athens: Ant. N. Sakkoulas Publishers.

Soderlund, G. (2005) 'Running from the Rescuers: New US Crusades against Sex Trafficking and the Rhetoric of Abolition', *NWSA Journal* 17: 64–87.

Spinellis, C.D. and M. Kranidioti (1995) 'Greek Crime Statistics', in J.M. Jehle and C. Lewis (eds), *Improving Criminal Justice Statistics: National Criminal Justice Perspectives*, pp. 67–88. Wiesbaden: KrimZ.

STOPNOW (n.d.) *Trafficking in Women and Children: Modern-day Slavery in Greece* (Leaflet). Athens: StopNow.

Sykiotou, A.P. (2009) 'Gendered Criminality: An Attempt towards a Critical Approach', in N.E. Courakis (ed.) *Gendered Criminality: A Penal and Criminological Approach to Gender* [in Greek], pp. 83–158. Athens: Ant. N. Sakkoulas Publishers.

Symeonidou-Kastanidou, E. (2003) 'Human Trafficking in International Context and its Criminalisation in Greek Law', in E. Symeonidou-Kastanidou (ed.) *The New Law 3064/2002 on Human Trafficking* [in Greek], pp. 11–50. Thessaloniki: Sakkoulas.

Symeonidou-Kastanidou, E. (2007) *Organised Crime and Terrorism: Contemporary Developments in the European and Greek Legal Order* [in Greek]. Thessaloniki: Sakkoulas.

Ta Nea (21 April 2008) 'Violent Fights for 5 Euros: War Climate in Manolada of Ilia after the Uprising of Foreign Workers Regarding Wages' [in Greek].

The A21 Campaign (n.d.) *The A21 Campaign. Abolishing Injustice in the 21st Century. Our Strategy*. Available online at: http://www.thea21campaign.org/index.php/en/home/our-strategy (Accessed 5 June 2009)

Tsarouchas, K. (10 March 2002) '600 million Euros the Turnover of Prostitution', *To Vima* [in Greek].

United Nations (2000) *Protocol to Prevent, Suppress and Punish Trafficking in Persons, especially Women and Children, supplementing the United Nations Convention against Transnational Organised Crime. Adopted by UN General Assembly resolution A/RES/55/67 of 15 November 2000*. Available online at: http://www.uncjin.org/Documents/Conventions/dcatoc/final_documents_2/convention_%20traff_eng.pdf

Van Steen, G. (2003) 'Margarita Papandreou: Bearing Gifts to the Greeks?', *Journal of Modern Greek Studies* 21: 245–283.

Varikas, E. (1993) 'Gender and National Identity in *fin de siècle* Greece', *Gender and History* 5: 269–283.

Vasilikou, K. (2007) *Female Migration and Human Rights* [in Greek]. Athens: Akadimia Athinon.

Xenakis, S. (2004) 'International Norm Diffusion and Organised Crime Policy: The Case of Greece', *Global Crime* 6: 345–373.

CLAUDIA ARADAU

Commentary

Human Trafficking and the Politics of Numbers

'Between 100,000 and 800,000 people are trafficked into the EU each year.' Thus starts a recent report by the House of Commons Human Affairs Committee about human trafficking in the UK (Home Affairs Committee, 2009). According to the US Annual State report, which takes up research conducted by the International Labour Organisation, out of the 12.3 million adults and children in forced and bonded labour at any time, 1.39 million are victims of commercial sexual servitude, both transnational and within countries (US Department of State, 2009). Media, policy-makers, and social scientists have increasingly focused on the numbers of victims of trafficking, attempting to derive the 'truth' about human trafficking from statistical methodologies. This concern with statistical measurement has emerged out of the problematisation of the knowability of numbers of trafficked persons. Human trafficking is seen as a phenomenon which is hidden, underground, criminal, in the shadows of legality, and, therefore, difficult to know and measure. 'How do you count something that is all underground?', asks Kristiina Kangaspunta, Chief of UNODC's Anti-Human Trafficking Unit. 'We can't go to official statistics because nobody knows about these crimes.' (UNODC, 2007)

    The uncertainty of knowledge has led to the rhetorical framing of trafficking as either a problem of 'large numbers' or of 'small numbers'. Large numbers have been used by policy-makers to justify counter-trafficking interventions. The magnitude of numbers functions as an emergency call to take extraordinary measures to tackle human trafficking. In contrast, small numbers have been mobilised by activists to oppose some of the measures justified by the politics of large numbers: police raids, repressive measures against migrants, blanket suspicion of sex workers. 'Only a minority of sex workers have been trafficked!' is the title of a recent project on sex workers in London (Mai, 2009). Human trafficking is made actionable for the purposes of governance through the problematisation of its numerical extent. How many people are trafficked to a particular country, how many victims are identified, how many are rescued and assisted?

The chapter by Georgios Papanicolaou and Paraskevi Bouklis on the construction of the counter-trafficking regime in Greece offers an interesting perspective on these debates as it considers official statistics on human trafficking by the Hellenic police in Greece.[1] At the same time, the authors are concerned with the conditions of possibility of the sudden emergence of human trafficking on the political agenda in Greece at the turn of the 21st century. They trace the imbrication and, later on, fusion of notions of organised crime, human trafficking, and prostitution. Thus, they offer another important contribution to the debates about the 'truth' of human trafficking. The mobilisation of numbers in the fight against trafficking globally works in conjunction with a politics of classification and categorisation. The abstraction of numbers is underpinned by particular categorisations of what human trafficking is and classifications of who counts as a victim of trafficking. To be counted is both to be accounted for and to be valued in particular ways. In this discussion piece, I place Papanicolaou and Bouklis' analysis in the context of counter-trafficking regimes internationally, particularly in the UK and Europe, with the purpose of exploring what the politics of numbers discounts while counting, and what it effaces while categorising.[2]

1   For a discussion of how a security continuum is created between human trafficking, migration, prostitution, and organised crime in the EU, see Aradau (2008).
2   I use 'regime' here in Foucault's (1980: 131) sense of a regime of truth: 'Each society has its regime of truth, its "general politics" of truth – that is, the types of discourse it accepts and makes function as true.'

Counting Victims: Large Numbers

Numbers are central to modern knowledge of the world, and statistics have long been a privileged way of knowing the social. The predominance of statistics in establishing a regime of truth about a particular social problem has been intimately linked to the policing mechanisms of the state finance and to military interests. This drive for knowledge fostered by statistical methods is even more relevant in relation to social problems characterised by radical uncertainty. Human trafficking is one of the social problems rife with uncertainty. As the UK Threat Assessment Report by the Serious Organised Crime Agency (2009) indicates, 'the nature of human trafficking makes it harder to identify and therefore gauge'. The uncertainties associated with human trafficking, its 'hidden' nature, have not deterred from a politics of numbers, from counting as a means of legitimating what needs to be done about trafficking. Rather, they have strengthened the injunction to knowledge through numbers by sharpening methodologies, gathering data, and 'raising awareness' amongst professionals and the public to the phenomenon of trafficking. Two strategies have been pursued to counter the problem of uncertainty concerning human trafficking: on the one hand, human trafficking has been placed in a continuum with other phenomena such as migration, prostitution, and organised crime (with numerical importance being derived from the latter), and, on the other hand, counting numbers has become a widespread technology pursued by the actors involved in the field of counter-trafficking.

Rather than knowable and researchable on its own, human trafficking is known through derivation from other social and political problems. Although definitions of human trafficking attempt to set it apart from migration, organised crime, and prostitution, trafficking is repeatedly subsumed under these categories. In Europe in particular, the creation of a continuum between human trafficking, organised crime, migration, and prostitution has been possible through the integration of human trafficking within an overarching concern with security (Aradau, 2008). Thus, the EU Hague Programme on the area of freedom, security, and justice reinforced the securitisation of human trafficking by enjoining member states to develop a more effective approach to 'cross-border problems such as illegal migration, trafficking in and smuggling of human beings, terrorism and organised crime, as well as the prevention thereof' (Council of the European Union, 2004: 3). Migration, organised crime and prostitution are taken as the starting points in the analysis of trafficking. This derivation creates continuity between social and political problems allowing for existing actors to act upon human trafficking, too.

At the same time, human trafficking cannot be exhausted by the reality of migration, prostitution, and organised crime. Thus, human trafficking appears to require movement of people across borders; it is nonetheless distinguished from human smuggling by the supplement of labour exploitation (be it in the domestic field, sex work, agriculture, construction work, and so on). Human trafficking requires modes of facilitation of movement (transport, papers, border crossings) that appear to be placed under the heading of organised crime; however, victims of trafficking need to be dis-identified from these networks as victims of human rights abuses and crime. The 2009/2010 UK Threat Assessment Report has coined the new terminology of 'organised immigration crime' under which it subsumes both human trafficking and human smuggling (Serious Organised Crime Agency (SOCA), 2009). Human trafficking is and is not irregular migration, is and is not organised crime, is and is not prostitution. It is equated to all these social problems with the important proviso that the women involved are to a certain extent dis-identified from stories of illegal migration, organised crime, and prostitution inasmuch as it has been the 'use of force, fraud or coercion' (UN, 2000) that has turned them into unwilling and exploited illegal migrants or prostitutes. This minimal difference can buttress claims of extra funding, new action, and improved governance technologies alongside or replacing existing ones.

The derivation of human trafficking from irregular migration, organised crime, and prostitution is underpinned by a politics of large numbers which seamlessly counts foreign migrants, sex workers, or criminals as susceptible to human trafficking. 'About 8,000 women work in off-street prostitution in London alone, 80 percent of whom are foreign nationals', claims a report by the Home Affairs Committee in the UK House of

Commons (2009). While the link between human trafficking and foreign nationals working in the sex industry is not made explicit, there is an implicit extension of human trafficking to encompass migrants. Counting victims in these discourses relies on the implicit assumption that foreign equals vulnerability. The use of police raids has reinforced the discursive link in practice as migrants working in the sex industry are detained on suspicion of having been trafficked. Despite the pernicious effects that raids have had on sex workers and migrants, they are still promoted as a measure of choice in the fight against human trafficking. The politics of large numbers mobilises raids alongside referrals of victims to NGOs without making any differentiation between their potential effects.

Human trafficking has also been associated with the 'large numbers' of organised crime. Here, the politics of large numbers concerns profits that are generated from criminal activities. According to the ILO, the profits that are generated annually from forced commercial sexual exploitation as a result of trafficking are of 27.8 billion US dollars (Belser, 2005). Human trafficking is often placed in the top-three hierarchy of profits from international organised crime after arms dealing and drugs. The emphasis on profits and the representation of organised crime as undermining the social cohesion and security of European societies reasserts the need for police action and state intervention to tackle trafficking.

What the politics of large numbers fails to mention is that human trafficking might be the result of state action, from migration control to the criminalisation of sex work, and socio-economic conditions. Whilst legal and political practices have increasingly tightened the linkages between human trafficking, irregular migration, prostitution, and organised crime (as the authors of this chapter also evidence in the case of Greece), academic work has increasingly shown human trafficking to be the effect of practices of governance. Kyle and Koslowski (2001) have pointed out that some migrant smugglers are more akin to the historical free traders of an earlier era. They denounce existing studies of human smuggling for using a particularly ahistorical concept of organised crime that allows no conceptual space for analysing the organisational sources of transnational human smuggling. Similarly, in the case of human trafficking in Greece, as Papanicolaou and Bouklis remind us, the data offered by the Hellenic

Police do not support an idea of large Mafia-type organisational structures. Moreover, these are embedded in an indigenous circuit of exploitation where bars, night clubs, and strip clubs are an important part of the whole process of trafficking.

Many scholars have put forward the idea that trafficking is an unintended consequence of restrictive migration policies and of the efforts to curb illegal entry and illegal employment of migrants. Khalid Koser (1998) has pointed out that the activities of smugglers and traffickers have flourished in the context of tightening political restrictions. Given that legal channels of migration are more and more reduced or restricted to specific categories such as highly skilled migrants, other types of migrants have recourse to mediating parties. EU visa regimes and restrictive immigration regulation work in favour of the third-party organisers of trafficking as a supplementary migration system or an alternative to the EU system (Andrijasevic, 2003).

However, the use of 'large numbers' in the problematisation of trafficking has been extremely resilient. Counting and classification are 'technologies of government' (Rose and Miller, 1992) which give prominence to particular categories whilst effacing others. Counting victims of trafficking also entails deciding on what counts and what does not count as important in the governance of trafficking. The politics of large numbers relies on categorisations that reinforce imaginaries of the 'dangerous other' which are difficult to unmake. Thus, even when representations of organised crime are challenged by representations of the 'other' as indigenous, these 'others' can be categorised anew as 'new citizens', the ones who recruit from the poor countries they escaped themselves (Bales and Soodalter, 2009).

Discounting Numbers: Affective Politics

Alongside the politics of large numbers with its statistics and discursive derivation, there is also a politics of small numbers. As Arjun Appadurai has remarked, small numbers are troubling for liberalism. Not only is liberal political theory based upon the legitimacy of large numbers (as aggregates of individuals), but small numbers can raise questions of dissidence, conspiracy, internal enemies, traitors, and not least elitism (Appadurai, 2006). Thus, the prospect of small numbers associated with victims of trafficking is unsettling for counter-trafficking regimes.

The numbers of identified and assisted victims of trafficking gathered by NGOs, police, and international organisations often reveal small numbers. As the authors of the chapter show in the case of Greece, the numbers of assisted victims have tended to vary little and have remained small over the years. In the UK, the numbers claimed by the Operation Pentameter, the UK's biggest investigation on sex trafficking, have also been exposed as 'small' and even negligible in comparison to the extent of the operation and costs entailed (Davies, 20 October 2009). Small numbers need, therefore, to be consistently discounted from the regime of truth of large numbers. They are seen as the result of insufficient administrative measures and legal procedures to tackle trafficking. The small number of prosecutions or assisted victims does not raise questions about the usefulness of raids, but is taken to be a token of their insufficiency. Moreover, small numbers are discounted by what I call 'affective politics' of human trafficking. The intensive suffering that victims experience at the hands of traffickers is opposed to extensive numbers. As the UK Minister Harriet Harman has put in response to debates about the accuracy of numbers regarding human trafficking:

> We have to make it absolutely clear that, although we do not know the exact numbers, we have never based our case for concern on the overall numbers; it is enough if even one woman has been kidnapped, brought across borders to this country, and bought and sold like a modern-day slave. (Harman, 3 December 2009)

Harman's comment is a rebuttal of claims about 'small numbers' of identified victims of trafficking on the basis of an affective politics of human trafficking-as-modern slavery. The representation of human trafficking as abhorrent slavery has rapidly gained acceptance in the media, governments, NGOs, and the collective imaginary. Internationally, human trafficking is considered a modern form of slavery:

As unimaginable as it seems, slavery and bondage still persist in the early 21st century. Millions of people around the world still suffer in silence in slave-like situations
of forced labour and commercial sexual exploitation from which they cannot free
themselves. Trafficking in persons is one of the greatest human rights challenges of
our time. (US Department of State, 2003)

Slavery is generally understood to mean ownership of a person and horrific
exploitation. What is predominant in analyses of slavery is the element
of unfreedom, of trade that leads to ownership, and the appalling consequences the 'sale' of human beings entails.

Slavery has been used by NGOs, experts, and academics to draw
attention to unacceptable practices at the heart of modern societies. This
representation of trafficking has particularly led the debates on counter-
trafficking policies in the direction of human rights and victimhood. In
the UNHCR definition, slavery and slavery-like practices cover a variety of
human rights violations. In the context of human trafficking, the representation of slavery has been upheld by many radical feminists, those who see
prostitution as sexual slavery. What counts in this representation is not the
distinction between forced and voluntary labour, but the understanding
of prostitution as slavery. In that sense, human trafficking is an abuse of
human rights that is made possible by patriarchal power relations. When
a woman is trafficked and sexually exploited, she is denied the 'most basic
human rights, and in the worst case, ... their right to life, as prostitution
and sexual exploitation have devastating health and quality-of-life effects
on its victims' (von Struensee, 2002). Nonetheless, many NGOs and international organisations that have taken up the representation of slavery do
not engage in debates about prostitution. What they point out is the de-
humanisation that victims of trafficking endure, the denial of agency and
freedom, and the pervasive violence to which they are subjected.

Stories of victimhood and terrible suffering, whether narrated through
the voice of NGOs or by the victims of trafficking themselves, appear to
re-enact images of abjection, those who have become politically disquali-
fied from life and have been projected to spaces beyond the law (Agamben,
1998). Amnesty International, as many other NGOs involved in counter-
trafficking campaigns, has argued that women are 'systematically subjected

to torture, including rape and other forms of cruel, inhuman, and degrading treatment' (Amnesty International, 2004). Women's confessionary stories are renditions of 'bare life', lived outside the law where life can be sacrificed with impunity:

> He beat and raped me constantly for three days, to the point while I was lying in blood and urine while tied to the bed. He then brought two of his friends who raped me, put out cigarette butts on me, and cut me with razors. (Barbir Mladinovic, 15 June 2006)

The accounts of victims of trafficking render them as bare, depoliticised life, life which exists beyond the law. Their existence 'beyond the law' renders them vulnerable to what Judith Butler (2006: 65) has called the 'petty sovereigns', the traffickers who can function in this space beyond the law.

Affective narratives and imageries of suffering have been mobilised to inform a 'different' politics, a politics that does not treat women as lives in abjection, but extracts them from categories of illegal migrants, prostitutes, and criminals, and represents them as suffering victims. The stories of suffering and human rights abuses have been exposed as unstable, either leading to 'half-hearted protection' (Pearson, 2002) or being unable to lift the suspicion of autonomous projects of migration and prostitution from victims of trafficking. The literature on human trafficking has shown the impossibility to clearly and definitively dis-identify victims of trafficking from migrants and prostitutes (Aradau, 2004, 2008; O'Connell Davidson, 2006).

The impossibility to extract victims of trafficking from the latter categories leads to a permanent suspicion about the status of their life. Despite the continual attempt to differentiate victims of trafficking from other illegal migrants, this distinction remains unstable. Trafficked women are eventually *voluntarily* returned home after having testified against their traffickers and having undergone more or less extended periods of *rehabilitation*. Instead of deportation, voluntary return. Instead of detention centres, rehabilitation shelters. Instead of illegal migrants, victims. Although deployed upon supposedly different categories of subjects, the measures employed appear as hardly different. In the shift from the indiscriminate securitisation of all illegal migrants to an emphasis on the human rights of victims of trafficking – a shift made possible by the mobilisation of NGOs in the anti-trafficking struggle –, what appears to change is rather the form of incarceration or the mode of normalisation. The logic of their removal from the space of the political community they attempted to enter irregularly remains the same.

This apparently paradoxical junction of a discourse of slavery, and one of removal and rehabilitation, can be understood from the perspective of what I have called the 'affective intensification' of human trafficking. The equation of human trafficking with slavery is not really actionable for the purposes of governance, as the action that slavery requires is abolition. Despite the discursive collapse of trafficking and slavery, abolition does not appear as the adequate action to tackle human trafficking. The affective intensification of the 'slavery' discourse is intimately connected with therapeutic practices which presuppose victims of trafficking as emotionally unstable and psychologically vulnerable (for a discussion see Aradau, 2004, 2008). The affect of intense suffering brings about practices of clinical risk which try to locate factors of vulnerability. Rather than being characterised by suspension of existing legal frameworks and political practices, counter-trafficking has entailed the proliferation of regulation and intervention. For the purposes of governance, human trafficking is represented as a risk which can be managed and prevented. As victims of trafficking and psychologically vulnerable, women are to be helped through education and various forms of psychological counselling to become self-sufficient and autonomous subjects who act in accordance with governmental premises. The purpose of psychological therapy is to 're-constitute subjects who autonomously make appropriate (from the point of view of international governance) decisions' (Harrington, 2005: 193). Thus, victims of trafficking are expected to develop a new image of themselves, testify against their traffickers, return to their countries of origin, and undertake productive work.

Given the affective politics of trafficking, small numbers do not suspend the regime of truth of counter-trafficking, but can be re-appropriated within it. Where the politics of large numbers fails, an affective politics is mobilised to buttress the regime of truth. Affective politics does not suspend counting: rather than counting extensionality, it counts (and values) intensification. Therefore, it simultaneously discounts forms of violence and exploitation that do not fit the affective narrative of the slave-victim, subject to raw suffering and deprived of agency. Destabilising the regime of truth of counter-trafficking might be best served by pointing out its effects, what it discounts and devalues, rather than trying to buttress a countervailing politics of small numbers.

References

Agamben, G. (1998) *Homo Sacer: Sovereign Power and Bare Life*. Stanford, CA: Stanford University Press.

Amnesty International (2004) *'So Does It Mean That We Have Rights?' Protecting the Human Rights of Women and Girls Trafficked for Forced Prostitution in Kosovo*. Available online at: http://web.amnesty.org/ library/index/ ENGEUR/700102004 (Accessed 5 August 2006)

Andrijasevic, R. (2003) 'The Difference Borders Make: Legality, Migration and Trafficking in Italy among Eastern European Women in Prostitution', in S. Ahmed, C. Castaneda, A. Fortier and M. Sheller (eds) *Uprootings/Regroundings: Questions of Home and Migration*, pp. 251–272. Oxford: Berg.

Appadurai, A. (2006) *Fear of Small Numbers: An Essay on the Geography of Anger*. Durham, NC: Duke University Press.

Aradau, C. (2004) 'The Perverse Politics of Four-Letter Words: Risk and Pity in the Securitisation of Human Trafficking', *Millennium: Journal of International Studies* 33(2): 251–277.

Aradau, C. (2008) *Rethinking Trafficking in Women: Politics out of Security*. Basingstoke: Palgrave Macmillan.

Bales, K. and R. Soodalter (2009) *The Slave Next Door: Human Trafficking and Slavery in America Today*. Berkeley, CA: University of California Press.

Barbir Mladinovic, A. (15 June 2006) *Croatia: A Human Trafficking Victim Speaks with Rfe/Rl*. Available online at http://www.thewarproject.org/ node/10086. (Accessed 5 August 2006)

Belser, P. (2005) *Forced Labour and Human Trafficking: Estimating the Profits*. Geneva: International Labour Organisation.

Butler, J. (2006) *Precarious Life: The Powers of Mourning and Violence*. London: Verso.

Council of the European Union (2004) *The Hague Programme: Strengthening Free-dom, Security and Justice in the European Union*. Available online at: http://www.eu.int/comm/justice_home/doc_centre/doc/hague_programme_en.pdf. (Accessed 16 January 2006)

Davies, N. (2009) 'Inquiry Fails to Find Single Trafficker Who Forced Anybody into Prostitution', *The Guardian*, 20 October.

Foucault, M. (1980) 'Truth and Power', in C. Gordon (ed.) *Power/Knowledge: Selected Interviews and Other Writings, 1972–1977*, pp. 109–133. New York: Pantheon Books.

Harman, H. (3 December 2009) *Human Trafficking: Women and Equality*, House of Commons Debate. Available online at: http://www.theyworkforyou.com / debates/?id=2009-12-03b.1276.5. (Accessed 11 January 2010)

Harrington, C. (2005) 'The Politics of Rescue: Peacekeeping and Anti-Trafficking Programmes in Bosnia-Herzegovina and Kosovo', *International Feminist Journal of Politics* 7(2): 175–206.

Home Affairs Committee (2009) *The Trade in Human Beings: Human Trafficking in the UK*. London: House of Commons.

Koser, K. (1998) 'Out of the Frying Pan and into the Fire: A Case Study of Illegality Amongst Asylum-Seekers', in K. Koser and H. Lutz (eds) *The New Migration in Europe: Social Constructions and Social Realities*, pp. 185–198. London: Macmillan Press.

Kyle, D. and R. Koslowski (2001) 'Introduction', in D. Kyle and R. Koslowski (eds) *Global Human Smuggling: Comparative Perspectives*, pp. 1–25. Baltimore: Johns Hopkins University Press.

Mai, N. (2009) *ESRC Project: Migrants in the UK Sex Industry*. London: London Metropolitan University.

Pearson, E. (2002) 'Half-Hearted Protection: What Does Victim Protection Really Mean for Victims of Trafficking in Europe?', *Gender and Development* 10(1): 56–59.

Rose, N. and P. Miller (1992) 'Political Power Beyond the State: Problematics of Government', *British Journal of Sociology* 43(2): 172–205.

Serious Organised Crime Agency (SOCA) (2009) *The UK Threat Assessment of Organised Crime 2009/2010*. London: SOCA.

UN (2000) *Protocol to Prevent, Suppress and Punish Trafficking in Persons, Especially Women and Children, Supplementing the United Nations Convention against Transnational Organised Crime*. Available online at: http://www.uncjin.org/ Documents/Conventions/dcatoc/final_documents_2/convention_%20traff_eng.pdf. (Accessed 20 August 2003)

UNODC (26 March 2007) *UNODC Launches Global Initiative to Fight Human Trafficking*. Available online at: http://www.unodc.org/unodc/press_release _2007_03_26.html. (Accessed 20 August 2003)

US Department of State (2003) *Trafficking in Persons Report*. Available online at: http://www.state.gov/g/tip/rls/tiprpt/2003/. (Accessed 20 August 2003)

US Department of State (2009) *Trafficking in Persons Report*. Washington, DC: Department of State.

von Struensee, V. (2002) 'Sex Trafficking: A Plea for Action', *European Law Journal* 6(4): 379–407.

EFI AVDELA

Honour, Violence and Crime

It is well known that Greece constitutes one of the major fields for anthropological research on the concept of 'honour' as an organising principle of social relations, which has long been considered a typical feature of 'Mediterranean' societies. One of the first and leading studies to underscore the social and political significance of 'honour' was carried out by British social anthropologist John Campbell, who researched the Sarakatsani, a nomadic mountain community of Epirus between 1954–1955 (Campbell, 1964). According to Campbell, family ties were of great significance to the Sarakatsani, while animosity and competitiveness prevailed between families not related by kinship or marriage. This social organisation was supported by a system of social values based on the concepts of honour, power, and pride. For the Sarakatsani, 'honour' was the recognition of the value of a person both by others and by oneself. Everyone had honour, men as well as women, but it was conditioned upon different, gendered attitudes and qualities. While a man was judged by his ability to protect the honour of his family, a woman's honour was conditional upon disciplining her sexuality. Individual honour was directly related to family honour. Whoever suffered an affront to his or her honour was obligated to restore it, even by resorting to violence. Otherwise, this person and his or her family would be 'shamed' and would lose their reputation and prestige. Thus, the honour of a family depended on the degree of prestige, integrity, and social value which the community accorded to its members.

Campbell and other social anthropologists (e.g., Friedl, 1962; Peristiany, 1965a, 1965b; Pitt-Rivers, 1977; Davies, 1977) created the field of so-called 'Mediterranean anthropology' in the 1960s and 1970s. Mediterranean anthropology and its various proponents constitute the basic point of reference for all historical studies dealing with 'honour' as it relates to

'violence' and 'crime' in a variety of geographical, historical and social contexts. Thus, the relationship between the three terms that form the title of
this chapter, is often taken for granted. In what follows, and focusing specifically on the case of Greece, I argue against such an approach. I begin by
commenting on each one of these terms, and then consider what is known
about the affront to honour as a motive for violent crimes in Greece, from
the late nineteenth century to the beginning of the twenty-first, focusing
especially on the aftermath of the Civil War (of 1946–1949), in relation to
which more in-depth research is available. The argument developed is that
the concept of honour is not static, but rather dynamic and changing. The
same violent crimes for which perpetrators evoked an affronted honour
varied in meaning as well as in frequency from the mid-nineteenth century up to the early 1960s. The post-civil-war years were characterised by
a public debate on 'honour crimes' and the management of interpersonal
violence, which, in these particular circumstances, led to the disassociation
of 'honour' from 'violence' by the end of the 1960s, and, as a consequence
of this, to the end of 'honour crimes'.

Concepts and Meanings

It should be noted at this early juncture that the terms 'honour', 'violence',
and 'crime' do not constitute analytical categories, hence the reader should
consider them as being in quotation marks throughout the chapter. What
this indicates is that their meaning is not fixed, but rather contextually
shaped, changing over time, among social groups, and between geographical areas and cultures.

The idea that crime and criminality are historically constructed and
that the cultural meanings of 'crime' are transformed with time is undoubtedly as much a truism for historians of crime and criminal justice as it is
among criminologists and jurists. Equally historically bounded are the
institutional provisions against what is conceived as crime in a specific

historical context, but also the social obsessions and fears that lead to the transformation of penal policies (Perrot, 1975). Historians also agree that penal definitions and popular beliefs and practices do not always coincide. For example, the popular symbolic dimensions of interpersonal violence, for instance the codes of agonistic masculinity usually identified with honour, hegemonic among rural as well as working-class men, became penalised in periods of acute social transformation (Wiener, 1998; Avdela, 2010).

To be sure, violence is an important component in the study of crime, but not all violence is considered criminal, and the distinction between legal and illegal forms of violence changes over time, as the example of domestic violence demonstrates most tellingly. Most researchers agree that violence is part of everyday life. War and peace, public and private, the state and individuals, bodies and symbols; these are all inscribed in a 'continuum of violence', albeit highly contextualised, gendered and non-unified (Scheper-Hughes and Bourgois, 2004; D'Cruze and Rao, 2004).

Violence has often been associated with honour. Historians have, since the 1990s, extensively used the concept of honour to interpret interpersonal conflicts in a variety of geographical, historical, and cultural settings (Wyatt-Brown, 1982; Spierenburg, 1998a; Johnson and Lipsett-Rivera, 1998; Reddy, 1997; Gallant, 2000; Caulfield, 2000; Avdela, 2002a, 2002b). Most would agree that the concept of honour is socially diverse and runs through gender identities, but that its meaning is highly contextual. Honour as a middle-class code, expressed by the duel in nineteenth-century Europe (Frevert, 1995; Nay, 1993; Reddy, 1997; Spierenburg, 1998a), is not identical to plebeian 'honour contests', that is, violent clashes caused by competitive masculinity throughout the modern period (Gallant, 2000; Spierenburg, 1998b). It is not always clear precisely what constituted the crucial factors for the decrease of 'honour-related' crimes and the growing disassociation of honour from violence. For some, it is an illustration of the 'civilising process', and it is linked to the growing accessibility of the juridical system; for others, it is more related to processes of cultural transformation in times of acute social change.

At any rate, it is noteworthy that historical interest in honour today is in direct contrast to that of anthropologists. According to the British and American anthropologists, who, in the 1960s and 1970s, established the Mediterranean as a 'cultural area' characterised by the social values of 'honour and shame', interpersonal violence, or the threat of it, was a crucial component of social relations, and an important factor of social and cultural stability and reproduction. However, subsequent work in the 1980s criticised the idea of a Mediterranean concept of honour as essentialist and ethnocentric (Herzfeld, 1980, 1985, 1987; Wikam, 1984; Pina-Cabral, 1989; Goddard, 1987; Maher, 2001). In the 1990s, these criticisms led to the deconstruction of the concept of honour through the theoretical shift from values to emotions (Abu-Lughod, 1985; Abu-Lughod and Lutz, 1990; Papataxiarchis, 1994). Few historians followed anthropologists in these theoretical and methodological shifts. Many continue to identify the 'code of honour' – and the violence that it entails – with pre-modern, or not yet modernised, societies, in a diachronic as well as synchronic sense. Based on schematic crystallisations of the long and vivid debates in social anthropology, they reproduce positions that anthropologists no longer maintain.[1]

In the remainder of the chapter, I have adopted the current anthropological conceptualisation of honour as a culturally and historically determined emotion, as a discourse on the self, produced in social interaction and signified in culturally specific ways. Construed as an emotion, honour does not constitute a static code of public social practice, but a potential mental construct, which structures the distinction between public and private as gendered domains. Part of a historical 'emotional regime', linked to specific forms of emotional management, honour is expressed through claims in present-tense, first-person emotional formulations, which act upon the world in historically changing ways, while they are interwoven with contextualised public mechanisms of emotional restraint (Reddy 2001: 111–132; Avdela, 2002b, 2007). In other words, I consider violent crimes as 'honour-related' only when 'honour' – or what was perceived in each historical context as its synonym – is claimed as a motive by those involved in the specific act.

1   For a recent survey and assessment of 'Mediterranean anthropology', see Albera *et al.* (2001). For historical studies using an essentialised and homogenised concept of honour, see Caulfield (2000), Baker *et al.* (1999), and Smith (2004). For critics of the historiographical uses of honour, see Johnson and Lipsett-Rivera (1998), Twinam (1998), Carroll (2007), and Avdela *et al.* (2010).

Offence, Affront to Respectability, and Violent Crimes

Fragmentary statistical data as well as scattered and disparate juridical records make it difficult to draw an accurate picture either of the evolution of criminal violence since the creation of the Greek state (1833), or the types and motives of violent crimes (Avdela, 2008). However, according to the existing evidence, mainly press entries, throughout the nineteenth century and up to the end of the inter-war years, crimes against the person – which comprised the majority of all offences (Benveniste, 1994; Karouzou, 2005) – involved those whom Spierenburg terms 'intimates' and 'acquaintances' (Spierenburg, 1994: 710). The main motive for this kind of violent crimes seems to be a perceived offence or affront to the self, even if the term 'honour' was rarely used as such. The American diplomat and writer Charles Tuckerman, in his 1872 book *Greeks of Today*, noted that the alleged increase in violent crimes in the 1860s was due to the 'code of honour', but he did not explain this claim further. In the 1880s, the Athenian press repeatedly reported fights between men as a result of verbal insults, and noted that they became increasingly lethal, not least because of the growing substitution of the traditional knife with firearms (Gallant, 1997: 10–11).

Violent confrontations between males were common. In the Ionian islands under British dominion, in Athens in the mid-nineteenth and again at the end of that century, as well as in early twentieth-century Lefkas, verbal insults escalated into brawls, arguments, and stabbings (Gallant, 1997, 2000, 2002; Kopsida-Vrettou, 1998). In rural areas, these confrotations were often linked to long-term conflicts regarding property; in the urban setting, they took place either outside taverns and bars or in the neighbouring public streets. They concerned men from the same social environment, whose reputations and thus their place in the community depended upon their ability to protect their personal and familial 'honour'. Any affront, be it trespassing field boundaries, stealing animal stock, verbal insults, or the disgrace of a female family member, entailed the obligation to retaliate, even in a bloody manner, in order to restore honour and therefore maintain – for the person involved as much as for his entire family

– respectability and status in the community (Campbell, 1964). These were incidents of 'plebeian honour contests' related to the cultural construction of hegemonic masculinity in rural societies as well as in urban low strata, and which have been documented in various historical contexts (Johnson and Lipsett-Riviera, 1998; Spierenburg, 1998b, Boschi, 1998; Boyer, 1998; Graham, 1998; Gallant, 2000).

Historians of Greek populations have attributed the decrease in 'knife fights' or other types of violent 'masculinity contests' to social, cultural, and institutional transformations (e.g., urbanisation, effective state mechanisms, social diversification, migration, changes in accepted gender attitudes) that resulted in a more individualised concept of honour, an afront to which could find restitution in court, as well as to new masculine ideals not so much based on physical force (Gallant 1997, 2000). But historians have also identified these same processes, at least in the short term, as being responsible for an increase in violent crimes involving some affront to honour. These processes, it is said, produced new social hierarchies and made individuals, especially men, more fragile and sensitive to whatever might constitute a challenge to masculine identity, and, therefore, more ready to prove their worth when the occasion arose, even resorting to acts of violence (Gallant, 1997; Safilios-Rothschild, 1969).

We know very little about non-plebeian concepts of 'honour' before the end of the nineteenth century. Duelling was rare, but female sexuality seems to have been the motive for a number of cases of interpersonal violence, for which perpetrators invoked the affront to their family's respectability and integrity by the victim. Especially the cases of women defending their affronted honour on their own were highly unusual. At the end of the century, the *Ladies' Journal* – the first Greek weekly to be written entirely by women and devoted to promoting female emancipation (Varika, 1987; Psarra, 1999) – urged the state to 'punish those who violate their promise of marriage' (Anonymous, 1888b), a usual motive for 'honour crimes' throughout the period in question. The journal even congratulated the jurors who acquitted a young woman for killing her lover because he abandoned her: 'The jurors ... are, of course, aware of the moral depravity of certain regular villains, who destroy with premeditation the reputation of honest families as well as the life and happiness of unfortunate innocent souls' (Anonymous, 1888a).

Cases of interpersonal violence revolving around female sexuality constituted the bulk of Greek 'honour crimes' or 'crimes for reasons of honour', and they became increasingly visible in the daily press over the course of the twentieth century. However, as we shall see, their meaning, their configuration, and their frequency have also changed with time.

Twentieth-century 'Honour Crimes'

'Honour crimes' never constituted a formal category of Greek penal law. What distinguished these acts from other types of interpersonal violence was that their perpetrators claimed to have been motivated by the will to restitute their personal and familial honour, which presumably had been affronted by the victim's conduct. As such, they were gender-bound, in the sense that they rested on particular gender subjectivities. In the majority of cases, the perpetrators were male, as were most of the victims. Women were more often victims rather than perpetrators of honour crimes, but they did occasionally commit such acts (Avdela, 2002b).

Very little is known of honour crimes in the early twentieth century. It is only through the press that the issue can be approached, since, as already mentioned, they did not constitute a legal category and criminal records remained fragmentary until the establishment of the new Penal Code in 1950. However, there is evidence that, during the first half of the century, sororicide constituted the most common type of honour crime. Identified with the popular strata (urban as well as rural), these 'honour killings' seemed to be self-explanatory whenever reported in the press. For instance, at the turn of the century, commenting tangentially on the recent case of a brother killing his sister, the distinguished editor of the intellectual journal *Noumas* wrote: '[T]here is not much one can say. As terrible as it is, it also has its bright side, since it proves us that the feeling of family honour is still alive among the working classes, a feeling [...] which remains sacrosanct to the Greek people and serves to conceal certain other flaws' (T[angopoulos], 1906).

In the course of the inter-war period, cases of honour crimes appeared regularly in the daily press. Their configuration, however, became increasingly varied. Sororicide came under attack for the first time. Intellectuals repeatedly denounced men who claimed the dishonourable behaviour of their kinswomen to be the motive behind killing them, denunciations that were strongly supported by the feminist press of the time (Anonymous, 1925; Th[eodoropoulou], 1932). However, the vast majority of honour crimes in the inter-war period, but also after the war, concerned males: men killing or gravely injuring other men for 'having seduced' their kinswoman, 'refusing to legalise their union', 'breaching the promise to marry her', 'abandoning her', and so forth. Irrespective of their frequency, they were considered 'minor incidents' in the inter-war period, deserving only a brief mention; for the ascending urban middle classes, they represented the undesirable but unavoidable proof of tradition's grip on Greek society.

Despite the variety of circumstances surrounding honour crimes, they were treated in a wholesale fashion, as having occurred 'for reasons of honour'. Doing so served as a 'hegemonic commonplace' (Angenot, 1989): whoever understood what 'reasons of honour' meant without requiring further explanation, belonged to the same cultural community. But this cultural community was soon to be contested, for the first time during the post-civil-war years, when honour crimes became the focus of an unprecedented public debate.

Post-war 'Honour rimes':
Rhetorical Forms and Cultural Scenarios

During the 1950s and 1960s, the hundreds of violent crimes committed all over the country 'for reasons of honour' appeared in the daily press of Athens.[2] This was hardly a new phenomenon. However, in the period

---

2   The press, but also the existence of systematic, even if not always easily accessible, criminal records, make this period ideal for the study of violent crimes. For what

following the end of the Civil War, 'honour crimes' not only increased significantly; they also became the focal point of a public debate over the management of interpersonal violence, which was associated with the duress of the 1940s and was identified with a supposedly disquieting rise in 'criminality' over subsequent decades. Questioning the organisation of justice as well as family and social relations within Greek society at the time, the debate surrounding honour crimes gave rise, through successive redefinitions, popular as well as scholarly, of the concept of honour, to the delegitimisation of its association with violence. The process of redefining honour, in pace with wider social transformations, is part of a larger concern regarding the features and specific values of Greek society during this period. It is, in fact, a process of cultural transformation.

The news about an honour crime usually reported the various justifications provided by perpetrators for their respective acts. For example, the news about Takis Bokas, a conscript from the village Georganades Trikalon, who on 16 October 1950 stabbed and killed his fellow-villager Efstratios Gavriil 'for reasons of honour', conveyed the perpetrator's statement that he 'was forced to do this deed because the victim had corrupted his sister' (*Acropolis*, 17 September 1950).[3] In fact, during this period, for a homicide or an attempted homicide to be reported as an honour crime the perpetrator had to invoke 'reasons of honour' for his or her act.

Typically, the news about a honour crime was brief, with no other information than the names of those involved and the location where the incident took place, often a village or a provincial town. Narratives were more detailed at times, especially if they had taken place in Athens or if they were particularly controversial, that is, if the perpetrator's claim concerning his or her affronted 'honour' did not carry sufficient evidentiary weight. Such, for example, was the case of the brothers Apostolos and Antonis Lakopoulos, from the village of Salades in the region of Artas. On the night of 15

---

follows, see further Avdela (2002a, 2002b, 2007, 2008). These publications are based on research on a number of dailies published in Athens between 1949 and 1967 as well as on trial records, from the archives of several criminal courts around the country from 1950 to 1967.

3   All names in criminal cases are pseudonyms.

July 1954, the two brothers stabbed and killed their fellow-villager Antonis Sismanis, twenty-eight, near the railway station in Athens, in order to 'wash the shame out of their family'. They accused him of refusing to marry their sister after having 'corrupted' her. The case created a sensation in the capital and covered several front columns, especially after the victim's relatives questioned the validity of the claim during the trial by casting doubt on the morality of Lakopoulos' sister (*Kathimerini*, 16 July 1954).

Motives were expounded in the news through specific rhetorical forms that represented the variety of justifications given by perpetrators invoking 'reasons of honour' for their crimes. In this sense, they specified a common cultural code, a 'hegemonic commonplace'. All honour crimes appeared to revolve around sexuality and marriage. 'He had corrupted her'; 'he refused to legalise their relations'; 'he broke his promise to marry'; 'he abandoned her'; 'she maintained illicit relations'; 'she conducted a debauched life'; 'he/ she suspected her/him of having sexual relations' – such rhetorical forms corresponded to the various types of affront to which the crime constituted a response, and of which the victim was presented as 'guilty'. As such, they formed stories, namely, coherent narratives based on a distinctive range of possible causalities, the *cultural scenarios* of honour crimes. Their distinctive characteristic, indeed, what turned them into *cultural scenarios*, was the self-evident, almost trivial nature of those justifications, recognisable by everyone involved: the perpetrator, the victim, the public, the police, and the court of justice.[4]

In most cases, the subject of news reporting was the victim of the criminal act, and his or her affront to the perpertrator's honour. When the subject of news reporting was the perpetrator, the wording commonly conveyed ambivalence as to the unavoidable nature of the violent reaction. It is noteworthy, however, that the husband's violence, presumably the main cause of female homicides during this period (Avdela, 2008), was only occasionally presented in the press as having 'legitimate' motives, hence such interchangeable qualifications as 'family drama', 'crime of jealousy', and 'crime of passion'. These, indeed, were the most ambivalent cases in that the 'reasons of honour' claimed by perpetrators were subject to dispute.

4   For different approaches to the notion of 'scenario', see Burke (2005).

As in previous years, acts of violence as a response to affronted honour were not exclusively perpetrated by men. In the post-civil-war years, a significant number of 'crimes of honour' were committed by women who, after having been abandoned following a sexual relationship based on a marriage promise, attacked their former lovers, sometimes with the intention to kill, but often to injure, mostly by throwing acid in their faces. These women often lived in the city and could not count on the protection of their kinsmen. For example, in June 1959, Niki Sotiropoulou, twenty-five, from Aigio, threw acid at her fellow-townsman, Ioannis Vourakis, twenty-eight, a landowner. She claimed to have done so 'for reasons of honour', in order 'to take revenge on her beloved for having abandoned her after he corrupted her' (*Vradini*, 19 June 1958, 20 June 1958, 21 June 1958).

The Court of Reputation: The Role of Witness Testimonies

As mentioned earlier, what was distinctive about 'honour crimes' in post-war Greece was the invocation of honour as the fundamental social value and motive for the violent act. What this meant was commonly understood by all parties involved (the perpetrator, the victim, the public, the police, and the judiciary), irrespective of whether they accepted the association of honour with violence. This is why news of honour crimes generated stronger emotions than any other sensational issue at the time. Moreover, honour crimes related to concerns commonly shared by the broader public: the family and the relationships within it. After all, those engaging in crimes of honour were not seen as 'common criminals'; they were rather men (and occasionally women) perceived to have momentarily lost their self-control as a consequence of an affront to their honour.

What was thus at stake in the corresponding trials, including witness testimonies, was not to establish the guilt of the perpetrator; this was an accepted fact to which perpetrators themselves had already confessed. The issue was the motive – whether the invocation of the insult against one's honour was valid, either with respect to the behaviour of the victim or with respect to the reputation of the perpetrator. In assessing the claims made, judges first needed to gauge the 'character' or 'worth' of the individuals in question, of the perpetrator as much as the victim. To this end, witnesses were called upon to comment on either party: their public image, their reputation in the broader 'society' of the locality, and so on. 'The village believes that there were no relations between the victim and the defendant's wife, he killed him for no reason', affirmed the witness for the defence at the trial of Pandelis Mathioudakis, who in 1957 in the village Mytsika killed his fellow-villager Efstratios Travlos, for having an affair with his wife. But two witnesses for the prosecution testified otherwise: 'The entire village knew about the relationship' (General State Archives, 1958).

Crucially, witness testimonies also concerned the 'character' of those women who would find themselves at the centre for the dispute (e.g., the 'corrupted' sister of an avenging brother). Judges relied on such testimonies in order to assess whether or not perpetrators had really acted 'for reasons of honour'. A woman of no honour in the community was not worth killing another man for. But equally, a woman's conduct could impel her kinsman to turn against her. 'The whole of Aegaleo knows of the victim's conduct; the defendant was ashamed to show himself in public', declared a witness for the prosecution in the trial of Charilaos Theofilou, who in 1958 killed his sister, Despoina Drakati, twenty, for 'conducting a debauched life'. In effect, his testimony rendered him a witness for the defence (General State Archives, 1958).

In fact, witness testimonies in trials of honour crimes confirm what anthropologists have termed 'the court of reputation', or 'the all-power-fulness of public opinion' (Pitt-Rivers, 1965: 27; Peristiany, 1965a: 11). The community assessed the individuals concerned according to their overall behaviour as well as according to the family to which they belonged. This assessment was deeply gendered and referred to the common values shared by all community members. The turmoil of the period had caused significant rifts in the self-evident character of this 'community of values', especially with respect to populations migrating from the village to the city, where they often veiled their old values with a new, 'modern' type of behaviour, without, however, the former losing their grip. Going beyond the distinction between public and private, witness testimonies manipulated the social identities of those involved in an honour crime, and, in this way, linked each case within a wider framework of sociality, beliefs, and social values.

'Honour Crimes' in the Courtroom: The Role of the Jury

The body which decided whether the circumstances of a homicide, including cases of 'honour crimes', might qualify as mitigating was the jury. This
verdict formed the basis upon which the court eventually passed its sentence.[5] The concern that jurors exhibited leniency towards perpetrators
of honour crimes, a concern first raised at the beginning of the century,
resurfaced with vigour in public debates during the 1950s and 1960s. Public
prosecutors, alongside journalists and other commentators, criticised juries
for failing to express 'the public feeling of justice' when they accepted 'ret-
rograde' claims as justifications of violent crime. What is more, by the end
of the 1950s, it was no longer certain that perpetrators and jurors actually
shared a common value system, e.g., that they perceived honour in the same
way. What was thus contested, for the first time, was not only whether
the perpetrator had the right to invoke offended honour as a mitigating
circumstance with regard to the criminal act, but, more importantly, the
very emotion that the perpetrator put forward as his or her motive, i.e.,
the shame and turmoil felt at the insult, which compelled him or her to
use violence (Avdela, 2007).

It is not possible to factually substantiate the charges against the jury
for leniency in cases of honour crimes. Based on the information available, one might discern a commonly shared system of cultural values in
cases where the jury accepted that the victim's conduct at the time of the
incident functioned to confuse, completely or partially, the perpetrator.
'Guilty of manslaughter ..., but in a state of complete confusion', was the
jury's verdict in the case of Periklis Gravias, who in 1953, at his home in an
Athenian neighbourhood, murdered his daughter's fiancé, because he kept
breaking his promise to marry her. The verdict recognised that Gravias was
'enraged by this behaviour of [the victim], by which yet another calamity
was being forced upon his family, which, from a moral standpoint, had
collapsed to such a degree that he could not distinguish the injustice of

---

5   Such felonious offences as homicide, attempted homicide, and bodily harm, were
    tried at the time in specialised felony courts called *Kakourgiodikeia*. See further
    Papageorgiou (1988).

his action, and, being in such a mental state, he committed the offence in question.' Based on this verdict, Gravias was 'exempted from any penalty' (General State Archives, 1953).

But, in fact, the matter may be quite secondary. The way in which jurors were perceived by judges, journalists and others, had little to do with their actual severity or leniency, no matter what our difficulties in assessing it today. The fact that their attitude became, during the period under investigation, the subject of public debate is more than anything else indicative of the cultural transformation that is characteristic of the time. In the juridical domain, this cultural transformation took the form of a decisive break with the consensus that jurors were by definition representative of *sensus juris communis*. The question that lay at the centre of this debate was to what extent perpetrators and jurors shared common values and recognised common emotions. Not only was this common ground not considered self-evident any longer, but the question was raised as to whether it was even desirable to secure the public feeling of justice and the public's confidence in justice, not to mention whether this common ground could ever actually exist.

The End of 'Honour Crimes'

In the course of the 1960s, the news about honour crimes became scarcer and scarcer. Even when homicides or serious injuries for 'reasons of honour' were reported in the press, a question mark systematically followed the standard rhetorical form. An affront to one's honour was now less commonly claimed as a motive by perpetrators of acts of interpersonal violence. In courts, judges were more willing to exhaust the maximum sentences and less prepared to accept the 'fit of rage' generated by the affront to honour as a mitigating circumstance. Apparently, the public debate about the alleged leniency of the jurors was effective.[6]

6   It is worth noting that one of the first acts of the military regime that seized power on 21 April 1967, was to convert the jury system into a mixed jury and judge court

The disassociation of honour and violence, which took place and was completed during the 1960s, was complex. It was certainly related to the social and political mutations characteristic of the period: urbanisation; internal and external migration; unequal but unprecedented economic growth; the context of political polarisation and a massive social protest movement (Close, 2002). In the course of these processes, honour was all the more construed as an individual rather than as a family emotion, identified by the Greek word *filotimo* (love of honour), which would henceforth replace the word *timi* (honour), invoked until then by the perpetrators of 'honour crimes'. The end of 'honour crimes' did not mean that killing ceased occurring in Greece; in fact, until the late 1980s, homicides remained an affair between intimates or acquaintances, and men continued to predominate as perpetrators as well as victims (Chimbos, 1993; Gallant, 1995). It did, however, mean that perpetrators of violent crimes no longer invoked 'reasons of honour' for their acts. Honour crimes came to be seen as relics of the past, and claims of affront to honour were viewed as insensible and meaningless.

Lately, there has been growing concern in Europe about 'honour crimes' related to immigrant Muslim communities in various European countries (European Conference Report, 2004; Welchman and Hossain, 2006). Greece is not one of them, contrary to what a recent report of the Research Centre of Women's Affairs would have us believe. According to the report, certain native or immigrant communities in Greece were at risk of 'honour-related violence', in spite of the fact that no relevant evidence was provided. The report also classified domestic violence (e.g., wife and children battery, marital rape) as 'honour-based' (Institute of Equality, 2004; also Backer *et al.*, 1999). However, this diffusion of the concept of 'honour' to include any form of gender-power relations obscures not only the historically specific configurations of 'honour crimes', but also the historical processes which, in Greece, led to the abolition of 'honour' as a justification for interpersonal violence.

(Papageorgiou, 1988). In this way, the constitutional constraint that so many jurists had previously lamented was overcome once and for all: by the abolition of the constitution itself.

References

Abu-Lughod, L. (1985) 'Honour and the Sentiments of Loss in a Bedouin Society', *American Ethnologist* 12(2): 245–261.

Abu-Lughod, L. and C.A. Lutz (1990) 'Introduction: Emotion, Discourse, and the Politics of Everyday Life', in C.A. Lutz and L. Abu-Lughod (eds) *Language and the Politics of Emotion*, pp. 1–23. New York and Paris: Cambridge University Press and Éditions de la Maison des Sciences de l'Homme.

Albera, D., A. Blok and C. Bromberger (eds) (2001) *L'Anthropologie de la Méditerranée*. Paris: Maisonneuve & Larose, Maison Méditerranéenne des Sciences de l'Homme.

Angenot, M. (1989) '"La Fin d'un Sexe": Le Discours sur les Femmes en 1889', *Romantisme* 63(1): 5–22.

Anonymous (1888a) 'Miscellaneous' [in Greek], *Efimeris ton Kyrion* 66: 6–7.

Anonymous (1888b) 'Punish Those who Violate their Promise of Marriage' [in Greek], *Efimeris ton Kyrion* 71: 1–2.

Anonymous (1925) 'News' [in Greek], *O Agonas tis Gynaikas* 20: 9.

ATCA, Thessaloniki Assessors (1961) *Archives of the Thessaloniki Court of Appeal, Thessaloniki Mixed Jury and Judge Court, Thessaloniki Assessors' Records and Judgements* Nos. 61–63/16–18.2.

Avdela, E. (2002a) '"Pour Cause d'Honneur": Violence Interpersonnelle et Rapports de Genre en Grèce dans les Années 1950–1960', in C. Bard, F. Chauvard, M. Perrot and J.-G. Petit (eds) *Femmes et Justice Pénale, XIXe–XXe Siècles*, pp. 163–171. Rennes: Presses Universitaires de Rennes.

Avdela, E. (2002b) *'For Reasons of Honour': Violence, Emotions and Values in Post-Civil-War Greece* [in Greek]. Athens: Nefeli.

Avdela, E. (2007) 'Emotions on Trial: Judging Crimes of Honour in Post-Civil War Greece', *Crime Histoire & Société/Crime, History & Society* 10(2): 33–52.

Avdela, E. (2008) 'Crimes Violents et Homicides dans la Société Grecque (XIXe–XXe Siècles): L'État de la Recherche', in L. Mucchielli and P. Spierenburg (eds), *Histoire de l'Homicide en Europe de la Moyen Age a Nos Jours*, pp. 109–129. Paris: La Découverte.

Avdela, E. (2010) 'Making Sense of "Hideous Crimes": Contested Masculinities and the Cultural Remaking of Gendered Sociality in Post-Civil War Greece', in E. Avdela, S. D'Cruze and J. Rowbotham (eds) *Problems of Crime and Violence in Europe, 1780–2000: Essays in Criminal Justice*, pp 281–310. London: Edwin Mellen Press.

Avdela, E., D'Cruze, S. and J. Rowbotham (2010) 'Introduction: De-Centering Violence History', in E. Avdela, S. D'Cruze and J. Rowbotham (eds), *Crime, Violence and the Modern State, 1780–2000: Greece and Western Europe*, pp. 1–40. London: Edwin Mellen Press.

Baker, N.V., Gregware, P.R. and M.A. Cassidy (1999) 'Family Killing Fields: Honour Rationales in the Murder of Women', *Violence Against Women* 5(2): 164–184.

Benveniste, R. (1994) *The Penal Repression of Juvenile Delinquency in the Nineteenth Century (1833–1911)* [in Greek]. Athens-Komotini: Ant. N. Sakkoulas Publishers.

Boschi, D. (1998) 'Homicide and Knife Fighting in Rome, 1845–1914', in P. Spierenburg (ed.) *Men and Violence: Masculinity, Honour Codes and Violent Rituals in Europe and America, 17th-20th Centuries*, pp. 128–158. Columbus, OH: Ohio State University Press.

Boyer, R. (1998) 'Honour among Plebeians: Male Sangre and Social Reputation', in L.L. Johnson and S. Lipsett-Rivera (eds) *The Faces of Honour: Sex, Shame, and Violence in Colonial Latin America*, pp. 152–178. Albuquerque: University of New Mexico Press.

Burke, P. (2005) 'Performing History: The Importance of Occasions', *Rethinking History* 9(1): 35–52.

Campbell, J.K. (1964) *Honour, Family, and Patronage: A Study of Institutions and Moral Values in a Greek Mountain Community*. New York and Oxford: Oxford University Press.

Carroll, S. (2007) 'Introduction', in S. Carroll (ed.) *Cultures of Violence: Interpersonal Violence in Historical Perspective*, pp. 1–43. Basingstoke: Palgrave Macmillan.

Caulfield, S. (2000) *In Defence of Honour: Sexual Morality, Modernity, and Nation in Early-Twentieth-Century Brazil*. Durham and London: Duke University Press.

Chimbos, P.D. (1993) 'A Study of Patterns in Criminal Homicides in Greece', *International Journal of Comparative Sociology* 34(3–4): 260–271.

Davis, J. (1977) *People of the Mediterranean. An Essay in Comparative Social Anthropology*. London: Routledge & Kegan Paul.

D'Cruze, S. and A. Rao (2004) 'Violence and the Vulnerabilities of Gender', *Gender & History* 16(3): 495–512.

Close, D. (2002) *Greece since 1945*. London, New York, Tokyo: Longman–Pearson Education Limited.

European Conference Report (2004) *Honour-related Violence within a Global Perspective: Mitigation and Prevention in Europe*. SOCRATES–GRUNDVIG PROGRAMME–CLIMBING UP, 'For a supported and shared life "Climbing Up" of Women Victims of Violence', Stockholm 7–8 October. Available

online at: http://www.stockport.ac.uk/climbingup/Documents/GreekLegis-
lationDom.doc

Friedl, E. (1962) *Vasilika: A Village in Modern Greece*. New York: Holt, Rinehart &
Winston.

Frevert, U. (1995) *Men of Honour: A Social and Cultural History of the Duel*. Oxford:
Oxford University Press.

Gallant, T.W. (1995) 'Collective Action and Atomistic Actors: Labour Unions, Strikes,
and Crime in Greece in the Post-War Era', in T. Stavrou and D. Constas (eds)
Greece Toward the 21st Century, pp. 149–190. Baltimore: John Hopkins University Press.

Gallant, T.W. (1997) 'Murder in a Mediterranean City: Homicide Trends in Athens,
1850–1936', *Journal of the Hellenic Diaspora* 23(2): 7–28.

Gallant, T.W. (2000) 'Honour, Masculinity, and Ritual Knife Fighting in Nineteenth-
Century Greece', *The American Historical Review* 105(2): 359–382.

Gallant, T.W. (2002) *Experiencing Dominion: Culture, Identity, and Power in the British Mediterranean*. Notre Dame, Indiana: University of Notre Dame Press.

Goddard, V. (1987) 'Honour and Shame: The Control of Women's Sexuality and
Group Identity in Naples', in P. Caplan (ed.) *The Cultural Construction of Sexuality*, pp. 166–192. London: Tavistock Publications.

Graham, S. (1998) 'Honour among Slaves', in L.L. Johnson and S. Lipsett-Rivera
(eds) *The Faces of Honour: Sex, Shame, and Violence in Colonial Latin America*,
pp. 201–228. Albuquerque: University of New Mexico Press.

GSA, Athens Assessors (1953) *Athens Assessors' Records and Judgements: Volume 56
Nos. 43a, 44, 45, 46/23–29.11*. General State Archives, Court Archives, Athens
Mixed Jury and Judge Court.

GSA, Athens Assessors (1955) *Athens Assessors' Records and Judgements: Volume 59,
Nos. 19, 20, 20a, 21, 22, 23, 24/16–18.2*. General State Archives, Court Archives,
Athens Mixed Jury and Judge Court.

GSA, Athens Assessors (1958) *Athens Assessors' Records and Judgements, Volume 65,
Nos. 10, 11, 12/4.2*. General State Archives, Court Archives, Athens Mixed Jury
and Judge Court.

GSA, Athens Assessors (1963) *Athens Assessors' Records and Judgements, Volume 75,
Nos. 31, 32, 33, 34/16–17.5*. General State Archives, Court Archives, Athens Mixed
Jury and Judge Court.

Herzfeld, M. (1980) 'Honour and Shame: Problems in the Comparative Analysis of
Moral Systems', *Man* 15(2): 339–351.

Herzfeld, M. (1985) *The Poetics of Manhood: Contest and Identity in a Cretan Mountain Village*. Princeton: Princeton University Press.

Herzfeld, M. (1987) *Anthropology through the Looking-Glass: Critical Ethnography in the Margins of Europe*. Cambridge: Cambridge University Press.

Institute of Equality (2004) *Honour-based Violence – Greece: Status Report*. SOC-RATES–GRUNDVIG PROGRAMME–CLIMBING UP: 'For a Supported and Shared Life "Climbing Up" of Women Victims of Violence', provided by the Research Centre of Women's Affairs, Athens, October 2004. Available online at: www.hera2001.com/violenciasporhonour/upload/doc92_final%20 shehrezad_form_eng.doc

Johnson, L.L. and S. Lipsett-Rivera (eds) (1998) *The Faces of Honour: Sex, Shame, and Violence in Colonial Latin America*. Albuquerque: University of New Mexico Press.

Karouzou, E. (2005) *Definitions: Crime and the Criminal* [in Greek]. Unpublished paper presented at the Postgraduate Programme in Contemporary European and Greek History, University of Crete, Rethymno.

Kopsida-Vrettou, P. (1998) *Crime and its Social Specifications: Lefkada 1900–1940* [in Greek]. Athens: Ant. N. Sakkoulas Publishers.

Kressel, G.M. (1981) 'Sororicide/Filiacide: Homicide for Family Honour', *Current Anthropology* 22(2): 141–158.

Maher, V. (2001) 'How Do you Translate Pudeur? From Table Manners to Eugenics', in D. Albera, A. Blok, and C. Bromberger (eds) *L'Anthropologie de la Méditerranée*, pp. 157–177. Paris: Maisonneuve & Larose, Maison Méditerranéenne des Sciences de l'Homme.

Melas, S. (1932) 'Their Profession', *Athinaika Nea*, 21 June [in Greek].

Nay, R.A. (1993) *Masculinity and Male Codes of Honour in Modern France*. Oxford: Oxford University Press.

Papageorgiou, G. (1988) *Felony Courts, Mixed Jury and Judge Courts, Mixed Jury and Judge Courts of Appeal, Three- and Five-member Courts of Appeal* [in Greek]. Athens-Komotini: Ant. N. Sakkoulas Publishers.

Papataxiarchis, E. (1994) 'Emotions et Stratégies d'Autonomie en Grèce Égéenne', *Terrain* 22: 5–20.

Peristiany, J.G. (1965a) 'Introduction', in J.G. Peristiany (ed.) *Honour and Shame: The Values of Mediterranean Society*, pp. 9–18. London: Weidenfeld and Nicolson.

Peristiany, J.G. (ed.) (1965b) *Honour and Shame: The Values of Mediterranean Society*. London: Weidenfeld and Nicolson.

Perrot, M. (1975) 'Délinquance et Système Pénitentiaire en France au XIXe Siècle', *Annales ESC* 30(1): 67–94.

Pina-Cabral, J. (1989) 'The Mediterranean as a Category of Regional Comparison: A Critical View', *Current Anthropology* 30(3): 399–406.

Pitt-Rivers, J. (1965) 'Honour and Social Status', in J.G. Peristiany (ed.) *Honour and Shame: The Values of Mediterranean Society*, pp. 19–77. London: Weidenfeld and Nicolson.

Pitt-Rivers, J. (1977) *The Fate of Shechem, or the Politics of Sex: Essays in the Anthropology of the Mediterranean*. Cambridge: Cambridge University Press.

Psarra, A. (1999) 'Addendum: The Novel of Emancipation or the "Wise" Utopia of Kallirroe Parren', in K. Parren (ed.) *The Emancipated Woman* [in Greek], pp. 407–486. Athens: Ekati.

Reddy, W.M. (1997) *The Invisible Code: Honour and Sentiment in Post-Revolutionary France, 1814–1848*. Berkeley, CA: University of California Press.

Reddy, W.M. (2001) *The Navigation of Feeling: A Framework for the History of Emotions*. Cambridge: Cambridge University Press.

Safilios-Rothschild, C. (1969) '"Honour" Crimes in Contemporary Greece', *British Journal of Sociology* 20(2): 205–218.

Scheper-Hughes, N. and P. Bourgois (2004) 'Introduction: Making Sense of Violence', in N. Scheper-Hughes and P. Bourgois (eds) *Violence in War and Peace: An Anthology*, pp. 1–31. London and New York: Blackwell Publishing.

Smith, A. (2004) 'Murder in Jerba: Honour, Shame and Hospitality among Maltese in Ottoman Tunisia', *History and Anthropology* 15(2): 107–132.

Spierenburg, P. (1994) 'Faces of Violence: Homicide Trends and Cultural Meanings: Amsterdam, 1431–1816', *Journal of Social History* 27(4): 701–716.

Spierenburg, P. (1998a) 'Masculinity, Violence, and Honour: An Introduction', in P. Spierenburg (ed.) *Men and Violence: Masculinity, Honour Codes and Violent Rituals in Europe and America, 17th-20th Centuries*, pp. 1–29. Columbus, OH: Ohio State University Press.

Spierenburg, P. (1998b) 'Knife Fighting and Popular Codes of Honour in Early Modern Amsterdam', in P. Spierenburg (ed.) *Men and Violence: Masculinity, Honour Codes and Violent Rituals in Europe and America, 17th-20th Centuries*, pp. 103–127. Columbus, OH: Ohio State University Press.

T[angopoulos], D.P. (1906) 'Appearances and Realities' [in Greek], *O Noumas* 180.

Th[eodoropoulou], A. (1932) 'Their Profession' [in Greek], *O Agonas tis Gynaikas* 158: 1–2.

Twinam, A. (1998) 'The Negotiation of Honour: Elites, Sexuality, and Illegitimacy in Eighteenth-Century Spanish America', in L.L. Johnson and S. Lipsett-Rivera (eds) *The Faces of Honour. Sex, Shame, and Violence in Colonial Latin America*, pp. 68–102. Albuquerque: University of New Mexico Press.

Varika, E. (1987) *The Ladies' Revolt: The Origin of Feminist Consciousness in Greece, 1833–1907* [in Greek]. Athens: Foundation for Research and Culture of the Commercial Bank of Greece.

Welchman, L. and S. Hossain (eds) (2006) *'Honour' Crimes, Paradigms and Violence against Women*. London: Zed Books.

Wiener, M.J. (1998) 'The Victorian Criminalisation of Men', in P. Spierenburg (ed.) *Men and Violence: Masculinity, Honour Codes and Violent Rituals in Europe and America, 17th-20th Centuries*, pp. 197–212. Columbus, OH: Ohio State University Press.

Wikam, U. (1984) 'Shame and Honour: A Contestable Pair', *Man* 19(4): 635–652.

Wyatt-Brown, B. (1982) *Southern Honour: Ethics and Behaviour in the Old South*. New York: Oxford University Press.

PIETER SPIERENBURG

Commentary

Efi Avdela discusses a set of interesting offences in which honour played a leading role, embedding this in an analysis of changing public perceptions concerning these acts of violence. She rightly stresses the problematic aspects of several concepts, that of crime in particular. What is defined as criminal or lawful changes over time, depending not only on formal legislation, but also on the views of various social groups. Acts of violence, she continues, are not always considered as crimes. Indeed, in societies where it is widely understood that a breach of a man's honour requires some kind of violent reaction, third parties, including to some extent the authorities, often accept this physical retaliation as legitimate. The main focus of Avdela's chapter is on post-civil-war Greece, when the law refused to accept violent reactions to offended honour, yet allowed juries to take mitigating circumstances into account. Notably, these required defendants to maintain that the insult to their honour had brought about a fit of uncontrollable rage. A further remarkable element in Avdela's contribution concerns the relative frequency with which women acted as perpetrators of honour-related attacks.

Scholars once assumed that the honour-violence complex was part of a typically Mediterranean culture. Frank Henderson Stewart (1994) already devoted a chapter of his book to reject such a close connection and, without referring to him, Avdela agrees. In fact, traditional notions of honour lived on longer in many Mediterranean communities than they did elsewhere, which allowed anthropologists to observe them in action by the mid-twentieth century. From Stewart's study it becomes clear, furthermore, that honour is an elusive subject. He set himself to the formidable task of establishing, for all societies at all times, what honour actually is, and concluded that it is best defined as a right. The honourable person,

Stewart explains, has certain rights, particularly to respect. In order to prove his case, he moves back and forth through history and from there to the contemporary Bedouins, in an analysis that finally appears as a dead end. By contrast, I find it more fruitful to ask questions such as 'what do you have to be or to do in order to be called honourable?' 'How does one lose or gain honour?' The answers to these questions lead us to conclude, again just as Avdela does, that honour changes over time.

One of the most conspicuous features that changes over time is precisely honour's relationship with violence. Far from constant, this relationship can either be very strong or nearly absent. The latter is the case, for example, in the academic world of today and the not so distant past, where honour is nevertheless important. That can be illustrated by an anecdote. A colleague of mine, embarking on a study of honour, started by collecting a list of books that had the word in their title. He was surprised by the large number of titles he found, but he soon discovered that most of them sounded like 'essays written in honour of professor X at his 60th birthday.' We may assume that the professors in question, unlike some of their nineteenth-century predecessors, were not prone to duelling. By contrast, the honour of a man of the Sarakatsani, as studied by Campbell, depended heavily on one's capacity for physical protection.

It was the historical anthropologist Anton Blok (1980; revised in Blok 2001: 173–209) who subjected the research on Mediterranean people, among which his own conducted in Sicily, to a comparative analysis. He argued that the honour-violence link was part of a broader association of honour (especially but not exclusively male honour) with the physical person or, to put it differently, the body. Honour was expressed in terms of the symbolic functions connected with the human body: blood, the heart, genitals, the head, and the right hand. Physical contact could be rewarding or humiliating depending on the context. Sicilian *virtu*, for example, implied virility accompanied by strength, influence, and power. Even if you could not prevent your cattle from being stolen, this was an encroachment upon your honour. The bodies of animals played their part as well, with human virility being associated with strong and awe-inspiring species. Animal symbolism was connected in particular with horns. Originally, the horns associated with a cuckold referred to those of male goats, which allow other males with their females. By contrast, rams continually fight each other over access to females. Hence honour concerned a sexual symbolism, but this was tied inextricably with issues of violence and domination.

Since Blok first published his analysis, the body-related concept of honour, has been explored by numerous historians of medieval and early modern Europe. Robert Muchembled (1989), for example, confirmed in his study of sixteenth-century Artois that physical contact was humiliating or rewarding depending on the context. If a stranger came near to another man within arm's length, this was interpreted as an act of hostility. Claude Gauvard (1991) saw honour involved in nearly every act of violence committed in medieval France. Removing a man's hat, for example, or meddling with it otherwise was often taken as an insult that could lead to a fight. Historians of early modern Germany and Scandinavia came to similar conclusions in studies published since the mid-1990s. Thus, male sociability in taverns included alcohol consumption and merriment, but a wrong word or gesture could change the atmosphere into hostility that might escalate into violence. In rural areas, conflicts over land use, a material issue at first sight, sometimes lingered on for years, with the contestants' honour at stake during every single confrontation. This was no different in England, but perhaps the most remarkable feature of English historiography in this respect is its focus on women. Female honour has received even more attention there than in other European countries. Yet, everywhere in early modern Europe, female honour was not only upheld by men, whether brothers or husbands. The reputation of women was always an important issue among themselves, being discussed within the gossip circuit.

Based on this vast literature, we can now say with confidence that the body-related concept of honour was not at all typically Mediterranean. It was once widespread in Europe, but in many parts it is no longer that prevalent. Traditional honour was equally important, as Avdela indicates, for men of the nineteenth-century US South. On the other hand, I would not follow Avdela in her insistence to consider as honour cases only those confrontations in which a perpetrator explicitly says to have acted for reasons of honour. That may be an appropriate method for post-civil-war Greece, but it is not adopted by most historians of early modern Europe. They often recognise the honourific features of violence indirectly, as these are implicit

in activities such as reacting to insults or adhering to ritual patterns. I have
done the same in my publications based on Amsterdam court records. It is
clear, for example, that participants and bystanders acknowledged a knife
fight as honourable only when it was a one-on-one confrontation, even
though this is explicitly referred to just a few times. A related but separate question is whether or not we should single out honour as a separate
motivational category. Some historians distinguish fights for honour from
fights over property rights, for example. Schwerhoff (2004) rejects such a
classification and I agree with him on this point. Honour could be equally
involved in violent conflicts over grazing sheep or negotiating prices.

As indicated above, the marginalisation of the body-related concept
of honour did not mean that honour *per se* became less important. What
happened in Europe at the end of the early modern period was that honour
changed – a change that eroded its intimate connection with male violence.
The body ceased to be the primary source of honour. The literary scholar
George Fenwick Jones (1959) was among the first to express the idea of a
transformation of honour. He spoke of a change of emphasis from external
to internal honour, completed by the mid-eighteenth century and univer-
sally accepted as an ideal before the end of the nineteenth century. During
this transformation of meaning, honour shifted from denoting respect,
deference, prestige, rank, or superiority to denoting admirable conduct,
personal integrity, or an inner sense of right and wrong. Jones investigated
this for German literature, but similar developments appear to have taken
place in other European countries. Blok (1980: 225–227) makes reference
to Jones as support for his hypothesis that the body-related concept of
honour is especially prevalent where and when a stable monopoly of force
is absent, which implies that this concept becomes more marginal as processes of state formation proceed. The persistence of traditional honour in
Mediterranean communities was due to the lesser penetration of state institutions in these communities even by the mid-twentieth century. Although
Blok criticises Jones for his dichotomous opposition of external vs. internal
honour, emphasising that we are dealing with long-term developments, he
concludes by positing a transformation from 'honour' to 'conscience'. In
a similar vein, American historians speak of a contrast between Southern
'honour' and Northern 'dignity'.

If we want to underline that any change which took place was gradual and part of long-term societal transformations, it is better to avoid such dichotomies and to use a processual concept. Instead of being replaced by something else, honour changed in character. I have called this process the 'spiritualisation of honour'. One of its conspicuous features was the emergence of the peaceful man as a cultural model. By the late eighteenth century, a considerable proportion of Europe's upper and middle classes accepted that a man could be both honourable and non-violent (even though duelling persisted until the First World War). Increasingly, male honour came to be based on a reputation for moral conduct and economic solidity. This transformation has to be investigated in greater detail (see further Spierenburg, 2008: 108–111). There is still another reason for speaking of a transformation within honour, rather than its replacement by something else. Even within the core of Europe after 1800, the traditional, body-related concept of honour has never been entirely absent. We can observe periodic upsurges, most notably in recent times related to immigration from outside Europe. Under the influence of American ghetto culture, traditional honour nowadays is usually called respect.

Thus, the history of changes in honour becomes increasingly international. For this reason, it would be incorrect to state that a country like Greece simply underwent the same development as in Northern Europe, but at a slower pace. In some respects, honourific violence in post-1800 Greece was different from that practiced throughout early modern Europe. Amsterdam knife fighters, for example, fought over all kind of insults. If someone called a young brave a 'boy', he would show by his skillful handling of the knife that he was not. Honourific violence as discussed by Avdela, at least when it was lethal, almost always revolved around women's sexuality. This was already the case with the knife fights, studied by Gallant, on the Ionian islands in the nineteenth century, and there is another modern parallel. Turkish immigrants to the Netherlands distinguish between their *seref* (reputation, relative) and their *namus* (honour, absolute). They kill only for *namus* and, here too, it has always to do with women's sexuality. As in some of Avdela's cases, the victim of an honour killing may be a woman of the perpetrator's own family, but more often it is the man from another family on whom the blame is laid. At times, the killer's family adapts their view of reality, by presenting an unwanted relationship as rape (van Eck, 2002). Perhaps, in countries and communities where the belief that honour can only be repaired through violence persists in the nineteenth and twentieth centuries, honour is increasingly restricted to the sphere of women's sexuality. Or perhaps this feature is typically Mediterranean after all. In any case, there are few examples in early modern Europe of men killing a dishonourable woman of their own family.

Finally, among Avdela's cases, there were some in which a woman was not the victim but the perpetrator. This as well as a few other characteristics make them a parallel to yet another modern phenomenon, that of *crime passionnel*. The term was a popular, not a legal concept, that gained currency in France and neighbouring countries from the late nineteenth century onward. Its prerequisites were the expansion of the jury trial and the growing importance of forensic experts. According to popular understanding, *crime passionnel* meant killing for love, more specifically out of jealousy or disappointment. While juries never pronounced automatic acquittals, they tended to excuse the defendant's deed, because they could imagine themselves in her or his shoes. For their part, psychiatrists often concluded toward diminished responsibility. Blinded by love, jealousy, or hatred induced by passion, the defendant was an obvious candidate for a plea of temporary insanity. In the public mind, women – and elegant ladies at that – were especially prone to *crime passionnel*. In fact, most passionate killers had working-class backgrounds and the majority consisted of men. Yet, female offenders were overrepresented compared to the total criminality of the period. Even more important, *crime passionnel* was not straightforwardly modern, since old honour lurked in the background, for male as well as female offenders. In particular, women who threw vitriol (sulphuric acid) into their victim's face often targeted the new woman rather than the man who had deceived or deserted her (Spierenburg, 2008: 187–192).

Avdela's cases of vitriol throwing prove that this originally French custom had reached Greece by the 1950s. On the other hand, the Greek press reserved the term 'crime of passion' for husbands who attacked their (allegedly) unfaithful wives, considering this as less acceptable than a 'true' crime of honour. The parallel between Northern European *crimes passionnels* around 1900 and Greek honour crimes in the mid-twentieth century, however, lies in two elements recurrent in all cases in Avdela's chapter: the sympathetic jury and the overwhelming emotion that offended honour produced. The first is clear enough. The second is a little harder to evaluate, since Avdela does not discuss the role of defence lawyers or forensic experts. Presumably, defendants knew or were told that offended honour alone was not (legally) sufficient to convince jurors and judges, but that it had to be accompanied by a sudden fit of rage, and they duly complied. Here, too, instead of just slower change, we are confronted with an intriguing mix of old and new.

References

Blok, A. (1980) 'Eer en de Fysieke Persoon', *Tijdschrift voor Sociale Geschiedenis* 18: 211–230.

Blok, A. (2001) *Honour and Violence*. Cambridge: Polity.

Gauvard, C. (1991) '*De grace especial*': *Crime, état et société en France à la fin du Moyen Age*. Paris: Publications de la Sorbonne.

Jones, G.F. (1959) *Honour in German literature*. North Carolina: University of North Carolina Press.

Muchembled, R. (1989) *La violence au village: Sociabilité et comportements populaires en Artois du 15e au 17e siècle*. Turnhout: Brepols Publishers.

Schwerhoff, G. (2004) 'Social Control of Violence, Violence as Social Control: The Case of Early Modern Germany', in H. Roodenburg and P. Spierenburg (eds) *Social Control in Europe, Vol. 1, 1500–1800*, pp. 220–246. Columbus: Ohio State University Press.

Spierenburg, P. (2008) *A History of Murder: Personal Violence in Europe from the Middle Ages to the Present*. Cambridge: Polity.

Stewart, F.H. (1994) *Honour*. London: University of Chicago Press.

van Eck, C. (2001) *Door bloed gezuiverd: Eerwraak bij Turken in Nederland*. Amsterdam: Bert Bakker.

PART III

Reactions to Crime

VALSAMIS MITSILEGAS[1]

The Impact of the European Union on the Criminal Justice System

The past decade has witnessed a plethora of legislative and other measures in criminal matters at European Union level. Often developed in synergy with international initiatives in the field, these measures have the potential to have a significant impact on the domestic criminal justice systems of the EU member states. The aim of this chapter is to examine the impact of EU criminal law and policy on the Greek criminal justice system. In doing so, the analysis will focus on legislative and operational action undertaken by the Greek authorities in response to EU requirements in the criminal justice field. Domestic responses will be viewed in the context of the broader, ongoing debate taking place in Greece in the post-dictatorship era on the relationship between security and the protection of fundamental rights in the development of criminal justice measures. In this context, the impact of Union law and policy on the Greek criminal justice system will be examined at three levels. The first substantive part of the chapter will focus on criminalisation, namely, the impact of EU measures on the introduction of new criminal offences in the Greek legal order and the strengthening of the penal enforcement framework. This part will be followed by an analysis of the impact of the EU on domestic administrative and operational structures. The third substantive part will focus on the impact of the incorporation in the Greek criminal justice system of the principle of mutual recognition in criminal matters in the EU, as exemplified by the implementation of the European Arrest Warrant.

1   I am indebted to Professor Maria Kaiafa-Gbandi for her invaluable assistance in the preparation of this chapter. I would also like to thank the editors for their patience and comments, and Anna Damaskou for her research assistance. The chapter was finalised in January 2009.

The Impact on Substantive Criminal Law

This part will examine the impact of EU law and policy on Greek substantive criminal law. It will focus on the process of criminalisation of conduct related to aspects of organised crime, terrorism, and money laundering. In this context, the part will be divided into two sections. The first section will examine the criminalisation of conduct related to organised crime and terrorism. The two issues will be examined together, as the offences in question have been largely interrelated in the development of Greek criminal law in the field. The second section will focus on the related, but separate, issue of the criminalisation of money laundering, a younger offence dictated largely by the globalisation of criminal law. In order to assess the impact of EU law and policy on the introduction of these criminal offences in the Greek criminal justice system, it is essential to examine the context of the development of responses in both the European Union and in Greece. The relationship between Union initiatives and Greek law and policy must be viewed in the light of the evolution of European integration in criminal matters, on the one hand, and in the light of the evolution of the integration of Greece into the Community and then Union system, on the other. In this context, emphasis will be placed on the positioning of both the Union and Greece with regard to evolving global security concerns dictating the creation of new criminal offences and the strengthening of the penal enforcement system.

Organised Crime and Terrorism

European responses to terrorism had emerged already in the 1970s, in the days of the European Economic Community (EEC). Although the Treaty of Rome did not contain any express legal basis for the development of Community legislative action in the field, concerns with regard to the spread of terrorism and radicalisation in Europe led to the establishment of informal networks of co-operation between authorities in

EEC Member States, exemplified in particular by the establishment of the TREVI Group. TREVI continued functioning in the 1980s, when Greece entered the Community. Its remit broadened that decade to include *inter alia* drug trafficking, thus reflecting the shift in the global securitisation discourse from counter-terrorism to the 'war on drugs'. This emphasis on drug trafficking as a security threat was also reflected by the participation of the Community in international initiatives aimed at combating drug trafficking, in particular the United Nations Drug Trafficking Convention of 1988. In the 1990s, the 'war on drugs' was extended to the fight against transnational organised crime, which emerged as a primary threat to the global securitisation vocabulary that decade. In Europe, the priority of fighting organised crime was justified in particular in the light of phenomena such as increased market integration and political events (e.g., the fall of the Berlin Wall) which led to Western fears of instability in the East. In this context, the 1990s witnessed the transformation of the European Community to the European Union, which was granted (primarily under the third pillar) powers to legislate in criminal matters. Indeed, the adoption of the Maastricht Treaty saw the gradual adoption of a number of legally binding measures related to organised crime, as well as the adoption of a series of related policy action plans. EU action in the field intensified at the end of the decade, with the entry into force of the Amsterdam Treaty and the strengthening of the political impetus for enhanced EU action in Justice and Home Affairs, including serious and organised crime. The '00s saw these measures multiply, with a new security focus replacing the prioritisation of organised crime counter-measures. In the post-9/11 world, the 'war on terror' has taken centre stage (Mitsilegas *et al.*, 2003; Mitsilegas, 2009a).

This evolution of global and EU security concerns and responses over time is to a great extent – but with some important variations – reflected in the development of Greek law in the field. Greek anti-terrorism legislation was introduced as early as 1978, when Law 774/1978 'on the suppression of terrorism and the protection of democracy' was passed (Kassimeris, 2001; Manoledakis, 2007; Livos, 2007). The law criminalised the conduct of two people acting in concert, who have been carrying arms or explosives, and have intended to commit or have committed a series of offences. This

law can be seen, as a specialised counter-terrorism instrument, to reflect
the prevalent European security concerns at the time. Although Greece
was not yet a member of the EEC, the legislation was justified by the conservative Government of *Nea Dimokratia* on the grounds that Greece was
still a fragile democracy and on the need to take into account the work of
European bodies on counter-terrorism (Kassimeris, 2001: 159–160). On
the other hand, the law was heavily criticised by the opposition parties. The
(then anti-EEC) socialists of *PASOK* claimed that the law was contrary to
the rule of law and aiming to control protest and to use the security services for law enforcement. It also argued that legislation was the product
of foreign political pressure (namely, by Germany) and was used in order
to achieve accession to the Community (ibid.: 162–163). Similar concerns
were voiced by the communists of *KKE*, while the then centre party of
EDIK also voiced civil liberties concerns (ibid.: 163).

Two main features of reaction to counter-terrorism law can be discerned here: a reaction on the ground that terrorism law jeopardises civil
liberties by criminalising protest and by enhancing the power of the State;
and a reaction on the ground that terrorism law is 'foreign', a product of
political pressure from abroad (Europe or the US). Both these reactions
are perhaps not surprising in the context of Greece in the 1970s, with
the country emerging from a seven-year military dictatorship. However,
it is noteworthy that reactions on both these grounds have proved to be
enduring in the evolution of relevant legislation in Greece since the 1970s.
Reactions at the time led to Law 774/1978 being abolished by the PASOK
Government when it came to power in the 1980s. PASOK argued that
such counter-terrorism measures are not justified given that in Greece
terrorism was not likely to take the fork of action experienced in Italy and
Germany in the 1970s, and stressed the danger to civil liberties. Moreover,
in an argument which would be repeated in the debate over subsequent
laws on terrorism and organised crime, it was argued that the general provisions of criminal law were adequate to address this phenomenon, with
no need arising for specific counter-terrorism legislation (ibid.: 170; see
also Livos, 2007: 194).

Counter-terrorism concerns were subsequently reflected in legislation
criminalising acts by criminal organisations. Law 1916/90 'on the protection

of society from organised crime' was adopted again by a Nea Dimokratia Government, notably not in response to a relevant Community measure. The law was adopted to address a series of violent attacks occurring in the late 1980s (including a fatal attack against the Nea Dimokratia Parliamentary Spokesman Pavlos Bakoyannis), and was justified as necessary to protect citizens and democratic institutions, with references also being made to developments in the Council of Europe (Kassimeris, 2001: 175–176). It is noteworthy that the law did not expressly refer to terrorism – rather, it used the term 'organised crime' in the title and criminal organisations in the text. However, it also included provisions banning the media from publicising statements by criminal groups, a provision which effectively 'photographed' the publication by the Greek press of statements by terrorist groups (see Manoledakis, 2002: 4; Livos, 2007: 195). It has thus been argued that the term 'organised crime' in the 1990 law was devised in order to sidestep left-wing protest, with organised crime acting as a substitute for terrorism for domestic purposes (Xenakis, 2004: 348). Unsurprisingly, the legislation was met by fierce criticism by the press and by opposition parties. The latter argued that the law infringed freedom of the press and that it encouraged spying and reporting on fellow citizens (*hafiedismos* in Greek, a term strongly reminiscent of the country's authoritarian past; see Kassimeris, 2001: 180). PASOK committed itself to abolish the law as soon as they became government, and indeed they did so in 1993. In the explanatory report to Law 2172/1993, which abolished the 1990 law, it was again stated that the general provisions of Greek criminal law were sufficient to deal with conduct criminalised in the 1990 law, and that this fact constituted a systemic advantage, rather than a disadvantage for the Greek legal system (but see Livos, 2007: 63, 201).

Greece thus moved in the 1990s without a specific legislation on organised crime. At the same time, combating organised crime was becoming a priority for the European Union, with various policy initiatives aiming at ensuring the exchange of strategic and personal data between member states being put forward, and participation in a criminal organisation being criminalised in 1998 (Mitsilegas, 2001). This EU-wide criminalisation of participation in a criminal organisation was reiterated in greater detail in the 2000 United Nations Convention on Transnational Organised Crime (the

Palermo Convention). Demands for more systematic and accurate information on organised crime in Greece, as well as for a more strategic approach to the phenomenon, resulted in the establishment of various committees at national level over time and in the attention – at least at the presentational level – of the submission of organised crime statistics to EU bodies (Lambropoulou, 2003). In 1998, there was a sudden change in Greek organised crime reports, with organised crime instances in Greece appearing explicitly in the relevant Greek reports. While some commentators argue that this change was cosmetic, representing merely a change in the categorisation of cases of criminality by the Greek authorities (ibid.: 81–82), others argue that it represented a change of perception by the Greek authorities, namely, an acceptance that organised crime exists (Livos, 2007). Subsequently, the PASOK government (which had abolished both the 1978 and the 1990 legislation on terrorism/organised crime) set up in 2000 a committee to study the development of legislation on organised crime.

The work of the Committee and the passing of the legislation more generally have proven to be turbulent. Discussions for new domestic legislation on organised crime had to reconcile serious civil liberties concerns by the lawmakers with the need to comply with international commitments. Added complexity arose in light of the fact that the governing party keen to pass legislation now was the party which had traditionally rejected specific legislation on terrorism and organised crime, and had abolished earlier law (Xenakis, 2004: 349). Moreover, attempts to pass legislation on organised crime were again viewed by some as bowing to pressure by foreign power centres (albeit not so much by the EU as by the US and the UK; Manoledakis, 2002: 8; Xenakis, 2004: 361). Concerns led prominent members of the law-making committee (including a number of academics, Manoledakis being one of them) to resign, and the law was ultimately passed with the support of Nea Dimokratia, then in the opposition. However, only 20 Greek MPs (out of 300) voted for the legislation (see Manoledakis, 2002: 9; Xenakis, 2004: 350–351). Even with this diminished legitimacy, Law 2928/2001 or the 'amendment of provisions of the Criminal Code and the Code of Criminal Procedure and other provisions for the protection of the citizen from criminal acts of criminal organisations' was passed.

Law 2928/2001 introduced a detailed and comprehensive framework dealing with organised crime. It is noteworthy that again the emphasis was on the conduct of criminal organisations, and not on terrorism. However, acts branded as terrorist could be included in the criminalisation of such conduct (Livos, 2007: 204). This was confirmed by the trial in 2003 of members of the notorious 17 November organisation (on which see further Xenakis, this collection), who were convicted on the basis of Article 187 of the Greek Criminal Code as amended by Law 2928/2001. Article 187 was amended to introduce heavy custodial penalties (of a maximum of ten years) for the establishment or membership of a structured group of particular duration intending the commission of a list of criminal offences enumerated therein. The wording of the EU Joint Action was thus followed closely, but the Greek legislator used a list rather than a penalty threshold to define the offences committed by a group for the purposes of the law. Law 2928/2001 also introduced new provisions *inter alia* on mitigating circumstances, the extension of jurisdiction for organised crime, the abolition of trial by jury, and enabling DNA testing (Symeonidou-Kastanidou, 2005). The law has been criticised for unduly extending the realm of punitiveness by introducing very broad criminal offences (including offences which potentially criminalise thought; ibid.: 36–38) and for blurring the boundaries between common criminal law offences and the so-called 'political' offences which are protected by the Greek Constitution (Kyritsis, 2005). It is undoubtable, however, that compliance with EU and UN imperatives has had a significant impact on the domestic criminal justice system, with new criminal offences and enforcement measures being introduced.

Notwithstanding the passage of this law in 2001 and its potential to also include conduct by terrorist groups, sustained pressure has been placed on successive Greek governments to implement terrorism-specific measures adopted at EU-level post-9/11. Of particular priority in this context has been the implementation in Greece of the Framework Decision on the European Arrest Warrant (examined below) and of the Framework Decision to combat terrorism. With the deadline for the implementation of these two instruments having passed, the Greek authorities were placed under considerable pressure to enact legislation, particularly in light of the approaching date of the 2004 Athens Olympics.[2] Legislation to implement the two Framework Decisions was thus tabled by a Nea Dimokratia government (succeeding PASOK earlier that year) in the summer of 2004. The legislative proposals caused a heated debate, primarily on civil liberties grounds, but also on the grounds that legislation was again pushed through due to 'foreign' pressure dictating counter-terrorism action in light of the 2004 Athens Olympics. The government, on the other hand, stressed the need to comply with obligations undertaken at EU level and stressed that implementation of the Framework Decisions in question had been long overdue.[3]

Law 3251/2004 on the 'European Arrest Warrant, the amendment of law 2928/2001 on criminal organisations and other provisions' was eventually adopted in June 2004. Its explanatory report stressed the will of Greece to contribute actively to the formulation of a common European policy against international terrorism within the remit of an area of freedom, security, and justice (see also Livos, 2007: 209). It introduced, amongst other things, a new article into the Greek Criminal Code, Article 187A (for an extensive analysis of which, see Kaiafa-Gbandi, 2005). This provision defined and criminalised a terrorist act using a number of the elements of the offence introduced in the EU Framework Decision (commission of offences in order to seriously damage a country or an international organisation, and intending to intimidate a population or to unduly compel a public authority or international organisation to perform or to abstain from any act or to seriously harm or destroy the fundamental constitutional, political, and economic structures of an organisation). Like the 2001 Law, Article 187A included a list of offences as terrorist offences – in this context, the Greek legislator attempted to 'translate' the conduct described in the list included in the Framework Decision to offences under the Greek Criminal Code. It also criminalised a series of related acts, including threatening to commit a terrorist offence, directing a terrorist organisation (punishable with a minimum custodial sentence of ten years), and establishing or participating in such an organisation. Moreover, and

2   See *The Independent*, 8 June 2004.
3   See *Parliamentary Debates* of 22 and 23 June 2004.

beyond the requirements of EU law, Article 8 of the Criminal Code was amended to introduce extraterritorial jurisdiction for terrorist acts under Article 187A. As a safeguard to these extensive provisions, Article 187A stated that it is not a terrorist act to commit one or more of the offences mentioned therein if these are 'political offences' or if they constitute the exercise of a fundamental right enshrined in the Greek Constitution or the ECHR.[4]

Article 187A introduced a series of extremely heavy penalties for terrorist offences. In this respect, there were a number of differences between the Greek law and the EU Framework Decision. Whereas, for example, the Framework Decision provided for the punishment of participation in a terrorist group by custodial sentences of a 'minimum maximum' of not less than fifteen years, the Greek legislator adopted a slightly different approach and provided for the punishment of such conduct by custodial sentences of a minimum of ten years. Also, the Framework Decision provided for the punishment of directing a terrorist group by a minimum maximum custodial sentence of eight years, whereas Greek law provided for a minimum maximum custodial sentence of ten years. More generally, terrorist acts became punishable in Greek law (depending on the offence) with a minimum custodial sentence of three years, a penalty threshold that was not introduced as such in the Framework Decision. Indeed, as the European Commission has noted, this amounts to the abolition of the dual criminality requirement for terrorist offences for the purposes of the European Arrest Warrant (European Commission, 2006: 26).

As well as punishing terrorist acts with severe penalties, Law 3251/2004 thus introduced a number of very significant changes to the criminalisation of terrorism in Greece. First of all, it is noteworthy that Article 187A made clear reference to the concept of a 'terrorist group' and a 'terrorist

---

4 The wording of the Greek law in this case is more detailed and more specific to the domestic constitutional context and the constitutional tradition of the protection of 'political offences' than to the Framework Decision. Article 1(2) of the latter contains a rather general wording stating that the Framework Decision will not have the effect of altering the obligation to respect fundamental rights and fundamental legal principles as enshrined in Article 6 of the Treaty on the European Union.

act'. These concepts were thereby firmly introduced in the Greek criminal justice system. Secondly, the extension of criminalisation is notable. In conjunction with Law 2928/2001 (Kaiafa-Gbandi, 2005: 872), Law 3251/2004 criminalised individual terrorist acts without making them dependent upon the existence of an organisation (Symeonidou-Kastanidou, 2005: 130; Livos, 2007: 210). Using the vague and broad elements of the Framework Decision (on which see Symeonidou-Kastanidou, 2005), it extended criminalisation to a series of related acts, such as directing a terrorist group or threatening to commit a terrorist act, and thus covered a wide range of stages, from preparation to commission to the concealment of a terrorist act (Kaiafa-Gbandi, 2005: 872). It also extended criminalisation via the introduction of extraterritorial jurisdiction for terrorist acts. While the law did take into account domestic concerns not to criminalise the so-called 'political offences' and to safeguard fundamental rights, it was not clear how these provisions would be interpreted in practice.[5] This new legal framework was justified in order to achieve compliance with Union law. The Greek legislator implemented Union law in detail, and efforts have since been made to adjust the EU requirements to the Greek legal system. Implementation of the terrorism Framework Decision was judged to be more than adequate by the European Commission (2006). Compliance with Union law has therefore led to fundamental changes to the domestic criminal justice system.

Money Laundering

Elsewhere, I have characterised the perceived threat by money laundering as a 'chameleon' threat (Mitsilegas, 2003a). Money laundering countermeasures have developed relatively recently both globally and within the EU. Since the introduction of the first major global anti-money laundering standards in the late 1980s, the global and EU anti-money laundering

---

5   It has been reported that the anti-terrorism law was recently used to prosecute high-school student protesters (see *Eleftherotypia*, 10 January 2009).

framework has been constantly expanding, with the criminalisation of money laundering being stretched to address the various security concerns over time: while in the 1980s the focus had been on the proceeds of drug trafficking (in line with the 'war on drugs'), in the 1990s attention shifted more broadly to the need to combat proceeds from serious and organised crime in general. Post-9/11, the anti-money laundering legal and regulatory framework has been expanded to also aim at countering terrorist finance. EU law and policy has been evolving along these lines in order to accommodate changing security concerns and the resulting global standards. Global standards including the 1988 UN Drug Trafficking Convention and the 1990 40 Recommendations by the Financial Action Task Force (FATF) led to the adoption of the first Money Laundering Directive in 1991. Amendments to global standards (in particular the FATF Recommendations) led to the adoption of the second Money Laundering Directive in 2001 (Mitsilegas, 2003b). And further amendments (including 'war on terror' considerations) led to the adoption, in 2005, of the third money laundering Directive (Mitsilegas and Gilmore, 2007).

In terms of the implementation of these measures, EU member states have been required to introduce new criminal justice and regulatory concepts into their domestic legal systems. This challenge was compounded by the constant evolution of these measures, which meant that member states undertook the obligation to implement, within a period of less than fifteen years, three very substantial anti-money laundering Directives. On all three occasions, such implementation has proven to be difficult for Greece: Greek implementing law was adopted *after* the implementation deadline of the relevant Directives, whilst adjustment of Greek law and administration to the EU anti-money laundering requirements has been slow.

In the criminal justice sphere, considerable difficulties have been encountered with regard to the introduction of money laundering offences into Greek criminal law. These offences, as introduced in the 1990s, have been criticised as overtly broad and vague, and as imposing more intense criminalisation (in terms of both scope and sanctions) than the EU requirements (see further Kaiafa-Gbandi, 2007; Symeonidou-Kastanidou, 2007). This uncertainty with regard to the legislative implementation has led to a high level of uncertainty by the courts, which – at least in the early years of implementation – have often interpreted money laundering offences very broadly, to include everyday conduct lacking the sophistication of the money laundering process, and which could be prosecuted under separate – and simpler – offences under the Greek Criminal Code (see further Symeonidou-Kastanidou, 2005). The state of the Greek criminal law after the implementation of the second money laundering Directive and at the time when Greece was under the obligation to implement the third money laundering Directive was summed up by the FATF as follows:

> [I]n the criminal law area, ... Greece has adopted a large set of repressive measures that generally lack the precision and quality that is required by international and domestic law in order to impose efficient AML/CFT systems. (FATF, 2007: 48)

The year 2008 saw the Nea Dimokratia government called for to address both the scathing comments published by the FATF in its 2007 evaluation and the delay in implementing the third money laundering Directive. Against this background, a new anti-money laundering draft law was tabled in the summer of 2008. According to its explanatory report, the aim of the legislation was four-fold: to implement the third Directive; to implement FATF requirements; to introduce a number of new, domestically-inspired provisions; and to consolidate existing law. However, as in the case of legislation against terrorism and organised crime, the draft law was subject to sustained criticism by academics, law practitioners and politicians. Academic and practitioner reactions continued (as with earlier anti-money laundering legislation) to focus on the broad criminalisation of everyday conduct under money laundering law and on the change in the relationship between the individual and the State which the anti-money laundering reporting duties (extended after the second money laundering Directive to lawyers) would entail. Civil liberties concerns were also raised by left-wing MPs during the passage of the Bill in Parliament, with KKE also making the 'foreign pressure' claim, namely, that the law was intended to create a favourable impression that Greece is taking action against money laundering. However, objections to the Bill had also a further political dimension. Opposition parties, in particular PASOK, accused the government that the real reason for the adoption of this law was to replace the Head of the

Greek FIU (Financial Intelligence Unit) – this would be done by changing the law to require that the Head of the FIU is an active member of the judiciary, rather than a retired judge as with the Head at the time. Changes to the nature and composition of the FIU were deemed unconstitutional and the passage of the law (which was examined together with unrelated legislation on collective bargaining and the remuneration and promotions of judges) was deemed to be rushed in order to serve political expediency on the part of the government. The latter dismissed these arguments by evoking the need to implement EU and FATF requirements.

Law 3691/2008 was published in August 2008. It is a detailed and lengthy statute, with some 53 sections devoted to anti-money laundering measures. Major changes have been introduced with regard to the Greek administrative and operational structures aimed at countering money laundering (including the FIU), which will be discussed in detail in the next part of this chapter. In terms of the money laundering criminal offences, the law aligned to a great extent the definition of money laundering with the one included in the Third Directive. It also amended the definition of terrorist finance to this effect. The main differences with the Directive are the explicit inclusion into the definition of money laundering of the 'use of the financial system by the placing or movement of proceeds of crime in order to give to these proceeds the appearance of legality' (this stress to the *process* of money laundering may be justified as guidance to the courts as regards the differences of money laundering from ordinary property crimes such as handling of stolen goods); the requirement of pecuniary benefit for certain offences to be considered as money laundering predicates; and the extension of the offence of terrorist finance to also include (along with the provision or collection of funds) the provision of information or material means for terrorist offences. The Greek law goes further than the Directive in specifying that custodial sentences will be imposed for non-reporting of suspicious transactions and in expressly criminalising own funds money laundering. The latest Greek criminal law on money laundering is thus detailed, and at times (in an attempt to address FATF concerns) stricter than EU requirements. It is the third attempt to introduce the – admittedly rather broad and contested – criminalisation of money laundering into the Greek legal system. It remains to be seen whether the new provisions will help to raise awareness and understanding of money laundering processes in practitioners and courts, and how the money laundering offences will be defined by the latter.

Administrative and Operational Implementation

Administrative and operational implementation of EU criminal law can be viewed at three levels: at the level of the accommodation in the domestic legal system of the work of EU criminal law bodies such as Europol and Eurojust (on which see further Mitsilegas, 2009); at the level of the accommodation of EU criminal law measures related to 'horizontal' police and judicial co-operation in criminal matters; and at the level of the accommodation in the domestic legal order of EU enforcement measures with regard to specific offences. This part of the chapter will focus primarily on the administrative implementation of the EU anti-money laundering measures.

Implementation to address Co-operation with EU bodies

Greece has established a centralised model of police cooperation. The body responsible for such co-operation in Greece is the International Police Co-operation Division at the Greek Police Headquarters. It is responsible for the communication between the Greek Police and the Ministry of Interior, on the one hand, and international organisations, on the other. It is also the Greek contact point in relation to Interpol, SIRENE, and Europol, being the Europol National Unit. As regards Eurojust, Greece passed legislation to implement the 2002 Eurojust Decision only in 2008. The implementing law specifies that the Eurojust member for Greece must be a judge or a prosecutor in the Court of First Instance or above with a mandate of three years, renewable for another three. As regards the powers of the national member, however, the law is largely a copy of the Eurojust Decision. In light of this choice, the picture as to the powers of the Euro-just national member in the Greek jurisdiction and the relations between the national member and the domestic prosecutors remain unclear. The two national members for Greece seconded to Eurojust have thus far been both relatively junior prosecutors (Eurojust, 2003: 56; Eurojust, 2005: 103). Greece has used Eurojust for co-ordination meetings, and the number of cases in which it has been involved either as a requesting or as a requested country has mainly been on the rise since the start of Eurojust operations (Eurojust, 2003: 30, 32; Eurojust, 2005: 31, 19).

Implementation to address Horizontal Police and Judicial Cooperation in Criminal Matters

With regard to the accommodation of horizontal cooperation measures in the Greek criminal justice system, Greece has been very slow in ratifying the 2000 EU mutual legal assistance Convention and in implementing the Framework Decision on joint investigation teams. On the other hand, following increased pressure from the EU, Greece has now implemented the Framework Decision on the European Arrest Warrant (on which more in the next part). Here it must be noted that Greece has designated a central authority for the purposes of issuing European Arrest Warrants and (in cases where Greece acts as an executing State) for the purposes of receiving Warrants, arresting, and detaining the requested person, submitting the case to the competent judicial authority and executing the court's decision to surrender.[6] This central authority is the Public Prosecutor at the Court of Appeal. In cases where the requested person consents to surrender, the

---

6   However, according to Article 3 of the implementing law, the Greek Ministry of Justice can also act as a conduit for the transmission and reception of European Arrest Warrants. It may be entitled to keep statistics. These tasks are performed by the Department of Special Criminal Cases and International Judicial Co-operation in Criminal Cases, within the Legislative Co-ordination and Special International Legal Relations General Directorate.

competence to decide on the execution of the European Arrest Warrant lies with the Presiding Judge of the Court of Appeal. In cases of non-consent, the competent authority is a Judicial Council composed of three Court of Appeal judges. Their decision may be appealed in the Supreme Court (Council of the European Union, 2008: 6–7).

The recent evaluation report on the Greek implementation of the European Arrest Warrant (where more on these arrangements can be found) has noted, however, that regular systematic coordination between the different prosecution offices throughout Greece is lacking. The evaluators also raised the issue of lack of specialisation in judges with regard to working with European Arrest Warrants, the lack of training and the de facto centralisation of the system of issuing of Warrants in Athens (with more than two-thirds of issuing warrants emanating from the Public Prosecutor's Office at the Athens Court of Appeal, even though this office is only one of fifteen authorities competent to issue Warrants in the country; ibid.: 32–33). The evaluators also noted that, with regard to the execution of European Arrest Warrants, more than two-thirds of the Warrants received by Greece in 2007 were assigned to three Public Prosecutor's Offices (Athens, Thessaloniki, and Thrace; ibid.: 33).

*Implementation to address the Enforcement of
EU Criminal Law Requirements*

A field where the operational and administrative implementation of EU requirements has proven to be challenging in the Greek context involves money laundering counter-measures. Beyond the various legislative requirements, this could be discerned by the various evaluations of Greece – in particular the 2007 evaluation – that there existed neither a clear picture or awareness of the money laundering phenomenon in the country nor a clear strategy or method to counter it. The 2008 legislation was an attempt to address these concerns through the establishment of a number of new administrative structures. The Ministry of Finance henceforth acts as the central co-ordination authority for the implementation of this law and represents the country in international fora. A high-level anti-money laundering and terrorist finance strategy committee is established, located within the Ministry of Finance and with the participation of officials also from the Ministry of the Interior (i.e., the police), the Ministries of Foreign Affairs, Justice, and Shipping Affairs, the Greek FIU, the Bank of Greece, and other financial authorities (along with strategic and policy guidelines, a task of this committee is to monitor the compliance of Greece with international standards). An authority responsible for the consultation of the private sector is also established. The authority is chaired by the secretary of the Greek Banking Association and is tasked *inter alia* with providing guidelines to the professions and persons covered by the law with regard to its implementation. It is evident that these measures are there to show that Greece is taking its anti-money laundering obligations seriously: they are aimed to enhance co-ordination between the various authorities, to raise awareness of money laundering and its counter-measures, and to promote a coherent anti-money laundering strategy.

However, the major change introduced by the 2008 anti-money laundering law has undoubtedly been in the nature and powers of the Greek FIU (which is responsible for receiving and analysing suspicious transaction reports from the private sector). In the first anti-money laundering law of 1995, Greece had chosen to introduce the 'independent' model of an FIU, which consisted of a committee from various ministries and financial authorities (for a typology of FIUs and the features of the Greek model, see Mitsilegas, 1999). This model was changed with the 2005 anti-money laundering law, which boosted the powers of the unit (for an analysis, see Daniil, 2008). However, this did not stop the very severe criticism of Greece by the FATF in the 2007 evaluation. Greece was found to be noncompliant with the FATF Recommendation on FIUs, with the Report noting a number of serious shortcomings including the absence of guidance from the FIU to reporting parties; severe technological gaps and shortcomings; gaps in the exchange of information with other authorities; lack of staff; and absence of systematic work (with the Report stating that action relies upon 'the intuitive decision of FIU members'). More importantly, the FATF team raised concerns with regard to the operational independence and autonomy of the FIU, including concerns with regard to possible conflicts of interest (FATF, 2007).

The 2008 law aimed to address these concerns by totally revising the law on FIUs. The new Greek FIU is a Committee under the supervision of the Finance Minister. Its Chairperson is a high-ranking active prosecutor and its members come from a number of ministries and financial supervision authorities (including the Bank of Greece). The Committee has been given sweeping powers of investigation, data collection, and co-operation with other authorities.[7] The law also provides for the staffing of the FIU with up to fifty new staff. This provision has been criticised on political grounds (as an attempt to replace the Head of the previous FIU), constitutional grounds (in that the FIU is chaired by an active prosecutor), and criminal procedure grounds (as extensive powers of criminal investigation are given to an administrative authority) (Daniil, 2008). On paper, it addresses to the letter the FATF recommendations, and the less detailed EU requirements, although these may conflict with the internal structure of the criminal justice system. It seems that, in attempting to secure compliance with international fora, this relationship has not been thought through extensively by the legislator. However, as is evident from the 2007 FATF evaluation report, the requested compliance is not a matter of law, but a matter of practice. It is also a matter of achieving awareness of the money laundering phenomenon, prioritisation of action against it by the authorities concerned, and co-ordination between the competent authorities.[8] It remains to be seen how the role of the Greek FIU will develop in this context.

7   Note that there is a separate FIU for lawyers, i.e., a Committee of Lawyers consisting of five members and appointed by the Plenary of the Chairpersons of the Greek Bar Associations. This FIU receives suspicious transaction reports from lawyers and has been established – in line with the Directive provisions – in order to safeguard the independence of the legal profession and to address fears that the imposition of reporting duties to lawyers will undermine the administration of justice and the right to a fair trial.
8   The FATF Evaluation Report also noted the lack of co-ordination between national law enforcement authorities responsible for the fight against money laundering (paragraph 259). For an overview of the Greek structures in this context see part 2.6 of the Report.

Implementing Mutual Recognition

Calls for the application of the principle of mutual recognition – already tried in the context of the EU internal market – in the field of EU criminal law appeared in the late 1990s, particularly during the UK Presidency of the Union in 1998, and were reflected in detail in the 1999 European Council Tampere Conclusions which provided an impetus for new legislative action in the field of EU Justice and Home Affairs. Mutual recognition was for some an alternative, for others a complementary mechanism, to harmonisation in criminal matters in the European Union. In an era when the Commission was actively promoting harmonisation (if not uniformity) of EU criminal law, most notably via the *Corpus Juris* project, more sceptical member states were pushing forward mutual recognition as an alternative (its main advantage being that, by accepting to recognise judicial decisions from courts in another member state, they would not have to change their domestic law, something that could happen if they would have to implement a harmonising EU criminal law measure). At the same time, for pro-integration advocates, mutual recognition would provide a way out of the prospect of legislative stagnation in EU criminal law (accentuated by the unanimity requirement for voting in the Council on third-pillar matters, which could mean in practice that sceptical member states could block harmonisation initiatives): not only would it lead to the adoption of some EU criminal law (as exemplified by the adoption of the European Arrest Warrant in 2001), but also, if the example of mutual recognition in the internal market were to be followed, mutual recognition would lead to the adoption of complementary minimum harmonisation standards aiming at creating a level playing field among member states (Mitsilegas, 2006a).

Mutual recognition in criminal matters would involve the recognition and execution by a judge in the receiving (or, according to EU terminology, the 'executing') member state of a judicial decision by a court in the sending (or the 'issuing') member state. The main features of this process are speed, automaticity, and a minimum of formality. The executing judge would receive the mutual recognition request via a pro-forma form (completed by the issuing judge). In principle, the executing judge should not look behind the form and accept the request without asking too many questions. As the EU institutions have repeatedly pointed out in the negotiations of the various EU mutual recognition measures, the basis of mutual recognition is mutual trust in the criminal justice systems of member states. This perceived mutual trust should thus lead to quasi-automatic enforcement. But in practice the 'no questions asked' mutual recognition effectively consists of a 'journey into the unknown' for the executing judge who is in essence being asked to accept almost blindly a decision which stems from the judicial, legal, and constitutional tradition of another EU member state (Mitsilegas, 2006b).

The first – and most talked about – example of mutual recognition in criminal matters in the European Union has been the Framework Decision on the European Arrest Warrant. The application of the mutual recognition principle in the case of the European Arrest Warrant raised a number of constitutional concerns across the European Union (Mitsilegas, 2006b, 2009a). A major concern relates to the principle of legality, which is deemed to be threatened by the abolition of dual criminality for a wide range of offences. This could lead to the authorities of a member state employing their criminal law enforcement mechanism in order to arrest and surrender an individual for conduct which is not an offence under its domestic law. Legality concerns are inextricably linked in this context with issues of legitimacy and trust, most notably regarding the bond between the State and its citizens. The lack of legitimacy may be an issue particularly in light of the fact that, on the basis of mutual recognition, a court in a member state must accept decisions stemming from standards and laws in the adoption of which the public of the executing State played no part, and of which it has limited, if any, knowledge. Further constitutional concerns were raised on the specific issue of the surrender of own nationals which the European Arrest Warrant allows but several national Constitutions expressly prohibited. Last, but not least, a major issue regarding the implementation of the European Arrest Warrant concerned the protection of fundamental rights, especially the rights of the individual subject to surrender in another member state before and (crucially) after surrender. It is here that the concept of mutual trust seems to have been challenged most strongly, with a number of concerns voiced regarding the capacity and ability of a number of EU member states to safeguard effectively the rights of the defendant in their domestic criminal justice systems (see further Mitsilegas, 2006b, 2009a).

The Framework Decision on the European Arrest Warrant is, at the time of writing, the only mutual recognition instrument which Greece has implemented. The implementation of other measures dictating the mutual recognition of orders related to financial matters (such as freezing orders, financial penalties, or confiscation) is still pending, although the implementation deadline has now passed. The constitutional issues analysed above have also appeared under various guises in the process of the implementation of the European Arrest Warrant Framework Decision in Greece. Concerns were raised already at the stage of the negotiations of the Framework Decision in Brussels, when the Greek government had to reconcile the need of reaching agreement swiftly in the run up to 9/11 with the need to be seen to protect domestic constitutional principles and civil liberties (Andreou, 2003). Particular concerns in negotiations centered on the application of the European Arrest Warrant to acts related to political or labour law rights, especially rights related to freedom of expression and association, and the impact of such developments on the Greek constitution and civil liberties (see, e.g., *To Vima*, 18 November 2001).

Unanimous agreement to the European Arrest Warrant Framework Decision was reached in December 2001, with the text itself published in the Official Gazette of the Hellenic Republic in the summer of 2002. However, Greece was again slow to implement the Framework Decision in its domestic legal order. With the deadline for implementation having passed (this was the end of 2003), and as seen above, Greece was placed under increasing pressure – intensified in light of the organisation of the 2004 Athens Olympics – to take steps towards implementation. A draft bill was eventually tabled before Parliament in the summer of 2004, aimed at implementing both the European Arrest Warrant and the Framework Decisions on terrorism. Attempts to implement the Framework Decision were met again with severe criticism by academics (see in particular Bekas, 2007) and parliamentarians from all opposition parties mainly on three grounds: the abolition of dual criminality for a list of offences; allowing the surrender of own nationals; and extending the State's punitive reach by facilitating surrender. The government responded to this criticism by stressing that the legislator applied the discretion granted to member states by Framework Decisions to adjust their content to the domestic context, and introduced a series of protective provisions for individuals. It was also argued that the Greek Constitution did not prohibit the surrender of own nationals and that, in any case, it would prevail. Finally, the government pointed out that there was no further leeway from the EU with regard to the implementation of the Framework Decision which was overdue (ibid.).

The Framework Decision on the European Arrest Warrant was eventually implemented by Law 3251/2004. Some 38 sections of the domestic law were devoted to such implementation. The Greek law followed a similar, albeit not identical, structure to that of the Framework Decision. The first part on 'general provisions' contains a provision on the definition of the Framework Decision (article 1 in both EU and domestic law) and a provision on the content and type of the European Arrest Warrant (which comes only in Article 8 of the Framework Decision). The Greek legislator chose to continue by dividing the Framework Decision provisions on the surrender procedure into various more specific parts. Chapter 2 deals with the issuing and transmission of the European Arrest Warrant (articles 4–8), while chapter 3 (the bulk of the implementing law) deals with the execution of the Warrant (articles 9–29). The latter chapter incorporates details with regard to the abolition of dual criminality and the grounds of non-execution which appear at an earlier stage in the Framework Decision. The fourth chapter is devoted to the surrender process itself (articles 30–32), while the fifth and sixth chapters follow the structure of the Framework Decision by dealing with the effects of the surrender (articles 33–36) and final provisions (articles 37–39), respectively. According to the Explanatory Memorandum to the Act, the deviation from the structure of the Framework Decision was deemed necessary to facilitate the application of the law in the domestic system. This is, indeed, a clearer structure than that of the Framework Decision, highlighting the different stages of the European Arrest Warrant process.

The administrative arrangements for the issuing and execution of European Arrest Warrants in Greece were examined in the previous part of this chapter. More generally, the Greek legislator chose to stay close to the wording of the Framework Decision. A characteristic example is the enumeration of the list of acts for which dual criminality has been abolished, which constitutes largely a verbatim translation from the Framework Decision, rather than attempting to translate them into criminal conduct as described in the Greek criminal law. This strategy has led to negative comments in the recent evaluation report of Greece's implementation of the European Arrest Warrant, which states that the Greek implementing law is, to a large extent, a copy-and-paste of the Framework Decision and that, in using this technique, it seems that the legislator did not pay full attention to the relationship with regulations and practices in other fields of criminal law which interact with the handling of European Arrest Warrants (European Commission, 2006: 31). There have been cases, however, where the Greek implementing law has gone beyond Framework Decision requirements. These have occurred in order to assuage civil liberties concerns, and involve extending the possibility of non-execution of a Warrant by a Greek judge. Optional grounds for refusal have been translated into mandatory grounds in the Greek law, while the general human rights safeguard in the Preamble to the Framework Decision has been introduced as a mandatory ground for refusal in the Greek law.[9]

The Greek implementing law does not contain a ground for refusal with regard to the surrender of own nationals. This issue of constitutional significance has been inevitably raised before the Greek courts in their handling of European Arrest Warrants. In this context, it is noteworthy that in a recent judgment the Greek Supreme Court confirmed earlier case law stating that the surrender of own nationals is not contrary to the Greek Constitution. This is one of a number of court decisions clarifying elements of the implementation of the European Arrest Warrant and facilitating its application (see further Mitsilegas, 2009b). The reasoning

9   Article 11(e) prohibits surrender if a Warrant has been issued for the purpose of prosecuting or punishing a person on the grounds of sex, race, religion, ethnic origin, nationality, language, political opinions, sexual orientation *and action to promote freedom*. The latter, italicised element does not appear in the Framework Decision, but has been introduced to reflect the Greek constitutional tradition.

of the Court is significant in this context, as it accepts (as the Court of
Justice in Luxembourg has done in the context of EU criminal law cases)
that there exists mutual trust between EU member states, adding essentially
that fundamental rights are respected throughout the Union. According
to the Court,

> the prohibition of extradition or surrender of own nationals in another Member State
> of the European Union does not emanate from the Constitution, nor has it any other
> ground for existence today between the EU member states[.] ... [T]he provision of
> the new law is *lex specialis*[.] ... [W]ithin the European Union member states, mutual
> trust has developed which is based on the respect for fundamental rights and the
> rule of law[.] ... [T]he historical reasons for such prohibition, namely, the obliga-
> tion of the State to protect its citizens and more specifically their protection from
> the adversity of a trial in a foreign and alien legal environment, but also the existing
> mistrust towards foreign judicial authorities, *is no longer justified especially within
> the framework of the European Union*. (Decision 558/2007 of the Supreme Court, as
> published in *Poinika Chronika* (2007: 597); my translation, emphasis added)

Conclusion

The implementation of EU criminal law measures into the Greek criminal
justice system has proven to be far from a straightforward task. A number
of EU measures in the field have not been implemented at all. Those measures which have been implemented saw implementation taking place very
slowly, with the relevant legislation being adopted in the majority of cases
after the expiry of the transposition deadline. Even in these cases, legislative
implementation has not always amounted to meaningful implementation
on the ground. While some noteworthy attempts have been made by the
Greek legislator to use the discretion offered by European law in order to
adjust EU requirements to the particular features of the domestic criminal
justice system, other occasions saw the Greek authorities largely copying
EU standards into the domestic statute book (at times in light of the time

pressure to introduce legislation which had been long overdue). Unsurprisingly, this approach has led to difficulties in achieving meaningful implementation and developing an approach which would bridge effectively the EU requirements with the specificities of the Greek criminal justice system. It has amounted at times to a rather superficial (although detailed) accommodation of EU standards, which has inevitably led to doubts with regard to whether combating serious organised crime is a priority for the Greek authorities. Prime example in this regard has been the accommodation of EU anti-money laundering requirements, where more than fifteen years after the deadline of the introduction of the first generation of anti-money laundering measures, the Greek legal system still appears to be struggling with very basic elements of the EU and global regime.

Having said that, on paper at least, the impact of the EU on the Greek criminal justice system has been far reaching. With all the caveats expressed above, a detailed anti-money laundering framework has been consolidated and developed. Greece, for the first time, has introduced specific far-reaching offences on terrorism and organised crime. Although the bulk of EU measures on mutual recognition in criminal matters have not been implemented, there has been extensive implementation of the Framework Decision on the European Arrest Warrant in the Greek legal system. And the country does participate in Europol and, not inactively, in Eurojust. Three points are worth highlighting in this respect. The first is that, while criticism on civil liberties grounds has been sustained throughout the past four decades, the tone and content of this criticism has changed: resistance focusing on the fear of the 'authoritarian state' in the 1970s and 1980s has gradually been replaced over the past two decades by an opposition discourse centering on proportionality and the need to reconcile security with freedom. The second point involves the 'foreign' factor: while anti-terrorism law has been constantly opposed on the grounds that it constitutes foreign intervention in the country, there is a growing awareness that the commitments undertaken by the Greek Government in Brussels must be honoured. This is a sign of maturity with regard to both the Greek political system and the state of Greece's EU membership. The third point involves the application of these measures on the ground. It transpires that, on a number of occasions, it has been the practitioners (and not the politicians or academics) who have boosted the implementation of EU standards in Greece, in particular when having to deal with their colleagues in other EU member states. A prime example is that of judges, who, in cases concerning the (highly controversial) European Arrest Warrant, have not hesitated to find ways of accommodating the EU co-operation requirements into the Greek constitutional and criminal justice system. It remains to be seen whether it will be the judges who will ultimately render meaningful the legislative transposition of measures on organised crime and terrorism.

References

Andreou, G. (2003) 'The European Arrest Warrant Negotiations: Negotiations of the Greek Position at Domestic Level', *Negotiating European Issues: National Strategies and Priorities Occasional Paper* 4.2–11.03. Available online at http://www.oeue.net/papers/greece-negotiationsontheeurope.pdf

Bekas, G. (2007) 'Political Choices and the Law: The Extradition-Transfer-Surrender of the Defendant and the European Arrest Warrant' [in Greek], *Poinikos Logos*: 549–557.

Council of the European Union (3 December 2008) *The Practical Application of the European Arrest Warrant and Corresponding Surrender Procedures Between Member State-Report on Greece*. Evaluation Report on the Fourth Round of Mutual Evaluations, Doc. 13416/2/08 REV 2. Brussels: Council of Europe.

Daniil, G. (2008) 'Thoughts with Regard to Certain Provisions of Law 3424/2005 Amending Law 2331/1995' [in Greek], *Poiniki Dikaiosyni*: 472–482.

Eurojust (2003) *Eurojust Annual Report 2003*. The Hague: Eurojust.

Eurojust (2005) *Eurojust Annual Report 2005*. The Hague: Eurojust.

European Commission (2006) *Annex to the Report from the Commission based on Article 11 of the Council Framework Decision of 13 June 2002 on Combating Terrorism*. Staff Working Document, SEC 1463. Brussels: European Commission.

Financial Action Task Force (2007) *Third Mutual Evaluation on Anti-Money Laundering and Combating the Financing of Terrorism: Greece*. Paris: FATF/OECD.

Kaiafa-Gbandi, M. (2005) 'The Delimitation of the Criminal Offence of Terrorism and the Challenges of a Criminal Law based on the Rule of Law' [in Greek], *Poinika Chronika*: 865–879.

Kaiafa-Gbandi, M. (2007) 'The Criminal Law Anti-Money Laundering Framework: Between International, European and National Legislation' [in Greek], in Association of Greek Penologists (ed.) *Money Laundering: 'Clean' or Free Society?* [in Greek], pp. 53–100. Athens: Ant. N. Sakkoulas Publishers.

Kassimeris, G. (2001) *Europe's Last Red Terrorists*. London: Hurst.

Kyritsis, D. (2005) 'Terrorism and Political Crime: Proposals for a Categorisation' [in Greek], *Poinika Chronika*: 490–499.

Lambropoulou, E. (2003) 'Criminal "Organisations" in Greece and Public Policy: From Non-Real to Hyper-Real?', *International Journal of the Sociology of Law* 31(1): 69–87.

Livos, N. (2007) *Organised Crime and Special Interrogation Acts* [in Greek]. Thessaloniki: P.N. Sakkoulas.

Manoledakis, I. (2002) *Security and Freedom* [in Greek]. Athens-Thessaloniki: Sakkoulas.

Mitsilegas, V. (1999) 'New Forms of Transnational Policing: The Emergence of Financial Intelligence Units in the European Union and the Challenges for Human Rights-Part 1', *Journal of Money Laundering Control* 3(2): 147–160.

Mitsilegas, V. (2001) 'Defining Organised Crime in the European Union: The Limits of European Criminal Law in an Area of Freedom, Security and Justice', *European Law Review* 26(6): 565–581.

Mitsilegas, V. (2003a) 'Countering the Chameleon Threat of Dirty Money: "Hard" and "Soft" Law in the Emergence of a Global Regime against Money Laundering and Terrorist Finance', in A. Edwards and P. Gill (eds) *Transnational Organised Crime: Perspectives on Global Security*, pp. 195–211. Oxford: Routledge.

Mitsilegas, V. (2003b) *Money Laundering Counter-Measures in the European Union: A New Paradigm of Security Governance versus Fundamental Legal Principles*. The Hague: Kluwer Law International.

Mitsilegas, V. (2006a) 'Trust-building Measures in the European Judicial Area in Criminal Matters: Issues of Competence, Legitimacy and Inter-institutional Balance', in S. Carrera and T. Balzacq (eds) *Security versus Freedom? A Challenge for Europe's Future*, pp. 279–289. Aldershot: Ashgate.

Mitsilegas, V. (2006b) 'The Constitutional Implications of Mutual Recognition in Criminal Matters in the European Union', *Common Market Law Review* 43(5): 1277–1311.

Mitsilegas, V. (2009a) *EU Criminal Law*. Oxford: Hart.

Mitsilegas, V. (2009b) 'The Reception of the Principle of Mutual Recognition in the Criminal Justice Systems of Member States: The Case of Greece', in G. van Tiggelen, L. Surano and A. Weymbergh (eds) *The Future of Mutual Recognition in Criminal Matters*, pp. 175–188. Brussels: Éditions de l'Université de Bruxelles.

Mitsilegas, V. and B. Gilmore (2007) 'The EU Legislative Framework against Money
    Laundering and Terrorist Finance: A Critical Analysis in the Light of Evolv-
    ing Global Standards', *International and Comparative Law Quarterly* 56(1):
    119–141.
Mitsilegas, V., Monar, J. and W. Rees (2003) *The European Union and Internal Secu-
    rity*. Basingstoke: Palgrave Macmillan.
Symeonidou-Kastanidou, E. (2005) *Organised Crime and Terrorism* [in Greek]. Ath-
    ens-Thessaloniki: Sakkoulas.
Symeonidou-Kastanidou, E. (2007) 'The Offence of Money Laundering after Law
    3424/2005: Interpretative Proposals' [in Greek], *Poiniki Dikaiosyni*: 606–618.
Xenakis, S. 'International Norm Diffusion and Organised Crime Policy: The Case
    of Greece', *Global Crime* 6(3–4): 345–373.

MONICA DEN BOER

Commentary

Valsamis Mitsilegas is extremely well equipped to deal with the legal interaction between Justice and Home Affairs instruments that have been adopted in the EU and their impact on the Greek criminal justice system. His four-year period as legal adviser to the House of Lords European Union Committee has bolstered and expanded his knowledge about a variety of topics related to police and judicial co-operation in criminal matters, including EU responses to terrorism and organised crime, border and immigration issues, and civil liberties.

Mitsilegas begins his chapter with stating its aim, namely, the examination of the impact of EU criminal law and policy on the Greek criminal justice system. He studies this impact at three levels: the criminalisation and the introduction of new criminal offences in the Greek legal order; the impact of the EU on the internal administrative and operational structures; and the impact of the incorporation of the 'mutual recognition' principle in the Greek criminal justice system. Strikingly, Mitsilegas starts with the assumption that EU law has the 'potential' to have a significant impact, whereas I would have argued that the EU has become an unavoidable tissue which is gradually being weaved into the national criminal codes of the member states.

The ouverture is succeeded by a firm demarcation of the fields which are affected by EU instruments, namely, organised crime, terrorism, and money laundering. Not only are these typically forms of serious transnational crime, they are also the types of criminal offences about which member states would argue that pooling sovereignty and resources would be instrumental in undermining them. In the absence of harmonised (and binding) definitions, there may still be divergences between the perception of member states of what they view as crimes that ought to be subsumed under the new rules.

'Organised crime', for instance, includes a very wide category of offences, ranging from trafficking in human beings to the forgery of the Euro. And beyond the fields selected by Mitsilegas, there is an increasing number of offences that are also subject to EU instruments, including offences in the fields of public order, the environment, or ICT. Coincidentally, Mitsilegas explains the widening EU crime-control agenda against the background of shifting securitisation discourses, which in a way 'absorb' new security elements into the realm of the EU and transform them into instruments and mandates for the relevant agencies (particularly Europol and Eurojust).

When speaking of the impact of EU counter-terrorism instruments – most of which were evoked in the wake of 9/11 – on the legislation in Greece, one can observe the differences with some other member states. Unlike countries like the Netherlands, for instance, which did not suffer from a structural presence of a separatist 'domestic' terrorist organisation, Greece already had an anti-terrorism law since 1978, and hence the impact of EU legislation was, perhaps, less dramatic. In that sense, Greece resembles member states like Spain, the United Kingdom, and Germany, all of which had anti-terrorism legislation prior to the entry into force of the EU Framework Decision on terrorism. Another dimension which is relevant is the level of discussion and scrutiny in the national parliament: in Greece – and Mitsilegas gives a very interesting account of this –, the debate about the possible infringement of civil liberties as well as the empowerment of the central state was rather fierce. The raw nerve underlying this active parliamentary scrutiny of EU-instruments relates to the country's authoritarian past (see, e.g., Samatas, this collection), where a mass-file bureaucratic system was held on those who did not act in conformity with the anti-communist regime. The new reality in the EU is that surveillance instruments have been adopted at rapid speed. Several binding instruments in this field can be used for law enforcement and criminal justice purposes, such as the data-systems (SIS, VIS, EIS and Eurodac), the Directive on the Retention of Telecommunication Data, the Passenger Name Record agreement, ECHELON, the Prüm Treaty (which allows the exchange of DNA-data and fingerprints), and, through Europol, the exchange of strategic and personal data with the law enforcement authorities of the USA. In short, having come away from a dictatorial regime, these instruments of control by surveillance may have evoked emotional and political sentiments in the Greek context.

Whilst Europe was in the grip of new security challenges, such as organised crime, Greece remained without specific legislation on organised crime until the 1990s. But perhaps this can also be explained by the relatively late gathering of the momentum, namely in 1997, when the first EU-wide Action Plan on Organised Crime was adopted. Also, we should take into account that Europol only became operational by 1 July 1999. The salient aspect is not only that Greece was relatively late with the introduction of anti-organised crime legislation, but that it unleashed turbulent domestic debates in high-level committees, that eventually even perspired in the resignation of prominent members. The European Convention on Mutual Legal Assistance (2000) and the EU Framework Decision on Joint Investigation Teams (2002) are binding legal instruments which have opened a wide array of practical instruments to the police and the judiciary for the establishment of cross-border operations, and which could have been used effectively in the fight against organised crime. However, with respect to these practical instruments, Mitsilegas notes that Greece has been relatively slow.

Moreover, the partnership of Greece in the Schengen Convention (1999), which was fully effected by 26 March 2000 through the common operation of external border controls and the abolition of internal border controls, must have brought several legal and policy changes with it, including the setting up of a National Schengen Information System and a SIRENE bureau, the introduction of cross-border police competences such as surveillance, hot-pursuit and controlled delivery, and the gathering of data on international crimes, including data on people with an intention to perpetrate serious crimes. Hence, as a result of the Schengen Implementing Convention (1990), several changes were introduced in the Greek criminal justice system, including aspects of the precautionary anti-crime logic. Although it would have been on the verge of the remit of Mitsilegas' contribution, it would have been interesting to read his view on the way in which the Schengen acquis – which was lifted into the Treaty on European Union in 1997 by virtue of a protocol – has impacted upon the Greek criminal justice system, and to share his reflections on whether or not Schengen has been a 'mixed blessing' for Greek citizens. To me, it seems that Greece's geopolitical position brings up particular challenges in view of controlling irregular migration: have the EU instruments, including the Schengen regulations, led to a regulatory cocktail which has allowed a spill-over between migration law and criminal law (Samatas, 2003)? What is the Greek political position within the Euro-Mediterranean complex? Have the Greek calls for a creation of an EU Coastal Guard been answered? Frontex elaborated a maritime control strategy in view of the needs of Malta, Cyprus, Greece, Italy and Spain to control illegal migration at sea[1] and more recently, an agreement was signed between the Greek government and Frontex in order to curb irregular migration at the complex borders of Greece, and it was given the necessary equipment in order to step up these border controls. What are its specific stakes in neighbouring countries like Albania, Bulgaria, FYROM, and Turkey, onto which a differentiated border regime (Apap and Tchorbadjiyska, 2010) will have to be applied if and when they fully enter the Schengen zone, and all of which generate complex crime control issues in the areas of corruption and organised crime? What are the predominant threads in the Greek threat analysis of the relationship between illegal immigration, on the one hand, and stolen identity documents, the trafficking of women and children, and corruption of government officials, on the other hand (Baldwin-Edwards, 2004; Geddes and Lazarou, n.d.; see further Xenakis, this collection)?

In a centrally directed criminal justice system like Greece's, taking on the changes desired by the EU action plans and instruments may be easier than in de-concentrated police systems like those in the Netherlands and the United Kingdom. The anti-organised crime strategy of the EU has been coined on the philosophy that member states ought to refurbish their criminal justice system in a fashion which allows easy mutual co-operation through centrally co-ordinated channels of communication, usually

---

1   Note, however, that the EU Agency for the Management of External Border Controls FRONTEX performed several actions under the POSEIDON programme. In the second phase of this combined maritime, land, and aerial surveillance programme, 673 illegal immigrants were apprehended, and there was a 'remarkable increase in the number of facilitators' in human smuggling operations. Turkey did not participate in POSEIDON, despite an invitation to do so. At the time of writing, a first Frontex Operational Office (FOO) is soon to be opened in Piraeus, Greece, which is to provide regionally-based support, e.g., for joint operations.

accommodated within the State Departments of the Interior or Justice or the national police agencies. Central authorities have been designated for issuing EU Arrest Warrants; the Greek Police Headquarters have the International Police Co-operation Division, which is responsible for the communication between the Greek Ministry of Interior and the Police, and the external communications with international law enforcement organisations, including Interpol and Europol. But compared to international police co-operation, Greece is behind schedule when it concerns international judicial co-operation in criminal matters through Eurojust. This observation calls for a comparative analysis with other member states and makes one yearn for an analysis of the Greek position on the desirability of a European Public Prosecution Office, which may eventually be built from Eurojust.

The chapter does not cover the forms of multi-agency co-operation between law enforcement agencies (e.g., police, immigration authorities, and tax revenue authories) in the field of organised crime and terrorism, which is a strategy strongly driven by the EU Action Plans against organised crime. Several EU member states have built experience with multi-agency co-operation, such as with the Serious Organised Crime Agency (SOCA) in the United Kingdom and the Anti-Mafia Directorate in Italy. Moreover, it would be interesting to know how the Greek law enforcement agencies contribute to Europol with annual reports and threat assessments on organised crime, whether they see any benefit in this EU agency, and what their strategic priorities are in view of combating organised crime within different multilateral forums, including Europol, Interpol, and SECI.[2] The South-Eastern area is seen by Europol and other law enforcement bodies as a fertile and major hub for organised crime (Matei, 2009). Have

---

2   SECI is the South East Co-operation Initiative. The SECI Regional Center for Combating Trans-border Crime, headquartered in Bucharest, Romania, was launched in 2000, in which police and customs liaison officers from 13 states (Albania, Bosnia and Herzegovina, Bulgaria, Croatia, Greece, Hungary, Former Yugoslav Republic of Macedonia, Moldova, Montenegro, Romania, Serbia, Slovenia and Turkey) work together in direct cooperation, coordinate joint investigations, and facilitate information exchange.

the new EU instruments, including the agreements between Europol and Albania, contributed to higher crime detection and the forging of mutual trust relationships between the Greek criminal justice authorities and their counterparts in neighbouring countries?

Interestingly, Mitsilegas highlights a few instances where Greece was late with the implementation of new instruments, particularly the Framework Decision on the European Arrest Warrant and the Framework Decision to Combat Terrorism. It is generally known that the implementation of so-called 'third-pillar' instruments tends to be a tedious process: the European Commission has regularly been in despair about the slack implementation of instruments, even if they were binding upon national law, like the two framework decisions discussed by Mitsilegas. If the passing of deadlines is paralleled by fierce parliamentary discussions, as has been the case in Greece, it can only be read as a healthy sign of vivid reflection. I would welcome an analysis of how the implementation speed of instruments in the field of police and judicial co-operation in criminal matters is affected by the new decision-making rules in the Lisbon Treaty, and how the limitation of national sovereignty on non-operational matters has been perceived in Greece. Have these changes stirred up the debate in the Greek parliament, and if so, what were the main concerns?

Meanwhile, however, according to Mitsilegas, the way in which Greece has implemented the Framework Decision on terrorism 'has been judged to be more than adequate', and compliance has led to fundamental changes in the Greek criminal justice system. In terms of political realism, the question is to what extent Greece is potentially subject to terrorist attacks by violent Jihadists; some assessments argue that Greece is not a major haven as the country does not have many Muslim immigrants (ibid.). Nevertheless, Article 8 of the Greek criminal code has even moved beyond the requirements of EU law. In sum, Greece has been a good pupil though somewhat lenient on the deadlines (also with respect to the EU directives on money laundering, where on all three occasions, the Greek implementing law was adopted after the deadline). Again, in the field of money laundering, the Greek law goes further than the Directive, and introduces wider criminalisation as well as sanctions for the non-reporting of suspicious transactions. Unclear to me is why the Greek parliament has apparently wanted this to happen, which somehow seems in contrast with the opposition against the framework decisions. Perhaps it is related to the relatively pro-integrationist stance of Greece, which was demonstrated when the European Convention was at play.

Since the entry into force of the Maastricht Treaty on European Union in 1993, a few hundred Justice and Home Affairs instruments have been adopted by the Council, and those have been dispersed through the national criminal justice systems. However, with a high volume of soft law, one is left wondering whether and to which extent recommendations and action plans have given any pressing impetus to the convergence of criminal justice systems. Any measurable effect will be hard to find empirically, though Mitsilegas uses a persuasive argument towards the end of his exposé: it is the practitioners on the ground, he writes, who will turn the EU criminal justice space into a reality. An important success factor indeed resides within national law enforcement bureaucracies. Do they see European co-operation as beneficial and as a means to cost-reduction or rather *vice versa*? Can criminal justice co-operation in Europe acquire any real sense beyond the interpretation of legal texts, and can its merit be shown to Greek citizens and national law enforcement officials? What is the perception of the Greek police and judiciary of the application of human rights standards on practices of cross-border co-operation? Though Mitsilegas addresses crucial issues with regard to accountability and legitimacy, this level of empirical analysis remains latent within his eloquent contribution.

References

Apap, J. and A. Tchorbadjiyska (2004) *What about the Neighbours? The Impact of Schengen along the EU's External Borders*, CEPS Working Document No. 2010. Available online at: http://unpan1.un.org/intradoc/groups/public/documents/ UNTC/UNPAN018877.pdf (Accessed 30 May 2010)

Baldwin-Edwards, M. (2004) *The Changing Mosaic of Changing Mediterranean Migrations*, Migration Information Source. Available online at: http://www.migration-information.org/feature/display.cfm?ID=230 (Accessed 30 May 2010)

Geddes, A. and E. Lazarou (n.d.) *Europeanisation of Migration Policy and Narratives of Migration Management: The Case of Greece*. Paper in ESRC series 'Multi-Level Governance in South-East Europe (SEE) – Institutional Innovation and Adaptation in Croatia, Greece, Macedonia and Slovenia'. Available online at: http://www.sps.ed.ac.uk/__data/assets/word_doc/0015/2014/Lazarou.doc (Accessed 30 May 2010)

Matei, F.C. (2009) *Combating Terrorism and Organised Crime: South Eastern Europe Collective Approaches*, Research Paper No. 133, Research Institute for European and American Studies. Available online at: www.google.nl/search?q=threat+assessment+europol+organized+crime+greece+2009&hl=nl&start=20&sa=N (Accessed 30 May 2010)

Samatas, M. (2003) 'Greece in Schengenland: Blessing or Anathema for Citizens' and Foreigners' Rights?', *Journal of Ethnic and Migration Studies* 29(1): 141–156.

MINAS SAMATAS

Surveillance

Surveillance Legacy, Modernisation and Controversy in Contemporary Greece

This chapter is an overview of surveillance modernisation in contemporary Greece. Particular attention is paid to the influential role played, in different ways, by the terrorist attacks in New York on 9/11 and by the Olympic Games held in Athens in 2004. The aim is to explore the dynamics of surveillance in 'post-authoritarian' Greek society as a revealing case for surveillance studies. For, whilst most western countries approach and use surveillance as a major means of crime control, counter-terrorism, and security, Greece is a country in which state and police surveillance still arouse a good deal of controversy and resistance. In no small part, this is due to the authoritarian legacy of the post-civil war police state and the military junta (1950–1974). Indeed, the process of surveillance modernisation is analysed below, not through a technocentric focus on the staggering expansion of electronic surveillance in both the public and private fields, but through a socio-historical and political focus on how surveillance is legimated, promoted, and/or restricted in a given society (Samatas, 2004, 2005).

The chapter begins with a brief discussion of the legacy of authoritarian surveillance in Greece, the remembrance of which still raises suspicions amongst the Greek citizenry of state surveillance as a threat to privacy and civil liberties. The focus then shifts to the modernisation of surveillance in contemporary Greece in relation, first, to Greece's accession to the Schengen Treaty and the Schengen Information System, and second, to the Athens 2004 Olympic Games, the first summer Olympics following 9/11. Also examined are the serious controversies over the post-Games use of surveillance cameras installed for the Olympics, foreign intervention for counter-terrorism and surveillance purposes, and the purported inefficiency of the Greek police to date. The chapter concludes by analysing the ambivalent impact of the authoritarian legacy upon surveillance in Greece; firstly, as both barrier to surveillance modernisation and shield for civil liberties and the protection of privacy, and secondly, as inspiration for resistance to official surveillance, despite increasing apathy towards private surveillance and data collection.

The Authoritarian Surveillance Legacy

In contemporary democratic societies, surveillance by public and private institutions is considered legitimate in cases of care, security, and control, where the rights of surveilled subjects are respected (Lyon, 1994; Lianos, 2003). In Greece, however, surveillance by the state is popularly demonised in its entirety, even if for public safety, taxes, or traffic control (Samatas, 2008). There is widespread sensitivity and vigilance concerning any official monitoring and filing, which inhibits the modernisation and expansion of surveillance policies and practices.

This anti-surveillance attitude of the Greek people can be attributed to the prolonged era of police surveillance, from the end of the civil war to the fall of the military dictatorship (1950–1974). The anticommunist panoptic system in post-war Greece, even if without computers and other electronic devices, employed informers across the country to continuously update the extensive police files on the citizenry. The technology of political control, imported from the US, included such methods as the issuing of 'certificates of civic mindedness' and 'loyalty statements', designed to enforce loyalty and conformity (*ethnikofrosyni*) to the anticommunist regime (Samatas, 1986). This system was partly abolished after the dictatorship, in 1974, when the Greek Communist Party (KKE) was legalised. Most police surveillance files continued to be updated until 1981, but were subsequently officially denounced by the first Panhellenic Socialist Movement (PASOK) government of Andreas Papandreou, and were burned in 1989 as a symbolic act of distantiation from the past by a coalition government (see further Eliou, 1989; Samatas, 1993, 2004; *Ios*, 2007a).

Nevertheless, public hostility towards official surveillance has endured. Greek citizens, deprived for a long time of any protection for their private socio-political views, have learned to mistrust personal data collection by the state, even if for legitimate purposes. Especially as concerns the older generation, which has experienced the authoritarian political control surveillance, the problem is not so much the watching (*parakolouthisi*), i.e., 'face-to-face surveillance', as it is the 'filing' (*fakeloma*) of personal data, or 'file-based, bureaucratic surveillance' (Lyon, 2007: 76–83). The latter is always perceived in Greece in negative terms, as a process that can entail sanctions and discrimination detrimental for life chances, not just for the individual directly surveilled, but for extended family members, too (Samatas, 1986).

Even in the midst of liberal politics today, citizens mistrust the collection of personal data by the state. This is not merely due to the legacy of authoritarian surveillance, but is also a consequence of the negligence and possibly corruption of official bodies, which often violate the right to privacy (Samatas, 2004: 133–143). As I have sought to outline below, privacy and data protection have been considerably improved in recent years, especially following the introduction of a new privacy law and the establishment of the Greek Data Protection Authority in 1997. Yet there remains a serious deficiency in data protection amongst the private sector, telecommunications, and the internet, as has been admitted by both the Data Protection Authority and the Telecommunications Privacy Authority (Samatas, 2008, 2009a).

Surveillance Modernisation and 'Europeanisation' in Greece

The Schengen Treaty and Information System

In September 1996, the PASOK government of Costas Simitis ratified the Schengen Treaty, which enhanced the flow of police information within the EU in order to counter crime, terrorism, and illegal immigration. After long delays for technical, legal, and political reasons, Greece became a full signatory to the Treaty on 26 March 2000, when the Schengen Information System (SIS) was implemented in Greece (Samatas, 2003a). SIS is the basic EU electronic surveillance network for the collection and processing of various data, and is comprised of a central electronic database (central SIS) located in Strasbourg and a network of national SIS data banks (SIRENE) in each member-state (Lewis, 2005: 106–108).

A precondition of the implementation of SIS in Greece was the incorporation into national law of the European Directive 95/46/EC, which set new standards for the protection of personal data in EU member states. This step was achieved with the introduction of the law 2472 in 1997. The new law has not been without controversy, however, since it allows authorities to process 'sensitive' personal data for a host of reasons, including national security, defence, and public order. Such provisions, in combination with those of the Schengen Treaty (and in particular Article 99, which provides that information be held where a person gives reason for suspicion that they may commit serious offences in the future), serve to legitimate preventative surveillance by the police of their 'usual suspects'. Given the legacy described above, fears have been raised as to the potential misuse of the new law at the expense of human rights and civil liberties (Samatas, 2003).

The Greek Data Protection Authority

Another important consequence of the signing of the Schengen Treaty has been the institution of a Greek Data Protection Authority (DPA). The DPA, whose independence is guaranteed under the Constitution, was established in 1997 under the Law 2472 (see further www.dpa.gr). Staffed by academics, jurists, and judges, the DPA strives to avoid being a mere decorative board for legitimation purposes, and instead to function as an effective deterrent and safeguard against the exploitation of personal data by both state and private bodies. Having the authority to check the blacklists of the Greek Schengen Bureau, the DPA crosses out the names of Greek citizens and aliens who are listed as 'suspects' without adequate evidence.

Soon after its establishment, the Greek DPA fought and won against the powerful Greek Orthodox Church in the hard battle over the issue of identity cards. With its Decision 510 on 15 May 2000, the DPA ruled in support of the removal of religious affiliation from the new national identity cards. This led to legal challenges and massive protests supported by the Church, which served to undermine public support for the DPA (see *Ios*, 2007a; Samatas, 2004: 136). The DPA has also fought hard to restrict the use of CCTV cameras installed as part of the security system for the Olympic Games of 2004 in Athens. In general, it has proved unable to control the mushrooming of CCTV more widely, largely due to operational difficulties and limited personnel (see the statements of the DPA's first chief, Konstantinos Dafermos, in *To Vima*, 12 January 2000). Nevertheless, the DPA is considered to be an active, and often 'disturbing', independent authority that struggles to enforce Greek and European privacy protection laws, even against governmental surveillance policies.

The Surveillance Impact of the Athens 2004 Olympics

Following 9/11 and in anticipation of the Athens 2004 Olympics, Greece came under immense international pressure to ensure the safety of the Games by way of enhancing surveillance measures in general and counter-terrorism measures in particular.

The Draconian 'Anti-terrorist law'

American and British pressures, including threats to boycott the Games, led the Greek Parliament to introduce the so-called 'anti-terrorist law' 2928 in 2002. Better known as the 'terror law' (*tromonomos*), the new law encouraged spying on fellow citizens, provided monetary incentives for police informers, introduced non-jury criminal trials, limited the right of appeal, allowed for DNA testing without prior consent, enhanced police powers of infiltration and surveillance, and provided for severe prison sentences for members of terrorist organisations and criminal gangs. On the basis of this draconian law, and with the assistance of Scotland Yard, members of the terrorist group November 17 (17N) were arrested and sentenced to imprisonment in 2003 (see further Xenakis, this collection).

The Olympics 'Super-panopticon' Project and the SAIC-SIEMENS C4I Surveillance System

In the aftermath of 9/11, the Athens 2004 Olympics became a testing ground for the latest anti-terrorist panoptic technology, and 'the biggest security operation in peacetime Europe', as it was advertised by the American Society for Industrial Security (ASIS, 2006). Regardless of costs and efficiency, Greece was impelled to participate in a new international security alliance and to buy the most up-to-date security and surveillance technology available, typically made in the US and the European Union, in order to secure the support and confidence of its international counterparts. A seven-nation 'Olympics Advisory Security Team' was established, comprising of France, Germany, Israel, Spain, the US, Britain, and Australia, to provide intelligence and training. Even NATO, the FBI, the CIA, and the British MI6 were actively involved (Samatas, 2007). Faced with warnings that the Games could be a prime target for international terrorists, there was little domestic opposition to NATO and foreign involvement. Hence, Athens as the Olympic capital was transformed into what might be described as an arena of 'urban panopticism' (Gray, 2003), or a 'fortified urban space' (Coaffee, 2003: 15), with a highly sophisticated surveillance security system to shield the Games from land, air, and sea against domestic and international terrorism.

A security system resembling a 'super-panopticon' (Foucault, 1977; Simon, 2005) was prescribed, involving an electronic nexus of cameras, vehicle-tracking devices, and blimps, with continuous online linking of common databases and communications to provide real-time images and updates of available resources to a central command. More specifically, mass electronic surveillance was integrated with 'dataveillance' through data links and the matching of SIS blacklists with those of Europol. All these interconnected systems were expected to facilitate decision-making far from the front lines of policing. The Athens Olympics 'super-panopticon' was based on the C4I system of the SAIC-Siemens consortium, which was originally intended for military use. C4I, an acronym for 'command, control, communications, and integration' (see www.C4I.org), was designed to concentrate all information and allow management of information by way of a vast network of computers, as well as 1,250 interconnected CCTV cameras all over the Athens metropolitan area, running 24 hours a day. The CCTV systems were linked by a surveillance network of mobile sets (TETRA), which received images and sound in real time by 22,160 security staff, and was coordinated by a central information security station (*Ta Nea*, 20 March 2004).

However, whilst the C4I system's software was supposed to concentrate signals from all sensors into a single nerve centre linked with 30 subsystems, it became a technical nightmare because of its enormous complexity (Samatas, 2007). For SAIC, marrying the systems to the central piece of software, the Command Decision Support System (CDSS) that formed the backbone of C4I, proved impossible. During the Games, the CDSS repeatedly crashed and was unable to support the expected 800 users at the main command centre (*Athens News*, 4 March 2005). The technical problems of C4I (SAIC, 2006) were not only hidden from the public, but were lost in the increasingly overt presence of surveillance cameras, the noisy blimp, and the conventional monitoring carried out by the police and the armed forces. This produced a show of 'spectacular security' (Boyle and Haggerty, 2008) that was heralded by the Greek media as a representation of absolute security. In this way, the image of Olympic security was successfully managed so that both the public and potential terrorists were kept ignorant of C4I's failure (Samatas, 2007).

The C4I system was belatedly contracted and implemented, and was delivered seriously flawed only a few weeks prior to the commencement of the Games. Furthermore, the system failed to work even long after the Games were over (*Athens News*, 18 February 2005). Greek officials were nervous that they were being given a faulty security apparatus in return for an extraordinary sum of money. The Greek government had already spent over $750 million on security before the Games began, almost triple the amount Australians spent on the Games in Sydney in 2000 (*Athens News*, 9 June 2004). Final acceptance of the system by the Greek state, which would include payment in full, was set for 1 October 2005. This deadline was not met, and the government is still in negotiations with SAIC to decide how much of the cost to accept and pay for. A tentative acceptance of C4I by the Ministry of Public Order and SAIC was signed on 29 March 2007. After several modifications to the original agreement, the total cost of the system was lowered from 259,032,250 Euros to 245,640,871 Euros, 75 percent of which has already been paid to SAIC.

Five years after the Athens 2004 Games and almost a year after the Beijing Olympics, the Greek government has not yet signed the final acceptance of the C4I system. Its final cost will exceed 250 million Euros, despite the fact that C4I was deficient, it did not work during the Olympics, and after such long delays it will not include several subsystems that are now of little use to Greece. Prospects for a definitive settlement are gloomy so long as judicial investigations are ongoing into the C4I deal as part of a bribery scandal involving Siemens. After a German court condemned Siemens' involvement in a bribes-for-contracts scandal that spanned several countries, Greek prosecutors also found enough evidence to suggest that the Greek state was defrauded during the purchase of the multi-million-Euro C4I Olympic security system. The Greek branch of the German electronics giant, which was the subcontractor on the C4I project, allegedly made under-the-table payments worth hundreds of millions of Euros to Greek politicians of both major political parties, as well as to senior officials, in order to secure lucrative contracts (*Kathimerini*, 24 January 2009).

The Controversy over the Post-Games Use of Surveillance Cameras

Although the costly C4I system proved a failure, much of what the Greek governments had sought in its purchase was not only to avoid a potential boycott of the Games, but also the enhancement of policing on a long-term basis (*Athens News*, 23 July 2004). The Greek Police (ELAS) was pleased with its new digital, wireless encrypted, multi-channel communication system, TETRA (Terrestrial Trunked Radio); four years later, however, TETRA, the only C4I subsystem which had actually functioned properly since the Olympics, is also dysfunctional (*To Vima*, 4 July 2008). In addition to TETRA, the Olympic surveillance 'dowry' includes the C4I Subsystem 17, consisting of the aforementioned 1,200 CCTV surveillance cameras on the roads of Attica, equipped with Intelligent Traffic System (ITS), or 'Traficon'. This subsystem has the potential to monitor and evaluate all categories of incidents of traffic control, similar to the N-System in Japan (Abe, 2004).

The extraordinary cost of the Olympic C4I system pushed the Government to insist on its continued use after the Olympics, not only for traffic control, but also for security and anti-terrorism. Whilst the Greek public had largely accepted the need for extra security and surveillance systems during the Olympics, they saw no serious reason to continue sacrificing their hard-earned civil liberties after the Games. Political parties of the opposition, civil society groups, legal experts, intellectuals, and students all vividly expressed their opposition to the post-Olympics use of surveillance cameras (see Samatas, 2008; and *Ios*, 2007b). In May 2004, the DPA approved the request of the Greek police to operate CCTV cameras on the streets during the 'operational phase' of the Olympics, so long as they were utilised according to its basic Directive 1122 on CCTV systems (26 September 2000), and would not be used after the conclusion of the Games (DPA, 3 May 2004). The European Union Data Protection Authority also suggested that the Olympic panoptic systems be either sold or rented to other states organising mega-events (*To Vima*, 23 May 2006).

After the Games, in November 2004, the DPA ruled in favour of the continued use of CCTV cameras on the streets for a period of six months, on the condition that they would serve solely traffic control purposes (DPA, 24 November 2004). Following an inspection, the DPA stated in its 2004 annual report that the presence of police CCTV cameras was not accompanied by warning signage for the public, nor were they all situated in appropriate locations. Subsequent to the DPA inspection, signage was put in place by the police, but no cameras were moved or incapacitated. The Ministry of Public Order submitted a further request to the DPA that the use of police CCTV cameras be extended beyond the set deadline of 18 May 2005 for both traffic control and the prevention or repression of crime and terrorism. Despite pressure from the Ministry, the DPA only approved the use of cameras for traffic control, and deemed unconstitutional their proposed use for security and counter-terrorism purposes. The DPA Decision 58/2005 of 12 August 2005 issued rules severely restricting the use of surveillance cameras in public areas, in accordance with EU regulations (Grass, 2004). The Decision cited the principle of proportionality between means and ends in policing, as well as a UK Home Office study (Gill and Spriggs, 2005), which suggested that CCTV is ineffective in securing large public spaces. It also cited the judgement 2765/2005 of the Court of First Instance of Patras that the operation of CCTV systems in public spaces is in contradiction with the right to privacy guaranteed by the Greek Constitution and should therefore be limited. Nevertheless, the DPA has left a loophole in its decision, which allows monitoring for purposes other than traffic control in case of emergencies or other special occasions characterised as 'security events' (*Rizospastis*, 23 August 2005).

The DPA decision of 12 August 2005 disappointed everyone: the police, the Government, opposition parties, and anti-surveillance NGOs. In parliament, left-wing parties claimed that the cameras were targeting protesters during demonstrations for record-keeping, and asserted also that US and British law enforcement authorities had access to Greek police surveillance data. The government contested the DPA ruling, arguing that national security concerns should take precedence over the privacy rights of citizens, and took the issue to the Council of State, the country's highest administrative court. The Council of State, according to a ruling made public on 7 August 2006, approved the extended use of police CCTV cameras until May 2007, but again only for traffic monitoring in Athens (*Kathimerini*, 8 August 2006). Meanwhile, in snap inspections on 12 and 24 May 2006, the DPA found that 13 of the 32 Olympic CCTV cameras were working illegally and imposed a 3,000-Euro fine on the Public Order Ministry (*Athens News*, 26 January 2007). This fine, however symbolic, was ratified by the Council of State, and proved an irritant to the government, which did not hide its annoyance with the DPA on that and other occasions (Samatas, 2008).

Soon afterwards, the US embassy in Athens – a super-guarded complex in the centre of the city – was proved to be a vulnerable fortress indeed by a rocket-propelled grenade launched against it by a new Greek terrorist group on 12 January 2007 (see further Xenakis, this collection). The rocket demythologised the efficiency of the security systems and the CCTV cameras monitoring the area around the embassy. As previously proven by the terrorist attacks in New York and London, security cameras cannot prevent terrorist acts, although they may assist in the identification of terrorists *ex post facto* (Monahan, 2006: 6–7). Neither Greek nor FBI agents who examined CCTV footage from the embassy's cameras, however, could identify the culprits in this case (*Kathimerini*, 17 January 2007). Despite (or, perhaps, because of) this, the New Democracy (ND) government felt this was an opportune moment to intensify its call for the Olympic cameras to be activated for security purposes. Also, in early 2007, the government promoted the use of CCTV in sports stadia to combat hooliganism (*Sunday Eleftherotypia*, 7 April 2007). The Ministry of Transport and the Greek National Railways Organisation (OSE) also announced that CCTV would be installed in all new trains.

Amidst renewed controversy over the official uses of surveillance cameras, the DPA once more gave the police a fine of 3,000 Euros, on 8 October 2007, for using traffic cameras to monitor a student protest in Athens earlier that year, for failing to operate 49 police cameras with software that blurs people's faces, and for retaining data from some of the cameras for more than seven days, in contravention of privacy rules. The DPA also expressed its opposition to the permission accorded by Supreme Court prosecutor Giorgos Sanidas to the police on 30 October 2007 to record protest marches and sports events with traffic cameras, and to use the footage as court evidence if criminal acts were committed. Finally, on 19 November 2007, the President and five members of the Greek DPA resigned in protest at the decision of the government to allow police CCTV cameras to monitor the political rallies of commemorating the student revolt against the military dictatorship. Early the following year, the government appointed a new staff to the DPA, which has lately legalised the use of CCTV in private spaces, including schools and churches under certain restrictions.

Although one cannot speak of an organised anti-surveillance movement in contemporary Greece, there is certainly a growing degree of everyday resistance, such as is found in many other surveillance societies
(Gilliom, 2006: 120–122; Lyon, 2007: 166–171). In Greece, besides the
DPA, opposition parties (including the far-right LAOS party), senior
Greek legal experts, civil liberties organisations, and various other civil
society groups, have strongly condemned the post-Games use of Olympic
surveillance cameras (Samatas, 2008). This anti-surveillance resistance has
taken various forms, including blinding cameras with black hoods, ripping
off their cables, spray-painting their lenses, bringing down CCTV poles,
and arson (*Ios*, 2007b). CCTV cameras have been blinded, not only by
young radicals, but also by the mayors of the Athens districts of Nikea,
Galatsi, and Halandri, as well as by union leaders. According to *Kathi-*
merini (9 October 2007), out of 550 traffic cameras installed in Athens
during 2004, only 198 were maintained for subsequent use by the police;
yet, because arsonists had damaged 110 of these, the police in 2007 could
only use 88 cameras to monitor traffic. 'Officers said that it costs around
20,000 Euros to repair just one camera, but often, by the time one is fixed,
another is set on fire' (*Ios*, 2007b).

Communications Interceptions and Covert Foreign Anti-terrorist Operations in Greece

The Phone-tapping Scandal

On 2 February 2006, the Greek government announced that the mobile
phones of the then Prime Minister Kostas Karamanlis, of the Ministers
of Foreign Affairs, Defence, Public Order, and Justice, as well as of many
other top government, military, and security officials, had been tapped
during the Athens 2004 Olympics and for nearly a year thereafter. It was
also revealed that the phone-tapping began prior to the Games and probably

continued until 7 March 2005, when it was discovered, but it had not been possible to identify who was behind the unlawful surveillance (Prevelakis and Spinellis, 2007). All investigations ended by January 2008, without revealing the identity and the motives of the culprits. A study conducted by the Greek polling group VPRC found that the public was severely shocked by the revelations and doubtful as to the efficiency of state institutions to safeguard both security and privacy (*Sunday Eleftherotypia*, 5 February 2006; see also Samatas, 2010).

The government, the judiciary, the investigating authorities, and the phone company involved (Vodafone) evoked national security risks in defence of withholding evidence on the case. In December 2006, the Greek Communications Privacy Protection Authority (ADAE) fined the Greek branch of Vodafone 76 million Euros for involvement in the illegal wiretapping, whilst, more recently, the Court of First Instance in Athens ordered Vodafone to compensate one of the victims of the phone-tapping with 50,000 Euros (*Eleftherotypia*, 24 April 2009). The dominant interpretation is that the phone-tapping was organised by the US secret services for reasons related to the problems of the C4I and the more general mistrust of the Greek government and its Olympic security system (Kiesling, 2006; see further Samatas, 2010).

CIA 'Rendition' Flights

According to media reports, following 9/11, the CIA organised secret 'rendition' flights in which Muslims were kidnapped from the streets of Europe and taken to various prisons in over 25 countries, where they were held without trial. Of the 15 CIA flights to Greece, 14 were in 2002 and one just before the Athens 2004 Olympics, according to the MEGA TV Channel documentary programme 'Fakeloi' (19 May 2005). During the period 2002–2004, following surveillance, 12 Muslims were kidnapped by CIA agents from Greece. Most of them have been freed, but some have disappeared without trace (see *To Vima*, 3 July 2005).

The Abduction of Pakistani Immigrants

The British Secret Intelligence Service MI6 had sent to the Greek government a long list of individuals suspected of involvement in the terrorist attacks on the London underground on 7 July 2005. The list appeared to contain the names of Pakistani immigrants in Greece, who had made phone calls to their relatives and friends in London in the timeframe preceding the attacks. Subsequently, in July and August that year, the Greek authorities pursued the questioning of 5,342 immigrants, whilst a further 2,172 were investigated and 1,221 were arrested for reasons other than terrorism (6 of them were deported).

Plain-clothed security agents, apparently at the behest of MI6, kidnapped 28 Pakistani men from Athens, Oinofyta, and Ioannina. The men were held in secret locations, denied legal advice, questioned, and subjected to violence. Athens lawyer Frangiskos Ragoussis submitted a report to parliament on the alleged abductions, and urged the authorities to investigate. The kidnappings were confirmed in January 2006 by the then Minister of Public Order Giorgos Voulgarakis in his testimony to a parliamentary committee (see *Statewatch.org* article no. 269, 20 January 2006). The public prosecutors department of the Court of First Instance of Athens took over the investigation. The prosecutor, Nikos Degaitis, filed abduction charges against 'unknown persons' after establishing that the abductions actually took place. The case is still open at the time of writing, without any apparent prospect for clarification.

The Inefficiency of the Greek Police and Foreign Anti-terrorist Assistance

The inability of the Greek police to enforce an efficient security and surveillance system against crime and terrorism has encouraged foreign interference before, during, and after the Athens 2004 Olympics.

After the events of 9/11, and in preparation of the Games, counter-terrorist intervention in Greece by the US and Britain increased. The US State Department and the US Embassy in Athens had previously pressured Greek governments to investigate specific terrorist suspects, but these leads had proved incorrect. In June 2001, following the murder of the British military attaché Stephen Saunders by the terrorist group November 17 (17N), a group of police from Scotland Yard arrived in Greece, and began assisting their Greek counterparts in methodical analysis (including the use of computerised systems) that contributed to the arrest of 17N members in 2003. The British also proposed the broadening of surveillance through CCTV systems, as well as automatic number plate readers (ANPR) and new phone-tapping powers for mobile phone communications, which would be covered by pertinent legislation. Furthermore, taking up a British recommendation, the Greek police established an anonymous information hotline, encouraging cooperation between citizens and the police, which was not, however, fruitful given common mistrust of the police amongst the Greek public. In brief, the intervention of the British police significantly contributed to the modernisation and efficiency of the counter-terrorist efforts of the Greek police and the successful policing of the Athens 2004 Olympics.

After the Games, however, the unprecedented security blanket that had been cast over Greece, was lifted. With the 17N terrorists behind bars and the Olympics over, the new government appeared to take its eye off public security, either through complacency, incompetence, or fear of being accused of authoritarianism. According to the main opposition party, PASOK, the police department responsible for combating terrorism was actually dismantled by the New Democracy government. Out of around 800 counter-terrorism staff in 2004, there remained only 14 in 2009 (see the statements of PASOK spokesman Giorgos Papakonstantinou at www.in.gr/news on 18 June 2009). During 2007 and 2008, the Ministry of Public Order (renamed by the incoming PASOK government the Ministry of Citizen Protection) and the police proved unable to enforce law and order in the face of frequent violent incidents in central Athens. In fact, despite being the most heavily policed area of Athens, the city centre routinely experienced fires set by dozens of hooded anarchists, whilst riot police

(MAT) would keep watch from a distance (*Kathimerini*, 9 March 2007). The MAT blamed DPA restrictions on the use of CCTV for facilitating the unrest, even though police cameras alone would not have sufficed to enforce law and order.

Counter-terrorism experts from Scotland Yard returned to Athens on 16 March 2009 to once more advise their Greek counterparts on how to tackle what was described as an emerging terror threat and burgeoning crime in the capital. This followed the fatal shooting of a teenager by a policeman in December 2008, which, combined with frequent police brutality, sparked riots throughout the country. That the police appeared either unable or unwilling to put a halt to the vandalism and looting which often accompanied the riots, seemed to encourage an exacerbation of lawlessness, including the rise of new terrorist organisations.

This time, Scotland Yard experts proposed, firstly, the use of surveillance cameras to crack down on rising crime in the capital, and their installation outside police stations to discourage potential troublemakers. The Government Council on Foreign Policy and Defence (KYSEA) approved the use of surveillance cameras; it was reportedly decided that the first cameras to be activated would be those used during the Athens 2004 Olympics. Footage recorded on the cameras would be kept on file. The last time such a proposal had been made, the DPA had rejected it on the grounds that it would constitute an invasion of privacy. Experts from Scotland Yard also proposed the enhancement of phone-tapping technologies, and the creation of a national DNA bank that would store the genetic information of those arrested by the Greek police. The creation of a DNA bank had been considered by the Greek police in the past, but was eventually shelved. Under the new proposals, the authorities would be able to retain all data, rather than being obliged to destroy them at the end of each criminal investigation. Finally, the experts recommended that the Greek police reassemble their counter-terror intelligence-gathering capacities, and consolidate their police stations by retaining in post trained officers for longer and reducing a number of precincts (from about 1,000 to 400) in order to free police time for investigations and neighbourhood foot patrols (*Kathimerini*, 30 March 2009).

The above recommendations involved a number of measures (e.g., 24-hour CCTV surveillance, a national DNA bank, phone-tappings, and internet monitoring) that would overturn restrictions imposed by both the DPA and the Telecommunications Privacy Protection Authority (ADAE). The restrictions were bypassed in July 2009, during the summer session of Parliament, in the urgent move to legislate following the assassination of a police officer, Nektarios Savas, by a new terrorist group on 17 June that year (see further Xenakis, this collection). The government also passed a new law which provided that prison sentences be doubled for those found guilty of vandalising property whilst concealing their identity with hoods or masks of any type. After a public outcry over its repressive character, however, the incoming PASOK government announced in October 2009 its intention to repeal the law (*Kathimerini*, 24 October 2009). By the time of publication, the law had not yet been repealed.

Concluding Remarks

The abolition of the notorious anti-communist police files reflected the democratisation of the country in the 1980s. On the other hand, the Schengen Treaty and SIS have contributed to the 'Europeanisation' of Greece in the 1990s, just as the Athens 2004 Olympics contributed to its globalisation in the post-9/11 era. A vivid legacy of authoritarian surveillance and its accompanying concerns have worked to counterbalance these developments. However exaggerated these fears, they have sustained a useful vigilance against an encroaching 'panopticism', including such controversial developments as the EU data retention directive (Mitrou, 2010), and moves towards the construction of a maximum-security suprastate within a 'fortress Europe' (Maas, 2005; Hayes, 2010; Samatas, 2003a, 2009).

Aside from the impact of the EU and Schengen, the Athens 2004 Olympics, under the heavy shadow of 9/11, had a catalytic impact upon surveillance in Greece. Not only did the country relinquish sovereignty to a multinational alliance in order to ensure the security of the Games, it also almost bankrupted itself to host a successful Olympiad, spending $15 billion. The security budget dramatically inflated the costs; $1.5 billion was spent on security, including the faulty C4I surveillance system that became notorious for its place in a political corruption scandal. A non-financial, but equally heavy, cost was the phone-tappings scandal which hit the security façade of the Greek government (Samatas, 2011, forthcoming).

It is perhaps an irony that Greece was ranked first amongst 47 countries for its level of privacy protection in a study conducted in 2007 by the Electronic Privacy Information Center (EPIC) and Privacy International (PI). Greece was accorded the best privacy protection record (3.1 out of 4), with adequate safeguards against privacy abuse, thanks to its Constitutional protection and enforcement of privacy rights, as well as its position on identity cards, biometrics, visual surveillance, and democratic safeguards. It was only with regard to communications interceptions that Greece was accorded a low score, due to the aforementioned phone-tappings scandal and the ease by which phone and internet interceptions may be made by authorities and private intruders alike. In light of the more recent anti-terrorist legislative developments, however, it is doubtful whether Greece will score so highly in such surveys in the future.

At the same time, analysts and the media in Greece point to the existence of a 'surveillance paradox': whilst there is a popular sensitivity, vigilance, and resistance to state surveillance, Greeks show a conspicuous apathy towards private surveillance. Such indifference is particularly acute amongst many young Greeks born long after the end of the military dictatorship in 1974. Surveys show that, whilst many express concern about police cameras, they care less about privacy related to internet and mobile phone use, easily provide personal data for commercial purposes, and are comfortable watching 'Big Brother'-type reality shows on TV. Such apathy, as I have argued elsewhere (Samatas, 2005), is not absent amongst those of middle-age and older generations who directly experienced the authoritarian surveillance.

Legitimate 'institutional surveillance' in a democratic state presupposes trust and confidence in public institutions, based upon the protection of privacy and the respect of human rights (Offe, 1999; Lianos, 2003). This form of trust has never really existed in contemporary Greece. Indeed, the controversy over the use of CCTV by the Greek state reflects an embedded mistrust and lack of confidence that Greek citizens still have in official surveillance practices, evident also in comparison with their European counterparts, even 35 years after the collapse of the country's dictatorship.[1] The tenacity of the legitimacy crisis underlines the urgent necessity for reforms that will cultivate trust between the Greek state and its citizens.

References

Abe, K. (2004) 'Everyday Policing in Japan: Surveillance, Media, Government and Public Opinion', *International Sociology* 19(2): 215–231.

American Society for Industrial Security (ASIS) (2006) *ASIS January 2006 Newsletter, San Diego Chapter*. Available online at: www.asis-sandiego.org/newsletters/ pdffiles/ 2006_01.pdf (Accessed 20 August 2008)

Barlett, D.L. and J.B. Steele (March 2007) 'Secrets: Washington's $8 Billion Shadow', *Vanity Fair*.

Boyle, P. and K.D. Haggerty (2008) 'Spectacular Security: Mega-Events and the Security Complex', in J. Castro-Rea (ed.) *Our North America*. Edmonton: University of Alberta Press.

Clarke, R.A. (1994) 'The Digital Persona and its Application to Data Surveillance', *The Information Society* 10(2): 77–92.

Coaffee, J. (2003) *Terrorism, Risk and the City: The Making of a Contemporary Urban Landscape*. Aldershot: Ashgate.

1   According to the Eurobarometer survey on Data Protection that was conducted in January 2008 in the 27 EU member-states, whilst most EU citizens consider the fight against international terrorism to be an acceptable reason why to restrict data protection rights, Greeks express the highest levels of suspicion towards any provisions that would allow authorities to relax data protection laws. See http://europa. eu/rapid/pressReleasesAction.do?reference and www.in.gr/news (17 April 2008). Also, most Greek citizens express mistrust towards nearly all governmental institutions, the Church, and the mass media. See http://www.publicissue.gr/wp-content/ uploads/2008/12/institutions_2.pdf

Coleman, R. (2004) 'Reclaiming the Streets: CCTV, Neoliberalism and the Mystification of Social Division in Liverpool, UK', *Surveillance & Society* 2(3): 293–309.

Electronic Privacy Information Center (EPIC) and Privacy International (PI) (11 February 2006) *Leading Surveillance Societies in the EU and the World*. Available online at: http://www.privacyinternational.org/article.shtml (Accessed 16 August 2007)

Eliou, F. (1989) *The Files* [in Greek]. Athens: Themelio.

Foucault, M. (1977) *Discipline and Punish: The Birth of Prison*. New York: Vintage.

Gill, M. and A. Spriggs (2005) *Assessing the Impact of CCTV*, Home Office Research Study No. 292. London: HMSO.

Gilliom, J. (2006) 'Struggling with Surveillance: Resistance, Consciousness, and Identity', in K.D. Haggerty and R. Ericson (eds) *The New Politics of Surveillance and Visibility*, pp. 111–140. Toronto: University of Toronto Press.

Gras, M. (2004) 'The Legal Regulation of CCTV in Europe', *Surveillance & Society* 2(3): 216–229.

Gray, M. (2003) 'Urban Surveillance and Panopticism: Will We Recognise the Facial Recognition Society?', *Surveillance & Society* 1(3): 314–330.

Hayes, B. (2010) 'Surveillance vs Democracy in the EU: When the Security Industry and the European Research Agenda Become One', in K.D. Haggerty and M. Samatas (eds) *Surveillance and Democracy*, pp. 148–170. London: Routledge.

Hellenic Data Protection Authority (DPA) (2004) *Opinion 4/May 3, 2004* and *Decision 63/2004 on CCTV cameras on the Attica road network*. Available online at: http://www.dpa.gr/Documents/Eng/CCTV%20cameras

Ios reporters (2007a) 'Authority Without Principles', *Sunday Eleftherotypia* (21 January) [in Greek].

Ios reporters (2007b) 'Why Are Cameras Burnt? The New Constitutional Article 1-1-4', *Sunday Eleftherotypia* (7 January) [in Greek].

Kiesling, J.B. (20 March 2006) 'An Olympian Scandal', *The Nation*.

Lewis, N. (2005) 'Expanding Surveillance: Connecting Biometric Information Systems to International Police Cooperation', in E. Zureik and S.M. Devon (eds) *Global Surveillance and Policing*, pp. 97–112. Cullompton: Willan.

Lianos, M. (2003) 'Social Control after Foucault', *Surveillance and Society* 1(3): 412–430.

Lyon, D. (2001) *Surveillance Society: Monitoring Everyday Life*. Buckingham: Open University Press.

Lyon, D. (2003) *Surveillance after September 11*. Cambridge: Polity.

Lyon, D. (2006) 'Why Where You Are Matters: Mundane Mobilities, Transparent Technologies, and Digital Discrimination', in T. Monahan (ed.) *Surveillance and Security: Technological Politics and Power in Everyday Life*, pp. 209–224. London and New York: Routledge.

Lyon, D. (2007) *Surveillance Studies: An Overview*. Cambridge: Polity.

Maas, W. (2005) 'Freedom of Movement inside "Fortress Europe"', in E. Zureik and S.M. Devon (eds) *Global Surveillance and Policing*, pp. 233–246. Cullompton: Willan.

Mitrou, L. (2010) 'The Impact of Communications Data Retention on Fundamental Rights and Democracy: The Case of the EU Data Retention Directive', in K.D. Haggerty and M. Samatas (eds) *Surveillance and Democracy*, pp. 127–147. London: Routledge.

Monahan, T. (ed.) (2006) *Surveillance and Security*. New York: Routledge.

Offe, C. (1999) 'How Can We Trust Our Fellow Citizens?', in M.E. Warren (ed.) *Democracy and Trust*, pp. 42–87. Cambridge: Cambridge University Press.

Prevelakis, V. and D. Spinellis (2007) 'The Athens Affair', *Spectrum* 44(7): 26–33.

SAIC (2006) *A Gold-Medal Achievement: SAIC and the 2004 Summer Olympic Games in Athens*. Available online at: www.asis-sandiego.org/newsletters/pdffiles/2006_01.pdf

Samatas, M. (1986) 'Greek McCarthyism: A Comparative Assessment of Greek Post-Civil War Repressive Anti-Communism and the US Truman-McCarthy Era', *Journal of the Hellenic Diaspora* 13(3–4): 5–75.

Samatas, M. (1993) 'The Populist Phase of an Underdeveloped Surveillance Society: Political Surveillance in Post-Authoritarian Greece', *Journal of the Hellenic Diaspora* 19(1): 31–70.

Samatas, M. (2003) 'Greece in "Schengenland": Blessing or Anathema for Citizens and Foreigners' Rights?', *Journal of Ethnic and Migration Studies* 29(1): 141–156.

Samatas, M. (2004) *Surveillance in Greece: From Anti-Communist to Consumer Surveillance*. New York: Pella.

Samatas, M. (2005) 'Studying Surveillance in Greece: Methodological and Other Problems related to an Authoritarian Surveillance Culture', *Surveillance & Society* 3(2–3): 181–197.

Samatas, M. (2007) 'Security and Surveillance in the Athens 2004 Olympics: Some Lessons from a Troubled Story', *International Criminal Justice Review* 17(3): 220–238.

Samatas, M. (2008) 'From Thought-Control to Traffic-Control: CCTV Politics of Expansion and Resistance in Post-Olympics Greece', in M. Deflem (ed.) *Surveillance and Governance: Crime Control and Beyond*, pp. 345–369. Bingley: Emerald Publishing.

Samatas, M (2010) 'The Greek Olympic Phone-Tapping Scandal: A Defenceless State and a Weak Democracy', in K.D. Haggerty and M. Samatas (eds) *Surveillance and Democracy*, pp. 213–230. London: Routledge.

Samatas, M. (2011, forthcoming) 'Surveilling the Athens 2004 Olympics', in C. Bennett and K. Haggerty (eds) *Security Games: Surveillance and Control at Mega-Events*. London: Routledge.

Sidel, M. (2004) *More Secure Less Free? Antiterrorism Policy and Civil Liberties after September 11*. Michigan: University of Michigan Press.

Simon, B. (2005) 'The Return of Panopticism: Supervision, Subjection and the New Surveillance', *Surveillance & Society* 3(1): 1–20.

Sutton, A. and D. Wilson (2004) 'Open-Street CCTV in Australia: The Politics of Resistance and Expansion', *Surveillance & Society* 2(3): 310–322.

KEVIN D. HAGGERTY

Commentary

Surveillance Legacies

By appearing in this collection, I open myself to accusations of being at best an interloper and at worst an imposter. In a collection dedicated to developments in Greece, I lamentably have just once visited that splendid country, and am only faintly familiar with its fabled history. That said, as someone interested in surveillance, for some years now I have been reading the works of Professor Minas Samatas, who has become the foremost authority on surveillance in Greece (see Samatas, 2004). Studying his contribution to this collection, I was intrigued by his assessment of some lingering consequences of the anti-communist surveillance conducted after Greece's post-civil war and military junta. Those authorities cultivated a complex network of informants to feed a regime of bureaucratic monitoring – a system which aspired to politically appraise every Greek citizen. How officials classified a citizen on such files profoundly influenced that individual's life chances. Particularly fascinating is how Greeks continue to deplore bureaucratic recording, or filing (*fakeloma*) systems, even after those files were symbolically destroyed. This antipathy is not confined to being wary of unambiguously coercive state surveillance, but extends to all manners of data collection, including forms of benign or even potentially progressive administrative scrutiny.

While Samatas describes a distinctive Greek history, his analysis points to a more fundamental issue, and one that has been insufficiently addressed in the critical literature on surveillance. That is, the Greeks' continuing discomfort with filing systems is one example of a surveillance legacy, and it is this question of legacies that I would like to foreground here. Doing so introduces into discussions of surveillance a mid-range temporal horizon, one that splits the difference between how such practices are usually framed; orientations that now tend to alternate between pragmatic attentiveness to the immediate implications of a surveillance measure, or speculations about the distant future that can veer towards a form of science fiction (Nellis, 2009). My aim is to encourage analysts to contemplate the midpoint, to foreground a temporal span of perhaps fifty years. Whilst this is ultimately an arbitrary figure, it is nonetheless useful, because it offers sufficient critical distance to allow us to evaluate how changes introduced several decades ago have transformed our present. This is particularly opportune now, given that time is passing and the opening of archives allows us to critically assess some of the larger social consequences of how the totalitarian regimes of the 20th century used surveillance to repress their citizens (Funder, 2003; Garton Ash, 1997; Schmeidel, 2008). Looking forward, a timeframe of several decades encourages commentators to contemplate the larger implications of contemporary surveillance initiatives, but in a future that remains recognisable.

My inclination in thinking about surveillance legacies – and surveillance, more generally – is to acknowledge the potential benefits of surveillance, whilst accentuating the inherent dangers of our frantic embrace of a world where monitoring becomes daily an ever-more dominant organisational practice. Such an orientation has both a political and an academic rationale. Politically, it allows us to detail the potentially disempowering and coercive effects of surveillance. This is vital given that most of the influential voices in public discussions of surveillance – outside of a small cadre of overburdened and legally circumscribed privacy advocates (Bennett, 2008) – have institutional interests which tend to result in them cavalierly dismissing, denying, or downplaying the undesirable attributes of surveillance.

Academically, attending to the more disquieting potentialities of surveillance accentuates a much wider range of social implications than are typically part of public discussion. The starting point here is to recognise that surveillance does not simply involve watching from afar. Instead, surveillance is routinely a vehicle for change, in that it aims to transform, at a minimum, the phenomena being observed (Haggerty and Ericson, 2006).

Such changes tend to be approached in at least two different fashions. First, there are the proclaimed modifications that advocates believe will result from a surveillance measure, such as transformations in driving behaviour or student achievement. A substantial programme evaluation enterprise tries to assess the scope and direction of any such changes. Second, and more central to my concerns here, there are a host of broader but typically less desirable (although often entirely predictable) changes that surveillance measures can introduce to such things as culture, politics, institutional trust, and interpersonal relations. Rather than present a fully developed analysis of these developments, I will use this opportunity to introduce one crucial axis along which we can productively start to think about surveillance legacies. In particular, I would like to discuss some potential legacies related to the technological character of much contemporary surveillance.

Whilst face-to-face scrutiny is an inherent part of social life (Goffman, 1959), such informal inspection is now enhanced and sometimes supplanted by technologies with explicit or derived surveillance capabilities. What long-term impacts will such devices have? To address this question, we must first recognise that technological surveillance systems tend to be comparatively durable, which makes it imperative to see past the claims that these devices might produce immediate gains in efficiency, control, or profit (and so on), to recognise that the more monumental dynamic concerns how, cable-by-cable, camera-by-camera, and database-by-database, we are unwittingly constructing an ever-more comprehensive and integrated technological surveillance architecture (Graham, 2002). The sheer number of devices which now contain a surveillance application is simply too numerous to begin to enumerate. Suffice to say that almost daily the media run a story about how different aspects of the world are being made more perceptible because of the introduction (or integration) of some system of cameras, databases, sensors, or scanners.

Once installed, these devices tend to remain, meaning that the surveillance inherent in their design will extend well into the future. Samatas provides a small but telling example of a technological legacy of surveillance in his analysis of the Athens Olympics. As the first Games after the September 11th terrorist attacks, and with a security budget of $1.5 billion, these Games were then at the forefront of attempts to incorporate technological surveillance into mega-event security. This included a command and control system that deployed over 1,000 new surveillance cameras installed in and around Olympic venues. After the Games ended, this system was re-deployed to monitor urban traffic, producing a distinctive technological surveillance legacy in some Greek cities (Samatas, 2007). In itself, the comparative immutability of surveillance technologies is not necessarily troubling. The issue becomes more disconcerting, but more speculative, when we connect lasting surveillance infrastructures with broader dynamics in regulating deviance. One unassailable truth repeatedly demonstrated by generations of study in the sociology of deviance is that deviance is an extraordinarily malleable category (Sumner, 1994). Such variability is apparent cross-culturally, as different societies often stigmatise or criminalise starkly different behaviours. It is also apparent historically within the same society, where over time the identical behaviour has sometimes been alternatively condemned, tolerated, or even encouraged (and *vice versa*).

We can, therefore, expect that current normative positions will, over time, change. A host of our own personal behaviours, including the opinions we express, medical treatments we undergo, images we enjoy, products we ingest, beliefs we espouse, books we buy, and locations we visit (both physical and informational), now seem innocuous. Should, in the near future, however, there arise a confluence of factors that make it politically expedient, morally righteous, and/or financially profitable to censor such actions, officials in advanced Western societies will have at their disposal a system of monitoring the likes of which has never before existed in human history. The conspicuous cautionary example here is Nazi Germany, where officials drew upon a bureaucratic infrastructure that classified, amongst other things, people's occupations, residences, and religion, making it comparatively easy for the Nazis to identify and round-up undesired categories of humanity (Bauman, 1989; Black, 2001; Götz and Roth, 2004). If, as Giddens (1987: 302) has noted, '[t]he possibilities of totalitarian rule depend upon the existence of societies in which the state can successfully penetrate the day-to-day activities of most of its subject populations,' it is worth emphasising that the Nazis' technical infrastructure of domestic surveillance was rudimentary by contemporary standards.

There are other significant, although perhaps less alarming, legacies to contemplate pertain to how an elaborate surveillance infrastructure might alter the dynamics of deviance and normality beyond how it could be coordinated to tyrannise stigmatised groups. Here the starting point is to identify the subtle cultural transformations that are apt to follow from the fact that new surveillance technologies now allow us to see more, and in more detail, of other people's behaviours. Many of these behaviours were formerly understood to be intimate, private, or so unremarkable as to be unworthy of public scrutiny. In his recent book, *The Peep Diaries*, Niedviecki (2009) charts the emergence of a voyeuristic culture obsessed with using new information technologies to watch other people's often prosaic activities, and with displaying their own comparable behaviour (see also Koskela, 2004).

The consequences of our technologised ability to see ever-more of other people's behaviour are apt to cut at least two ways. On the one hand, there is the prospect that emerging dynamics of exposure and revelation could normalise or de-exoticise behaviours that were previously understood to be alternatively tantalising or distasteful; attitudes encouraged by how such things previously remained unseen and hence unfamiliar. For many, any liberalisation in such attitudes would be seen as a progressive development, as new opportunities to humanise the people engaging in such behaviours, which could challenge unhealthy forms of stigmatisation. The other related possibility is that the sheer scope of phenomena on public display will simply re-calibrate contemporary benchmarks of deviance downward. Here we take a lead from Durkheim's famous assertion that, even in a society of saints, some otherwise virtuous individuals will be censored due to the necessary social functions served by deviance (Durkheim, 1938; Erikson, 1966). Why this point is germane to thinking about surveillance is because the comprehensive technological monitoring of an expanding range of social life is (thankfully) apt to reveal that there are very few of the egregious behaviours which initially justify introducing most monitoring systems (such as child abduction, terrorism, and the like). The cameras will also reveal, however, that there is a tremendous amount of routine low-level deviance (Gabor, 1994). We can expect that the simple technological exposure of such behaviour will help problematise such otherwise unremarkable acts, in a process that we might deem the 'banalisation of surveillance.'

Such banalisation appears to be already emerging in the United Kingdom. There local authorities have turned the country's formidable infrastructure of security cameras to use in assorted prosaic regulatory efforts designed to deal with such things as people putting their garbage out on the wrong day, not cleaning up after their dog, urinating in public, littering, delivering newspapers without a licence, smoking under-age, posting flyers, and driving in an anti-social manner. While such acts can detract from the quality of urban life, bringing the full weight of the state's prodigious surveillance infrastructure to bear on such behaviours appears to be a disproportionate regulatory response. As evidence that this involves a banalisation process at work, officials are conducting this monitoring under legal authority derived from legislation designed to track terrorists. All of this exemplifies how a relatively permanent surveillance infrastructure can produce a legacy of re-calibrated standards of deviance and energised micro-regulatory projects, developments attributable in large part to how malleable standards of deviance interact with the emergence of new technological regimes of visibility to both detect such behaviour and make them potentially actionable.

All of these technologies also have financial costs. The exact dollar figures involved in designing, installing, staffing, and maintaining the plethora of state and private surveillance systems is impossible to discern, but is obviously enormous. Whilst it is conceivable that some agencies might dismantle some of these surveillance infrastructures because of some future financial crises, the knowledge these devices produce is now so engrained in the warp and woof of institutional practice that it is uncertain that they could function in their absence. Why it is germane to contemplate such financial costs in terms of a surveillance legacy is because such investments represent opportunity costs. The funds dedicated to surveillance technologies come from an always limited pool, and could have been directed elsewhere, raising the question of what types of alternative programming and resource allocation are being curtailed or forsaken in favour of ever-more surveillance initiatives.

Moreover, it is not just dollars that we can count among the limited resources dedicated to surveillance. One gets a sense of this from recent developments at the US National Security Agency (NSA), which is the arm of the American security establishment that analyses signal data, such as telephone and email messages. The greater technological ability to monitor such information has seen the NSA storm to the front of American's war on terror. Given secrecy restrictions, it is hard to determine the exact scope of the NSA's data collection projects, but James Bamford (2009) quotes a report that, by 2015, the amount of sensor data the NSA could be processing would increase to the level of Yottabytes, which roughly equals about a Septillion (1,000,000,000,000,000,000,000,000) pages of text. For anyone anxious about surveillance legacies, these numbers are simultaneously awe-inspiring and chilling. To compile and analyse this data deluge requires both enormous supercomputers, and the electricity to run them. The NSA now faces the pragmatic problem that these devices are such a drain on the electrical grid that they produce brownouts (Aid, 2009). Again, this raises the question of opportunity costs, and how such energy might have alternatively been deployed or conserved if it were not ploughed into the insatiable maw of the NSA's informational Leviathan?

Attentive readers will note that, in this brief discussion of some technological legacies of surveillance, I have strayed into questions of culture, economics, and even electrical utilities. Some might suggest that these are actually different legacies and that I confuse matters by introducing them all here. Instead, my sense is that anyone who commences by focusing on a single surveillance legacy will inevitably find themselves branching outward to address phenomena far-removed from their initial starting point. The social world routinely defies attempts to cleave-off the financial from the cultural, from the political, from the scientific, and so on (Latour, 1993). Surveillance legacies are diverse, and cut across our familiar analytical categories and disciplinary boundaries. Given such heterogeneity, I have only attempted to broach the smallest smattering of such legacies here. Even a casual consideration of the topic points us towards contemplating larger dynamics pertaining to culture, trust, gender, resistance, racialisation, and a plethora of other topics. My hope is that, by foregrounding the issue of surveillance legacies, scholars interested in both the history of surveillance and its possible futures will take up the challenge of giving these issues the sustained attention they deserve.

References

Aid, M. (2009) *The Secret Sentry: The Untold History of the National Security Agency*. London: Bloomsbury.

Bamford, J. (2009) *Who's in Big Brother's Database?* New York: New York Review of Books.

Bauman, Z. (1989) *Modernity and the Holocaust*. New York: Cornell University Press.

Bennett, C. (2008) *The Privacy Advocates: Resisting the Spread of Surveillance*. Cambridge, MA: MIT Press.

Black, E. (2001) *IBM and the Holocaust: The Strategic Alliance Between Nazi Germany and America's Most Powerful Corporation*. New York: Crown Publishers.

Durkheim, E. (1938) 'Rules for Distinguishing the Normal from the Pathological', in *The Rules of Sociological Method*. London: Free Press of Glencoe.

Erikson, K. (1966) *Wayward Puritans: A Study in the Sociology of Deviance*. New York: MacMillan.

Funder, A. (2003) *Stasiland: True Stories from Behind the Berlin Wall*. London: Granta.

Gabor, T. (1994) *Everybody Does It! Crime by the Public*. Toronto: University of Toronto Press.

Garton Ash, T. (1997) *The File: A Personal History*. New York: Vintage.

Giddens, A. (1987) *The Nation-State and Violence*. Cambridge: Polity.

Goffman, E. (1959) *The Presentation of Self in Everyday Life*. Harmondsworth: Penguin.

Götz, A. and K.H. Roth (2004) *The Nazi Census: Identification and Control in the Third Reich*. Philadelphia: Temple University Press.

Graham, S. (2002) 'CCTV: The Stealthy Emergence of a Fifth Utility', *Planning Theory and Practice* 3: 237–241.

Haggerty, K.D. and R.V. Ericson (2006) 'The New Politics of Surveillance and Visibility', in K.D. Haggerty and R.V. Ericson (eds) *The New Politics of Surveillance and Visibility*. Toronto: University of Toronto Press.

Koskela, H. (2004) 'Webcams, TV Shows and Mobile Phones: Empowering Exhibitionism', *Surveillance and Society* 2: 199–215.

Latour, B. (1993) *We Have Never Been Modern*. Cambridge, MA: Harvard University Press.

Nellis, M. (2009) 'Since "Nineteen Eighty-Four": Representations of Surveillance in Literary Fiction', in B. Goold and D. Neyland (eds) *New Directions in Surveillance and Privacy*. London: Willan.

Niedzviecki, H. (2009) *The Peep Diaries: How We're Learning to Love Watching Ourselves and Our Neighbors*. San Francisco: City Lights.

Samatas, M. (2004) *Surveillance in Greece: From Anti-Communist to Consumer Surveillance*. New York: Pella.

Samatas, M. (2007) 'Security and Surveillance in the Athens 2004 Olympics: Some Lessons from a Troubled Story', *International Criminal Justice Review* 17: 220–238.

Schmeidel, J.C. (2008) *Stasi*. London: Routledge.

Sumner, C. (1994) *The Sociology of Deviance: An Obituary*. Buckingham: Open University Press.

SOPHIE VIDALI

Police and Policing

This chapter addresses the system of police and policing in Greece. It begins by highlighting the wider socio-political framework and key historical events that have played a determining role in shaping the development, central features, and structural organisation of the police and policing in the country. The analysis goes on to discuss pertinent reforms to police and policing, before turning to consider the discretional power of the police, police deviance, police culture, discipline and institutional control, and the institutional and actual aspects of police personnel enrolment, as well as the profile of police officers.

The analysis is limited exclusively to the State Police and specifically to the history and current developments of the Hellenic Police corps. The Hellenic Police is the main police corps in Greece and is relatively newly formed. It was instituted in 1984 by the unification of the pre-existing corps of the Gendarmerie and *Astynomia Poleon* (City Police). Under Article 8 of Law 2800/2000, the Hellenic Police is the national body responsible for maintaining public peace and order, ensuring that the lives of citizens are unhindered, preventing and countering criminality, and protecting the democratic regime and constitutional order (a function attended to by both public and State security police). Beyond the State police *stricto sensu*, other police forces include the Hellenic Coast Guard, the Special Controls' Service (widely known as the Economic Crime Corps), the Municipal Police, and the Rural police (Law 3585/2007), as well as private police agencies (see further Papanicolaou, 2006). It is the Hellenic Police, however, that holds primary responsibility for crime control.

Policing has only recently emerged as a subject of criminological interest in Greece. In part, this has been due to a dominant positivism (Lambropoulou, 2005; see also Newburn and Reiner, 2007: 910), in combination with a number of particular sociopolitical trends (on which more below) which have together shaped the development of social science research in the country (see further Tsoukalas, 1984). Thus, policing has been studied through the fields of criminalistics (e.g., Gardikas, 1964; Alexiadis, 2003) or public law (e.g., Tachos, 1990). Even if this perspective has largely changed since the 1990s, academic interest in police and policing could not be considered to have been constant. Space limits here do not permit greater analysis of the relevant literature of recent years. It should be noted, however, that it has mainly focused on evaluating the competency of police practice, organisational structure, educational training, and the necessity of reforms to each (Kampanakis, 2003; Stergioulis, 2001; Panousis, 1999; Panousis and Vidali, 2001; Papakonstantis, 2003), on police co-operation (Stergioulis, 2001), on public security more generally (Papatheodorou, 2005), on the values and culture of the police force (Papakonstantis, 2003), and on police and policing from a political economy perspective (Vidali, 2007a; Rigakos and Papanicolaou, 2003). From the end of the 2004 Olympic Games until December 2009, the question of police reform found itself once again ignored by both public and scientific debate, despite expanding crime problems and an increase in abusive policing.

Although the development of the Greek police force followed continental models as well as – in part – that of Britain, critical to understanding its evolution is its moulding by a different sociopolitical history to that of its counterparts in developed, industrialised European countries (Vidali 2007a; Rigakos and Papanicolaou, 2003). Specific social, political, and economic conditions relating to the development of the country have, since the 19th century, constituted the determining context to the development of police and policing in Greece and its particular path (Vidali, 2007a: 615). Further attention to such matters is essential in order to appreciate the extent to which historical influences are relevant to the features, attitudes, and ineffectiveness of the police today, as well as to the issue of security in Greece more generally; and first of these is the necessity to shed light on the police system and its historical development.

The Police and the Political History of Policing

Comparative Perspectives

With the founding of the Kingdom of Greece in 1833, the Greek police system was created in accordance with the 19th-century continental model that was prevalent at that time (Rigakos and Papanicolaou, 2003; Vidali, 2007a; see further Emsley, 1991). The Gendarmerie, in operation between 1833 and 1984, was part of the Armed Forces, and was responsible for state security, crime control, and the maintenance of law and order across the extensive rural and mountainous areas of the country. The Municipal Police, in operation between 1836 and 1893, was responsible for keeping the peace in urban areas, enforcing market regulations and administrative rules. This was a civilian corps, accountable to local municipal authorities. Later, in the cities of Athens and Piraeus, the Municipal Police were substituted with Administrative Police.

Police forces in Greece were strongly involved in politics and were utilised by political power elites in the country. The Municipal Police and, later, the Administrative Police, were conditioned by the interference in personnel recruitment of political parties and their clientele (Vidali, 2007a: 292). The Gendarmerie had historically been linked to the regime consolidation interests of the monarchy (Petropoulos, 1997) and, until the outbreak of the Second World War, to the repression of social banditry and social revolts (Petropoulos, 1997; Koliopoulos, 1996; Vidali, 2007a). Similar, actually, to experience of continental Europe (see Emsley, 1991), the Gendarmerie became the main force of social integration and con-solidation of the nation-state until the interwar period. Moreover, specific security needs related to revolts against the King, to social banditry, and to cross-border criminality, had led to the relatively short-lived establishment of specialised paramilitary and police corps during the 19th century: the Mountain Police and National Guards. Their violent and abusive practices against peasants and their own move towards banditism ensured the hostil-ity of citizens and their distrust toward state institutions.

Despite multiple reforms of a secondary nature and changes to the organisational structural of police forces in Greece during the 19th and 20th centuries, there were a limited number of structural reforms to the system of policing until 1984, as discussed below. An important but under-analysed reform was one related to the establishment of the first intelligence police institution in Athens via the creation of the Administrative Police (as noted above and discussed further below). The institution of the latter had been determined both by the increasing need for greater police knowledge of order and security issues in the expanding urban areas of the Greek capital, and by the influence of wider European revolutionary trends in that period.

In 1893, however, the system of policing underwent profound reform. Law ΒΡΠΗ/1893 put to an end the responsibility of local authorities for police and policing, abolished the existing civilian police corps (the Administrative Police and the Municipal Police), and established a new corps, the *Astyfylaki* (City Police) which was placed under the authority of the Armed Forces; the system of policing had been completely militarised (i.e., made accountable to the Armed Forces; see further discussion below). The significance of this reform should be evaluated against the background of the emergence of the first governments by bourgeoisie parties in Greece and, in time, the forthcoming Olympic Games.

By the end of the 19th century, the increasing probability of Greece's involvement in war had shaped state policy towards the effectiveness of enforcement by the Armed Forces. The *Astyfylaki* was abolished in 1906 by Law ΓΡΞΕ/1906. From 1906 to 1984, the Gendarmerie dominated the Greek police system, even if later a new civilian corps, the *Astynomia Poleon* (City Police), was created in 1920 (by Law 2461/1920). From 1920 until 1984, four cities came under the authority of *Astynomia Poleon*: Patras, Corfu, Piraeus and Athens (see further Vidali, 2007b).

Several complicated and conflicting historical, political, and socio-economic circumstances further determined the development, organisational structure, and crime control policies of the police during the 19th and 20th centuries. Between 1920 and 1974, they effected the differentiation of the institutional role and position of the Greek police system in comparison with its counterparts in Western countries. In particular, the fundamental contradiction between the formal purposes of the institution and the socio-political reality, the specific processes of social integration that pertained in Greece, and the relationship between the Armed Forces and the political system, all shaped the division between the formal/legal aims of the police and its real functions, effecting processes of criminalisation, the occupational culture of the police, and patterns and policies of crime control. These factors are analysed immediately below.

Institutional Framework and Political Reality

The relationship between the centre and the periphery within capitalistic development (see Lea and Young, 1993) is critical to explaining the relationship between the institutional framework and political reality in Greece, as well as its effects on prevention and security policies and agencies. Included amongst the typical effects of that peripherality has been the structural dislocation between liberal institutions and their authoritarian or deviant development. In most cases, legislative and institutional reforms concerning prevention and security were not the result of long-term social conflict, ideological-political debate, or cultural trends in Greece, but instead (even authoritarian) transplantations or imitations of foreign institutions. Such reforms were further shaped by the real primary aim of the police: the protection of the interests of the King and powerful political groups, rather than the security of citizens. Hostility between police and citizenry, distrust toward institutions, and coercive and abusive policing as a unique form of population control, were the main effects of these processes. During the interwar period, criminalisation and crime control had been further politicised and conditioned by anti-communism and the political control of citizens which, in the name of national security, became the first goal of the police. Between the 1930s and the mid-1970s, the question of state security was fashioned by the State Security establishment.

Apart from internal sociopolitical processes, the relationship between Greece and the developed countries, on which it had been politically and economically dependent during previous years, was also of primary relevance. Throughout those years, the interference in Greek political and security affairs of the so-called 'Great Powers' during the 19th century (the British until 1949, and then the US from 1949 onwards), and the consequences of the Cold War, further shaped Greek security policies and, until the 1980s, ensured the disjuncture between the legal aims and actual targets of the police. The establishment of a democratic regime in 1974, European integration, new trends in police cooperation, and the globalisation of crime policies, served to change the features and orientations of the Greek police system over the last 25 years.

The broader sociopolitical context, to which brief reference has already been made, had permitted the prominent military character and repressive patterns of policing. Even the civilianisation influence – proper first to the British and then to the US – had been used to ensure the political control of the social classes *stricto sensu* and the elimination of political threats. This has not gone unexplained: according to some scholars, the influence of foreign countries in crime prevention and security policies amounted to the transferral to Greece first of British patterns of colonial policies and then of US policies of control as employed over other countries and territories (Vidali, 2007a: 322, 371, 390; Fatouros, 1984: 442–445; see further Emsley, 1991: 160; Senior, 1997: 77, 97–98). These trends had a double effect: on the one hand, they contributed to the forced modernisation of the police system; on the other, in association with the problems of the Greek political system, they had supported its deviation from typical liberal capitalistic forms of social control.

A plethora of examples link crime control policies in Greece to colonial and/or imperialist politics; amongst them, the above-mentioned Administrative Police in Athens and the specific measures of crime policy against banditry during the same period (both reflecting British influence) (see Vidali, 2007a: 322; Papadopoulos, 1977: 165–166). The protection of French and (mainly) British commercial interests in the Balkan region played a pivotal role in this perspective (ibid.: 160). Nevertheless, the clienteles of political parties and the strong political disputes of the 19th century also conditioned trends in crime prevention and security.

Subsequently, during the 1920s, the British Police Mission (the London Metropolitan Police Mission) played a determining role in the foundation of the *Astynomia Poleon*, which it also administered and directed until 1929 (with Sir Frederick Halliday becoming its first Chief). A less discussed aspect of British involvement in the interwar period is that the London Metropolitan Police had itself at that time been administered by armed forces personnel (Emsley, 1991: 160; Senior, 1997: 77). Their involvement in the institution of the *Astynomia Poleon* therefore reduces the significance of prevailing rhetoric concerning the civilian character of that corps. In fact, the *Astynomia Poleon* was a centralised corps (and not a local police) that had been strongly linked to the control of urban populations and spaces and to the expansion of undercover policing, in a period in which political policing and anti-communism became typical features and aims of the police forces in Greece.

Furthermore, after the establishment of the US mission in Greece in 1949, the police system and its modernisation passed to its control. In the 1960s, the unconstitutional growth in the autonomy of police sections from governmental direction and the use of extra-institutional paramilitary policing was directed by US services in association with supporters of the Greek Armed Forces, the King, and politicians of the extreme-right (Meynaud, 2002: 470; Samatas, 2004: 300; Mazower, 1997: 146–147). Political policing and the technological modernisation of the police during the Cold War was conditioned and directed almost officially by US politics in the field (Fatouros, 1984: 422). There were reactions, however, by the Greek Armed Forces to any British or US proposals to abolish the accountability of the police to the Armed Forces, which had set in place the post-war development of the police in Greece (Antoniou, 1967). The political events that took place from then until the dictatorship's fall in 1974 disarticulated the system and discipline of the police. Over all these years, state crimes in various forms had neutralised law enforcement and become part of policies of order maintenance.

The Expansion of the Nation-state and Social Integration

The next determinant of the different path taken by Greece to that of other European countries relates to processes of social integration. State policies and the continuous expansion or change of the state's borders until 1948 were both significant in this respect. Security and crime control policies became a constant means by which new populations were socially and nationally integrated. The institution of the Greek Kingdom in 1833, and every further acquisition of new territories, had been followed by the criminalisation of the existing system of social, economic, and power relations in those areas and, consequently, of particular social groups (Vidali, 2007a: 276, 406, 472). This approach is not inexplicable.

The criminalisation of social questions became a constant part of the process of social integration until the 1970s. In the first instance, critical to this was the question of rural banditry which, until the interwar period, was linked to the reactions to the disarticulation of the economy of nomad cattle-raising communities in mountainous regions (Vidali, 2007a: 311, 406). First legislated in 1870, the repressive policy against banditry had long-term effects on the process of social integration accompanying Greece's modernisation. Its main principles and strategies were further elaborated in the 1920s, 1930s, and 1940s, and had constituted an exceptional security-based model of social control that effected tough policing and massive criminalisation of social groups (including, amongst others, bandits, political opponents, bohemian musicians (*rebetes*), and hashish users). Besides criminalisation, the main principles of this policy could be summarised as the militarisation of crime-control policies and agencies, the forced collaboration between police and the community, the construction of wider social consent, and, at least in the post-war era, the institutionalisation of a system of differentiated social control in dangerous regions of the country by their division into specific zones of prohibition and surveillance (ibid.). The application and re-elaboration of this model against bandits, Royalists and Republicans, and communists above all, elevated political policing to a key means of delimiting social exclusion and inclusion until the fall of dictatorship.

In particular, apart from the question of banditry and the reactions of leading local groups and political parties to authoritarian policies pursued by the monarchy (Petropoulos, 1997), the specific form of economic development experienced by the country also contributed to the distinctive social integration processes in evidence until the interwar period. The prevalence of the rural economy (Petmezas, 2009), the lack of large-scale industry, the extensiveness of self-employment and of the small enterprise sector in Athens and Piraeus and, furthermore, numerous economic crises (Leontidou, 1989; Tsokopoulos, 1984, Giannitsiotis, 2006), all functioned to prevent the subordination of labour to capital. For these reasons, unlike the processes experienced by developed European states (see, e.g., Melossi, 1990: 88; Taylor, 1999: 100), the economy in Greece did not stimulate the massive transformation of formerly rural human resources into an industrial labour force. Consequently, social integration could not take forms similar to those of industrialised countries (Vidali, 2007a: 341, 474–475). From the same perspective it is possible to explain not only the underdevelopment of the penitentiary system in Greece and the leading role of the police in social control and social integration (for both police officers and citizens), but also the extensive dimensions of political clientelism in the country.

During the first half of the 20th century, the effects of country's repeated involvement in wars (the Balkan Wars, the First World War, and the Asia Minor War involving the massacre and expulsion of Greeks) were to change Greek society, creating new questions of social integration and social marginalisation. The entrenched intra-class conflict between the bourgeois Royalists and Republicans (a conflict known as the 'National Schism', which lasted between 1916 and 1934) could not permit a liberal solution to the increasing demands of the labour classes and marginalised social groups. The aforementioned exceptional security model of population control constituted an alternative 'solution' to the question of social integration (Chatziiosif, 2003). The Metaxas Dictatorship of 1936–1941, the Nazi Occupation of 1941–1944, and the civil war of 1945–1949, served to consolidate a Security State that lasted until 1974. Social control was identified with political control and with national security. In that context, on the basis of anti-communist criteria, the specific political nature of penal legislation and its enforcement had determined access to social and economic institutions.

The Political System, the Armed Forces, and the Police

The third aspect of Greek particularism in comparison to other Western developed states concerns the relationship between the political system and the armed forces, especially the involvement of the Greek Armed Forces in political life as an autonomous part of the political system from the interwar period onwards. This shift was supported by factors related to the structure of political system itself and their consequences. In particular, extensive political patronage (Petropoulos, 1997), which had affected the achievement of extra-institutional consensus by Greek governments (Charalambis, 1989: 96), the deviations from standard parliamentarism by the political system (Alivisatos, 1983: 65), and the intra-bourgeois conflict previously noted between Royalists and Republicans (Chatziiosif, 2003: 62; Mazower, 1997: 137), had further conditioned the development of the police and policing. The influence of these factors on the historical rivalry between the two police forces – which has been described as litigation for control over the state's Security Services (Antoniou, 1964) – was critical.

In these circumstances, the Armed Forces increased their mediating influence in politics and established themselves as an autonomous source of power within the political system. They controlled social order and, indeed, governed the country through dictatorships in specific periods (i.e., between 1924 to 1925, 1936 to 1941, and 1967 to 1974). The particular implications of the influence of the Armed Forces in political life also related to the governance of security, political policing, and to reform of the police personnel system. The emergence of security measures under the so-called 'Social Regime' during the interwar period had led to the formation of temporary detached paramilitary battalions in 1923, named after the Hunter Battalions, similar to the National Guards of the 19th century. Civilians also participated in the paramilitary battalions (Vidali, 2007a: 423).

During the Nazi Occupation this 'tradition' was revived (ibid.) and contributed to the institution of Greek Security Battalions in order to combat the left-wing resistance and communists. The Battalions were accountable to the Nazi authorities and to the Gendarmerie. This trend had conditioned further the police's personnel renovation system, not least since the personnel of the Gendarmerie and City Police decreased dramatically (Margaritis, 2001: 223; see also below). After liberation in 1944, the former personnel of the Security Battalions were enrolled in the newly-formed National Guard. Their personnel, as well as the personnel of other local security squads that were created during what became known as the 'White Terror' (1945), were mainly recruited as police officers by the Gendarmerie (ibid.; Vidali, 2007b: 588; Kostopoulos, 2005), and had become actively involved in the Civil War.

The effects of these flows in the personnel of police forces are extremely important if one takes into account the following: that since 1938, any officer considered to be a liberal would have been discharged from duty; that because of the Second World War, the Nazi occupation, and the Battle of Athens in December 1944, police personnel numbers shrank dramatically in the years 1940 to 1944 (Margaritis, 2001: 223; Antoniou, 1965); and that since 1946, enrolment to the police had been directly curtailed by nationalistic and political criteria decreed by law, allowing recruitment to the police of members of extreme right-wing and former paramilitary groups, as well as of former Nazi collaborators (Mazower, 1997). Simultaneously, anyone who had participated in leftist resistance, or who could not be classified as a nationalist anti-communist, was excluded from the recruitment process (Vidali, 2007b: 540, 588; Kostopoulos, 2005). Until 1981, and as with the public sector more generally, enrolment to the police was conditional upon the presentation of a certificate of social beliefs (according to Resolution Θ of 1946 and the stipulations of Law 516/1948). Through this certification process, political beliefs became subject to penal control (Alivisatos, 1983: 474, 480).

From the end of the Civil War in 1949 until 1984, the system of policing remained officially unchanged. The police and policing had been almost totally conditioned by the outcome of the civil war and Cold War politics. In that context, the primacy given to militarised crime control and political policing had resulted in the underdevelopment of civilian and local police corps (which were abolished at the end of 19th century, as noted above). Political policing had been given additional support by a less-researched variable; organised criminality on the part of the state. During the 1960s, the illegal operational autonomy of police departments allowed them the organisation and control of extra-governmental para-police; extreme right-wing groups composed of underworld figures, poor petty criminals, and former Nazi collaborators. These groups were used in violent political provocations and the commission of political murders (Lentakis, 2000; Petridis, 1995). Moreover, the increasing empowerment of the youth and the working classes had further 'stimulated' the rise of politically violent and abusive policing against them as a normal and, indeed, the exclusive function of the police (Vidali, 2007b: 662; Mazower, 1997: 135). In turn, these trends had also shaped the educational system and occupational culture of the police. The dictatorship of 1967 to 1974 saw the further degeneration of police forces as law enforcers.

Criminality and the Cold War

A final distinguishing feature of the Greek experience that contrasts with those of other European states during the post-war era relates to explanations of low crime rates. The primacy given to political policing contributed to the underestimation of the crime problem in Greece (Vidali, 2007b: 681). The relationship between crime reporting and the dark figure of criminality, especially state criminality, is crucial here. In general, criminality in Greece did not match the trends of developed industrialised countries in this period (Spinellis, 1971: 670). Felonies represented an insignificant part of reported criminality. The data of *Astynomia Poleon* for the period 1956–1960 reported 40 robberies and 19 felony thefts in Athens in total (Vidali, 2007b: 682–693, 1010).

Low and static crime rates, the overrepresentation of misdemeanours, the low rates of felonies, the absence of drug abuse and trafficking reports, and the increasing rates of profiteering and crimes related to market regulations, together comprised the map of criminality over the years 1956 to 1965. Studies are available that document the expansion of interpersonal violence for 'motives of honour' (Avdela, 2002) and the extensiveness of crimes related to brothels and prostitution control (Lazos, 2002: 100) over roughly the same timeframe. Contrary to official reports, 'crimes against state authority' present a different picture: during 1957 to 1966, rates of crimes committed 'against the internal security of the state' increased by 59.3 per cent (see Vidali, 2007b: 685). Furthermore, the extended grey zone of crimes committed by the state forced political policing to be ranked above the policing of common criminality.

During the dictatorship, police abuses of power, illegal detentions, the disarticulation of the hierarchical system of discipline amongst the police (i.e., the denial of obedience by lower-ranking to higher-ranking officers), and the widespread organisation of torture by officers of the police and armed forces as a normal feature of political controls, revealed the extensiveness of state crimes (Haritos-Fatouros, 2003; Korovesis, 1970). As typical in such circumstances (see Kleinning, 1996: 67, 72), violence had become part of the professional life of the policeman, and the occupational culture and system of policing was inevitably affected (Vidali, 2007b: 707, 719). As has been documented, even after the restoration of democracy in 1974, new generations of policemen continued to reproduce the values and practices of this period (Alivizatos, 1983a: 630; Zianikas, 1992: 108).

In sum, it should be noted that the police performed an instrumental role designed to ensure the reproduction of the political system during the 19th and 20th centuries. Moreover, the police became a constitutive and active factor in consolidating authoritarian regimes. It is for this reason that the relationship between police effectiveness and respect for, and enforcement of, human rights standards has become a critical issue since the establishment of democracy in Greece.

Police, Policing and the Democratic state

Despite the establishment of democracy in 1974, the accountability of the police to the Constitution and to the authority of legal government remained at the centre of public debates. By the beginning of 1980s, and in combination with increasing crime rates (see Vidali, 2007b: 773–774, 831; compare Courakis, 1991: 36; and see also Cheliotis and Xenakis, this collection), wider sociopolitical and economic changes, the radicalisation of social demands, repressive policing, the abuse of police power (Vidali 2007b: 813), and the ineffectiveness and ideological rigidity of the police (Papakonstantis, 2003: 101), led to greater demands for the democratisation and reform of the police.

After the electoral victory of the social democratic party PASOK in 1981, a key reform instituted changes to the police system: with Law 1481/1984, the Gendarmerie and *Astynomia Poleon* were abolished. Their personnel were transferred to a new corps, the Hellenic Police, with a system that was strongly resonant of the bureaucratic model of the Gendarmerie (Papakonstantis, 2003). The democratisation and demilitarisation of the police became fundamental subjects of government policy as increasing crime rates became more and more a public issue. The restoration of state and government control over the police, and the consolidation of the first mission of the police as the protection of the democratic constitutional regime, amounted to the most influential principle institutionalised by the reform of 1984. Apart from democratisation *per se*, police-community relations, abusive policing, and police ineffectiveness became constant public themes, notwithstanding the succession of reforms adopted.

Democratisation and Demilitarisation: Meanings and Contexts

Since 1984, the democratisation, demilitarisation, and effectiveness of the police became the targets of various reforms. At this point it is necessary to clarify some pertinent concepts. The democratisation of the police took various forms and meanings throughout the years, as reflected in their very frequency. During a first stage that lasted until 1984, democratisation was identified with the discharging of supporters and collaborators of the dictatorship from police service. In a second stage, from 1984 to 1994, democratisation assumed a different significance, being associated with the accountability of the police to government and to the demilitarisation of the police (that is to say, the liberation of the police from control by the Armed Forces and their civilianisation through the equalisation of employment conditions with those of other state employees). The freeing of the police from control by the Armed Forces was implemented with the abolition of the police headquarters by Law 1481/1984. Police chiefs became directly accountable to the Minister of Public Order, who then directly controlled crime policy and the administration of the police. This development would be reconsidered many years later, and police's headquarters were reinstituted by Law 2800/2000.

However the military 'nature' of the Hellenic Police was also reconfirmed by a set of other regulations. Namely, the participation of generals of the Armed Forces in the selection of the chief of the Hellenic Police (Presidential Decree 24/1997), the obligatory participation of police personnel in national defence under exceptional circumstances, the institutionalisation of ambiguity concerning the military or civilian character of the police, and the ideological orientations typified in the 'competencies and official assignments' of police personnel (Presidential Decree 141/1991).

A recent sequence of administrative reforms revealed the difficulties in managing the relationship between the police and government. The fusion of the Ministry of Public Order with that of the Interior (Presidential Decree 205/2007), and then the establishment of a position of Vice-Minister of Public Order in 2009, demonstrated the divergent approaches of political leadership on the matter of managing the police. A significant move towards greater civilianisation was nevertheless instigated by Law 1481/1984, which abolished restrictions concerning the employment status of personnel, the necessity of authorisation for those policemen wishing to marry foreign women or prohibiting marriage with those of communists 'origin'. Moreover, the eight-hour working day was established and the obligation to spend nights in camp ended. Police trade unions were legalised ten years later by Law 2265/1994, when the system of admission to the corps was also reformed and rationalised; under Law 2226/1994, admission to the police required successful participation in national Higher Education general exams.

During the 1990s, increasing concern about police effectiveness deflected attention from issues of democratisation and demilitarisation. This change may be explained by reference to the so-called 'managerial turn' in crime control policies. In this context, demands for democratisation and demilitarisation have been substituted by those for police effectiveness. This has mainly been considered a technical question to be resolved by law enforcement, without considering the influence of the occupational culture of the police or other pertinent variables. The connection between the organisational structure, territorial distribution, and the negative effect of the military character of the police was long underestimated in official and scientific discourses, even if the administrative and territorial decentralisation of police departments in the late 1980s constituted a significant effort towards that direction (as discussed further below).

Police Organisation and Policing Strategies

Structures and Modernisation Policies of the Hellenic Police

The Hellenic Police is structured by so-called leading or central services, which govern and control the police and peripheral regional services. Regional policing is structured by three main hierarchical levels: the General Directorate of the Police (responsible for a whole region), the Police Directorate (responsible at the prefectural level), and the Police Department (responsible at the municipal or local level). With the aim of increasing the effectiveness of policing, reforms adopted over the late 1980s and 1990s sought to address the issue of authority over local police departments and the apportioning of responsibilities between the Ministry of Public Order and the Security Police.[1]

---

1   According to the continental and Greek organisational structure of the police, the term 'security' is associated mainly with the 'Security Police', which corresponds to investigative and undercover policing, whilst operative enterprise sections of the police are denoted by terms such as 'security units' and 'guards'. For the purpose of this chapter, the term 'Security Police' is used to indicate the Intelligence and Investigation Police, and the term 'Unit' or 'Guard' for operative sections. It should be mentioned that the protection and enforcement of national security is the competence of the National Intelligence Service (E.Y.P.), which is the body that corresponds to the CIA and the Intelligence Service.

The first effort at decentralisation concentrated on the regions of Attica and Thessaloniki. It provided for the territorial proliferation of existing police departments and for the creation of specialised departments at a local level with administrative and financial autonomy. The distribution of local police force duties, local crime-control policy, and the management of annual funds became totally dependent on the responsibility of and administration by the local Department Chief. The effects of this reform had never been evaluated properly, but a recent study (Vidali, 2007a: 809) found that the following year crime rates had exploded. On the one hand, police reforms could not safely be directly related to the increase in crime rates. On the other hand, it is known that the intensification of the territorial presence of the police could not reduce crime (Goldblatt and Lewis, 1998: 67), but could increase the reporting of crimes (Lea and Young, 1993: 167). Moreover, the creation of specialised departments had favoured the selective functioning of the police through the intensification of policing of specific forms of crime and social groups (Bittner, 1990: 169).

In particular, the rates of some forms of crimes had distinctly increased in 1988 in comparison to the previous year, and some (such as offences posing danger to the commons and offences against property) could be immediately related to the reform adopted (Vidali, 2007b: 828, 1044). Crimes related to violations of specific penal laws also increased (i.e., crimes related to public health, illegal arms, drugs, gambling, and violations of building construction rules), but the rise was, in this case, related to policing intensification (ibid.: 1042). Over the same period, police violence against citizens during stop and searches, riots, illegal detentions in police departments, raids in dangerous urban areas, or searches for terrorist suspects increased dramatically. The intensification of the territorial presence of the police, violent policing, and the lack of collaboration between police departments, all contributed to the unsuccessfulness of this reform (ibid.: 818–819; Papakonstantis, 2003: 131–132, 179). Nevertheless, the less-discussed and lateral political effects of the reform concerned the policies of the PASOK government to obtain consensus amongst the police personnel. The proliferation of autonomous police departments had increased the numbers of mid-level Head Officers. The groups of officers that had benefitted by the reform (as they unexpectedly climbed police ranks) and who could consequently be expected to consent to further governmental decisions had probably grown. At the same time, the reform had caused a disjuncture in the power of the (oldest) Heads of the Police Directorates to control the (inferior) ordinary administration of Police Departments.

Managerialism

The election of the right-wing party *Nea Dimokratia* (New Democracy), in government between 1990 and 1993, was framed by increasing concerns about the policing of national borders. Additionally, the massive influx of migrants to Greece during the 1990s, combined with an increase in drugs trafficking, the intensification of Greek terrorist attacks, and new security policies pursued by the United Nations and the European Communities, rendered the control of cross-border crime, terrorism, and police cooperation the central objectives of crime policy. The strengthening of security measures in border regions, the reorganisation of police presence in those areas (Presidential Decree 291/1991), and the enforcement of the Anti-terrorism Department were included amongst the main innovations of those years. Through these efforts, a first version of situational crime prevention policy was adopted, if tacitly, on a national level. Moreover, Presidential Decree 141/1991 set out the reform of the 'competences and official assignments' of the police. These trends should be evaluated with reference to increasing crime problems and the first appearance of organised crime in Greece since the 1920s.

Following the expansion of market economy, the issue of immigration and its association with the growth of criminality (see Karydis, 1996, and this collection), and international trends in security policies (on which see Pallida, 2000; Wacquant, 2000), in the mid-1990s the shifting focus of policing was accompanied by a growing authoritarianism. Belief in the need for a new style of management of police forces became prevalent amongst policy-makers at the Ministry of Public Order. In Greece, the managerial turn in policing coincided with the consolidation of modernisation trends in politics, the change of orientation on the part of social democratic governments towards the market economy, and the growth of the market society and consumerism (Chalaris, 2005). These new approaches broke with previous strategies of crime control by adopting the goal of transforming policing into a consensual and effective process of crime control through the continuous management of street problems in collaboration with the community (Papakonstantis, 2003).

Presidential Decrees 97/1995, 260/1995, and 334/1995 provided for the intensification and reorganisation of police foot patrols, the organisational restructuring of the General Directorates, and the trialling of large new divisions named 'Multiforce Police Departments' (MPD), which would unify three to four Departments. The autonomy previously enjoyed by Departments was abolished and they were made accountable to the Head of the MPD. The reforms overturned the ordering of the local police, dislocated the autonomy of individual Departments and the management of power relations at local levels (ibid.: 303), and reduced the influence and role of Security Police Departments in the police system (Vidali, 2007b).

As a managerial initiative, it failed: the reform proposals had been rejected by the police bureaucracy and, compounded by changes to the leadership of the Public Order Ministry, revisions to the proposed reforms ensured that critics of its logic and necessity stymied some its effects. Additionally, the reforms served to stimulate new tensions between the centre and the periphery of the police force (Papakonstantis, 2003: 298, 303).[2] Notwithstanding internal criticisms, the enforcement of the reforms was

2   These tensions are typical of the relations evident between local interests and the state in continental Europe (as in France, according to Ferret, 2004). In France (as well as in Greece), 'the territorial organisation of state power through powerful state representatives at the local level – the territorial bureaucracies –, is one crucial factor of power relations within the space of the state. [...] The relations between the central state and the periphery are asymmetric and unequal contrary to Anglo-Saxon countries' (ibid.). The particularity of Greece is that this tension between centre and periphery was historically determined by extra-institutional local interests, which influenced the effectiveness of local state agencies. As concerns the police, determinant influences were networks of crime tolerance development inside local territories that were founded on factors such as personal relations and the interests of local politicians. The autonomy of police departments could affect a similar process of local power control acquisitions by regulating issues of order. Whoever had enforced their position of power inside police through the previous structural reforms, now had to react to the re-centralisation of police structures.

disastrous all the same, resulting in intensified patrols, the use of 'stop-and-search' by newly-formed 'Special Control Squads' (SCS), managed by the Special Controls Police Department (SCPD) (established by Presidential Decree 216/ 1995), and the targeting of minorities such as the Roma (Vidali, 2007a: 881). Unexpected outcomes of the reforms included a swift rise in recorded crime rates (Papatheodorou, 2005: 187), fear of crime, police violence, and increased public hostility towards the force in over-policed areas. According to subsequent official reflection on the subject, the primacy given to street policing in major urban areas indeed reflected more the control of public spaces than the control of criminality *per se* (see Vidali, 2007b).

Community Policing: The Greek Version

With the emergence of a moral panic about increasing crime rates, further provoked by a number of serious incidences relating to the criminal activities of recidivist offenders, the public demanded greater security provision. In response, crime-prevention policy turned to promoting police-community relations as a means of attending to feelings of public insecurity. From 1999 onwards, community policing and its European varieties thus became a core issue concerning policing, public safety, and security in Greece. The leading role of the state in prevention and community relations (see further Crawford, 1997) and the production of security via police-community collaboration (see Skolnick and Bailey, 1986: 212) constitute some of the main principles of this widely-known model of policing. Policing, rather than the police, were accordingly to be transformed, a transformation which became the core goal of pertinent reforms in Greece until 2004.

Whilst subdivisional police structures at the local level remained untouched, operational units and departments proliferated, and soft street policing was promoted. On the other hand (and as mentioned above), the control of illegal immigration and cross-border criminality became constant foci of policing. Two new specific services were developed in this regard, the personnel of which are subject to different conditions of enrolment in comparison to the rest of the police. In 1998, Law 2622 established a specific Border Guard Police Service (BGPS) for the purposes of migration control. The next year saw Law 2734 introduce a Special Guard Service (SGS), with the primary remit of protecting sites seen as potential targets, such as public buildings, banks, and metro stations, but which would later come to assume ordinary policing duties.

Supporting the implementation of new preventive policies was a well-organised public communications policy and related initiatives involving community responsibilisation and police-community relations. Amongst these have been the establishment of Local Council Crime Prevention groups (Law 2713/1999; see further Papatheodorou, 2005), in which local communities and municipal authorities participate; a shift in police training to lay greater emphasis on such values (including, for example, pilot projects wherein social workers and psychologists are stationed in police Departments); and the establishment of the 'Neighbourhood Policeman' as a mediator between the local police Department and the community (as stipulated by Presidential Decree 254/2003). Whilst the continuous efforts to modernise the police do appear to have effected some change in police attitudes and middle-class feelings about the police, and although the impact of these reforms have yet to be systematically evaluated (whether by the state or by the academic community), given the broader characteristics of security discourse in the country such changes do not appear to have been consolidated.

The Latent Securitarian Turn

The most interesting aspect of the period of the 1990s is that behind the discourse of community policing, coercive policing had continued to expand. The securitarian turn was fuelled both by the above-mentioned policies, as well as the domestic and international concerns about terrorism, organised crime, migration, and international police co-operation (see further the contributions to this collection by Mitsilegas, Samatas, and Xenakis). Typical examples of the intensification of coercive policing were 'hot-spot' controls and arrests targeting marginalised groups (from prostitutes and homosexuals, to those suspected of being anarchists, to immigrants and Roma (Greek Ombudsman, 2004: 78; 2008)). At the institutional level, the securitarian turn in policing was identifiable by changes to the leadership of the police concerning the re-institution of Police Headquarters, and by the influence this subsequently had on police reforms.

Prominent factors motivating the securitarian turn of crime policy since the 2000s have been the issues of terrorism in Greece (see Bossis, 2003; also Xenakis, this collection) and the security demands related to the 2004 Olympic Games in Athens (Panousis, 2007), both of which coincided with the re-establishment of the Hellenic Police Headquarters. In reinstituting the Headquarters, a dimension of police administration in Greece that had been related to the dictatorship was thereby removed, and a new effort to centralise crime-control policies and the organisation of the police was launched. Whilst there may be no direct connection between the re-establishment of the Headquarters and the securitarian turn of crime policies, and although the re-election of New Democracy to government in 2004 also played its part, it is evident that the securitarian turn occurred after the Headquarters were reformed.

The primary reforms introduced by the securitarian turn were the administrative centralisation of the police, the proliferation of operational units designed to target particular social groups, and the informal institutionalisation of discretional abusive policing against vulnerable sections of society (and immigrants especially). The aftermath of the re-institution of the Police Headquarters soon saw the growth of new Directorates (according to Presidential Decree 1/2001), rationalised by international and domestic developments, including urban expansion. It also saw the proliferation of Security Police Departments specialising in illegal immigration control ('ISPD'), and the restructuring of those focused upon organised crime. In 2004, in the regional area of Attica alone, 96 Security Police Departments were newly established, and there has been further growth since then (implying a return to the pre-1998 institutional regime of the police). Security Police Departments, responsible for countering organised crime and including undercover policing actions, became centralised structures, accountable only to the corresponding Police Directorate (according to Presidential Decrees 2/2004 and 48/2006). Undercover policing efforts were reinforced due to concerns about rising crime rates (and particularly concerns about organised crime), and were further enhanced by the upgraded administrative status of the Security Police Departments (a consequence also of the reforms of the mid-1990s).

Meanwhile, the proliferation of special squads targeting 'special' areas and crimes built upon that of the 1990s, when the SCPD, BGPS, and SGS units had been founded. In 2006, the BGPS saw its name and remit expanded to encompass illegal immigration control, its powers now extending to the investigation and arrest of those involved (according to Presidential Decree 189/2006). The power of the SGS was also broadened to incorporate regular policing duties (in line with Law 2838/2000). Additionally, eleven raid units named 'Criminality Prevention and Repression Squads' (CPRS) were established in Athens and Thessaloniki to intervene in 'intensive problem' areas, such as Roma settlements and immigrant dwellings. In countering common criminality, groups such as the SCPD used methods associated more with anti-terrorism policing, and its policing efforts appeared focused more on marginalised groups rather on serious crime itself. The institution of these units should be understood in the context of the growth in marginalised urban populations and their subjection to differentiated control (Vidali, 2007a).

Problem-oriented Policing and beyond

The groundwork for the securitarian turn described above (on securitisation more generally, see Loader, 2002) appears to have been set in place by a number of institutional changes to the police as well as wider developments in the political arena. The intensification of pressure to address the challenge posed by domestic terrorism (see further Bossis, 2003), in addition to new security demands imposed by the responsibility of hosting the 2004 Olympic Games, was claimed to be the official motivation behind the shift in Greek crime control policy (Panousis, 2007). The shift was officially proclaimed shortly after the re-establishment of the Headquarters of the Hellenic Police, an institutional change which would empower the police in shaping crime-control policies. Subsequently, the police saw further administrative centralisation, the proliferation of squads targeting particular areas and crimes, and the informal institutionalisation of discretional abusive power against vulnerable subjects (particularly migrants). In 2004, the newly-elected New Democracy government announced its intention to institute 'problem-oriented policing' (Ministry of Interior,

22 January 2008). Police forces were 'removed' from the streets and were refocused upon urban nuclei of disorder with militaristic interventions and raids (see, e.g., *Eleftherotypia*, 25 May 2007). This policy halted any attempt to redress the military culture of the police and reinforced the increasingly problematic character of the discretionary power of the police.

Evaluating the Reforms

None of the above-mentioned reforms brought about their expected results. The (even liberal) transplantation of policies from abroad without any amendment (Vidali, 2007a: 86), and the influence of conservative cultures associated more with a military style of policing (Papakonstantis, 2003: 238), played a critical role in this outcome. It should also be mentioned that liberalisation and soft policing, which were adopted by the end of the 1990s, reflected only part of police work; namely, that of policing the streets and neighbourhoods. Despite the rhetoric, double-talk characterised 'community policing' in the case of Greece. More generally, military-style policing (on which see further Lea and Young, 1993: 188) of marginalised groups remained a constant. The historical processes determining the occupational culture of the Greek police inhibited the integration of any liberal reformist ideas amongst police personnel. By the end of 1990s, the rise of racist attitudes in Greece only fuelled the expansion of, and demand for, repressive policing against marginalised groups and immigrants (see Antonopoulos, 2006), and consolidated racist attitudes amongst the police. The lack of concrete, long-term crime policy-planning, its dependence on short-term politics, its limitation to temporary transplantations of EU directives, and its coincidence with a sequence of revelations of crimes of the powerful (including state crimes), provoked a general atmosphere of dissatisfaction with the police that was reflected in fear of crime and demands for greater security. The use of policing to confront social problems in turn reinforced the militaristic and abusive attitudes and actions of the police.

Discretion, Deviance, Culture

The discretionary powers of the police determine its effectiveness, legality, culture (even if not uniformly), and relations with citizens (Ianni-Reuss and Ianni, 1983/2005; Paoline, 2004; McLaughlin, 2001; Manning, 1975/2008). Abuse of discretionary power results in human rights violations such as illegal detention (Greek Ombudsman, 2004: 25). Abuses and illegal police actions are shaped by the types of duties routinely carried out by the police; namely, a range of practices including controls, stop-and-search operations, and arrests, largely targeting marginalised groups (ibid.: 28). In Greece, arbitrary police practices and racist attitudes are 'normalised' by reference to the discretionary power of the police, as confirmed by various reports of the Greek Ombudsman (ibid., 2007) and other bodies such as Amnesty International (2009), and highlighted by a number of incidents that received public attention in recent years.

Cases of Abuse

One such example involved 28 Pakistanis denouncing their abduction shortly after the London bombings by persons who claimed to be police officers (see further www.in.gr, 11 May 2006; also Samatas, this collection). Another case concerned video recordings made by Greek policemen in 2005 and 2006, subsequently posted on the internet (in February 2007), of seven police officers from the Omonia Police Department in Athens abusing two Albanian youths in custody following their arrest for drug dealing, including ordering them to repeatedly hit each other (Magistrate's Court Decision 326/2008). A further case related to footage taken by a television reporter, which showed the public grievous beating of a Cypriot student in Thessaloniki by a group of CRPS officers with covered faces on 17 November 2006. The injuries to the student were initially attributed by the Ministry of Public Order to the individual falling onto a public plant box, but the case soon became a public scandal once the serious injuries of the student and the unprovoked nature of the attack were revealed (*Eleftherotypia*, 17 December 2008).

In each of these three cases, the conclusion to police disciplinary hearings and decisions by the Courts was lenient. Reflecting what Cohen (2001: 201) terms a 'state of denial' as to the institutional nature of police abuse of power – a reaction that appears to be typical of police organisations (see further Skolnick and Fyfe, 1993/2005) –, responsibility was attributed to the individual deviance of police officers. It thus comes as no surprise that abusive policing has become a more widespread and normalised form of policing and riot control, its use being extended to actions against middle-class demonstrators and activists. Most notably, on 6 December 2008, unsuspecting 15-year-old student Alexandros Grigoropoulos was shot fatally by a Special Guard, an incident that sparked over a month of unprecedented demonstrations and rioting across Greece, events themselves marked by violence against civilians and police officers alike, as well as property damage estimated at 1 billion Euros (US State Department, 2009). With regard to police actions during these protests, there were many reports of ill-treatment, arbitrary arrests, prosecutions, and detentions (including of adolescents), and denial of prompt legal assistance (see further Amnesty International, 2009). Two years later, in October 2010, the officer who shot Grigoropoulos was sentenced to life imprisonment (whilst his patrol partner received ten years of imprisonment for complicity).

Corruption

The nature of police work places officers in situations where they are vulnerable to being seduced by corruption (see Reiner, 1995; Kleining, 1996). Police corruption in Greece has been identified as a complex phenomenon related both to the structure and functions of state institutions as such, but also associated with broader cultural attitudes and practices (see Lambropoulou, 2006), for example the impunity of those involved in corruption. The extensiveness of police corruption is hinted at by the results of a survey of police officers (POASY, 2006), where a remarkable 17.7 percent said they believed that cases of corruption go unreported, whilst 68.6 percent stated that they themselves only reported some cases of corruption. Reasons cited for tolerance of corruption related to lack of trust in institutional structures (38.3 percent), solidarity amongst colleagues (39.9 percent), fear of negative personal repercussions and involvement (44.9 percent), indifference (17.4 percent), and lack of documented evidence (2.9 percent). A somewhat different picture is painted in official reports, which focus on personal responsibility. In 2006, 79 police officers were prosecuted for crimes largely related to the violation of duties and falsifying documentation, but also to drugs trafficking. Police criminality is described as personal, occasional, and not organised, motivated by rational choice and opportunity (Internal Affairs Directorate, 2007). Despite this, however, police have been reported to have collaborative relations with blackmailers, organised crime figures, and illegal prostitution networks (see, e.g., *To Vima*, 24 September 2006).

Police Culture

Occupational culture here refers to the effect of processes of group socialisation within the police; general values and work and institutional routines (McLaughlin, 2001). The occupational culture of the Hellenic Police is not politically neutral. Abuses of power, for example, are linked to a discriminatory and conservative subculture, itself a residue from the militarised antecedents of the force. Despite limited research into the relationship between police culture, political ideology, and abuse of power, the relationship between these three factors has been apparent in cases of police abuse that have come to light after riots and stop-and-search operations, as well as in cases such as that of Grigoropoulos. In the latter case, for example, the alleged dangerousness and deviance of the victim – argued to be 'proved' by his bourgeois background, his school performance, and preferred leisure activities – were cited by the lawyer defending the police officer on trial (*Ta Nea*, 11 December 2008). The recent trends of scapegoating and police abuse of power in Greece suggest that militaristic policing assumes the additional dimension of a vendetta against the usual targets (from, for example, rioters, to hooligans, to immigrants) that are fuelled by notions of honour and reputation amongst the police, rather than by concerns for law enforcement. Not only is the conservatism of the force evident from their broadly held conviction that diversity undermines police effectiveness and their opposition to the de-militarisation of the police (POASY, 2004), it is also manifested in the impunity and tolerance accorded to discretionary abuses committed by police officers. Facing cases of abuse by police officers, police authorities have refused to recognise the occurrence of abuses or impose significant or any disciplinary penalties in such cases, and the Greek courts have shown overwhelming reluctance to apply the Greek penal provisions relating to torture. Of course, culture and attitudes amongst the police are not homogenous. Progressive police perspectives can be found in the reactions of their trade unions to cases of police violence that have come to light in recent years (*Eleftherotypia*, 11 May 2007). Moreover, in proposals for reform, and in denunciations of abuse cases and the authoritarian turn in police discipline and rules of service, police trade unions have underlined the differences of culture across the force.

Police Discipline and Institutional Control

Institutional measures to counter police deviance and disciplinary violations are governed by the Disciplinary Law for Police Personnel (Presidential Decree 120/2008). The meaning of police discipline provided therein, in conformity with constitutional and other legal provisions, is that officers execute obediently, promptly, and without objections, the orders of superiors, even if the order is suspected to be illegal by the subordinate officer (who, in such cases, is allowed to register their opposition before obeying nonetheless; ibid.). Disciplinary penalties range from dismissal from the corps, 2–6 months temporary discharge from the corps, 15 days-4 months suspension, to a pecuniary penalty of up to three basic monthly wages, and reprimand.

Disciplinary authority extend to penal violations committed by police officers, notwithstanding the fact that the disciplinary process is independent and autonomous from any trial. As a prerequisite for cases to go to inquest of trial, allegations against police officers are required to be submitted in written form, and to be signed by the individual reporting the case. Where the final verdict of a penal case points to evidence of acts constituting disciplinary offences, a disciplinary process will be launched since differences between penal and disciplinary sentences necessitate a separate disciplinary procedure. Police involvement in common crimes is punished relatively severely: felonies and misdemeanours, and crimes related to violation of specific laws concerning cattle theft, drugs, aliens, antiquities, smuggling, and fire arms (punishable with penalties of imprisonment of over one year in duration), provoke the disciplinary penalty of dismissal from service.

Aside from the general structure of disciplinary controls, the Internal Affairs Directorate (IAD) also exerts control over specific forms of police criminality (Law 2713/1999). The latter, a product of the managerial turn in police administration (see Papanicolaou, 2006: 82), has a remit over crimes committed by police personnel relating to fraud, corruption, forgery, drugs, aliens, gambling, guns, antiquities, and smuggling, and as an organisation is obliged to present annual reports to the competent Parliamentary Commission. Since 2003, moreover, the authority of the IAD has extended to the entire personnel of the public sector. Additionally, the Greek Ombudsman, as a body unrelated to that of the police, is also involved in police discipline since it gathers information and allegations by citizens concerning violations committed by any public servant, including the police.

In conclusion, whereas the institutional and legal framework governing police discipline should be considered sufficient, such provisions are unable to prevent abuses on the part of police officers. In theory, it is the educational system of the police that should be the primary means by which abuses by the police are prevented.

Becoming a Police Officer

Admission to the corps

Law 2226/1994 sought to rationalise the recruitment process for police personnel, freeing it from political bias (Stergioulis, 2001) and raising the expected educational entry level of new recruits, and to upgrade the quality of personnel. According to that Law, extra-institutional 'exceptional' recruitment procedures were abolished (see further Rigakos and Papanicolaou, 2003). Nevertheless, this general rule was relaxed in order to staff two of the new corps, the BGPS and SGS, for which enrolment has followed a different admissions process. Employees of the latter – who have tended to be low-skilled and many of which are former members of the Special Forces of the Greek military – receive a shorter training of 4 to 6 months and, as a result, were initially graded as temporary personnel (i.e., with five-year contracts). More recently, however, BGPS and SGS personnel have seen their status equalised with that of the regular police force and their duties extend correspondingly, a move that has been accompanied by a rise in cases of violent or risky policing. SGS personnel are exclusively allowed to be 'rented' to other public and private bodies (such as the metro consortium, banks, and government ministries), associated operational costs being carried by the private hirer in such circumstances. This system has been the subject of considerable criticism by individual police and police unions.

Education for Regular Personnel

Education for regular police personnel is led by the Hellenic Police Academy, and divided between a School for Officers, which offers a four-year programme that is the equivalent of a university degree, and a School for Policemen, which offers a more basic two-year programme for personnel that will become non-commissioned officers. For reasons of space, a full critique of the police educational system will not be set out here, but it is important to note that some of its dysfunctions may be attributed to the quality of the civilian training staff, given that doctoral or masters level qualifications are not prerequisite to teaching at the Academy (even if they are considered an asset; see further Presidential Decree 113/2008). In general, the professional standards of the civilian personnel at the Academy do not meet those of higher education. The principal emphasis of teaching is the generation of technical, and mainly practical, knowledge about law and order, whilst the teaching of theory is underemphasised. Furthermore, in many cases the programme of study is prematurely terminated when specific security demands require additional personnel. The inadequacy of the system is confirmed by the results of surveys commissioned by Panhellenic Federation of Police Employees (POASY) published in 2004 and 2006: a majority of police personnel believe that neither their primary police education (60.6 percent), nor subsequent seminars and training (58.8 percent) helped them to effectively carry out their duties (POASY, 2004, 2006).

A Profile of the Police

The number of police personnel in Greece is not easy to calculate. There are no reliable published official data concerning the number of police employees, so figures suggested by official and media sources cannot be verified. Notwithstanding this caveat, from official data published on the web (on www.astynomia.gr), it appears that there are 71,500 police employees in Greece, i.e., one police officer per 156.6 citizens. The majority of police personnel are male, non-commissioned officers, while women are estimated to comprise 13 percent of total police personnel, constituting 5,500 of the police workforce. According to recent research based on trade union data (POASY, 2006), the gender ratio is even less balanced; 89.2 percent are male, and 10.8 percent female. Discrimination against the employment of women in the police force was only overturned relatively recently by Presidential Decree 90/2003, which nevertheless continued to allow for the exclusion of women from the force on certain grounds, including gynaecological disorders. The prospect of hiring immigrant personnel has been very controversial, and discrimination has been reported against female, homosexual, disabled, and younger employees. Despite official support to diversity agendas, these have proved to be a very low priority for human resource managers. Indeed, traditional stereotypes of gender and social health – common to broader Greek society – are prevalent and continue to be reproduced amongst the force (see further POASY, 2004).

Employment Satisfaction

Police officers in Greece report being sufficiently satisfied by their profession, and satisfaction is recorded to be highest amongst female and older personnel. Those that claim to be more satisfied also tend to consider the behaviour of the police toward citizens as unproblematic. Another interesting finding is that those who have had longer periods of police service tend to consider favourably the behaviour of their colleagues towards citizens (55.1 percent), while 64.6 percent of the youngest policemen who have been in service less than 10 years, and the 59.9 percent of those who have 10 to 20 years experience of serving in the police, affirm that they are not satisfied by their colleagues' behaviour. A large proportion of police personnel do not appear to feel fulfilled with the main tasks involved in police duties. Only the 38 percent of those questioned agreed that they were satisfied by the main tasks of their position. Reasons cited for job dissatisfaction were insufficient levels of information concerning principal police duties (23 percent), levels of bureaucracy (80.4 percent), and the limited powers legally accorded to police officers for the effective execution of their work (40 percent). Of those surveyed, 24.8 percent claimed that they had received orders whose application would result in the unfair treatment of citizens. Over 60 percent affirmed that they work intensively, 40 percent stating that they work more hours than those allocated and consequently cannot fulfill their duties satisfactorily. Last but not least, 67.1 percent of those questioned considered the system of professional evaluation and hierarchical promotion to be unfair and to be influenced by extra-institutional variables (POASY, 2004, 2006).

Conclusion

Amongst all the reforms and trends explored in this chapter, a particular problem has been evident throughout; namely, the militarised model of policing. Indeed, militarised policing is an increasingly prevalent means of controlling the effects of social changes and one that seems destined to become entrenched as rates of social exclusion rise. This is particularly so for a country such as Greece that has had relatively little historical experience of the civilian model of policing. Policies of crime control will probably continue to be determined by extra-institutional forces, rather than by formal organisational and legal frameworks. To understand those extra-institutional forces we need to turn to the power of the market and its crises.

References

Alexiadis, S. (2003) *Criminalistics* [in Greek]. Thessaloniki: Sakkoulas.

Alivisatos, N. (1983) *Political Institutions in Crisis, 1922–1974: Aspects of the Greek Experience* [in Greek]. Athens: Themelio.

Amnesty International (2005) *Out of the Spotlight: The Rights of Foreigners and Minorities are Still a Grey Area*, Report, AI Index: EUR 25/016/2005. London: Amnesty International.

Amnesty International (2009) *Greece: Alleged Abuses in the Policing of Demonstrations*, Report, AI Index EUR25/001/2009. London: Amnesty International.

Amnesty International and International Helsinki Federation (2002) *Greece: In the Shadow of Impunity – Ill-treatment and the Misuse of Firearms*, Report, AI Index: EUR 25/022/2002. London: Amnesty International.

Antoniou, K. (1964) *History of the Greek Royal Gendarmerie, 1833–1967* [in Greek]. Athens: G. Ladias & Co.

Antonopoulos, G.A. (2006) 'Greece: Policing Racist Violence in the "Fenceless Vineyard"', *Race & Class* 48: 92–100.

Astynomia Poleon Headquarters (1962) *Astynomia Poleon: 40 Years* [in Greek]. Athens: Astynomia Poleon.

Avdela, E. (2002) *For Reasons of Honour* [in Greek]. Athens: Nefeli.

Bayley, D.H. (1994) *Police for the Future*. New York and Oxford: Oxford University Press.

Bittner, E. (1990/2005) 'Florence Nightingale in Pursuit of Willie Sutton: A Theory of the Police', in T. Newburn (ed.) *Policing: Key Readings*, pp. 150–172. Cullompton: Willan.

Bossis, M. (2003) 'The Mysteries of Terrorism and Political Violence in Greece', in M. Van Leeuwen (ed.) *Confronting Terrorism: European Experiences, Threat Perceptions and Policies*, pp. 129–146. Hague: Kluwer Law International.

Chalaris, G. (2005) 'Greece in the Frame of Globalisation', in G. Agioritis (ed.) *Economic Changes and Social Contradictions in Greece* [in Greek], pp. 27–58. Athens: Typothito Dardanos.

Charalambis, D. (1985) *Armed Forces and Political Power: The Structure of Power in Post-Civil War Greece* [in Greek]. Athens: Exantas.

Charalambis, D. (1989) *Clientelist Relationships and Populism: The Extra-Institutional Consensus to the Greek Political System* [in Greek]. Athens: Exantas.

Charitos-Fatouros, M. (2003) *The Torturer as an Instrument of State Power* [in Greek]. Athens: Ellinika Grammata.

Chatziiosif, C. (2003) 'Parliament and Dictatorship', in C. Chatiziiosif (ed.) *History of 20th-century Greece* [in Greek], pp. 37–123. Athens: Vivliorama.

Cohen, S. (1993/2000) 'Human Rights and Crimes of the State: The Culture of Denial', in J. Muncie, E. McLaughlin and M. Langan (eds) *Criminological Perspectives: A Reader*, pp. 489–507. London: Sage.

Cohen, S. (2001) *States of Denial: Knowing about Atrocities and Suffering*. Cambridge: Polity.

Council of Europe (2008) *Report to the Government of Greece*, CPT/Inf. 3. Strasbourg: Council of Europe. Available online at: http: www.cpt.coe.int/documents/ grc/2008–03-inf-eng.pdf

Crawford, A. (1997) *The Local Governance of Crime*. Oxford: Clarendon Press.

Dahrendorf, R. (1985) *Law and Order*. London: Stevens & Sons.

Emsley, C. (1999) *Gendarmes and the State in Nineteenth-Century Europe*. Oxford: Oxford University Press.

Emsley, C. (1991) 'Police Forces and Public Order in England and France during the Interwar Years', in C. Emsley and B. Weinberger (eds) *Politics, Professionalism and Public Order, 1850–1940*, pp. 159–186. New York and London: Greenwood Press.

Fatouros, A. (1984) 'The Construction of an Official Interference Network: USA in Greece, 1947–1948', in *Greece during 1940–1950: A Nation in Crisis* [in Greek]. Athens: Themelio.

Ferret, J. (2004) 'The State, Policing, and "Old Continental Europe": Managing the Local/National Divide', *Policing and Society* 14: 49–65.

Gardikas, K. (1964) *Criminology: The Criminal Police System* [in Greek]. Athens: Tzaka.

Giannitsiotis, J. (2006) *Piraeus' Social History: The Constitution of the Bourgeoisie Class, 1860–1910* [in Greek]. Athens: Nefeli.

Goldblatt, P. and C. Lewis (eds) (1998) *Reducing Offending: An Assessment of Research Evidence on Ways of Dealing with Offending Behaviour*, Research Study No. 187. London: HMSO.

Greek Ombudsman (2004) *Disciplinary-Administrative Charges, Investigations against Police Officers*, Special Report, July 2004 [in Greek]. Athens: Greek Ombudsman.

Greek Ombudsman (2008) *Annual Report 2007* [in Greek]. Athens: Greek Ombudsman.

Greek Royal Gendarmerie Headquarters (1967) *Gendarmerie Report, 1965–1966*. Athens: Greek Royal Gendarmerie.

Ianni-Reuss, E. and F.A.J. Ianni (1983/2005) 'Street Cops and Management Cops: The Two Cultures of Policing', in T. Newburn (ed.) *Policing: Key Readings*, pp. 297–314. Cullompton: Willan.

Kampanakis, J. (2003) 'Profession: Policeman' [in Greek], *Poiniki Dikaiosyni* 12: 1370–1372.

Kleining, J. (1996) *The Ethics of Policing*. New York: Cambridge University Press.

Klockars, C.B. (1988/2005) 'The Rhetoric of Community Policing', in T. Newburn (ed.) *Policing: Key Readings*, pp. 442–495. Cullompton: Willan.

Koliopoulos, I. (1996) *Brigandage in Greece* [in Greek]. Thessaloniki: Paratiritis.

Korovesis, P. (1970) *The Method: A Personal Account of the Tortures in Greece*. London: Allison & Busby.

Kostopoulos, T. (2005) *The Self-Censored Memory: Security Battalions and Post-War National Beliefs* [in Greek]. Athens: Filistor.

Lambropoulou, E. (2005) 'Crime, Criminal Justice and Criminology in Greece', *European Journal of Criminology* 2: 211–247.

Lambropoulou, E. (2006) 'Crime and Culture: Crime as a Cultural Problem – Greek Report'. Available online at: http://www.uni-konstanz.de/crimeandculture/docs/

Lazos, G. (2002) *Prostitution and Transnational Trafficking in Modern Greece, Vol. 1: The Prostitute* [in Greek]. Athens: Kastaniotis.

Lentakis, A. (2000) *Extra-Governmental Groups and the April 21st Group* [in Greek]. Athens: Proskinio.

Loader, I. (2002) 'Policing, Securitisation and Democratisation in Europe', *Criminal Justice* 2: 125–153.

Manning, P. (1978/2005) 'The Police: Mandate, Strategies and Appearances', in T. Newburn (ed.) *Policing: Key Readings*, pp. 191–215. Cullompton: Willan.

Margaritis, G. (2001) *History of the Greek Civil War, 1946–1949* [in Greek]. Athens: Vivliorama.

Mazower, M. (1997) 'Policing the Anti-Communist State in Greece', in M. Mazower (ed.) *The Policing of Politics in the Twentieth Century*, pp. 129–150. Oxford: Berghahn Books.

McLaughlin, E. (2001) 'Key Issues in Policework', in E. McLaughlin and J. Muncie (eds) *Controlling Crime*, pp. 53–100. London: Sage.

Melossi, D. (1990) *The State of Social Control*. Cambridge: Polity.

Meynaud, J. (2002) *Political Powers in Greece, 1946–1965* [in Greek]. Athens: Savalas.

Ministry of Interior (22 January 2008) 'Presentation points of the Minister of Interior Prokopis Pavlopoulos to the Govermental Committee concerning the three-year programme on political public order and security' [Press release in Greek]. Available online at: www.ypesdt.gr/index.php?option=0z0_content&lang=& perform=view&id=232&Itemid=279ts

Newburn, T. (2007) *Criminology*. Collumpton: Willan.

Newburn, T. and R. Reiner (2007) 'Policing and the Police', in M. Maguire, R. Morgan and R. Reiner (eds) *The Oxford Handbook of Criminology*, pp. 910–952. Oxford: Oxford University Press.

Pallida, S. (2000) *Polizia Postmoderna: Etnografia del Nuovo Controllo Sociale*. Milano: Feltrinelli, Interzone.

Panousis, G. (1999) 'Police Education and their Anti-Criminal/Social Mission', in N. Courakis (ed.) *Anti-crime Policy II* [in Greek], pp. 357–372. Athens-Komotini: Ant. N. Sakkoulas Publishers.

Panousis, G. (2007) *Criminogenic and Criminoproductive Risks* [in Greek]. Athens: Nomiki Vivliothiki.

Panousis, G. and S. Vidali (eds) (2001) *Texts on the Police and Policing* [in Greek]. Athens-Komotini: Ant. N. Publishers.

Paoline, E.A. (2004) 'Shedding Light on Police Culture: An Examination of Officers' Occupational Attitudes', *Police Quarterly* 7: 205–236.

Papadopoulos, S. (1977) 'The Crimean War and Hellenism' [in Greek], *History of Hellenic Nation* 13: 143–168.

Papakonstantis (2003) *Hellenic Police: Organisation, Policy, Ideology* [in Greek]. Athens: Nomiki Vivliothiki.

Papanicolaou, G. (2006) 'Greece', in T. Jones and T. Newburn (eds) *Plural Policing*, pp. 77–97. London and New York: Routledge.

Papatheodorou, T. (2005) *Public Security and Anti-crime Policy: A Comparative Approach* [in Greek]. Athens: Nomiki Vivliothiki.

Petmezas, S. (2003) 'Rural Economy', in C. Chatziiosif (ed.) *History of 20th-century Greece* [in Greek], pp. 189–249. Athens: Vivliorama.

Petridis, P. (1995) *The Lambrakis Murder: Unedited Documents* [in Greek]. Athens: Proskinio.

Petropoulos, G. (1997) *Politics and Creation of the State in the Kingdom of Greece, 1833–1843* [in Greek]. Athens: National Bank Foundation.

Panhellenic Federation of Police Employees (POASY) (2004) *Research on Diversity in the Hellenic Police* [in Greek]. Available online at: http://www.poasy.gr/arthra-melet/ereunapolimorfias.pdf

POASY (2006) Hellenic Police: Personnel: Satisfaction Measurement [in Greek]. Available online at http://www.inamete.gr/UserPages/index.aspx

Reiner, R. (1995) 'Policing and the Police', in M. Maguire, R. Morgan and R. Reiner (eds) *The Oxford Handbook of Criminology*, pp. 705–772. Oxford: Oxford University Press.

Rigakos, G.S. and G. Papanicolaou (2003) 'The Political Economy of Greek Policing: Between Neo-Liberalism and the Sovereign State', *Policing and Society* 13: 271–304.

Samatas, M. (2004) *Surveillance in Greece: From Anticommunist to Consumer Surveillance*. New York: Pella.

Senior, H. (1997) *Constabulary: The Rise of Police Institutions in Britain, the Commonwealth and the United States*. Toronto and Oxford: Dundurn Press.

Skolnick, J.H. and D.H. Baley (1986) *The New Blue Line: Police Innovation in Six American Cities*. New York: The Free Press.

Skolnick, J. and J. Fyfe (1993/2005) 'The Beating of Rodney King', in T. Newburn (ed.) *Policing: Key Readings*, pp. 568–579. Cullompton: Willan.

Spinellis, C.D. (1972) 'Survey on Fluctuating Criminality in Greece between 1960 and 1970' [in Greek], *Poinika Chronika*, 11: 657–676.

Stergioulis, E. (2001) *The Greek Police during the Post-Dictatorship Era, 1975–1995* [in Greek]. Athens: Nomiki Vivliothiki.

Tachos, A. (1990) *Public Order Law* [in Greek]. Thessaloniki: Sakkoulas.

Taylor, I. (1999) *Crime in Context: A Critical Criminology of Market Societies*. Cambridge: Polity.

Tsoukalas, K. (1984) 'The Civil-war Ideological Influence', in *Greece during 1940–1950: A Nation in Crisis*, pp. 561–594. [in Greek]. Athens: Themelio.

US State Department (2009) *Country Report on Human Rights Practices: Greece.* Available online at: http://www.state.gov/g/drl/rls/hrrpt/

Vergopoulos, K. (1984) 'The Formation of the New Bourgeoisie Class', in *Greece during 1940–1950: A Nation in Crisis*, pp. 529–560 [in Greek]. Athens: Themelio.

Vidali, S. (2007a) *Crime Control and State Police: Ruptures and Continuities in Crime Policy, Volumes I and II* [in Greek]. Athens-Komotini: Ant. N. Sakkoulas Publishers.

Vidali, S. (2007b) 'Criminology: Under Re-determination or Extinction?', in S. Georgoulas (ed.) *Criminology in Greece Today: A Volume in Honour of Stergios Alexiadis* [in Greek], pp. 79–94. Athens: KΨM.

Wacquant, L. (2000) *Parola d'Ordine, Toleranza Zero: La Trasformazione dello Stato Penale nella Sociata Liberale.* Milan: Feltrinelli, Interzone.

Zianikas, C. (1992) *The Invisible Side of the Police* [in Greek]. Athens: Gnosis.

ROB I. MAWBY

Commentary

The Greek Police in Context

As Sophie Vidali notes, criminology in Greece, although scarcely new-born, is barely into adolescence, and sociological analysis of the police is minimal. Equally, international scholars have paid scant attention to the question of policing in Greece, the honourable exception being Rigakos and Papanicolaou's (2003) review. Nevertheless, it is widely accepted that, while public police systems across the world share common characteristics, different *ideal types* can be distinguished. This chapter thus aims to assess the history and more recent development of the Greek police in a cross-national context.

Elsewhere I have argued that the public police can be distinguished in terms of its *legitimacy, structure,* and *function* (Mawby, 1990, 2008). Legitimacy implies that the police are granted special authority by those in power, whether this is an elite within the society, an occupying force, or the community as a whole. Structure implies that the police is organised, with some degree of specialisation and with a code of practice within which, for example, the extent to which the use of force is legitimate is specified. However, the extent of organisation or specialisation, and the types of force considered appropriate, will vary. Finally, function implies that the role of the police is concentrated on the maintenance of law and order and the prevention and detection of offences, but there might be considerable differences in the balance between these, and in the extent to which other duties are assigned to the police.

In comparing the police according to these three criteria, I have suggested a typology of police systems, distinguishing five *ideal types*: Anglo-

American police; Continental European police; colonial police; communist police; and Far-Eastern police. Clearly, there are vast parts of the world that are excluded from this typology, and often considerable differences between countries classified together. However, the typology provides a useful way of contextualising on a country-by-country basis and of identifying change. The following sections address the Greek police and its correspondence to the continental European model, both historically and since 1984.

The Continental Model and the Greek police prior to 1984

Discussions of an alleged Continental European policing system have a long history, and Fosdick's (1969) account of continental police at the beginning of the twentieth century is the first of many attempts to identify key characteristics of the police systems of continental Europe (see, for example, Bayley, 1975, 1979; Emsley, 1999). In terms of function, the role of the police in continental societies has traditionally tended to be wide-ranging, with a particular emphasis upon political control, termed 'high policing' in the French context, in addition to crime control. Following Chapman (1970), continental systems have also been associated with a range of administrative responsibilities, with relatively less emphasis on welfare or service functions. However, there is a marked difference between the French, Italian, and Spanish police, on the one hand, as classic examples of this *ideal type*, and their counterparts in countries such as the Netherlands or Scandinavia, on the other hand.

The need for strong policing might imply that continental police systems would also be characterised as centralised and paramilitary, but this was not always the case. For example, Iceland and Switzerland have, respectively, district and canton-based systems, and the Netherlands reorganised in 1993 into 25 regional forces (Interpol, 1992; Jones, 1995). Similarly, in Germany, most police are based in the counties (*Länders*). At the other extreme, a few countries, including Sweden and the Irish Republic, have one centralised, national force. What is more characteristic of the traditional continental model, though, is a structure whereby one centralised, militaristic force is counterbalanced by either a second or by a medley of local city forces. The French, Italian, and Spanish police may traditionally be identified most fully with the model: in each case the maintenance of at least two police forces allowing governments to ensure that no one institution achieved too much power. While the police in most continental countries carry firearms, it is also the case that, in many countries, there is at least one centralised force that evidences significantly greater militaristic qualities. In France, for example, the *Police Nationale* traditionally came under the Ministry of the Interior, whereas the *Gendarmerie* has been a military force under the Ministry of Defence, with a two-tier entry system, barrack accommodation, and impressive armaments. The *carabinieri* operated in much the same way in Italy, as did the *guardia civil* in Spain.

In the past, continental police systems were also distinguished in terms of their lack of public accountability, being directly responsible to the head of state. While this is less easily reconciled with the liberal democracies of postwar Europe, it is still the case that public accountability is more restricted in countries where the police are more centralised and militaristic. Even here, though, there are exceptions, with Sweden, for example, incorporating a local accountability mechanism within its centralised structure (Akermo, 1986).

An assessment of the Greek police as it developed after gaining independence from the Ottoman Empire, suggests that the system was steeped in the Continental European tradition. This was partly the result of external influence, partly the law-and-order problems prioritised by the new hegemony. The creation of the Greek State in 1830 owed much to the influence of the major European powers: Britain, France, and Russia. Prioritising the importance of Greece as the European boundary for Christianity, they saw a strong central government supported by a powerful paramilitary police as crucial to long term stability. The *Chorofylake*, formed in 1833 and initially headed by a Frenchman, was modelled on the French *gendarmerie* and charged with the task of supporting the army in protecting the fledgling state from insurrection. The Chorofylake remained the major policing agency for the next 150 years, adapting and being reformed to meet new challenges perceived to threaten public order. For example, while it continued to be used against the hordes of bandits that thrived outside the growing cities, it was also variously used to counter the emerging 'threat' of communism, to assert Greek sovereignty in newly 'acquired' territories, as a guard for prisoners of war, and as a operational section of the military (Rigakos and Papanicolaou, 2003).

However, the prioritisation of high policing meant that the Chorofy-lake seemed unwilling or unable to deal with conventional crime problems, most notably in the expanding cities. As a result, municipal police forces were created in the late nineteenth century. Initially under local control, largely untrained, funded by local taxation, and seen as the mayors' private armies, they failed to gain credibility and eventually came under the control of the army. They were disbanded in 1906, but then, in 1920, a national force was reconstituted to cover the main cities and the island of Corfu. Known as the *Astynomia Poleon*, with a British chief, the Astynomia Poleon aimed to be a civilian force, modelled on the London Metropolitan Police, with its own training system and a pay structure designed to present it as a more professional alternative to the Chorofylake.

To a certain extent, the establishment of separate forces, a gendarmerie to police rural Greece and a civilian urban equivalent, paralleled developments in many other European countries. The Chorofylake was clearly the more militaristic, being part of the army, but both forces were armed and explicitly conservative and anti-communist. The latter tendency was reinforced in the immediate postwar period as the police were positioned as a force against communism, both internally, where wartime communist resistance to Nazi control became marginalised as the postwar government made the communist party illegal, and externally where the communist National Liberation Front (EAM) drew support from Albania, Yugoslavia, and Bulgaria. The role of Britain and, especially, the US through the Truman Doctrine, was crucial in this respect. Both the Hellenic National Intelligence Service (KYP) and the LOK Special Forces were allegedly supported by the US. The latter was actively involved in the 1967 coup that led to the Military Dictatorship of the Colonels (1967–1974) and a further shift towards paramilitary policing with the creation of the Greek Military Police.

The creation of the civilian *Hellenic Police* in 1984 was thus built on the foundations of a centralised and militaristic police system, mandated to uphold right-wing governments, with little or no broader accountability. In reviewing and assessing the police in democratic Greece, the question arises, as in the former Warsaw Pact countries (Mawby, 1999a), as to how far dramatic changes to the political system have been reflected in changes to the police.

Changes to the Police:
The Example of the Hellenic Police since 1984

The example of Sweden is illustrative of the fluidity of change throughout Europe. Sweden moved towards a national structure in 1965, with the National Police Act 1984 providing the basis of the current centralised framework. Elsewhere, however, policing has become more localised in some respects, as illustrated through the extension of local police units in France (Journes, 1993; Kania, 1989), as well as in Italy and Spain. Other changes include the removal of a range of non-crime responsibilities from the police in France under the Mitterand presidency, and a similar reduction in broader responsibilities imposed on West Germany by the Allies (Fairchild, 1988). However, while it is tempting to see these as indicative of a convergence across Europe, there is little evidence of any consistency here. Rather, it appears that governments have used their autonomy to respond to national issues where they arise, or have been pressured in specific directions by powerful external influences such as by the US. For example, in Germany, the significance of the national police has faded as border patrols have become less necessary, and the Dutch system, never excessively centralised, was changed due to controversy over area variations in police funding (Wiebrens, 1990), and is now structured in a way that is more akin to England and Wales (Jones, 1995). In contrast, former Warsaw Pact countries have been supported by the US, for example through senior officer training programmes, in their concerns to uphold strong government and tackle crime and disorder problems prioritised by the US (Marenin, 1998).

There are, clearly, marked differences between the police from different nations of continental Europe. That said, pressures towards harmonisation have emanated from the European Community, supported by European and international law, and from Europol. The formation of CEPOL as a pan-European agency charged with harmonising police education and training has proved another structure to support policy transfer (Jaschke *et al.*, 2007). As the above examples illustrate, moreover, all police systems are subject to change. The modern police contrast starkly with the police of newly industrialising societies, and indeed the police today differ from their predecessors of the 1980s or 1990s. Some of these changes are brought on by internal pressures, others by external influences, and many by a mixture of both. External influences are particularly important in postmodern society. The 'global village' brings senior police managers and politicians closer to their contemporaries from other countries, and police innovations are more readily exported from one country to another than was the case even 30 years ago (Jones and Newburn, 2006).

Regime change at first sight appears to be an example of where internal changes might bring about police reform. However, even here external influences are important. Two examples well illustrate this. Firstly, the social, economic, and political changes that occurred in former Warsaw pact countries were themselves influenced by external factors, and the police models advocated by the newly emerging political parties at the time were defined by their understanding of what 'democratic policing' as practiced in the west actually involved (Mawby, 1999a). External influences then became more direct as western countries attempted to influence the form of police reform, through secondments and training (Marenin, 1998; Mawby, 1999a). Secondly, regime changes whereby former colonial societies achieved independence were dependent upon the occupying power acceding independence (albeit often reluctantly), and the subsequent creation of 'new police' for 'new democracies' involved colonial powers in directly advising the new governments. Somewhat ironically, for example, the British government established the Knowhow Foundation to fund democratic policing initiatives in its former colonies, which it had previously denied any form of 'democratic' or 'community' policing. Interestingly, the Knowhow Foundation was subsequently modified to provide finance for initiatives in partnership with post-communist countries.

However, the examples of post-communist and post-colonial countries illustrate not only change, but the power of impediments to change (Pino and Wiatrowski, 2006). In Russia and its former satellites, changes to the police have been less radical than many expected (Beck *et al.*, 2006; Galeotti, 2003; Mawby, 1999a; Pustintsev, 2000), at least partly due to the threats to social order posed by rapid social and economic change and the role of the reformed media in keeping crime and disorder at the top of the agenda. In post-colonial societies, similarly, conflict and disorder after independence sometimes led the new regimes to preserve the social control functions of the colonial police (Arnold, 1986). There is, consequently, no guarantee that regime change will result in significant change to the police system. It is important to bear this in mind in evaluating the Greek situation, where, as a crucial part of the move towards a new democracy, the socialist government of Andreas Papandreou, elected in 1981, prioritised a reformed police system.

The structure of the new police was encapsulated in the 1984 Act, whereby the Chorofylake and Astynomia Poleon were merged into the new Hellenic Police. Unlike in post-communist societies (Mawby, 1999a), though, there was no dramatic change to police personnel. However, as Rigakos and Papanicolaou (2003: 286) note, this new police system was intended to become a 'genuine social service'. But, as in former Warsaw Pact countries, with no unequivocal model as to what 'democratic policing' might entail, and with limitations to the extent to which radical change was practicable, the ensuing structure contained a hybrid mix of its forbearers, with innovations constrained by political and social expediency. Thus, while it was answerable to a new Ministry of Public Order, the Hellenic Police continued the centralised, militaristic tradition of the Chorofylake, the latter justified with reference to the universal mantra of a 'war on crime' and the only slightly less common assumption that the military model was a safeguard against corruption.[1] The importance of this militaristic blueprint is underlined by Rigakos and Papanicolaou (2003: 286) in a telling quote from the Ministry:

[1]   Interestingly, one also used in the USA (Mawby, 1999b).

Special organisation firstly means that police units are capable of undertaking operations against the criminal or those disrupting the public order, operations similar to those undertaken by the Army against the enemy. It also means that the services and the personnel are equipped with appropriate means (weapons, machinery, vehicles, communications) for the execution of these operations. Finally, it means that the police officers are trained and commanded with special hierarchical subordination and disciplinary rules, so that they are capable of fighting the daily battles, which constitute this continuous war.

In one sense, any justification for such a model appears weak. Thus Greece had, and continues to have, a relatively low crime rate. The International Crime Victim Survey (ICVS), which included Greece for the first time in 2003/2004, ranked the rate for most crimes as well below average, albeit levels of fear were higher than in most other countries (van Dijk *et al.*, 2008; see also Cheliotis and Xenakis, this collection). It is, rather, the political dimension that continues to define the need for strong policing. This incorporates at least three elements:

The Terrorist Threat: despite the communist party achieving legal status in 1974, concern over the threat from radical factions, especially of the left, has underpinned varying governments' psyches (Bossis 2003; Mazower 1997). One example is the operation of November 17 (N17), a Revolutionary Organisation established in 1975 that took its name from the day in 1973 when the Greek military junta sent tanks into Athens Polytechnic School to put down a student uprising, resulting in twenty student deaths. N17 has been held responsible for at least twenty-three assassinations and over 140 attacks, including the murder of a British defence attaché in Athens in 2000 (see further Xenakis, this collection; also Biliouri and Makarenko, 2002; Buhayer, 2002). The threat from terrorist groups achieved particular saliency during the Athens Olympics of 2004 (Philpott, 2004), but has been underpinned in the long term by Greece's uneasy relationship with Turkey (Rigakos and Papanicolaou, 2003).

Illegal Immigration: given its strategic position, the threat of illegal immigration, especially from Albania and Africa (and earlier from Romania and Bulgaria), with Greece an entry point into the EU, has been a dominant theme, as Vidali has noted herein.

Drugs: as with illegal immigration, Greece's adherence to Schengen meant that its position on the trading routes whereby illegal drugs were brought across Europe came under particular scrutiny, especially where drugs were brought into the country along with illegal immigrants.

These concerns chime significantly with those of Greece's external allies within Europe and the US. In the latter case, as in Japan and South Korea, it is clear that US support for community-oriented policing might be outweighed by foreign policy concerns, be these political or related to international crime (Aldous, 1997; Lee, 1990). Examples of UK support for increased security include: security at the 2004 Olympics, when an international committee, comprising, in addition to Greece, the United States, Britain, Australia, Israel, Spain, France, and Germany, was established to oversee the security effort (Philpott, 2004); also following the murder of the British attaché in 2000, the London Metropolitan Police Service's Specialist Operations Department became involved in training the Hellenic Police, including holding joint anti-terrorism exercises (Buhayer, 2002).

Reflecting such concerns, as Vidali and Rigakos and Papanicolaou (2003) note, a number of developments in the past fifteen years have been aimed at toughening security responses, including:

- The reformulation of the Special Suppressive Anti-Terrorist Unit (EKAM), originally introduced in 1978, when the Hellenic Police was created.
- The creation of the Border Guard Police Service (BGPS) in 1998 to tackle illegal immigration.
- The formation of the Special Guard Service (SGS) in 1999 to protect sensitive sights from terrorist attacks.
- The introduction of Criminality Prevention and Repression Squads (CPRS), with a particular focus on Romas and illegal immigrants.
- The creation of the Department of Police Special Controls (DPSC) in 1995 with Special Controls Squads (SCS), mainly active in areas of social deprivation.

There have, of course, been counter-trends. Thus, while Greece's police system continues to be dominated by the state sector (Papanicolaou, 2006), there has, as in France, been a growth in locally-based public sector services (Ferret, 2004; Rigakos and Papanicolaou, 2003). Nevertheless, the Greek police have maintained their tradition as a powerful, centralised, and militaristic organisation. It is against this backcloth that we need to contextualise the response to incidents such as the fatal shooting of Alexis Grigoropoulos in December 2008, that provoked riots both at the time and a year later,[2] and the confrontations on the streets of Greece's major cities following the financial crisis in the Spring of 2010. More broadly, it is illustrated in the feelings of the Greek population, expressed in the ICVS. The ICVS measures public perceptions of the police in three ways: whether or not victims report crimes to the police; if they do, how they rate the police response; and for all those surveyed, whether they feel the police do a good job in controlling crime in their area. On each criterion, the Greek police scored badly in 2003/2004. For example, only 28 percent of victims expressed satisfaction with police response to their crime, under half the survey's average, while only 57 percent of respondents thought the police did a good job in controlling crime locally, again well below the average of 70 percent (van Dijk *et al.*, 2008; see also Cheliotis and Xenakis, this collection).

Elsewhere I have compared police systems in terms of whether they are control-dominated or community-oriented (Mawby, 2010). By the latter, I mean a system where the main function of the police is to provide a public service that addresses the wider needs of the community. Maintaining order is important, but the emphasis is more on crime as symptomatic of community problems than as an affront to authority. This model assumes that the police is accorded considerable legitimacy by local communities, ideally by being organised and managed locally, with barriers between police and public minimal. It is this model, perhaps, to which the Papandreou government aspired when it talked of making the police a genuine social service. However, it seems to bear scant resemblance to the realities of policing in Greece in 2010.

2   See www.msnbc.msn.com/id/34298556/ns/world_news-europe, accessed on 2 May 2010.

Discussion

This brief review of the Greek police systems in a worldwide context illustrates the extent to which the Greek police system grew out of the Continental European ideal of a wide ranging, all-powerful, and centralised gendarmerie. However, while all police systems are subject to change, and policy transfer within the global village has become common, some modern police systems are more resistant to change than others. The examples of post-communist and post-colonial countries illustrate the difficulties associated with police reform, even after regime change. In the case of Greece, the new democratic government of 1981 created what it saw as a new democratic police. However, the pressures of the past, combined with internal and external pressures on social order, mean that changes have been less ambitious than might have been anticipated. As in former Warsaw Pact countries, strong policing in the face of perceived threats to social stability have taken precedence over any progress towards a community-oriented system.

Police systems are closely embedded in the wider structure and culture of their societies, and are susceptible to external influences. They are resistant to change, even when regimes change, and even a change of personnel does not guarantee that the system itself can be transformed. It is, therefore, scarcely surprising that the more modest agenda undertaken by the 1981 Greek government failed to radically change the police. Hopefully, this review of police in different societies aids our understanding of the nature of the Greek police in an international context and alerts us to the pressures against change.

References

Akermo, K.E. (1986) 'Organisational Changes and Remodelling of the Swedish police', *Canadian Police College Journal* 10(4): 245–63.

Aldous, C. (1997) *The Police in Occupation Japan: Control, Corruption and Resistance to Reform*. London: Routledge.

Anderson, D.M. and D. Killingray (eds) (1992) *Policing and Decolonisation*. Manchester: Manchester University Press.

Arnold, D. (1986) *Police Power and Colonial Rule: Madras 1859–1947*. Oxford: Oxford University Press.

Bayley, D.H. (1975) 'The Police and Political Developments in Europe', in C. Tilley (ed.) *The Formation of Nation States in Europe*, pp. 328–379. Princeton, NJ: Princeton University Press.

Bayley, D.H. (1979) 'Police Function, Structure and Control in Western Europe and North America: Comparative Historical Studies', in N. Morris and M. Tonry (eds) *Crime and Justice: An Annual Review of Research*, pp. 109–143. Chicago: University of Chicago Press.

Beck, A., Chistyakova, Y. and A. Robertson (2006) *Police Reform in Post-Soviet Societies*. Abingdon: Routledge.

Biliouri, D. and T. Makarenko (2002) 'Is this the End of 17N?', *Jane's Intelligence Review* 14(9): 6–10.

Bossis, M. (2003) 'The Mysteries of Terrorism and Political Violence in Greece', in M. Van Leeuven (ed.) *Confronting Terrorism: European Experiences, Threat Perceptions and Policies*, pp. 129–146. Hague, London, New York: Kluwer Law International.

Buhayer, C. (2002) 'UK's Role in Boosting Greek Counterterrorism Capabilities', *Jane's Intelligence Review* 14(9): 11–13.

Chapman, B. (1970) *Police State*. London: Pall Mall Press.

Emsley, C. (1999) *Gendarmes and the State in Nineteenth-Century Europe*. Oxford: Oxford University Press.

Fosdick, R.B. (1969) *European Police Systems*. Montelair, NJ: Patterson Smith.

Galeotti, M. (2003) 'Russian Police Reform: Centralisation, Paramilitarisation and Modernisation', *Crime & Justice International* 19(70): 17–19.

Interpol (1992) 'Netherlands', *Police* November: 20–21.

Jaschke, H-G., Bjorgo, T., del Barrio Romero, F., Kwanten, C., Mawby, R. and M. Pagon (2007) *Perspectives on Police Science in Europe*. Bramshill: CEPOL.

Jones, T. (1995) *Policing and Democracy in the Netherlands*. London: Policy Studies Institute.

Jones, T. and T. Newburn (2006) *Policy Transfer and Criminal Justice*. Maidenhead: Open University Press.

Journes, C. (1993) 'The Structure of the French Police System: Is the French Police a National Force?', *International Journal of the Sociology of Law* 21(3): 281–287.

Kania, R.R.E. (1989) 'The French Municipal Police Experiment', *Police Studies* 12: 125–131.

Lee, S.Y. (1990) 'Morning Calm, Rising Sun: National Character and Policing in South Korea and in Japan', *Police Studies* 13: 91–110.

Marenin, O. (1998) 'United States Police Assistance to Emerging Democracies', *Policing and Society* 8: 153–167.

Mawby, R.I. (1990) *Comparative Policing Issues: The British and American Experience in International Perspective.* London: Routledge.

Mawby, R.I. (1999a) 'The Changing Face of Policing in Central and Eastern Europe', *International Journal of Police Science and Management* 2(3): 199–216.

Mawby, R.I. (ed.) (1999b) *Policing Across the World: Issues for the Twenty-first Century.* London: UCL Press.

Mawby, R.I. (2008) 'Models of Policing', in T. Newburn (ed.) *Handbook of Policing*, 2nd edn., pp. 17–46. Cullompton: Willan.

Mawby, R.I. (2010) 'World Policing Models', in M. Natarajan (ed.) *Introduction to International Crime and Justice*, Revised edn., pp. 409–415. New York: McGraw-Hill.

Mazower, M. (1997) 'Policing the Anti-Communist State in Greece', in M. Mazower (ed.) *The Policing of Politics in the Twentieth Century*, pp. 129–150. Oxford: Berghahn Books.

Papanicolaou, G. (2006) 'Greece', in T. Jones and T. Newburn (eds) *Plural Policing*, pp. 77–97. London and New York: Routledge.

Philpott, D. (2004) 'Security Challenge: Athens Olympics 2004', *Homeland Defense Journal* 2(3): 13–20.

Pino, N. and M.D. Wiatrowski (2006) *Democratic Policing in Transitional and Developing Countries.* Aldershot: Ashgate.

Pustintsev, B. (2000) 'Police Reform in Russia: Obstacles and Opportunities', *Policing and Society* 10(1): 79–90.

Rigakos, G.S. and G. Papanicolaou (2003) 'The Political Economy of Greek Policing: Between Neo-Liberalism and the Sovereign State', *Policing and Society* 13(3): 271–304.

van Dijk, J., van Kesteren, J. and P. Smit (2008) *Criminal Victimisation in International Perspective: Key Findings from the 2004–2005 ICVS and EU ICS.* The Hague: Boom Legal Publishers.

Wiebrens, C. (1990) 'Police Personnel Reallocation: The Dutch Case', *Policing and Society* 1(1): 57–76.

ANGELIKA PITSELA

Youth Justice and Probation

Juvenile Delinquency in Greece

Until the 1980s, crime rates in Greece, including rates of juvenile delinquency, stood at a very low level. Since then, however, public debate and academic and practitioner conferences have turned attention to the prevention and treatment of juvenile delinquency, in response to rising levels of recorded juvenile delinquency (Courakis, 1999). According to police statistics, there has been a steady increase in the number of juvenile delinquents over recent decades. The situation has not in reality been much of a dramatic shift, since violent crimes (homicide, robbery, rape, and bodily injury) still constitute only a small part of crimes committed by juveniles. Indeed, most recorded offences in Greece are traffic offences: the 'crime problem' in Greece is mainly a problem of traffic offences (see also Cheliotis and Xenakis, this collection). When traffic offences are excluded from crime analysis, the most frequently recorded crimes committed by young persons are crimes against property. It is also worth mentioning that recent years have seen a significant increase in recorded cases of illegal entry into the country, as well as beggary, offences which are in turn related to police practices (Spinellis and Tsitsoura, 2006: 314). It would not be an exaggeration to state that juvenile delinquency in Greece almost exhaustively pertains to traffic law violations and crimes against property (and theft in particular). Drug-related offences and violent crimes are on the rise, but remain at low levels in comparison to other countries (see Neubacher *et al.*, 2004). The increase in the number of offences committed by juveniles and known to the police is not, however, reflected in court statistics (Spinellis and Tsitsoura, 2006: 313). The latter show a reduction in the number of minors brought to trial in recent years (see further Papageorgiou, this collection).

Against this background, the present chapter seeks to provide an overview of the treatment of juveniles under Greek law, recent amendments to the rights and processes affecting juvenile justice, and the persistent procedural and legal deficiencies of the juvenile justice system. As presented below, the system appears increasingly to be recognising the rights of minors in principle, but has to date lacked the infrastructure, training, and support to ensure that principles are systematically put into practice. In conclusion, therefore, this chapter draws attention to a number of key areas of the juvenile justice system and associated body of law in which reform is still sorely needed.

The Juvenile Courts System

Juvenile courts were first established in Greece in the 20th century. They were initially proscribed by Article 100 of the Greek Constitution of 1927, and, subsequently, the Code of Criminal Procedure of 1950 clearly stated that felonies committed by juveniles should not be tried by criminal courts composed of judges and jurors, but rather by Juvenile Courts of First Instance and Appeal, which the Code established. The Greek Criminal Code of 1950 entered into force on 1 January 1951, and from then until 2003, its provisions concerning young delinquents essentially remained in place (see further Chaidou, 2002). Act 3189/2003 on the 'Reform of Criminal Legislation on Minors and other provisions', which came into force on 21 October 2003, amended the 8th chapter of the General Part of Penal Code (PC). According to the explanatory report accompanying the Act, this reform was influenced by legislative developments in Greece and internationally (from the provisions of Article 21 paragraphs 1 and 3 of the Greek Constitution, to the United Nations Convention on the Rights of the Child, the European Convention on the Exercise of Children's Rights, and other non-binding, or 'soft law', international legal instruments such as the United Nations Standard Minimum Rules for the Administration of Juvenile Justice, and the Recommendation of the Committee of Ministers of the Council of Europe R(87)20 on Social Reactions to Juvenile Delinquency), as well as other socio-political changes (see further Spinellis and Tsitsoura, 2006; Spinellis, 2007).

The Greek juvenile justice system has traditionally emphasised the education, protection, support, and reintegration of the minor. Of these principles, and for more than half a century, education has been the predominant value. This much is evident from the educational measures provided for juvenile delinquents as a primary response to their predicament. The recent legislative reform cited above was no exception to this approach, and aimed to strengthen not only the principle of education, but also the rule of law ('due process'), care for crime victims, and the reintegration of juveniles into society. The modernisation of the juvenile justice system in Greece arrived with the adoption of measures that treat the deprivation of liberty as a measure of last resort, including the development of a large variety of non-custodial measures and other diversionary options at the prosecutorial stage, consideration of the victim's interests, the abolition of indeterminate sentences, and the extension of the right to appeal to a higher judicial body, each of which have illustrated the system's orientation towards a 'balanced justice model' (see further Courakis, 2003: 254; Spinellis, 2007: 174, 197).

More specifically, Greek legislation took into consideration the results of criminological studies explicitly incorporated in the United Nations Standard Minimum Rules for the Administration of Juvenile Justice ('The Beijing Rules'), the provisions of the Convention on the Rights of the Child (CRC), and the concluding observations made by the United Nations Committee on the Rights of the Child (CRC/C/15/Add.170: UN CRC 2002) with respect to the first report submitted by the Greek government to that body in 2000 (CRC/C/28/Add.17: UN CRC, 2000) (see further Spinellis and Tsitsoura, 2006: 316). The age at which an individual is considered to have the capacity to commit offences and to appear at a youth (or juvenile) court was raised from seven to eight years, the minimum age of criminal responsibility was raised from twelve to thirteen years, and the age of full criminal responsibility was raised from seventeen to eighteen years. Minors are defined accordingly as those persons who are between eight and eighteen years of age at the time the offence is committed. This addresses the concern raised by the UN Committee on the Rights of the Child that Greek penal law considered to be minor to be a child under the age of 17, in contrast to Greek civil law, which set the age limit of 18 (UN CRC, 2002: 6). The range of non-custodial educational or reformatory measures available was substantially expanded. A wide variety of possible alternatives to institutional care and the deprivation of liberty were introduced, the most significant being victim-offender mediation, community service, and education and training orders. In addition, the court decision would also specify the maximum duration of the imposed educational measure, while a periodic review of its necessity by the court would take place one year (at the latest) after such measure was imposed.

Victims' interests were first taken into consideration through the introduction of mediation between the minor offender and the victim to allow for the expression of an apology and the extra-judicial settlement of the dispute, along with compensation or other forms of restoration for the harm caused to the victim. Non-custodial therapeutic measures applicable to minors in need of particular treatment were introduced and, in particular, the attendance of a counselling-therapeutic program by the minor if addicted to drug use. This was an important change to the law given that Greece has recently seen a considerable increase in the number of juveniles accused of having infringed drug-related criminal law. The relatively indeterminate period of confinement in a correctional institution for juveniles was abolished (see Recommendation R(87)20 on Social Reactions to Juvenile Delinquency, paragraph 12), and replaced by a determinate period. Diversionary options at the prosecutorial stage were also introduced (see Article 45A of the Code of Criminal Procedure). If a minor has committed a petty offence or a misdemeanour, the public prosecutor may refrain from criminal prosecution if, from examination of the circumstances under which the act was committed and the personality of the minor, the prosecutor is convinced that prosecution is not necessary in order to prevent the minor from reoffending. Alternatively, the prosecutor can impose one or more of the non-custodial educational measures provided by law (Article 122 PC) or order the payment of a sum of money (up to 1,000 Euros) to a community or other non-profit organisation by the minor.

There have also been some moves to upgrade and strengthen the functions of the juvenile probation service. The Committee on the Rights of the Child had commented on the 'lack of a sufficient number of probation officers in all cities and regions of the country', recommending that the number of trained probation officers be increased (UN CRC, 2002: 22). Further duties have since been allocated to pertinent personnel with the aim of increasing the effectiveness of care and supervision for minors that find themselves in front of the justice system. Probation officers are now responsible, *inter alia*, for finding a foster family and carrying out mediation. They may also contribute to the effective implementation of a diversion from trial at the prosecutorial stage by instigating an inquiry into the personality and social surroundings of the minor who is alleged to have infringed criminal law, and by submitting a report to the prosecutor expressing their view on the case and, if considered necessary, the appropriate non-custodial measure to be imposed. The legal position of juveniles has been strengthened through the widening of opportunities to appeal against sentences imposing a period of detention in a Young Offenders Institution, irrespectively of the duration of such detention. The Committee on the Rights of the Child had raised concerns that the right of appeal in the Greek juvenile justice system was restricted to sentences of imprisonment of more than one year and, amongst other recommendations, had called for Greece to ensure respect for non-restricted rights of appeal (UN CRC, 2002: 22). The right of appeal is no longer restricted to sentences of imprisonment of more than one year, but was not subsequently extended to apply to any decision imposing an educational or a therapeutic measure upon a juvenile offender. Under Greek law, a higher judicial body cannot review these decisions even though, according to Article 40(2) CRC, every adjudicated child has the right of appeal (see also Committee on the Rights of the Child, General Comment No. 10(2007), Children's Rights in Juvenile Justice, CRC/C/GC/10).

An Overview of Contemporary Youth Justice Legislation

Greece does not have a separate statute addressing youth justice. Within the Penal Code, however, there is a particular chapter containing provisions on minors. Most of these concern the sanctions that may be imposed on juvenile offenders, whilst issues relating to youth courts and criminal proceedings against minors are regulated by the Constitution (Article 96), the Code of Criminal Procedure (CCP), and by the Statute on the Organisation of the Judiciary. Moreover, there are a number of provisions in the Correctional Code specifically concerning young detainees (Act 2776/1999). A series of other provisions related to youth justice are contained in the legislation establishing the juvenile probation service (Act 2793/1954 on Setting up the Youth Court's Probation Service, Act 378/1976 on the Establishment of the Juvenile Probation Service, and Presidential Decrees 49/1979 on the Functions of the Juvenile Probation Service and 36/2000 on the Organisation of the Ministry of Justice).

A number of international sources of law also impinge on the Greek justice system. The most important treaties concerning youth justice are the United Nations Convention on the Rights of the Child of 1989, the International Covenant on Civil and Political Rights of 1966, the Optional Protocol to the Convention on the Rights of the Child on the Sale of Children, Child Prostitution and Child Pornography of 2002, and the European Convention on Human Rights of 1950 (the latter does not contain any further specific provisions related to young offenders, but has been the basis for the development of some leading safeguards for criminal proceedings against juveniles through the right to a fair trial by the European Court of Human Rights). After their ratification by Greece, all international treaties form an integral part of domestic law and prevail against any contradictory provision of domestic law (Article 28 of the Greek Constitution). For example, the Convention on the Rights of the Child became part of Greek domestic law upon its ratification in 1992 (Act 2101) and since then has been directly enforceable by Greek courts in the course of administering youth justice.

Age Groups and Criminal Responsibility

Chapter 8 of the General Part of the Greek Criminal Code distinguishes between two different age groups of minors:

a) Persons aged 8 to 12 years: this age group are not considered criminally responsible for any act or omission. They can be subjected only to educational or therapeutic measures. Although persons between 8 and 12 years old who are alleged to have infringed the criminal law are criminally irresponsible, however, they are still liable to prosecution (Spinellis, 2007: 175). These young persons are subject to the exclusive jurisdiction of one-member juvenile courts (Article 113 CCP).

b) Persons aged 13 to 18 years (i.e., juveniles): this age group may be judged either criminally irresponsible or responsible for any act or omission. Above the age of the total absence of criminal responsibility but below the age of criminal majority, a juvenile may be subjected to educational or therapeutic measures, or to detention in a Young Offenders Institution. A juvenile may be subjected to the same educational or therapeutic measures as a person of between 8 and 12 years old if the court does not consider that he/she should be submitted to penal correction in an institution. Detention in a Young Offenders Institution may be imposed on a juvenile if the court finds – from the examination of the circumstances of the case and personality of the offender – that his/her penal correction is required in order to deter him/her from committing further offences. In an exceptional case such as this, the juvenile must be considered criminally liable.

Persons below eight years of age (i.e., 'infants') are not subject to criminal law. They are considered to have absolutely no capacity to infringe criminal law and hence are not subject to the jurisdiction of juvenile courts, but are subject to the jurisdiction of civil courts (see further Pitsela, 2004). Those over eighteen years of age, on the other hand, are subject to full adult criminal responsibility. All adult offenders are subject to the jurisdiction of ordinary criminal courts, although those who were minors at the time the criminal act was committed are referred to youth courts (see below). If, at the time of the commission of an offence, a person is between 18 and 20 years of age (inclusive), the court may impose a mitigated sentence according to the provisions of Article 83 PC. Thus, whilst young adults are subject to adult criminal law, the court has discretion to impose a lenient sentence (Spinellis and Spinellis, 1999: 7). Life imprisonment can nevertheless be imposed upon young adults if the court does not recognise the mitigating condition of post-juvenile age.

Sanctions

When juvenile offenders are not deemed criminally liable for a criminal act, they can either be dealt with outside of the court system or be prosecuted, and the youth court can impose a (non-custodial or custodial) measure. If the juvenile is deemed to be criminally liable, the youth court can impose detention in a Young Offenders Institution, or other criminal sanctions (in accordance with Articles 130 and 131 PC). Greek law enforcement structure is based on the legality principle, which means that, with rare exceptions (i.e., for petty offences such as traffic law violations), the police have no discretionary power in passing the case to the office of the public prosecutor. The prosecutor's powers are also regulated by the legality principle, and prosecution is thus mandatory; as a general rule, prosecutors are obliged to prosecute every reported offence, provided that the report is not manifestly ill-founded (see Articles 43, 47, and 50 CCP; however, see also cases of abstinence from prosecution in Article 45 CCP, Article 344 PC, Act 3500/2006 on 'Combating Domestic Violence and other provisions', and Act 3459/2006 on drug-related legislation; Brienen and Hoegen, 2000: 397; Dellidou, 2007: 104). The 'principle of opportunity', or the 'expediency principle', is also recognised in cases involving juveniles (i.e., the introduction of diversionary options under Act 3189/2003). In accordance with Article 45A CCP, the prosecutor may decide that in cases of petty offences and misdemeanours no prosecution is necessary to prevent the juvenile from reoffending and, hence, may take no further action against the juvenile. Furthermore, the prosecutor may decide that, while no prosecution is necessary, further action should be taken (e.g., the imposition of a non-custodial educational measure such as a victim-offender mediation scheme, or payment of a certain monetary sum to a community or other non-profit organisation). The prosecutor may dismiss proceedings without seeking the permission of a judge, regardless of whether or not the juvenile is a first-time offender.

There are no official statistics available about the number of out-of-court measures that have been imposed by prosecutors. According to my own research, the number of juvenile offenders who are diverted from criminal prosecution proceedings is insignificant. In Athens, the prosecutor for juveniles decided to largely abstain from prosecution and to place minors under probation in few cases, whilst in Thessaloniki there has been no such development. The lack of progress in the latter area may be explained by the fact that the prosecutor in Thessaloniki does not work exclusively on juvenile cases, and the resulting heavy workload and pressure upon the prosecutor means that they dedicate insufficient time to juvenile cases. This situation stands in stark contrast to the provision under Greek law that juvenile prosecutors in the country's largest cities should deal exclusively with juvenile cases and be specially qualified for this purpose. There are also no official statistics available about the number of minor offenders who have been prosecuted. Official statistics from the Ministry of Justice show only the number of juvenile offenders that were subjected to educational or therapeutic measures, that were convicted and sent to detention in a Young Offenders Institution, or were convicted and subjected to mitigated penalties under adult criminal law (according to Articles 130 and 131 PC). Available data shows that courts rarely impose the sentence of detention in a Young Offenders Institution, and more usually impose educational measures in cases involving juvenile offenders (see further Papageorgiou, this collection).

When a juvenile offender is prosecuted, the court can impose a series of measures, but a pre-sentence report, prepared by a juvenile probation officer, is first required. Juvenile probation officers provide assistance to the juvenile court judge by investigating the personality and social environment of the minor accused of having committed an offence, and proposes an appropriate response for each juvenile. Until 2003, before the enactment of the new law, courts did not have many options in dealing with young offenders. Probation was not extensively imposed due to the very limited number of probation officers (Lambropoulou, 2001: 33, 53). The new law has not yet been fully implemented, in part due to the fact of staffing deficiencies; on the one hand, the number of juvenile probation officers responsible for supervising and guiding the juvenile under adjudication is still very limited, and, on the other, juvenile prosecutors outside Athens have yet to be appointed. Equally, there is insufficient familiarisation amongst existing staff with the use of alternative measures such as diverting from trial, mediation and other forms of restorative justice, or social, psychological, educational, or training programmes. Courts have thus shown themselves to be very reluctant to impose these new measures (Spinellis and Tsitsoura, 2006: 322; Papadopoulou, 2006). The objective of measures applied to minors is their education, rehabilitation, and social reintegration, with a view to preventing reoffending (Rupp-Diakojanni, 1990; Pasiotopoulou-Poulea, 1986). The measures which can be imposed by a juvenile court range from the educational to the therapeutic, and from detention in a Young Offenders Institution to conditional release and moderated forms of penalties provided by adult criminal law, each of which is outlined below.

Educational Measures

The courts have a wide range of discretion in dealing with juvenile offenders. The use of educational measures does not presuppose the criminal responsibility of the juvenile. Educational measures may be applied regardless of the total absence of criminal responsibility for all minors of between 8 and 18 years of age. According to Article 122 PC, educational measures are the following: a reprimand; placement of the minor under the responsible care of parents or guardians; placement of the minor under the responsible care of a foster family; placement of the minor under the care of a 'Society for the Protection of Minors', a children's institution, or a probation officer; mediation between the juvenile offender and the victim to allow the expression of an apology and extra-judicial settlement of the repercussions of the act; compensation of the victim or any other means of restoring or eliminating the consequences of the act; community service; attendance of social or psychological support programmes in state, municipal, communal, or private agencies; attendance of vocational or other educational training programmes; attendance of traffic education programmes; and placement of the minor in an appropriate state, municipal, communal, or private educational institution. This list of the main educational measures for minor offenders may be supplemented by additional obligations related to the lifestyle or education of the minor. Furthermore, in exceptional cases, the court can impose two or more of the aforementioned non-custodial measures (Article 122 PC).

The last-mentioned measure entails deprivation of liberty and is the sole custodial educational measure in the Greek youth justice system, It can only be served by boys aged between 8 and 18 years old, and only in state institutions, since appropriate municipal, communal, or private educational establishments do not exist. In practice, the minimum duration of custodial placement is six months. The sole such educational institution for girls was based in Athens until 1997, when it was closed down due to its high running costs and the small number of inmates, and as a result of the favouring of an out-of-detention-centre approach to the treatment of young delinquents. Today, only one appropriately tailored educational institution exists in Greece. The institution, which is public, was hosting only 12 male minors in October 2008. It is run by the Ministry of Justice and its mandate is to 'educate, socially support, and provide vocational training and education' for delinquent minors, most of whom are juveniles.

According to Article 17 of Act 2298/1995, irrespective of the commission of a criminal offence, a minor aged between 7 and 18 years old is also subject to welfare measures, including custodial placement, against his/her will but with the parental consent, when the minor faces problems of social integration, meaning that he/she lives with persons who commit offences habitually or professionally (i.e., children at risk of becoming involved in criminal activities). The minor can be held by an educational institution only following a request or consent by their parents or guardians. A request by parents or guardians is addressed to the public prosecutor or to competent police authorities (local to the minor's place of residence), who will submit it to the juvenile judge. The juvenile judge is then called upon to issue a decision as to whether such measures should be imposed. In their decision, judges are obliged to consider the personality and social background of the minor, as well as the opinion of the juvenile probation officer who is in charge of the social investigation. The juvenile judge must also discharge the measure whenever the preceding request or consent is withdrawn, or in accordance with the opinion of the directorship of the educational institution if the reasons supporting the measure's application become invalid. In any case, the young person is discharged when they complete 18 years of age. Minors of different ages are thus treated differently where criminal acts are concerned, but similarly when they face problems of social integration.

Therapeutic Measures

Such measures are applied in cases where minors require particular treatment, especially when they suffer from certain types of mental or physical health problems, or are drug addicts and cannot cease drug-use by themselves, and commit an offence. Once again, the application of therapeutic measures does not presuppose the criminal responsibility of the minor. Article 123 PC sets out an exhaustive list of the therapeutic measures for minor offenders: placement of the minor under the responsible care of parents, guardians or a foster family; placement of the minor under the care of a 'Society for the Protection of Minors' or a juvenile probation officer; attendance by the minor of a counseling-therapeutic program; and placement of the minor in a therapeutic or other appropriate institution. The aforementioned measures are applied after diagnosis and advice by a specialised team of doctors, psychologists, and social workers. In exceptional cases, the court may make attendance of a counseling-therapeutic program compulsory in combination with the minor's placement under the responsible care of parents, guardians, a foster family, a 'Society for the Protection of Minors', or a juvenile probation officer. When the minor is a drug addict, the court seeks expert psychiatric opinion before deciding on the appropriate therapeutic measures to be taken. In practice, the placement of the minor in a therapeutic or other appropriate institution (the sole custodial therapeutic measure) is very rarely applied.

Detention in a Young Offenders Institution

The only prison sentence provided for under the Greek youth justice system is detention in a Young Offenders Institution, meaning either confinement in a correctional institute for juveniles or youth, or detention in a juvenile prison facility or a special institution for youngsters. The court orders detention in a Young Offenders Institution only if, after investigating the circumstances under which the act was committed and the personality of the juvenile, the court deems that his/her penal correction is necessary in order to prevent him/her from reoffending. In the court's decision, the duration of detention is specified (Article 127 PC). Until 1996, the majority of sentences imposing detention in a Young Offenders Institution were between six months and one year. Only in rare instances did the maximum duration exceed five years. The number of young people sentenced to detention has been relatively low (approximately 50–60 juveniles per year; see further Papageorgiou, this collection). Since 1998, however, this figure has been rising; in particular, the number of young prisoners detained for more than five years has increased. By 2006, for example, according to the National Statistical Service of Greece, 80 percent of young prisoners in Greek Young Offenders Institutions were serving a sentence lasting over five years.

Article 12 of the Correctional Code identifies young detainees as persons between 13 and 21 years of age. Young detainees (as a rule, persons up to 21 years of age but, exceptionally, up to 25 years of age) are kept in special institutions for young offenders or units in common correctional institutions separate from other adult detainees. There are currently three young offender institutions in Greece for males: a so-called 'rural penitentiary institution for juveniles' in Kassabeteia, Almyros Volou, and two special institutions for young offenders in Avlona, Attica, and in the city of Volos (the latter only for young aliens, most of whom are Albanian). There are also two small units for the detention of young male inmates in the adult prisons of Korydallos (near Athens) and Diavata (near Thessaloniki). There are no special facilities for young women offenders in Greece (for various aspects of the Greek juvenile prison system, see Spinellis and Spinellis, 1999: 46; Pitsela, 2003; Neubacher *et al.*, 2003: 17; Pitsela and Sagel-Grande, 2003:

352; Pitsela and Sagel-Grande, 2004: 208). Semi-custodial institutions or open detention facilities without any or with minimal security measures have not been established. In the facilities for young prisoners, juveniles are the minority and young adults the majority. All institutions offer primary and/or secondary education. It is worth noting that education in the Greek prisons has a status equivalent to that of work with respect to the favourable calculation of sentence duration. Namely, one day of education is equated with two days of the prison sentence served. Various educational and social reintegration programmes exist to prepare the offender for his/her return to the outside community. Nevertheless, official efforts are primarily focused upon the secure custody of prisoners, whether adults or young offenders. Greece has an acute problem with prison overcrowding (Spinellis, 1998; see further Cheliotis, this collection). Prison occupancy in Greece is one of the highest among member-states of the Council of Europe. Amongst both pre-trial and sentenced prison populations, foreigners are significantly over-represented (see further discussion in Cheliotis and Xenakis, this collection; see also UN CRC, 2002). Special institutions for young offenders are also overcrowded, if not to the same extent as the rest of Greek prisons.

Conditional Release

The juvenile court may release on parole an offender serving a detention sentence at a Young Offenders Institution. The conditional or early release (parole) of juvenile offenders is possible once half of the detention sentence has been served (see further Cheliotis, this collection).

Moderated Forms of Penalties provided by Adult Criminal Law

The sole penalty for juveniles is the detention in a Young Offender Institution, if they are brought to trial before completing 18 years of age. Article 130 PC allows that, if the offender was a juvenile at the time of the criminal act was committed but has become a young adult before the court's decision, moderated penalties provided by adult criminal law can be applied, in accordance with the provisions of Article 83 PC. Moreover, if a juvenile sentenced to detention in a Young Offenders Institution has completed 18 years of age prior to the commencement of execution of his/her sentence, the trial court may substitute the sentence with a moderated form of the statutory penalty for the offence under adult criminal law. If the person sentenced is over twenty-one years of age, it is mandatory that the detention sentence in a Young Offenders Institution be substituted (Article 131 PC). In applying adult criminal law, the court may impose either an imprisonment sentence that may range in duration from 10 days to 20 years, or a pecuniary penalty. A life sentence may not be imposed for a crime committed by a person aged less than 18 years, regardless of their age at the time of their trial or sentence. It appears that juvenile court judges prefer to use the sanctions system of adult criminal law, but it is not clear whether this practice results in more severe punishment (see further Pitsela, 1997: 166).

Youth Courts

Article 96 of the Greek Constitution sets out that special laws regulate matters relating to juvenile courts, for which the provisions of Articles 93 and 97 may not be applied. According to Article 97 of the Greek Constitution, felonies should be tried by criminal courts, composed of a majority of regular judges and jurors. Article 93 of the Greek Constitution declares that the sessions of the courts of law shall be public. Offences which would qualify as felonies if committed by adults, are not tried by criminal courts composed of professional and lay judges when committed by juveniles, but instead by juvenile courts (Mylonopoulos, 1993: 180). Moreover, public participation in juvenile court hearings is restricted to the parties directly involved in the trial, their legal counsels, juvenile probation officers, and parents or guardians and representatives of the 'Society for the Protection of Minors' (Article 1 of the Act 3315/1955). The juvenile justice system and juvenile courts have jurisdiction over all young persons aged between 8 and 18 years old at the time the offence was committed. The administration of juvenile justice is carried out by a one-member and a three-member Juvenile Court of First Instance, and a three-member Juvenile Court of Appeal. The three-member Juvenile Court has jurisdiction over offences that are punishable by detention in a Young Offenders Institution for at least five years. The one-member Juvenile Court has jurisdiction over cases involving all other offences. The overwhelming majority of minor offenders treated by juvenile courts have their cases adjudicated at the lowest level of the juvenile court hierarchy (one-member juvenile courts).

Transferring Juveniles to Adult Courts

Juvenile courts deal with all juvenile criminal cases apart from those where juveniles are co-accused with adults. When minors have participated in the commission of a felony or a petty offence by an adult, prosecution is always separate for them and is managed by a juvenile court. The juvenile court has jurisdiction over all petty offences and felonies as well as misdemeanours committed by juveniles younger than 15 years of age. Concerning misdemeanours committed by juveniles older than 15 years (and as exception), however, it is common for all accomplices to be tried by an adult criminal court if the public prosecutor or the judicial council considers justice to be better served that way. According to data from the National Statistical Service of Greece, the number of juveniles sentenced by adult criminal courts constitutes a small percentage (no more than 12 percent) of the total number of juveniles prosecuted each year.

Pre-trial Detention

Although minors aged between 8 and 12 years old are liable to criminal prosecution, they are deemed criminally irresponsible and cannot be subject to either restrictive measures or detention pending trial. Restrictive measures as well as pre-trial detention can be applied to juveniles aged between 13 and 18 years old, however. According to the provision of Article 282 CCP, restrictive measures mainly comprise remand on bail, the offender's obligation to appear at intervals before an examining judge or other authority, the prohibition of passage or residence in a certain place or abroad, and the prohibition of associations or encounters with certain persons. Pre-trial detention may also be ordered if the accused has violated the restrictive measures imposed on him/her (Article 298 CCP). Pre-trial detention is intended to be a measure of last resort, restricted to the most serious crimes, in conformity with the provision of Article 37 of the Convention on the Rights of the Child. It should be imposed only if there are no other non-custodial options. Additionally, the accused juvenile should only be placed in detention pending trial only if, for the respective crime, a penalty of at least 10 years of imprisonment is provided by law and regardless of the duration of the measures that are likely to be imposed in the given case (Article 282 CCP). Consequently, pre-trial detention is to be imposed upon juveniles (only) when the alleged crime is a felony that would carry a sentence of 10 years or more. Empirical research nevertheless shows that pre-trial detention is not often used as a measure of last resort, nor for the shortest appropriate period of time (Article 37 CRC). Indeed, the large number of pre-trial detainees was a key concern raised in 2002 by the UN Committee on the Rights of the Child in its observations on Greece (UN CRC, 2002: 21). In 2005 and 2006, the average duration of juvenile pre-trial detention was between 6 and 7 months. Furthermore, whilst pre-trial juvenile detainees in Greece are kept separately from adults (either in a separate institution for juveniles or in a separate section of an adult institution, in conformity with Article 37 CRC, Article 10 ICCPR, and Rule 13.4 of the Beijing Rules), young pre-trial detainees are not kept separate from young convicts (in contrast with Rule 17 of the UN 'Rules for the Protection of Juveniles Deprived of their Liberty', also known as the 'Havana Rules').

The Juvenile Probation Service

The Juvenile Probation Service in Greece is operated on a regional basis by the Ministry of Justice and a section of the juvenile courts. It is staffed by civil servants that come from various scientific fields, such as law, psychology, social science, and social work. Probation officers are appointed by juvenile courts and may be given instructions by the juvenile judge for their activities. As a rule, no volunteers are engaged by the Greek juvenile justice system. Officers submit to the court a so-called 'social inquiry report' for all minor offenders, which provides evidence of the physical, intellectual, emotional, moral, and social development of the minor, their background, living conditions, and the circumstances of the offence (see further Spinellis, 2007: 180, 184). The report is confidential and does not constitute part of the criminal file. Access is only granted to the judge and the minor's parents or guardians. Juvenile probation officers are also responsible for supervising and guiding the adjudicated person in accordance with the court order, and to report regularly to the court. In reality, juvenile probation officers have a tremendous caseload and are very limited in number. This jeopardises the potential success of the new educational measures introduced by the Act 3189/2003; courts appear reluctant to introduce the measures given that problems of staffing and expertise are compounded by the lack of available suitable programmes.

At the same time that new dynamics that are developing within Greek society have led to the readjustment and re-examination of the responsibilities and expectations of juvenile probation officers, officers themselves have called for their role to be upgraded in legal provisions and their contribution to criminal procedure to be recharacterised as essential (to ensure, for example, that the absence of a 'social inquiry report' should lead to the postponement of a trial). Committees of Juvenile Probation Officers have been established to develop concrete proposals along these lines, including the creation of a code of conduct for juvenile probation officers.

Conclusion: Outlook and recommendations

Over recent decades, the position of juveniles within the law has received greater attention by academics and practitioners alike. International co-operation has also facilitated the dissemination of knowledge and awareness about this field. The early 2000s saw the legal position of children in Greece advance with the adoption of a series of legal instruments such as Act 3094/2003 on the Ombudsman, Act 3500/2006 on Combating Domestic Violence, and the establishment of associated institutions. In particular, the 2003 Act established an independent administrative 'Ombudsman for the Child', a department of the Greek Ombudsman with a mission to protect and promote the rights of minors. Whilst Greek legislation concerning youth justice and its implementation appears to be oriented more towards rehabilitation and education than punitiveness or retribution, it is clear that its provisions are not being fully implemented. Recent legislative developments have constituted a step forward in protecting the interest of children facing the law, but there remain a number of issues which need further reform. To emphasise this point and help focus attention on the practical challenges that lie ahead, by way of conclusion this chapter offers a non-exhaustive review of some of the key reforms required.

The implementation of non-custodial measures focusing on social re-integration should be extended to the 25th year of age (instead of the 18th or the 21st year of age under a specially justified decision, as provided currently by law) after the pertinent request by the person concerned. Equally, the 20-year upper limit for detention in a Young Offenders Institution should be reduced. The concerns raised by the UN Committee on the Rights of the Child on this point were subsequently taken into account by the working group preparing the draft law on 'Reform of Criminal Legislation on Minors and other provisions' (Act 3189/2003), suggesting an upper limit of 10 years. The 20-year provision remained in place, however, despite the fact that its negative implications for personal liberty are well known both to Greek society and the Greek Parliament.

Given the introduction to juvenile criminal law of a wide variety of non-custodial educational measures, the sanctions system of juvenile criminal law needs to be extended to incorporate cases involving young adults. Judges, prosecutors, probation officers, correctional officers, lawyers, police officers, and indeed all professionals involved in the administration of youth justice, should be properly trained in order to cater for the needs of young offenders and cope with contemporary challenges. Although this point was made by the UN Committee on the Rights of the Child and is provided by numerous non-binding international legal instruments, it is still needed and yet to be sufficiently addressed. In addition, youth courts should be competent to dismiss proceedings before the hearing stage ends. The role and duties of the juvenile probation service in relation to the newly introduced procedure of diverting from trial should be further clarified.

In the one-member juvenile court, the presence of a defence lawyer is rare. The participation of legal counsel in the criminal proceedings needs to be strengthened through an *ex officio* appointment that is free-of-charge for minors who may face detention (see further Pitsela, 2000: 139). Pre-trial detention should be abolished in the case of juveniles under the age of 14, particularly in light of its negative impact upon the emotional, psychological, and social development of the child. Finally, efforts must be made to create a unified and comprehensive body of legislation regarding youth justice; provisions concerning youth justice in Greece are scattered across various legal sources (Spinellis, 2007: 174). Needless to say, it remains to be seen if, or when, any of these reforms will be taken up.

References

Akritidou, M., Antonopoulou, M. and A. Pitsela (2007) 'Greece', in A.M. van Kalmthout, F.B.A.M. Hofstee-van der Meulen and F. Dünkel (eds) *Foreigners in European Prisons*, pp. 392–424 and 953–957. Nijmegen: Wolf Legal Publishers.

Androulakis, N. (1980) 'Strafrecht', in K.-D. Grothusen (ed.) *Südosteuropa-Handbuch Vol. 3: Griechenland*, pp. 138–146. Göttingen: Vandenhoeck & Ruprecht.

Brienen, M.E.I. and E.H. Hoegen (2000) *Victims of Crime in 22 European Criminal Justice Systems. The Implementation of Recommendation (85) 11 of the Council of Europe on the Position of the Victim in the Framework of Criminal Law and Procedure*. Nijmegen: Wolf Legal Productions in cooperation with the Global Law Association.

Chaidou, A. (2002) 'Griechenland', in H.-J. Albrecht and M. Kilchling (eds) *Jugendstrafrecht in Europa*, pp. 191–203. Freiburg i.Br.: MPI für Ausländisches und Internationales Strafrecht.

Courakis, N. (1994) 'Alternative Penal Sanctions in Greece', *The Journal of Asset Protection and Financial Crime* 2: 257–264.

Courakis, N. (1999) *Juvenile Delinquents and Society*. Athens-Komotini: Ant. N. Sakkoulas Publishers.

Courakis, N. (2003) 'A Typology of Juvenile Justice Systems in Europe', in A. Manganas (ed.) *Human Rights, Crime, Criminal Policy: Essays in Honour of Alice Yotopoulos-Marangopoulos, Volume A*, pp. 251–273. Athens: Nomiki Vivliothiki.

Dellidou, Z. (2007) 'The Investigative Stage of the Criminal Process in Greece', in E. Cape, J. Hodgson, E. Prakke and T. Spronken (eds) *Suspects in Europe. Procedural Rights at the Investigative Stage of the Criminal Process in the European Union*, pp. 101–128. Antwerp-Oxford: Intersentia.

Frangoulis, S. (1994) *Freiheit durch Arbeit. Die Institution der 'wohltätigen' Anrechnung von Arbeitstagen auf die Freiheitsstrafe in Griechenland*. Jur. Diss. Marburg: N.G. Elwert.

Ioannou, K.M. (1996) 'The Application of the European Convention on Human Rights in the Greek Legal Order', *Hellenic Review of European Law* 16: 223–250.

Lambropoulou, E. (1993) 'Umwandlung der Freiheitsstrafe als kriminalpolitisches Modell? Zur Diskrepanz von Verurteilungen und Inhaftierungen in Griechenland', *Monatsschrift für Kriminologie und Strafrechtsreform* 76: 91–100.

Lambropoulou, E. (2001) 'The "End" of Correctional Policy and the Management of the Correctional "Problem" in Greece', *European Journal of Crime, Criminal Law and Criminal Justice* 9(1): 33–55.

Lambropoulou, E. (2005) 'Crime, Criminal Justice and Criminology in Greece', *European Journal of Criminology* 2(2): 211–247.

Mangakis, G.A. (1959) 'Das griechische Strafrecht. Allgemeiner Teil', in E. Mezger, A. Schönke, H.-H. Jescheck (eds) *Das ausländische Strafrecht der Gegenwart Vol. 3*, pp. 257–323. Berlin: Duncker & Humblot.

Mangakis, G.A. (1973) 'Introduction to the Greek Penal Law', in *The Greek Penal Code* (transl. N.B. Lolis), pp. 1–33. London: F.B. Rothman Co., Sweet & Maxwell.

Meurer, D. (1994) 'Freiheit durch Arbeit nach griechischem Strafrecht', in M. Busch, G. Edel and H. Müller-Dietz (eds) *Gefängnis und Gesellschaft. Gedächtnisschrift für Albert Krebs*, pp. 78–94. Pfaffenweiler: Centaurus.

Mylonopoulos, C. (1993) 'The Criminal Procedure System in Greece', in C. van den Wyngaert (ed.) *Criminal Procedures Systems in the European Community*, pp. 163–183. London: Butterworths.

Neubacher, F., Walter, M. and A. Pitsela (2003) 'Jugendstrafvollzug im deutsch-griechischen Vergleich – Ergebnisse einer Befragung', *Zeitschrift für Strafvollzug und Straffälligenhilfe* 52: 17–24.

Neubacher, F., Filou, M., Pitsela, A. and M. Walter (2004) 'Jugendkriminalität in Deutschland und Griechenland – Registrierung, Verarbeitung, Ausfilterung', *Zeitschrift für Jugendkriminalrecht und Jugendhilfe* 1: 63–72.

Papadopoulou, P. (2006) 'Victim-Offender Mediation for Minors in Greece', *Newsletter of the European Forum for Restorative Justice* 7(1): 1–3.

Pasiotopoulou-Poulea, M. (1986) *Rechtsfolgen der Straftat eines Jugendlichen im griechischen materiellen Jugendstrafrecht*. Jur. Diss. München.

Philippides, T. (1954) 'Das System der Strafen und sichernden Maßregeln im Griechischen StGB vom 1.1.1951', *Zeitschrift für die gesamte Strafrechtswissenschaft* 66: 408–422.

Philippides, T. (1958) 'Der Einfluß der deutschen Strafrechtswissenschaft in Griechenland', *Zeitschrift für die gesamte Strafrechtswissenschaft* 70: 291–313.

Pitsela, A. (1988) 'Greece', in A.M. van Kalmthout and P.J.P. Tak (eds) *Sanctions-Systems in the Member-States of the Council of Europe. Part I. Deprivation of Liberty, Community Service and Other Substitutes*, pp. 149–170. Deventer: Kluwer.

Pitsela, A. (1997) 'Griechenland', in F. Dünkel, A. van Kalmthout and H. Schüler-Springorum (eds) *Entwicklungstendenzen und Reformstrategien im Jugendstrafrecht im europäischen Vergleich*, pp. 155–191. Mönchengladbach: Forum.

Pitsela, A. (1998) 'Jugendgerichtsbarkeit und Jugenddelinquenz in Griechenland', in H.-J. Albrecht, F. Dünkel, H.-J. Kerner, J. Kürzinger, H. Schöch and K. Sessar (eds) *Internationale Perspektiven in Kriminologie und Strafrecht. Festschrift für Günther Kaiser*, pp. 1085–1107. Berlin: Duncker & Humblot.

Pitsela, A. (2000) 'Vorschläge für einen rationalen Umgang mit der Jugenddelinquenz', in C. Prittwitz and I. Manoledakis (eds) *Strafrechtsprobleme an der Jahrtausendwende*, pp. 131–144. Baden-Baden: Nomos.

Pitsela, A. (2003) 'Jugendstrafvollzug', in Bremer Institut für Kriminalpolitik (ed.) *Quo Vadis III. Innovative Wege zur nachhaltigen Reintegration straffälliger Menschen–Reformmodelle in den EU-Staaten*. Bremen: Eigenverlag.

Pitsela, A. (2004) 'Greece. Criminal Responsibility of Minors in the National and International Legal Orders', *Revue Internationale de Droit Pénal* 75: 355–378.

Pitsela, A. and I. Sagel-Grande (2003) 'Jugendliche Straftäter in deutschen, griechischen und niederländischen Strafanstalten–Ergebnisse einer mündlichen Befragung von Jugendlichen in drei europäischen Ländern', *Zeitschrift für Strafvollzug und Straffälligenhilfe* 52: 352–357.

Pitsela, A. and A. Sagel-Grande (2004) 'Jugendstrafrechtliche Sanktionen mit Freiheitsentzug in Griechenland und in den Niederlanden', *Zeitschrift für Strafvollzug und Straffälligenhilfe* 53: 208–217.

Rupp-Diakojanni, T. (1990) *Die Schuldfähigkeit Jugendlicher innerhalb der jugendstrafrechtlichen Systematik*. Jur. Diss. Pfaffenweiler: Centaurus.

Spinellis, C.D. (1998) 'Attacking Prison Overcrowding in Greece: A Task of Sisyphus?', in H.-J. Albrecht, F. Dünkel, H.-J. Kerner, J. Kürzinger, H. Schöch and K. Sessar (eds) *Internationale Perspektiven in Kriminologie und Strafrecht. Festschrift für Günther Kaiser*, pp. 1273–1289. Berlin: Duncker & Humblot.

Spinellis, C.D. (2007) 'The Juvenile Justice System in Greece', in V. Patanè (ed.) *European Juvenile Justice Systems, Volume 1*, pp. 171–199. Milano: A. Giuffrè.

Spinellis, C.D. and D.D. Spinellis (2002) 'Sanctions Imposed, Sanctions Executed: Who Benefits from the Discrepancy?', *Hellenic Review of European Law* 55: 311–345.

Spinellis, C.D. and A. Tsitsoura (2006) 'The Emerging Juvenile Justice System in Greece', in J. Junger-Tas and S.H. Decker (eds) *International Handbook of Juvenile Justice*, pp. 309–324. Dordrecht: Springer.

Spinellis, D.D. (1993) 'Criminal Law and Procedure', in K.D. Kerameus and P.J. Kozyris (eds) *Introduction to Greek Law*, pp. 339–365. Deventer: Kluwer.

Spinellis, D.D. and C.D. Spinellis (1999) *Criminal Justice System in Greece*. Helsinki: HEUNI.

Tsitsoura, A.M. (2002) 'Community Sanctions and Measures in Greece', in H.-J. Albrecht and A. van Kalmthout (eds) *Community Sanctions and Measures in Europe and North America*, pp. 271–283. Freiburg i.Br.: Max Planck Institut für ausländisches und internationales Strafrecht.

UN Committee on the Rights of the Child (2002) *Consideration of Reports Submitted by State Parties under Article 44 of the Convention: Concluding Observations of the Committee on the Rights of the Child: Greece*, 29th Session, 1 February, CRC/C/15/Add.170. Available online at: http://www.unhchr.ch/tbs/doc.nsf/%28Symbol%29/CRC.C.15.Add.170.En?OpenDocument

JOHN MUNCIE

Commentary

Comparative Juvenile Justice

There is little or no existing work comparing Greek juvenile justice with other countries. The case of Greece is ignored in three major comparative texts (Muncie and Goldson, 2006; Winterdyck, 2002; Tonry and Doob, 2004) and afforded a descriptive summary in just one (Spinellis and Tsitsoura in Junger-Tas and Decker, 2006). The aspiration of comparative juvenile justice studies is typically one of discovering if there is anything distinctive about particular jurisdictions and whether it is divergent from or convergent with broader international trends and conventions. From a policy point of view, such research is often driven by the frequently asked question of 'what can be learnt from the experiences of others?' From a theoretical point of view, it is inspired by assessments of 'how far individual nation states can hang on to their own sovereignty in the face of global economics and international legal obligations?' Seeking answers to any of these questions is, however, far from straightforward. And why should we want to make such comparisons? If the aim is to identify 'effective practice', we must continually ask 'effective for whom?' and 'by what standards?' And even if 'effective practice' can be identified, is it capable of being transferred readily and successfully from one jurisdiction to another?

Comparative youth justice in general is notably underdeveloped. Existing studies are typically jurisdiction-specific descriptions. Any attempt to compare is beset by myriad issues. The classification and recording of crime differ between jurisdictions, and different countries have developed different judicial systems for defining and dealing with young offenders. Ages of criminal responsibility differ markedly. Different means are used to record imprisonment. What is classified as penal custody in one country may not be in others, though regimes may be similar. The existence of specialised detention centres, training schools, treatment regimes, reception centres, closed care institutions and so on, may all hold young people against their will, but may not be automatically entered in penal statistics. Not all countries collect the same data on the same age groups and populations. None seem to do so within the same time periods. Some do not collect any data at all. There are few reliable statistical comparators. Linguistic differences in how the categories of 'minor', 'juvenile', child', and 'young offender' are defined and implemented further hinder any attempt to ensure a sound comparative base. Furthermore, juvenile justice systems often appear in a state of constant flux, managing a mix of rationales from child protection, education, welfare, restoration, and rehabilitation, to due process, just deserts, and retributive punishment (Muncie, 2005). Such flux makes it difficult to assess broad trends, particularly when relying on descriptive snapshots of powers and procedures taken at any one particular time.

Nevertheless there is a widespread assumption that, throughout most Western jurisdictions, formative principles of 'child welfare' have, particularly since the 1970s, been undermined by various principles of 'justice'. By the 1990s, retributive justice appeared to be in ascendance, with the penal population of young people growing worldwide amidst a burgeoning 'culture of control'. Through various measures of 'adulteration', young people are also now assumed to be more likely to find a decline in their special status as in need of care and protection, and to be seen as more in need of punishment through which they will face up to the consequences of their own actions. However, such developments stand in some opposition to counter-movements designed to further rather than diminish children's rights. Of note is the 1989 UN Convention on the Rights of the Child which stresses the importance of incorporating a rights consciousness into juvenile justice reform by, for example, establishing an age of criminal responsibility relative to developmental capacity, encouraging participation in decision-making, providing access to legal representation, protecting children from capital or degrading punishment, and ensuring that arrest, detention, and imprisonment are measures of last resort. Above all, the Convention emphasises that the well-being of those aged under 18 should be a primary consideration. It has been ratified by over 190 countries. But ratification does not necessarily mean implementation.

These issues clearly resonate with Pitsela's account of juvenile justice in Greece. Its 2003 legislation appears a direct response to some of the concerns of the UN Committee. But at the same time, child incarceration rates appear to be growing amidst (an all too familiar) moral panic about youth offending. As noted above, it is difficult to give any precise answer to whether any one jurisdiction (including Greece) is, or has been able, to counter any global trend towards punitiveness. Our often sole measure is one of comparative penal statistics. In 2008, it was estimated that Greece imprisoned (adults and juveniles) at a rate of 109 per 100,000 of population. This appeared to be just above average for neighbouring Southern European countries when compared to Italy (92) and FYROM (107), but below Turkey (142) and Albania (159). However, both absolute numbers and the prison population rate had doubled since 1997 (Walmsley, 2008; see also Cheliotis, this collection). The Council of Europe Penal Statistics for 2008 record that Greece held 491 prisoners under the age of 18. Again, this appears to compare favourably with the likes of Turkey, Germany, and England and Wales, and places Greece on a par with Poland and Romania, but far exceeds numbers incarcerated in the Scandinavian countries (Council of Europe, 2010). These bald figures, however, reveal very little. When estimated as a rate per 1,000 under 18 populations, Greece does appear as relatively punitive (see Table 1).

The UN Committee reports provide perhaps the only other 'reliable' means of comparing 'effective practice'. But the latest such report for Greece was published in 2002, and some of its concerns (as Pitsela notes) have been at least partially addressed. These concerns were, however, detailed and damning: that children are protected by the juvenile justice system only up to age 17; at the prosecution of children for begging; at the lack of respect for juvenile justice standards with regard to arrest and detention proceedings, including the occasional detention of children with adults; at the proportionally high number of children from distinct ethnic, religious, linguistic, and cultural groups involved in juvenile justice proceedings, especially involving arrest and imprisonment; that the right of children to legal representation or other appropriate assistance is not always systematically guaranteed; at the large number of juveniles detained pending trial, on non-felony offences, in spite of the fact that domestic legislation prohibits such detention unless the alleged crime is one that would carry a sentence

of 10 years' imprisonment or more; at delays in judicial proceedings leading to long periods of pre-trial detention; that, under the law, children can
be given a sentence of 20 years' imprisonment; that the right of appeal is
restricted to sentences of imprisonment of more than one year; at the lack
of a sufficient number of probation officers in all cities and regions of the
country (UN Committee, 2002).

Greece's response to these concerns appears to have been somewhat
piecemeal. But this is far from uncommon. Certainly, the UN Committee is adamant that

> many States parties still have a long way to go in achieving full compliance with CRC
> [Committee on the Rights of the Child], e.g., in the areas of procedural rights, the
> development and implementation of measures for dealing with children in conflict
> with the law without resorting to judicial proceedings, and the use of deprivation
> of liberty only as a measure of last resort. [...] The Committee is equally concerned
> about the lack of information on the measures that States parties have taken to
> prevent children from coming into conflict with the law. This may be the result
> of a lack of a comprehensive policy for the field of juvenile justice. This may also
> explain why many States parties are providing only very limited statistical data on
> the treatment of children in conflict with the law (UN Committee on the Rights
> of the Child, 2007: 1).

As other jurisdiction-specific reports for Western Europe conclude, there
remain pan-European concerns for the increasing criminalisation of young
people and in particular the disproportionate arrest and detention of juvenile minorities (especially the Roma and traveller communities) (Muncie,
2008). Greece is not alone in supporting a system that appears to produce racialised outcomes. As Pitsela records, Greece has incorporated the
UNCRC into its domestic law, but concerns remain (despite the 2003
legislation) about increasing rates of imprisonment and for longer periods.
The full range of diversionary measures does not appear to have been fully
taken up whether through lack of practitioner training or political will.

In this regard, the case of Greece underlines the need of the comparative researcher to clearly distinguish between *policy as rhetoric*, *policy as
codified*, and *policy as implemented*. These are *critically* different facets of
the policy process, subject to different fields of power, interest, knowledge,

and values. Juvenile justice in any jurisdiction appears constantly to be undergoing political 'doctoring' to manage the 'mix' between educative and diversionary measures, and punitive responses and sanctions. But comparative research also has to note that such 'doctoring' is evident *within* jurisdictions as well as between them. As Fergusson (2007) has pointed out, any attempt to assess degrees of international divergence and convergence must also take account of 'internal' differences between what is presented publicly to be politically acceptable; what can be enshrined in policy directives which are open to public scrutiny; and how policy and legal prescription are interpreted through the localised practice knowledge bases of youth justice workers, probation officers, social workers, and other para-professionals. National governments might strive to maintain broad control over an infinitely complex network of agencies and interventions, but are continually faced by disparate, partially autonomous managers and practitioners who retain an ability to interpret legislation and directives in diverse, and sometimes unpredictable or unintended ways (Goldson and Hughes, 2010).

The precise nature of any juvenile justice system is then contingent on a variety of national, regional, and local conditions – such as cultural history; political commitment to expansionism or diversion; media toleration of children and young people; and the extent of autonomy afforded to professional initiative and discretion. These issues will seriously affect any assessment of whether Greece (or any other jurisdiction) is actually moving toward a fully rights-compliant system of juvenile justice.

Country	Under-18-year-olds in custody	Rate per 1,000 under-18 population
Netherlands	2,038 (07/06)	0.57
England and Wales	2,927 (06/07)	0.25
Germany	3,448 (10/06)	0.23
Greece	434 (09/06)	0.22
Spain (under 21)	1,520 (05/07)	0.20
Scotland	188 (09/04)	0.17
N. Ireland	76 (09/04)	0.16
Austria	161 (05/07)	0.10
Portugal (under 19)	140 (12/06)	0.06
Ireland	52 (04/06)	0.05
France	572 (09/06)	0.04
Switzerland	52 (09/06)	0.03
Italy	275 (12/06)	0.02
Norway	10 (06/07)	0.009
Belgium	19 (08/06)	0.008
Sweden	14 (10/06)	0.007
Denmark	3 (07/07)	0.002
Finland	3 (05/07)	0.002

Table 1   Estimated number of juveniles in penal custody:
Western Europe, 2004–2007 (at various dates)
Source: Adapted from Muncie (2008: 116)

References

Council of Europe (2010) *Annual Penal Statistics, SPACE 1 2008 Survey*, Strasbourg: Council of Europe.

Fergusson, R. (2007) 'Making Sense of the Melting Pot: Multiple Discourses in Youth Justice Policy', *Youth Justice* 7(3): 179–194.

Goldson, B, and G. Hughes (2010) 'Sociological Criminology and Youth Justice: Comparative Analysis and Academic Intervention', *Criminology & Criminal Justice* 10(2): 211–230.

Muncie, J. (2005) 'The Globalisation of Crime Control – The Case of Youth and Juvenile Justice: Neo-Liberalism, Policy Convergence and International Conventions', *Theoretical Criminology* 9(1): 35–64.

Muncie, J. (2008) 'The Punitive Turn in Juvenile Justice: Cultures of Control and Rights Compliance in Western Europe and the USA', *Youth Justice* 8(2): 107–121.

Muncie, J. and B. Goldson (eds) (2006) *Comparative Youth Justice: Critical Issues*. London: Sage.

Spinellis, C.D. and A. Tsitsoura (2006) 'The Emerging Juvenile Justice System in Greece', in J. Junger-Tas and S.H. Decker (eds) *International Handbook of Juvenile Justice*, pp. 309–324. Dordrecht: Springer.

Tonry, M. and A. Doob (eds) (2004) 'Youth Crime and Youth Justice: Comparative and Cross-National Perspectives', *Crime and Justice, Vol. 31*. Chicago: Chicago University Press.

United Nations Committee on the Rights of the Child (2002) *Consideration of Reports Submitted by State Parties under Article 44 of the Convention: Concluding Observations of the Committee on the Rights of the Child – Greece*, 29th Session, 1 February, CRC/C/15/Add.170. Geneva: United Nations.

United Nations Committee on the Rights of the Child (2007) *Children's Rights in Juvenile Justice*, 44th Session General Comment No 10. CRC/C/GC/10. Geneva: United Nations.

Walmsley, R. (2008) *World Prison Population List*, 8th edn. London: International Centre for Prison Studies.

Winterdyk, J. (ed.) (2002) *Juvenile Justice Systems: International Perspectives*, 2nd edn. Toronto: Canadian Scholars Press.

CHARIS PAPACHARALAMBOUS

The Adult Judicial System

This chapter offers an overview of the adult judicial system in Greece, highlighting the tensions between theory and institutional frameworks, on the one hand, and the law in practice, on the other. It is suggested here that legal doctrine offers an important insight into the logic of institutional frameworks as well as the paradoxes of the law's implementation on the ground. Equally, however, in order to appreciate the development of legal doctrine in the Greek context, it is necessary to recognise the particular historical conditions which have played a role in its conditioning. The first section of this chapter thus offers a synopsis of the evolution of Greek legal doctrine since the second half of the twentieth century situated against the backdrop of political upheaval. The focus then turns to the institutional framework of the adult judicial system – from the structures wherein judges and prosecutors are governed, to the management of caseload through to trial – with reference to the specific legal principles that underpin it. The final section seeks to underscore a number of key challenges facing the Greek adult judicial system today: the controversial question of political influence, infrastructural weaknesses, and the difficulties of balancing security and human rights in prison settings.

General Principles of Greek Legal Doctrine

Aside from respecting human dignity and its derivative principles (e.g., access to justice, the presumption of innocence, and the right to a fair trial), the Greek penal system is also committed to such principles as the search for the material truth, the need for fully reasoned judgment, the swift conclusion of proceedings, an adversarial system of trial, and proportionality. The principle of proportionality is legally safeguarded (Code of Criminal Procedure [CCP], Articles 282 et seq.) and is crucial to the debate concerning coercive measures during the pre-trial stage (e.g., pre-trial detention, on which see further Cheliotis, this collection). Indeed, the use of coercive measures, as dictated by austere judicial decisions or orders, often appears to constitute a form of pre-emptive 'crypto-penalty' (Karras, 1998; on the relation of the principle of proportionality to pre-trial detention, see Dalakouras, 1993; Margaritis, 1995: 152–158).

After the Second World War, and following the end of the Civil War (of 1946–1949), Greek legal doctrine was firmly supportive of the status quo and acquiescent towards a political climate dominated by violent ideological prejudice against the Left, remaining silent or even apologetic in the face of evidence of concentration camps, systematic killings, rapes, and torture. Over the ensuing decades, vicious anti-Leftist legislation (e.g., Laws 375/1936 and 509/1947; see further Samatas, this collection) also remained untouched by any thoroughgoing academic critique. Only after the fall of the military dictatorship of 1967–1974 were political crimes and the penal system given any serious scholarly attention (Papacharalambous, 1998; see also Mazower, 2003; Alivisatos, 1995).

German idealism had provided the bedrock to Greek penal thought, which grew increasingly politically independent, even though it still demonstrated a reluctance to engage in deeper reflectivity of any kind (on this distinction, see Hassemer, 1980: 19–22).[1] Mirroring this intellectual influence, a new theoretical trend emerged in Greek penal scholarship during the 1970s and 1980s (and was particularly associated with the School of Law

---

1   German thought has been prevalent in Greek penal rationale and law due to the dominance of the former in the continental tradition of civil law, as well as the perceived superiority of German scholarship. Greek civil law has also been influenced by jurisprudence from other jurisdictions, including France (see further Mangakis, 2005: 4–5; Giannides, 2007: 769). The dominance of German thought in Greece is likely to have stemmed, in part, from Germany's direct influence over the country via the imposition of a Bavarian monarch in 1832, shortly after Greece had won its war of independence from the Turks.

at the Aristotle University of Thessaloniki), which promoted a so-called *theory of the 'legal good'*, referring to social value rather than 'legal interest' in the Anglo-Saxon sense of the term. The theory was underpinned by legal positivism, and sought to demystify state authoritarianism and limit the expansion of punitiveness. On the one hand, this approach challenged many ideological tenets of legal theory as had been traditionally applied in Greece, and encouraged legal interpretations to be more sensitive to the principle of the 'rule of law', thus also serving to salvage some of the discipline's lost democratic credentials (see, e.g., Manoledakis, 1996: 122–129).

The fact that a great part of contemporary Greek criminal case-law refers to this theory illustrates the way in which the judiciary has adapted to, and absorbed, this shift in penal thought. This development has been counterbalanced, however, by the emergence of an inflexible dogma which has resurrected an inflexibly materialistic approach to law, marginalising reflectivity upon subjective or 'cultural' conditions that affect its interpretation. According to this logic, the corporeal origin of every criminal act is presupposed and privileged in legal judgement, whilst the motivational aspect of the criminal act is relegated to a fully secondary concern (see, e.g., Giannides, 2005: 139).

As regards the aims of penal sanctions, there has been little change since the 1980s, when retribution was replaced by special and general preventive goals. These goals were adopted not so much for their deterrent (or 'negative') aspect, but rather as 'positive' preconditions for the reintegration of the offender into society and the enhancement of lawfulness more broadly (see Courakis, 2005: 826–831). The balance between retribution and rehabilitation has not always been an optimal one, however, from over-facilitating the granting of conditional release for certain cases, on the one hand (but see also Cheliotis, this collection), to limiting release and rehabilitation opportunities for 'drug dealers' (e.g., by Law 2943/2001) and submitting to populist and symbolic politics, on the other hand (Papacharalambous, 1999, 2003c).

Since the late 1990s, meanwhile, the margins of Greek legal scholarship have seen growing interest in systems theory. This trend has drawn on Luhmann to re-analyse the Greek criminal justice system with a perspective that emphasises the 'normative' dimension of crime. Scholarship in this area has sought to re-vindicate the sense of objective wrongdoing and its punishment without dependence upon materialist accounts, and to overcome the 'modernist' distinction between a purely objective sense of wrongdoing and a subjective sense of guilt. It is an approach which has offered useful insights into issues such as the limits to deliberation and discursive communication in legal proceedings, the judicial decision as a mode of reducing social complexity, law as a binary code system, and the autarkic character of law as a self-referential system (Papacharalambous, 1993, 1994, 2003a; Vathiotis, 1999).

At the same time, mainstream scholarship has remained preoccupied with the clash between idealist and realist approaches, and with critiques of systems theory. This focus may be regarded not only as a symptom of Greek epistemological provincialism. It also points to a problem inherent in systems theory itself; namely, the simple transposition into legal theory of views which treat society as 'social mechanics', stripped of reflection upon the normative, cultural, or political dimensions that are crucial to understanding criminal justice. This problem has been enhanced in Greece by politically conservative (and even reactionary) readings of the theory intended to give a fashionable gloss to the new authoritarianism of right-wing politics. Traditionalist rejection and right-wing distortion of systems theory may be countered, however, by the enhancement of its normative dimension (for example, by focusing on political engagement to ensure social protection against heinous crimes), and thereby engaging with its political potential.

Despite the fact that systems theory has largely been read in Greece rather conservatively, it is interesting to note that so-called 'enemy penology' (Jakobs, 2005) has been almost totally rejected by Greek scholars (see, e.g., Manoledakis, 2007; Giannides, 2007; Kaiafa-Gbandi, 2005; Pavlou, 2008; Vathiotis, 2007). In sum, the argument in support of this model is that certain categories of criminals, because of the dangerousness they pose and level of public concern about them, must be fought as 'enemies' rather than policed as citizens and in accordance with safeguards and procedural guarantees of standard penal law. To the extent that the 'enemy penology' model is merely a means of rationalising state brutality, which itself undermines the rule of law, its rejection by Greek theorists is understandable (Papacharalambous, 2002b, 2003a, 2008). However, the rejection of the model in Greece does not seem to result from thorough political reflection. The same holds for so-called 'zero tolerance' measures, which are also portrayed as bound exclusively to a static conservatism. In both cases, mainstream liberal criminal law and policy discourse argues away the political element in legal theorising, conserving for itself an alleged political 'virginity', freedom from 'value-laden' thought, and 'tolerance' (Papacharalambous, 2007).

But the reality tells another story. 'Liberal' trends in criminal policy have been promoting the replacement of individualised treatment with the management of social aggregates (see Lambropoulou, 1991: 121–134). The punitive turn amongst Western states since the 1970s has been well described by Garland (2001) and Christie (1996) (see further Sack, 2005), a reality which corresponds to some aspects of the Greek situation. Indicative is the growing harshness of the Greek penal system, spanning the systematic groundless denial of temporary release to prisoners, increasing restrictions to the granting of parole, the systematic detention and expulsion of irregular migrants, and the obstruction of oversight of prisons by the Ombudsman (see further Cheliotis, this collection). Equally illustrative is the authoritarianism of the 2001 Law against terrorism (see further Mitsilegas, this collection), which passed despite strong political controversy and in full disdain of critical expert opinion. The episode offered a stark and powerful lesson on the political underpinnings of law combating 'internal enemies'.[2] Praxis belies what appears to be rejected in penal law theory, revealing once more the paradox of 'legal ideology': scholarly rhetorical abhorrence for

2   In Greece, 'organised crime' is addressed by way of an overly austere, pre-emptive and catch-all provision (Article 187 of the Penal Code), in which its entrepreneurial features are omitted from definition, thereby facilitating its analytical merging with terrorism and the construction of a conspiratorial notion of 'hyper-crime'. A later distinct provision (Article 187A of the Penal Code) aimed to distinguish so-called 'terrorist acts' (see further Anagnostopoulos, 2002; Costaras, 2000: 79–80; Kaiafa-Gbandi, 2005b: 1445; Kareklas and Papacharalambous, 2001: 117–118; Papacharalambous, 1992, 2001, 2002a, 2003b; Symeonidou-Kastanidou, 1990; 2002; 2004; 2006; 2007; Tzannetis, 2001). Special Investigative Techniques against organised crime (and principally against terrorism), provided for by Article 253A CCP, have lacked precision and practicality, such as measures for witness protection (see indicatively Dalakouras, 2001: 1023–1029; Papacharalambous, 2003d: 1055–1064; Samios, 2001; Spirákos, 2001; Vathiotis, 2001: 1048–1053).

the 'enemy penology' may conceal its actual acceptance in practice, and practice that is not acknowledged by theory can thereby be perpetuated as impure contingency.

The Greek Adult Penal System: Institutional Framework

In theory, the judiciary in Greece is independent and subject only to the Constitution.[3] According to the separation of powers, no judges (or prosecutors) can participate in public administration or in government. Criminal courts generally hold public hearings (unless unfeasible due to issues of privacy, the protection of minors, or of 'social mores'). As to the question of media presence in the courtroom, the Greek legislator has tried to balance the contradictory interests of privacy and the right to information, on the one hand, with those of judicial independence and impartiality, on the other hand, by only allowing media presence in exceptional circumstances (see further Spinellis, 1993; Karras, 1998). Criminal court decisions must be reasoned and the publication of minority opinion is mandatory (Karras, 1998; Androulakis, 1998).

Judges and prosecutors are supervised by higher-ranking colleagues and the Prosecutor of the Supreme Court. The former are appointed for life, serving until the age of 65 (or 67, in case of senior judges). Appointments are made by presidential decree, and both appointments and promotions require a decision by the High Judicial Council. Appointments may be refused if an individual seeking appointment has received convictions for certain crimes, or has been subject to disciplinary dismissal on moral or health-related grounds. Members of the judiciary are forbidden from holding a second job, participating in strike activity, holding strong partisan views of a political nature, and membership of secret organisations.

3   For further details, see Articles 87 et seq. and 93 et seq. of the Greek Constitution, and the Law regarding the courts, the judiciary, and the CCP (Law 1756/1988).

Where judges or prosecutors are suspected of a breach of their duties, and depending on the circumstances, they may be indicted by the Minister of Justice, the Supreme Court, or the Prosecutor of the Court of Appeal. Judges and prosecutors of the Supreme Court may be tried by the Supreme Disciplinary Council, whilst the plenary assembly of the Council of State (the equivalent of the High Court for cases of administrative law) decides upon their definitive dismissal. The decisions of the Council can be legally challenged by the person facing judgment, and the Minister of Justice may refer the issue to the Plenary of the Supreme Court. Providing oversight for the judiciary as a whole are a number of supervisory bodies (see further Christoforides, 2003).

In terms of court competencies, minor and more serious misdemeanours are tried by one-member or three-member tribunals of the first instance, whilst juries are present in cases involving core felonies such as manslaughter or rape. The mainstay of Greek penal justice remains three-member appeal courts, which practically judge most severe forms of criminality such as drug trafficking and organised crime. Appeals, normally relating to the suspension of a sentence, are addressed to higher courts. Local judicial competence is determined in accordance with the place where the event took place or by the place of residence of the accused. Where legal errors have been made, revision is possible (and so is the re-launch or proceedings, in exceptional cases where new evidence is available; Articles 525 et seq. of CCP). Finally, in the case of unlawful detentions, compensation is provided for (Articles 533 et seq. CCP; see further Karras, 1998).

The opening of the pre-trial stage indicates that the indictment has been set in motion. Before indictment, the preliminary investigation functions to filter out vague or legally unfounded allegations. The police investigation plays a particularly important role in determining the urgency and strength of the prosecution's case. During the pre-trial stage, procedures must be written, secrecy maintained from third parties, proportionality protected, self-incrimination prohibited, and, of course, the presumption of innocence upheld. The pre-trial stage sees the effort to balance effective prosecution and fairness with citizens' rights, although the secretive or 'intimate' procedure by which prosecution is pursued is prone to undermining the latter. On the one hand, effective prosecutions are pursued by

intensively intrusive investigations (from organised crime-tracing techniques, to quasi-mandatory testing of DNA samples in cases of violent or
sexual crimes). On the other hand, citizens' rights are primarily supported
by a system of exclusionary rules and prohibitions relating to constitutional
and penal provisions (such as the prohibition of torture, the confidentiality
of witnesses' testimonies, the requirement that an aggravating testimony
by an individual who is also accused be corroborated, and the formalities
required for house searches; see Karras, 1998; Spinellis, 2001b).

Case filtering is also carried out by councils after the pre-trial stage and
before trial: they may exonerate, defer the case to a trial chamber, or order
supplementary investigations. Judges of the councils of Appeal Courts
may bypass the councils of first-instance courts, and even make definitive
decisions concerning some categories of cases, such as organised crime and
serious economic crimes, thereby preventing the convicted individual from
appealing through the Supreme Court. This is officially justified by the need
to accelerate judicial processes, but critics point to the symbolic politics
looming behind such logic, which acts against the individual's right to be
heard. It has also been argued that this practice of excluding applications
for such appeals has impeded the development of thorough legal reasoning
by the Supreme Court on serious doctrinal questions related to organised
crime (Karras, 1998: 544–554; Anagnostopoulos, 2002: 41–43).

The trial itself is governed by the principles of public, oral, and adversarial proceedings, and by direct process, which requires the 'proximity'
of evidence (direct confirmations or manifestations are preferable than
indirect inferences, such as an eye-witness rather than a hearsay witness).
Testimonies provided in the pre-trial stage are not permitted to be substituted by their readings during the trial. According to the principle of
'moral proof', the judge is bound to make their decision on the grounds of
reasoned legal opinion, the integrity of which is controlled by the Supreme
Court. 'Moral proof' finds its limit in the exclusionary rule of Article 177(2)
of the CCP: evidence obtained through the commission of a crime is not
taken into account for a conviction, unless the court decides otherwise
on the basis of an exceptional reasoned opinion where the case involves a
felony punishable with life imprisonment (Karras, 1998; Spinellis, 2001a;
Tzannetis, 1998).

Concluding Comments: The System in Practice

As dictated by law (and noted above), the Minister of Justice is sporadically involved in matters concerning the judiciary. Despite the fact that the major political parties often blame one another on this issue, it cannot be clearly determined whether such involvement may constitute political interference, since it is hard to discern substantive claims from the usual sensationalism of political 'dogfights'. The alleged role of bar associations in lobbying to influence judicial processes has also yet to be confirmed 'beyond reasonable doubt'. Aside from the question of influence, the main problems faced by the Greek penal system relate to its administration and to delays in particular. These are caused by shortcomings of infrastructure combined with an extreme workload, which is in turn exacerbated by the excessive use of custodial sentences and a lack of alternative forms of dispute settlement (such as extended filtering of allegations, and the underuse of mediation). Certain legislative efforts have been made in response. For example, Law 3346/2005 provided for the retroactive commutation of sentences for misdemeanours where incarceration had not been served; the release on parole of individuals sentenced for misdemeanours if the sentence did not exceed two years (or even then, if one third of the sentence had already been served; see further Cheliotis, this collection); and the cancellation of short sentences (up to six months) that had not yet been served.

Turning to the role of the prosecutor in the Greek adult penal system, their main duties span pressing charges, initiating and overseeing pertinent investigations, ordering arrests in the case of crimes apprehended *in flagranti*, submitting legal remedies as and when required, and bearing responsibility for the execution of sentences (Karras, 1998: 199–212, 857–860). Prosecutors specifically charged with the execution of sentences oversee the operation of individual prison establishments, including monitoring order (in collaboration with a specialised corps of the Ministry of Justice; Articles 1–5 of Law 3090/2002) and ensuring the protection of prisoners' rights. Such prosecutors also participate on the Board of each prison, which is responsible, amongst other things, for the granting of temporary release.

As illustrated by the common role of prosecutors in resolving hunger strikes amongst prisoners, however, their commitments appear to be primarily oriented towards prison security rather than prisoner rights (see further Panousis 2003: 616–617; but also Koulouris 2003: 618).

More generally, recent years have seen a significant rise in convictions.[4] Cheliotis (this collection) elaborates that the use of long-term imprisonment has been expanding rapidly since 1990. Whilst, for example, prison admissions on remand have fallen, admissions to the prison for long terms have increased disproportionately. According to Karydis (this collection), the fact that non-Greeks are over-represented amongst prisoners in Greece is to be explained by reference to biases in the decision-making process at the sentencing stage (see also Cheliotis and Xenakis, this collection). It could be argued – and it is indeed argued by Mitsilegas (this collection) – that Greek penal policy and practice should be assessed in conjunction with influential international initiatives such as those taken by the European Union. With a view to producing more holistic accounts and, perhaps, help shape penal matters to a greater degree than has been possible to date, future scholarship should heed this plea.

References

Alivisatos, N. (1995) *Political Institutions in Crisis, 1922–1974. Aspects of the Greek Experience* [in Greek]. Athens: Themelio.

4   Contributing to this has been organised crime (which was, to a significant degree, 'imported' into the country), as it gave rise to new types of offences (from extortions to 'death contracts'), and caused an increase in juvenile delinquency (but see also Xenakis, this collection). This is shown through studies that have also, nevertheless, stressed the importance of fear of crime (on which see further Cheliotis and Xenakis, this collection; also Papatheodorou, 2005: 210–233; Courakis, 2000: 175–184; Zarafonitou, 2000). Since the 1990s, corruption has also become a crucial problem, especially in the earlier part of the decade concerning misuse of EU subsidies, broadly known as the 'Eurofraud cases' (CPCR, 1995; on corruption in Greece more generally, see Lambropoulou, this collection).

Anagnostopoulos, I. (2002) 'The Draft Law on Organised Crime: Modernisation or Decomposition of Liberal Penal Law?', in Northern Greek Jurists' Association (ed.) *The Draft Law on the Combating of Organised Crime* [in Greek], pp. 35–52. Athens-Thessaloniki: Sakkoulas.

Androulakis, N.K. (1998) *Substantiation and Judicial Control as Components of Criminal Evidence* [in Greek]. Athens: P.N. Sakkoulas.

Cheliotis, L.K. (2006) 'Demystifying Risk Management: A Process Evaluation of the Prisoners' Home Leave Scheme in Greece', *Criminology & Criminal Justice* 6: 163–195.

Christoforides, C.-E. (2003) *The Delivery of Penal Justice* [in Greek]. Athens: P.N. Sakkoulas.

Costaras, A. (2000) 'The Notion, Typification and Problematic of Sanctions against Organised Crime', in Hellenic Association of Penal Law (ed.) *Organised Crime from the viewpoint of Penal Law* [in Greek], pp. 69–89. Athens: P.N. Sakkoulas.

Courakis, N. (2005) 'Introductory Remarks on Articles 50–78 of the Penal Code', in N. Androulakis, G.A. Mangakis, I. Manoledakis, D. Spinellis, K. Stamatis and A. Psarouda-Benaki (ed.) *Systematic Commentary on the Penal Code* [in Greek], pp. 797–841. Athens: P.N. Sakkoulas.

Dalakouras, T. (1993) *The Proportionality Principle and Measures of Procedural Coercion* [in Greek]. Athens-Komotini: Ant. N. Sakkoulas Publishers.

Giannides, I. (2005) 'Article 14 PC', in N. Androulakis, G.A. Mangakis, I. Manoledakis, D. Spinellis, K. Stamatis and A. Psarouda-Benaki (ed.) *Systematic Commentary on the Penal Code* [in Greek], pp. 131–182. Athens: P.N. Sakkoulas.

Giannides, I. (2007) 'The New Legitimisation of Penal law and the End of Classical Dogma' [in Greek], *Poinika Chronika* 9: 769–775.

Hassemer, W. (1980) *Theory and Sociology of Crime* [in German]. Frankfurt am Main: Europäische Verlagsgesellschaft.

Jakobs, G. (2005) 'The Penal Law of the Citizen and the Penal Law of the Foe' [in Greek], *Poiniki Dikaiosyni* 7: 868–877.

Kaiafa-Gbandi, M. (2005) 'Delimiting Terrorist Wrongdoing and the Challenges for a Penal Law Governed by the Rule of Law', *Poinika Chronika* 10: 865–879.

Kareklas, S. and C. Papacharalambous (2001) 'Greek report', in A. Eser and J. Arnold (eds) *Penal Law as Reaction to Systemic Wrongdoing* [in German]. Freiburg i.B.: Max-Planck-Institut für ausländisches und internationales Srafrecht.

Karras, A. (1998) *Criminal Procedure Law* [in Greek]. Athens: Ant. N. Sakkoulas Publishers.

Koulouris, N. (2003) 'Internal Rules of Prisons of Type A and B' [in Greek], *Poiniki Dikaiosyni* 6: 617–618.

Lambropoulou, E. (1991) '"Tackling" the Correctional Problem through Greek Correctional Policy: More of the Same or the Same is Different?' [in Greek], *Hellenic Review of Criminology* 5–10: 117–139.

Mangakis, G.-A. (2005) 'Introduction', in N. Androulakis, G.A. Mangakis, I. Manoledakis, D. Spinellis, K. Stamatis and A. Psarouda-Benaki (ed.) *Systematic Commentary on the Penal Code* [in Greek], pp. 1–8. Athens: P.N. Sakkoulas.

Manoledakis, I. (1996) *Penal Law: Articles 1–49 PC, General Part* [in Greek]. Thessaloniki: Sakkoulas.

Manoledakis, I. (2007) 'Penal Law: Continuous Influences and Maintenance of its Character' [in Greek], *Poiniki Dikaiosyni* 11: 1311–1314.

Margaritis, M. (1995) 'Pretrial Detention', in Northern Greek Jurists' Association (ed.) *The Recent Amendments to the Penal Code and the Penal Procedure Code* [in Greek], pp. 127–159. Thessaloniki: Sakkoulas.

Mazower, M. (2003) 'Three Forms of Political Justice: Greece, 1944–45', in M. Mazower (ed.) *After the War was Over* [in Greek], pp. 33–51. Athens: Alexandreia.

Panousis, G. (2003) '"External" or Internal Prison Rules?' [in Greek], *Poiniki Dikaiosyni* 6: 616–617.

Papacharalambous, C. (1992) 'Law 1916/1990: A Case of Symbolic Penal Legislation' [in Greek], *Yperaspisi* 2: 1357–1377.

Papacharalambous, C. (1993) 'Strafprozessuale Szene und Entscheidung: Ein rechtstheoretischer Beitrag', *Rechtstheorie* 24: 353–373.

Papacharalambous, C. (1994) 'A Strategic Project in Penal Law?', in N. Courakis (ed.) *Anti-crime Policy* [in Greek], pp. 151–169. Athens-Komotini: Ant. N. Sakkoulas Publishers.

Papacharalambous, C. (1998) 'The Structure of Penal Institutions concerning Political Offences according to the former and existing Penal Laws' [in Greek], *Poinika Chronika* 5: 436–447.

Papacharalambous, C. (1999) 'The Article 106 P.C. between the Good Behaviour of the Prisoner and the "Bad" Behaviour of the Legislator' [in Greek], *Poinika Chronika* 49(6): 501–515.

Papacharalambous, C. (2001) 'The Draft Law of the Ministry of Justice on Organised Crime: An "*aberratio ictus*" with Incalculable "Collateral Damages"?' [in Greek], *Poiniki Dikaiosyni* 3: 285–292.

Papacharalambous, C. (2002a) 'Remarks on the Provisions of the Draft Law of the Ministry of Justice on "Criminal Organisations"', in Northern Greek Jurists' Association (ed.) *The Draft Law on the Combating of Organised Crime* [in Greek], pp. 53–68. Athens-Thessaloniki: Sakkoulas.

Papacharalambous, D. (2002b) 'The Penal Law of the "Foe": The European Arrest Warrant, Terrorism and Exceptional Anti-terrorist Legislation in the US' [in Greek], *Poiniki Dikaiosyni* 2: 189–195.

Papacharalambous, C. (2003a) *Naturalism and Normative Approach* [in Greek]. Athens-Thessaloniki: Sakkoulas.

Papacharalambous, C. (2003b) 'Political Crime and Terrorism' [in Greek], *Poiniki Dikaiosyni* 3: 311–320.

Papacharalambous, C. (2003c) 'Drugs: Prevention and Rehabilitation – Recent Legislative Developments' [in Greek], *Poiniki Dikaiosyni* 12: 1373–1378.

Papacharalambous, C. (2003d) 'Clearing up Organised Crime: The Problem of Interrogation Techniques' [in Greek], in *Essays in Honour of Alice Yotopoulos-Marangopoulos: Human Rights, Crime, Criminal Policy*, pp. 1047–1064. Athens/Brussels: Nomiki Vivliothiki/Bruylant.

Papacharalambous, C. (2007) 'The Penal Law of the "Foe": Beyond Liberalism' [in Greek], *Poinikos Logos* 3: 819–824.

Papacharalambous, C. (2008) 'Mass Democracy à la Guantánamo and Carl Schmitt', *Dikaiomata tou Anthropou* 37: 27–78.

Papatheodorou, T. (2005) *Public Security and Anti-crime Policy: A Comparative Approach* [in Greek]. Athens: Nomiki Vivliothiki.

Pavlou, S. (2008) 'European Union and European Convention on Human Rights' [in Greek], *Poinika Chronika* 2: 97–111.

Sack, F. (2005) *Feinstrafrecht: Auf dem Wege zu einer anderen Kriminalpolitik?* Available online at: http://www.cilip.de/presse/2005/sack_druck.htm

Samios, T. (2001) 'Interrogation Acts regarding Criminal Organisations', *Poinika Chronika* 11: 1034–1044.

Spinellis, D.D. (1993) 'Criminal Law and Procedure', in K.D. Kerameus and P.J. Kozyris (eds) *Introduction to Greek Law*, pp. 339–365. Deventer: Kluwer.

Spinellis, D.D. (2001a) 'Admissibility and Free evaluation of Evidence in the Greek Penal Procedure' [in Greek], in D.D. Spinellis (ed.) *Studies in the Penal Sciences*, pp. 289–301. Athens-Komotini: Ant. N. Sakkoulas Publishers.

Spinellis, D.D. (2001b) 'Beweisverbote im griechischen Strafprozeßrecht', in D.D. Spinellis (ed.) *Studies in the Penal Sciences*, pp. 303–319. Athens-Komotini: Ant. N. Sakkoulas Publishers.

Spirakos, D. (2001) 'The Correlation and Combination of Personal Data in the Fight against Organised Crime' [in Greek], *Poinika Chronika* 11: 1030–1033.

Symeonidou-Kastanidou, E. (1990) *The Notion of the Professional and Habitual Crime* [in Greek]. Thessaloniki: Sakkoulas.

Symeonidou-Kastanidou, E. (2002) 'Remarks on the Provisions of the Draft Law of the Ministry of Justice on "Criminal Organisations"', in Northern Greek Jurists' Association (ed.) *The Draft Law on the Combating of Organised Crime* [in Greek], pp. 69–94. Athens-Thessaloniki: Sakkoulas.

Symeonidou-Kastanidou, E. (2004) 'The Law on the European Arrest Warrant and the Combating of Terrorism' [in Greek], *Poiniki Dikaiosyni* 7: 773–786.

Symeonidou-Kastanidou, E. (2006) 'For a New Definition of Organised Crime in the European Union' [in Greek], *Poinika Chronika* 10: 865–873.

Symeonidou-Kastanidou, E. (2007) 'The Terrorist Crime: The Provisions of Law 3251/2004 and their Importance in the Context of our Penal System', in E. Symeonidou-Kastanidou (ed.) *Organised Crime and Terrorism: Contemporary Developments in European and Greek Legal Orders* [in Greek], pp. 151–165. Athens-Thessaloniki: Sakkoulas.

Tzannetis, A. (1998) 'Obtaining Evidence Illegally' [in Greek], *Poinika Chronika* 2: 105–109.

Tzannetis, A. (2001) 'The Notion of Criminal Organisation according to the New Article 187 PC' [in Greek], *Poinika Chronika* 11: 1016–1022.

Vathiotis, K. (1999) *The Prohibition of Retroaction and Objective Imputation* [in Greek]. Athens: P.N. Sakkoulas.

Vathiotis, K. (2001) 'The Protection of Witnesses according to Article 9 of Law 2928/2001' [in Greek], *Poinika Chronika* 11: 1045–1053.

Vathiotis, K. (2007) 'Confronting the "Enemy" of the Legal Order in the Context of Contemporary Anti-crime Policy', in S. Georgoulas (ed.) *Criminology in Greece Today: A Volume in Honour of Stergios Alexiadis* [in Greek], pp. 327–342. Athens: KΨM.

Zarafonitou, C. (2000) 'Fear of Crime: Research Findings and Contemporary Problematisations', in I. Daskalaki, P. Papadopoulou, D. Tsamparli, I. Tsiganou and E. Fronimou (eds) *Criminals and Victims at the Doorstep of the 21st Century* [in Greek], pp. 491–509. Athens: EKKE.

NICOLA PADFIELD

Commentary

It was a pleasure to be asked to respond to this chapter, not least because I knew I would learn more from it than I currently know about the Greek criminal justice/judicial system, but also because I knew I would also gain a useful insight into how a Greek academic saw the Greek criminal justice/judicial system. It was not a surprise that, in a book entitled *Crime and Punishment in Contemporary Greece: International Comparative Perspectives*, there should be a chapter entitled *The Adult Judicial System*. A first reading of the chapter, however, was somewhat surprising for this English lawyer. The first part is theoretical, but grounded in the reality of the recent history of Greece. How much we take for granted in England! No revolution since the 17th century, and a democratic system which, despite its evident flaws, apparently shuffles onwards without imminent collapse. There are, of course, some wonderful critical histories (Gattrell (1996) and Emsley (2005) are my favourites), but we do not have the backdrop of political upheaval which so dramatically introduces this chapter, and doubtless hangs over the book, a constant reminder of a very recent past. We take our history for granted, and this is evident in most books on the English legal system, which do not adequately acknowledge that they are but a 'photograph' of a system at just one moment in history (the best acknowledge history, of course: Malleson and Moules (2010) and Darbyshire (2009) offer brief but accurate accounts).

This chapter then moves swiftly to the 'general principles of Greek legal doctrine'. The reader is now introduced to the theory of 'the legal good', 'systems theory', and 'enemy penology'. Again, a surprise: it forced me to consider how a similar chapter would start in an equivalent English collection. For my part, an introduction to general principles would have started with due process, or a human rights perspective (see Padfield, 2008,

2010). Ashworth (2009) starts his textbook on the *Principles of Criminal Law* with the principle of autonomy, which he identifies as lying at the foundation of criminal liability: individuals in general have the capacity and free will to make meaningful choices, and this individual autonomy should be respected by others and the legal system. Elsewhere, Ashworth (2000: 253) identifies four interlinked principles which form the principled core of the criminal law:

- The criminal law should be used, and used only, to censure persons for substantial wrongdoing.
- Criminal laws should be enforced with respect for equal treatment and proportionality.
- Persons accused of substantial wrongdoing ought to be afforded the protections appropriate to those charged with criminal offences; i.e., at least the minimum protections declared by Articles 6.2 and 6.3 of the European Convention on Human Rights.
- Maximum sentences and effective sentence levels should be proportionate to the seriousness of the wrongdoing.

This is one approach. Sanders and Young (2006) prefer to measure their analysis of the criminal justice process against their core values centred on the 'enhancement of freedom'. Where does Papacharalambous start? I welcome his acknowledgement that theory, law, and practice do not walk hand in hand. Law in books (Codes of Criminal Procedure and the like) rarely reflects law on the ground. But I am concerned to read that practice that is not acknowledged by theory can be perpetuated as 'impure contingency'. Surely theory should not be used to justify bad practice? Or is Papacharalambous simply suggesting that practice should be based on sound theory (and not the other way around)? I would welcome further exploration of the criteria against which he seeks to measure the Greek judicial system. I am surprised that he leaves the human rights agenda to others to apply, and that his later descriptive sections are not more critical.

The chapter then moves the reader on to the main part of the chapter: the institutional framework of the judicial system. This still starts with 'theory': in theory, the judiciary is independent. Theory is being used here in a rather different sense: in the earlier section, we were looking at theories which justified or explained the conceptual background to criminal justice. Here we are looking at basic constitutional principles. There are, of course, threats to judicial independence everywhere. In many countries, the main threats are financial and political corruption. In the UK, the threats are, as Le Sueur puts it, of 'populist tabloid newspapers, which delight in personalised attacks on judges oblivious to the risks of undermining public confidence in the administration of justice and the rule of law; and the tendency, since the 1990s, for some government ministers to disparage judges and judgments which are regarded as politically inconvenient' (Le Sueur, 2008: 652). What are the real pressures on judicial independence in Greece? We are offered some tantalising hints in this chapter, but are left with many questions concerning the selection, training, pay, and promotion of judges in Greece. For example, who sits on, or appoints, the High Judicial Council? Can you really have a number of supervisory bodies 'providing oversight' for the judiciary? If so, do we need them in the UK? 'Judges and prosecutors are supervised by higher-ranking colleagues and the Prosecutor of the Supreme Court', but in what way are they supervised? Is this a limp appraisal system, or does pay and promotion depend on this supervision? How does Papacharalambous assess the system? How often have judges actually been dismissed?

Of course, there are fundamental differences between the judge in Greece and the judge in the UK: judges in England are traditionally fiercely independent of both the legislature and the executive, not least in order (in theory) to protect the citizen against an over-mighty state. Perhaps in Greece, the judiciary remains subordinate to its political masters? In France, for example, as Hodgson puts it, 'the executive would claim to protect citizens from the excesses of a non-elected judiciary' (Hodgson, 2005: 18). Does the Greek judiciary share the strong collegial ethos of the French *magistrature*, which seems to accept its subordinate non-elected position, an ethos which sits uncomfortably alongside the traditional 'independence' of the English judiciary?[1]

---

1   The position is changing in England as the judiciary develop a more collective ethos due, in part, to the drive for more consistency and better training.

The fact that prosecutors and judges can be considered in the same breath is, of course, a shock only for the anglophile lawyer: it is part of a 'civil law' tradition to 'blur' what for us is a fundamental distinction. It is certainly of interest to consider the architecture of a typical court in comparative perspective. In the English court, the prosecutor and defence sit as equals in the body of the court, and only the judge is raised on the bench. How does it work in Greece? And where is the suspect symbolically placed: not I hope hidden at the back, as is so often the case in the English Crown Court? There is a vast literature on English judges: from the famous classics by Lee (1988) and Griffiths (1997), to Stevens' more cautious analysis (2002). Have Greek judges been subjected to similar analysis? And there are judges and judges, of course: the English magistrate is a very different creature to the appellate judge: can one find such contrasts in Greece?

The chapter now moves on at dizzying speed. It touches on some crucial topics: criminal courts 'generally' hold public hearings (unless 'unfeasible' due to issues of privacy, the protection of minors, or of social mores). How fascinating: is this often challenged? What makes publicity 'unfeasible'? Is there a copious case law: journalists challenging their right to report cases; suspects or witnesses seeking to establish their right to privacy? Clearly the rules are different in Greece to England (see *Reklos v Greece* (2009) EMLR 16).

The brief summary of Greek criminal procedure raises further questions. How well does the pre-trial procedure described really safeguard the suspect's rights? How much empirical research has been carried out into 'case filtering'? Is there evidence of discrimination or indeed malpractice? As an outsider, I am keen to know what official or other empirical data exist on these issues. There is a tantalising paragraph on rules of evidence: what does Greek law today do with the all too common problem of, for example, witnesses too frightened to give evidence? Does it allow anonymous witnesses or hearsay evidence? Does it give practical protection to frightened witnesses?

The Greek court hierarchy can easily remain something of a confusion for the foreign observer. We are told, for example, that 'the mainstay of Greek penal justice remains three-member appeal courts'. In what sense are these appeal courts, or courts of first instance, and in what sense the mainstay? Is there usually just one level of appeal? What cases are likely to go to the Court of Cassation or Supreme Court? Can a convicted person appeal as of right? Most importantly, what are his rights to (free) legal aid? The role of the lawyer is surprisingly absent from this chapter: when he or she appears in the conclusion, we are told simply that '[t]he alleged role of bar associations to influence judicial processes has ... yet to be confirmed[.]' Surely the role of the lawyer is constantly to bite at the heels of the judicial process in order to ensure justice for his or her client? Are Greek lawyers effective? If not, why not? It was a surprise that the lawyer does not appear, either as underpaid saint or avaricious schemer (doubtless the Greek system has both, but most practising lawyers sit somewhere on the sliding scale between the two?).

Papacharalambous suggests alternative forms of dispute settlement as a solution to the 'extreme workload' faced by the courts. The role of mediation in criminal justice has huge potential, of course, but also huge dangers. What is the scope in Greek criminal procedure for plea bargains and plea negotiations? Can the prosecutor impose fines as well as supervise the execution of judicially imposed sentences? It is a pity that the book did not have a whole chapter on sentencing: we have a few short lines in the conclusion on sentencing and the execution of sentences. I asked to see the Table of Contents to see what information I could mine elsewhere. The structure of the book is fascinating. The first part on 'experiencing crime' focuses interestingly on fear, public perceptions, media, and also 'youth and crime'. The second part raises perhaps predictable topical issues: corruption, serious crime, trafficking, drugs, and so on. It is only when we get to the final section on reactions to crime where we come face to face with the institutional players. I was amused to think that the judicial system and judges had to wait their turn, to appear in the penultimate chapter of this collection. And truth be told, I actually want to be asked to review another piece of work: not just a chapter, but a whole book which subjects the Greek criminal justice process to a critically theoretical or, for me as important, a realistically critical analysis.

References

Ashworth, A. (2000) 'Is the Criminal Law a Lost Cause?', *Law Quarterly Review* 116: 225–256.

Ashworth, A. (2009) *Principles of Criminal Law*, 6th edn. Oxford: Oxford University Press.

Darbyshire, P. (2009) *The English Legal System*, 9th edn. London: Sweet & Maxwell.

Emsley, C. (2004) *Crime and Society in England 1970–1900*, 3rd edn. London: Longman.

Gattrell, V. (1996) *The Hanging Tree: Execution and the English People, 1770–1868*. Oxford: Oxford University Press.

Griffiths, J. (1997) *The Politics of the Judiciary*, 5th edn. London: Fontana Press.

Hodgson, J. (2005) *French Criminal Justice: A Comparative Account of the Investigation and Prosecution of Crime in France*. Oxford: Hart Publishing.

Lee, S. (1988) *Judging Judges*. London: Faber & Faber.

Le Sueur, A. (2008) 'Judicial Independence', in P. Cane and J. Conaghan (eds) *The New Oxford Companion to Law*. Oxford: Oxford University Press.

Malleson, K. and R. Moules (2010) *The Legal System*, 4th edn. Oxford: Oxford University Press.

Padfield, N. (2008) *Text and Materials on the Criminal Justice Process*, 4th edn. Oxford: Oxford University Press.

Padfield, N. (2010) *Criminal Law*, 7th edn. Oxford: Oxford University Press.

Sanders, A. and R. Young (2006) *Criminal Justice*, 3rd edn. Oxford: Oxford University Press.

Stevens, R. (2002) *The English Judges: Their Role in the Changing Constitution*. Oxford: Hart Publishing.

LEONIDAS K. CHELIOTIS

Prisons and Parole

Recent years have witnessed an immense growth in the use of imprisonment in Greece. Overcrowding in prison establishments is staggering and living conditions are deplorable, turning unrest and even riots into commonplace occurrences. With international watchdogs and national pressure groups joining prisoners in the chorus of outcry, the Greek state has been promising to effectuate fundamental reforms, including a decisive turn towards decarceration. This is meant mainly in the twofold sense of promoting diversionary alternatives at the pre-sentencing and sentencing stages, on the one hand, and enhancing parole opportunities for those behind bars, on the other. Promises, however, have proved to be sheer rhetoric.

This chapter begins by addressing the issue of how to gauge the scale of imprisonment in contemporary Greece. With reference to heretofore ignored indicators (i.e., annual prisoner caseloads and annual prison admissions), it is revealed that rates of imprisonment in the country are higher than commonly reported.[1] Moving from description to explanation, it is further shown that imprisonment under conviction has risen at a faster pace than pre-trial detention; that the inflation of imprisonment under conviction has resulted from a tremendous rise in the duration of stay in prison, more so than from a rise in the rate of prison admissions as such; that the extended duration of stay in prison under conviction has stemmed from the increasing length of custodial sentences and the parallel shrinking of rates of discharge; and that the upward trend in the use of imprisonment for longer periods can be traced to the so-dubbed 'liberal' 1980s.

---

1 This is without taking into account immigration detention; an issue of great importance, but one not addressed in this chapter for reasons of space (see further Cheliotis, 2012b).

Prisons

Sources of Data on Imprisonment

Although not themselves devoid of substantive gaps and methodological pitfalls, the yearbooks compiled and published by the National Statistical Service of Greece (NSSG) constitute the most comprehensive and reliable source of information about past and current imprisonment trends in the country. Secondary works, however, fall far short of exhausting NSSG data or reading them with accuracy. For instance, secondary literature usually relies on one-day snapshots alone (at times also on rather irregular snapshots), to the exclusion of annual caseloads of prisoners and annual totals of admissions to the prison.[2] Evidently, this leaves one in the dark as to the number of offenders held in custody over the course of a year, the number of offenders sent to prison by the courts over that year, and the length of their stay in prison (read further Muncie and Sparks, 1991: 92–93). Likewise, what is read as total prisoner population typically refers to the convict population only, despite explicit or implicit claims that the analysis concerns both convicted and remand prisoners. This is no small error, as remand prisoners in Greece comprise one-third to one-quarter of the total prison population (see Table 1) and the vast majority of them

2   This information is either readily available in the yearbooks published by NSSG or easily computable on the basis of the data available in NSSG yearbooks. The term 'caseload' refers to the total number of cases of offenders (whether convicts or pre-trial detainees) held in custody during a given year. To put it differently, the caseload of offenders held in custody during a given year is the sum total of the number of prisoners remaining in custody at the end of the previous year and the number of prisoners admitted to the prison system during the year at issue. On occasion, multiple cases may regard single individuals who were, for example, discharged, readmitted, and discharged again within the same year. Precisely due to the possibility of duplication or multiple counts (a possibility that remains small due to common court delays and the ever-increasing length of stay in prison), the terms 'caseload' and 'cases of offenders held in custody' are preferred here to 'yearly totals of *individual* prisoners held in custody', which is the description employed erroneously by NSSG and others.

are kept in the same facilities as convicted prisoners. What is more, the average length of remand detention (that is, 365 days) much exceeds the minimum custodial sentence, and has been reported to rank highest in the EU (Commission of the European Communities, 29 August 2006; see also later).

Whether by relying solely on one-day snapshots or by missing the prison population on remand, secondary works understate the overall scale and severity of imprisonment. Precisely because it is judged in proportion to such understated measurements of imprisonment, the extent to which non-custodial alternatives are implemented in practice is exaggerated. Ultimately, if not necessarily by design, secondary scholarship on imprisonment joins company with misrepresentations of crime as an epidemic (see further Cheliotis and Xenakis, this collection) to legitimate the further aggrandisement and harshening of the prison system under the popular banner of public safety. In much the same vein, high recidivism rates are attributed, not to the expansion of imprisonment and the contemporaneous reduction in the use of decarcerative schemes, but to what is henceforth seen as the insufficient employment of the former and the overgenerous application of the latter.

It is against this background that the following section offers a summary of basic findings from a reanalysis of NSSG data on the rates of imprisonment, focusing specifically on annual caseloads of prisoners and annual totals of admissions to the prison.

Rates of Imprisonment: 1980–2006

After a modest overall decline during the 1980s, imprisonment in Greece has known an explosive growth over the last two decades. Between 1980 and 1989, the annual total caseload of prisoners (including pre-trial detainees) fell by 6 percent, from 11,455 (or 119 per 100,000 inhabitants) to 10,763 (or 107 per 100,000 inhabitants). This was because of a drop in the caseload of convicted prisoners, significant enough to overshadow the contemporaneous rise in the caseload of pre-trial detainees. On the one hand, the caseload of pre-trial detainees increased by 22.8 percent between 1980 and 1989, from

3,269 (or 34 per 100,000 inhabitants) to 4,015 (or 40 per 100,000 inhabitants), with the proportion of cases of pre-trial detainees amongst the total prisoner caseload also rising, from 28.5 percent to 37.3 percent. On the other hand, the caseload of convicted prisoners fell by 17.5 percent, from 8,186 (or 85 per 100,000 inhabitants) in 1980 to 6,748 (or 67 per 100,000 inhabitants) in 1989. Correspondingly, the share of cases of convicted prisoners amongst the total prisoner caseload fell from 71.4 percent to 62.6 percent, although they still represented the majority (see further Table 1).

The overall fall in the annual total caseload of prisoners reflected an important 22.4 percent drop in prison admissions: from 8,490 (or 88 per 100,000 inhabitants) in 1980 to 6,585 (or 65 per 100,000 inhabitants) in 1989. Again, whilst there was a 6.9 percent rise in the total of admissions of pre-trial detainees, from 2,644 (or 27 per 100,000 inhabitants) to 2,828 (or 28 per 100,000 inhabitants), and whilst the proportion of prison admissions of pre-trial detainees amongst the total of admissions of all prisoners increased from 31.1 percent to 42.9 percent, the total of admissions of convicted prisoners fell by an impressive 35.7 percent, from 5,846 (or 61 per 100,000 inhabitants) in 1980 to 3,757 (or 37 per 100,000 inhabitants) in 1989. The share of admissions of convicted prisoners amongst the total of prisoner admissions dropped from 68.8 percent to 57 percent, but nevertheless amounted to the majority (see further Table 2).

Trends were overturned between 1990 and 2006. The annual total caseload of prisoners (including pre-trial detainees) rose by 52.6 percent, from 11,835 (or 116 per 100,000 inhabitants) to 18,070 (or 162 per 100,000 inhabitants). This is not so much because of the rise in the caseload of pre-trial detainees, as in that of convicted prisoners. The caseload of pre-trial detainees increased by 15.3 percent between 1990 and 2006, from 4,247 (or 42 per 100,000 inhabitants) to 4,900 (or 44 per 100,000 inhabitants), but the proportion of cases of pre-trial detainees amongst the total prisoner caseload fell, from 35.8 percent to 27.1 percent. By contrast, the caseload of convicted prisoners rose by a massive 73.5 percent, from 7,588 (or 75 per 100,000 inhabitants) in 1990 to 13,170 in 2006 (amounting to a rate of 118 per 100,000 inhabitants). Correspondingly, the share of cases of convicted prisoners amongst the total prisoner caseload increased from 64.1 percent in 1990 to 72.8 percent in 2006 (see further Table 1).

As one would expect, prison admissions have also been on the rise. The annual total of admissions grew by 13.2 percent between 1990 and 2006, from 7,242 (or 71 per 100,000 inhabitants) to 8,199 (to 73 per 100,000 inhabitants). The rise, in this case, is modest and relates to convicted prisoners only. Unlike what is commonly assumed, the total of admissions of pre-trial detainees is on the decline. Between 1990 and 2006, it fell by 32.1 percent, from 2,690 (or 26 per 100,000 inhabitants) to 1,824 (or 16 per 100,000 inhabitants), whilst the proportion of prison admissions of pre-trial detainees amongst the total of admissions of all prisoners dropped from 37.1 percent to 22.2 percent. The total of admissions of convicted prisoners, on the other hand, rose by an impressive 40 percent, from 4,552 (or 45 per 100,000 inhabitants) in 1990 to 6,375 (or 60 per 100,000 inhabitants) in 2006, whilst the share of admissions of convicted prisoners amongst the total of prisoner admissions increased from 62.8 percent to 77.7 percent (see further Table 2).

Some additional comments by way of clarification and qualification are in order. As concerns the period 1980–1989, the modest decline in the annual total caseload of prisoners does not appear congruent with the overall decline in prison admissions, given that the former was exceeded by the latter nearly fourfold. Similarly, the fall in the annual total caseload of convicted prisoners only equalled half the fall in prison admissions under conviction, whilst the annual total caseload of pre-trial detainees rose at a rate four times higher than the rate of prison admissions on remand. Finally, although both the caseload and prison admissions of convicted prisoners fell when the caseload and prison admissions of pre-trial detainees increased, the share both of cases and admissions of convicted prisoners remained the bulk amongst the corresponding totals. Turning to the period 1990–2006, prison admissions do not alone suffice to account for the growth in the caseload of prisoners, nor can the rise in prison admissions under conviction alone adequately explain the increased caseload of convicted prisoners. Most notably, the drop in prison admissions on remand appears to contradict the rise in the caseload of pre-trial detainees.

The key variable here is duration of stay in prison, which is to be analysed by reference to the length of custodial sentences (or, in the case of pre-trial detainees, the length of time spent in custody awaiting trial) and the levels of early discharge from prison, particularly on parole. Indeed, once attention turns to these variables, it is revealed that penal punitiveness in Greece was already undergoing an upward course in the 1980s – a decade commonly associated with a more 'liberal' approach to penal matters (see further Cheliotis and Xenakis, this collection).[3]

Duration of Stay in Prison, Length of Custodial Sentences, and Length of Pre-trial Detention

During the period 1980–1989, the average length of stay in prison under conviction knew a significant 47 percent rise, from 3.8 months to 5.6 months. In terms of custodial sentences, there was a fall in the caseload of prisoners sentenced to terms of less than a month (by 69.5 percent, from 1,555 to 474), between one and six months (by 58 percent, from 1,899 to 796), and between six and twelve months (by 19.9 percent, from 1,208 to 967). But there was a large expansion in the caseload of prisoners sentenced to a term of five to twenty years (by 77.2 percent, from 874 to 1,549), accompanied by an increase in the caseloads of prisoners sentenced to a term of one to three years (by 15.7 percent, from 1,607 to 1,860), three to five years (by 4.3 percent, from 854 to 891), and life imprisonment (by 12.5 percent, from 167 to 188). In 1989, the caseload of prisoners sentenced to a term of one to three years was the highest (27.5 percent), followed closely by the caseload of prisoners sentenced to a term of five to twenty years (22.9 percent).

Turning to the annual totals of offenders admitted to the prison during the period 1980–1989, there was a fall for terms of less than a month (by 70.9 percent, from 1,540 to 448), one to six months (by 60.7 percent, from

---

3   One could also draw attention to the rise in the use of pre-trial detention during the 1980s, as this gave way to the rapid expansion in the use of imprisonment under conviction from 1990 onwards, which marked a qualitative rather than merely quantitative development. In much the same vein, one could point to the consistent over-representation of working-class populations in the caseload of convicted prisoners, notwithstanding widening ethno-national disparities (see further below).

1,725 to 677), six to twelve months (by 19.8 percent, from 958 to 768), three to five years (by 8.4 percent, from 390 to 357), and life imprisonment (by 40 percent, from 25 to 15). But again, there was a large expansion in the total number of offenders admitted to the prison for a term of five to twenty years (by 78.2 percent, from 198 to 353), accompanied by an important rise in the number of offenders admitted to the prison for a term of one to three years (by 23.5 percent, from 989 to 1,222). Of the totals of offenders admitted to the prison in 1989, the highest was by far for a term of one to three years (29.8 percent). Not, then, that the judiciary was more liberal in their use of custodial sentences during the 1980s, but their traditionally punitive mentality (on which see further Cheliotis, 2010) manifested itself in the expanding use of long custodial sentences, more so than in the use of custodial sentences as such.

As regards the period 1990–2006, the average length of stay in prison under conviction underwent a meteoric 1,337 percent rise, from 5.1 months to 73.3 months (or 6.1 years). In terms of custodial sentences, there was a fall in the caseload of prisoners sentenced to terms of less than a month (by 76.6 percent, from 476 to 111), between six and twelve months (by 17.4 percent, from 1,201 to 991), and between one to three years (by 31.5 percent, from 2,788 to 1,909). But there was a huge expansion in the caseload of prisoners sentenced to terms of one to six months (by 122.4 percent, from 616 to 1,370), three to five years (by 323.3 percent, from 616 to 2,608), five to twenty years (by 332.7 percent, from 1,246 to 5,392), and life imprisonment (by 155.1 percent, from 270 to 689). The caseload of prisoners sentenced to a term of five to twenty years was by far the highest (40.9 percent) in 2006.

Turning to the annual totals of offenders admitted to the prison during the period 1990–2006, there was a fall for terms of less than a month (by 77.7 percent, from 462 to 103), between six and twelve months (by 19.8 percent, from 947 to 759), and between one to three years (by 35.6 percent, from 2,003 to 1,289). But again, there was a huge expansion in the total number of offenders admitted to the prison for a term of one to six months (by 127.1 percent, from 535 to 1,215), three to five years (by 699.4 percent, from 186 to 1,478), and five to twenty years (by 305.3 percent, from 374 to 1,516). Overall, admissions to the prison for a term of life imprisonment remained stable. Of the totals of prisoners admitted to the prison in 2006, the highest were for terms of five to twenty years (23.7 percent), three to five years (23.1 percent), one to three years (20.2 percent), and one to six months (19 percent). Unlike, then, what we saw earlier with regard to imprisonment under conviction in general, the periods 1980–1989 and 1990–2006 are characterised by a notable continuity as to the duration of stay in prison under conviction and the length of custodial sentences served. More specifically, there has been a durable parallel trend towards longer stays in prison under conviction and the use of ever-longer custodial sentences; a trend which gathered momentum during the 1980s and exploded since (especially in the 2000s).

As far as the duration of pre-trial detention is concerned, NSSG data are available only for the period 1998–2006. What is shown is, on the one hand, a small drop in the duration of stay in prison for one to three months (from 19.6 percent to 17.6 percent of the annual caseload of pre-trial detainees) and for three to six months (from 26.2 percent to 22.1 percent of the annual caseload of pre-trial detainees). On the other hand, there was a somewhat more notable rise in the duration of stay in prison for twelve to eighteen months (from 9.5 percent to 14.2 percent of the annual caseload of pre-trial detainees), accompanied by an insignificant rise in the duration of stay in prison for six to twelve months (from 36.7 percent to 37.9 of the annual caseload of pre-trial detainees) (see further Pitsela, 2009: 453). It has been reported that the average duration of pre-trial detention stood at twelve months in 2003 (Commission of the European Communities, 29 August 2006).

Clues to long-term trends in the duration of pre-trial detention can be gained by juxtaposing prison admissions on remand with the caseload of discharges of pre-trial detainees. From 1980 to 1989, whereas the total of admissions of pre-trial detainees rose by 6.9 percent, the annual caseload of discharges of pre-trial detainees fell as such by 6.8 percent, and by 24.1 percent in proportion to the annual caseload of pre-trial detainees. With more pre-trial detainees entering prison and their likelihood of being discharged reduced by a quarter, it is safe to conclude that the duration of pre-trial detention increased. From 1990 to 2006, whereas the total of admissions of pre-trial detainees fell by 32.1 percent, the annual caseload of discharges of pre-trial detainees fell as such by 28.4 percent, and by 38 percent in proportion to the annual caseload of pre-trial detainees. Here the likelihood of pre-trial detainees being discharged decreased to a greater extent than the flow of pre-trial detainees into prison, which allows for concluding that the duration of pre-trial detention continued rising overall.

Composition of the Prisoner Population: Main Conviction Offence and Basic Socio-demographic Characteristics

Whilst NSSG data on the criminal justice and basic socio-demographic characteristics of pre-trial detainees are lacking, this is not the case with regard to convicted prisoners.

During the period 1980–1989, the most common main offence of which prisoners had been convicted fell under the broad category of property offences (e.g., burglary, theft, and robbery). Indeed, the pertinent rate rose from 22.8 percent in 1980 to 34.1 percent in 1989. Other major offence categories included drug-related crimes (e.g., illicit drug use, drug trafficking), whose proportion in the total caseload rose from 7.6 percent to 12.8 percent; so-called 'crimes against life' (e.g., homicide), whose proportion rose from 8.2 percent to 10 percent; and bodily harm, whose proportion fell from 6.7 percent to 4.1 percent. Turning to the period 1990–2006, drug-related crimes became the most common main conviction offence, with the pertinent rate rising from 14.2 percent to 32.3 percent. The increase was most marked for drug trafficking (a crime often committed by drug addicts and systematically conflated by judges with possession of small quantities of drugs), which exploded from 56.8 percent to 94.2 percent as a proportion in the caseload of convicted drug offenders, and from 8.1 percent to 30.5 percent as a proportion in the total caseload of convicted prisoners. In 2006, 44.9 percent of convicted drug traffickers were themselves drug users. Other major offence categories included property offences, whose proportion in the total caseload fell from 28 percent in 1990 to 25 percent in 2006; crimes against life, whose proportion fell from 9 percent to 6.7 percent; and bodily harm, whose proportion fell from 3.3 percent to 1.9 percent. Special mention needs to be made of illegal entry into, departure from, or stay in the country, which grew to become one of the most common offence categories amongst convicted prisoners (and non-Greeks in particular). From 1993, when relevant NSSG data first became available, to 2006, it rose as a proportion in the total caseload from 6.9 percent to 13.9 percent.

With insignificant variation over time, cases of convicted prisoners in Greece are overwhelmingly of male and adult individuals (e.g., 93.4 percent and 99.2 percent of the total prisoner cascload in 2006, respectively). As regards the nationality of convicted prisoners in the total caseload, however, the temporal variation is striking. Between 1996 and 2006, for example, the annual total caseload of non-Greek convicts rose by 140.5 percent, from 2,253 (or 404 per 100,000 non-Greek inhabitants) to 5,420 (or 559 per 100,000 non-Greek inhabitants).[4] Correspondingly, the proportion of non-Greeks amongst the total caseload of convicts increased from 25.3 percent to 41.1 percent. This is four times higher than the estimated proportion of non-Greeks in the general population of Greece, but the level and nature of their criminal involvement fails to justify the discrepancy (see further Cheliotis and Xenakis, this collection). In 2006, and reflecting a long-standing upward trend, the majority (52.4 percent) of non-Greek convicted prisoners were of Albanian origin. During the same

4   NSSG data on cases and prison admissions of non-Greek convicts were first made available in 1996. Snapshot measurements for earlier years show that the proportion of non-Greeks amongst the total prison population nearly doubled from 1983 to 1993, rising from 11.6 percent to 22.7 percent, and by 126.2 percent in terms of absolute numbers (Spinellis *et al.*, 1996: 166–167). Courakis *et al.* cite a report written by the then Vice-Chairman of the Prosecutors' Union, Eleftherios Vortselas, to show that the proportion of non-Greeks amongst the total prison population stood at 22 percent in 1994, and that the majority of non-Greek prisoners were of Albanian origin. Albanian prisoners, the cited report concludes, 'are indeed particularly disobedient' (Courakis *et al.*, 1995: 310, my translation). An interesting aside: having climbed through the ranks to become Vice-Prosecutor of the Supreme Court, Vortselas was heavily accused in 2008 of obstructing the prosecution of his 'spiritual father', Abbot Ephraim, during investigations of the Vatopedi land-exchange scandal that rocked Greece and the then conservative government in particular (*Eleftherotypia*, 17 September 2008; on the Vatopedi scandal, see Xenakis, this collection).

period (1996–2006), the annual total caseload of Greek convicts increased by 16.8 percent, from 6,632 (or 65 per 100,000 Greek inhabitants) to 7,750 (or 76 per 100,000 Greek inhabitants), yet fell in reference to the annual total of cases of convicted prisoners, from 74.6 percent to 58.8 percent (see further Cheliotis and Xenakis, this collection).

Finally, the majority of convicted prisoners are of working-class extraction, as illustrated *inter alia* by their occupational and educational background. In 1980, for instance, 57.4 percent in the caseload of convicted prisoners had been previously employed as skilled or unskilled labourers, or as service workers. The rate did not change by 1989, but rose from 59.2 percent in 1990 to 67 percent in 2006.[5] In 1993, when official data were first collected on the educational level of prisoners, 61 percent in the caseload of convicted prisoners were either illiterate or had only completed primary education; a rate which increased to 75.4 percent by 2006. Foreign convicts are vastly overrepresented in terms of working-class occupations, but not necessarily in terms of poor educational history (see, e.g., Aloskofis, 2005).

The Prison Estate

The Greek prison estate currently comprises 34 establishments, of which there are three main types. First are the 'general' prisons, subdivided into 'type A' (for remand prisoners, debtors, and short-term convicts) and 'type B' (for long-term convicts and lifers). Second are the 'special' prisons, spanning agricultural units, young offender institutions, and the central storage and supply centre. And third are the 'therapeutic' prisons, subdivided into 'general hospitals', 'psychiatric clinics', and 'drug rehabilitation units'. There are 24 general prisons (15 of type A and 9 of type B), 7 special prisons (3 agricultural units, 3 young offender institutions, and the central storage and supply centre), and 3 therapeutic prisons (a general hospital, a psychiatric

---

5   Recent changes in the classification of employment categories may have slightly inflated the numbers for 2006.

clinic, and a drug rehabilitation unit). Women are held in two prisons, one of type A and the other of type B. Albeit the largest by a narrow margin, the Male Prison of Korydallos (located in the prefecture of Piraeus, outside Athens) is by far the most populated establishment in the country, holding around one-fifth to one-sixth of the total prison population at any given time (see also below).

The operation of prisons in Greece is coordinated centrally by the Ministry of Justice and various of its bodies, including, amongst others, the General Directorate of Correctional Policy, the Central Committee of Prisoner Transfers, and the Scientific Board of Prisons. The latter consists of eleven members, six of whom academics and one a 'specialist scientist', their formal role being to provide the Minister with independent suggestions and opinions on any aspect of prison policy (see further Panousis, 2008). In light of spectacular security failures (the most well-known of which are two helicopter escapes by the same two prisoners, from the same prison, and within the space of three years), a Secretariat of Prison Security has been formed and given increasing prominence in recent years.

As far as the inspection of Greek prisons is concerned, every establishment is served by a prosecutor, whose role is to ensure that rules and regulations are fully observed, and to monitor the fair treatment and welfare of prisoners. Prosecutorial input, however, tends to fixate on security concerns at the expense of prisoners' rights. A unit of external inspectors was established in 2001, flatteringly called 'untouchables' and 'Rambos' by government-friendly media of the day. But the unit never really got off the ground, not least due to gross understaffing (with only four individuals in place, one of which a retired member of the judiciary). At the same time, under the pretext of enforcing the strict letter of the law, ministerial authorities of all colours have restricted access to prisons for lawyer associations, medical NGOs, the Greek Ombudsman, academic researchers, and MPs (see further Cheliotis, 2012a).

Conditions of Imprisonment and Prisoner Health

The surge in prisoner numbers has been the primary stimulus of severe overcrowding in the Greek prison system. Despite the addition of new prisons and the construction of extra accommodation at existing sites in recent years, overcrowding has persisted. During the period 1994–2009, the total certified accommodation rose by 133.8 percent, from 3,892 to 9,103, compared to a 70.4 percent increase in the total prisoner population (as measured in annual one-day snapshot censuses by the Ministry of Justice). The ratio of prisoners to certified accommodation was thus brought down from 1.76 to 1.28, but the problem still pertains. Nowhere is this more evident than in the Male Prison of Korydallos. With its certified accommodation standing at 800 prisoners, the Male Prison of Korydallos held 2,018 prisoners on 1 January 2009; a ratio of 2.52.

Partly as a consequence of overcrowding, and partly due to a continuing lack of state provision, conditions of imprisonment are deplorable. A number of academic studies chime with prisoner allegations and reports by the media, national pressure groups, and international watchdog organisations that Greek prisons are plagued by insufficient floor space, limited sanitation, lack of ventilation and hot water, unsuitable room temperature, and poor hygiene. Moreover, healthcare provision in Greek prisons has long been minimal, despite the high the prevalence of serious transmittable diseases (e.g., hepatitis B and C) and mental disorders amongst prisoner populations. The rates of deliberate self-harm (e.g., wrist-cutting), suicide, and death more generally are also high; indeed, the officially recorded incidence of prisoner deaths has risen at a faster pace than imprisonment itself. Prisoner use of prescribed and illicit drugs is alarmingly common, especially as regards injection drugs, and drug abuse appears to account for the bulk of prisoner deaths (ibid.).

The overall picture emerging from inside the opaque world of Greek prisons is one of degrading and inhumane treatment that aggravates prisoners' pre-existing disadvantages and furthers their social marginalisation. It is thus a bitter irony that the Ministry of Justice was renamed in 2009 the Ministry of Justice, Transparency, and Human Rights.

Parole[6]

Parole has long been deployed as a no-cost tool for curbing overcrowding in the antiquated prisons of the country and a 'carrot-and-stick' mechanism of incentivising orderly behaviour amongst prisoners.[7] Owing to political considerations of the elites in office and the centralisation of decision-making powers in the hands of a traditionally punitive judiciary, however, harsh legal and practical restrictions have been placed upon the granting of parole. This has not simply crippled the capacity of the scheme to bring down overcrowding. The attendant frustration amongst prisoners over degrading conditions of captivity combines with resentment for the lack of promised rewards in exchange for compliant conduct to erode the effectiveness of parole as a means of pre-empting prison unrest. Indeed, prisoner riots and hunger strikes started becoming commonplace occurrences in the early 1980s, the prime demand being the expansion of opportunities for parole. The Greek state first responded by forming inquiry committees of 'specialists', many of whom simply advocated the holistic import of provisions from jurisdictions elsewhere. One way or another, a string of reforms was produced in the 1990s and early 2000s, giving rise eventually to the parole system which is in place today.

Before turning to those reforms and the current era, the discussion is put into context by reference to a reanalysis of NSSG data on the use of parole in Greece over the last three decades or so.

6   The terms 'parole', 'conditional release', and 'release on licence' are used interchangeably throughout the chapter. On the early history of parole in Greece, see Cheliotis (2010).

7   The same holds true in relation to similar schemes such as temporary release (on which see Cheliotis, 2005, 2006a).

Data on the Use of Parole: The 1980s

During the period 1980–1989, the annual caseload of convicted and remand prisoners released for any reason dropped by 26.3 percent, from 8,301 to 6,110, which was also a significant fall in proportion to the annual caseload of convicted and remand prisoners, from 72.4 percent to 56.7 percent. To differentiate between convicted and remand prisoners, the annual caseload of convicted prisoners discharged for any reason decreased by 35.3 percent during the period 1980–1989, from 5,701 to 3,688, which was also an important fall in proportion to the annual caseload of convicted prisoners, from 69.6 percent to 54.6 percent. As concerns remand prisoners, the annual caseload of discharges for any reason during the same period fell by 6.8 percent, from 2,600 to 2,422, and from 79.5 percent to 60.3 percent in proportion to the annual caseload of remand prisoners. During the 1980s, then, the drop in the rate of discharge for any reason combined with the rise in the rate of prison admissions for longer periods to offset the significant drop in the rate of prison admissions as a whole, thereby also arresting the decline in the total caseload of prisoners.

As concerns specifically the caseload of convicted prisoners released on parole, it increased by 17.8 percent between 1980 and 1989, from 381 to 449, but this was only a small rise in proportion to the caseload of convicted prisoners, from 4.6 percent to 6.6 percent.[8] One might deduce that the judiciary (Local Misdemeanours Councils in the case of parole, as elaborated later) exhibited far greater propensity to pass long custodial sentences than to grant release on parole, and that parole eligibility was delayed in good part due to the ever-increasing length of custodial sentences. Karydis and Koulouris (2002) go on to suggest that lengthier sentences may well be the means by which judges manage to control the release process before even offenders are put behind bars. Alas, these themes have yet to be subjected to thorough and methodologically reliable empirical scrutiny.

Turning to the period 1990–2006, the annual caseload of convicted and remand prisoners released for any reason increased by 16.9 percent,

8   Data for this period are not available on remand prisoners released on parole.

from 6,607 to 7,725, but fell in proportion to the annual caseload of convicted and remand prisoners, from 55.8 percent to 42.7 percent. To differentiate between convicted and remand prisoners, the annual caseload of convicted prisoners discharged for any reason increased by 46.1 percent during the period 1990–2006, from 4,021 to 5,876, but fell in proportion to the annual caseload of convicted prisoners, from 52.9 percent to 44.6 percent. As concerns remand prisoners, the annual caseload of discharges for any reason during the same period fell by 28.4 percent, from 2,586 to 1,849, and from 60.8 percent to 37.7 percent in proportion to the annual caseload of remand prisoners. In conclusion, the rise in the rate of discharge for any reason has proved too low to put a halt to the increase in the caseload of prisoners.

Particularly as regards the caseload of convicted and remand prisoners released on parole, it increased by 17.8 percent between 1998 and 2006, from 3,035 to 3,578, but fell in proportion to the annual caseload of convicted and remand prisoners, from 21.8 to 19.8. During the same period, the caseload of convicted prisoners released on parole rose by 17.4 percent, from 2,515 to 2,954, but dropped in proportion to the caseload of convicted prisoners, from 24.8 percent to 22.4 percent. The caseload of remand prisoners released on parole increased by 20 percent, from 520 to 624, but fell in proportion to the caseload of remand prisoners, from 14.2 percent to 12.7 percent.[9] It seems reasonable to deduce that the judiciary remains far less likely to grant release on parole than to pass long custodial sentences or to order remand detention, and that parole eligibility is delayed due to the ever-increasing length of required stay in prison.

The picture is complicated when attention is focused specifically on parole rates of convicted prisoners. The caseload of convicted prisoners released on parole knew a huge 392.3 percent increase between 1990 and 2006, from 600 to 2,954, which was also a very significant rise in proportion to the annual total caseload of convicted prisoners, from 7.9 to 22.4 percent. Whilst, in other words, the caseload of convicted prisoners nearly doubled, the caseload of convicted prisoners released on parole quadrupled.

9   Data for earlier years are not available or calculable.

But this trend has not been consistent over time; indeed, it has been slightly reversed in recent years. In any case, parole alone could not have put a halt to the rise in the caseload of convicted prisoners. Although release on parole has become the most common reason for discharge of convicts, rising as a percentile proportion of the caseload of all discharges from 14.9 in 1990 to 50.3 in 2006, the remaining reasons for discharge either fell or rose insignificantly during the same period (largely as a consequence of the lengthening duration of custodial sentences passed). As percentile proportions of the caseload of all discharges of convicts, discharge due to expiry of sentence fell from 19.8 to 5.8, discharge due to conversion of sentence fell from 39.6 to 19.5, discharge due to work-related 'good-time' credits rose from 8.8 to 9.5, and discharge due to other legal reasons fell from 16.7 to 14.7.

Legislative Reforms and the Use of Parole since the 1990s

We are now in a position to address the reforms of the law on parole since the 1990s, as well as the practical effects, if any, that those reforms have generated in turn.[10] In November 1991, the maximum term required before parole eligibility was reduced to three-fifths of the sentence for the general prison population and to half of the sentence for prisoners aged over seventy. Owing to conservative resistance on the part of the judiciary, however, the use of conditional release actually fell. The caseload of convicted prisoners released on licence, for example, decreased by 25.4 percent, from 440 (or 6.1 percent of the total annual caseload of convicted and remand prisoners released) in 1991 to 328 (or 4.2 percent of the total annual caseload of

---

10   In those cases where laws were ratified within the first half of the calendar year (January–June), statistical comparisons are between the preceding year and the year when the law at issue was ratified. In those cases where laws were ratified within the second half of the calendar year (July–December), statistical comparisons are between the year when the law at issue was ratified and the year that follows. The underlying principle is that the practical effects of legislative reforms will become clearer if examined over sufficient time (i.e., at least six months subsequent to their ratification).

convicted and remand prisoners released) in 1992. The corresponding rate *vis-à-vis* all reasons for release of convicted prisoners dropped from 9.6 percent in 1991 to 7.2 percent in 1992. What is more, prison admissions of convicted and remand prisoners concurrently rose by a significant 16.1 percent, from 7,462 (or 73 per 100,000 inhabitants) in 1991 to 8,880 (or 86 per 100,000 inhabitants) in 1992, thereby feeding a 13 percent rise in the caseload of convicted and remand prisoners, from 12,595 (or 123 per 100,000 inhabitants) in 1991 to 14,242 (or 137 per 100,000 inhabitants) in 1992 (see Tables 1 and 2). Further outbreaks of prison unrest were on their way.

In response, December 1993 witnessed the introduction of automatic early release for prisoners fulfilling the pertinent criteria, particularly that of orderly custodial behaviour. To be sure, this provision reinvigorated the control powers of prison officials, as they now appeared to hold the fate of prisoners tightly in their hands. At the same time, the judiciary was seemingly relegated to a mere 'approving body'. A good number of judges vocalised their opposition and many even actively resisted compliance with the law, continuing to process cases at will (Massouri, 2006: 287–288). As this caused further rioting in prisons, a new law was ratified in March 1994, whereby parole eligibility was extended to prisoners serving appealable sentences. The maximum term required before parole eligibility was reduced to two-fifths of the sentence for prisoners aged over seventy, and to eighteen years for lifers of the same age group. More importantly, the required minimum of stay in prison was brought down to two-fifths of the sentence for prisoners earning 'good-time' credits for participation in either educational and vocational training programmes or prison work. But, in actual practice, opportunities for placement onto 'good-time' schemes were so few that their function changed quickly from a means by which prisoners could expedite release to a powerful mechanism of prisoner control in the hands of allocating authorities in prison. Since the problem of overcrowding was thus bound to persist, the law also introduced a new, one-off, 'exceptional' type of automatic release, whereby short-term prisoners could be released at the one-quarter point of sentence.

As an immediate result, the caseload of convicted prisoners released on licence shot up by 382 percent, from 338 (or 4.2 percent of the total annual caseload of convicted and remand prisoners released) in 1993 to 1,630 (or

18.9 percent of the total annual caseload of convicted and remand prisoners released) in 1994. The corresponding rate *vis-à-vis* all reasons for release of convicted prisoners rose from 6.7 percent in 1993 to 28.1 percent in 1994. Meanwhile, however, judicial use of custody remained excessively high, which meant that imprisonment rates could only slightly be affected by the rise in the use of conditional release. More specifically, prison admissions of convicted and remand prisoners fell by 9.8 percent, from 8,402 (or 80 per 100,000 inhabitants) in 1993 to 7,580 (or 72 per 100,000 inhabitants) in 1994, yet remained high enough to confine the drop in the corresponding annual caseload to a mere 3 percent, from 14,847 (or 142 per 100,000 inhabitants) in 1993 to 14,390 (or 136 per 100,000 inhabitants) in 1994 (see Tables 1 and 2). The eruption of further prison unrest came as a logical consequence.

As if to undercut disparity in decision-making, a law ratified in March 1995 introduced two innovations. First, parole assessments were entrusted to three-member prison-based boards consisting of governors and specialist staff with a 'welfarist' mentality (for example, social workers, psychologists, criminologists). And second, prosecutors were assigned to individual prison establishments to supervise the internal operations thereof. But the very lack of specialist professionals, coupled with the punitive outlook predictably brought to the process by prosecutors, afforded prison governors abundant leeway to continue deploying parole as a tool of prisoner control. Judges, all the while, persisted in imposing their own preferences on the granting of early release, even as they were threatened with disciplinary proceedings by the Supreme Court (Massouri, 2006: 298–299). It comes as no surprise that the caseload of convicted prisoners released on licence dropped by 27.4 percent, from 1,630 (or 18.9 percent of the total annual caseload of convicted and remand prisoners released) in 1994 to 1,182 (or 14.7 percent of the total annual caseload of convicted and remand prisoners released) in 1995. The corresponding rate *vis-à-vis* all reasons for release of convicted prisoners fell from 28.1 percent in 1994 to 21.7 percent in 1995. Prison admissions of convicted and remand prisoners rose by 9.8 percent, from 7,580 (or 72 per 100,000 inhabitants) in 1994 to 8,326 (or 78 per 100,000 inhabitants) in 1995. An insignificant 3 percent drop can be observed in the corresponding annual caseload, from 14,390 (or 136 per 100,000 inhabitants) in 1994 to 13,944 (or 131 per 100,000 inhabitants) in 1995.

Further laws were ratified in June 1996 and September 2001, whereby parole eligibility was redefined according to length of sentence and seriousness of offence, respectively. With variation only in particulars, the provisions of these laws are still in force today. The most radical change in the law of 1996 was the abolition of a minimum term required of prisoners serving five years or less, whilst the maximum term required before eligibility was reduced to two-fifths of the sentence. For prisoners serving between five and twenty years, the minimum term required before eligibility was set at a third of the sentence, and the maximum term at three-fifths. The minimum term for lifers was set at sixteen years and the maximum remained twenty. Maximum terms were lowered to two-fifths of the sentence for prisoners serving between five and twenty years, and to sixteen years for lifers, in the case of prisoners over 70 years of age. Provisions were also made that prisoners aged over 65 earn double credit for each day spent in actual custody, and that juveniles (that is, persons aged between thirteen and eighteen) be eligible for conditional release at the one-third point of sentence.[11]

In 2001, the minimum and maximum terms before eligibility were, respectively, raised to two-thirds and four-fifths of the sentence for drug offenders serving between five and twenty years. The minimum term before eligibility was set at twenty-five years for prisoners serving a life sentence for a drug-dealing offence. A law passed in 2002 provided that foreigners subject to deportation orders following imprisonment are eligible for conditional release, but are to be deported immediately after conditional release is granted. When deportation is not possible, foreigners may stay in the country under conditional release. Subsequent legislation (on which more below) mandated that the minimum term before eligibility for those convicted of terrorist acts be 25 years, but set no minimum for prisoners convicted of high treason. At the same time, automatic release for reasons of ill health was extended to include prisoners diagnosed with one of the following: HIV/AIDS; long-term kidney failure which requires regular

---

11   Irrespective of age, each day of work in prison counts as one and a half days towards the sentence.

dialysis; resistant tuberculosis; quadriplegia; cirrhosis of the liver with a degree of disability that exceeds 67 percent; elderly dementia at the age of eighty or over; final-stage malignant neoplasms (cancer). But the list was drafted in such a way as to disqualify controversial cases: from a half-blind and nearly deaf amputee Savvas Xiros, captive member of the terrorist group November 17, to elderly and terminally ill junta officers still alive in prison (see, for example, Ministry of Justice, 26 November 2008).

At the time of writing, applications for conditional release are submitted by prison governors to Local Misdemeanours Councils one month prior to the eligibility date.[12] If the applicant is deemed unsuitable for release, prison governors may also submit to the Council a pertinent account, along with a report drafted by the social services authorities of the establishment. At least ten days prior to the hearing, prisoners are invited to attend, whether in person or via their chosen legal representative. Despite expressing concerns over what they depict as their declining role in the decision-making process, judges enjoy as wide discretion as ever. On the one hand, the law provides for the grant of conditional release as a general rule, and stipulates that negative decisions can only be an exceptional means by which to prevent further re-offending, in which case the burden of proof rests with the judiciary. On the other hand, risk of re-offending is to be assessed by resort to subjective court rulings. This is why risk assessments remain tightly and exclusively tied to such a slippery criterion as that of 'custodial behaviour', even though it bears a tenuous link to recidivism. It is indicative that, whilst most judges equate good custodial behaviour with the absence of prior disciplinary record, there is no consensus as to whether past failure to comply with the conditions of home leave should count against the applicant (Massouri, 2006: 340–341).

In the event of conditional release being granted, conditions may be imposed upon the parolee regarding his or her 'lifestyle and especially his or her place of residence'. These conditions may be revoked or modified upon the request of the parolee. As concerns adult prisoners, if the remainder

---

12   Juvenile cases are dealt with in three-member juvenile tribunals (see further Pitsela, this collection).

of the sentence to be served is three years or less, the licence stays in force for three years. If the remainder of the sentence to be served exceeds three years, the licence stays in force until the entire sentence has expired. In the case of lifers, the licence stays in force for ten years. As concerns juvenile prisoners, the licence stays in force until the entire sentence has expired. Responsible for the supervision of parolees is the newly established body of probation officers (on which more shortly). The law draws a technical distinction between recall and suspension of conditional release. Licences are *recalled*, by the Local Misdemeanours Council following the recommendation of the supervising authorities, when parolees fail to abide by the conditions imposed. In such cases, the time spent on licence does not count towards the sentence. Licences are *suspended* when parolees commit premeditated offences punishable by imprisonment for a term longer than six months. In such cases, parolees are returned to prison to serve both the new sentence and the whole of the period between release on licence and the expiry of the original sentence.

Thanks to the law of 1996, the caseload of convicted prisoners released on licence rose by an impressive 47.6 percent within a single year, from 1,182 (or 14.7 percent of the total annual caseload of convicted and remand prisoners released) in 1995 to 1,745 (or 22 percent of the total annual caseload of convicted and remand prisoners released) in 1996. The corresponding rate *vis-à-vis* all reasons for release of convicted prisoners increased from 21.7 percent in 1995 to 33.6 percent in 1996. All the while, prison admissions of convicted and remand prisoners fell by 9.6 percent, from 8,326 (or 78 per 100,000 inhabitants) in 1995 to 7,524 (or 70 per 100,000 inhabitants) in 1996. The corresponding annual caseload dropped by 4.7 percent, from 13,944 (or 131 per 100,000 inhabitants) in 1995 to 13,281 (or 124 per 100,000 inhabitants) in 1996. To assess the impact of the 1996 reform on a longer-term basis, the caseload of convicted prisoners released on licence rose by 116.5 percent, from 1,182 (or 14.7 percent of the total annual caseload of convicted and remand prisoners released) in 1995 to 2,560 (or 35 percent of the total annual caseload of convicted and remand prisoners released) in 2000. The corresponding rate *vis-à-vis* all reasons for release of convicted prisoners increased from 21.7 percent in 1995 to 45.1 percent in 2000. Over the same period, prison admissions of convicted and remand prisoners saw a slight increase of 2.8 percent, from 8,326 (or 78 per 100,000 inhabitants) in 1995 to 8,563 (or 78 per 100,000 inhabitants) in 2000. The corresponding annual caseload rose by 5.4 percent, from 13,944 (or 131 per 100,000 inhabitants) in 1995 to 14,708 (or 109 per 100,000 inhabitants) in 2000 (see Tables 1 and 2). It is reasonable to conclude that the rather modest increase in the use of custodial sentences, on the one hand, and the significant rise in the use of conditional release, on the other hand, helped minimise the growth of the prisoner caseload during 1995–2000.

Turning to the impact of the law of 2001, the caseload of convicted prisoners released on licence fell by 5.4 percent, from 2,639 (or 31 percent of the total annual caseload of convicted and remand prisoners released) in 2001 to 2,497 (or 30.5 percent of the total annual caseload of convicted and remand prisoners released). The corresponding rate *vis-à-vis* all reasons for release of convicted prisoners fell from 40.2 percent in 2001 to 38.1 percent in 2002. Concurrently, the annual total caseload of convicted and remand prisoners remained essentially static (falling from 16,446 (or 150 per 100,000 inhabitants) in 2001 to 16,444 (or 150 per 100,000 inhabitants) in 2002).[13] On a longer-term basis, the caseload of convicted prisoners released on licence rose by 11.9 percent, from 2,639 (or 31 percent of the total annual caseload of convicted and remand prisoners released) in 2001 to 2,954 (or 38 percent of the total annual caseload of convicted and remand prisoners released) in 2006. The corresponding rate *vis-à-vis* all reasons for release of convicted prisoners increased from 40.2 percent in 2001 to 50.3 in 2006. At the same time, the annual caseload of convicted and remand prisoners rose by 9.8 percent, from 16,446 (or 150 per 100,000 inhabitants) in 2001 to 18,070 (or 162 per 100,000 inhabitants) in 2006 (see Tables 1 and 2). In stark contrast, then, with the previous six years, the rise in the use of conditional release proved insufficient to prevent a significant growth in the prisoner caseload, even as prison admissions fell.

13 For reasons relating to the accuracy of the data for the year 2001, reference is not made to admissions data in this case (see further Table 2).

The 2008 Prison Riots and Parole

The prison system of Greece was shaken to its roots in November 2008. For eighteen consecutive days, some 6,000 prisoners, or half of the prison population at the time, either abstained from prison food or, as became increasingly the case, went on complete hunger strike. During this time, two prisoner deaths were reported, one attempted suicide, whilst tens of others sewed their lips together. It was a desperate mass protest directed against the underuse and unfair administration of parole and temporary release, overcrowded and degrading conditions, inadequate medical provision, and abusive prison staff, to name but a few of the grievances. A significant minority amongst the Greek public sympathised with the protesters. With marches and motorbike rallies through city centres, demonstrations outside prisons, open-air concerts featuring well-known Greek artists, and internet blogging, supporters joined prisoners in calling not only for reforms, but also for the eventual abolition of prisons (Cheliotis and Xenakis, 2008). Opposition extended outside the country's borders, as the then Minister of Finance Yorgos Alogoskoufis discovered at the London School of Economics, where he came under sustained egg-pelting from Greek anti-prison agitators.

The government responded spasmodically. A new law was passed within less than a month, introducing various measures of a one-off character.[14] Most notably, the maximum term before eligibility for discretionary conditional release was lowered from four-fifths to three-fifths of the sentence for prisoners serving drug-related sentences between five and twenty years.[15] Prisoners convicted of serious organised drug dealing were exempted, but the authorities declared emphatically that the remaining

14   The sole exception was the aforementioned provisions for early release on grounds of ill health, which were given a permanent character.

15   In December 2009, and largely in response to prisoner protests in eight establishments one month earlier, the then newly elected centre-left government of PASOK passed a number of permanent amendments to the legal provisions concerning conditional release. Crucially, the amendments included lowering the maximum term before eligibility for discretionary conditional release to three-fifths of the sentence for prisoners serving drug-related sentences between five and twenty years. The applicability of the amendments, however, is likely to be plagued by the same problems encountered with the 2008 law (on which more in a moment).

two-thirds (or 4,900) of drug convicts would still benefit from the new law (Ministry of Justice, 19 November 2008). Further provisions included the automatic conditional release of misdemeanour offenders (after serving a fifth of sentences up to two years or a third of sentences over two years) and the discretionary conversion of sentences up to five years into monetary penalties at a minimum rate of 3 Euros per day. Eligible prisoners lacking the necessary financial resources were given the alternative to opt for early release on a community work order.

Following what was described as a thorough examination of the records of all 12,315 offenders held in prison at the time, the Minister of Justice, Sotiris Hadjigakis, announced that 5,500 were to be released by April 2009 at the latest (*Kathimerini*, 1 January 2009). Of those, 3,720 were to be released imminently so that they could 'spend Christmas and New Year's with their significant others'. All this, Hadjigakis asserted in a speech he gave to parliament, was a gesture of '[Aristotelian] leniency', 'sin-forgiving', and 'benefaction', a 'second chance [to petty offenders] to start their lives afresh' (Ministry of Justice, 25 November 2008). Official predictions were made concurrently that the overall capacity of the prison estate would quickly overtake the number of prisoners behind bars (8,243 vs. 6,815, respectively, by April 2009; Ministry of Justice, 26 November 2008).

But it was only by way of heuristic analogy that state authorities compared the promised reduction of the prison population by half to 'closing down three large prison establishments' (*Kathimerini*, 1 January 2009). Prison population forecasts were based on the two-fold assumption that the courts would suddenly cease passing custodial sentences (for releases and releases alone could hardly ever suffice to bring the prison population down to 6,815), and that the use of early release would expand according to plan. If the former was false by definition, the latter was bound to be disproved very soon. Anticipating the obvious, Hadjigakis coupled his discourse of generosity and open-heartedness with stern assurances that four new prison establishments (or an additional 1,290 places) would be ready to operate before the end of 2009 (ibid.; see also below).[16]

16 It is worth noting here that, during his time at the Ministry of Justice, Hadjigakis was alleged to have made sure that a branch of *Themis Kataskevastiki*, a construction company affiliated with and supervised by the Ministry, opened in his home city

Indeed, the new law was replete with self-defeating features. Though referred to as the major 'beneficiaries' of the new law, petty drug-possession offenders could only rarely fall under the provisions for conditional release at the three-fifth point of sentence. The reason was that most had been penalised so harshly by sentencing courts as to be convicted of serious organised drug dealing (a phenomenon on which see further Lambropoulou, 2003). Not dissimilarly, the conversion of prison sentences into monetary penalties was a real possibility solely for the tiny minority of prisoners who could find the financial means required. For want of a permit to stay in the country, the majority of foreign prisoners were not even entitled to a tax number (similar to a UK Schedule D number), the latter being a necessary prerequisite for the conversion of their prison sentence into a monetary penalty. The alternative to opt for community work was essentially a non-option, given that opportunities for work of this kind were few and far between. To top it all off: with its discretionary powers untouched, the judiciary could in any case ensure that 'front-door' entries would not be offset by 'back-door' conversions of sentences into monetary penalties or community work orders.[17]

Further difficulties were to be found beyond the narrow confines of the law. Leaving aside the pockets of public sympathy to prisoners and their struggles, the broader socio-political climate could not have been less conducive to the application of decarcerative reforms on the shopfloor. Before the new law was even ratified formally, the fatal shooting of unsuspecting fifteen-year-old Alexandros Grigoropoulos by a police officer sparkled three weeks of violent civil unrest across Greece. Unwilling to address the root causes of the crisis (that is, a mixture of police brutality and impunity, political corruption, unemployment and precarious labour, and degraded education), the Greek government spoke of 'acts of blind violence' resulting from 'the exploitation of the anxieties of the youth by extreme elements'

(and electoral prefecture) of Trikala. It was also alleged that all staff appointed there were offspring or other relatives of members of the same political party as Hadjigakis (i.e., New Democracy) (*O Kosmos tou Ependyti*, 25–26 January 2009). The affair was subsequently discussed in parliament.

17   This is not to negate the possibility of professional resistance (on which see further Cheliotis, 2006b), only to doubt the degree of its applicability in the case at issue.

(*Athens News Agency*, 12 December 2008). Pledges to exhibit 'zero-tolerance' and restore 'law and order' followed suit (read, for example, *The Sunday Times*, 14 December 2008). The cacophony of warring voices must have sounded like music in the ears of judges, for they were now abler than ever to legitimate and enhance their long-standing punitive stance.

It comes as no surprise that a mere 370 prisoners were released under the new law by the end of 2008 (Ministry of Justice, 29 December 2008), and only 968 by 10 April 2009 (*Eleftherotypia*, 10 April 2009), not to mention that most of them would have been released under previous law anyway. Nikos Dendias, who took over as Minister of Justice in the meantime, was forced to admit to what he termed a 'partial failure'. Of which, however, he also absolved himself and his predecessor by blaming the missed target on a 'tragic mistake in the calculations owing to the lack of a dedicated statistical service at the ministry' (ibid., my translation). Explaining away failures is deeply ingrained in everyday practice throughout contemporary Greece. As Herzfeld says of Greek bureaucrats, for instance, 'the buck-passing is consistent: clerk to supervisors, registrar to superiors, deputy mayor to mayor, mayor to prefect and minister' (Herzfeld, 1992: 92). And minister to no-one, we may now add.

Parole and 'Re-entry'

At first sight, more constructive steps seem to have been taken towards helping parolees in the transition between imprisonment and discharge. Following a thirteen-year period of gestation, for example, the establishment of a nationwide probation agency entrusted with responsibilities for aftercare supervision was finally brought into effect in 2004. Ever since, however, street-level practice has been fraught with difficulties, from ill-defined duties for practitioners and their lack of training to understaffing and disproportionately high caseloads (see further Giovanoglou, 2006: 204–213). It is plausible to suggest that the small but growing body of probation officers is mainly preoccupied with running routine checks on parolees for technical infractions, more so than with demanding tasks of a welfarist, aftercare orientation (for example, assistance in securing employment, housing, or placement onto professional training schemes).

The emerging gap is said to have been filled by a private-law, state-supervised organisation named EPANODOS, meaning 're-entry', which was inaugurated amidst great fanfare in 2007. In this case, too, however, there is a yawning abyss between theory and practice. It is not so much that EPANODOS suffers from insufficient resources (certainly human and possibly financial), nor the flawed presumption underlying its rhetoric (and reflected in its very name) that prisoners were once included in mainstream society. It is principally that the organisation itself lacks conviction in the possibility of rehabilitation for the vast majority of prisoners. In a paper presented at the re-training programme of the National School of Judges in 2005, for example, the academician later appointed head of EPANODOS declared that the problems faced by young prisoners in seeking employment after discharge 'appear insurmountable'. In good part, he went on to explain by reference to a self-exonerative conventional wisdom, this is due to chronic drug addiction and the attribute of 'laziness' instilled into the youth as a result of their incarceration, to such an extent that they would rather choose prison over life on the outside. If there is any rehabilitative hope for young prisoners, he concluded, it is to be placed mainly with the youngest of them, 'there where the branch is not yet crooked' (Courakis, 2005: 11, my translation). Were all this to be true, then riots and hunger strikes would merely be games by which 'lost causes' break their monotony, rather than generalised struggles for dignity and freedom.

But there is more. Although high fear of crime amongst Greeks remains stubbornly disproportionate to the objective risk of victimisation (see Cheliotis and Xenakis, this collection), the head of EPANODOS led the publication of a state-funded manual instructing 'active citizens' as to the 'best practices' of minimising vulnerability: from installing bolt-type locks on home doors and avoiding riding in elevators with strangers, to parking cars tightly adjacent to pavement edges lest thieves plan to tow vehicles away (see Courakis, ed., 2006: 21–42). It requires quite a stretch of the imagination to believe that such an organisation can actually help prisoners find their way back into a community that never wished to incorporate them anyway (see further Cheliotis and Xenakis, this collection). It is, instead, more likely that the function of EPANODOS is to provide an evermore punitive system with a veneer of humanism – a 'human face', as the suggestive buzzword of the day has it. Indeed, purportedly in opposition to such efforts to beautify penality, a group of self-dubbed anarchists went so far as to violently interrupt a conference organised by EPANODOS in central Athens in February 2009.

Concluding Remarks

There is no inherent contradiction in the fact that legal and practical restrictions on parole fuel unrest in prisons and beyond, or that mixing increased surveillance of parolees with inadequate provisions to them is destined to push recall and suspension rates higher, or that rises in the use of imprisonment may well be causally related to recidivism (see, for example, Cheliotis, 2008, 2009). The buck for the failure of penality, in this case, is passed to the victims. Cohen puts the point astutely when he writes that, in the same way as the health industry attributes iatrogenic illness to purported faults of patients, so crime-control ideologues blame systemic failure on offenders, be they captive or otherwise. 'A special group of offenders is particularly to blame: the incorrigibles, the hard cores, the career criminals who so ungratefully persist in keeping recidivism rates so high. If only they would cooperate!' (Cohen, 1985: 169). Ultimately, and utterly paradoxically, the misfires of penality legitimate its own existence, aggrandisement, and harshening at the expense of decarceration, but also subtly in support of social control more broadly (see further Cheliotis and Xenakis, this collection; Cheliotis, 2010 and 2011).

Year	Total caseload of prisoners		Caseload of convicted prisoners			Caseload of remand prisoners		
	n.	per 100,000 inhabitants	n.	%	per 100,000 inhabitants	n.	%	per 100,000 inhabitants
1980	11,455	119	8,186	71.4	85	3,269	28.5	34
1981	10,306	106	7,200	69.8	74	3,106	30.1	32
1982	9,602	98	6,417	66.8	66	3,185	33.1	33
1983	10,110	103	7,043	69.6	72	3,067	30.3	31
1984	10,082	102	7,214	71.5	73	2,868	28.4	29
1985	9,114	92	6,198	68.0	62	2,916	31.9	29
1986	9,818	99	6,420	65.3	64	3,398	34.6	34
1987	10,536	105	6,960	66.0	70	3,566	33.9	36
1988	10,422	104	6,921	66.4	69	3,501	33.5	35
1989	10,763	107	6,748	62.6	67	4,015	37.3	40
1990	11,835	116	7,588	64.1	75	4,247	35.8	42
1991	12,595	123	7,992	63.4	78	4,603	36.5	45
1992	14,242	137	8,649	60.7	83	5,593	39.2	54
1993	14,847	142	9,866	66.4	94	4,981	33.5	48
1994	14,390	136	9,883	68.6	93	4,507	31.3	43
1995	13,944	131	9,377	67.2	88	4,567	32.7	43
1996	13,380	125	8,885	66.4	83	4,495	33.5	42
1997	13,344	124	8,997	67.4	83	4,347	32.5	40
1998	13,912	128	10,130	72.8	93	3,782	27.1	35
1999	13,409	123	9,910	73.9	91	3,499	26.0	32
2000	14,708	134	11,555	78.5	106	3,153	21.4	29
2001	16,446	150	12,687	77.1	116	3,759	22.8	34
2002	16,444	150	12,684	77.1	115	3,760	22.8	34

2003	17,191	156	12,889	74.9	117	4,302	25.0	39
2004	17,227	156	12,634	73.3	114	4,593	26.6	42
2005	17,869	161	13,082	73.2	118	4,787	26.7	43
2006	18,070	162	13,170	72.8	118	4,900	27.1	44

Table 1 Caseload of convicted and remand prisoners in Greece, 1980–2006; the incidence rate of imprisonment under conviction and remand per 100,000 inhabitants in Greece, 1980–2006.
Sources of primary data: National Statistical Service of Greece (NSSG), Statistical Yearbook and Justice Statistics. The data were compiled and analysed by the author. Note: Data for the years 2002, 2003, and 2004 are based on NSSG estimates, as they were published originally. The latest (2007) statistical yearbook of the NSSG provides slightly different estimates that hardly affect the analysis. Annual incidence rates of imprisonment per 100,000 inhabitants are rounded, and were calculated on the basis of NSSG estimates of the country's total population on 30 June each year.

| Year | Total number of admissions | | Admissions of convicted prisoners | | | Admissions of remand prisoners | | |
	n.	per 100,000 inhabitants	n.	%	per 100,000 inhabitants	n.	%	per 100,000 inhabitants
1980	8,490	88	5,846	68.8	61	2,644	31.1	27
1981	7,171	73	4,728	65.9	49	2,443	34.0	25
1982	6,561	67	4,156	63.3	42	2,405	36.6	25
1983	6,959	71	4,880	70.1	50	2,079	29.8	21
1984	6,393	65	4,559	71.3	46	1,834	28.6	19
1985	5,690	57	3,620	63.6	36	2,070	36.3	21
1986	6,435	65	4,048	62.9	41	2,387	37.0	24
1987	6,832	68	4,239	62.0	42	2,593	37.9	26
1988	6,613	66	4,131	62.4	41	2,482	37.5	25
1989	6,585	65	3,757	57.0	37	2,828	42.9	28
1990	7,242	71	4,552	62.8	45	2,690	37.1	26

1991	7,462	73	4,455	59.7	43	3,007	40.2	29
1992	8,880	86	5,250	59.1	51	3,630	40.8	35
1993	8,402	80	5,779	68.7	55	2,623	31.2	25
1994	7,580	72	5,099	67.2	47	2,481	32.7	24
1995	8,326	78	5,429	65.2	51	2,897	34.7	28
1996	7,524	70	5,015	66.6	47	2,509	33.3	23
1997	8,105	75	5,504	67.9	51	2,601	32.0	24
1998	7,819	72	6,035	77.1	56	1,784	22.8	16
1999	6,403	59	5,308	82.8	49	1,095	17.1	10
2000	8,563	78	7,142	83.4	65	1,421	16.5	13
2001	11,921	108	8,901	74.6	81	3,020	25.3	27
2002	8,473	77	6,610	78.0	60	1,863	21.9	17
2003	9,347	84	6,803	72.7	62	2,544	27.2	23
2004	9,057	82	6,485	71.6	58	2,572	28.3	25
2005	8,851	79	6,702	75.7	60	2,149	24.2	19
2006	8,199	73	6,375	77.7	60	1,824	22.2	16

Table 2 Prison admissions of convicted and remand prisoners in Greece, 1980–2006; the incidence rate of prison admission under conviction and remand per 100,000 inhabitants in Greece, 1980–2006.

Sources of primary data: National Statistical Service of Greece (NSSG), Statistical Yearbook and Justice Statistics. The data were compiled and analysed by the author.
Notes: Data for the years 2002, 2003, and 2004 are based on NSSG estimates, as they were published originally. The latest (2007) statistical yearbook of the NSSG provides slightly different estimates that hardly affect the analysis. Data for the year 2001 should be treated with caution: the calculations on which they are based, use data for the year 2000 that do not include 2,036 cases of convicted prisoners and 777 cases of remand prisoners about whom no information was provided by the authorities in charge. Annual incidence rates per 100,000 inhabitants are rounded, and were calculated on the basis of NSSG estimates of the country's total population on 30 June each year.

References

Aloskofis, W. (2005) *Social and Penal Situation of Prisoners in the Judicial Prison of Korydallos: Differences between Natives and Foreigners* [in Greek]. Report submitted to the Ministry of Justice.

Athens News Agency (12 December 2008) 'Greek Prime Minister Calls for an End to "Acts of Blind Violence"'.

Cheliotis, L.K. (2005) 'The Prison Furlough Programme in Greece: Findings from a Research Project in the Male Prison of Korydallos', *Punishment & Society* 7(2): 201–215.

Cheliotis, L.K. (2006a) 'Demystifying Risk Management: A Process Evaluation of the Prisoners' Home Leave Scheme in Greece', *Criminology & Criminal Justice* 6(2): 163–195.

Cheliotis, L.K. (2006b) 'How Iron is the Iron Cage of New Penology? The Role of Human Agency in the Implementation of Criminal Justice Policy', *Punishment & Society* 8(3): 313–340.

Cheliotis, L.K. (2008) 'Reconsidering the Effectiveness of Temporary Release: A Systematic Review', *Aggression and Violent Behavior* 13(3): 153–168.

Cheliotis, L.K. (2009) 'Before the Next Storm: Some Evidence-based Reminders about Temporary Release', *International Journal of Offender Therapy and Comparative Criminology* 53(4): 420–432.

Cheliotis, L.K. (2010) 'Greece', in N. Padfield, D. van Zyl Smit and F. Dünkel (eds) *Release from Prison: European Policy and Practice*, pp. 213–236. Cullompton: Willan.

Cheliotis, L.K. (2011) 'Governing through the Looking-Glass: Neoliberalism, Managerialism and the Psychopolitics of Crime Control' [in Italian], *Studi sulla questione criminale* 6(1): 47–94.

Cheliotis, L.K. (2012a) 'Suffering at the Hands of the State: Conditions of Imprisonment and Prisoner Health in Contemporary Greece', *European Journal of Criminology* 9(1): 1–25.

Cheliotis, L.K. (2012b) 'Matter out of Place: Immigration Detention in Greece', *European Journal of Criminology* 9(6).

Cheliotis, L.K. and S. Xenakis (2008) 'Public Support for Prison Protests: Greece in the Spotlight', *Statewatch: Monitoring the State and Civil Liberties in Europe* (20 November 2008). Available online at: http://www.statewatch.org/news/2008/nov/greece-prison-protests.pdf (Accessed 9 June 2009)

Cohen, S. (1985) *Visions of Social Control*. Cambridge: Polity.

Commission of the European Communities (29 August 2006) *Commission Staff Working Document, Accompanying Document to the Proposal for a Council Framework Decision on the European Supervision Order in Pre-trial Procedures between Member States of the European Union: Impact Assessment.* Available online at: http://ec.europa.eu/justice_home/doc_centre/criminal/recognition/docs/ sec_2006_1079_en.pdf (Accessed 16 June 2009)

Courakis, N.E. (2005) 'Recidivism Problems of Young Prisoners: Findings from a Follow-up Study', paper presented at the 12th Re-training Programme of the National School of Judges, Komotini, 11–14 October [in Greek]. Available online at: http://www.law.uoa.gr/crime-research/nearoiapofylakizomenoi.pdf (Accessed 8 June 2009)

Courakis, N.E. (ed.) (2006) *In Order for us to Feel Safe in a Society of Active Citizens: A Practical Manual for the Lawful Protection of Citizens from Everyday Lawbreaking* [in Greek]. Athens-Komotini: Ant. N. Sakkoulas Publishers.

Courakis, N., Milioni, F. and Student Research Group of the Athens Law School (1995) *Research in Greek Prisons: The Juvenile Correctional Establishments of Korydallos and Kassavetia.* Athens-Komitini: Ant. N. Sakkoulas Publishers.

Eleftherotypia (17 September 2008) 'In the Morning… Enemies, in the Evening Together' [in Greek].

Eleftherotypia (10 April 2009) 'Dendias: The Project of Releases Failed' [in Greek].

Giovanoglou, S. (2006) *Institutional Problems of Social Reintegration of Released Prisoners* [in Greek]. Athens-Thessaloniki: Sakkoulas.

Herzfeld, M. (1992) *The Social Production of Indifference: Exploring the Symbolic Roots of Western Bureaucracy.* Chicago and London: University of Chicago Press.

Karydis, V. and N. Koulouris (2002) 'Conditional Release: A Ship without Governor and Destination?' [in Greek], *Poiniki Dikaiosyni* 49: 504–506.

Kathimerini (1 January 2009) '"Ticket of leave" for Hundreds of Prisoners' [in Greek].

Lambropoulou, E. (2003) 'Drug Policy in Greece: A Balance between Enforcement and Persuasion', *European Journal of Crime, Criminal Law and Criminal Justice* 11(1): 18–39.

Massouri, G.S. (2006) *The Introduction and Development of Conditional Release for Adults in Greece as Idiosyncratic Pardon* [in Greek]. Athens-Komotini: Ant. N. Sakkoulas Publishers.

Ministry of Justice (19 November 2008) 'Final Provisions for a Modern Correctional System' [Press release in Greek].

Ministry of Justice (25 November 2008) 'The goal of the Ministry of Justice is that 3,720 prisoners released under the beneficiary provisions spend holidays with their families' [Press release in Greek].

Ministry of Justice (26 November 2008) 'The social programme for the correctional system was ratified unanimously by the governmental committee' [Press release in Greek].

Ministry of Justice (29 December 2008) 'Prisoner discharges' [Press release in Greek].

Muncie, J. and R. Sparks (1991) 'Expansion and Contraction in European Penal Systems', in J. Muncie and R. Sparks (eds) *Imprisonment: European Perspectives*, pp. 89–106. New York: Harvester Wheatsheaf.

O Kosmos tou Ependyti (25–26 January 2009) 'Vote Contractor Sotiris Hadjigakis' [in Greek].

Panousis, G. (2008) 'Central Scientific Board of Prisons: A First Account (1996–2002)', in S. Vidali and P. Zagoura (eds) *Counselling and Prison* [in Greek], pp. 121–140. Athens-Komotini: Ant. N. Sakkoulas Publishers.

Pitsela, A. (2009) 'Greece', in M.K. van Kalmhout, M.M. Knapen and C. Morgenstern (eds) *Pre-trial Detention in the European Union: An Analysis of Minimum Standards in Pre-trial Detention and the Grounds for Regular Review in the Member States of the EU*, pp. 437–464. Nijmegen: Wolf Legal Publishers.

Spinellis, C.D., Angelopoulou, K. and N. Koulouris (1996) 'Foreign Detainees in Greek Prisons: A New Challenge to the Guardians of Human Rights', in R. Matthews and P. Francis (eds) *Prisons 2000: An International Perspective on the Current State and Future of Imprisonment*, pp. 163–178. Basingstoke and London: Macmillan Press.

The Sunday Times (14 December 2008) 'Greek Riots Spark Fear of Europe in Flames'.

ROY D. KING

Commentary

Prisons and Parole in Greece: A Familiar Story

That the prison and parole systems in Greece are in a state of disarray comes as no great surprise. Greece is in good company. When I last looked (King, 2007), I categorised Greece, along with Austria, Spain, Ireland and Hungary, in the group of nations with the second highest rate of growth in imprisonment per 100,000 population. The comparison was based on snapshot data from the *World Prison Population Lists*, for the period between the first edition (Walmsley, 1999) and sixth edition (Walmsley, 2005), and it meant that Greece had moved from being a low user of imprisonment (those with imprisonment rates below 75 per 100,000) to a moderate user (with rates up to 150 per 100,000).[1] In that comparison, Greece was joined, somewhat surprisingly, by Finland and Sweden, which had similar rates of growth, with Norway not far behind, although all of the Nordic countries remained low users of imprisonment overall. The Netherlands, however, traditionally a model of punitive restraint, had exceeded the Greek rate of growth and had likewise moved from low use to moderate use.

This is not the place for a detailed debate on the statistics, but Cheliotis' re-analysis of the official data from the National Statistical Service of Greece suggests that the figures supplied by the Greek Ministry of Justice to the compilers of the *World Prison Population Lists* may be a considerable

---

1   The categories themselves are obviously artificial and arbitrary, and intended merely to aid comparison: in addition to low and moderate use, I defined 'high use' as countries with rates between 151 and 225 per 100,000, 'very high' as 226–300 per 100,000, and 'extremely high' as those with rates exceeding 300 per 100,000.

underestimate, particularly in regard to pre-trial detainees.[2] On the nearest comparable dates, for 2005, Walmsley (2007) cites 9,984 prisoners including pre-trial detainees, producing a rate of 90 per 100,000 against a total population of 11.1 million, whereas Cheliotis' caseload figure of 17,869 (79 percent higher) suggests a rate of 161 per 100,000, which would place Greece in the high use category rather than the moderate use. Assuming the same differential for the latest available data for 2008 (Walmsley, 2009), one might speculate that the actual prison population might be as high as 22,000 (rather than the officially cited 12,300), producing a rate of 195 per 100,000 rather than 109 – though it has to be said this may be a speculation too far.

It is not just Greece that suffers from a poor reporting of statistics. There are many jurisdictions around the world where the prison authorities would find it hard to come up with any sort of figures for prison populations apart from occasional spot counts of doubtful accuracy. England and Wales, by contrast, probably has the longest history of any country of collecting and reporting reliable statistics both of annual receptions into custody and of the prison population on an average daily basis, with a detailed breakdown of prisoners by legal category and length of sentence, as well as sex, age, and ethnicity among other variables. It is true that the Annual Reports and Accounts of the Prison Service, now incorporated into the Annual Report of the National Offender Management Service, have come to resemble those of commercial businesses and no longer contain the more interesting criminological and penological data – but most of those data are still available for those prepared to search the websites, and in some respects, thanks to the internet, are more widely available to the general public. Thus, the Ministry of Justice website publishes monthly tables of the population in custody (once distributed in hard copy to those on the mailing list) as well as a weekly *Prison Population and Accommodation Briefing*. And so, for example, according to the monthly tables for May

2   Of course, Greece is probably not alone in providing figures to the World Prison Population Lists that may be hard to interpret. All international comparisons in this regard, including my own, have to be treated with a suitable degree of caution.

2010, we know that there was a total of 85,460 persons in custody, of whom 81,062 were males and 4,398 were females, about one sixth of these (just under 16 percent) were people remanded in custody either to await trial (about 10 percent) or sentence (about 5.5 percent). Incarceration rates in England and Wales, and Greece, therefore appear to be of the same order of magnititude between 150 and 200 per 100,000 population – higher than most other members of the European Union, with only Poland, Estonia, Latvia, and Lithuania having significantly higher incarceration rates.

Greece, evidently, has a much higher proportion of the prison population in custody on remand (between a quarter and a third of the total compared to about a sixth in England and Wales), almost certainly as a result of the high average length of stay in prison (365 days) which, as Cheliotis notes, is the longest in the EU. But the throughput of remand prisoners in England and Wales, most of them remanded for short periods, nevertheless creates significant problems for the Prison Service. The 81,700 or so receptions into custody of remands and trials prisoners in 2008 (Ministry of Justice, 2009a) had somehow to be accommodated separately from convicted and sentenced prisoners in accordance with international prison rules and domestic delegated legislation. But accommodation in the prison estate is relatively inelastic and the 'rights' to separate accommodation for the unconvicted, along with other rights of those 'presumed innocent until proven guilty', have always been predicated upon what is 'reasonably' possible in the 'defensible' view of the prison governor. Some decades ago, it was demonstrated that the exercise of such rights could result in worse conditions than those which prevailed for convicted prisoners (King and Morgan, 1975). Today, the Prison Service has moved on and English prisons are no longer the dirty, foul smelling, unhygienic places that once they were. Although conditions for remand prisoners no longer warrant paragraphs, or pages in annual reports, and although prison governors may do their best, where the physical structure of their prison permits, to effect real separation between the different classes of prisoner, it is often not possible to do so. It is doubtful whether the rights, as opposed to the needs, of remand prisoners are better met now than they have ever been – although they may now be asked more politely whether they are prepared to share cells with convicted prisoners.

Cheliotis reports a prison population which rose by 52.6 percent between 1990 and 2006, driven largely by substantial increases in the length of sentences for convicted prisoners. During a broadly comparable period – 1995 to 2009 –, the prison population of England and Wales grew even more dramatically by 66 percent. The picture is complex, but for present purposes it is sufficient to note that the main drivers have been policy changes and new legislation which have led, first, to increased sentence lengths, including the introduction of mandatory minimum and increased maximum sentences, and the new indeterminate sentence of Imprisonment for Public Protection; and second, tougher enforcement regimes which have meant increasing numbers of offenders being imprisoned for breach of non-custodial sentences and prisoners recalled to custody for failing to comply with the conditions of their parole licences (for a more detailed analysis, see, for example, Ministry of Justice, 2009b). That these astonishing rates of increase in the prison population have taken place alongside very much smaller proportionate increases in official crime rates in Greece (see Cheliotis and Xenakis, this collection), and alongside steadily falling crime rates in England and Wales, where the British Crime Survey crime rate peaked in 1995 and the officially police-recorded crime rate peaked in 1992, is quite remarkable. Although there are always some who argue that it is the increasing use of imprisonment that brings about the reduction in crime, the truth is that crime rates have much more to do with social and economic conditions, on the one hand, and the opportunities to commit crime, on the other. As Wacquant (2009) and others have persuasively argued, there is simply no convincing evidence of a correlation between the levels of crime and rates of incarceration. There has unquestionably been a 'talking up' of the use of imprisonment in many parts of the world. What we see in prisons today owes much to the pusillanimity or unscrupulousness of politicians, searching for the votes of a public in whose minds an unrealistic fear of crime has been fostered by irresponsible sections of the media and the intense publicity they give to the worst crimes, as well as their denunciation of all attempts at reform as being 'soft on crime'. Moreover, in both Greece and England and Wales, this process has seen increasing proportions of the prison populations who are addicted to drugs, with consequent problems about diseases such as hepatitis and HIV/AIDS, and large numbers of prisoners who have mental health problems, poor levels of literacy, and so on.

Although the statistics of imprisonment provide some of the context in which to understand what is going on, statistics alone do not a prison system make. No more do bricks and mortar. The 34 prisons in Greece are crowded, from Cheliotis' description, far more so than the 124 public and 11 private sector prisons in England and Wales. Whilst the prison population on 16 July 2010 (two days before writing this commentary) stood at 85,117 and the useable operational capacity of the system was listed as 87,844 places, this conceals the fact that there were many pockets of significant overcrowding in the system.[3] HMP (Her Majesty's Prison) Altcourse, for example, which has a CNA (Certified Normal Accommodation) of 794 places held 1,234 prisoners, and at Wandsworth, with 1,107 places and 1,651 prisoners, almost all prisoners were doubled up in cells intended for single occupation. This pales into insignificance compared to the crowding in the Male Prison of Korydallos where Cheliotis reports a population of 2,018 held in accommodation intended for 800 (though that, in turn, is short of the levels found in Kresty or Burtyka in the Russian Federation (King, 1994) or the former prison, now thankfully demolished, at Carandiru in São Paulo (Varella, 1999) – and, indeed, in prisons in many other parts of the world). Cheliotis, nevertheless, lists a catalogue of poor conditions, from limited sanitation, to lack of hygiene, to minimal access to medical care. It is at this point that the similarities between the prison systems of Greece and England and Wales begin to break down.

Most of the matters discussed so far are matters over which the prison authorities have little control, and prison systems need to be judged by how they respond to the circumstances in which they find themselves. Whereas, according to Cheliotis, 'ministerial authorities of all colours have restricted access to prisons for lawyer associations, medical NGOs, the Greek Ombudsman, academic researchers, and MPs', and whereas Greece, like so many systems around the world relies upon a possibly overworked, or understaffed, but in any case ineffective, system of oversight by public

---

3   It has to be said that there will be some unavoidable, but relatively minor, inaccuracies in the population data, and that the definitions of usable operational capacity depend upon subjective judgements rather than legally enforceable space standards. See King and Morgan (1980) for a detailed analysis of the problems of interpreting CNA (Certified Normal Accommodation) and other measures of prison capacity.

prosecutors whose 'input tends to fixate on security concerns', the prison system in England and Wales has become progressively more open and is surrounded by a plethora of comparatively well-staffed bodies to examine its activities, from Independent Monitoring Boards attached to each prison to national bodies such as the Prisons and Probation Ombudsman and the independent HM Inspectorate of Prisons. Both systems are subject to periodic visits from the Committee for the Prevention of Torture.

Moreover, over a period of nearly fifty years, the system has been exposed to research from academic researchers (Morris *et al.*, 1963; King and Elliott, 1977; Genders and Player, 1995; Sparks *et al.*, 1996; King and McDermott, 1995; Liebling, 1992, 2004; Crewe, 2009, to list just some of the major studies), who have accumulated a considerable body of knowledge concerning both the sociology of the prison and ways of evaluating prison performance. It would be idle to pretend that the relationship between researchers and prison adminitrators has always been an easy one. It has not. But over the years, in a faltering progress, the relationship has changed from suspicion to one close to mutual respect for each other's needs and problems – and there is little doubt that research has gained from the increasing openness and administrators have gained from constructive criticism and advice.

It would similarly be folly to assume that everything within the prison estate in England and Wales is good and well. Clearly it is not. The Prison Service has been buffeted by events beyond its control, and has been the subject of almost constant reorganisation, transformed by the mixed blessing of New Public Management. Since 2004, it has been struggling with the implementation of the National Offender Management Service, which has sought to integrate the prison and probation services in an attempt to provide end-to-end management of offenders – an organisational process now more or less complete and one which has been more traumatic for probation than for prisons. It remains to be seen whether end-to-end management of offenders becomes an effective reality on the ground and whether it produces improvements in what are currently very high levels of re-offending. But it is important to keep a sense of perspective and to acknowledge, as the outgoing Chief Inspector of Prisons, Anne Owers, did in her valedictory lecture to the Prison Reform Trust, that things are much better than they were: 'Over the last nine years, there is no doubt that prisons became better places – better able to keep prisoners safe, provide a decent environment, offer some purposeful activity, and provide some resettlement opportunities' (Owers, 2010: 9).

Parole has a much shorter history in England and Wales than in Greece, dating only since the Criminal Justice Act 1967, although before then all prisoners could receive remission of one-third of their sentence, notionally for good behaviour, and they were then released, for the most part without supervision in the community.[4] Space precludes any detailed consideration of the many complex changes that the parole system has undergone since its inception (but see West, 1972; Padfield, 2002; Padfield *et al.*, 2010), or any point-for-point comparison with the very different system which operates in Greece. At the same time, those very complexities make it difficult to provide a brief, and meaningful, overview. But some general points are worth making. The first, perhaps, is that, whilst the period awaiting parole decisions can be very anxiety-provoking for prisoners, the system has never generated the kind of response which Cheliotis reports for Greece in November 2008 of mass hunger strikes in protest at the underuse and unfair administration of parole (although in the 1970s, 1980s, and again in 1990, there were spectacular prison riots and disturbances about prison conditions in England and Wales). Indeed, prisoners have, if anything, been rather docile in the face of the many changes which have made their chances of release more problematic.[5] Crewe (2009) has documented the way in which a variety of measures, including the need to earn 'privileges' and demonstrate reduced risk of further offending in order to get parole, have become very effective ways of controlling prisoner behaviours.

4   In reality, the remission was automatic, although prisoners could lose some of their remission if they committed offences against prison discipline. Some prisoners did receive compulsory aftercare from the probation service and others could get voluntary support from various Discharged Prisoners Aid Societies.

5   It was remarkable, for example, that, when the Home Secretary changed the rules to restrict the parole eligibility of some longer-sentence prisoners in 1983 – thus giving them 'less to lose' –, the situation was managed without major troubles.

Secondly, whereas parole in Greece, though justified by high-minded rhetoric which remained just that, has been at least partly used as a 'low-cost tool for curbing overcrowding' in prisons, albeit not very effectively, this has only ever been a modest latent function of the parole system in England and Wales. In Greece, the hurried response to the hunger strikes in 2008 and the review of the records of all prisoners which suggested that 3,720 prisoners were due for imminent release, was reminiscent of the periodic amnesties found in some former Soviet systems, although it seems that, in the event, the number of releases was significantly lower. By contrast, the early rhetoric on parole in England and Wales was genuinely based on a belief in rehabilitation, and the expectation that prisoners reached a point in their sentences when further detention would be both costly and possibly counter-productive. In such circumstances, the interests of all would be better served by supervision in the community. Any relief to the problem of crowding was essentially a by-product. One recent overt attempt at using early release to relieve pressure on the prison system met with fierce political and media resistance, and was shortlived. Thus, an End of Custody Licence scheme which allowed minor offenders to be released up to a modest 18 days early, introduced in June 2007, was abandoned in March 2010.

Thirdly, the organisational structures of parole in the two countries appear to have been located in different parts of the criminal justice system, and whilst there have been dramatic changes to parole in England and Wales, the two systems remain very different in operation. In Greece, the parole process has been, and remains, essentially a judicial function, with applications for conditional release passed from prison governors to Local Misdemeanours Councils which operate their discretion very conservatively. These Councils also make recall decisions. Some attempts have been made to undercut disparities in decision-making by establishing prison-based boards to make parole assessments, but without much apparent impact. In England and Wales, a national Parole Board of some 16 members was established under an independent chairman appointed by the Home Secretary. The Board was initially assisted by Local Review Committees, again comprising independent members, who undertook an initial assessment and made their recommendations to the Parole Board.

The process was one of reaching an executive rather than a judicial decision, and the role of the Parole Board was essentially advisory: whilst the Home Secretary could not release prisoners on parole without a recommendation from the Board, s/he was free to reject any of the Board's positive recommendations as s/he thought fit.

Over the succeeding decades, both the role of the Parole Board and the nature of its activities changed dramatically. In 1991, the Local Review Committees were abolished and the Board was given the power to direct the release of some prisoners. Prisoners were given the right to see and comment on their dossiers, and to be provided with the reasons for the parole decision (for many years the Board had refused to give reasons in case they were challenged). Three years later, what had until then been a purely paper process was given a slightly more human aspect with the introduction of face-to-face interviews between the parole applicant and a member of the Board.[6] Judicial reviews and cases determined in the European Court of Human Rights had led to a steadily increasing pressure for the Board to become a court-like body exercising a judicial rather than an executive function, and, in 1991, discretionary life sentence prisoners became entitled to a formal oral hearing. Most importantly, under the Criminal Justice Act 2003, parole became automatic for most determinate sentence prisoners at the halfway stage of their sentence, with the role of the Board in those cases limited to the review of recall decisions. At the same time, the Board was given sole responsibility for dealing with release decisions for prisoners under the new (and now notorious) sentence of Imprisonment for Public Protection, whereby certain eligible offenders received a tariff period of custody justified by the gravity of the current offence, but could be held in custody indefinitely unless they were able to demonstrate to the Parole Board that their risk of further serious offences had been reduced – making them, for all practical purposes, life sentence prisoners. The early justifications of parole in terms of rehabilitation had finally given

---

6   Sadly, interviews were abandoned some ten years later, ostensibly on grounds that they added little to the parole decision but really on grounds of cost. Face-to-face contact was resumed, however, in the increasing number of oral hearings.

way to a situation where its sole concern was the management of risk in a risk-averse society. In the process, the Board has grown from its original 16 members of whom three were judges, to a body, as at March 2010, with 216 members under the chairmanship of a judge, with 73 judicial members in all and 30 psychiatrists amongst its number. At the time of writing, the final resting place for the Parole Board has yet to be determined: once in an uneasy relationship with the Home Office and more recently the Ministry of Justice, it seeks closer integration with HM Courts Service.

The introduction of the sentence of Imprisonment for Public Protection (IPP) has produced major problems for both the prison and parole systems. The Parole Board can only recommend release in such cases when the risk has been reduced. Since the sentence is imposed on the basis of fixed criteria, it is often difficult to know what the baseline risk was. Assessing risk and the reduction of risk is not an exact science. The proxy for *actual* risk reduction becomes, in effect, the completion of an offending behaviour course *intended* to reduce risk. But since the tariff for such offenders is often relatively short, there is often insufficient time for them to complete an appropriate course before their parole review – with the result that the Parole Board has no option but to put the case back for further review after two years (see further Padfield, 2002). The introduction of a growing number of offending behaviour courses has been one of the relative success stories of the Prison Service over the last decade, but the service is obliged to give IPP prisoners priority for such courses, thus making them less available to the already large population of life sentence prisoners and possibly many determinate sentence prisoners who may have greater needs. This, together with the difficulty of recruiting sufficient judges required to chair oral hearings, partly accounts for why only about 130 of the almost 6,000 IPP prisoners now in the system have so far been released.

Conclusion

At the time of writing, both Greece and the United Kingdom face a straitened economic future, following the so-called 'credit crunch': Greece, under pressure from the EU and the IMF, as the first country in the Euro zone to feel the pinch; England and Wales under a government-imposed regime of expenditure cuts by a newly elected coalition in which the dominant party is ideologically opposed to the public sector in virtually all its forms. How these will play out in terms of their prison and parole systems in a context of risk aversion and a continuing penal populism, remains to be seen. What is absolutely clear is that, unless both countries first take control of prison population growth and then systematically reverse it, there can be no progress whatever in prisons and parole. Indeed, without changes to sentencing policy that would reduce the demand for prison places sufficiently to begin taking prisons out of the system completely, expenditure cuts of the order of 25 percent which have been demanded in England, can only be at the expense of much-needed programmes and constructive activities and a reduction in hours out of cells. One imagines that expenditure cuts in Greece will only make a bad situation worse.

If, on the other hand, changes to sentencing and early release policies were to have a significant impact on the size of the prison population, then in England and Wales, at least, the expertise is there to ensure that a smaller prison and parole system could be much more effective. Greece, on the evidence presented here, it would seem, has much further to go. Not only does it need to control the growth of the prison population, but it also has to open up the system to independent inspection and systematic research, and then to heed the outcomes of that process. There are those of us, the present writer included, who have argued that most countries cannot afford the levels of expenditure which they waste on prisons and imprisonment, and that sooner or later politicians, the mass media, and the public will have to learn to live with realistic policies that are evidence-based. If not now, when?

References

Crewe, B. (2009) *The Prisoner Society*. Oxford: Clarendon Press.

Genders, E. and E. Player (1995) *Grendon: A Study of a Therapeutic Prison*. Oxford: Clarendon Press.

King, R.D. (1994) 'Russian Prisons after Perestroika: End of the Gulag?', *British Journal of Criminology* 34 (Special Issue): 62–82.

King, R.D. (2007) 'Imprisonment: Some International Comparisons and the Need to Revisit Panopticism', in Y. Jewkes (ed.) *Handbook on Prisons*, pp. 329–355. Cullompton: Willan.

King, R.D. and R. Morgan (1975) *A Taste of Prison: Custodial Conditions for Trial and Remand Prisoners*. London: Routledge and Kegan Paul.

King, R.D. and R. Morgan (1980) *The Future of the Prison System*. Farnborough: Gower Publishing.

King, R.D. and K. Elliott (1977) *Albany: Birth of a Prison – End of an Era*. London: Routledge and Kegan Paul.

King, R.D. and K. McDermott (1995) *The State of Our Prisons*. Oxford: Clarendon Press.

Liebling, A. (1992) *Suicides in Prison*. London: Routledge.

Liebling, A. (assisted by Helen Arnold) (2004) *Prisons and their Moral Performance: A Study of Values, Quality and Prison Life*. Oxford: Clarendon Press.

Ministry of Justice (2009a) *Offender Management Caseload Statistics 2008*, Ministry of Justice Statistics Bulletin. Available online at: www.justice.gov.uk

Ministry of Justice (2009b) *Story of the Prison Population 1995–2009, England and Wales*, Ministry of Justice Statistics Bulletin. Available online at: www.justice.gov.uk

Morris, T., Morris, P. and B. Barer (1963) *Pentonville: A Sociological Study of an English Prison*. London: Routledge and Kegan Paul.

Owers, A. (2010) *Lecture to the Prison Reform Trust*. Available online at: www.justice.gov.uk

Padfield, N. (2002) *Beyond the Tariff: Human Rights and the Release of Life Sentence Prisoners*. Cullompton: Willan.

Padfield, N., van Zyl Smit, D. and F. Dünkel (2010) *Release from Prison: European Policy and Practice*. Cullompton: Willan.

Sparks, R., Bottoms, A.E. and W. Hay (1996) *Prisons and the Problem of Order*. Oxford: Clarendon Press.

Varella, D. (1999) *Estação Carandiru*. São Paulo: Companhia das Letras.

Wacquant, L. (2009) *Punishing the Poor: The Neoliberal Government of Social Insecurity*. Durham and London: Duke University Press.

Walmsley, R. (1999) *World Prison Population List (1st edn.)*. London: Home Office Research, Development and Statistics Division.

Walmsley, R. (2000) *World Prison Population List (2nd edn.)*. London: International Centre for Prison Studies.

Walmsley, R. (2005) *World Prison Population List (6th edn.)*. London: International Centre for Prison Studies.

Walmsley, R. (2007) *World Prison Population List (7th edn.)*. London: International Centre for Prison Studies.

West, D. (1972) *The Future of Parole*. London: Duckworth.

Notes on contributors

CLAUDIA ARADAU is Lecturer in International Studies at The Open University, UK, and Research Director of the Securities Programme at the Centre for Citizenship, Identities and Governance. She is the author of *Rethinking Trafficking in Women: Politics out of Security* (2010), and is currently working on a co-authored book (with Rens van Munster) on the politics of catastrophe.

EFI AVDELA is Professor of Contemporary History at the Department of History and Archaeology, University of Crete, Greece. She specialises in social and cultural 20th-century Greek history. She has published in several languages on gender history, the history of work and social movements, history teaching, and the history of violence, crime and criminal justice. Her current project concerns youth and delinquency in post-civil-war Greece.

MARGARET E. BEARE served as the first Director of the Nathanson Centre for the Study of Organised Crime and Corruption (now called the Nathanson Centre on Transnational Human Rights, Crime and Security) located within Osgoode Hall Law School, York University, Toronto, Canada, from 1996 to 2006. She holds the position of Professor within the Sociology Department and within Osgoode Hall Law School. Her books include work on organised crime, money laundering, policing, and social justice issues.

TREVOR BENNETT is Professor of Criminology and Director of the Centre for Criminology at the University of Glamorgan, UK. Before this, he was Senior Lecturer and Deputy Director of the Institute of Criminology at the University of Cambridge and Fellow of Wolfson College. He has published widely in the areas of policing, crime prevention, offender behaviour, and drug misuse. His most recent book on drug misuse is *Drug-crime Connections* (2007), co-authored with Katy Holloway.

DIDIER BIGO is Professor at the Department of War Studies, King's College London, UK, and MCU Research Professor at Sciences-Po, Paris. He is co-editor, with Rob Walker, of *International Political Sociology* (one of the journals of the International Studies Association) and editor of the French journal *Cultures et Conflits*. He is responsible for Work Package 1 of INEX, a project on internal and external security, funded under the 7th Framework Programme of the European Commission.

PARASKEVI S. BOUKLIS is a PhD candidate at the Department of Law, London School of Economics and Political Science, UK, having previously studied criminology at the same institution, and sociology and criminology at Panteion University, Greece. Her research interests are in victimology, particularly in relation to criminal law and human rights. She has been the Chief Editor of Kodikas Publications in Athens since 2000, and has published two books of poetry, *Poetic Cause* (2001) and *Medea Plath* (2006).

PETER BRATSIS teaches political theory at the University of Salford, UK. He is the author of *Everyday Life and the State* (2006) and co-editor (with Stanley Aronowitz) of *Paradigm Lost: State Theory Reconsidered* (2002). He is an editor of the journal *Situations: Project of the Radical Imagination*, and book review editor of the *Journal of Modern Greek Studies*.

LEONIDAS K. CHELIOTIS is Lecturer and Deputy Director of the Centre for Criminal Justice at the School of Law, Queen Mary, University of London. He holds MPhil and PhD degrees from the University of Cambridge (his doctoral thesis was awarded the 2010 Nigel Walker Prize by the Cambridge Institute of Criminology), and has been elected to a Visiting Fellowship at the Centre for Criminology, University of Oxford, and a Visiting Scholarship at the Centre for the Study of Law and Society, University of California, Berkeley. He is an Associate Editor of the *European Journal of Criminology*, and the editor of *The Arts of Imprisonment: Control, Resistance and Empowerment* (2012) and *Roots, Rites and Sites of Resistance: The Banality of Good* (2010). He is currently working on a monograph provisionally entitled *The Punitive Heart: Neoliberal Capitalism and the Psychopolitics of Crime Control*.

CAROLYN CÔTÉ-LUSSIER is a PhD candidate in the Methodology Institute at the London School of Economics and Political Science, UK. She has an MA in Criminology from the University of Toronto. Her doctoral dissertation uses experimental social psychology to study social stereotypes about criminals and how these stereotypes relate to psychological needs, political ideology, and policy preferences such as support for harsh criminal justice policy.

MONICA DEN BOER holds the Police Academy Chair on Comparative Public Administration, specialising in the Internationalisation of the Police Function, at the VU University Amsterdam, the Netherlands. She formerly held academic posts at Tilburg University, the European Institute of Public Administration, the Netherlands Institute for the Study of Crime and Law Enforcement, Edinburgh University, and the European University Institute. Her publications include several books, chapters, and articles on the subject of European law enforcement co-operation, with a more recent focus on the ethical aspects of international security governance. She is a member of the Dutch Advisory Board on International Affairs, and has served as Vice-Chair of the Board of the Clingendael Institute of International Relations in The Hague.

MONICA GERBER is a PhD candidate in the Methodology Institute at the London School of Economics and Political Science, UK. Prior to this, she gained an MSc in Social Research Methods at the same university. Her research is on punitive attitudes from a social-psychological perspective. She is currently conducting studies testing the motivational basis of punitive attitudes and the extent to which punishment may serve a system-justifying function.

KEVIN D. HAGGERTY is Professor of Sociology and Criminology at the University of Alberta, Canada, and a member of the executive team for the *New Transparency* Major Collaborative Research Initiative. He is editor of the *Canadian Journal of Sociology* and book review editor of the international journal *Surveillance and Society*. In addition to his numerous published articles, he has authored *Making Crime Count* (2001), co-authored (with Richard V. Ericson) *Policing the Risk Society* (1997), and co-edited (with Richard V. Ericson) *The New Politics of Surveillance and Visibility* (2006).

JONATHAN JACKSON is Senior Lecturer in Research Methods and member of the Mannheim Centre for Criminology at the London School of Economics and Political Science, UK. His research centres on public attitudes towards crime, policing and punishment. He is currently involved in a number of comparative studies, including a European Commission-funded project into trust in the police and the legitimacy of legal authorities, a European Social Survey module on the same topic, and a Universidad Católica de Chile-funded project into punitive sentiment in Santiago. Recent publications include *Social Order and the Fear of Crime in Contemporary Times* (co-authored with Stephen Farrall and Emily Gray) and articles in *Criminology*, the *Journal of Research in Crime and Delinquency*, *The British Journal of Criminology*, the *British Journal of Sociology*, *Risk Analysis* and the *European Sociological Review*.

VASSILIS KARYDIS is Professor at the Department of Social and Educational Policy, University of the Peloponnese, Greece. Since February 2010, he is Deputy Greek Ombudsman for Human Rights. He has published the books *Criminality and Social Control in the USSR* (1991), *Criminality of Immigrants in Greece* (1996), *The Hidden Criminality: National Victim Survey* (2004), and *Visions of Social Control in Greece: Penal Justice, Moral Panics* (2010). He is a member of the Steering Committee of the European Group for the Study of Deviance and Social Control, and of the ERASMUS Network *Critical Criminology and Criminal Justice Systems in Europe*.

ROY D. KING is Emeritus Professor of Criminology and Criminal Justice in the University of Wales, UK. From 2004 to 2011, he was Honourary Senior Research Fellow at the Institute of Criminology, University of Cambridge, where he directed the MSt Programme in Applied Criminology, Penology and Management. He was a founder member of the Parole Board for England and Wales from 1967 to 1971, and again served as a criminologist member from 2001 to 2006.

EFFI LAMBROPOULOU is Professor of Criminology at the Department of Sociology, Panteion University, Greece. She received an LLB from the University of Athens, and conducted postgraduate studies in the sociology of criminal law and criminology at the Universities of Bielefeld and Freiburg i.Br., earning a PhD from the latter. Between 1983 and 1987, she worked with the Criminological Research Group at the Max-Planck Institute for Foreign and International Criminal Law, Freiburg. Her research and teaching interests span social control, the sociology of criminal law, the mass media, corrections, police and policing, drug policies, and corruption.

ROB I. MAWBY is Professor of Criminology and Criminal Justice. He worked at the universities of Sheffield, Leeds, Bradford, and Plymouth, before semi-retiring to a visiting chair at the University of Gloucestershire, UK. His interests include policing and victimology, especially in a cross-national context, burglary, tourism and crime, and crime reduction. He was the UK representative on CEPOL's Special Expert Committee on Police Science in the EU (2005–2007). He is editor of *Crime Prevention and Community Safety: An International Journal*, and has published numerous articles and books, the most recent being *Policing Across the World: Issues for the Twenty-first Century* (1999), *Burglary* (2001), *Burglary* (second series, 2007), *Police Science Perspectives: Towards a European Approach* (co-authored, 2009) and *Rural Policing and Policing the Rural* (co-authored, 2010).

VALSAMIS MITSILEGAS is Professor of European Criminal Law at the School of Law, Queen Mary, University of London, UK. From 2001 to 2005 he was legal adviser to the House of Lords European Union Committee. He is a regular consultant to parliaments, governments, EU institutions, international organisations, and NGOs, and is a member of the Management Committee of the European Criminal Law Academic Network (ECLAN). He has published widely in the field of EU law and in the field of law, security and trasnational crime. His latest monograph is *EU Criminal Law* (2009).

JOHN MUNCIE is Professor of Criminology and Director of the International Centre for Comparative Criminological Research (ICCCR) at the Open University, UK. He is the author of the best-selling text *Youth and Crime* (3rd edition, 2009). His most recent research is on the impact of devolution, globalisation and international conventions on the formulation of law and penal policy for young people in the UK and Western Europe. He has published widely on issues in comparative youth justice and children's rights, including the co-edited companion volumes *Youth Crime and Justice* and *Comparative Youth Justice* (2006). He is editor (with Barry Goldson) of *Youth Justice: An International Journal*.

NICOLA PADFIELD is Senior Lecturer at the Faculty of Law, University of Cambridge, UK. A barrister by training, she has published widely on criminal law, sentencing, and criminal justice. Her books include *The Criminal Justice Process: Text and Materials* (4th edition, 2008); *Criminal Law* (6th edition, 2008); *Beyond the Tariff: Human Rights and the Release of Life Sentence Prisoners* (2002); and *A Guide to the Proceeds of Crime Act 2002* (with S. Biggs and S. Farrell, 2002). She has edited other collections of essays, and is editor of *Archbold Review*. She sits as a Recorder (part-time judge) in the Crown Court, and is a Bencher of the Middle Temple.

GIANNIS PANOUSIS is Professor of Criminology at the Faculty of Communication and Mass Media Studies, National and Kapodistrian University of Athens (EKPA), Greece. He was Rector of the Democritus University of Thrace between 1994 and 1997, Dean of the Faculty of Communication and Mass Media Studies at EKPA between 2001 and 2005, and General Secretary of the General Secretariat for Greeks Abroad in 1996.

CHARIS PAPACHARALAMBOUS is Assistant Professor of Criminal Law at the University of Cyprus. He holds a PhD in Penal Law and Legal Theory from the Goethe University in Frankfurt. He has worked as a legal advisor to the Greek Ministry of Justice on matters of criminal law, and as Senior Investigator at the Greek Ombudsman's Section on the Protection of Human Rights. He is the author of three monographs and various articles on criminal law.

IOANNIS PAPAGEORGIOU is a PhD candidate in Criminology at the University of Edinburgh, UK. His doctoral work focuses on the expansion of prison privatisation in the UK from the perspective of political philosophy and state theory in particular. He holds an LLB from the University of Athens, and an MSc in Criminology and Criminal Justice from the University of Edinburgh. He is a qualified lawyer of the Athens Bar Association with experience in company and criminal law.

GEORGIOS PAPANICOLAOU is Lecturer in Criminology at Teesside University, UK, having previously studied Law and Penal Sciences at the University of Athens, Greece, and Criminology and Criminal Justice at the University of Edinburgh, Scotland. His interests include the study of policing, particularly of transnational policing and the control of transnational 'organised crime' within a materialist state theory framework. His book entitled *Transnational Policing and Sex Trafficking in Southeast Europe: Policing the Imperialist Chain* was published in 2011.

ANGELIKA PITSELA is Associate Professor of Criminology and Penology at the School of Law, Aristotle University of Thessaloniki, Greece. She holds an LLB from the same university, and a PhD from the School of Law, Albert-Ludwig University of Freiburg.

ROBERT REINER is Professor of Criminology in the Law Department, London School of Economics and Political Science, UK. He is author of *The Blue-Coated Worker* (1978/2010), *The Politics of the Police* (1985/2010), *Chief Constables* (1991), and *Law and Order: An Honest Citizen's Guide to Crime and Control* (2007). He has edited *Beyond Law and Order* (with M. Cross, 1991), *Accountable Policing* (with S. Spencer, 1993), *Policing* (1996), and *The Oxford Handbook of Criminology* (with M. Maguire and R. Morgan, 1994/2007). He was President of the British Society of Criminology during the period 1993–1996. He was Director of the LSE Mannheim Centre for Criminology (1995–1998) and Acting Director (2009–1010).

VINCENZO RUGGIERO is Professor of Sociology and Director of the Crime and Conflict Research Centre at Middlesex University in London, UK. His research interests include social theory, urban sociology, comparative criminology and social movements. His work has been widely published in several languages, and his books include *Penal Abolitionism* (2010), *Social Movements: A Reader* (2008), *Understanding Political Violence* (2006),

Crime in Literature (2003), *Movements in the City* (2001), *Crime and Markets* (2000), *The New European Criminology* (1998), *Organised and Corporate Crime in Europe* (1996), *European Penal Systems* (1995) and *Eurodrugs* (1995).

MINAS SAMATAS is Associate Professor of Political Sociology at the Department of Sociology, University of Crete, Greece. He holds an MA and a PhD in Sociology from the New School for Social Research, New York, USA. He is the author of *Surveillance in Greece: From Anticommunist to Consumer Surveillance* (2004), co-editor (with Kevin Haggerty) of *Surveillance and Democracy* (2010), and the Greek representative on the Managing Committee of the European research network 'Living in Surveillance Societies' (LiSS).

PIETER SPIERENBURG is Professor of Historical Criminology at the Erasmus University, Rotterdam, the Netherlands. He has held Visiting Professorships at Carnegie Mellon University, Pittsburgh, USA, and the University of California at Berkeley, USA. His books include *The Spectacle of Suffering: Executions and the Evolution of Repression: From a Preindustrial Metropolis to the European Experience* (1984/2008), *The Prison Experience: Disciplinary Institutions and their Inmates in Early Modern Europe* (1991/2007), *De Verbroken Betovering: Mentaliteit en Cultuur in Preïndustrieel Europa* (1998), *Written in Blood: Fatal Attraction in Enlightenment Amsterdam* (2004), and *A History of Murder: Personal Violence in Europe from the Middle Ages to the Present* (2008).

MICHAEL TONRY is Professor of Law and Public Policy, and Director of the Institute on Crime and Public Policy, University of Minnesota, USA. He is also a Senior Fellow in the Netherlands Institute for the Study of Crime and Law Enforcement.

JOANNA TSIGANOU is Director of Research and Deputy Director of the Institute of Political Sociology at the Greek National Centre for Social Research (EKKE) in Athens, Greece. Originally a lawyer, she obtained her PhD in the Sociology of Crime and Deviance from the London School of

Economics and Political Science in 1988, and has worked as a Researcher at EKKE since 1994. Her main fields of research are in the sociology of law, sociology of crime and deviance, and social institutions. She has authored and co-authored a number of national and international scholarly publications, and is presently involved in research projects addressing issues of safety, migration, and violence.

SOPHIE VIDALI is Associate Professor of Criminology and Crime Policy at the Department of Social Administration, Democritus University of Thrace, Greece. She worked for several years at the National Statistical Service of Greece, has been a chief scientific coordinator for research projects conducted by the National Organisation against Drugs in Greece, and has participated in workgroups of the Ministry of Public Order on police and crime policy. She is the author of books and articles on police and policing, state crime, nightlife and crime, organised crime, prison life, criminal statistics, and critical criminology.

SAPPHO XENAKIS is Marie Curie Intra-European Fellow of the European Commission (7th Framework Programme), based at the Hellenic Foundation for European and Foreign Policy (ELIAMEP) in Athens, Greece. She is also an Associate of the South East European Studies programme at St Antony's College, University of Oxford. She holds a DPhil in International Relations from the University of Oxford, and undergraduate and masters degrees in International Relations from the London School of Economics and Political Science. Her research addresses the dynamics of state power and international policy transfer in the field of security, with particular reference to transnational organised crime, terrorism, and corruption. In 2011, she was the winner of the Young Criminologist Award of the European Society of Criminology.